Reimagining the Educated Citizen

REIMAGINING THE EDUCATED CITIZEN

*Creole Pedagogies in the
Transatlantic World:
1685–1896*

Petra Munro Hendry

University of Michigan Press
Ann Arbor

For questions or permissions, please contact um.press.perms@umich.edu

Published in the United States of America by the
University of Michigan Press
Manufactured in the United States of America
Printed on acid-free paper
First published September 2023

A CIP catalog record for this book is available from the British Library.

Library of Congress Cataloging-in-Publication data has been applied for.

DOI: https://doi.org/10.3998/mpub.12562601

ISBN: 978-0-472-07639-0 (hard : alk. paper)
ISBN: 978-0-472-05639-2 (paper : alk. paper)
ISBN: 978-0-472-22129-5 (ebook)

The author and publisher would like to thank Taylor & Francis for permission to reproduce copyright material. A small portion of chapter 5 appeared in "'Listen to the Voice of Reason': *The New Orleans Tribune* as Advocate for Public Integrated Education 1864–1870," with Kristi Richard Melancon, *History of Education* 44, no. 3 (2015): 293–315.

The portrait on the cover of the book *Creole Boy with a Moth* was completed by Julien Hudson (1811–1844) in 1835. Julien Hudson, a free man of color born in New Orleans, is the second documented painter of African American heritage in the United States to work prior to the Civil War. He was not only an artist known for his portraits, but a teacher in New Orleans in the late 1830s.

To my parents
William and Gisela Munro

Contents

List of Illustrations   ix

List of Abbreviations   xi

Acknowledgments   xiii

Introduction: Practicing History   1

ONE Transatlantic Educational Spaces: Remapping the Word
and the World   30

TWO Counter-Enlightenment Pedagogical Ruptures:
The Ursulines in Colonial Louisiana   98

THREE Remapping the "Unthinkable:" The Haitian Revolution,
White Citizenship, and the Common School Movement   163

FOUR A Curriculum of Imagination: Counterpublic Spaces
in the Age of Segregation, 1841–1868   237

FIVE The New Orleans Tribune and The Crusader:
Interracial Community-Based Texts   288

Epilogue   338

Notes   343

Bibliography   411

Index   441

Digital materials related to this title can be found on the Fulcrum platform
via the following citable URL: https://doi.org/10.3998/mpub.12562601

Illustrations

Figure 1. French Colonial Territories in the Americas   6
Figure 2. French Colonial North America 1600–1763   72
Figure 3. Kaskaskia in Upper Louisiana, 1720s   74
Figure 4. Jesuit Missions in Lower Louisiana, 1720s–1763   88
Figure 5. Jesuit Plantation in New Orleans, 1720s–1763   90
Figure 6. The Blessed Virgin of the Ursuline Convent   120
Figure 7. 1732 New Orleans   144
Figure 8. Hospital Wing of Ursuline Convent   146
Figure 9. Ursuline Convent Grounds 1734–1752   149
Figure 10. New Orleans Schools, 1811   182
Figure 11. Organic Regulations of the College of Orleans   190
Figure 12. College d'Orléans, 1812   191
Figure 13. New Orleans Schools, 1822   194
Figure 14. Gazette de la Louisiane, Sept 16, 1822   201
Figure 15. Joseph Lakanal   203
Figure 16. Countries and years in which slavery was abolished
in Caribbean   220
Figure 17. Map of New Orleans schools, 1842   230
Figure 18. Perserverance Masonic Lodge No.4   273
Figure 19. Masonic Statement of Germania Lodge No.46, 1848   278
Figure 20. Alboin Turgée   319
Figure 21. Rudolphe Desdunes   331

Abbreviations

AANO	Archives of the Archdiocese of New Orleans
AC	Archives de Colonies, Archives Nationales de France, Paris
ADC	Archives du Calvados, Caen, France
ARCTU	Amistad Research Center, Tulane University, New Orleans
ASHFNO	Archives of the Sisters of the Holy Family, New Orleans
AUNPO	Archives of the Ursuline Nuns of the Parish of New Orleans, Historic New Orleans Collection
CHA	Cammie Henry Archives, Northwestern University, Louisiana
CRC	Charles B. Roussève Collection
HNOC	Historic New Orleans Collection, New Orleans
HTML	Howard-Tilton Memorial Library, Tulane University, New Orleans
JR	Jesuit Relations
LHQ	Louisiana Historical Quarterly
LUANO	Loyola University Archives, New Orleans
NONA	New Orleans Notarial Archives
OPSB	Orleans Parish School Board
RSC	Records of the Superior Council of Louisiana
UCAC	Ursuline Convent Archives, Caen, France
UNOA	University of New Orleans Archives, New Orleans
UVA	University of Virginia Archives

Acknowledgments

My initial interest in the educational history of the Gulf South was the result of moving to Baton Rouge in 1991 to begin a tenure track job at Louisiana State University in the College of Education. Consequently, I learned that the oldest publicly funded Black high school in the deep South, McKinley High founded in 1927, was less than a mile from the campus. I was captivated by the history of the school and wanted to learn more about the African American struggle for public education in my newly adopted home state. Little did I know where that journey would lead me. More than fifteen years ago, I took an unprecedented step in academia when I shifted the focus of my research in educational theory and philosophy to engage in historical research examining the impact of the transatlantic world and specifically the French colonial period on the history of education in Louisiana. I am grateful for funding from several sources that allowed me to travel and conduct research including: a Regents Award to Louisiana Artists and Scholars; the Center for French and Francophone Studies, Louisiana State University; and a Woest Fellowship in the Arts and Humanities, Historic New Orleans Collection.

Like all scholarship, this research would not have been possible without the generosity and assistance of a great many people. A great debt is owed to the numerous archivists and staff members whose knowledge and assistance made this work possible. In particular the staff at the Historic New Orleans Collection, especially Daniel Hammer, Erin Greenwald, Mary Lou Eichhorn, Robert Ticknor, Eric Seiferth, and Jennifer Navarre; Hill Memorial Library at Louisiana State University, with special thanks to

Germain Bienvenu and Hans Rasmussen; Emilie Loumas and Katie Vest at the Archives of the Archdiocese in New Orleans; Brad Petitfils, who facilitated my work at the Loyola University Archives in New Orleans; Mary Linn Wernet at the Cammie G. Henry Research Center at Northwestern University in Natchitoches; Lisa Moore at the Amistad Center at Tulane University; Marie Noëlle Vivier at the Bibliotheque Caen; Sister Marie-Therese Lagon of the Ursuline Convent in Caen; and Sister Marie-Andree Jegou in Paris at the Ursuline Convent. Sister Donna Hyndman OSU, at the Ursuline Academy in New Orleans, provided access to materials and shared her deep knowledge of the treasures in the Ursuline Museum.

The people who have provided support, conversation, feedback, and critique is long. I am grateful to Emily Clark who agreed to meet with me at P.J.'s coffee shop near Tulane at the start of this research and encouraged my research from the beginning. Shannon Dawdy was equally gracious when I asked if I could volunteer at the archeological dig she was conducting at the old Ursuline Convent in New Orleans, which gave me my first real insights into the value and importance of material culture. Essential feedback was received from those who commented on papers at conferences, especially at the Louisiana Historical Society and at the American Educational Research Association Conference. They include: James D. Anderson, Emily Clark, Raphael Cassimere, Mark Fernandez, Erin Greenwald, Virginia Gould, Alecia Long, Michael Pasquier, Paul E. Hoffman, Gaines Foster, William Pinar, and Hong Yu Wang.

Numerous graduate students helped me to think more deeply about my work in the graduate seminars in which we engaged. They include: Robyn Andermann, Paul Eaton, Thomas Eldringhoff, Seth Eisworth, Shaofei Han, Kirsten Edwards, Dana Hart, Roderick Jenkins, Danielle Klein, Nicholas Mitchell, Reagan Mitchell, Berlisha Morton, Brad Petitfils, Nicholas Ng-A-Fook, Donna Porche-Frilot, Kristi Richard Melancon, David Robinson-Morris, Kaori Shimizu, and Heather Stone. I am fortunate to benefit from having colleagues across the country in a variety of disciplines (African American studies, curriculum theory, history, education, French, women's and gender studies, anthropology, and geography), whose insights have enhanced my work tremendously and whose support has been critical. They include: Lisa Delpit, Jay Edwards, Richard Fossey, Walter Gershon, Rob Helfenbein, Joyce Jackson, Kate Jensen, Michelle Masse, Janet Miller, Roland Mitchell, Nicholas Ng-A-Fook, Katrina Sanders, Maud Walsh, Molly Quinn, and Annie Winnfield.

Many people have read all or part of the manuscript and provided essential feedback. Donna Porche-Frilot deserves special thanks for her fearless editing of several conference papers on the Ursulines and Sisters of the Holy Family that eventually became parts of chapters in this book. She was also an exceptional research partner in exploring the New Orleans archives as we searched to gain a deeper understanding of the role of education among Catholic women educator activists. Kristi Richard Melancon introduced me to the riches of the *New Orleans Tribune* as a site for exploring the meanings of public education to a radical, interracial, transatlantic group of activists in the era of the Civil War. Our research and writing together have contributed immeasurably to chapter 5 of this book. Robyn Andermann and Libby Neidenbach were also invaluable research and writing partners who contributed to my understandings of "public" education in the territorial and early American period of Louisiana, especially the impact of the Haitian Revolution. Our collaboration was foundational for the development of my ideas in chapter 3. Thanks also go to Sam Rocha and Nicholas Ng-A-Fook for taking the time to read and provide feedback on chapter 1. Their insightful and honest feedback was greatly appreciated.

Two colleagues, Jackie Bach and Laura Choate, deserve special recognition given that they have read and reread the manuscript several times. Not only have they provided critical feedback, but they have done so with the unconditional support that allowed me to continue to write even in the toughest of moments. Our writing retreats and many celebratory lunches provided me the spaces to rejuvenate and reflect on all the small steps I was accomplishing on the way to the finish line. I am grateful as well to my dear friends Marie and Mike Rourke, who provided a peaceful retreat at their St. Francisville home where I could write undisturbed. On many long walks, Marie listened attentively as I talked through the stories I was trying to tell. Many thanks to both of you. A special thanks also to my dear colleague and friend Molly Quinn, who cotaught the course "Theorizing Curriculum History: Rethinking the Enlightenment, Education, and Louisiana's Franco-Afro-Creole Protest Tradition" in which many spirited discussions helped refine my ideas and thinking.

Several editors also provided essential feedback in the final stages of writing. They are Benjamin Choate, Karin deGravelles, June Pulliam, and Carol Schanche. Two anonymous reviewers also provided critical feedback that strengthened the manuscript in significant ways. Many thanks to Judy Riffel for help with translations of documents from French to English. At the University of Michigan Press, Senior Acquisitions Editor, Elizabeth Demers supported this project from the beginning and was always gracious and generous in providing the necessary feedback that turned the original manuscript into a book. My grateful thanks also go to Haley Winkle who provided assistance as I worked through the various stages of publication, as well as Danielle Coty-Fattal my publicity manager, Mary Hashman my production editor, and my excellent copyeditor, Drew Bryan. I thank them all for making this book come to life.

All this would not be possible without the support of my family. My parents, William and Gisela Munro, to whom this book is dedicated, have supported me unconditionally. Their boundless love provided the foundation for all that I have accomplished. I only wish my mother were still with us to see this project completed. My father, at age ninety-one, asks every day, "When will the book be done?" He can't imagine how much that question means to me and how it keeps me going back again and again to my computer. My husband John has sacrificed so much in order that I could devote endless hours a day writing. He also provided excellent company as I traveled to archives, conferences, and research sites in the United States, Canada, France, and Spain. Most importantly, his love has sustained me in the most difficult of times. While my parents made this book possible, my inspiration has been the future generations of our wonderfully blended family. Our grandchildren, Ben (Ashley), Brant (Erin), Grace, Brady, Anna (Wilson), Clay, Mae, Lauren, Emma Claire, Grant, Harrison, Banks, as well as great-grandchildren Mallie Ann, Hudd, and John Todd are the light of my life who have made Louisiana my home.

Introduction

Practicing History

Doucet and Madame Hoffman

On August 9, 1741, Madame Marie Ann Hoffman made her way downriver from the German Coast to the Place d'armes in New Orleans, where she entered the court of the Superior Council of Louisiana.[1] Unlike many court cases of the time, this was not a matter of a runaway slave.[2] She was the plaintiff in a court case in which she petitioned the Superior Council for the return of her property, a young enslaved African male, Doucet, from a Monsieur Pierrer Delisle de Dupart (also spelled Dupare), who had been contracted to provide an apprenticeship for the enslaved boy. Madame Hoffman testified that baptism funds had been specifically designated for Doucet, which were to serve to instruct the child. While apprenticeships had a long history in Europe, starting in the fourteenth century, the contract signed between Madame Hoffman and Monsieur Dupart differed from traditional apprenticeship arrangements in one significant way. According to Madame Hoffman's testimony, Monsieur Dupart had "undertaken to teach him to read and write during two years and then to teach him his trade in three years which would be the space of five years."[3] The inclusion of reading and writing, skills usually associated with the upper classes in this time, marked not only a significant shift from an oral to a written culture, but also illustrates how literacy was increasingly necessary to a growing market economy and being extended to larger segments of the population. A system of apprenticeships began in colonial

New Orleans as early as 1727, and by the 1740s many apprenticeship contracts included reading and writing, indicating a shift in apprenticeships from informal to formal learning. That this type of education was extended to the enslaved is significant because it demonstrates the lack of prohibitions against literacy among the enslaved in the early French colonial period. While Doucet should have learned to read and write, Marie testified that M. Dupart had not taught Doucet "the least thing" and demanded his return and compensation in the sum of four hundred livres. The court ruled in her favor, and she was compensated in full.

While the archival evidence of this particular educational endeavor ends without further traces, the legal records of this court transaction provide a fruitful window into the culture of education in early colonial Louisiana. For many of the struggling colonists in Louisiana, like Marie Ann Hoffman and her husband, the apprenticeship system served to provide skilled artisans desperately needed for the economic growth of the struggling colony. For most of the young boys in the colony, who could not afford tutors or travel abroad to France for an education, apprenticeships functioned as a primary means to get an education, especially if one was poor, orphaned, illegitimate, or enslaved.[4] Apprenticeship contracts were not limited exclusively to training in a trade, but in many cases stipulated that the master teach the apprentice writing, reading, and arithmetic.[5]

One of the primary arguments of this book, despite popular (mis)conceptions otherwise, is that New France—particularly colonial and antebellum Louisiana—has had a "long history" of education. Doucet is one of numerous documented cases in which enslaved persons were apprenticed to learn a trade as well as read and write.[6] While we do not know how many actually learned to read or write, we do know that they were not prohibited from reading and writing and that many slave masters saw literacy as critical to the productivity of enslaved peoples, making them more effective workers.[7] Unlike other colonies, Louisiana did not pass laws against teaching enslaved persons to read and write until the 1830s. In the British colony of South Carolina, for example, shortly after a revolt of enslaved Africans known as the Stono rebellion of 1739, the Negro Act of 1740 was passed, restricting not only slave assembly and movement, but also education. While enslaved Africans could still learn to read or draw, teaching enslaved persons to write was strictly forbidden. The leader of the revolt, Jemmy, was a literate Kongolese slave who sought freedom in Spanish Florida, where enslaved Africans from the British colonies were promised land and freedom if they settled in St. Augustine. Unlike many histories of education that portray education in the South as absent until after the Civil

War, this book maintains that when we reposition the history of education within the continual movement of people and creolization processes that circulated through the transatlantic world, new avenues emerge from which to understand the complex ways in which education was taken up, appropriated, and reimagined as a tool of both freedom and oppression.

Not only does this book suggest a long history of education in Louisiana, in part driven by the agency of the enslaved, who saw liberty and literacy linked in their desire to be acknowledged as full human beings, but Madame Hoffman's judicial case also helps us to gain insight into the worldviews of the French colonists regarding race, class, and gender. As Doucet's case suggests, the first generation of French colonists clearly saw literacy and slavery as compatible and, in fact, desirable. In this preplantation society, cash-strapped colonists relied on earning income from enslaved Africans, who were skilled in a variety of trades and were employed as carters, coopers, masons, carpenters, and caulkers.[8] Enslaved artisans were in great demand. Marie knew the value of a skilled, literate enslaved African in the colonial New Orleans frontier exchange economy, whether for her own household or to be leased out for additional income. While we do not know if Doucet ever learned to read or write, this experience would have shaped his understanding of the importance of literacy.

Another important feature that might not seem obvious, given rights that we take for granted, is that Madame Hoffman was allowed to petition and testify in court. This was not a right that women in the British or Spanish colonies were guaranteed. This case clearly reveals that public spaces, like the court system, in Louisiana were spaces occupied by women and the enslaved, as well as men.[9] In other words, even those most marginalized in colonial society had access to public spaces in which they could learn the apparatuses of power engaged by the dominant culture. While Doucet did not appear in court, enslaved persons in Louisiana, under the Code Noir, had certain legal rights including the right to testify when accused. Under the revised 1685 Code Noir of 1724, the rights of the enslaved were extended when they were granted the authority to act as witnesses.[10] But the enslaved could not bring suit in either civil or criminal cases, although their masters could bring suit for them. Though the Code Noir functioned primarily as a means of controlling enslaved persons, it did allow for them to testify under certain conditions in the same public courts as white men and women, as well as free blacks. As Sophie White has suggested, "these laws gave the enslaved a place in which to speak as well as the space to sketch out, and stretch out, their own narratives."[11] Although it still did not provide equal treatment, the judicial system provided opportunities for enslaved persons to learn the culture of power: the legal system, the hierarchies of colonial authority, and the ways in which race, freedom, and literacy were being constructed in the early modern Atlantic world.[12] This education was invaluable in learning the spaces in which enslaved persons could take advantage of what Michel de Certeau has called the "strategies" of those in power in order to bend them to their own purposes.[13] Enslaved persons used knowledge of this culture of power to seek freedom and "challenge the different variants of racial prejudice and exclusion" that undergirded the emerging constructs of race, ethnicity, and freedom.[14]

Marie Turpin

After several weeks traveling down the Mississippi River from Kaskaskia (just south of present-day St. Louis) in the Upper Louisiana Territory in the latter part of 1747, Marie Turpin, age eighteen, of mixed French-Illinois heritage, arrived in New Orleans, where she entered the Ursuline convent school as a fee-paying boarding student with the desire to become a professed nun. Marie, a devout Catholic and already literate, was older than most of the students, who had entered as boarding students at a much earlier age. Her French father, Louis, recently widowed, was deeply devoted to his daughter and had been reluctant to let her leave home. Given that she had never experienced convent life, he encouraged her to first become a student before making her profession, hopeful that she would perhaps change her mind and return to Kaskaskia. In July of 1749, after fourteen months as a student, however, Marie was as determined as ever to begin her novitiate and formally requested that she be allowed to do so. While her request to begin her novitiate was granted, her designation would not be as a choir nun; instead she would become a converse nun, an inferior status to that of the full position of a choir nun.

These designations were indicative of the Ursulines retention of a social hierarchy transmitted from France in which class—based on wealth, education, and occupation—was the primary factor in the social organization of their religious order. Two converse nuns had traveled to New Orleans from France with the Ursulines in 1727, but both returned to France within six months because of the harsh climate and primitive conditions. At the time Marie arrived at the Ursuline convent, there were eleven choir nuns but no converse nuns. While both converse and choir nuns took vows of poverty, chastity, and obedience, only choir nuns took the fourth vow of education. For all practical purposes, as a converse nun, Marie would be a domestic worker and would not be allowed either to teach or sing in the choir. These restrictions did not dampen her desires to lead a spiritual life, and in November of 1751, after twenty months as a novitiate, she took her final vows, completing her metamorphosis into Sister St. Marthe, the third converse nun in the New Orleans Ursuline convent.

This transformation of Marie from a young French-Illinois girl from the Illinois country in Upper Louisiana, to a French, Catholic nun in New Orleans might sound remarkable and exceptional. And on one level it is. What is remarkable is the agency that Marie exercised in negotiating her Illinois-French, Catholic, literate identity to give it her own meaning. Her desire to be a woman religious was born of a long-entangled history of intracolonial economic, political, social, sexual, and cultural networks among French settlers, enslaved peoples of African descent, and Indigenous peoples that circulated throughout the transatlantic. This transatlantic world was a space of high mobility, with cultural encounters and exchanges between various diasporas resulting in continually shifting identities and new hybrid identities.[15] This was particularly the case in regard to the French transatlantic colonial period in the Americas (Figure 1). Kaskaskia was part of a vast agro-urban zone that extended from the Great Lakes in Canada to the Gulf of Mexico and the Caribbean and from the Alleghenies to the Rocky Mountains. French imperial desires and colonial visions were always mitigated by local intracolonial relations, conditions, and influences. Reading the narrative of Marie's life in and through the circulating, pulsating spaces of the hybrid, fluid, and indeterminate transatlantic world provides ruptures in dominant ideologies that have typically relegated a life like Marie's within the spaces of the binaries of colonizer/colonized.

Marie was not the first Indigenous girl to attend school at the Ursuline convent. In fact, the original calling of the Ursulines as missionaries in the New World was to minister among the Indigenous peoples. Upon arriving in New Orleans, they had welcomed *all* girls and women as students, including Indigenous girls, local French girls, and both enslaved and free African girls. It was social and economic rank, not race or ethnicity, that determined who would be a boarding student, extern (day) student, or afternoon Catechism student. There is evidence (to be discussed in further detail in chapter 2) that when the Ursulines arrived in New Orleans, numerous Indigenous girls and women attended the Catechism classes, and at least two Indigenous girls attended as boarders between 1729 and 1739. At the time Marie entered the boarding school, her niece, Marianne Chauvin (also of French-Illinois descent), was also a boarding student. Marianne was the daughter of Marie's half-sister, Marie Ann Danis, who

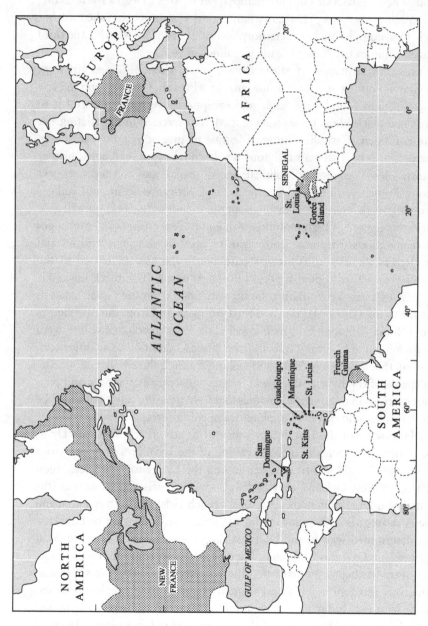

Figure 1. Map of French Colonial Territories in the Americas. Drawn by Mary Lee Eggart.

was from their mother's first marriage to the Frenchman Charles Danis and who had married into the prominent Chauvin family of New Orleans. These interracial, interreligious, and transatlantic familial networks across place, space, and time must have fortified Marie's cosmopolitan worldview, in which she engaged the moral/spiritual authority of the Catholic Church as central to making meaning of her life as a subject of her own making.

Marie was born in Kaskaskia in 1729 to Louis Turpin, a French Canadian who had established himself as one of the wealthiest inhabitants and merchants in the Illinois Country, and Dorothée Mechip8e8a, an Illinois Catholic convert known for her piety.[16] Her parent's twenty-three-year marriage was by all French accounts a successful one, in which they built the largest house in the village, schooled their children in reading and writing, and were devout Catholics. The Upper Louisiana Territory in many aspects epitomized successful French colonial policy, especially in relation to Indigenous conversion and Frenchification. The Illinois nation had been one of the few in the Upper Louisiana region (stretching from current day St. Louis through the Great Lakes to Canada) to become Catholic converts and allies of the French. Colonial policy in New France encouraged intermarriage between French and Indigenous peoples as a means of Frenchifying the Indians, although, as has been recently articulated, it also worked to make Frenchmen Indigenous.[17]

It is not hard to imagine that Marie, as a young girl, saw her world as intimately connected to both her Illinois culture and history, as well as that of the French. The Jesuits who had arrived among the Illinois in the 1670s had developed the mission of the Immaculate Conception in Kaskaskia in 1703 and initially attracted many of the surrounding Illinois due to the potential of increased trade. Given the resistance of the Illinois to learn French, Marie would have sung hymns and heard sermons in the Illinois Anishinabe (Algonquian) language.[18] Being raised in a devout Catholic family, her education was entrusted to Father Antoine-Robert Le Boulanger (also spelled Boullenger), who served as Jesuit curate at Kaskaskia from 1719 to 1744. Father Boulanger saw education as critical to conversion, but more importantly education was the central component in establishing a universal, global church in which all people would be united in a common humanity. He had longed for a group of Ursulines from Quebec or New Orleans, where his sister Sr. Ste. Angelique (Marie-Anne Boulanger) was assistant mother, to open a convent school in Kaskaskia, but this was not to be. It was he who provided Marie with religious instruction and most likely planted the seed regarding her entering the vocation.[19] Marie was the product of a cosmopolitan upbringing in which she could imagine her life through multiple prisms. We can only speculate as to how she understood her decision to become a religious sister in the Ursuline order. We do know, however, that she used the cultural/religious interaction between the Illinois and French to create a new life for herself. Central to that creation was education.

Marie's story provides a window into the complex social networks of the Lower and Upper Mississippi Valley in which the Ursulines were intricately embedded. Marie was situated at the crossroads of this thriving network of economic, social, religious, and cultural exchanges between Indigenous, European, and African actors. For most of the colonial period, Indigenous nations and peoples retained their sovereignty and always outnumbered the French colonists. Far from being "colonized," Indigenous peoples lived in proximity with Europeans, and the groups eventually developed an interdependence through economic, familial, military, and educational relations that defied official imperial policies. As Kathleen Duval has articulated, "In reality, the French had little power, and the Mississippi valley remained largely an Indian-defined and Indian controlled place through the end of the eighteenth century."[20]

Marie's arrival in New Orleans coincided with increased fear among the French settlers due to heightened tensions among the Choctaw, who had long been the most powerful trade partner of the French in the Lower Mississippi Valley network of alliances and a military partner of the French against the British and Chickasaws. The Choctaw Civil War of 1747, which pitted Eastern and Western Choctaw against each other, had recently broken out, with the French and British each supporting one faction of the Choctaw in their quest for more colonial power. Not long after Marie arrived in the spring of 1748, the Western Choctaw warriors, supported by the British, attacked the German settlement outside of New Orleans, killing a settler and taking his daughter, wife, and five enslaved Africans. There is no doubt that these attacks invoked the memories of the Natchez Revolt in 1729 by many of the New Orleans colonists. Thus while networks of relations with Indigenous peoples were critical to the survival of the neglected colony of New Orleans, local French and German settlers also lived with some trepidation given the often tenuous, ever shifting relations with local tribes. Given the colonists' fears of warfare, and the Ursulines' dependence on the colonists for support, it could be speculated that the Ursulines had to weigh carefully their decision to take Marie in as a fully professed choir nun.

Likewise, it is hard to imagine, given that the nuns were barely sustaining themselves at the convent in New Orleans, that Marie chose, and the choice was hers to make, to continue as a nun after her time as a boarding student. It is tempting to read Marie's life and the Ursulines through the lens of the master narrative of colonizer/colonized, master/slave, or Christian/savage. By shifting the view to a long history of education within the transatlantic world, however, new spaces emerge in which both Marie's and the Ursulines choices takes on potential multiple meanings. Marie's entry into the Ursuline convent as a nun and wearing the habit signified her as fully French and educated. This status allowed Marie to construct her subjectivity as a mixed-race woman as fully human through taking up the identity of a Catholic religious woman. And, for the Ursulines, her entrance into the convent as a converse nun signified their ongoing commitment to the universal education of *all* girls and women. Marie's presence at the convent might, in the eyes of the sisters, have provided an avenue for further recruitment of local Indigenous girls, many of whom who had the convent in their line of sight from the market on the levee where they sold their goods. At the same time, the Ursulines had to negotiate the emerging racial, ethnic lines being drawn by local colonial authorities, whose desires were not based on heavenly wealth, but the wealth they hoped to acquire through the exploitation of peoples, land, and goods that fueled an emerging capitalist society. Regardless of the colonial authorities' priorities of economic wealth, which increasingly was based on race-based labor, the Ursulines' integrated, interracial convent school stood as a symbol of an alternative vision of a global, multiethnic conception of humanity that was often in direct opposition to the goals of colonial officials.

Marie took her final vows of obedience, chastity, and poverty in 1751 and served as a nun until her death in 1761. Marie would be the first and only *métissage* (mixed race) nun in the New Orleans convent. Her story sheds light not only on the Ursuline attempts to indoctrinate *all* girls and women in the Catholic faith but illuminates the complex ways in which transatlantic subjectivities shaped constructs of the educated subject that were being negotiated within the nexus of shifting, contradictory, and fluid class, racial, and ethnic identities/markers that circulated within French colonial Louisiana. Marie's story situates the New Orleans Ursulines within a larger circum–Caribbean–Mississippi Valley–Canadian circuit, a necessary move given that much of the scholarship regarding the Ursulines has relegated their impact to New Orleans, without taking into consideration the vastly larger global educational movement in which they emerged as female missionaries. As Marie's story shows, this was not a simple story of colonizer and colonized, but one in which agency and resistance were enacted as part of a complex network of tactics in which education was clearly recognized as central to being acknowledged as fully human. The Ursuline education tradition continues in New Orleans today, and the school is the longest continuously operating educational institution for women in United States history.

Pierre Roup

On November 3, 1827, Pierre Roup (1799–March 19, 1836) and his wife Catherine Coralie (1805–July 2, 1855) welcomed the birth of their son Charles.[21] At the time of his birth, they were residing comfortably in their recently built creole cottage at 1035 Rampart between Ursuline and St. Philip.[22] Pierre, like other free men of color, was an active and successful builder in the well-established Faubourg Tremé, and he owned property both on Esplanade Avenue and North Rampart. Pierre Roup was the son of Pierre Roup Sr. and Hélène Lesseige, both free people of color, who were originally from the French Caribbean colony of Saint Domingue, where they had experienced the tumultuous events of the Haitian revolution.[23] As part of the revolution, Pierre's father had seen the National Assembly of France grant full French citizenship to free men of color in 1791 with the restriction that those persons parents had also both been free. It was resistance to this decree that fueled tensions that ignited the full-blown revolution. While there is no conclusive evidence of when the family arrived in New Orleans, it can be surmised that Pierre and his parents might have been part of the group of refugees who fled Haiti in 1803, fearing that the Napoleonic invasion of 1802, which reinstituted slavery, would threaten their freedom. Seeking to maintain their status as free people, they fled to Santiago, Cuba, a Spanish colony. When France invaded Spain in 1809, however, the Spanish expelled thousands of Haitians, including Pierre and his family, who arrived in New Orleans circa 1809. As a young man, he was part of the largest wave of refugees from Saint Domingue to reach New Orleans, a wave that included 2,731 whites, 3,102 free people of color, and 3,226 enslaved Africans.[24] This large influx of free people of color arrived at a time when territorial Governor Claiborne was increasingly alarmed by the events of the revolution. He feared the internal security of the territory, given the ongoing revolutionary fervor throughout the region among free people of color and the enslaved for full emancipation and citizenship. Claiborne wrote in January, 1810,

> With a population so mixed and becoming more so every day by the press of emigration from Cuba and elsewhere, I must confess I am not without apprehensions that disorders and disturbances may

arise. The free men of color, in and near New Orleans, including those recently arrived from Cuba, capable of bearing arms, cannot be less than 800. Their conduct has hitherto been correct. But in a country like this, where the negro [*sic*] population is so considerable, they should be carefully watched.[25]

In the eyes of many Americans, enslaved and free people of color from Haiti/Saint Domingue were potential carriers of rebellion and discontent. Several rebellions and plots by enslaved Africans could be directly or indirectly traced to revolutionary events in Saint Domingue, including the 1795 Pointe Coupée rebellion in Louisiana, the 1812 Aponte Conspiracy in Spanish Cuba, and the enslaved Gabriel's plot in 1800 in Virginia.

The fear of radicalized elements seeking republican ideals had resulted in legislation in June of 1806 that forbade free men of color above the age of fifteen from Hispaniola and other French islands from settling in the Territory of Orleans. Less than a year later, this legislation was extended to all free persons of color regardless of origin. In 1809, when Pierre Roup, at age ten, most likely arrived, Governor Claiborne had been unable to enforce the ban on the admittance of free of people of color, and by January 1810 the mayor of New Orleans reported to Claiborne that 428 free men of color had taken up residence in the city. Pierre and his family were among these refugees, who now faced the challenge of maintaining their status as free men and obtaining the rights to citizenship.

Pierre and his family, who had experienced various degrees of freedom, and even citizenship, in Saint Domingue, Haiti, and Cuba, were now confronted with the prospect of re-enslavement, given that the territorial legislature had banned the settlement of newly arrived free men of color and called for their enslavement if they did not depart immediately. Although this ban was eventually ignored, the refugees' status was by no means assured. This was especially critical when in 1811, shortly after Pierre and his family arrived, the largest slave revolt in U.S. history took place upriver from New Orleans, apparently through a plot instigated by enslaved people, fugitive maroons, free people of color, and privateers. This revolutionary fervor of free men of color included not only the abolition of slavery but extended to supporting other revolutionary causes including fighting against the British in the War of 1812 and supporting republican revolutions in Mexico. In other words, some free men of color envisioned freedom and citizenship not tied solely to the nation-state, but as a global, universal right. This transatlantic activism was part of what has been termed the "hidden history of the Revolutionary Atlantic."[26]

While we cannot know with certainty the sympathies of Pierre Roup, it is clear that he was part of what Rebecca Scott has called the "regional variant of the long nineteenth century," in which the circulation of revolutionary ideas in the Atlantic and Caribbean circuits were produced and mobilized by free people of color and enslaved Africans to imagine freedom.[27] Young men like Pierre would have undoubtedly been privy to discussions of the male adults in his community who hoped that the young American republic would embody their rhetoric of equal rights by extending citizenship to free men of color who fought in the War of 1812. Jean Dolliole, a fellow builder who had served in the Spanish militia, was part of a larger contingent of free men of color who had extended their military services to the newly arrived American governor Claiborne in 1804 with the expressed confidence that the new government would assure their "personal and political" freedom.[28] When Andrew Jackson called on the free Afro-Creole militia to fight against the British in 1812, he appealed to freemen of color as "sons of freedom" and "fellow citizens."[29] Dolliole and others clearly expected that their participation in defending American national rights would garner their right to full citizenship and equal status. But this was not to be the case. No political recognition was extended to the Afro-Creole community after the Battle of New Orleans.

Pierre Roup, Jean Dolliole, and many of their fellow pioneering entrepreneurs contributed not only to the rapid growth of New Orleans suburbs, but were part of a growing social and political network of free men of color whose interests transcended economic advancement to include the pursuit of political rights including full citizenship in the new American nation. While military service had served as a significant vehicle for advancement to citizenship under both the French and Spanish colonial regimes for free men of color, the new American government, determined to maintain a slave society, sought to impose a dual racial order on the new Louisiana Territory. This new racial order required that the fluid and dynamic racial order that had characterized both French and Spanish Louisiana be harnessed to conform to an ideology of white supremacy.

Having been denied American citizenship, free men of color turned to the development of what Joanna Brooks calls "black counterpublics" as a means of fostering political activities that allowed them to reclaim their political subjectivity, despite their racial subordination, to imagine constructs of freedom and citizenship.[30] One of these avenues was participation in masonic activity in which they could envision their human dignity as part of the ideology of universal brotherhood. While secret and private, Freemasonry ironically provided free people of color a space in which to act as citizens of a brotherhood even though they were denied legal and political rights. Masonic lodges, like Persérvérance Lodge No. 4, were the product of an Atlantic and Caribbean rights consciousness that Rebecca Scott has maintained contributed to a vernacular ideology in which shared public space and public culture were the measure of social equality. Historian Craig Wilder has posited that for Blacks in early national America, Freemasonry was a primary venue through which they not only pursued their collective welfare, but also enacted a claim to public, civil society.[31]

Pierre Roup's story allows us to paint an intimate portrait of the complex layering of educational, political, and social activities of two Masonic lodges (Persérvérance Masonic Lodge No. 4 and Germania Lodge 46) that challenged dominant racial ideologies that restricted citizenship, and instead drew on the concept of universal brotherhood to challenge the very concept of citizenship as the product of nationhood. Pierre's story allows us to examine specifically how the ideal of "universal brotherhood" manifested itself in Masonic lodges as a "counterpublic" pedagogical space in which those excluded from "public" spaces could imagine citizenship. These interracial, multilingual, multinational Franco-Afro-Creole and German fraternal organizations are understood as sites of education that embodied what Stephen Kantrowitz has termed the "bonds of trust and even love across the color line."[32] The creation of a "universal brotherhood" extended political practice beyond "rights" and "citizenship" to envision a diasporic racial collectivity that displaced the nation-state as the site of production of the "educated subject." Alternatively, Freemasonry's concept of "universal brotherhood" allowed members to function as full citizens of an imagined brotherhood in which all men were equal. These imaginary spaces became material realities in the numerous educational and pedagogical practices that took root in the Masonic organizations of antebellum New Orleans.

The stories of Doucet, Madame Hoffman, Marie Turpin, and Pierre Roup provide no unitary historical narrative. They do, however, provide historically rooted *experiences* of how individuals are agents in taking up and reading elements of culture to both reproduce and transform them. This, I would argue, is the practice of history.[33] This agency reveals the many kinds of spaces in which constructs like gender, race, social discontinuities, rights, public spaces, diaspora, and borders were put in continual motion, circulating and reverberating through the Atlantic world. These stories as well as the many others presented in this book destabilize the well-tread narrative of a single system of modernity based on a dualistic structuring of the world into nation-states and European metropoles as colonizers and their colonies as colonized.[34] This supposed power binary has reduced not only the complexity of history but has restricted the spaces through which we can understand how everyday practices of history are engaged as processes to articulate one's humanity.

All three of the vignettes challenge dominant narratives of the history of education in the United States as an exclusive project of Western modernity. Alternatively, what emerges here is a complex picture/mosaic/bricolage of the processes of creolization in which the right to be understood as an educated subject, an emerging marker of one's humanity, was forged in multiple public spaces (apprenticeships, courts, convents, the Catholic Church, and Masonic lodges) of colonial and antebellum Louisiana. These shared spaces allowed for access to the cultures of power as well as exchanges among vastly diverse peoples. At best, the marginalized could create and use these spaces to imagine, negotiate, and appropriate meanings to make them their own. At worst, these spaces were used to exploit, silence, and dehumanize. Situating education within the complex, fluid processes of these transatlantic circulations means there is no grand narrative of education that emanates from Europe transported to the "New World," only local microhistories that emerge in a complex, multilingual, multiracial, transatlantic circuit. Consequently, I do not read backward from the "common school movement," to understand different trajectories of educational history, but alternatively I resist any unitary reading through diffracting the multiple lines of flights produced within the confluences of the transatlantic. This is the messy process of creolization, practicing culture/history/education that this book explores.

Reimagining the Educated Citizen takes the reader to the margins of empire, the transatlantic Gulf South, where Indigenous, French, African, and German colonists, indentured servants, enslaved peoples, free people of color, casket girls, prostitutes, sailors, pirates, and exiles negotiated their everyday lives through and in the spaces of emerging notions of the nation-state and its corollary the educated subject-citizen. By focusing on the Gulf South, this book seeks to disrupt early North American history by putting in motion narratives of education within the circuits of the transatlantic, specifically on the periphery of the Caribbean, to contribute to a broader historiographical trend aimed at decentering North America, and especially the English colonies, as the locus for the production of the educated citizen of the nation state.

This decentering requires a renewed perspective on how the languages, histories, and ideologies of education have contributed to formations of the educated subject as a citizen of the nation as opposed to a citizen without nations. First, the book calls for the development of a more complex "long" history of education, an alternative chronology so to speak, that acknowledges that current histories suffer from a teleological perspective in which the Anglo-Protestant "common school movement" is understood as the origin of public education. The opening vignettes spanning the early French colonial period to antebellum Louisiana suggest a much longer history of education that has traditionally been obscured when narratives of education in the South begin after the Civil War. As the stories of Doucet, Marie, and Pierre illuminate, they sought to create spaces in which their subjectivities acknowledged a common humanity born in shared public spaces. These spaces—courts, convents, churches, and Masonic lodges— while structured by social class, were fluid, hybrid spaces that signified to many a common humanity in which belonging, or citizenship, transgressed the emerging concept of the racialized/gendered nation. The concept of "public rights" as critical to human equality can be traced to the Code Noir of 1685, in which all colonial persons (French, enslaved, free people of color) were to be instructed and baptized in the Catholic religion. The "right" (or imposition) to become Catholic promoted in the Code Noir recognized that Africans were to be understood as members of a common Christian community. In addition, enslaved Africans freed under the 1685 Code Noir were granted full French citizenship rights. In effect, the Code Noir defined slavery as a legal, not a racial condition.[35] Consequently, I bracket this book between 1685 and 1896 (*Plessy vs Ferguson*) to punctuate the long history of the relationship between the constructs of public rights, the educated citizen, and human equality in the Gulf South transatlantic.

Second, by invoking the concept of "creole pedagogies," this book intends to underscore that ideas regarding the educated citizen were not exclusive to the northern United States, but that diverse, multiple, and rhizomatic ideologies regarding what constituted the educated citizen were born in the circulations of the transatlantic, but specifically in the Gulf South given its location at the vibrant nexus of the Mississippi River Valley and the circum-Caribbean. The term "creole" is used here to designate the inventive cultural, social, and political spaces that were born because of the processes of hybridization that shaped the transatlantic world.[36] As all three vignettes suggest, the actors in these stories were always part of the continual movement of ideas, cultures, and peoples in the transatlantic world that contributed to a transatlantic activism that envisioned freedom and human equality for all. The creole pedagogies in which they engaged (engendering the space of the courtroom, creating an interracial convent space, shifting the space of citizenship from the nation to a universal brotherhood) were imaginative interventions in the dominant curriculum of nation building. Doucet, Marie, and Pierre are troubadours or griots whose wandering stories continue to circulate, providing us with alternative subjectivities of what it means to be an educated subject and citizen.

Third, this renewed perspective challenges who counts as actors and what counts as agency in the story of education. How these actors shaped what it meant to be educated and how education functioned as a form of resistance to the inhumanity they experienced is the story this book tells. As Pierre's story suggests, citizenship was imagined without the nation, through the constructs of universal brotherhood, a form of creative resistance to the exclusive, racist nature of the construct of the nation-state. This counterpublic was one of many spaces created in response to exclusionary practices and ideologies that imposed racial and gender constraints on who could or could not count as educated and as a citizen. The counterpublics examined in this book were at times physical spaces (the Masonic lodges, the convent, the Catholic Institute for Indigent Orphans, Bayou Road School, College d'Orleans), but they also include imaginary spaces (literary works including *Les Cenelles*, the fictive letters written by free boys of color at the Catholic Institute, editorials in the *Tribune*, the first black daily newspaper in the United States), and the psychic spaces in which subjectivities that reinforced one's humanity were constructed on a daily basis in the everyday practices of history. These spatial tropes are creole pedagogies born in the fluid circulations of transatlantic flows that have long been in the shadows of history.

Reimagining Narrative

Traditional histories of education in the United States, while giving a brief nod to education in the colonial period, most often begin the story of education with the emergence of public schooling in nineteenth century New England.[37] Ellwood P. Cubberly, in his 1919 *Public Education in the United States*, states in the introduction to this classic that "education was a fruit of the movements which resulted from the Protestant Revolt of the sixteenth century. Back beyond this historic event the beginning student scarcely need go . . . much time, too, need not be spent on our development before the first quarter of the nineteenth century."[38] This narrative arc is deeply troubling in at least two regards. First is the ideological or cultural bias inherent in this arc. Cubberly clearly links the emergence of public education to the Protestant Reformation, in effect marginalizing Catholic, Judaic, and Islamic educational innovations of the Middle Ages and Renaissance. Protestantism, as an ideological framework or, as Emile Durkheim would suggest, as a set of cultural practices, produced education as individual, as rational, and as utilitarian.[39] Max Weber linked these practices as critical to the success of capitalism.[40] Second, this narrative arc, which traces the origins of nineteenth-century public education to Protestant colonial America, more specifically the Puritans, excludes multitudes of people and cultures. In effect, Indigenous, colonial French, and Spanish America (which were Catholic) are relegated to the margins even though they occupied the vast majority of the Americas. Recent trends in Atlantic history have emphasized the need to re-examine the conventional narrative plotting of a linear, diffusionist, Eurocentric development of the Americas to instead acknowledge the complex, creole, and multitudinous nature of the multiracial and multinational exchanges within the Atlantic world.[41] This has not been the case, however, with educational history. In other words, scant scholarship has taken up how the confluence of multiple intersecting cultures, languages, and ethnicities in the transatlantic world propelled human actions and interactions as a result of the desire to be understood as educable and fully human citizens.

I have argued elsewhere that we necessarily limit the vast possibilities for thinking about what it means to be educated when we equate education with schooling.[42] Schooling is an institution, whereas education is a broader conception of how one conceives culture and its aims.[43] Schools are not necessarily educational. Historians of American education overwhelmingly focus on the early nineteenth century, the point when, in the standard view, control of education was wrestled from the family and church by the state through the introduction of public education via schools. These historians implicitly argue that the only educational institutions worth studying are those that the state built and administered. Reducing education to schooling not only eliminates numerous sites of learning such as apprenticeships, Masonic lodges, and catechism classes, but effectively excludes much of the history of the revolutionary transatlantic in which the Atlantic proletariat (enslaved, indentured, Indigenous, free people of color, sailors, prostitutes, among others), what Peter Lindbaugh and Marcus Rediker describe as the "anonymous, nameless," expressed their vision of a common humanity based on an autonomous, democratic, multiracial social order.[44]

In contrast, the Enlightenment discourses of education and the invention of the modern school functioned to sort, classify, rank, and distribute children along a continuum of human worth and value.[45] Schools worked in the service and production of the constructs of emerging nation-states to produce rational, educated citizens of the nation who were defined as white, male, and propertied. Of course, this subjectivity was predicated on its opposite: the irrational, savage, and nonhuman subject. Education, like the constructs of liberty and rights, became racialized and then racist in the modern Atlantic world.[46] Histories of education in the United States continue to privilege the hegemonic Anglo-Protestant narrative of the "common school movement" as critical to the production of the democratic nation-state and its citizens. What is obscured is that the invention of the nation, as well as its corollary "rights" and "common schools," served to exclude all but white male citizens.

To challenge this exclusion, the "anonymous, nameless" required a "reimagined citizen" that transcended nations, borders, and boundaries by rejecting the intertwined constructs of nation, citizenship, race, and education that sought to discipline, divide, and dehumanize. The creole pedagogies described in this book explore alternative, obscured, and forgotten struggles to imagine education outside the construct of the nation-state by imagining education as a universal process of humanization. The suppression of this struggle has contributed to the reduction of education to schooling, an institution that continues today to dehumanize through disciplining bodies and subjectivities in the name of the nation through testing, ranking, sorting, labeling, and grading. Schools do not educate; instead they categorize students based on a hierarchy of value and worth for the purposes of reproducing social, racial, gender, economic, and class inequalities. All in the name of producing democratic citizens.

Schooling is a recent invention. The term was first used in the beginning of the seventeenth century to signal the institutionalization of mass education that emerged in part as a consequence of the Protestant Reformation and Catholic Counter Reformation.[47] The invention of schools has often been lauded as critical to emerging Enlightenment ideologies of reason and democracy because they extended education to a much larger segment of the population and were seen as critical to producing the citizens necessary to imagine nation-states. Scholars like Michel Foucault, however, have also maintained that schools emerged not in the interests of democratizing society but functioned instead as a form of control and surveillance that guaranteed the production of "normality" through stratification, measurement, and eventually testing as a means to determine "normal" development.[48] This "science of education" reduced learning to the mastery of knowledge, increasingly reduced to measurable bits and pieces of information that were served up in a linearized curriculum that allowed for the grading, ranking, and labeling of individual students. In other words, education under the influence of the Protestant Reformation, Enlightenment, and scientific revolution resulted in the production of the "normal" child whose trajectory from birth to adulthood was to move along a steady and stable developmental trajectory of stages.[49]

This fantasy of education as a linear, orderly, measurable gradation of developmental stages of intelligence and skills necessitated the construction of abnormality and irrationality through new categories, including savages, deviants, retards, imbeciles, idiots, morons, disabled, delinquents, dunces, and queers, among others. Schooling became a process of normalization through a technology of discipline, ranking, curriculum, objectives, method, lesson plans, and testing. This technology of education reflected both the emerging scientific view of the world and the language of the Protestant Reformation and marked a radical epistemological shift in which knowledge was no longer understood as critical to meaning making, but as a tool for mastery of the world and its people. Eurocentric, modernist ideologies of education, which for all practical purposes contributed to the dehumanization of vast swaths of people, were critical to the projects of imperialism, colonialism, slavery, capitalism, and the genocide of Indigenous peoples.

The hegemony of these ideologies, however, was not complete. Resistance to the emerging institutions of slavery, schools, the plantation, prisons, and hospitals as forms of dehumanization was ongoing throughout the transatlantic. The circum-Caribbean, a rich site of multiethnic, multilingual, and multiracial creolization in the eighteenth and nineteenth centuries, created fluid, hybrid, dynamic spaces that resulted not only in ongoing revolts, but forms of resistance through language, religion, foodways, and music that sought to validate people's humanity, history, and culture. While imperial designs were envisioned in the metropole, it was the local circumstances and desires embodied in everyday practices that took precedence. The practices I explore in this book are the rogue curriculums and creole pedagogies that have been obscured by the dominant narratives of education as schooling.

A Rogue Curriculum and Creole Pedagogies

I borrow the term *"rogue"* from Shannon Dawdy, an anthropologist who uses the term to describe French New Orleans during the colonial period. She surmises, "The idea of *rogue colonialism* provides a way of thinking about forms of agency beyond and beside those that follow the transcript of domination and resistance between colonizers and colonized. Rogues are improvisers."[50] This improvisation flourished due to the experimental nature of colonial projects in which people like Doucet, Marie Hoffman, Marie Turpin, and Pierre Roup could individually refashion themselves and collectively invent new institutions. I use the terms *rogue curriculum* and *transatlantic, creole pedagogies* to deploy a space that challenges the monumental history of colonialism, the nation, and citizenship and its corollary, education, as fixed, natural categories in our reading of history. A *rogue* curriculum, as a spatial practice, invokes historical imagination as an entangled web of irreducible relations across time and place.

In the space of a "transatlantic, creole pedagogical circuit" I reread the "commons" produced in the common school movement, the normative trope of educational history in the United States. This circuit has traditionally not been represented as a flowing, open system, but historically the exchanges in the Atlantic have been represented by the metaphor of the triangle. A map of the "triangle trade" traditionally shows how traders brought captives from West Africa to sell into slavery in the Caribbean and North America, picked up raw goods—notably sugar—and rum there, and brought this cargo back to Europe, where they exchanged their raw goods for manufactured goods, loading up their ships to trade for more captives, round and round again. What the Africans brought with them is not part of the map. The "triangle trade" is a linear, Euclidian mapping that assumes bound fixed routes that repeat the same pattern over and over again for several hundred years. The space is bound (much like the Africans on the ship) and does not allow for "repercussions": the resonances, the echoes, the reverberations of movement through space. The "triangle trade" as mapped does not make visible the memory, practices, or resistance that Africans, indentured servants, casket girls, French prostitutes, nuns, and Indigenous peoples engaged as they participated actively in the construction of cultural meanings throughout the circum-Caribbean. This active meaning making is the rogue curriculum invented to resist subjectivities of dehumanization.

As Susan Buck-Morss argues in *Hegel, Haiti and Universal History*, the collective experiences of concrete, particular human beings "fall out" of identifying monolithic categories like "nation," "race," and "civilization" (read "educated") that capture only a partial aspect of the subaltern as they travel across cultural boundaries, moving in and out of conceptual frames and in the process creating new ones. This creolization process resulted in new political-cultural subjectivities that rejected the organizing trope of the nation. Pierre Roup, who reimagined citizenship as a universal brotherhood embodied in Masonic lodges, created new creole subjectivities outside the racialized nation-state. These rogue curriculums and creole pedagogies require that we "recognize not only the contingency of historical events, but also the indeterminacy of the historical category by which we grasp them."[51]

Historians like Paul Gilroy have attempted specifically to grasp the diaspora of Africans across the Atlantic, leading him to also argue that identifying concepts like race or nation are inadequate to the task. The spatial signification of the "nation" functions as a "cut," a mechanism for the exclusion of bodies (Black, female, Indigenous, and poor), through which racial and gendered conceptions of nonhuman and noncitizen were produced. This book, much like the work of David Scott, argues that the spatial construct of the nation-state as a political, economic, and cultural unit has functioned as a "conscript of modernity."[52] Reading history through the space of the nation leaves intact a "modernist" teleological historical narrative in which preconstituted subjects, primarily white males, are engaged in "revolutionary" movements of transformation, whose final result is liberation. This reading fulfills fantasies of the normative tropes of resistance, revolution, liberation, and freedom, conscripts of modernity central to and bound by the space of the nation. What remains unseen and unread, however, are the stories like those of Marie, a *métissage* Illinois woman, who actively took up a Catholic, French subjectivity as a nun; this identity not only signified her as "human," but allowed her to disrupt the normative spatial and cultural relations in the convent. These micropractices were the rogue curriculums imagining other pedagogical spaces and places that constituted a common humanity.

This book suggests that the lived experience of the transatlantic, as an expanded social space shared by millions of heterogeneous, previously unconnected people, challenged every existing order of collective meaning of the modernist world. No cultural heritage, whether European or African, could be transported across the Atlantic without undergoing a radical transformation. Porosity characterized the existential boundaries of what was for all participants a fluid, entangled Atlantic world in which "histories were reimagined along human networks that were social, economic, sexual, and political all at once."[53] For these constellations of people, mutual recognition and entanglement was an unprecedented process of creolization that Édouard Glissant describes as an active, affirmative principle of cultural heterogeneity and innovation, a rogue curriculum.[54]

A transatlantic worldview situates history not as occurring within a state or part of a nation, but as a vibrant, rhizomatic, fractal, pulsating, hybrid assemblage of African, Caribbean, European, South American, and North

American intellectual exchanges. In other words, a dynamic system, not a triangle. This reconceptualization challenges the dominant geographic constructs of the nation-state as well as the dominant power relations associated with European colonialism as depicted in the spatial representations of the "triangle trade." An alternative metaphor to the nation-state embraced by Paul Gilroy is the image of "ships in motion across the spaces between Europe, America, Africa, and the Caribbean. The image of the ship—a living, micro-cultural, micro-political system in motion—focuses attention on the circulation of ideas and activists as well as the movement of key cultural and political artifacts."[55] Ships, as lived spaces, need to be thought of as cultural and political units rather than abstract embodiments of the triangular trade. The transatlantic spaces they produced were an entangled crisscrossing of movements and peoples, not commodities. At the heart of this transatlantic approach is the vital claim that the enslaved, indentured servants, sailors, and Indigenous populations "whose labor built much of the Atlantic world were also thinkers and political actors, and that at certain points they transformed and expanded the meaning of democracy."[56] Keenly attuned to shifting political currents, "Atlantic Creoles," during the age of revolution, were adept at interpreting and manipulating political ideologies and events to achieve freedom.[57] Ideas of freedom, democracy, and revolution were not borrowed from Europe and reconceived, but were invented and reinvented within this hybrid, creole crossroads, creating previously unimagined spaces for envisioning what Rebecca Scott has called a cosmopolitan tradition of transatlantic activism.[58]

This activism of educational and political thought reverberated particularly in direct relation to the Haitian Revolution, which in 1804 resulted in the first successful revolt of enslaved Africans to establish an independent black nation that was free of slavery. As Laurent DuBois has argued, the Haitian Revolution was more radically egalitarian than either the American or French Revolution:

> By creating a society in which all people, of all colors, were granted freedom and citizenship, the Haitian Revolution forever transformed the world. It was a central part of the destruction of slavery in the Americas, and therefore a crucial moment in the history of democracy, one that laid the foundation for the continuous struggles for human rights everywhere. In this sense we are all descendants of the Haitian Revolution, and responsible to these ancestors.[59]

The potential threat to white superiority sent shock waves through the United States that are still reverberating today. The possibility of black equality envisioned in the Haitian Revolution would threaten not only the institution of slavery, but the very construct of the nation based on race. This book takes the bold step of situating the Haitian Revolution within a larger transatlantic context as central to the racialization of American public education. I argue that it was the threat and fear of Black equality and citizenship that necessitated the production of the "white," male citizen through the common school movement.

C. L. R. James noted in his seminal work *The Black Jacobins* that the Haitian Revolution "would alter the fate of millions of men and shift the economic currents of three continents."[60] I maintain that the resonances and reverberations of the Haitian Revolution continue to circulate today in our racialized public schools. The Haitian Revolution reverberated throughout the Americas because the revolt against slavery was as significant as the "revolt" against the construct of the nation. That the nation has, in fact, become the dominant political community in modernity is beyond doubt. As Benedict Anderson reminds us in *Imagined Communities*, "the near-pathological character of nationalism, [has] its roots in fear and hatred of the Other, and in its affinities with racism."[61] To loosen the bonds or shackles of "slavery" was tantamount to removing the borders or boundaries of the nation. Blacks would no longer be slaves and noncitizens but would be "citizens" of the world. Haiti's revolution challenged the spaces and borders central to the construct of "citizen," what William Pinar has called the psychic violence of "civic virtue" embedded in notions of the nation and citizenship, by subverting the boundaries of citizenship as constituting whiteness.[62]

The concepts of the nation, nationality, and nationalism exist as profoundly powerful cultural artifacts. As Benedict Anderson has suggested, to understand the creation of these artifacts "we need to consider carefully how they have come into historical being, in what ways their meanings have changed over time, and why, today, they command such profound emotional legitimacy."[63] The radical displacement of the constructs of "race," "nation," and "citizen" by the Haitian Revolution created reverberations throughout the transatlantic. Situating colonial and antebellum Louisiana within the fluid, porous confluence of the transatlantic world, in which normative boundaries of space and place no longer make sense, provides ruptures within to reimagine Louisiana's history, as well as the grand narrative of American public education. This book is an "imaginative effort" in which I refuse the nation as the singular construct for imagining the normative tropes of modernist education. Alternatively, I envision a transatlantic entanglement whose processes of creolization are so intertwined that the nation becomes impossible to think. This book asks the reader to suspend dominant constructs of the nation, citizenship, and education as fixed, absolute categories that function as well-worn tracks in the narratives of history. Suspending these constructs allows us to envision the fluid, complex, and contradictory ways in which people at the street level carved out spaces in which they could embody their full humanity through reimagining the educated citizen.

Practicing History: Walking the Streets

> Every story [history] is a travel story–a spatial practice. . . . stories organize places through the displacements they "describe." . . . In short, *space is a practiced place.*
>
> Michel de Certeau, *The Practice of Everyday Life*, 116–17

My reading of history is situated in illuminating the micropractices of "everyday life," the social relations—the actual day-to-day encounters, practices, shared spaces and places, exchanges, and experiences—of the material world. De Certeau, in *The Practice of Everyday Life*, suggests that the street geometrically defined by urban planning is transformed into a space by walkers. These walkers make use of spaces that cannot be seen on a map. Their story begins on the ground level, with footsteps that are a spatial practice that determine the conditions of social life. According to de Certeau, "their swarming mass is an innumerable collection of singularities. Their intertwined paths give shape to spaces. They weave places together . . . they spatialize."[64] These practitioners live "down below," creating "pedestrian speech acts" that cannot be reduced to a graphic trail but instead constitute a "wandering of the semantic."[65] They lead us to a theory of everyday practices, of lived space. De Certeau further elaborates that "the everyday has a certain strangeness that does not surface, or whose surface is only its upper limit, outlining itself against the visible."[66] Normative modernist histories provide us with prefabricated spaces that adhere to a logic of representation. History's appearance of unity, of coherence, of order is predicated not on any direct correspondence to a reality but on the suppression of contradictory stories, those that do not comfortably fit into the geometrical spaces of histories visual, panoptic, or theoretical constructions. This suppression, this silencing, is what makes the myth of a *universal* history as we know it possible.

Like de Certeau, my practicing of history is concerned with the everyday, how subjectivities are enacted through the deployment of available, circulating, contradictory meanings. Meaning here operates not on the level of code or structure, but on that of the acts of ordinary language use, wanderings, doings, makings that construct the world through continual and practical creation and recreation over time. If we liken these pedestrian acts to spatial practices, then these wanderers walk not through time, but in indirect or errant trajectories obeying their own logic.[67] This logic is one that suspends linearity, causality, change, authorial intent, stability of meaning, human agency, and social determination as central to shaping history. And while the poststructural turn in history challenged many of these constructs by situating them in language, I maintain that it is time, place, and space that have remained constant and underanalyzed.[68]

For Henri Lefebvre, history is lived through *spatial codes* or systems of space, that are produced through relationships and interactions as opposed to structures. History has traditionally been conceptualized within *absolute* space, understood as a geometrical concept, simply that of an empty area. The work of Lefebvre in *The Production of Space* is particularly insightful in rendering space not a mathematical concept, but a "social space."[69] According to Lefebvre, "physical space has no 'reality' without the energy that is deployed within it."[70] Rejecting a simple expanding universe, Lefebvre proposes a much more complex theory in which energy travels in every direction. From this view, "a single centre of the universe, whether, original or final, is inconceivable. Energy-space-time condenses at an indefinite number of points (local space-times)."[71] This complexity of space makes historical *representation* impossible. In other words, there can be no unitary historical narrative when space is always on the move, multidimensional, shifting. History cannot be captured.

Alternatively, I understand history as a relational space or matrix in which we are suspended in a web of relationships so interconnected that the boundaries, categories, and monuments of modernism are made unintelligible. As I wrote this book, this relational history required me to read and interpret history through space and time to look for the connections and ruptures that have made a difference as opposed to reading for "progress." I looked for spatial shifts that imploded fixed boundaries of identity, nation, citizenship, freedom, and what it means to be educated and fully human. These slippages represent not another, different, subaltern truth, but instead function to suspend history as a relational web so entangled that it cannot be untethered. I have come to reimagine history as multidimensional, unknowable, incoherent, contradictory, and always in relationship. *Relational* space-time "is representative of the past, present and future swirling through and across space; rather than referring to what exists at a single point in time, it requires an aesthetic reading of history where mathematics, poetry and music converge if not merge."[72] To visualize history as space, not an "object" of study, or as a reference for some supposed reality, is to embrace history as a practice.

My practicing of history throughout the ten years of this project have thus been shaped by several fundamental beliefs. First, my goal as a historian is not representation. Instead, my work as a historian is an ethical responsibility to make visible under what conditions certain subjectivities are made possible and others impossible. As I have discussed above, this requires suspending the tropes of monumental narratives. In the case of this book, that required focusing not only on ordinary people but recognizing how space has been crucial to shaping history. For example, the space of colonial history has focused for a long time on the external linkages of colonies with their home countries to the neglect of internal relationships forged by the inhabitants. Yet the outcomes of colonization depended as much on how colonial and native inhabitants mapped their own day-to-day lives as upon the policies designed by official and commercial interests.

Second, remembering and writing about the lives of the dead is an ethical act. History has traditionally relied on the "archives" to portray an accurate picture of the actors of history. We cannot pretend, however, that the archive is impartial. Various perspectives and motives have shaped what is and what is not available as historical evidence. As Shirley Thompson reminds us, the archive is not a shrine and "we must not pretend that the archive is impartial."[73] Clearly, there are limitations of historical method. I have drawn on numerous archival records throughout my research, but I approach them not as holding nuggets of truth, but as another potential subjectivity. The archives are living, breathing spaces. They are not necessarily meant to be mined for facts but are spaces in which to understand how the narratives of some displace others. Archival work requires not so much reading, but listening to the echoes, reverberations of those who are not present.

Third, when history is understood as an ethical, relational practice, it resituates us across space and time to the entangled, multiple, rhizomatic threads of interconnectivity/intrarelationality that remind us of our common humanity. The power of history as a relational practice (as opposed to representation) is the force that must reorganize our way of being in the world and our relations to those past, present, and future. Resituating American educational history within the complex, circulating, vibrant nexus of the transatlantic world is a long overdue project given the intellectual, geographic, and cultural provincialism of the history of education. Practicing the history of education requires a deployment of history that

(a) engages history as a spatial practice no longer bound by the nation state, (b) complicates the hegemonic narrative of an Anglo-American history in which educational theories are rooted in reformed Protestantism and classical republicanism, (c) provides a genealogy of what makes possible and intelligible the constructs of modern schooling, and (d) historicizes the spatial, cultural, social, and religious discourses that have made "real" constructs of the educated citizen, public schooling and a technocratic curriculum. Each of the chapters, while situated within a larger macrohistory, is anchored by several microhistories of individuals who illuminate the day-to-day strategies of lived experience.

Practicing history as I wrote this book challenged me as a historian, educational/curriculum theorist/philosopher, and gender studies scholar to traverse across various and disparate geographies. While some might see this diffusion as a scholarly weakness, I believe that the complicated conversations between these fields allowed for a porosity and permeability in which *space* was created in which new relationships emerged. As Michel-Rolph Trouillot argues, "Historical representations—be they books, commercial exhibits or public commemorations—cannot be conceived only as vehicles for the transmission of knowledge. They must establish some relation to that knowledge."[74] Knowledge transmission as the purpose of history reduces narrative to a technocratic endeavor, one devoid of any ethical or relational dimensions.

In other words, history is not an object or a subject but rather an inter-relationship between "representational spaces and representations of space" and "their links to social practices."[75] For Marie Turpin the "convent" is a representational space in which women religious are perceived in specific ways given the social, gendered, religious, political, and racialized constructs in which that space was constructed. When Marie enters that space, her perception of herself as an Illinois woman who is also a French woman religious is lived in ways that radically alter the spaces of what it means to be French, Illinois, a religious sister, and educated. Consequently, my historiography is always in motion seeking out the ways in which historical agents navigate between, through, and in perceived, conceived, and lived space. To attempt to understand this ongoing process required me to envision a spatial/conceptual constellation much like a labyrinth in which past, present, and future were intertwined and where beginning and endings have no clear boundaries, resulting in a suspended state of the absent present in which there is never a stable position on which to perch.

This leveling of time shifted the ways I approached the sources on which I drew to understand the narratives of specific individuals. The past does not exist independently from the present, "the past is the past because there is a present, just as I can point to something *over there* only because I am *here*."[76] It was incumbent on me to both understand the ways in which the narratives I was constructing were inscribed in sources (archives, buildings, material objects) that already embodied silences, but also how my positionality had to take account of shifting meanings over time. This heterotemporal condition, "comprised of multiple pasts, presents and futures," required that I not privilege any one source.[77] While traces of past lives surface in the archives, they cannot be exhumed to tell history; instead they can prompt us to envision new relationships in the assemblage that is history. Instead, I travel through libraries, primary sources, secondary sources, archives, streets, museums, convents, archeological sites, fields, town squares, houses, and gardens with the expectation that each has a story to tell, a reverberating echo waiting to be heard. These relationships were often organic, unpredictable, and precarious. My readings of both the archives and secondary sources, across a range of academic fields, have been approached from an interdisciplinary perspective in which I seek to put into conversation a cacophony of voices.

In the pages that follow my intent is to introduce in each chapter several microhistories that provide a ground-level view of a specific moment in history. The microhistories I engage are not limited to individuals, but also include communities, events, and texts. Microhistories provide spaces to illuminate the dominant discourses made available to individuals, communities, or texts from which they make meaning. The actors in this book are understood as active meaning makers in the production of history. Given the dramatic and traumatic transatlantic cultural exchanges in which Indigenous, African, and European peoples were intertwined, these collisions were profound pedagogical moments. Pedagogy is a practice of learning. Learning to communicate, trade, go to war, navigate new environments, worship, and eat all resulted in a major restructuring of each culture, a process of creolization, that resulted in "distinct new world practices."[78] These are new creations resulting from "the encounter, the interference, the shock, the harmonies and the disharmonies among cultures."[79] And while creole culture and the processes of creolization have been detailed in the areas of language, material culture, religion, music, medical practices, and cuisine, education has been neglected. And yet, in the context of the vibrant transatlantic, making sense of the world and one's place in it was a continual process of creolization, in other words learning through creative invention and experimentation.

Creolization was often the product of resistance to ways of being and thinking that dehumanized those within the complex power dynamics of colonialism. The creole pedagogies that are examined in the following chapters suggest the ways in which not only education as a formal structure were reinvented, but how alternative spaces were created to signify who could be educated and the meanings they gave to education. In chapter 1, the first encounters between Indigenous peoples and Jesuit and Ursuline missionaries are viewed through a creole pedagogy of transcultural translation in which cross-cultural understanding was a complex multidimensional process that inevitably resulted in the transformation of all involved. Chapter 2 examines the production of the transatlantic educated subject in the Ursuline convent in New Orleans as a transgressive creole pedagogy of disorder in which the spatial constructs of the convent between 1736 and 1752 illuminate the complex networks of relationships among French (both teachers and students), African (enslaved and free students), and Indigenous peoples (students and choir nun) in which an Ursuline, female-centered spirituality pushed the limits of colonial and ecclesiastical policies. The silencing of the role of the Haitian Revolution in shaping American education as central to the production of the "white citizen" through the common school movement is the subject of chapter 3, which chronicles the creole pedagogy of counterpublic spaces that emerged among Afro-Creoles, French emigres, and enslaved Africans in New Orleans to contest the racialization of education. Chapter 4 highlights how a creole pedagogy of imagination was engaged by Afro-Creoles and other disenfranchised groups in schools and Masonic lodges to envision freedom in the increasingly repressive years leading up to the Civil War. Lastly, in chapter 5 the liminal spaces created by two texts, the *Tribune* and *Crusader*, are explored as a creole pedagogy engaged by an interracial coalition of radical activists who sought full equality in the era of Jim Crow.

I conclude this book by arguing that scholars need to reconsider the national narratives of American educational history that have been rooted in a northern, Anglo-Protestant, common school narrative of education and its dominance in perpetuating a singular curricular storyline. Louisiana's educational history contests not only the hegemony of the "common school" movement as the origins of "public" education, but it situates Louisiana as part of the transatlantic world that produced counterenlightenment ideologies of citizenship not bounded by the nation, race, or the law, but in a philosophy of equal rights that is produced in public spaces. Given the mounting challenges inherent in neoliberal, free market ideologies to constructs of the "public," the narratives in this book provide a timely intervention against the landscape of a seamless story of the Enlightenment's legacy concerning the nation, education, and citizenship in America, American history, and society.

ONE

Transatlantic Educational Spaces

Remapping the Word and the World

It is an unworthy thing to use one's Christian brother as a slave.

—Hyacinthe de Caen, Capuchin Missionary, 1640[1]

Fugitive slaves absent for a month should have their ears cut off
and be branded. For another month their hamstring would be
cut and they would be branded again. A third time they would be
executed.

Article 38 of the Code Noir, 1685

Article 38 of the French Code Noir makes abundantly clear that the
enslaved often resisted slavery by running away. And if they did not succeed in becoming free, they tried again and again, often choosing to die
rather than be re-enslaved. Physical mutilation of the slave body was a
visual reminder to other enslaved persons of the punishment for seeking
freedom. The Code Noir of 1685, the first French legal document to regulate slavery, reveals the tension between the mercantile interests of France's
colonial transatlantic empire, whose wealth increasingly depended on slave
labor, and the antislavery stance of many early French Catholic missionaries.[2] Hyacinthe de Caen represented a long line of Capuchin missionaries
who had denounced the enslavement of Africans.[3] The first Christianized
kingdom in Africa, the Kongo in 1506, became the site of fierce resistance
to slavery by the Capuchins in the 1640s.[4] The Capuchins demanded the
end of the slave trade, the freeing of all enslaved Africans, and the payment
of reparations, despite the argument advocated by colonial slave masters
that slavery ensured the salvation of Africans.[5]

Antislavery Catholic missionaries were eventually unsuccessful in abolishing slavery. By the 1640s, when the teaching orders of the Jesuits, and then the Ursulines in 1682, arrived in the French colonies of Martinique and Guadeloupe, state and colonial policies had shifted away from a focus on the conversion of Indigenous peoples and toward mercantile interests that relied on the slave trade as the crucial underpinning of the sugar plantation economy in the transatlantic market.[6] For the French crown, these islands served one purpose: to develop profitable plantations, based on enslaved labor, whose revenues would fill their coffers.[7] Once trading companies no longer provided funds, the Jesuits also acquired plantations using the labor of enslaved Africans to finance self-sufficient missions.[8] The economic and political growth of the Caribbean colonies eventually required an overall reorganization of French administration in order to centralize and unify a transatlantic France. It was in this context that the Code Noir of 1685 was issued by the Crown, drawing on well-established precedents in France regulating vagabonds, beggars, apprentices, children, and wives.[9]

Many French citizens condemned the Code Noir in strong terms. The practice of slavery was a significant departure from sixteenth- and early seventeenth-century French legal and philosophical principles. French thinkers, in this period, including Voltaire, considered slavery both a legal and moral aberration. In France, slavery was unlawful, and the French adopted the free-soil principle, which declared that any enslaved person who stepped on French soil was free. Since the early sixteenth century, Catholic theologians and missionaries on both sides of the Atlantic had been debating the compatibility of evangelization and enslavement of both Africans and Indigenous peoples in the Americas and the Caribbean. Hyacinthe de Caen opposed slavery by arguing that baptism conferred freedom to the Africans who had been forcibly transported to the French colonies. By the late seventeenth century, however, both French colonial authorities and the Catholic Church rationalized the enslavement of Africans by arguing that it was the primary vehicle for the conversion of pagans. The brutality of slavery, the "sacrifice of the body," was justified because it resulted in the saving of souls. By assimilating the enslaved into the Catholic community, the code also first and foremost sought to ensure social and political stability.[10] The irreconcilable constructs of chattel slavery and Christianity were nowhere more apparent than in the Code Noir of 1685.

The profound irony is that despite the many articles that spelled out the brutal enforcement of slavery through inhumane torture, punishment, and regulation, the Code Noir also guaranteed certain rights to enslaved peoples. The articles of the code addressed five aspects of slavery: religion, sexual relations and marriage, prohibitions, punishments, and freedom. The first eight articles are concerned with upholding the Roman Catholic Church as the only religion, including "expulsion of Jews from the colony" (Article I) and allowing "exercise of the Roman Catholic creed only" (Article III). Education was critical to this goal, and Article II "[m]akes it imperative on masters to impart religious instruction to their slaves." There is no doubt that religion in the Code Noir functioned as a strategy of control and assimilation through which the Crown attempted to incorporate enslaved people into the colonial social order by establishing slavery as a Christian institution. At the same time, because the enslaved were understood as Christian subjects, as moral/spiritual beings, they were invested with certain *rights*, including religious *instruction*, as well as participation in all the *public* sacraments of the Church (baptism, confirmation, marriage). According to the code, slave marriages were recognized by the Church, enslaved children were baptized in the Church, enslaved families were not to be separated through sale, and baptized slaves were to be buried in holy ground in cemeteries.

The Catholic education mandated in the Code Noir functioned to provide *public* spaces (churches, catechism classes, schools) in which enslaved persons, whether African or Indigenous, shared a communal setting that signified all as spiritual equals. In other words, the Code Noir provided access to one of the most important forms of cultural capital in the early French modern era: the public spaces of the universal, apostolic, Roman Catholic faith. The construct of the "public sphere" as foundational to the democratic nation-state was still in its infancy.[11] And while these ideas are often credited to European Enlightenment intellectuals, I maintain that it was in the pedagogical circuits of the transatlantic that the entangled notions of public rights, freedom, education, and eventually citizenship were continually being mapped and remapped by colonial officials, Indigenous peoples, enslaved Africans, Catholic missionaries, and colonists of all backgrounds.[12]

By moving beyond the narrow parameters of the European nation-state, we can see how the social and spatial geography of these public spaces of education created avenues for the enslaved and Indigenous peoples to assert their agency and humanity through a variety of tactics of resistance and accommodation. These public spaces provided ways to adapt and appropriate religious/spiritual beliefs to make them their own and, in some cases, to use the colonizers' religion as a cover for retaining their own practices and beliefs. Tracing these ruptures reorients the spatial topography of missionary efforts from conversion, a one-way pedagogy, to a creole pedagogy of transcultural translation that shifts our focus to understanding how *all* people embedded in colonial relations navigated their daily lives. Translation, as Tracy Neal Leavelle reminds us, involves active mediation between cultures and negotiations over meaning resulting in "diverse definitions and contrasting cultural expressions" intersecting to "produce novel interpretations and new meaning over time."[13] The convergence of the Jesuits, Ursuline, African, and Indigenous peoples, while often brutal, violent, and oppressive, also led to "new opportunities, new possibilities, and new ways of doing things for both Natives and newcomers."[14]

The missionary activity of the Jesuits and Ursulines in French colonial America was vastly diverse, ranging from missionary schools and plantations in the Caribbean and Gulf Coast to missionary communities in the Illinois territory and New France (Canada). But their vision of a global spiritual universalism united them in an educational endeavor that challenged the constructs of the emerging nation-state, often putting them in direct conflict with colonial authorities. The tensions between the French imperial plans of nation building and Catholic universalism signify part of a much larger cultural shift that emerged in Enlightenment political thought. Whereas the Catholic Church saw global expansion as part of their effort to create a universal system of education based in a collective, universal brotherhood, European states saw imperialism as central to bolstering the construct of the nation in which secularized notions of rights and citizenship guaranteed the individual. The eventual domination of secular nationalism and citizenship, as opposed to the Catholic notion of universal education, would profoundly shape constructions of American education.

The Code Noir of 1685 is the starting point for this book precisely because it embodies the complex tensions between the emerging social construction of slavery as a racial construct and the introduction of the first European attempt at mandated universal education based in the concepts of rights.[15] While the code was drafted by French legal scholars who drew on Roman jurisprudence, it was also influenced by Caribbean jurisprudence, which was shaped by emerging racial hierarchies seen as necessary to a plantation economy. Because Roman law was race blind, it has been argued that the Code Noir of 1685 understood slavery as a legal, not a racial, condition.[16] However, the code marks the transition from a premodern understanding of slavery as a legal institution to the emergence of a modernist understanding in which slavery is grounded in race and becomes the basis for understanding humanity along a natural hierarchy of value and worth, a perspective that would eventually be reproduced in modern American schooling through the common school movement. The code deprived enslaved people of any legal or political existence, but the instruction mandated by the Code Noir to enslaved Africans by the Catholic Church did signify them as spiritual and moral beings having certain rights. While the work of the Jesuits and Ursulines as missionaries in the seventeenth century among Indigenous and enslaved Africans was clearly situated within a colonial logic of assimilation, their mission of global, universal education simultaneously produced a counterdiscourse to dominant constructs of the enslaved and Native peoples as not fully human or educable.

This chapter looks at four transatlantic spaces in which a creole pedagogy of transcultural translation was at work: early Jesuit missionary activity in Canada, the missionary work of Marie de l'Incarnation who founded the Ursuline convent and school in Quebec in 1639, the Illinois mission at Kaskaskia from which Marie Turpin journeyed to New Orleans, and finally the missionary work of Father Paul Du Ru, the first Jesuit missionary in Louisiana in 1700. Their stories provide insight not only into the role that a transcultural translation pedagogy played in the utopian ideal of a universal Catholic Church through education, but they illuminate the complex ways in which emerging racial, gender, and ethnic subjectivities and caste systems were negotiated in the dynamic spaces of the transatlantic and the role that education played in both reifying and contesting these.[17] While not often understood as such, the Jesuit and Ursuline educational missions were ideally an attempt at establishing a global, universal form of education that would unite all people in a common humanity through the Catholic Church. The four spaces presented below do not seek to be representative of all missionary experiences across French colonial America; instead they illuminate specific microhistories of educational practices. Before moving onto these four transatlantic spaces, I briefly situate them within the larger contexts of the global educational reform movement of the Jesuit and Ursuline orders.

Global Educational Reform: The Teaching Orders of the Jesuits and Ursulines

The obligation to provide Catholic education to all who lived in the French empire, reinforced by the 1685 Code Noir, required a cadre of missionaries who could develop churches and schools, administer them, teach, and eventually provide teacher education. Ursuline and Jesuit missionaries took up this project. While Christians had been missionaries since the first Apostles of Jesus, the vehicle for the conversion of early Christians and pagan Romans was through oral traditions and transforming pagan rituals and beliefs to fit into early Christian belief systems. By the sixteenth century, the printing press, the Protestant Reformation, the Renaissance, the scientific revolution, and the gradual shift from an oral to a written culture brought about profound changes in concepts of missionary work through education.

At the center of the Protestant Reformation (1517–1648) was the notion of individual salvation through personal understanding of the Bible. Religious education prior to the Reformation had been oral. The focus on the word required access to literacy, which required the standardization of religious education for children. While medieval catechisms existed, it was Protestant reformers like Luther and Calvin who transformed the catechism into an inexpensive and portable text that was easy to teach and read.[18] Teaching catechism became tied to first communion by making memorization of the text a prerequisite. The Catholic Church quickly saw the necessity and advantages of adopting this same method, and in 1550 the first Catholic catechism was published. The French Jesuit Edmund Auger published the most popular catechism in 1563, which differed significantly from the Protestant catechism because two-thirds of it dealt with the sacraments. The sacraments, illuminated through ritual, were critical to shaping lifelong Catholic practices. For the Jesuits, morality could not be limited to the "word," but was embodied in ritual, a form of knowing that exceeded language.

It was the Jesuits, founded by Ignatius Loyola in 1540, who saw conversion as the primary mission of education, given the massive upheavals that were shaking the foundation of the Catholic Church. Not only was Protestantism challenging the hegemony of the Catholic Church, but the medieval world's focus on religion and the church as the ultimate answer to humanity's problems was being replaced by a vision that put man at the center of the world. For the Jesuits, who saw this as a struggle between good and evil, education became their sword, and the *world* was their classroom.[19] St. Ignatius established the first Jesuit school, "School of Grammar, Humanity, and Christian Doctrine, Free" in 1551, and within two years had 250 alumni. By the mid-seventeenth century, the Jesuits were running 444 schools across the globe. Young men entering the priesthood increasingly required an educational background, necessitating a standard plan for the society's educational institutions. In the 1580s, an initiative was undertaken to develop a document that would outline the educational program and philosophy of the Jesuits to be used in the seminary. In 1599, after several drafts and feedback from Jesuit teachers, the Ratio Studiorum, the official document for the Jesuit system of humanist education, was created.

The Ratio outlines the entire program of study with three purposes: teaching the humanities and arts, intertwining religious with secular studies, and forming the religious and moral character of students.[20] The Jesuits were the first to apply the ideals of a humanist education in a practical and systematic way. Renaissance humanism had focused on the study of literature dealing with what it means to be a human being.[21] That literature consisted of the Greek and especially Latin works of poetry, oratory, drama, and history that, when properly taught, were believed to develop an upright, articulate, and socially committed person. Their curriculum was designed specifically to help students navigate a complicated era that was shifting from a God-centered universe to a human-centered one. In implementing this vision, the Jesuits created the largest and most unified network of secondary schools that Europe had ever seen. In their desire to create a universal church, their schools were open to both clerical and lay students from any economic or social background. When the order was suppressed in 1773, the Jesuits had opened more than eight hundred schools in Europe and Latin America.

In 1685, the same year as the Code Noir, the Jesuits opened the first-ever teacher education institution in Reims, France. The notion that teachers had to be educated to teach was radical and marked a pedagogical shift from an understanding of humanist teaching as dialogue—a relational encounter or process—to understanding teaching as instruction, or knowledge transmission, a more technocratic or utilitarian view of education. The Jesuits sought a middle ground between their spiritual worldview and one that valued the vast explosion of scientific knowledge of the world.

In this effort, they were joined by the Ursulines, whose educational system for girls was influenced by the Jesuit system. The first Ursuline order, founded in Italy in 1532 by St. Angela Merici, marked a *revolution* in female religious life.[22] Previously, female orders had been cloistered, where they engaged in a single activity: prayer. Merici's Ursulines initially lived in the outside world and engaged in the *public* activity of teaching girls. They justified this radical departure from gender norms by arguing that Mary had been the first teacher of Jesus. Because mothers gave children their first religious training, it was only "natural" that young girls who were to become mothers needed to be educated in church doctrine. By 1598, after forty years of religious warfare, ardent French Catholics were committed to returning France to Catholicism, and the church welcomed a cadre of female teachers to further that goal. The convergence of female agency, the veneration of Mary, and the church's need for a massive missionary campaign provided a rationale for women to enter the public sphere of teaching. Small groups of pious laywomen in France began to offer instruction in Catholic doctrine, and over time many became Ursulines. By 1610, there were twenty-nine Ursuline communities in France. By 1700, there were more than three hundred communities, and 10 percent of all French women lived as avowed religious.[23]

Ursuline pedagogy distinguished itself radically from emerging concepts of modernist education that focused on knowledge transmission and that understood the student as an empty vessel. Ursuline education saw education not as "filling up" the child with knowledge, but as "drawing out" the unique dispositions of each child.[24] Ursuline understandings of the child were predicated on the belief that each child was already fully developed. In other words, children are not in need of being formed, they have already been fully constituted by God. There was nothing to put into the child that was not already potentially there. Teachers were not responsible for "teaching" children. Instead, they were to provide the unconditional love and nurturing that would allow for a child's potential to flourish. For the Ursulines, a student's potential developed *not* as the result of proper instructional method, but as the result of immersion in a community of faith that strove to embody divine love. This pedagogical vision was laid out in the *Règlements des religieuses Ursulines de la Congrégation de Paris* in 1705, in which students' individuality was predicated not on producing the autonomous individual subject through discipline, but on their immersion within a Catholic community.

Consequently, by the mid-seventeenth century, the Ursulines, like the Jesuits, were skeptical of Cartesian rationality, given that it was predicated on doubt, reason, and (most disturbing to them) the concept of the autonomous individual. The rejection of aspects of Cartesian thought by the Jesuits, as well as by the Ursulines, signified a profoundly radical departure from emerging modernist and, for the most part, Protestant conceptions of knowledge, curriculum, and schooling. As Michel Foucault has postulated, the shift to disciplinary power from sovereign power resulted in the emergence of the concept of the "individual" subject produced through the production of "docile bodies" in not only schools, but also hospitals, prisons, and mental institutions.[25] In particular, education shifted from dialogue between teachers side by side with students, to education in schools that sought to organize time and space as a disciplinary apparatus that would guarantee the construction of subjectivity as individual.

This "discovery" of "the geneses of individuals" was, according to Foucault, "correlative with the new techniques of power, and more specifically, with a new way of administering time and making it useful, by segmentation, seriation, synthesis and totalization."[26] Schools became disciplinary machines that were a mechanism for training through teaching, acquisition of knowledge through pedagogical activity, and reciprocal, hierarchized observation.[27] The invention of the "individual" through disciplinary institutions comes about through comparing (grades), differentiating (classes), imposing hierarchies (ranking), homogenizing (grade levels), and exclusion ("dropouts"); in short, it normalizes. This normalizing of a hierarchy of human worth and value through the production of the individual would become central to a caste system focused on constructing the "individual" subject of the nation through disciplinary power. This was indeed in stark contrast to the Jesuit and Ursuline production of the "universal" subject through the Catholic doctrine of a transcultural common humanity embodied in shared religious rituals.

This is to say that while the effects of power might be different, *all* education and knowledge is a form of power and control. For the Ursulines and Jesuits, this control was not about constructing the individual (this had already been done by God) but was directed to shaping a community that conformed to the "authority" of Catholic universalism, a shared set of cultural beliefs that were enacted *not* through "knowledge" or "disciplines," but through communal rituals and rites of passage. Thus while there was clearly the concept of an individual for the Ursulines and Jesuits, this was not the autonomous, rational individual that was emerging as the Enlightenment citizen of the modernist nation-state. The individual embedded in Ursuline and Jesuit thought and philosophy was, in fact, *not* independent, but existed only in relation to the collective, communal body of the church. Ursuline and Jesuit philosophy understood being and knowing as interrelated, not as separate entities. Consequently, they stood in direct opposition to modernist notions of education as an epistemological project that privileged "knowledge" instead of "love" as the purpose of education.

The Jesuits and Ursulines played not only a central role in the educational developments of early modern Europe, but were critical to its scholarly, scientific, educational, and political life.[28] This was in part due to the far-reaching Jesuit missionary tradition of *studying* local customs and languages, which Charlotte de Castelnau-l'Estoile has termed "Jesuit anthropology."[29] This contrasts with identifying them as "ethnographers" or "natural historians," given that the Jesuits would not have seen themselves as anthropologists or any kind of social scientists; these constructs had not yet been invented. What they did have was remarkable humanistic tools that they engaged to try and understand alterity. They constructed their knowledge of non-Christian peoples around the metaphor of "living books": a "stranger" was a book, which the missionaries needed to decipher, a work of cultural translation. The need and desire to know others was, of course, linked to religious goals: translating Christian messages, administering sacraments, fulfilling divine will. This process of transcultural translation, however, stands in stark contrast to Anglo-Protestant, especially Puritan, pedagogies of cultural transmission, or deficit pedagogy, which assumed that Indigenous peoples were deficient and ignorant.[30] The universalism of the Jesuit and Ursuline missionaries was in direct contrast to the hierarchical ordering of society that was central to the Puritans and that would eventually shape the caste-based evolution of the modern school in the United States.[31]

For the Puritans, the central facet of evangelization was the translation of devotional texts.[32] Protestants, given their emphasis on the word, initially promoted translation projects more vigorously than their Catholic counterparts. Protestant evangelization was one of imposing the word with little room for exchange of ideas. For Catholics, religious belief and experience resulted not only from the word, but also through ritual and other symbol systems creating spaces for the Jesuits to understand the experiences of Indigenous peoples. The characterization of Indigenous peoples as having only oral traditions has obscured the relationships that oral traditions had to material objects (wampum) and practices of reading, writing, and inscription embodied in them.[33] Catholic evangelization, not limited to the word, gave rise to the possibilities of syncretism that allowed for translation of religious beliefs that went both ways: Catholic saints were incorporated into Native belief systems, and elements of Indigenous ritual practice found their way into Catholic practice (this was also to be the case with Africans). This made possible to some degree a culture in which knowledge, values, and cosmologies were shared; something that was much more difficult in Puritan culture.[34]

The Jesuit and Ursuline missionary work of education has often been reduced to the binary of colonizer and colonized. I would suggest, though, that this simplistic reduction obscures the complex ways in which Jesuit and Ursuline education was engaged as a means of transcultural translation. I draw on Dominique Deslandres's concept of the "double setting" to rethink the binary of colonizer and colonized in relation to early missionary work in New France.[35] This concept allows for the possibility of a double pedagogy in which the French and Indigenous nations engaged in cultural exchange rather than just cultural imposition. Deslandres maintains that the work of conversion and civilizing "heathens" was a double mission that had as its focus not only the Indigenous nations of foreign lands, but the peasants in the French countryside as well, many of whom were still pagans (Celtics). In France at the end of the sixteenth century, Capuchin and Jesuit missionaries "literally patrolled the whole country, which they called the 'Black Indies of the interior' since they found there peasants as ignorant of the Christian faith as were the pagans of Canada, Constantinople, or Madagascar."[36]

Reframing the focus of the missionary gaze on all persons considered non-Catholic/heathen/pagan/*sauvage* resituates not only the spatial constructs of colonialism as transnational, but also the inherent racist underpinnings. Unlike other colonial missionaries in the Counter Reformation era, Catholic and Protestant alike, the Ursuline and Jesuit global educational mission discourse during the early modern period regarding Indigenous and African people was not based on inherent and immutable biological differences, but rather was focused on cultural deficiencies or differences (most notably in regard to religion). French conceptualizations of ethnicity were cultural rather than racial, with a special emphasis on religious instruction.[37] Extending religious instruction to all signaled not only the educability of all people, but also a form of equality through spiritual universalism. Peasants in France are compared with Caribs in the West Indies because of their shared pagan status, rather than because of their race. While race would eventually emerge as the primary category organizing society, this would not happen for another hundred years. This early global missionary work among the Ursulines and Jesuits cannot be reduced to a singular narrative of colonialism but must take account of the double setting of the interconnections between internal and external missionary activities, in which French peasants, Amerindians, and enslaved Africans would be united under the spiritual umbrella of the Catholic Church.

For the Jesuits, the process of transcultural translation is relational, an exchange between humans; in other words, translation seeks not just a copy of the original, but is its own creation, a process of creolization.[38] This process of translation suggests that interactions between the Jesuits, enslaved Africans, and Indigenous peoples, while in many cases multidimensional, are not reducible to a colonizer/colonized binary, but are more complex than these binaries can possibly recount. As Dwayne Donald has suggested, these cultural interactions resulting from settler colonial societies are a "shared condition wherein colonizers and colonized come to know each other very well."[39] Translation could be understood from an Indigenous perspective as articulated by Donald as métissage, meaning braiding, or the hybridization of identities as a result of colonialism and transcultural influences. This process, one that is still ongoing, is critical to "juxtaposing texts in such a way that highlights difference (racial, cultural, historical, sociopolitical, linguistic) without essentializing or erasing it, while simultaneously locating points of affinity."[40]

The Jesuits were famous for their particular flexibility in adapting to local conditions, customs, and belief systems, a strategy often labeled as "accommodation."[41] Beginning in 1552, when the first Jesuit missionary, St. Francis Xavier, traveled to India, then Japan and China, the Jesuits quickly realized that their teaching would not advance if they did not have a sound grounding in the language and culture of the Indigenous peoples. While the Jesuits infiltrated China, they also arrived in the Americas—Brazil in 1540 and Paraguay in 1587—where they established mission villages called *reductions*, in which Indigenous tribes were "settled" in order to "instruct" them in the Catholic faith, as well as in reading and writing. These villages were self-sufficient units that served not only to educate Indigenous peoples in Catholicism but were designed to assimilate them into French lifestyle norms. While imperial in design, these reductions also provided protection against Portuguese slavers, who often raided villages.

By the middle of the seventeenth century, the Jesuits had "laid their bones" in almost every country of the known world and on the shores of almost every sea.[42] They had received both praise and censure for the methods they developed in their conversion activity. In the Far East and the Americas, their activity reflected the spirit and practice of cultural flexibility or "accommodation" that governed the Jesuits' encounter with foreign cultures. The apostolic zeal of the Jesuit and Ursuline missionaries was grounded in the desire and necessity of conquering souls to establish a common humanity grounded in the universal Catholic Church. This vision of a new world order through Catholic education was a direct challenge to emerging modernist, Enlightenment ideologies in which the state would emerge as more powerful than the church; the individual, not community, would become the central organizing unit of society; and reason would replace faith as the primary epistemology. These shifting sands, or double settings, were the backdrop for missionary activity in which lives were clearly less coherent than is often imagined. In rethinking the lives of early modern missionaries in New France, Allan Greer (2011) has suggested, "When we look closely at individual Jesuit lives, we sometimes encounter far more uncertainty, internal contradiction, and a yearning sense of incompletion than the assured tone of the *Cartas annuas* or the *Jesuit Rela-*

tions would lead us to expect."[43] While clearly imperialist in design, the Jesuit and Ursuline focus on education sought to assimilate, not annihilate, thereby creating spaces for cultural exchange, appropriation, adaptation, creolization, and resistance among Indigenous and African peoples.

When the Jesuits first arrived in New France in 1609, they encountered the First Nations of the Anishinabe (Algonquin), Haudenosaunee (Iroquois), Innu (Montagnais), and Wendat (Huron) who lived in what is now considered the Eastern part of Canada: the Atlantic Coast, Saint Lawrence River, and Great Lakes region.[44] In addition to shared language, each nation had as its primary social unit the village, in which people were related by a clan kinship structure. For the most part, these villages were temporary and mobile, moving to the locations of the greatest food supply. The Anishinabe, with whom the French first made contact, were socially united by a strong totem/clan system, rather than the European-styled political concept of nationhood. The French would have to learn that power was not hierarchical, consolidated in one leader, but instead that power was cultivated through relationships with the numerous chiefs and clan leaders. Prior to European settlement, Indigenous people educated their children through communal, land-based, and experiential modes of learning and with holistic worldviews that would later clash with colonial settlers' dichotomies such as human/nonhuman, public/private, and rich/poor.[45]

The Jesuits established the first mission in Acadia in 1611, and in 1625 they arrived on the banks of the St. Lawrence River. While the effect of British colonization was being felt all along the Atlantic coast and into the Great Lakes region, Canada and the northeastern United States were still very much under the control of the First Nations. These Jesuit missionaries drew on the pedagogical innovations of their order for educational guidance. The Jesuits, shaped by Renaissance humanism, were scholars with a considerable interest in the study and collection of information about the human condition.[46] First, they began with the *study* of the language and culture of the Indigenous peoples, in essence becoming "students" of the language and recorders of myth and ritual.[47] The complexity of the Indigenous languages made assiduous study necessary in order to construct these languages in textual forms. This began with vocabulary collection and eventually the compilation of dictionaries. Second, the Jesuits, and eventually the Ursulines, produced written works that described the Indigenous people, as well as their own missionary activities. The *Relations des Jésuites de la Nouvelle-France* was an annual compilation of reports written by Jesuit missionaries to their superiors in Quebec or Montreal describing their work, which were then sent to France.[48] Printed beginning in

1632 and ending in 1673, the *Relations* provided graphic descriptions of the New World that many in Europe were eager to read. The *Relations* combined descriptions of the allegedly "savage" and "superstitious" practices of Native people with careful accounts of their economies, material culture, ritual practice, and political structures.[49] These richly detailed narratives inspired lay men and women in France to raise money for mission villages, colleges, hospitals, and a seminary, but first and foremost, these letters were designed to educate the French about their brothers and sisters.

Given France's initial neglect of the colony, the French missionaries were left on their own to pursue their mission of evangelization. In 1625, the Jesuits Jean de Brébeuf, Ennemond Massé, and Charles Lalemant arrived in Quebec. These Jesuits became involved in the Huron mission in 1626 and, in the tradition of the Jesuits, lived among the Huron peoples. According to Jérôme Lalemant, a missionary must first have "penetrated their thoughts . . . adapted himself to their manner of living and, when necessary, been a Barbarian with them."[50] This immersion in the culture was a prerequisite to the transcultural translation necessary for conversion. Studying the Indigenous belief systems, the Jesuits drew parallels between Catholicism and Indigenous practices, making connections to the mystical dimension and symbolism of Catholicism (pictures, bells, incense, candlelight), giving out religious medals as amulets, and promoting the benefits of the cult of relics. Brébeuf learned the Native language and created the first Huron-language dictionary. This first wave of missionary activity ended in 1629 with the occupation of Quebec by British forces. A permanent Jesuit presence would not occur until 1632.

Education as Transcultural Pedagogy: The Jesuits

> Would to God that those who can aid these poor souls and contribute something to their salvation could be here, if only for three days. I believe that a longing to help them would seize powerfully upon their souls. But let no one be astonished at these acts of barbarism. Before the faith was received in Germany, Spain, or England, those nations were not more civilized. Mind is not lacking among the Savages of Canada, but education and instruction.[51]

Father Paul Le Jeune (1591–1664), writing from Canada in the *Jesuit Relations* for his readers in France, suggests that there is a parallel between the lack of "civilization" of early Europeans and the Indigenous peoples of Canada. This deficit was not intelligence but lack of education in the Catholic faith. Father Le Jeune, named the superior of the Jesuit missions when they returned in 1632, was convinced that education was the key element in any attempt to spread the Catholic faith. One of his first initiatives was to open a seminary in Quebec. He was impressed by the Indigenous students who asked difficult questions issuing from what they saw as inconsistencies in Catholic theology. He wrote, "I confess they evince a great deal of intelligence, but I would not have believed that they could reason so well, especially in the matter of our belief."[52] Le Jeune's assessments of the Indigenous students were based not on constructs of race or underdevelopment but on the fact that he considered them pagan.

For Le Jeune, the road to conversion was through education and as the superior of the Jesuit missions from 1632 to 1639, he focused his energies on understanding how best to establish education among the Indigenous peoples.[53] Le Jeune, a Catholic convert, had been well prepared as a teacher. He entered his novitiate in 1613 and two year later began his studies in philosophy at the Collège Henri IV de la Flèche, where he studied with Father Massé, who had been among the first Jesuit missionaries to Canada from 1625 to 1629. After finishing his philosophical studies, Father Le Jeune was a teacher at the colleges in Rennes (1618–1619) and Bourges (1619–1622); he studied theology for four years at the Collège de Clermont in Paris, taught rhetoric at Nevers from 1626 to 1628, and did his third year of the novitiate at Rouen; in 1629–1630, he was once more professor of rhetoric, but this time at Caen. Like the other missionaries with whom he worked, as part of their missionary formation they were required to spend two years teaching.

With a deep personal understanding of the role of education in conversion, he focused his energies on establishing education. His first step was to immerse himself in the languages and cultures of the Indigenous peoples. Among his most well-known documented experiences are his travels in the winter of 1633–34 among the Innu (Montagnais). While his work during those six months did not result in mass conversions, it shaped his knowledge of Indigenous culture and customs in ways that would inform his vision for education. Given the egalitarianism and nonhierarchical nature of the Innu, the custom was that community problems were discussed in assemblies. Le Jeune believed that it was critical to attend Indigenous assemblies in which they could discuss worship, extend invitation to baptisms, and discredit the shamans, who were understood as teachers. In other words, the Jesuit priests were encouraged to learn the languages and live among the Innu, Wendat (Huron), and Anishinabe (Algonquin) in their villages.

The Mission de Sainte-Maire established in 1634 on Georgian Bay among the Wendat was considered by the Jesuits as the most successful until it was destroyed by the traditional enemies of the Wendat, the Haudenosaunee (Iroquois), in 1648–49.

At the same time, Le Jeune believed that it was imperative to end the nomadic way of life of the people in order to found European institutions such as schools, seminaries, and churches. Following the example of the Jesuits in Paraguay, he sought to establish "reductions," villages where local people were settled in agricultural communities under the control of the Jesuits. The first of these were the Sillery mission near Québec in 1637 and the Conception mission near Trois-Rivières; later, similar missions were started among the Wendat at Notre-Dame-de-Foy and Lorette, and among the Haudenosaunee at La Prairie de la Madeleine. None of these efforts were successful. The constant conflict between the French and the Haudenosaunee, and the epidemic diseases brought by the Europeans, essentially destroyed the Wendat.

Even less successful was Le Jeune's attempt to open a college/seminary for both Indigenous and French boys in Quebec. Notre-Dames-des-Anges opened in 1636 with five young Wendat students, who were followed by a dozen Innu and Anishinabe in 1638–39. Coincidently, 1636 also marked the founding of Harvard University in New England, which initially also allowed Indigenous students. While both religious institutions shared the common goal of perpetuating the Christian faith, their objectives were quite disparate and shed light on the different ideological foundations of these institutions of education. The primary mission of Harvard was to educate clergy who came from well-to-do Protestant families, as opposed to the Quebec seminary, which sought to educate young males of all classes and races, including Indigenous people. After first successes, the Quebec seminary failed as the young Indigenous boys resisted deculturalization and also died in great numbers due to infections brought by the Westerners. A second seminary was opened in Trois-Rivières but failed after one year. It became clear to the Jesuits that their efforts to convert the Indigenous peoples to Catholicism and to a French way of life had failed. Indigenous resistance to deculturization was pervasive.

Le Jeune and his fellow Jesuits did not limit their efforts in conversions and education to Indigenous peoples. While the first enslaved peoples had been Indigenous (mostly Pawnee), the first enslaved Africans arrived in 1629.[54] Although this was prior to the Code Noir, Le Jeune began including the children of the enslaved in the catechism classes he was teaching.[55] Catechism classes, usually held directly after mass, emphasized the sacraments, especially confession and communion, and were focused on practical religious behavior. Catechism classes began with prayer. As soon as the students entered the room, students were supposed to kneel, make the sign of the cross, and repeat a designated prayer. Lessons from the previous day were reviewed to make sure that the student still remembered them. The bulk of the hour centered around the new lesson. Teachers focused on the questions and responses as laid out in the catechism. In the teaching of the children of colonists, enslaved, and Indigenous peoples, Le Jeune and his fellow Jesuits relied not only on the catechism, but on singing hymns, biblical passages, and use of religious stories to convey Catholic religious beliefs and promote literacy. This commitment of the Jesuits to providing education to the enslaved would eventually contribute to the requirements for the Code Noir of 1685.

Despite their efforts, the Jesuits were unable to map their Christian worldview onto Indigenous worldviews. This was in part because, despite their immersion in the language and culture of the Indigenous peoples, there were concepts for which each had no language. And, despite the Jesuits' most determined efforts, most Indigenous peoples refused to abandon their place-based, holistic belief system through which they had made sense of their lives for centuries. Again, the Jesuits relied on a pedagogy that sought to understand the "other" through identifying similarities rather than differences as central to conversion. As followers of Aquinas, they believed in the relationship between faith and lived experience. In other words, faith did not require reason alone. Father Lalemont, fellow priest of Le Jeune, clearly saw the important role of experience or natural learning among the Wendat: "As regards Intelligence, they are in no wise inferior to Europeans and to those who dwell in France. I would never have believed that, without instruction, nature could have supplied a most ready and vigorous eloquence, which I have admired in many Hurons."[56]

By drawing on nature and grace, the Jesuits foregrounded the role of the senses (also an aid to meditation in the *Spiritual Exercises*) in knowledge. They not only had to rely on their own experience in these new cultures to make judgments, but they also realized they had to trust the experiences of the Indigenous peoples. In this regard, the Jesuits were prone to suspend judgment about Indigenous ways that were "novel or even offensive until they had acquired some purchase for understanding them."[57] In regard to learning the Indigenous languages, Jean de Brébeuf advised novice Jesuit missionaries: "The Huron language will be your Saint Thomas and your Aristotle; and clever man as you are, and speaking glibly among learned and capable persons, you must make up your mind to be for a long time mute among the Barbarians."[58]

The elevation of the Huron language to that of a philosophy suggests that the transcultural translation in which the Jesuits engaged required that they be students, willing to listen and engage the "other" as an intellectual equal. The mission experience of the Jesuits demanded adaptation and the reconsideration of traditional meanings of conversion, and even spirituality itself. Anya Mali maintains that in facing the idea of "newness" in the New World, missionaries "widened not only their knowledge of the world, but also their horizons of understanding, as they realized that traditional or preconceived categories could no longer account adequately for the new reality confronting them."[59] Openness to this destabilization made possible the reflexive, two-way, transcultural translation process that made attempts at genuine learning even possible.

Although the Jesuits, as has been suggested earlier, are often described as the first Western ethnographers, given their detailed attention and description of Indigenous cultures in the *Jesuit Relations*, their work cannot really be considered anthropological or ethnographic, given the very different understanding of culture they held. At the time the Jesuits wrote, neither the cultures of early modern Europe nor their respective members shared a single set of meanings and purposes with regard to culture, education, science, or religion. Rather than understand the educational work of the Jesuits and Ursulines as the transmission of a unified culture or set of ideas, my analysis assumes that the grand narratives of missionary work (saving souls, martyrdom, conversion) did not predetermine or define the experiences of colonizer or colonized, but instead that the processes of transcultural translation shaped experience in a multitude of disparate and indeterminable ways for both the Jesuits and the Indigenous peoples.

This was perhaps nowhere more apparent than in regard to the written word and alphabetic literacy that "was a foundational aspect of their interactions with Indigenous peoples as they worked to transform this space into a Catholic New France."[60] One strategy the Jesuits used in conversion was the exhibiting of their books and writings. They sought to establish "their books and the technology of writing as the sole source of past authority."[61] This, of course, conflicted directly with Indigenous peoples' use of oral traditions as authoritative narratives. Even though attempts at schooling had failed, the ongoing Jesuit presence with their emphasis on transcribing Indigenous languages, learning, and scholasticism continued to shape cultural relations during this period. As Thomas Peace has argued, "The central point is that alphabetic literacy and schooling—and the violent assimilative relationships that underpinned them—formed a basis for these early relationships developing from France's newly-achieved and more permanent presence in the region."[62]

These relationships must take account of the ways in which Indigenous peoples used schooling and literacy to their own advantage. For those few students who did attend, they often played intermediary roles between their own communities, religious orders, and the French. Engaging schooling for political, not religious, reasons reflects the ways in which Indigenous peoples began to appropriate education as a means to address colonial pressures on a number of different levels.[63] As the French colony grew both economically and in population, Indigenous peoples were increasingly under threat. Under these conditions, relations with both the Jesuits and Ursulines, who still at this point held an influential place in colonial society, was advantageous. This was particularly salient because both the Jesuits and Ursulines conducted instruction in religion, reading, and writing in Indigenous languages. In addition, they both had transcribed Indigenous languages into alphabetic scripts, creating grammars and dictionaries that were used as teaching tools for new missionaries, but were also becoming part of village life. While formal schooling had been a failure, the religious culture of the Jesuits and Ursulines, which focused on literacy, text, and schooling, would profoundly shape the agency of Indigenous peoples in taking control of their own education at the end of the eighteenth century.[64]

By 1658, resistance to Jesuit efforts to colonize resulted in increasing tensions as the Crown began to take charge of the loosely organized colony. They continued their efforts until 1687, when they abandoned their permanent posts in the Iroquois homeland. In June of 1659, the first Catholic bishop of New France, François de Montmorency de Laval, arrived in Quebec, with the title of bishop of Petraea. At the time of his arrival, Quebec numbered hardly five hundred French inhabitants and the whole of Canada was home to only twenty-two hundred French. During his time in Canada, Laval organized a complete system of education—primary, technical, and classical—and while French colonial policy shifted from religious conversion to promoting settlement by French colonists to maximize economic productivity, he founded the Quebec seminary (1663), connected to the Paris Seminary of Foreign Missions, to train young men for the priesthood.[65] In 1665, the seminary was affiliated with the Séminaire des Missions Étrangères de Paris. The Petit Séminaire, as it was named, opened in October 1668, accepting both Indigenous and French students who were going to study at the Collège des Jésuites.

In 1678, Laval also founded an industrial school at Saint Joachim, near Ste. Anne, to provide the colony with skilled farmers and artisans. He continued efforts to baptize and confirm French and Indigenous alike, and he was particularly vigilant in his attacks against the distribution of alcohol to the Indigenous peoples. His interventions against the trade in spirits included a meeting with Louis XIV in 1662, where Louis promised to forbid the trade. For all practical purposes the Jesuit missionaries were unsuccessful both in their educational endeavors and in curbing the devasting effects of the trade in alcohol. By 1700, the Jesuit missionaries had all but left the missions focusing their energies on maintaining their educational institutions in Quebec, Montreal, and Ottawa.[66] While the Jesuits struggled in their mission, the Ursulines who had arrived in Quebec in 1639, were forging new roles for women religious as missionaries.

New World Pedagogue: Marie de L'Incarnation and the Creation of a "New Eden"

> When I put my foot on the boat, it seemed to me I was entering Paradise, for I was taking the first step to risk my life for the love of him who gave it to me.
>
> —Marie de l'Incarnation, May 4, 1639

The paradise that Marie de l'Incarnation (1599–1672) envisioned was the New World. For Marie, this "garden of Eden" promised to restore the original purity of God's divine purpose of harmony and balance between humans and God. For this reunion, Marie was ready to risk her life, to suffer death, and this she did. Her death consisted of shedding her "old" self as laywoman, mother, and widow and translating herself into a "new" self as nun, student, teacher, mystic, and administrator. Marie de l'Incarnation was the first female missionary to New France, and in 1639 founded the oldest school for girls in the Americas, the Ursuline School in Quebec. Far removed from what many considered to be a declining Catholic Church in Europe and the imperial constraints of France, Marie envisioned a "new Eden" in which all people would live under one God, one government, and a single language.[67] Her vision was truly universal, including Jews, Muslims, and other non-Christians of Japan, China, India, and the Americas. It was based on the premise that all people were reasoning souls, educable, and part of God's grand design. From New France, Marie would also carry on an extensive correspondence with her son, Claude, whom she had left with relatives at the age of eleven to enter religious life. The letters exchanged between mother and son over the course of some thirty years (1640 to 1671) provide a window into the early history of New France, as well as the spiritual itinerary of one of the most celebrated mystics of the seventeenth century.[68] Her writings are unprecedented, given that most of the missionary writings in New France were composed by men. According to Mary Dunn, Marie de l'Incarnation's epistolary corpus discursively produces a colonial identity that escapes the neat binaries of self and other, thus disrupting the bifurcated image of the American *sauvage* as alternately and simultaneously "barbarous" and "noble."[69] Her body of writings provide not only a testimony of the encounter between a Western woman and Indigenous women, but they capture the ways in which this educational encounter resulted in an ideological destabilization of both Marie and Indigenous girls and women, which in turn created spaces for a pedagogy of transcultural translation.

Marie de l'Incarnation entered the Tours Ursuline convent in 1631 and began teaching young women in 1635. She claimed that the apostolic fire that burned inside her to teach in faraway lands had been revealed in a vision: "And the Holy Spirit, which possessed me, led me to say to the Eternal Father, 'I am learned enough [assez savant] to teach of [Christ] to all nations. Give me a voice powerful enough to be heard at the ends of the earth, to say that my divine Spouse is worthy of reigning and being loved by all hearts.'"[70]

Deflecting her own female agency by deferring to the Holy Spirit and passively being led to God enables her to tell God that she, a woman, is learned enough to teach. Her bold conviction that she was capable of educating "all nations" captures the universalizing approach rooted in the French Counter Reformation that was central to both the Ursulines and Jesuits. But her desire to have a powerful voice, heard "at the ends of the earth," clashed with the dominant conventions for women religious that restricted their role as educators to the private confines of the cloistered convent. Missionary work, going out into the world to teach Christianity, was by its very nature a public activity, one that was in direct opposition to the passive role of bodily submission and sacrifice central to the medieval piety practiced in enclosed convents. To take up the work of a missionary, a public teacher, outside the confines of the cloister was to transgress gender norms. But by relying on her inner voice, given to her by the Holy Spirit, Marie de l'Incarnation is not only able to convince herself that she is destined to become a teacher in New France, she is able to legitimate this new role for women with church authorities.

In successfully defending the Ursuline teaching apostolate from the limitations of the French Catholic Church and the Crown, Marie relied not only on her mystical callings. Earthly forces were also invested in her desires, including the Jesuits, who sought aid in evangelization, and lay-women who were called to travel to New France. Madeleine de La Peltrie, a French noblewoman, widowed at age twenty-five, also received a message that God wanted her to go to Canada to dedicate her life in service to the Indigenous peoples.[71] Upon learning about each other, Marie and Madame de la Peltrie began to plan the first Ursuline mission for Quebec, to convert young Indigenous girls to Christianity. At the heart of this missionary work was the educational work of translation, converting one set of cultural beliefs (in this case pagan and polytheistic) and meanings into another (Christian and monotheistic). For Marie, this pedagogy of conversion, or translation, was not an epistemological project, but an ontological project of universalism in which "religion makes all its subjects equal."[72] This shift from the role of women religious as contemplatives to demanding an active, public role as global missionaries and teachers was not only radical, given the gender norms of the time, but clearly marks the advent of teaching as "women's true profession" as much earlier than in normative histories of education.[73]

Marie, who sought to claim a role for the Ursulines as educators in New France, was of course aware of the long history of women's suppression as teachers; while the Pauline injunction in the seventeenth century had increased their roles as educators and ministers to the poor and ill, they continued to be forbidden by the church to participate in any *publicly* sanctioned role in evangelization. Consequently, while the Counter Reformation necessitated the work of Catholic women religious to counteract the rise of Protestantism through increased education, this progress of women into the public sphere traditionally reserved for men also resulted in backlashes and suspicion. For Marie de l'Incarnation, this resistance required rigorous counternarratives that legitimated the role of women in the public as well as her universalist educational project. She drew not only on early church history, in which women played an active role in the church as apostles, but from the traditions of religious universalists including Vincent Ferrer (1350–1419), Guillaume Postel (1510–1581), and Vincent de Paul (1581–1660), who envisioned a global common religion with one government and one language.[74]

Ultimately, according to Greenburg, Marie "had to leave France and travel to the ends of her world, Canada, a journey which is, as we have said, at one and the same time a voyage out (in space) and back in time (fantasy of returning to the primitive church) in order to escape those social contradictions that inhere in her."[75] Given the extreme societal pressures of conforming to gender norms, her actions and writings must be understood not so much in light of her positing religious truths, but as a reflection of how a very complex woman negotiated the contradictions of the social, sexual, and spiritual discourses of seventeenth-century French society, a society undergoing a tumultuous transition. The threat of women's increased influence and freedom resulted in constant tension between the church and women missionaries. How Marie negotiated this tension has been neglected as central to her pedagogical philosophy, which reflects the gendered dynamics she had to negotiate, as well as her encounter with Indigenous peoples. Below, I examine not only how Marie asserted her radical claim that teaching was a woman's profession, but also her development of a transcultural pedagogy that emerged through her creole, hybrid mysticism.

Creole, Hybrid Mysticisms

> No doubt I speak obscurely; and yet I see it clearly myself, even though it is impossible to express the thousandth part of the impressions and operations which my Divine Spouse has produced in my soul.
>
> —Marie de l'Incarnation, 1654[76]

> My study became a prayer, rendering the language no longer barbaric to me, but sweet.
>
> —Marie de l'Incarnation[77]

For Marie, words were inadequate to convey the invincible confidence she placed in her understanding of herself as an educator. As her autobiography makes clear, she drew on her mystical encounter with God to justify her claims to be an educator. For Marie, mystical encounters with the divine defied words; it was an ineffable state that "affords a divine nourishment which human language is unable to express, an intimacy and boldness, an inexplicable reciprocity of love between the Word and the soul."[78] This interactive relationship between the word and the soul, a new form of mysticism, was in part a product of the Counter Reformation response to the Protestant claim that divine knowledge was embedded in text, specifically the Bible. This focus on text, as well as literacy, emerged alongside the elaboration of a radically new Cartesian rationalist discourse in philosophy, which situated knowledge as external to the knower and discernable only through reason.[79] This modernist shift in understandings of knowledge differed significantly from Marie's, in which knowers (not knowledge) are already part of the wholeness of creation. These differences had profound implications for emerging understandings of education. While Marie saw the purpose of teaching as *drawing out* knowledge, modernist conceptions of teaching focused on *putting in* knowledge.[80] Marie saw her pedagogical imperative as instilling in young women, Anishinabe (Algonquin), Wendat (Huron), Haudenosaunee (Iroquois), and French, a pedagogical sensibility that did not abandon their own inner, spiritual, mystical knowing as irrelevant to emerging rationalist forms of knowing that were situated as external to the body. Her autobiography, considered to be among the finest spiritual literature of the day, makes explicit the idea of mystical love, or divine union, as a kind of springboard for active service, in particular teaching.[81] Teaching was not understood as any deliberate effort to affect learners, but understood strictly in terms of its effects on learners. In this sense, Marie's pedagogical imperative in teaching Indigenous girls was not strictly one of imposing knowledge, but of drawing out their ways of knowing as a starting point for developing a common spirituality.

Anya Mali suggests that the significance of spiritual identity in Catholic New France is still much less examined than that of the Puritans in New England. She maintains that "the spiritual expression of the New France missionaries is usually treated only in reference to general devotional themes or trends in Europe at the time."[82] This focus, she claims, ignores the ways in which the encounter with the Indigenous peoples impacted Marie's evolving spirituality. Central to Marie's autobiography are the chapters dealing with her struggles to make possible her missionary work in Canada and the conversion of pagan souls, as well as the opposition of church officials and family members to her missionary zeal. While a great deal of scholarship has focused on either her mysticism *or* her missionary work, it has been suggested that it was the reciprocal relationship between the two that resulted in her unique understandings of the conversion experience.[83] Her life was, in fact, marked by conversion experiences.

Born in Tours in 1599 as Marie Guyart, she was married at age seventeen to a silk merchant who died shortly after she gave birth to a son. At age twenty, a widow with a young infant, she managed the family business and began to experience mystical revelations. In 1631, she left behind her eleven-year-old son (Claude Martin, who eventually became a Benedictine) and entered the Ursuline convent in Tours.[84] This she considers her first conversion: her decision to leave her familial, worldly life and take up the life of contemplation as a cloistered nun. She refers to this as the turning point in her life that transformed her and initiated her into mystical life. Her own experience of conversion was to shape her attempts to convert, and her understanding of converting, Indigenous peoples to Catholicism, as well as her spiritual instruction of the nuns in her order.

Marie was well acquainted with the mystical traditions of her age. In 1601 in Paris, a small group of Spanish Carmelites introduced the teachings of Teresa of Ávila (1515–1582), who had reformed the order to an austere, contemplative one. Under Madame Acarie, fifty-five Carmelite convents were opened in France; these are seen as the precursors of the French, or Abstract, School of Mysticism that inspired Marie. Her confessor asked her to read the Spanish mystic Teresa of Ávila's spiritual autobiography, or *Vida*, which was one of the most widely read texts of the Counter Reformation. (Marie was later hailed by her Jesuit colleague Jérôme Lalemant as the Teresa of Canada.)[85] In the past, women religious had been barred from imitating Christ in his apostolic mission as a martyr, so they had to imitate his suffering through other means. While some embraced bodily mortification, poverty, and austerity, Marie saw the work of education, central to conversion, as a form of self-sacrifice.

Mystical traditions were embedded in both conversion (the call of God) and martyrdom (dying for God). The discourses of martyrdom drew on two models: The legends of the ancient Christian martyrs of Rome focused on the celebration of bodily assaults that are observed and described in order to function within the "economy of exemplarity."[86] The second form was that of the missionary martyr, especially that of the Jesuit missionary abroad. This model took the form of the medieval golden legend in which the exemplar of the wounded body bears witness to the truth of faith and makes salvation so readily available that it can convert all who look upon it. In 1627, twenty-six Catholic missionaries who were killed in Japan in 1597 were beatified. The torture and death of Jesuits in New France was reported in the Jesuit *Relations* with considerable detail.[87] Conversion of Indigenous peoples from the male Jesuit perspective was considered possible if, and only if, missionaries were persecuted and executed for their faith. For Marie, however, public martyrdom was impossible.

Martyrdom for the Ursulines required a new rhetoric that shifted the paradigm from one of suffering, torture, and death to martyrdom of the interior. This shifting to the interior and the practice of religious cloister (which prevents public martyrdom), according to Katherine Ibbett, signifies how the

locus of transmission of Christianity moves from the staged and public exemplarity of the glorious death to quieter scenes of pedagogy
and publication. In Marie's work the Christian sufferer is not on the
frontier but in the schoolyard: The essential work of these new martyrs, principally female, is education. . . . Conventional martyrdom
had always had something of the pedagogical about it, since it aims
to inspire those who look on to follow. But for Marie the realities
of the colonial convent make the reader and writer, not the torture
victim, into the privileged agent of religious transmission.[88]

Marie embraces not death, but the difficult task of learning Indigenous
languages, the laborious and tedious work undertaken in lexicography
and translation central to her creole pedagogy. Sacrifice is not in the form
of being tortured but in daily, hard work. In her letters home, she is making clear to the reader that the spread of Christianity will necessitate not
solitary action or death, but the long-term labor of religious women educators. This labor and suffering are documented in her letters to her son
and in her autobiography, providing an alternative site for martyrdom
for women, as well as rationale for women to be teachers. Marie's books,
like those of other colonial Ursulines and Jesuits, functioned as a physical site of saintly holiness in which martyrdom was inescapably a project
of publication. For Marie, martyrdom is embodied in a life of sacrifice as
teacher and mother; the difficult dailiness of life, not death, becomes the
suffering that marks the absolute commitment to God. Marie is able to
convert and translate the private (teaching) to the public (martyrdom).
This martyrdom functions to legitimate women's role as educators and
teachers in the public sphere.

   This interior martyrdom functions as an adaptation to the shifting
epistemological and ideological currents of the Enlightenment. It is the
mind, not the body; text, not contemplation; and reason, not faith, that
are the increasingly dominant tropes used to make sense of human experience. The decline of a distinctly female mystical tradition at the end of the
seventeenth century situated Marie in a nexus of conflicting discourses in
which spiritual experience was increasingly under suspicion, but also provided new meanings.[89] In shifting from bodily experience to textual experience as the signifier of knowledge (in this case divine knowledge), Marie
de l'Incarnation mediates not only the shifting epistemological terrain,
but in the process, she contributes to the Ursuline project of continually
remaking the pedagogical encounter that is the heart of education. In so
doing she ensures that women's experiences, despite the increasing focus

on rationality, will continue to be a legitimate site for education. According to Michel de Certeau, in sixteenth- and seventeenth-century Europe, the emerging modern scientific discourse reified the mystical as an object of inquiry in accordance with its own categories and methodologies. In fact, modern scientific discourse defined itself as the *not-that* of mysticism.[90] New religious orders, like the Ursulines, that were situated in the complex, contradictory gender discourses of the time were reluctant to embrace the traditional bodily practices of female mystics, which were increasingly seen as hysteria.[91] An epistemological shift moved from the conception of the body as existing in a premodern analogical relationship with the world—as a vessel penetrated with magical, occult, and divine presences—to a rational, organic, and medicalized perception of the body.

These tensions between signification of the body as irrational (female, pagan, other, possessed)—what had previously been elevated to mysticism—and the rational body (male, normative, independent) functioned as another type of cultural translation or conversion that gained momentum in New France. The Indigenous peoples, who were often characterized as worshiping false gods, superstitious, and at the extreme engaging in witchcraft, were in many ways no different than pagans in the French countryside or European women accused of witchcraft. No doubt this was not lost on Marie, who struggled with validating her own mystical experiences. And yet Marie had difficulty in understanding and accepting the basic cosmological beliefs of the Wendat (Huron) and Haudenosaunee (Iroquois) regarding the relationship between their dreams and the nature of their souls. Her discomfort was directed to the intensity with which they were guided and acted on their dreams after interpreting them with one another. While both parties shared a belief in the immortality of the soul, she found their conviction in obeying their dreams as superstitious and incompatible with Christianity.

For the Indigenous women who converted, however, this incompatibility was not necessarily a problem, given that they equated it with the self-examination and confessional skills that the Ursuline nuns exhibited. Likewise, female Indigenous converts who sought Catholic burials for family members often buried both Christian objects *and* grave gifts of wampum, beaver skins, and other items. For the Jesuits, these commodities were understood as property that had great value in the European system of inheritance. For those grieving the loss of a family member, gifts functioned as a way to honor the dead. This mixture of customs reflects a degree of hybridity of religious beliefs that signifies the ongoing agency of Indigenous women to not only resist the imposition of European ideologies, but to create a new role for themselves as religious practitioners within their own communities. Marie's choice to gloss over some of these inconsistencies in her descriptions of Indigenous conversions that she sent to France was no doubt deliberate, as she was determined to make a case for women missionaries through relegating stories of successful conversion. The success of a universalist pedagogy, from her point of view, depended on creating a public role for women religious as educators.

Women lay and religious missionaries, mostly of bourgeois or aristocratic lineage, not only demanded to emigrate to Canada on their own initiative, they did so in the face of suspicion or even straightforward hostility on the part of church and state.[92] In fact, in 1635, the Jesuit superior in Quebec, Père Paul Le Jeune, declared that he was deluged with nuns' demand to emigrate. He wrote in the *Relations*: "What amazes me is that a great number of nuns, consecrated to our Lord, who want to join the fight, surmount the fear natural to their sex to come to the aid of the poor daughters and poor wives of the savages."[93] In one account, a young woman entered by force a vessel bound from La Rochelle to Montreal, successfully stowing away and eventually entering the Ursuline convent in Quebec in 1646. For women, New France provided a site to challenge gender norms through creating and defining public spaces like religious and educational institutions.

When Marie and her companions—Madeleine de La Peltrie, Sister Marie de Saint Joseph, Sister Cécile de Sainte Croix, and Charlotte Barré (a converse nun)—arrived in Quebec in August of 1639, they arrived in what was a frontier village with only several hundred French residents. Upon reaching Quebec, the Ursulines, with land donated by the Company of New France and money for an Ursuline house and church provided by Madame de la Peltrie, were able to build a large, although rustic, compound with a convent, small church, birchbark cabins all surrounded by a low stockade of cedarwood. By 1650, the number of sisters had increased from four to fourteen, and by 1669, there were twenty-two (all were French, either from France or Quebec). Cloister was strictly enforced, so the female students were brought either by their French parents, Indigenous parents, or by the Jesuits. After the Iroquois war of 1649, which resulted from long-held tensions with the Huron over the fur trade, which decimated the Huron, the number of Huron girls at the Ursulines increased. By the 1660s, even the Iroquois women were sending their daughters.

From the start, both daughters of the French and those of Indigenous groups lived in the convent as boarding students. About twenty to fifty pupils, from age five to seventeen, usually lived in the convent. The

Ursulines provided instruction in religion, language, and domestic skills as part of the larger colonial project of *francization* (Frenchification), the official policy of France's plans for colonizing North America and asserting demographic and religious control over this vast region. The intent was to turn the Indigenous peoples into French subjects of the king: not only Catholic, but also linguistically, culturally, and legally French.[94] This policy of assimilation was never clearly defined but its goals were religious conversion to Christianity and cultural adaptation to French cultural norms.[95] This policy, embedded in the theory of monogenesis— the belief that all people shared a common origin—understands identity not as fixed but malleable. Whereas Indigenous peoples could become converted and Frenchified, this also meant that the French could become transformed by Indigenous culture.

The fluid and mutable understanding of the Jesuits and Ursulines toward culture at this time meant that they sought out the similarities in cultures, rather than the differences. This fluidity of identity meant that becoming French did not require the abandonment of Indigenous ways. For the Ursulines, this was further reinforced by the Catholic doctrine of spiritual universalism, which justified conversion but also suggested a moral equality between all human beings. To find this cultural common ground, it was necessary for the Ursulines to learn the languages of the local nations. They did this by learning from their students. Marie de Savonnières de Saint Joseph specialized in Wendat (Huron), Marie de l'Incarnation focused first on Anishinabe (Algonquin) and Innu (Montagnais), and by the 1660s she was speaking and teaching Haudenosaunee (Iroquois). She was often visited by various members of the Indigenous nations, missionaries, and colony officials. The Jesuits came for spiritual conferences, for the preaching given at retreats, and for the affairs regarding Indigenous peoples. Several governors sought her out as their spiritual advisor, and the Indigenous peoples were regular visitors in the parlor of the Ursulines. This continual slew of visitors coming and going to the convent for instruction, prayers, or meals provided many opportunities to learn and practice these new languages and learn the culture of the local nations, despite strict adherence to cloister. In other words, Marie created channels of communication with the outside world that brought people to her to be informed about the happenings in New France. Conversely, the Indigenous students functioned as important intermediaries between the Ursulines, French, and their home communities.[96]

This fluidity of exchange between the outside world and the inside world of the cloister clearly created a "hybrid" space in which there were adaptations and accommodations to Indigenous customs.[97] While the Ursulines focused on religious conversion, they were flexible in regard to adopting other forms of Frenchness. They supported the students' use of their own languages and foodways and they allowed for the alterations to some Catholic rituals and practices.[98] Multilingualism characterized the convent given that the sisters engaged in practicing their Indigenous language skills with the girls. And, within a few years, the Indigenous students were speaking, reading, and writing in French, as well as translating songs and writing letters in their Indigenous languages. Student names created "a badge of layered identity" through reflecting both Indigenous and French elements.[99] The adaptation of local foodways by the Ursulines, in part out of necessity, also provided continuity for the young girls when they arrived at the convent. They would regularly sit down to their traditional meal of sagamité, a corn-based stew, and moose. By 1669, the Crown renewed their push for Frenchification most strictly adhered to in regard to dress. The Indigenous girls, upon arrival at the convent, were stripped of their clothes, scrubbed (to remove the bear grease), and provided with French undergarments and dress. The girls' hair was styled to conform to French preferences, and they were clothed in red dresses, shoes, and mittens.[100] This process of cultural genocide -part of the policy of Frenchification— took place despite the Ursulines' attempts to implement a pedagogy of transcultural translation.

For the Ursulines, the liturgical life of the convent (prayers, mass, baptisms, feast days, singing, and processions) was the primary way to incorporate Indigenous girls and women into Catholic culture. And, of course, the central focus of the convent was on teaching the young girls (seminarians is what Marie called them) who would eventually become mothers. Ursuline classes centered on the elements of Christian belief, prayer, religious songs, and sacred practices, as well as on learning to speak French. At least some of the boarders were taught to read and write in French, and once the Ursulines had mastered the Indigneous languages, the students also learned to write in their mother tongues. Lessons were given in Anishinabee, Haudenosaunee, and French languages with the hope that the students who would return to their nations would begin teaching about the Christian God. Students also participated in the singing of hymns and prayers in all three languages. While language instruction, reading, and writing dominated the morning school hours, the afternoons were devoted to religion and to embroidery and painting. We can speculate that these artifacts of material culture most likely reflected a creolization of French and Indigenous materials, styles, and uses. One example is the appropriation of the Ursulines of making wampum necklaces for exchange and gifts.[101] Wampum was highly valued because of the effort to make the beads that are used to weave belts in which the Wendat record their living history or invite other nations to council.[102] They are in essence a textual form of communication in which the Ursulines also participated. Despite adhering to cloister, the Ursuline convent school was a site of cultural exchange, in many ways converting the cloister into a public space.

Marie fashioned public spaces and institutions not only in the convent school, but also through her writing, which was published and widely read in France. Marie's writing was first and foremost historical. Her historical writing covers the period from 1639 to 1672 and, according to Maria-Florine Bruneau, constitutes an important source of information for historians of New France and of the Indigenous peoples of the Northeast.[103] Her writing provided copious details that are not in *The Jesuit Relations*, a yearly publication from 1632 to 1673. Her writing, as a historian, had the impact of demonstrating the necessity of the Ursulines in New France.[104] In fact, her writing not only legitimated the mission of the Ursulines, but also helped to raise funds and to prove that her mission work was decreed by God. Writing for a broader audience in France, Marie challenged the normative conventions of female religious institutions, where writing traditionally took the form of chronicles of the order and hagiographies of their religious sisters. These works were usually not read outside the convents and addressed mostly the restricted history of a particular order.

Not only did Marie challenge the normative literary confines of women, she had to do so without being a threat to the Jesuits. Her historical writing included the domestic ingenuity of the women of the colony as well as that of the Haudenosaunee women. Her writing also allowed her to suggest new roles previously forbidden for women religious by relaying the successes she and her sisters had in preaching and teaching to not only Indigenous women, but to men. In her letters, she describes how the Wendat men, sometimes forty or fifty at a time, came to the convent to receive instruction in the guest parlor. Mother Marie de Saint Joseph had the mission of instructing them, and when the numbers grew too large, they would both instruct men and women in the birchbark cabins or in the convent yard.[105] Women teaching both sexes was a clear transgression of the Catholic Church's ban on women undertaking public preaching.

In the 1660s, she began publishing in the Indigenous languages. In Anishinabee, she composed catechisms, prayers, dictionaries, and a "big book of sacred history and holy things."[106] She produced a blended Wendat and Haudenosaunee dictionary, as well as a separate Haudenosaunee dictionary. These acts of translation might seem redundant given that the Jesuits had also produced catechisms, prayer books, and dictionaries. Undoubtedly, Marie believed that her translation projects added some gendered dimension to the linguistic and pedagogical projects that the Jesuits could not capture. These texts, while primarily produced for the teaching needs of her fellow Ursuline educators, could also have been used by the literate converts. As a female author writing for a female audience, she certainly would have tried to capture distinct uses of language or particular subjects that were unique to Indigenous women.

The *Vie de la vénérable mère Marie de l'Incarnation*, published in 1676, is in many ways typical of female spiritual narratives of the time, in that it fulfills the requirements of the autobiographical narrative of ecstatic female spirituality.[107] Noteworthy for two reasons, her autobiography gives a vivid view of the life of a French colonist in Quebec seen through the eyes of a woman who endured great physical and mental hardships. Additionally, the radical nature of the "female" missionary cannot be stressed enough. Marie not only challenged the accepted norms of public writing and preaching for women religious, but she did this through challenging the norms of *clausura*, which had kept women religious confined to the private sphere of the cloister. These challenges and adaptations were in part the result of what Bruneau has called a "geographic and anthropological decentering in the European consciousness," one result of the encounter between the Europeans and Indigenous peoples.[108] The *encounter narrative* written by Marie is one that sheds particular light on the meeting of the Western and Indigenous women, which is not present in the Jesuit texts and has rarely been noted. Bruneau maintains that the ideological and epistemological destabilization did not necessarily result in better understanding of the other, but clearly seeks to register the presence of otherness. Encounter with the other was not always one entered into from the position of superiority, but in fact was often a mutual experience of both difference and similarity.[109]

The face-to-face daily encounters between the Ursuline nuns and Indigenous people across time and space provided a rich variety of activities through which common and uncommon bonds were experienced. The Ursuline processions, singing, and sacramental rites could have held an emotional as well as an aesthetic appeal to the Indians. All the young girls at the school would have participated in the "choir ceremonies," the Good Friday liturgy, and story of Christ's Passion. Music and singing often functioned as bridges between the cultures and were seen as essential vehicles to conversion. The experiences with the Indigenous people led Marie to adjust her view of conversion to see it as an ongoing process rather than a single event, which in turn led her to develop new pedagogical approaches.

Marie began to see the function of language, imagery, ritual, and tradition in mediating faith, as well as the need to accommodate aspects of Indigenous custom where possible. In shared practices at the street level, fleeting moments of community were experienced. Again, the issue at hand is not whether Indigenous people were converting; religious beliefs are inherently amorphous, certainly not something that can be identified in any direct way. The larger pedagogy at work here, however, was the work of creating belief in a universal ideology that would unite all humans. One gesture suggesting this common regard for each other occurred after the 1650 fire that burned down and destroyed the Ursuline convent. Afraid that the Ursulines might abandon their mission and return to France, Chief Taiearonk of the Wendat addressed them, saying, "Courage, saintly maidens, do not let yourselves be overwhelmed by love for your family, and prove today that your affection for the poor Indians is an act of heavenly charity that is stronger than the bonds of nature."[110]

For the Ursulines, unlike the Jesuit fathers who lived in and traveled to Native villages, the encounter with Indigenous peoples took place within the contained enclosure of the convent. This was a hybrid space filled with diverse peoples (French, Innu, Anishinabee, Wendat, and Haudenosaunee), in which multiple languages were spoken, and in which cultures continually adapted and changed. Marie was able to interact on an intimate basis with the young girls in their dormitories, schoolrooms, chapel, and the convent yard. She spoke their language, shared in the daily rituals, and likened her own conversion to that of the young Indigenous girls. These similarities allowed her to believe in the universalizing impact of conversion. And while she describes several of the converts as having the "fervor" of the Christians of the early church, she later ruminated that of the hundreds of girls who had come to the convent, only a handful had become in her estimation true Catholics.[111] Unable to tolerate *clausura*, most of the girls went back to their villages, so the degree to which they practiced their new religious education cannot be determined. While some did minister and teach in their villages, not a single young girl had stayed at the convent with the intent to become a professed Ursuline.

The Ursuline Academy in Quebec, the oldest continuous educational institution for women in North America, still operates in Quebec.[112] For some it is a living testament to the durability of the universal vision of Marie de l'Incarnation, while for others it represents violent assimilative relationships and cultural genocide. This institution building by women religious was not without struggle. Not only did church and state male authorities see these women as threats to their authority, but their vision was radical because it treated all human beings as brothers and sisters. This basic premise of a universal humanity was at odds with the late seventeenth-century shifting views of what constituted social ills and how they should be addressed. The extension of the *grand renfermement* to Canada, in which poverty was increasingly understood as a social ill blamed on the individual that required remediation through centrally run institutions, was essentially rejected by women religious. Elizabeth Rapley maintains that two approaches to the question of public assistance existed side by side in seventeenth-century France.[113] The one treated poverty as a punishment from God and as a danger to social order; the other was more compassionate. This compassionate approach required not only care of both the soul and body, but a holistic approach that saw human beings as part of a universal family. Institution-building, however, was increasingly seen as the purview of the nation-state through which individuals could be regulated, monitored, and ordered along a hierarchy of human value and worth.

In this time of great flux, Jesuit missionary activity expanded from Canada down through the Great Lakes region and Mississippi River Valley to current-day Louisiana. Their goal of bringing Indigenous nations into the folds of the Catholic Church through missionary work added yet another dynamic to the ongoing shifting power relations. For the Jesuits, the empire they sought was not one based on the nation, but one grounded in Catholic universalism. These disparate goals would often put the Ursulines and Jesuits at odds with imperial policies and desires. But the expansion of missionary outposts into the borderlands and margins of France's empire, far from imperial eyes, allowed the Jesuits to pursue their educational vision unhindered by colonial mandates. The territories of the Mississippi Valley and the Gulf South provided ideal spaces in which to work undeterred by the imperial gaze.

The Middle Ground: Upper Louisiana and Marie Turpin

There remains no more, except to speak of the Calumet. There is nothing more mysterious or more respected among them. Less honor is paid to the Crown and scepters of Kings than the Savages bestow upon this. It seems to be the God of peace and war, the Arbiter of life and of death. It has but to be carried upon one's person and displayed, to enable one to walk safely through the midst of Enemies—who, in the hottest of the Fight, lay down

Their arms when it is shown. For That reason, the Illinois gave me one, to serve as a safeguard among all the Nations through whom I had to pass during my voyage.

—Father Jacques Marquette, June 1673[114]

The Illinois encounter with Jesuit Father Jacques Marquette (1637–1675), the first Jesuit to travel down the Mississippi River, was rooted in ways of understanding the world that were deeply ingrained in a cosmology about the nature of proper social relations. Shortly after Marquette and Jolliet arrived in Peoria, a city of over eight thousand, the great captain of the Illinois invited them to join him to watch a performance of the calumet ceremony. This ceremony was an elaborate ritual, engaging music (drumming, gourds, and flutes), dancing, singing, and miming in which warriors paraded to recount their victories. While individual feats were highlighted, this ritual also was a lesson in the collective history of the Illinois as a powerful nation who had arrived in the Mississippi Valley from the east the previous century, becoming the most powerful nation in the region. Clearly, the message was that the Illinois were a nation to be respected by the French. While the calumet ceremony taught history, the ritual was also a pedagogy that embodied relationship building through creating alliances that would ensure peaceful interactions. For the Illinois, like most of the nations of the Mississippi Valley, maintaining and extending a kinship network was essential to successful trade, political diplomacy, warfare, and marriage.[115]

Calumet ceremonialism was about building relationships. These alliances were sealed at the end of the ceremony when the great chief gave Father Marquette a pipe that signified the everlasting peace between the Illinois and French. But it was also a ceremony of misunderstanding. The Illinois saw the ritual as one of extending kinship through adopting the French. In other words, "the Illinois converted Marquette and Jolliet from strangers to members of the nation and forged a bond between themselves and the French empire."[116] Ironically, the French saw the ritual as forming an alliance in which the Illinois would become converts to Catholicism and would become subjects of the French.[117] While these misunderstandings clearly existed, they did not hinder the complex relationships between the Jesuits and the Illinois, given that they both needed each other in these times of tremendous upheaval and change. And, despite the Crown's resistance to colonizing outside Canada, the Jesuits were determined to expand their educational missionary work among the Indigenous peoples further south.

The expansion of the Jesuit pedagogical circuit into the Mississippi Valley was undertaken by Father Jacques Gravier (1651–1708), who re-established the Illinois mission begun by Father Marquette and Father Allouez. Gravier represented the ideal missionary Jesuit educator: well-educated, experienced in teaching in France, and having completed a teaching novitiate in the New World prior to taking on full missionary activities. Born in Moulins, France, Father Gravier attended the Jesuit College there before entering the Novitiate in 1670 at the College of Louis-le-Grand in Paris. After teaching in the College of Hesdin for five years, he studied philosophy in Paris, taught again for two years, and then attended theology school, where he was ordained. He arrived in Quebec in 1685 to teach at the Jesuit College and began missionary work at both Sillery and at Michilimackinac.[118] In 1689, fifteen years after the first Jesuit mission had been established by Marquette at Kaskaskia, Bishop Laval approved Jesuit missionary work among the Illinois, where Gravier settled in the village of the Peorias.

The Upper Mississippi Valley was home to the Illiniwek (the French transliteration was Illinois) Confederation, which was composed of twelve to thirteen tribes that stretched from Lake Michigan as far as Arkansas. Waterways in this region—the Illinois, Mississippi, Missouri, Ohio, Tennessee, and Wabash—linked this region, the "middle ground," to the South, the Great Plains, and the Great Lakes.[119] Having taken control of the central Mississippi Valley in the seventeenth century, the power of the Illinois lay in their ability to travel unencumbered from Lake Michigan west to the Plains and from Lake Superior to present-day Arkansas. This was still a remote area to the French, with few colonists, and its development was not a priority of the French empire. But it was precisely because the Illinois region was at the margins of the French empire and outside French authority that the Jesuits saw this as an ideal site to create a "primitive Christianity," much like the early Apostles.[120] Like previous Jesuit missionaries, their teaching mission did not require the Illinois to live as Frenchmen. Instead, they would live among the Illinois, learning their language, culture, and way of life. In these borderlands, far from the gaze of the French colonial government, the Jesuits sought to create their own ideal society, an Eden of sorts, in which education would hasten a universal spiritualism that would unify an increasingly diverse and multicultural society. While the Jesuits sought to unify all people through Catholicism, the Illinois saw the French as collaborators whom they could transform and incorporate into their nations.[121]

The Illinois had only recently moved into the Mississippi Valley region to occupy what had been Cahokia, the largest Indigenous city-state in North America. Originally the Illinois, part of the Great Lakes Anishinabee people, had lived in the area south of Lake Erie. Haudenosaunee expansionism into this region in the sixteenth century resulted in major demographic shifts in which the Illinois moved into the Mississippi Valley, colonizing the area of the Oneota. This required a radical change in lifestyle from woodland hunting to a bison-based economy supplemented by farming (corn, squash, fruit) and small game. The Illinois prospered, building a strong and complex network of cities. When Marquette first encountered them, there were fourteen distinct subgroups of about ten to fifteen thousand people; the five main groups included the Cahokia, Kaskaskia, Michegamea, Peoria, and Tamaroa.

The settlement of early French colonists in the Illinois country consisted mostly of fur trade merchants, *engages* (indentured servants), and *coureurs de bois* (illicit traders), many of whom did not settle permanently, but followed the fur trade migration patterns. By the 1730s, French-Creole colonial settlers, made up of *Canadiens*—those from the St. Lawrence Valley—made up the majority of the population. They sought "liberation and freedom" from French imperial policies through marrying local Indigenous women and mixing with Indigenous peoples.[122] The Illinois social organization was based on kinship, through which they divided the world into three arenas: the household, the community, and the outside world. Kinship was constituted not solely on biological family but also was established through intermarriage, adoption, and fictive kinship.

One form of fictive kinship was developed through trade relationships in which the *coureurs de bois* and trade merchants became kin. Trade was of course critical to the Illinois for increasing power, connecting people, and dealing with outsiders. They developed an expansive trading network that covered the lower Mississippi Valley (north to south) and from the Plains to the Algonquian (west to east). The Illinois occupied the strategic crossroads of this trade network from which they benefited economically as middlemen, building relationships that enhanced their power and stability. When the French arrived, the Illinois saw them as strangers who would be integrated into their trade networks and adopted into their kinship circles. Ironically, both the Jesuits and Illinois were proponents of conversion. For the Jesuits, conversion came through education; for the Illinois, through kinship networks.

While for different ends, both the Jesuits and Illinois desired transcultural assimilation, the Jesuits to establish a multicultural, multiethnic universal Catholicism and the Illinois to establish an alliance/kinship system that would secure their power. In the Illinois region, these interests, while not parallel, intersected in ways that allowed for an unprecedented collaboration between the French and Illinois for at least several generations. Historian Robert Morrissey suggests that this collaboration was based on the French colonists and Illinois developing "a flexible interracial order based on a huge network of kinship and fictive kinship linking together French and Native peoples."[123] Local agency, not imperial designs, shaped this community from the bottom up. This network was developed by the Illinois through fictive kinship practices, as discussed above, including the calumet, trade alliances, and intermarriage.[124] For the Jesuits, these networks were developed through the educational pedagogies of baptism, godparenting, and catechism, as well as intermarriage, which they promoted against official imperial policies. The story of Marie Turpin, introduced at the beginning of this book, also suggests that these networks were used by Illinois women for their own purposes.[125] In the case of Marie, the purpose was to travel to New Orleans, where she entered the Ursuline convent. While these networks were not to last, given the eventual racialization of French imperial policies through ideologies of racial purity through bloodlines and a ban on intermarriage, the Jesuits' pedagogical labor of universalism shaped the Upper Mississippi Valley for well over fifty years.[126]

By 1693, Father Gravier had established a permanent mission at Kaskaskia, one of five villages in the Illinois country, and was eventually appointed vicar general of the Illinois mission. Father Gravier, along with seven other priests, was at the forefront of developing relational networks, especially through intermarriage, that were central to intracultural community building.[127] Like earlier Jesuit missionaries who sought to teach the Indigenous people, these priest educators were an exceptional group of linguists who compiled studies of the Illinois languages, writing the most extensive Kaskaskia Illinois-French dictionary, as well as a catechism.[128] Learning the languages required immersion in Illinois life: accompanying the Illinois on their winter bison hunts, eating meals with them, and immersing themselves in all daily activities. Central to their pedagogy was the attempt to understand the Illinois language in all its complexity so that they could shape the three core texts, the Our Father, the Hail Mary, and the Apostle's Creed, to conform to the linguistic and cultural demands of the Illinois.[129] This required a collaborative effort in which Indigenous instructors were indispensable for accurate and efficient language study. This was not a project of mere translation, but one that resulted in shared experiences undertaken in the common quest for mutual transcultural understanding.

Over the course of six years, by 1696, Father Gravier is said to have baptized two thousand persons.[130] Father Marest was also vigilant in administering the rite of baptism, considered the first pedagogical step toward
conversion. Yet it was the daily rituals and prayers that demonstrated inter-
nalized Catholic beliefs. These daily rituals included daily mass followed
by instruction for those who were preparing for baptism who met at the
church prior to mass for practicing the signing of the cross, prayers, and
singing hymns. In the afternoon, those preparing for baptism returned for
catechism classes. In the evening, the community would gather again for
prayers, singing hymns, and instruction. Some might continue in their
own homes to learn and recite the rosary or sing hymns. According to
Tracy Leavelle, "Belief, faith, and knowledge may have been important,
but ritual action and performance assumed the paramount position in the
practice of Illinois Christianity."[131]

By 1707, the settlement at Kaskaskia counted twenty-two hundred
inhabitants, of whom all but forty were Catholics.[132] But while the Jesuits thought they were acquiring religious converts, the Illini understood
baptism not as a religious ritual, but one of fictive kinship in which they
were making strangers into kin. While they took up rituals of Catholicism as rites of kinship building, they retained their Native spirituality.
This was especially the case among the male Illinois, whose power in this
patrilineal society derived in part from their role as spiritual leaders. While
Illinois men were pragmatic Catholics, Illinois women were more likely to
practice Catholic spirituality in addition to embracing Catholic rituals.[133]
This can in part be attributed to the unequal gender relations among the
Illinois. Father Bienneteau wrote that "According to their customs, [Illi-
nois women] are the slaves of their brothers, who compel them to marry
whomsoever they choose, even men already married to another wife."[134]
For some Illinois women, French colonialism, particularly the Jesuit missionaries' offer of kinship through conversion, provided spaces in which
they had agency as women that was restricted among the Illinois. In one
of the many profound ironies of colonialism, becoming Catholic allowed
Illinois women access to power that they could bend to their own purposes.

A mutual goal of both the Jesuits and some Illinois women was to expand
the number of legitimate marriages in which both partners were Catholic.
While marriage between French fur trappers (*coureurs de bois*) and Native
women had a long history, these *métis* marriages were conducted in the
wife's Native village according to local marriage customs, with the husband
often living with her family to develop kinship connections. While the
Illinois saw these marriages (marriage "à la façon du pays") as essential for

developing trade alliances, the Jesuits saw them as a vehicle to stop French men from "going native." Devout Catholic Illinois women who married French traders were seen as central to keeping Catholic French men in the fold of the Catholic Church and to building the pious nuclear families critical to a Catholic society. Accordingly, the Jesuits focused their educational activity on Illinois women, whom they baptized and instructed through catechism to become pious, ardent Catholic women and mothers. Some, like Marie Turpin, rejected earthly marriage, taking up an identity of her own choosing. Upon marriage in the church, Illinois women left their village to live with their French husbands and were granted the same legal rights as French men and women, in essence becoming French. Illinois women saw advantages in these marriages for acting as brokers between two worlds: connecting the Illinois to a larger transatlantic economy while securing survival of their Native cultures. At the same time, for the Jesuits, this process of Frenchification accelerated their vision of a multiracial, multiethnic universal Catholic Church.

Father Gravier, while not initially successful with the conversion of Illinois men, found that the Illini women were more amenable to conversion. Jesuit teaching at this time stressed the cult of the Virgin Mary, emphasizing chastity and virginity, concepts unknown among the Illinois. Illinois women, although having few sexual sanctions, often choosing their partners and having lovers while married, also could be in unhappy polygamous marriages or in abusive relationships.[135] By adopting Catholicism and specifically abstinence, however, they derived religious authority and power as Catholics, allowing them to challenge gender norms and Indigenous elders whose power rested in visions and traditions.[136] These Catholic teachings provided them a form of agency and power within the nation that they had not had access to before. While this pleased the Jesuits, it infuriated the French traders and colonial officials who relied on French/Indian sexual relationships to cement trade, economic, and political relations. By converting to Catholicism, Illinois women were able to leverage celibacy and the sacrament of Christian marriage for their own means to acquire some authority and control over their lives. Intermarriage with Frenchmen also provided them with direct access to the power that marriage extended and enhanced.

For the Jesuits, intermarriage was initially a crucial catalyst of their missionary agenda. Not only did intermarriage promote conversion among Illinois women and create Catholic families, but devoted Illinois women brought lapsed Catholic Frenchman back into the fold of the church. Ironically, in this way, Illinois women aided the Jesuits in their role as educators, not only by ushering their children into the church but by re-educating their husbands. One such example is the case of Marie Rouensa, the daughter of the chief of the Kaskaskia Illinois.[137] After her conversion in 1694, she took up the role of teacher in evangelizing other Kaskaskia, especially other women and children, by using the copperplate engravings of Father Gravier to make intelligible the Old and New Testament to her fellow Illinois. Her desire was to remain celibate, never marry, and to devote herself fully to Christ. Her father, however, wanted her to marry a Frenchman, prominent fur trader Michel Accault, in order to build an alliance that would strengthen his power and the Illinois nation. She initially refused on the grounds that Accault was not a practicing Catholic. After reflection, Marie came to the conclusion that she could use this marriage as a vehicle for the conversion of others to Catholicism. She conceded to her father's wishes on the condition that Accault and her parents convert to Catholicism. Father Gravier's account in the *Relations* of this episode, in which Marie served as a catalyst for a myriad of conversions, including a wayward Frenchman, served to promote the practice of intermarriage, despite official government fear that intermarriage would result in Frenchmen going native.[138] Whatever success the Jesuits had in conversion, they owed much of it to Marie, who laid the foundation for a Catholic Kaskaskia community.

Interracial Catholic marriages became the basis for one of the most powerful pedagogies of the Catholic Church: godparenting. Following Catholic ritual, every child baptized was required to have a godmother and godfather who were responsible for their religious education. Through this type of fictive kinship, the responsibility for education was not solely reserved to the church or the parents, but was situated within a larger community. This dispersal of education through a community network not only situated education as a function of the community, not the individual, but created a web of relationships that strengthened the bonds of Catholic kinship.[139] The Jesuits continued to encourage intermarriage even after Louisiana's political elite began rejecting the strategy in the 1710s. Believing that the success of the colony was contingent on French families under French authority, the French colonial administration in 1716 banned French-Indigenous intermarriage. Despite the ban, the practice continued. Consequently, the fictive and nonfictive kinship networks that were seen by the Jesuits as the foundation of a universal Catholic community continued well into the late eighteenth century.[140] These networks were severely compromised when French officials, shortly after the ban on marriages, segregated the four permanent Jesuit mission villages: Cahokia (1699), Kaskaskia (1703), Fort Chartres (1719), and Prairie du Rocher (1722).[141]

The Kaskaskia moved away from the multiethnic French-Kaskaskia town; the Cahokia and Michigamea were removed from their French villages to form new villages several miles away. Only those Illinois who were considered French, by way of marriage or conversion, could stay in the now French villages. This change in policy reflected the emergence of race as a category for determining identity and interactions between different groups. Whereas the policy of Frenchification and conversion was predicated on the belief of the mutability and flexibility of identity, racial constructs were grounded in notions of a fixed identity. Some Illinois embraced the proposal, hoping it would protect their sovereignty and land. They lived in separate villages, resisted Catholicism, maintained their hunting lifestyle, and, despite the ban on interracial marriages, had Illinois women marry French men, creating multiethnic communities despite the protestations of missionaries and colonial officials.

While the Jesuit vision of a multiethnic, Catholic community was under attack, they stubbornly continued to promote the practice of intermarriage, engaging the support of Illinois women to do so. Between 1720 and 1765, however, priests performed only 13 French-Illinois marriages out of 272 weddings.[142] Baptisms and godparenting played an increasingly significant role in building kinship relations. In turn, they continued to function to facilitate education in various forms: within the family, in the Catholic Church, and in Catholic educational institutions. Despite the decline in intermarriages, in the 1740s—fifty years after the marriage of Marie Rouensa—Marie Turpin, a product of intermarriage, would attend the Ursuline convent school in New Orleans and become an Ursuline nun. Her niece also attended the Ursuline academy and married into a prominent French family in New Orleans. Family kinship networks mediated through and in the pedagogies of Catholic universalism and Illinois alliances continued to shape transatlantic communities in both Upper and Lower Louisiana regions, as well as throughout the transatlantic (Figure 2).

For the Jesuits and Illinois, these networks were essential to maintaining the alliances that protected them as they were being increasingly threatened by attacks from the Fox. Father Nicolas Ignace De Beaubois (1689–1770) became superior of the Illini mission in 1724.[143] Born in Orleans, France, he entered the society in 1706 and, after teaching in Rennes for three years, arrived in Canada in 1719 to complete his training as a missionary. A year later, in 1721, he was assigned as the parish priest in Kaskaskia in the Illinois country. Although the Illinois mission remained within the

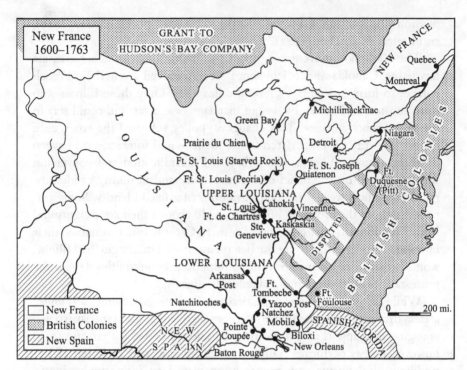

New France
1600–1763

GRANT TO
HUDSON'S BAY COMPANY

NEW FRANCE

Quebec

Montreal

Michilimackinac

Green Bay

Prairie du Chien

Ft. St. Louis (Starved Rock)

Ft. St. Louis (Peoria)

UPPER LOUISIANA

St. Louis   Cahokia   Vincennes
Ft. de Chartres
Ste.   Kaskaskia
Genevieve

LOWER LOUISIANA

Arkansas
Post   Ft.
Tombecbe
Natchitoches   Yazoo Post   Ft.
Natchez   Foulouse
Pointe   Mobile   SPANISH FLORIDA
Coupée   Biloxi
Baton Rouge   New Orleans

N E W

S P A I N

Detroit

Niagara

Ft. St. Joseph
Ouiatenon

Ft.
Duquesne
(Pitt)

B R I T I S H   C O L O N I E S

D I S P U T E D

New France
British Colonies
New Spain

0   200 mi.

Figure 2. Map of French Colonial North America 1600–1763. Drawn by Mary Lee Eggart.

jurisdiction of the Quebec diocese, military and civil jurisdiction had since 1717 been moved to the territory of Louisiana. An astute diplomat and shrewd fundraiser, Beaubois sought to maintain support for the missions by arranging for a delegation of Illinois to visit France. In late spring of 1725, Father Beaubois traveled to New Orleans from Kaskaskia with Chief Chicagou, a convert, and four other Illini chiefs from where they departed to France.[144] Their visit to Paris was discussed in the December 1725 issue of the *Mercure de France*. The chiefs met with King Louis XV on November 22. The *Mercure de France* reported that Chicagou made a speech to the young French king pledging allegiance to the Crown. The next day, the king took the chiefs on a rabbit hunt. It was while the chiefs were in Paris that Jean-Philippe Rameau, one of the most important French composers of the eighteenth century, attended a performance given by the Illinois at the *Theatre Italien*. At this performance, the Illinois danced three kinds of dance: the Peace, War and Victory dances. Rameau was inspired by this to write a rondeau for harpsichord entitled *Les Sauvages*, which was later used in his opéra-ballet *Les Indes galantes*, as the last of four Entrées. Situated on the borderlands of the French and Spanish colonies in North America, the opera describes a love story in which Zima, a young Indigenous girl, must choose between a French, a Spanish, and an Indigenous suitor and ends with the re-enactment of the calumet ceremony and the smoking of the peace pipe.[145] These types of transatlantic pedagogical exchanges put in motion a complex creolization of cultures that disrupts any unitary narratives of colonization as a hegemonic imposition of culture from Europe to the "New" world. Likewise, the Illinois "adoption" of Catholicism and knowledge of French diplomacy provided the necessary credibility to act as diplomats with their French allies to negotiate their own military plans.

By the 1730s, the Upper Mississippi Valley was the breadbasket of New France, providing the grain that was essential to the colonies' survival. The Jesuits had introduced wheat around 1700, and within a few years, they included tobacco, flax, and hemp. When Upper Louisiana was integrated into the official jurisdiction of Lower Louisiana in 1717, Governor Bienville hoped that increased agricultural production would feed both Lower Louisiana and the Caribbean. The Jesuits and the colonists in Kaskaskia relied on the labor of enslaved people of both Indigenous and African heritage for agricultural production.[146] French Jesuits had of course already been involved in the African slave trade and established plantations in the Caribbean. The first enslaved Africans arrived in New Orleans in 1719. By the 1720s, between sixteen and eighteen African and Indigenous enslaved peoples provided the forced labor in the Jesuit plantation fields and brewery at Kaskoskia (Figure 3).[147] While Indigenous slaves performed domestic labor, enslaved Africans worked largely in agriculture as field hands and ran the plantation's mill and brewery. Enslaved Africans and free men of color also worked as boatmen for the Company of the Indies navigating the river between New Orleans and Kaskaskia, ensuring not only commerce, but carrying news, gossip, letters, and newspapers from around the world.[148] While the importation of enslaved Africans to the Illinois country was limited, by 1726 enslaved Africans made up 25.1 percent of the population and 32.2 percent of the population in 1752.[149]

The Jesuit plantation on the Kaskaskia River and just two blocks from the Immaculate Conception Church was an integral part of the village. Given their zeal for creating a multiethnic, universal Catholic Church, as well as the requirements of the Code Noir of 1685, we can be certain that enslaved Africans, as well as Illinois and French villagers, attended mass together at Immaculate Conception. Enslaved Africans would have been baptized, received educational instruction through catechism, and been

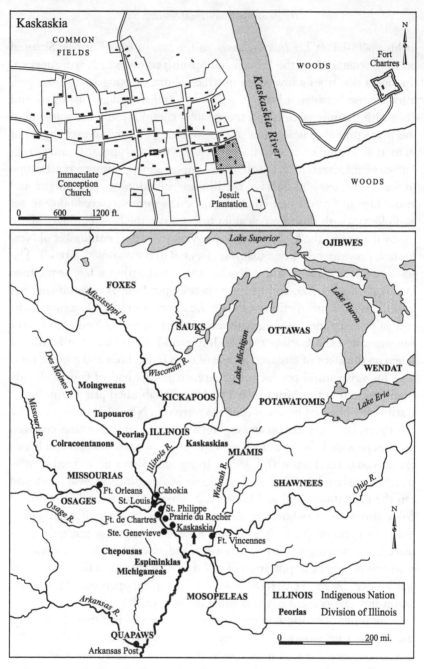

Figure 3. Map of Kaskaskia in Upper Louisiana, 1720s. Drawn by Mary Lee Eggart based on 1766 map titled "A Plan of Caskaskies." Adapted from image originally published in *The Present State of the European Settlements on the Mississippi*, by Capt. Philip Pittman, 1770.

married in the church. Father Francois Philibert Watrin, the last Jesuit priest among the Illinois before the Jesuit expulsion from New France in 1763, recalled the morning rituals in the village of Kaskaskia. "At sunrise, the bell rang for prayer and mass: the savages said prayers in their own language, and during the mass they chanted, to the air of the Roman chant, hymns and canticles, also translated into their language, with the suitable prayers; at the end of mass, the missionary catechized the children."[150]

Whether young enslaved African children would have participated alongside Illini-French children is speculation. But given the fluidity of race at this time, as well as the close-knit spatial relations within the village, enslaved Africans were visible members of the community and most certainly impacted it in numerous ways (food, material culture, religion, agriculture, music, language). This multiethnic, multilingual, multicultural space reflects the profound nature of the transatlantic pedagogical circuit.

By 1747, when the eighteen-year-old Marie Turpin left Kaskaskia for New Orleans, the Illinois country was situated at the crossroads of a thriving network of economic, social, religious, and cultural exchanges between Indigenous, European, and African actors. Marie was certainly not shocked by the site of the African boatman who would have guided their boat downriver to New Orleans. While the Illinois country has been considered back country by many, Kaskaskia was a cosmopolitan space within the transatlantic pedagogical circuit. The Mississippi River was the superhighway that connected these outposts through trade, marriage, military alliances, and Jesuit missionary educational activity. The prolific networks that emerged were built from the ground up, not by imperial design, thus making them difficult to control. Although French colonial policy was increasingly based on race, not kinship ties, the Jesuits, while accommodating racial norms to some degree, continued to provide education to all as a means of pursuing their vision of a universal Catholic Church.

While the Jesuits and Ursulines were establishing schools and universities in Canada and the Upper Mississippi Valley during the seventeenth century and early eighteenth century, the Lower Mississippi Valley remained a distant, unknown borderland to them. Up until this point, exploration of the Mississippi Valley had been initiated from Canada by Marquette, Jolliet, and La Salle. Unsuccessful in finding the mouth of the Mississippi from the north, the French minister of marine, Jérôme Phélypeaux, Comte de Pontchartrain, approved an expedition to locate the mouth of the Mississippi from the south, to establish a site there that could block entry to the river by France's rivals.

The famous thirty-eight-year-old Pierre Le Moyne, Sieur d'Iberville, from a well-established family in Montreal, was chosen to lead the first of three expeditions in search of the mouth of the Mississippi River from a gulf approach and to establish a permanent French settlement. The Mississippi provided not only a superhighway linking Canada, the Upper and Lower Mississippi Valley, and the Caribbean, but gave the French a strategic advantage over the Spanish and English by controlling the central artery of the North American continent.

Leaving from Brest in 1698, Pierre and his brother Jean-Baptiste Le Moyne, Sieur de Bienville, traveled along the Gulf coast relying on information from the Pascagoulas to find the mouth of the river. The delta provided no suitable site for a settlement, so the first French outpost was built at Fort Maurepas, on Biloxi Bay in present-day Ocean Springs. In his journal, Iberville remarks that "the Indians made maps of the whole country for me."[151] Iberville suggests that without Native geographical informants, he would have "discovered much less geography and perceived it in a far less insightful manner," which reflects the degree to which Indigenous knowledge was essential to the French colonial project.[152] While the grand design of French colonialism under Louis XVI envisioned a so-called "blank slate" on which they could write imperial designs of an "enlightened" empire, the actual everyday workings of the empire were very much dependent on negotiations and exchanges with the local Indigenous peoples, not on the imposition of French designs. On the ground, La Salle, who had described the "favourable disposition of the savages," was no doubt aware that the French would need the assistance of the Indigenous population in settling the Lower Louisiana territory.[153] Their intimate knowledge of the geography, ecosystems, and waterways was essential not only to French exploration of this region, but ultimately to French survival.

After returning to France, Iberville set out again in 1700 on his second voyage, determined to find a suitable site for a permanent settlement near the mouth of the Mississippi. Iberville refused to accept a missionary from the Foreign Missions in Quebec, choosing instead a Jesuit to accompany him with the purpose of establishing missions among the Indians.[154] Iberville knew that successful relations with the Indigenous peoples would require successful alliances, relationships he believed could be nurtured by the experienced Jesuits. Father Paul Du Ru joined them on this journey, staying in Louisiana for about two years and engaging in the first attempts to provide Catholic education to the Indigenous peoples of present-day Louisiana. His detailed journal written during this time, as well as that written by Iberville, later published in France, makes them the first European authors in Louisiana and contributors to the Republic of Letters.[155]

The Education of Father Paul Du Ru: Translation Pedagogy and Jesuit Mission in Louisiana

> I forgot to say that for two days I have been going to school to the
> old Savage to learn to speak the Bayagoula language.
>
> —Father Paul Du Ru, 1702[156]

Father Paul Du Ru might well be considered the founder of the first Jesuit mission and school in Louisiana. Yet the transcultural practices in which he engaged meant that Father Du Ru was not only a teacher, but also a student of the Indigenous peoples. As he recounted in his journal, *he* went to school in order to learn the Bayagoula language. While his motive was to gain a better understanding of the Bayagoula to convert them, these cultural exchanges ultimately functioned to radically change both the Jesuit missionary and the Bayagoula. What is unique about Father Paul Du Ru's journal is that it is not only one of the first detailed accounts of Indigenous peoples in Louisiana, but that it was never published as part of the *Jesuit Relations*. Father Du Ru was not writing for an audience in Europe, censoring what he said to portray a successful mission. He was writing for himself. This unadulterated narrative provides for all practical purposes a teacher memoir, a reflection of a first-year teacher.

Father Du Ru accompanied Pierre Le Moyne Iberville on his second voyage to the lower Mississippi (1700), where he served as the chaplain. Born on October 6, 1666, in Vernon, Du Ru had entered the society in Paris in 1686 (age twenty) and, upon completion, taught in the colleges of Quimper, Vannes, and Nevers, after which he took up five years of study in Paris. In 1699, he was chosen by his superiors for the mission in Louisiana. Arriving at Fort Maurepas (the first capital of Louisiana) on January 8, 1700, Father Du Ru traveled with Iberville, whose goal was to establish a fort on the Mississippi and to visit Indigenous villages up the river as far as the Red River, including the Bayagoula, the Houmas, Taensas, Natchez, and Colapissa. His journal provides a personal account of the expedition (February 1 to May 8, 1700). The journal has been overlooked as an important early document of Louisiana history, in part due to the simplistic nature of its style.[157] The daily notes of his activities and his firsthand impressions of and interactions with the landscape and people provide a unique view from the "ground" up.

While Du Ru had taught in France, he had no prior experience as a foreign missionary. To be a successful teacher, he knew he would have to learn multiple languages, including the Bayagoula language—Muskogean—as well as Houma, Choctaw, and Chickasaw. His lessons had already begun on the four-month journey from La Rochelle on board the *Renommé*, where Du Ru had traveled with a young Bayagoula boy whom Iberville had engaged on his first expedition to teach him the language. While Du Ru had learned some rudimentary knowledge of the language, he understood that he would have to "go to school."[158] Likewise, the Bayagoula, eager to form an alliance with the French for their own military and economic purposes, had sent a "teacher/*sauvage*," considered among the Bayagoula as an expert regarding knowledge of the country, to accompany Iberville's expedition to teach them their language and customs.[159] While their talk was initially more by gesture than by words, it was not long before Du Ru had learned "fifty of the most necessary words."[160] Within a month, Du Ru's knowledge of the Bayagoula language was sufficient to produce a rudimentary catechism.

Prior to European contact, the Bayagoula nation was west of the Mississippi about twenty-five miles south of Baton Rouge. The Bayagoula were part of a vast southeastern network of Indigenous trade and communication systems by land and water.[161] This was a dynamic world marked by constant movement and cultural exchanges in which the initial arrival of the Spanish and French Europeans in 1513 presented little threat, while offering opportunities to enhance trade relations. However, by 1700, the Bayagoula, a petite nation, had suffered not only from the diseases brought by Europeans, but also from the intertribal and colonial warfare caused by European rivalries. By 1650, it is estimated that only 3,000 Bayagoula remained; by 1699 when Iberville first arrived, epidemics had reduced the number to 1,250.

While no Jesuit missions had been established along the Gulf Coast at this time, Father Du Ru was part of the well-established global network of Jesuit educational missionary efforts in New France that extended from Quebec to Martinique.[162] Histories of encounters in New France have traditionally portrayed the "meeting" of European and Indigenous peoples as clashes in which Catholicism functioned as a form of social control and handmaiden to colonialism.[163] Alternatively, some historians have acknowledged the complexities of these encounters and highlighted the religious agency of Indigenous peoples and the everyday meanings they ascribed to their beliefs.[164] In other words, how religion is lived from the "ground up."[165] The Jesuits, as we have seen, were renowned for their flexibility in adapting to local conditions, customs, and belief systems, a strategy known as accommodation. This translation of oneself into another culture involved developing a local or transcultural Catholic terminology and literature, as well as religious rituals.[166] Drawing from Father Du Ru's journal, I examine the ways in which his work as an educator was a process of transcultural translation in which he and the Bayagoula became both students and teachers.

> Everybody dresses up to meet the Bayagoulas. Beards are trimmed and fresh linen put on.
> —Father Paul du Ru, Journal of Paul du Ru[167]

Iberville's expedition approached the Bayagoula with the respect due a sovereign nation. Du Ru's first impressions are ones that convey both rich description and awe:

> The landing begins. The whole bank is black with Savages who sing the calumet to us. We arrive thus in good form. After having embraced our people, it was necessary to respond to the embraces of the Savages, smoke the calumet and to go through all the other details of their ceremonial. I noticed three rather good looking chiefs and some well formed young people. This evening I went to the village which is more than six hundred years old. There is a huge plaza in the midst of it and at the end of this two temples of about equal size. The one belongs to the Mougoulachas, the other to the Bayagoulas, for the village is composed of these two tribes. The temples are made of thatch and are covered with cane mats. Their shape is quite like the dome of the portal of the Collège du Plessis.[168]

The calumet ceremony was an elaborate performative ritual engaging music (drumming, gourds, flutes), dancing, singing, and miming.[169] Prior to the calumet, the Bayagoula chief had passed his hands over his own face and chest and then over Iberville's and raised his hands to the sun and rubbed them together. This ritual signified the commingling of two people in which the chief bound the French into an ancient cosmological tradition of reciprocity, key to building newly established relationships. From the Bayagoula perspective, they had adopted the French, while the French saw the ritual as one in which the Bayagoula would become French and Catholic. For Father Du Ru, the syncretism of these performances allowed for the translation of seemingly universal human experiences across lines of cultural difference.[170]

Du Ru provided richly detailed descriptions of the social and public life of the Bayagoula. This included the plaza events such as the calumet, ball games (played by both women and men), dancing, feasts, weddings, and markets, which were public rituals that functioned to build community. Du Ru described the elaborate welcoming ceremony put on by the Bayagoula:

> [T]he singers have very soft voices and the dancers a very beautiful cadence. The women are of surprising modesty. They dance oppo-site their men, their bodies a little bent, their eyes cast down and marking the cadence admirably well with their bunches of feathers, so that it is only their hands that move. Flutes and drums set the measure. These are played by handsome young people with legs decorated with small gourds filled with stones with which they mark the cadence as we do with our castanets. After this entertainment, we were taken to dine at a camp which is at the edge of the river less than half a league from the village.[171]

He provides detailed descriptions of the village, its buildings, furnishings, and clothing, and the large earthen platform mounds that the Bayagoula were building.[172] Mound building had a long history among the cultures of the Mississippi Valley and signified important public buildings, like tem-ples for religious ceremonies, which held sacred objects and eternal fire.[173]

Like Catholic rituals and ceremonies, these performative acts were public enactments of values and beliefs that not only functioned to build commu-nity but were primary ways of teaching and reinforcing a shared culture. Observation of these rituals, comparing Native song and dance to balls, bal-lets, and opera, was central to the translation process through which Father Du Ru gained insights about the culture and beliefs of the Bayagoula.

Du Ru's lack of cultural superiority enabled him to recognize the rich culture of the Bayagoula: the elaborate rituals of hospitality, the long-developed history, political organization, architecture, education, and civility. This acknowledgment of Indigenous forms of courteous man-ners and orderly political life, called *civilité*, was unique to the Jesuits, who attributed these as signs that Christianity could take root.[174] He also found them open to his instruction.

> The barbarians, who seem to have only a very vague idea, readily accepted the idea that the sun is not a spirit. This makes it seem very probable that they do not adore it as the *Relations* say they do. As near as I can make out, their whole cult and religion is limited to the performance of their duties to their dead. This can easily be corrected by a little instruction.[175]

Du Ru sought not only to correct what he perceived as a false interpretation made by other Jesuits in the *Relations*, but suggests that instruction, as a form of remediation, would correct misunderstandings. In other words, Du Ru did not seek to replace the belief systems of the Indigenous peoples; instead, he sought through the process of translation to augment or amend their beliefs to conform to Catholicism.[176]

> I try to make them understand only a few things. They learn at least that the sky, the sun, the moon, and the stars are not spirits, that is gods, or Ougas, that is their chiefs, but that all these are creatures of a single Great Spirit or Great Chief whose home is up above in the sky. I left some images with certain old men and they promised to show them in the village. One of them who had a flux on his breast put his on the wound and gave me to understand that he expected it to heal him.[177]

Father Du Ru contrasts the notion of a single divine spirit to many spirits, while the old man compares the Catholic image perhaps to an amulet traditionally used among Indigenous peoples for healing. The shared belief that divine power can intercede to influence human pain and suffering linked the cosmologies of both the French and Bayagoula in a belief system where there was an understanding that humans were only one element in a larger cosmic design. The process of transcultural translation necessitated that Du Ru have a deep understanding of the worldview of the Bayagoula in order to identify those cultural elements to which the Catholic message could be translated. This religious syncretism, the "blending" of European and Indigenous spiritual practices, was grounded in accepting and tolerating Indigenous beliefs.[178] In this regard, Du Ru was a student, asking questions and conducting research with the aim of achieving cross-cultural understanding.

In his study of the customs and ways of life of the Indigenous peoples, Du Ru also visited the Natchez:

> There are two things about this village which I cannot cease to wonder at. One is the respect and obedience paid to the chief; the other is the gentleness and kindliness of all the Savages. We are living with them as with brothers. I should prefer to be alone at night in their midst than on Rue St. Jacques in Paris at nine o'clock in the evening.[179]

His reference to feeling safer among the Natchez than he would in Paris suggests that his positive appraisals of the Indigenous peoples provided a means to also critique his own French culture and society. Du Ru also notes the role of education received by the next in line as chief. He recalled:

> The chieftainess arrived and brought with her a supply of meal for us. She had a little prince following her whom she takes with her everywhere she goes; she is in charge of a man who serves as his tutor. The child is very pretty and already shows nobility in his countenance. Some day he will be the Grand Ouachilla and wear the crown with the same dignity as the present one.[180]

His favorable impression of many aspects of Indigenous life is more striking given the comments about his fellow French and Canadian travelers:

> It is hard to get our people together. Some go fishing at daybreak, others hunting. To-day is Sunday and it was necessary to have Mass very early so that all of the parishioners can attend. Several men carried on boisterously during Mass and I became indignant. In my discourse I was severe. French customs mean little to the Canadians, and they are more lawless than the others. . . . [M]ost difficult to control is the spirit of freedom which they acquire in the forest where they have no master over them.[181]

The process of religious education and reformation was not limited to Indigenous groups. Du Ru also saw his fellow Frenchman, who had "gone native," in need of renewed Catholic discipline. The need to evangelize *both* Indigenous peoples and the French, a double pedagogy, suggests that translation was not limited to the "other," in essence deconstructing rigid binaries of pagan/Christian, French/Native, and colonizer/colonized.

And while much is lauded regarding the customs of the Indigenous peoples, there is much that he does not and cannot understand. Du Ru writes:

> One of the evil customs of these Savages is to put away with the deceased all of his former possessions. Even the cabin where he lived is burned. It is said that among the Colapissas, the Natchez, and the Taensas, no chief dies without a dozen of his most loyal friends killing themselves to be buried with him.[182]

Du Ru's journal is filled simultaneously with awe and respect for some Indigenous customs and horror, even disgust, at others. To whatever degree he could not understand the ways of the Indigenous peoples, however, it did not constitute them as "uneducable." In other words, he understood them as capable of acquiring and producing knowledge, of educating and being educated.

Du Ru attempted to teach in a variety of ways, including baptism, using material culture (rosaries, crosses), and direct teaching through catechism.[183] While the use of images and text were central to catechism, by far the primary "teaching" tool was the use of rituals like baptism. Du Ru recalled,

> At Eight o'clock in the morning I baptized a little Savage, named Marly aged six or seven years with the full ceremonial of the church. He belongs to the village of the Onquilousas. M'Iberville was his godfather, and named him Pierre. This is the first baptism which I have had the honor of performing.[184]

The ritual of baptism, performed by Du Ru, would have been the simplest of the sacraments to perform, given that the use of water as symbolic of purification was a common element in both French and Bayagoula belief systems. For the Jesuits, unlike other missionary orders, the baptisms of Indigenous infants were critically important.[185] Baptism signified membership in the Catholic Church, and the absolution of original sin was a prerequisite for entering God's kingdom. The cosmological worldview of both Gulf Coast Natives and Catholic peoples shared a belief in an afterworld to which one could travel after death. For many tribes in the Lower Mississippi Valley, religious ceremonies and rituals were directed to pleasing the spirits with the hope of joining them after death. This syncretism regarding an afterlife was a point of translation in which rituals, like baptism, served to highlight shared beliefs.

Father Du Ru saw baptism, a rite of passage, as the first step toward a Catholic education. For the Bayagoula, baptism was a form of fictive kinship, given that Iberville (in the eyes of the Indigenous peoples the "chief") took on the role of "godfather" of this Native child.[186] For Catholics, the role of godfather is important because the godparent is tasked with the responsibility of making sure that the child receives a Catholic education. In the eyes of the Bayagoula, much like the Illinois, this ritual signified the establishment of a kinship bond critical to developing alliances. While

Father Du Ru understood baptism as a religious ritual and the Indigenous tribes understood it is a kinship ritual, through their translations, both understood baptism as a means of building relationships, fictive kinships that joined people in a common familial network. The ritual of baptism, like the Indigenous greetings and calumet ceremony described by Father Du Ru, suggests the willingness of both groups to engage in foreign rituals as a means of solidifying relations. It was this mutual engagement in rituals, rather than the imposition of one belief system or another, that expanded knowledge of one group about the other.[187]

These kinship rituals resulted not only in enhancing local relations, but they contributed to a network of relationships, as well as to communications and the flow of information that radiated throughout the lower Mississippi River Valley. On February 16, 1700, Iberville had begun building a fort and powder magazine on the cleared land of the former Quinipissas village (later New Orleans). In the evening, Henri Tonty (Tonti) arrived with eight men. Iberville wrote: "[T]he men with him [Tonty] are habitants, most of them from the Illinois and Tamarouas, who came on their own initiative to see what there might be to do here, in response to the letter M.de Sauvolle sent up there [saying] that if men came from upriver they would find work and would be welcomed here."[188]

Not only did the Illinois travel downriver to find paid labor, but they traded, exchanged information, and functioned as ambassadors. This vast "exchange" network between Indigenous peoples and the Jesuits that encompassed the Lower and Upper Mississippi Valley suggests a "continental" approach that emphasizes the transatlantic *collectivity* and *connectivity* in which kinship and alliance systems developed across vast cultural differences.[189] For the Jesuits, this was a primary way in which they sought to develop their vision of universal Catholicism through education.

It is impossible to determine to what degree the Bayagoula understood and embraced Catholic religious beliefs. What we do know is that they engaged in various rituals, ceremonies, and activities. By late March 1700, the Bayagoula, under the direction of Father Du Ru, were engaged in building a church. Father Du Ru describes the process:

> Our building progresses. Timber has been brought from every direction, but I do not yet know enough Bayagoula to make them place them as I wish. The chiefs themselves are working, a thing they do not always do on their own houses. One of them snatched a ball from the hands of a young man who was playing with it while the others worked and brought it to me in my tent. They understand

that they are not making the building for me but for the Great Nan-houlou and that it is in it that he will speak with me. They understand that the Great Nanhoulou is not seen because he has no body like man, that he has made all things, that he acts without hands, speaks without a tongue, and goes everywhere without feet. They know that every man is composed of body and soul, that the body dies, but the soul does not, that after a long period the souls will rejoin the dead bodies and that the bones in their temples will come to life, and that all men shall appear before the Great Nanhoulou, the good to dwell with him in heaven, and the evil to go under the earth where they shall burn in everlasting fire. . . . This is all that they know because it is all that I myself know in Bayagoula. They are as impatient to learn more as I am to teach them. The Savages give me to understand that my church will be finished in five days. This is all that I could wish so I wait upon their industry.[190]

The church upon completion would hold more than four hundred persons; clearly Du Ru had high hopes for the education of the Bayagoula.[191]

While Du Ru had hoped to convert the Bayagoula, their motivations for engaging with the Jesuits and participating in Catholic rituals are mere speculation. As a smaller tribe within the gulf region, they were continually threatened by other tribes, including the Houma and Chickasaw. The Chickasaw, who were engaged by the British, were continually conducting slave raids in the area to provide slaves for the British plantations in the Carolinas and West Indies. The alliance with the French served a practical purpose: an ally would strengthen their forces and provide protection. Du Ru records his conversations with the Bayagoula chief: "We talked politics chiefly, more by gesture than by words. He declared that his tribe expected us to avenge them for the wrongs that they have suffered from the Oumas."[192] In other words, the Bayagoula saw the French as an ally in settling disputes with various tribes These alliances were forms of fictive kinship, much like those of baptism and godparenting. In other words, these mutual cultural exchanges were pedagogies of relationship building in which cultural values and beliefs were transmitted. These fluid everyday exchanges encouraged what Daniel Usner has called "cultural osmosis" among the region's various inhabitants.[193] Social relations between the Jesuits and Bayagoula were fluid and organic, lived from the ground up, with little connection to the colonial designs originating in France that sought domination and control.

Ultimately, this cultural and economic exchange would also include

Africans. During his time among the Natchez, Father Du Ru wrote, "We have heard in all the villages here that quite a large group of negroes and of mulattoes, men and women, have deserted and are established in a separate district where they persist in their revolt."[194] While the first enslaved Africans were not brought to Louisiana until 1719, enslaved Africans from the British colony of South Carolina seeking freedom ran away, establishing permanent maroon communities in the area of the Natchez.[195] These were independent communities that were self-sufficient and outside the systems of government created by the Europeans. Communities like these signaled the agency and determination of enslaved peoples and the creation of creole communities in which Indigenous and African cultural exchanges formed another assemblage in the transatlantic pedagogical circuit. Father Du Ru's description of these maroon communities as sites of revolt brings attention not only to the resistance of enslaved Africans but to the potential collaboration between Indigenous and enslaved peoples in opposition to the French.

After his travels with Iberville, Father Du Ru returned to Fort Maurepas in Biloxi and then Mobile, where the fort was eventually transferred. Throughout 1701, Father Du Ru traveled the lower Mississippi Valley from the Red River to the gulf with two young Jesuit priests, Father de Limoges and Father Donge, helping them to establish missions. In the tradition of the Jesuits, both had been well-educated and had teaching experience. Father Joseph de Limoges (1668–1704) had taught for five years at Amiens and had taught one year of philosophy and four years of theology at the college of Louis le Grand, otherwise known as "The Jesuit College in Paris." In 1698, Limoges set out with Father Jean Mermet (1664–1716) for Canada, where they both began the requisite training as missionaries, learning the Indigenous languages and the ways of life among the Indigenous peoples and environs. In 1700, Father de Limoges joined Father Du Ru in Louisiana for a brief period of orientation before setting up a permanent mission among the Houma, who were at this time near the mouth of the Red River. Father Pierre Donge (1670–1702), after teaching for three years at the colleges of Blois and Rouen, was called to missionary work in Louisiana as well. He accompanied Iberville from France in late 1701 to Mobile, where he joined Father Du Ru at Fort Louis de La Louisiane and ministered to the French settlers and the surrounding Indigenous nations.[196] These missionaries began the first (yet short-lived) attempt to establish permanent mission schools in Louisiana.

By 1702, the Jesuits, with the support of the Le Moyne brothers, were successful in establishing several mission schools. The priests of the Quebec seminary, however, also wanted to establish themselves in Mobile. The bishop of Quebec, who held jurisdiction over all the land in New France, including the mouth of the Mississippi, was the rightful decision maker when it came to assigning missionaries and had declared the Seminary priests as the missionaries in this area. Disputes over missionary responsibilities between these two orders could not be resolved.[197] Father Du Ru returned to France in 1702 in hopes of reaching a resolution but failed to do so, and both Fathers de Limoges and Donge were recalled to France. Father Du Ru never returned to Louisiana. This marked the end of the first, brief missionary effort among the Jesuits in the lower Mississippi Valley. When Bienville became governor of Louisiana for the third time from 1718 to 1724, he would be instrumental in the Jesuits regaining a foothold in Louisiana, where they would remain as missionaries until their expulsion in 1763.

The Jesuits in New Orleans and Lower Louisiana

While the Company of the Indies was responsible for providing for the religious needs of the colonists, they had difficulty navigating among the competing religious orders.[198] Ultimately, with the urging of Bienville, the company turned to the Jesuits under the leadership of Father Beaubois, issuing a new contract in 1726 that gave them responsibility for Indigenous education throughout the Lower Mississippi Valley.[199] The Jesuits were given a house in New Orleans as their headquarters and instructed to limit their work to establishing missions throughout the Mississippi Valley, leaving the work of administering to the Catholics of New Orleans to the Capuchins. This would be the beginning of the first permanent Jesuit missionary presence in Louisiana. The Capuchins and the Jesuits, competing ecclesiastical bodies, both trying to survive in a colony that seemed always on the verge of collapse, were often embroiled in conflict. Consequently, it has been suggested that they attended "as much to economic development and political gamesmanship as to sacramental dispensation and moral legislation."[200]

Father Beaubois, after four years in Upper Louisiana among the Illinois, was named superior of the New Orleans Jesuit mission in 1725. Having just recently returned from France with the Illini delegation and having shown French imperial powers just how successful the Jesuits had been in converting the Illinois, he returned to France to seek support for the missions in Lower Louisiana, including a community of Ursulines. Father

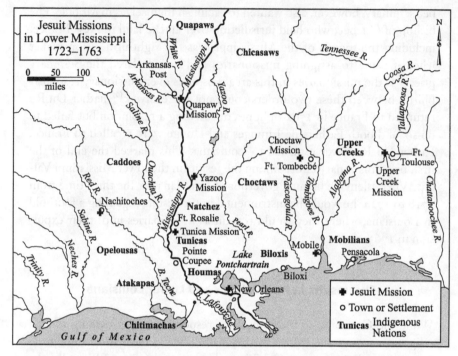

Jesuit Missions in Lower Mississippi 1723–1763

0 50 100
miles

Quapaws
Chicasaws
Tennessee R.
Coosa R.
Tallapoosa R.
White R.
Mississippi R.
Arkansas Post
Arkansas R.
Saline R.
Quapaw Mission
Yazoo R.
Caddoes
Ouachita R.
Red R.
Yazoo Mission
Choctaws
Choctaw Mission
Ft. Tombecbé
Upper Creeks
Ft. Toulouse
Upper Creek Mission
Alabama R.
Pascagoula R.
Tombigbee R.
Chattahoochee R.
Nachitoches
Sabine R.
Natchez
Ft. Rosalie
Tunica Mission
Tunicas
Pearl R.
Opelousas
Neches R.
Trinity R.
Pointe Coupee
Houmas
Lake Pontchartrain
Mobile
Mobilians
Pensacola
Biloxi
Atakapas
B. Teche
New Orleans
B. Lafourche
Chitimachas
Gulf of Mexico

✚ Jesuit Mission
○ Town or Settlement
Tunicas Indigenous Nations

Figure 4. Map of Jesuit Missions in Lower Louisiana, 1720s–1763. Drawn by Mary Lee Eggart.

Beaubois's time in France reaped rewards. He returned to New Orleans with six Jesuits who were each assigned to missions in Lower Louisiana (Figure 4).[201] These included missions among the Upper Creeks (Fort Toulouse), the Choctaw (Fort Tombeché), the Yazoo, the Arkansas, the Caddos at Natchitoches, and the Tunicas. These missions and schools were for the most part staffed by the Jesuits from 1727 to 1763.[202] As had been the custom of the Jesuits, they lived not at the nearby forts, but among the Indigenous peoples to learn the language and customs, as well as to provide education through catechism and conduct baptisms, marriages, and burials.

Between 1727 and 1763, when the Jesuits were expelled from Louisiana, there were, in addition to these original Jesuits recruited by Father Beaubois, twenty other Jesuits who taught and worked as missionaries. Ten of these twenty were assigned to Upper Louisiana and worked primarily among the Illinois at Kaskaskia, continuing the missionary work of Father Gravier and earlier missionaries. For a brief time in the 1740s, there were four Jesuits at Kaskaskia, indicating the continued need for priests/teachers among the villages of the Illinois. The Jesuit headquarters in New Orleans also housed Jesuits who ministered to local nations, including the Chitimacha, Houma, and later Choctaw. While the success of conversion was extremely limited, Indigenous peoples in Lower Louisiana, like the Illinois, formed alliances with the Jesuits through kinship rituals, trade, religious ceremonies, and education. These exchanges were forms of alliance building that sometimes resulted in mutual trust and a sense of responsibility to the other. The Jesuits often acted as conduits and go-betweens among the French and the Indigenous peoples to minimize misunderstandings or tensions. Access to French language, trade, culture, and religion also provided opportunities to use these institutions for their own purposes in a time of great upheaval within a rapidly changing and always contested colonial context.

While these posts ebbed and flowed, given the many challenges of the early French colonial period, an almost constant presence were the Jesuit priests. The Jesuit mission schools also functioned to connect a dispersed and disparate French colony through an educational network that traversed the whole of the Upper and Lower Mississippi Valley. Headquartered in New Orleans, the Jesuits, perhaps more so than the French colonial administration, provided the thin thread that functioned to facilitate cultural exchanges into a web of transatlantic alliances. While Indigenous relations with the Jesuits created alliances suited to their goals, it was the Jesuits prevalent in the backcountry of both Upper and Lower Louisiana whose ministrations facilitated the necessary relationships with the Indigenous peoples that helped the empire to function. With their knowledge of Indignenous cultures and languages, the Jesuits could act as a protective buffer, mediating misunderstandings and disputes between French and Indigenous peoples. In fact, the Jesuits protected the French from disgruntled Indigenous peoples, whose increasing reliance on alcohol and other French goods resulted in trade misunderstandings. By the 1720s, though, the Jesuits' economic resources were strained. Father Beaubois, given his experience in the Illinois country, recognized the possibility of turning to plantation agriculture, based on enslaved labor, to finance and maintain the missionary posts. It is a profound irony that in order to raise money to expand mission education, the Jesuits engaged in the brutal and dehumanizing institution of slavery.

While in France on his recruiting trip in April 1726, Beaubois completed the purchase of property just upriver from New Orleans belonging to Bienville, which included three enslaved Africans, on which he planned to establish a plantation to help finance the missions. The front of the plantation

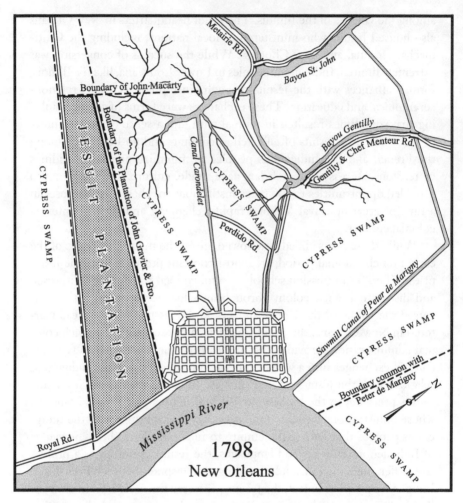

Figure 5. Map of Jesuit Plantation in New Orleans, 1720s–1763. Drawn by Mary Lee Eggart based on 1798 map of New Orleans in Bernard A. Cook, *Founded on Faith: A History of Loyola University New Orleans* (New Orleans: Loyola University, 2012), 11.

was about two-thirds of a mile along the river, and the property extended one and two-thirds miles back from the river (Figure 5). On route back to New Orleans, he purchased sixteen enslaved Africans in San Domingue for the plantation, nine of whom died before arriving. Father Beaubois, unlike earlier missionaries who opposed the institution, increasingly saw slavery not only as a means of conversion, but as an economic necessity for the financially pressed Jesuit missions. Given the lack of funding by the Crown, and driven by the need for money, Beaubois engaged in an ambitious vision for a prosperous plantation. The Catholic Church in Louisiana would now become complicit in the transatlantic slave trade and the institution of slavery. In fact, the Jesuits would become, along with the Ursulines, two of the largest slave-owning corporate entities in Louisiana during the French colonial period.[203] In essence, the Catholic Church in Louisiana increasingly relied on plantations and enslaved laborers for its growth and survival. While acknowledging the spiritual equality of enslaved Africans through baptism, catechism, marriage, and full participation in the church, they simultaneously saw African people as assets to be bought and sold.

While the Capuchins had started a small school in New Orleans in 1725, Beaubois was intent on establishing something larger.[204] Initially he had the support of Louis XV, who had proposed that a Jesuit college, whose curriculum would be equivalent to that of Harvard College at the time, be established in New Orleans. Beaubois believed that a full-fledged college might be premature, given that the city was still in its infancy with only 649 inhabitants. The proposal for a college came to nothing due to lack of funding. Instead, Beaubois focused his energies on developing the Jesuit plantation, which he envisioned as an agricultural college and experimental station for the colony. The plantation included a chapel (erected by the river near the intersections of present-day Gravier and Magazine), along with a house for the Jesuit fathers, warehouses for the storage of crops, work sheds, poultry houses, dovecotes, indigo curing sheds, a blacksmith shop, and houses for the enslaved population.[205] Beaubois planted orange and fig trees (introduced from Provence), indigo, tobacco, cotton, and sugar (brought from Hispaniola).[206] Produce from the plantation was sold on the open market or shipped to San Domingo or to France. Research, led by Beaubois, experimented with new methods of growing sugar cane and indigo and building canals; he also tried to devise a new type of cotton gin. Beaubois's agricultural research and experimentation was part of a larger Jesuit mission to develop knowledge of the natural sciences in Louisiana, which included François Le Maire (1675–1748), a scientist sent to Mobile in 1706 to gather observations, as well as Antoine Jean de Laval, who was send by the French Department of the Marine in 1720 to Mobile to chart the Gulf Coast and gather other scientific data, resulting in his 1728 publication of *Voyage de la Louisiana*.[207] The Jesuits clearly contributed to Enlightenment intellectual life in Louisiana as well as to building pedagogical circuits to France.

The Jesuits were part of the first generation of slaveholders in Louisiana's emerging slave economy. The first enslaved Africans had arrived in

1719, and in 1724, the 1685 Code Noir was updated, banning intermarriage and making it more difficult to free the enslaved. In the 1727 census, the Jesuits, like 78 percent of the slaveholders who lived between Point Coupee and New Orleans, had fewer than 20 slaves.[208] By 1763, when the Jesuits were expelled, they numbered 130 enslaved Africans.[209] The Jesuit mission in New Orleans had slowly shifted from the conversion of Indigenous peoples to that of enslaved Africans. This required new transcultural translations—the learning of new languages, religions, and cultures. Like Indigenous peoples, all slaves were required to be baptized, educated through catechism, and married and buried by the church. Forced to attend daily mass with all residents of the plantation, they learned hymns, recited prayers, and were exposed to scripture. These educational spaces like catechism classes, godparenting, and apprenticeships, provided spaces in which the enslaved could re-establish kinship systems that strengthened communal bonds within the enslaved community, as well as to appropriate these spaces and inscribe them with their own meaning. The Jesuit mission was a cross-cultural space that housed visitors from France, Canada, the Caribbean, and frequently the Illinois. As a nexus of the transatlantic, enslaved Africans participated in these encounters resulting in the emergence of cross-cultural practices that opened new spaces for cultural creativity, adaptation and resistance.

The New Orleans mission served as the "main campus" for the Jesuit missionaries throughout Louisiana and the Mississippi Valley. It was here that the Jesuit fathers from the various missions throughout Louisiana would return to gather supplies, letters from abroad, and books, and to rest from the work of the field. New missionaries from France would spend time here to complete their "teacher education training" by learning the rudiments of Indigenous languages and the use of catechisms, as well as survival skills necessary for living in remote areas before heading out to their posts. By 1740, colonial officials in New Orleans, including Governor Bienville, expressed their desire to have the Jesuits establish a college for the young men of the colony. Governor Bienville wrote in June of 1742 to the French government on behalf of the colonists advocating for a college, since it was "essential that there be one at least for the study of the classics, of Geometry, Geography, pilotage, and knowledge of religion."[210] While many of the colonists sent their sons back to France to be educated, this was not only costly, but risky; once in France, many of their sons did not return. Both Father Beaubois and Father Vitry advocated for the founding of a Jesuit college, but financial support for education was not the priority of the Crown.[211]

By 1763, when the Jesuits were expelled, the Indigenous population in the lower Mississippi River Valley had been decimated by disease and war. Those remaining invented new ways to resist colonization, including relocation, urban trade, maroonage, and continued diplomacy.[212] By the 1720s, the Bayagoulas, Mougoulachas, Chitimachas, Houmas, Taensas, and Colapissas had dwindled to a few families or had been absorbed by the more powerful Natchez and Choctaws. For these "petite nations," colonization had radically changed their world and the cosmology that explained it. New cosmologies emerged. Carson recounts:

> As one Taensa chief explained to a Jesuit missionary, there had once been a cave that was home to a white man, a red man and a black man. The white man left the cave first and found a good hunting ground. The red man left next, strayed off of the "good road" the white man had followed, and claimed a less abundant hunting ground, while the black man "got entirely lost in a very bad country." Since that time, the red man and the black man have been looking for the white man to restore them to the good road."[213]

The Taensa chief no longer saw himself as the power at the center of the sacred circle but as part of a larger colonial world. It is also a profound statement in regards to the transcultural relationships that the chief recognized the mistreatment and plight of the "black man."

Within these shifting landscapes, Native peoples adapted their lives by drawing on their vast knowledge of the geography, resources, and natural rhythms of the land, drawing French colonists into new circuits of trade and diplomacy, to both negotiate and resist colonialism. According to Carson, "the history of Louisiana is less a story of French imperialism and more an example of how chiefs and commoners managed the transformation of the Old World into the New."[214] The transcultural pedagogy of the Jesuits played a role in this transformation, although it was perhaps not what they had intended. The Jesuit and Ursuline approach to education as a process of transcultural translation contributed to both the cultural genocide of Indigenous cultures and way of life *and* the continual adaptation and reinvention of Indigenous people. In this regard, it reflects the nature of education as always embedded in power relations. Their endeavors in creating a transatlantic pedagogical circuit that intertwined Africa, the Caribbean, Lower Louisiana, Upper Louisiana, Canada, and France were radical given their vision of universal education for all, however, Indigenous peoples continue to experience the intergenerational historical harms from the violent history and legacy of European settler colonial injustices.

For all practical purposes, the intended educational efforts of the Jesuits and Ursulines among Indigenous peoples in both the Upper and Lower Mississippi Valley and in Canada were a failure, and in most cases extremely destructive to Indigenous lives and culture. While individual nations like the Wendat, Illinois, Apalachee, and Houma appropriated Catholicism in a myriad of diverse ways, the work of education among the Jesuits did not result in the creation of a utopian universal global community. Of course, this does not mean that education did not take place, just that the formal curriculum of catechism did not have the intended results. Jesuit language acquisition and anthropological writing, as well as medicinal, botanical, and biological scientific knowledge, resulted in increased knowledge about the New World, contributing to the emerging Enlightenment quest for knowledge. Simultaneously, the creole pedagogy of transcultural translation that took shape in the spaces of the transatlantic circuit resulted in the creative processes of hybridity. These exchanges produced new foods, clothing, language, music, frontier economies, and religions that remind us that education is always a creative process. The cultural interactions did not end here, though. In parallel to these complex acts of local translation, missionaries also "translated" cultural diversity in another direction, to the European Republic of Letters. In doing so, they hoped to defend their religious worldview in the context of the rapidly changing intellectual and political landscape of the Enlightenment.

While historians have vacillated between emphasizing either the pioneering character of the Jesuit missionaries as proto-anthropologists or their complicity in the colonial project through the forcible imposition of Eurocentric ideological agendas, there is growing awareness of the crucial importance of how Indigenous peoples acted as knowledge brokers and pursued their own personal agendas and cultural biases.[215] And while the vision of a new Garden of Eden did not take root as the Jesuits and Ursulines had hoped, the concept of *universalism*, that all human beings are inherently united in a common humanity with the *right* to be recognized as spiritual equals, circulated through the practices and spaces created in this transatlantic circuit. The right to be understood as spiritually and morally equal in the public spaces of the Catholic Church contributed to the long history of Indigenous and African protest for human equality that has continued through time and space. While the cultural genocide of Indigenous peoples and brutal system of slavery exploited bodies and minds in horrific, unthinkable ways, Africans and Indigenous peoples were resilient, creative, and persistent in resisting the dehumanizing effects of subjugation and slavery.

Reverberations

> As with all Indigenous Peoples, our existence and identity is tied
> to the lands and waters that gave birth to us. As the avarice of
> capitalism continues to devour our world, we wonder with our
> brothers and sisters around the globe, what will be left to pass on
> to our descendants?
>
> —Monique Verdin, Houma artist and activist, 2019[216]

For Indigenous peoples in Louisiana, education has either been used to exclude them or as a form of assimilation/deculturalization. After the Jesuit expulsion in 1763, access to formal education among Indigenous peoples severely declined. Ongoing slave raids conducted by the British, who hired Chickasaw warriors, decimated Indigenous groups in Louisiana, resulting in twenty to fifty thousand people being enslaved. The devasting consequences of this has led Monique Verdin, a Houma, to call this time the "Mississippian Shatter Zone."[217] Many tribes relocated to the sparsely populated Gulf Coast where new groups of people formed. When the Louisiana Purchase transferred control of the area from the French to the United States, only lands that had property titles registered with the French or Spanish authorities would be honored by the American government. Indigenous nations legitimate land rights were not recognized, meaning that many tribal identities were never acknowledged. "Unclaimed land" was transferred to the public domain, and the federal government began the process of surveying and selling the land to recoup the cost of the purchase. As a plantation slave economy expanded in the nineteenth century after the Haitian Revolution, many white settlers moved into south Louisiana, thereby dislocating Indigenous peoples and pushing them farther south into the bayous of Terrebonne, wetlands where they began making a living on the water. Given the hardening of the color line in the nineteenth century, Louisiana officially designated Indigenous peoples as "people of color," which meant they were considered Black. Given the racial segregation of schools, this meant that Indigenous peoples did not have access to education unless they attended segregated Black schools, which were woefully underfunded, inferior schools, or in some cases private Christian missionary schools that were opened specifically for Indigenous students.[218] Yet their determination to receive an education has never wavered. With the desegregation of schools in the 1960s, Indigenous groups and their tribal councils began to advocate for schools that acknowledge their unique history and education.

For the Point-au-Chien Tribe, located in Terrebonne and Lafourche parishes on the southeastern coast of the Gulf of Mexico and composed of descendants of the Chitimacha, Acolapissa, Atakapas, and Biloxi, that struggle continues today. Ironically, their fight is for a French-language school, a language that they were forbidden to speak when they started attending public schools. They are predominantly Catholic and French-speaking, seeing these as defining traits in their Indigenous cultural identity. As a community, they want the education their children receive to reflect not only their language, history, and culture but their place-based identity. This place they call home, the bayou wetlands, have been ravished for years due to oil and gas companies and by natural disasters like Hurricane Ida in 2020. After many years of grass-roots activism organized through the tribal council and executive committee, the École au-Chien French Immersion school opened its doors in the fall of 2022. The Louisiana Senate passed HB261 authorizing the creation of the school as a public school with a school board that is majority approved by the Point-au-Chien people. It will be the first publicly funded Indigenous French school in Louisiana.

Today there are only four federally recognized Indigenous tribes in Louisiana: the Chitimacha, the Jena Band of the Choctaw, the Coushatta tribe, and the Tunica-Biloxi. Both the Point-au-Chien and the Houma are recognized by the state, but not by the federal government. The Houma people, who are the largest surviving Indigenous group in Louisiana, numbering seventeen thousand, are still being denied federal recognition as a "tribe." Ironically, this is in part because they speak French and are Catholic, attributes that are not considered American "Indian." Like the Point-au-Chien, they have been denied access to public education. Historically, white and Black schools excluded Indigenous peoples, creating a tripartite system of segregation in Terrebonne and Lafourche parishes. Louisiana's educational exclusion of the Houma due to segregation resulted in the Houma not having access to public education until the 1950s.[219] In 1953, Daigleville school, a previously white school, was made an "Indian" elementary school for grades 1 through 8. Around 1957, Daigleville expanded its courses, making it a high school. Daigleville was then the only high school that offered education to the Indigenous community of Terrebonne Parish. While the school has been on the National Register of Historic Places since 2020, the United Houma Nation is working to obtain the building from the Terrebonne Parish School Board to renovate it as a historical tribute to the resilience of Indigenous peoples and embody the historical memories of generations of Indigenous peoples who were and continue to be marginalized and traumatized by centuries of educational injustice.

Indigenous peoples in Canada have launched the largest class action suit in Canadian history in regards to the legacy of Indian residential schools in the nineteenth century. The Truth and Reconciliation Committee was formed with the purpose of collecting the stories and experiences of residential school survivors to address the ongoing impacts of intergenerational trauma. Nicholas Ng-A-Fook, Patrick Philips, Mark T. S. Currie, and Jackson Pind, Canadian scholars whose work is situated within the "so-called era of reconciliation," suggest that the dominant narratives of the history of education have been ones of "great forgetting."[220] The erasure of complex and troubling colonial educational histories, including that of the Jesuits and Ursulines, has allowed for the production of an American educational history that locates colonialism in the past rather than the present. This not only obscures the ongoing colonialism that persists in the education system but also the Jesuit and Ursuline vision of education as a public right that signified a universal common humanity.

Counter-Enlightenment Pedagogical Ruptures

The Ursulines in Colonial Louisiana

> My dear Father, when one is certain of doing God's will, one
> values as nothing the opinions of men. Many people considered
> our enterprise as folly, but what is folly in the eyes of the world is
> wisdom in the eyes of the Lord.
>
> —Marie Madeleine Hachard, October 1727[1]

The "folly" that the twenty-three-year-old French postulate Marie Madeleine Hachard refers to in the letter to her father in Rouen, France, is the
Ursuline missionary enterprise to French colonial New Orleans, believed
by many to be the "Devil's Empire."[2] Founded only nine years prior to the
arrival of Marie and her eleven Ursuline companions at the capital of Louisiana, New Orleans had already garnered a reputation in France of being
a disorderly city that was on the brink of failure due to both economic and
moral corruption. Marie's ardent desire to join the Ursulines in establishing a religious house in this "Babylon" was clearly seen by many as folly or
even outright madness. The colony was considered by most in the metropole a failure that should be abandoned. What possible good could this
group of women religious do in a city that required Enlightenment order
and reason? Marie's use of the word "folly," however, is a gesturing to her
understanding, like Erasmus, that in the end, folly is the heart of reason.[3]
True madness is to rely solely on knowledge, or the "opinions of men."
These tensions between Marie's absolute faith in God and the emerging
Enlightenment faith in reason are brought to life in the five letters Marie

Hachard wrote to her father, Jacques Hachard, which he subsequently published in France. These letters not only reflect the struggle between faith and reason, but also anticipate the profound impact on understandings of education that these shifting sands would engender.

Published in France in 1728 under the title *Relation du voyage des dames religieuses Ursuline* (Relation of the Voyage of the Ursuline Nuns), Marie's eloquent letters not only give the reader a "street level" view of colonial New Orleans, but they convey the heart-wrenching agonies of a young woman's decision to trust her faith at the very time when "official public attention had turned from salvation in heaven to reformation on earth."[4] Support for religious orders—specifically active, self-governing teaching orders like the Ursulines, who had sizable wealth—had begun to decline in France after 1689. Despite faltering support from the French Crown, the Ursulines saw the missionary work of educating young women in New France as a way to reinvent and revitalize their teaching order, whose educational mission had been underway for almost two hundred years. For Marie there was no better site to negotiate the "shifting sands" of faith and reason than in the promised land of the Mississippi Valley.[5] Her certainty stands in stark contrast to the modernist shifts in the relation between the sacred and the profane. Yet looking back on Marie's story, what is astonishing is that her certainty of faith was never inevitable.

Marie Hachard: Rebellious Daughter and Dutiful Teacher

Born in Rouen, the youngest of seven children in 1704, Marie Hachard was by no means encouraged by her parents to enter religious life. Given that five of their children had already consecrated their lives to Christ it was most likely hoped that Marie would marry, have children, and remain close to home.[6] Well-educated and high-spirited, Marie showed a proclivity to devotion at a young age, often waking in the night to pray and taking her first communion at the young age of ten. When, at the age of eighteen her parents arranged an advantageous marriage, she adamantly refused.[7] Her first attempt at entering religious life among the sisters of St. Francis was thwarted by her confessor, Father de Houppeville, who assured her that this was not what God wanted for her. She languished for two more years until she heard rumors that three sisters from the Ursuline house in Rouen had been chosen by the Company of the Indies to found a new order in the Province of Louisiana.

Marie was no doubt familiar with accounts of New France, and specifically Louisiana. She most likely would have had access to the Jesuit *Relations*, a serialized collection of letters from Jesuit missionaries that were Europe's earliest genre of colonial literature. Given her devout spiritual nature, it is likely that Marie might have been introduced to the published letters of Marie de l'Incarnation, the Ursuline missionary whose nuns were described by the Jesuits as "Amazons." These fearless women were described by Marie de l'Incarnation as "*Canadoises*," missionaries who were physically strong, healthy, young, tenacious, self-sacrificing, and brave, whose stories of converting young Indigenous girls captivated the imaginations of those who saw New France as critical to propagating the one and true faith in post-Reformation France.[8] The Ursulines constructed a narrative in which they were central to the missionary history of the Catholic Church and in which God sent Angela Merici (the foundress of the Ursuline order), as another Deborah, to recall His people.[9] In 1673, Marie-Augustine de Sainte-Paule Pommereu, the Ursuline archivist at the Rue St. Jacques convent in Paris, constructed her own history of the order that featured the Ursulines of New France and demonstrated how they completed a long lineage of crusaders including St. Ursula, "the Archangel of the Apocalypse," Angela Merici, their "spiritual mother," and Marie de l'Incarnation, the "enterprising Christian Amazon" with Solomon-like strength.[10] For a young woman whose mind was set on serving God, these narratives of heroic women would surely have fueled not only her desire but provided a historical narrative in which she could name and legitimate her ambitions.

We can never know with certainty what fueled Marie's passion for missionary work as a teacher. It might have been the desire for adventure, the mystique of foreign lands, or her deep belief that she was called to meet the needs of the poor inhabitants of Louisiana. It is perhaps not astonishing though that a young girl, especially from Rouen, would have envisioned herself as taking an active role in shaping a "New World." Rouen was part of an extensive transatlantic commercial network that had developed during the sixteenth century after the economic devastation of the Hundred Years War. A major French port, the city was made up of wealthy, international wholesale merchants from Spain, Italy, and Holland who had since the early sixteenth century become part of an expansive transatlantic commercial network that linked Europe, Africa, and the New World. Rouen ships went to the Baltic to fish for herring, to Newfoundland for cod, to Portugal for salt, to Spain for wool, and to Brazil for brazilwood. The textile industry, which had started in the fifteenth century, developed a robust trade with Rome and extended as far away as the Canary Islands, West

Indies, Brazil, Canada, and India. Trade with Africa and the New World became a lucrative sector of Rouen's commerce as the city became a redistribution center for exotic new products.[11]

Also dominating the Rouen economy was the Senegal trading company, whose primary commodity was enslaved persons from Africa. The French had explored the Senegal River as early as the middle of the fifteenth century. It was merchant associates from Rouen who in 1638 established the first trading post on the Senegal River. Twenty year later, St. Louis became the first permanent town as well as the base of the emerging economy in enslaved persons and gold. From 1723 to 1731 the Company of the Indies delivered thirteen slave ships with 3,396 enslaved persons to Louisiana from the Senegambian region.[12] The majority of these were from the Bambara and Wolof peoples, who would be critical in Louisiana to developing both rice and indigo and serving as the primary navigators of the Mississippi River, where Marie would eventually encounter them as they took her up the river from Balize to New Orleans.

By the early seventeenth century Rouen was the second largest city in France; the city's economy rested on a wide base that included manufacturing and government administration as well as commerce. As the largest and wealthiest city and the capital of Normandy, Rouen was the center of political, legal, and ecclesiastical administration for the province and royal governments in Normandy, and it dominated the surrounding town, villages, and countryside.[13] The power of the state, as well as the significance of secular affairs, grew during this period of explosive commerce. From the late medieval period, the state began to play an increasing role in everyday life through its administrators, who collected taxes, recruited soldiers, dispensed justice, and enforced order.[14] Provincial governments like those in Rouen reflected these changes through rapid growth in educational institutions to supply the administrators needed to provide the increased regulation of the state.

Marie's father, a procurer in the Chamber of Accounts in Rouen, was one of the new bureaucrats. From his position monitoring the city's finances, he had a vantage point from which he could see the increasing international networks that were not only forming the basis of a new class of merchant bourgeoisie, but a rapidly developing transatlantic society. As an international crossroads, Rouen developed as an intellectual and cultural center of Europe that was at the forefront of the emerging printing and publishing industry in the sixteenth century. Literacy rates, especially in Rouen, had been steadily increasing not only as a consequence of the Reformation and Counter Reformation, but as a result of the state's increased demand for trained officials to manage the state's growing regulatory functions. Rouen as France's "second city" became known as a site for learning, much of which was conducted by religious orders. By 1550, the city was home to numerous religious orders, including the Dominicans, Carmelites, Augustinians, and Franciscans, as well as three wealthy nonmendicant religious houses: the Abbey of Saint Ouen, the Priory of Saint Lô, and the Hôtel-de-Dieu-de-la-Madeleine. In 1593, in response to the threat of the rise of Protestantism, the Jesuit College or Collège de Bourbon opened and quickly became the most important institution in Rouen in this period. Within a decade, eighteen hundred students were enrolled, receiving the characteristic Jesuit education, at once theologically orthodox and pedagogically innovative.[15] It was an education designed to reinvigorate the church by producing pedagogues who would be the universal foot soldiers of the church.

The truly universal nature of this mission is apparent by the inclusion of indigenous peoples from New France at the college. Shortly after the arrival of the Jesuits in New France, they sent young Wendat (Huron) males to Rouen to be educated for the priesthood. The presence of Wendat at the college was designed not only to create a cadre of Indigenous priests, but also for young Frenchmen at the college to learn about the Indigenous peoples of New France in preparation for their future lives as missionaries. Antoine Daniel from Dieppe in Normandy is one such example. While attending the Jesuit College, he became acquainted with and taught a young Wendat student who had been sent to France for his education. Daniel became interested in the Wendat mission and joined Jean De Brébeuf, a fellow Jesuit graduate, when he returned to Canada in 1632 in his second attempt to evangelize the Wendat.[16] Daniel set up a seminary in Quebec to train young Wendat for the priesthood. Then from 1637 he worked for ten years on Lake Huron and had not long settled in Teanaostaye when he and his Wendat parishioners were killed by the Haudenosaunee. The stories of Jesuit martyrdom in New France fueled devotion among pious Catholics who sought to re-establish the strength of the Catholic Church after the Wars of Religion.

The Hachard family, as both a deeply devout Catholic family and part of the nobility, undoubtedly understood the potential role of the Jesuits in New France in not only reinventing Catholicism as *the* universal church, but in solidifying a strong imperial government that would uphold this faith. Marie was most likely familiar with the Jesuit missionaries and martyrs from Rouen whose stories had been recorded in the Jesuit *Relations*, the annual accounts sent back from the Canadian Jesuits to its Paris office. Travel narratives about New France that began to be published in the mid-

1700s and gained increasing popularity in the late seventeenth century, conveyed a particularly challenging situation for Indian conversion south of Canada in the Mississippi Valley. Given that no published accounts of Louisiana were in circulation at the time Marie was contemplating her future, her vision of Louisiana most likely was shaped by her awareness of the many stories she had heard about the missionaries in Canada and the efforts to convert the Indigenous peoples.

Marie Hachard, exceptionally bright, well-educated, and with a large dowry, had choices. It is of course difficult to know what motivated Marie Hachard's fervent desire to engage in missionary activity in the New World. Mission activity, or apostolic work, was central to Catholicism and its belief in universalism. Since the Protestant Reformation, missionary activity had been directed not only toward the "New World" but was also focused on France. The reconversion of Protestants was critical, but just as important was education in rural Catholic areas of France that were lacking in literacy. Catholicism was, at best, superficially understood by rural peasants, and religious practices were rituals that reflected a hybrid of belief systems and cosmologies. The role of magic and folk religion was still pervasive in the everyday life of communities and families.[17] Visual symbols, rituals, processions, and interpreting pictures, not reading or writing, continued to mediate religious experience for the majority of people in France in the early eighteenth century.

For a young girl seeking mission or even adventure, Marie actually did not have to travel that far. Clearly, there was much "missionary" work to be engaged in right at home. Not only did Protestantism continue to be a threat, but a downturn in the economy left city streets flooded with forlorn peasants, abandoned children, hungry thieves, prostitutes, beggars, and those on the brink of trying to hold on to their sanity. In the 1720s, religious women were increasingly being directed by the state away from education; instead, they were encouraged to manage the work of taking care of the sick, the poor, and the outcasts of society. Education, the previous domain of women and men religious, was slowly seen as the purview of the state. The state's drive for secular control over its citizens led to national campaigns that sought to structure education under government control.[18] This shift of education from the control of religious orders to the state clearly unsettled the Jesuits and Ursulines who, up until this time, had provided the only unified educational system in France. Most disturbing, though, was the implications of this shift for the purposes of education. The state saw education as a technical endeavor to serve the needs of an emerging nation-state, whereas the Ursulines and Jesuits saw education as essential for developing a spiritual economy that had little concern with earthly life.[19]

For the Ursulines, and perhaps for young Marie, the significance of this shift must have been deeply disturbing. Education was increasingly understood as a secular endeavor whose primary purpose was to secure a hardworking, industrious, and loyal citizen to the nation-state.[20] This utilitarian view of education stood not only in direct opposition to the Ursuline vision of education, in which the "opinions of men" were seen as insignificant in the larger cosmos of the divine, but to the important role attributed to the education of girls by the Ursulines. The publication of Francois Fénelon's *Treatise on the Education of Girls* in 1687 signaled a radical shift in the education of girls to reflect the emerging social function of women as responsible for the governance of families.[21] While Fénelon's specific educational reforms never had sweeping success, the shift in cultural norms regarding the role of women as limited to the domestic, private sphere was part of larger ideological changes in gender roles that constituted Enlightenment thought. These shifts that required that women be relegated to the private, domestic sphere not only threatened the very basis of Ursuline pedagogy, in which women were to be teachers, but ultimately resulted in increasing regulation and scrutiny of convents. Given that the Ursulines had played a public, active role throughout the seventeenth century as leaders in educational reform for girls, this was a radical threat to their mission.

The shifting image of women religious was in stark contrast to the significant place that they had garnered in seventeenth-century France.[22] Female convents had dominated city landscapes where they owned large amounts of property, had ties to wealthy, noble families through their patrons, and, in the case of the Ursulines, dominated female education. The Ursulines, in particular, occupied an increasingly "public" space and sphere of influence that would eventually conflict not only with the anticlericalism of the philosophies of the Enlightenment, but with Enlightenment roles for women that relegated them from the public sphere to the private realm, in which the "natural" relationship between mother and child stood at the moral center of domestic life.[23]

While Ursuline pedagogy elevated women as teachers, given that Mary was the first teacher of Jesus, this pedagogical role was not based on essentialized, biological roles of nurturance. The emerging discourses of a "natural" relationship between mother and child that increasingly circulated through eighteenth-century novels, pedagogical works, and social treatises contributed to a view of asexual nuns as "unnatural." Simultaneously, rumors of uncontrolled passion, abuse of authority, and the perversion of the sacred arena of the convent all contributed to the very concept of celibacy and devotion to God as "unnatural" while also raising questions regarding the appropriateness of women religious as pedagogues.[24] The fact that women religious became "suspect" provided the state with the rationale to take over the control of schools run by women religious. Alternatively, the state encouraged the development of *petite écoles* whose purpose was not the construction of the Catholic subject, but was instead increasingly focused on constructing a secular subject that was a hard-working citizen of the nation. The poor were increasingly treated as *workers* and not moral human beings. This was in direct contrast to the Ursuline pedagogy, which continued to focus on spiritual universalism as the heart of subjectivity.

The suspicion that convents would influence young girls to choose the cloister over marriage, or make young girls "too" bookish, ironically, came from the ranks of their own. Françoise d'Aubignè, Marquise de Maintenon had attended the Ursuline convent school at Rue St. Jacque in Paris. In 1686, with the support of Louis XIV, she established the *Maison Royale de Saint Louis* at Saint-Cyr. This girl's school for the daughters of nobility would become a model for female education throughout the eighteenth century. Interestingly, it was her friendship with Fénelon that shaped her vision of social reform through female education. Like Fénelon, Maintenon hoped to produce noble girls who were hard-working and skilled in the domestic arts, household management, and finances. Letter writing and conversation skills were omitted from the curriculum for fear that they would encourage young girls to partake in courtly life. For Maintenon, the family was the "source of both individual and social salvation."[25] The creation of a privatized nuclear family or "cult of family," along with the enormous centralization and concentration of power, which bolstered the growth of the absolutist state, were critical factors in shifting conceptualizations of gender roles in France.[26] These significant cultural shifts had profound implications for women. As Natalie Zemon Davis has argued, the avenues for women's freedom in this period of "modernization" and "enlightenment" were foreclosed rather than expanded with the rise of the modern nation-state, secular culture, private property, and even Protestantism.[27] No longer was the Catholic Church, particularly its religious orders, seen as the primary site of salvation, but the family, regulated by the state through "public" education, would ensure a stable, moral, and virtuous society. These shifting sands were clearly recognized by the Ursulines, who began to see their role as major educational reformers of the seventeenth century challenged.

This threat clearly influenced their ambitions to participate in mission-ary work in foreign lands, where they could distance themselves in order to circumvent the increasingly restrictive roles for women in France. These missions—Quebec (1639), Martinique (1681), New Orleans (1727), and Pondicherry, India (1738)—were, as has been suggested by Heidi Keller-Lapp, part of a larger political/ecclesiastical resistance movement within absolutist France. The Ursulines sought to protect their teaching aposto-late from the French Catholic Church and the Crown by engaging in mis-sionary work overseas that would allow them to maintain a "public" role in society as well as reinvent their order.[28]

Ironically, the Enlightenment "public" increasingly excluded women, whose "power" or "influence" was relegated to the domestic sphere.[29] For women religious, this shift to the "domestic" sphere manifested itself in the cloistering of all women's religious orders as decreed in the Council of Trent. Ursuline orders were now forced to either cloister or become purely secular communities devoted to charity work. This division was central to the gendered construction of a public/private binary in which the pub-lic sphere was increasingly understood as male and secular, and authority was relegated by the state, as opposed to the private sphere, which was understood as female, religious, and limited in authority. Many Ursulines resisted this shift as a threat to their well-established educational mission and the authority of their institutions. This state "reform" of education away from women religious was resisted by many Ursuline orders, who saw this as a clear attempt to undermine their authority as educational leaders.

The Ursuline sisters of Rouen were one such group who resisted these educational reforms. A renowned convent, the Ursulines had established themselves in Rouen in 1624, reaching their peak number of yearly profes-sions, twenty-five, in 1628. By 1700, there were only seven new entrants.[30] One of these was Marie Tranchepain, a young convert from Protestantism, who had long dreamed of taking up missionary work in the New World. Raised in a family of devote Huguenots, Marie Tranchepain encountered immense pressure from her family regarding her decision to convert to Catholicism. Despite this resistance she entered the Ursuline convent determined to follow the path of Marie de l'Incarnation and engage in missionary work, a pursuit that took twenty-seven years to be fulfilled. It was the recently appointed superior of the Jesuits in New Orleans, Father Nicolas Ignace de Beaubois (1689–1770), of the newly designated mission district within the diocese of Quebec—*Missio Ludovisiana*—who wrote, at the request of Governor Bienville, to Mother Tranchepain regarding the desperate need for a religious order in the new colony to look after the military hospital and start a school. In 1726, the ambitious Father de Beaubois traveled to France not only to seek more support for the missionary activity of the Jesuits among the Indigenous peoples in the Lower Mississippi Valley, but to finalize the arrangements for the Ursuline mission.

Since 1723, the colonial administration in New Orleans had written repeatedly to the Company of the Indies asking for an order of religious women to assist with the institution of the hospital, which was critical to the physical and mental health required for a prosperous and well-ordered French city.[31] It was not a teaching order that the Company of the Indies desired. And in fact, it was the need for nurses in colonial Louisiana that would provide the initial momentum that would result in the Ursuline mission to New Orleans.[32] The company had hoped to entice the practically oriented Grey Nuns or the Filles de la Charité (Daughters of Charity), but to no avail. Father de Beaubois, who favored the Ursulines, proved himself a tough negotiator in dealings with the Company of the Indies, which by charter was supposed to provide financially for parishes and missions in its monopoly colony. Finally, the company administrators and Jesuit authorities (including Beaubois) agreed upon a contract in February of 1726. The company pledged fixed sums per annum, and contributions for travel and supplies.

Given the shared educational mission in New France of the Jesuits and Ursulines to Indigenous conversion, as well as their long history of friendly relations, it is not surprising that Father de Beaubois thought of the Ursulines as perfect allies in the evangelization of Louisiana's Indigenous people. If he could secure the favor of the Company of the Indies by convincing the Ursulines to take up the additional work of nursing, he hoped the Jesuits would clearly benefit through an expanded influence in shaping New France's educational mission. Seeing an opportunity to secure the Ursulines, Beaubois traveled to France in 1726, where he visited the Ursuline convent in Rouen. When Father de Beaubois appeared at the doors of the convent, Marie Tranchepain's lifelong dream was in her grasp. Word spread quickly among other Ursuline convents regarding the plans for a mission in Louisiana, and within a few short weeks, twelve sisters from the regions of Normandy and Brittany had been recruited.

Marie Hachard recounted in her first letter to her father,

> You know, my dear father, that I believe that I have already had the honor of telling you that it is the Reverend Father de Beaubois of the Company of the Jesuits who formed the noble project of our establishment in New Orleans. This missionary is full of zeal and

wisdom. You would not believe the number of obstacles he had to overcome to make this project succeed. He obtained everything with the help of God.

You also know, my father, that our Reverend Mother Tranchepain, chosen to be superior; Mother Judde, chosen the Assistant; and Mother Boulenger, chosen as treasurer, went ahead of us to Paris to make arrangements, in the name of our little community, with the gentlemen of the Company of the Indies. These men, very zealous for religion, treated us with the greatest respect. The foundation seemed to us equally solid and advantageous.[33]

February 27, 1727, Lorient, France

The Ursulines did not approach these negotiations lightly. At age forty-seven, Marie Tranchepain (1680–1733), after a twenty-year wait, was determined to make the necessary provisions that would result in a successful educational mission. Her assistant, Sister Judde (?–1731), despite strenuous objection from her family in Rouen, was determined to go to Louisiana. And, forty-one-year-old Sister Boulanger (1686–1766) no doubt sought to follow in the footsteps of her brother, Father Boulanger, who like Father de Beaubois served at the Jesuit Illinois Mission in Kaskaskia.[34] As cloistered nuns, the mother superior had to request special permission from the clerical authorities to travel overland to Paris to meet with company officials to negotiate their contract.

On September 13, 1726 in the hotel of the Company of the Indies in Paris, Mother Superior Tranchepain and Sister Boulanger, as treasurer, met with the Abbé Gilles Bernard Raguet, the religious director of the Company of the Indies, and company officials to prepare an agreement for the new convent in Louisiana. With the support of the mother superior of the Rue St. Jacque in Paris, Sister Bruscoly, the twenty-eight-article treaty between the Ursulines and the Company of the Indies was signed on September 13, 1726.[35] Five days later, the agreement was confirmed by the royal order, signed by Louis XIV and his minister Philippeaux. The agreement stipulated first and foremost that the sisters were to take care of the royal hospital in New Orleans and *only* if time permitted could they undertake the education of girls in the colony. The company was to provide for the maintenance and upkeep of the hospital, provide housing, and pay a stipend for the upkeep and subsistence for six nuns. This financial aid was critical, given that the sisters would not be able to transfer their dowries and were setting out as independent agents or "company girls." For all practical purposes they were cut off financially from their motherhouses in France and responsible for their own finances. This financial burden would prove to have a major impact on shaping the culture of their lives in New France.

Like Marie de l'Incarnation before them, the Ursulines saw missionary work in New France as a means not only to circumvent the restraints of claustration, but to reinvent their central role as educators, and to do so on a global scale. Marie Hachard clearly envisioned herself as one in a long tradition of educators. With monastic life becoming ever less fashionable by the time Marie was contemplating her future, given the challenges that women religious in France were facing, she was likely one of only a handful of women considering entry into life at the Ursuline convent in Rouen in 1720s. Marie was clearly not dissuaded by the decreasing popularity of religious life, nor the rumors of illicit behaviors, or shifting gender norms that depicted women religious as unnatural. What is clear is that Marie was convinced beyond any doubt that her destiny was in Louisiana. Now all she had to do was convince the Ursulines that, despite being only twenty years of age, she had the strength of character for such an ambitious undertaking. She clearly was persuasive, since in the spring of 1726 she was admitted as a postulate. After three months of scrupulous examination as a novitiate, she had impressed the Ursulines with her piety and humility; what remained was the heart-wrenching task of receiving consent from her parents.[36] Both were staunchly opposed to relinquishing a daughter not only to convent life, but also to a foreign mission, knowing they would most likely never see her again. Once again it seemed that Marie's plans were to be thwarted, not least by her own thoughts of the pain she would cause her parents by leaving them. In the end, her parents relented, perhaps comforted by the promise that Marie would at least be able to write to them until her full profession. Little did she know (or perhaps she did) that the five letters she would send to her father would establish her as part of the burgeoning Republic of Letters. These letters, published in 1727, were widely read throughout France to satisfy an increasing interest in the New World, and they were constitutive of the Enlightenment's emerging concept of the "public" sphere.

Marie could not wait to reach Louisiana, "the blessed country for which I long as if it were the Promised Land."[37] Finally, on Thursday, October 24, 1726, Marie boarded the Paris coach with Sister St. François Xavier (?–1728), an Ursuline from Le Havre, and the thirty-year-old Sister Cavalier (1697–1742), an Ursuline from the Elboeuf convent, just outside Rouen, both of whom were experienced teachers. Sister St. François Xavier, much like Marie Hachard, had faced staunch opposition from her family regarding her decision to enter religious life and was only able to do so once her mother had died. And like Marie Tranchepain, she had long desired to undertake missionary work, praying to St. Francis Xavier to assist her in fulfilling her desires. Hearing that Father de Beaubois was planning for a community of Ursulines in Louisiana, she wrote asking permission to join them. They readily agreed, but to Sister St. François Xavier's dismay, her mother superior staunchly opposed her request, writing to both Father de Beaubois and Mother Superior Tranchepain that she could not possibly undertake mission work given her poor health. In the end her perseverance prevailed, though she did die within the first year of being in Louisiana. Sister Cavalier from Elboeuf had also always desired to become a missionary and at age thirty was already a well-seasoned teacher.

Despite poor roads, the three sisters reached the Paris coach stop in three days, where they were greeted by an extern of the Ursuline convent of Rue St. Jacques. While the three sisters hoped to spend only a few days in Paris, Marie was extremely distressed to hear that they would most likely be staying for longer than a month because their sailing vessel was not ready. The three Ursulines were given a warm welcome by the mother superior of the Rue St. Jacque in Paris, Sister Bruscoly, whose kindness and generosity tempted Marie to stay in Paris "in that earthly paradise."[38] They were showered with gifts for their new convent, including many books that would form one of the first libraries in New Orleans.[39] But despite Marie's growing attachments to the comforts of this, the most illustrious of the Ursuline houses, she was convinced of God's will for her. On December 8, earlier that they had anticipated, Marie, her two companions, and two Jesuit missionaries who would work in the Illinois country, the Reverend Father Étienne Doutreleau and Brother Philippe Crucy, departed after mass on the five o'clock Brittany coach to Rennes.[40] First stop was Versailles, where Marie had her first glimpse of Louis XIV's palace, the opulence of which was so disturbing to her it almost drove her to mortification. The eight-day trip to Rennes is described as a harrowing journey through bad weather, muddy roads, and stories of robberies, but also one filled with laughter, joking, and congeniality. Upon arriving in Rennes, the Ursulines and their Jesuit travel companions were invited to visit the Jesuit college. They then moved on to Hennebont to join Mother Superior Tranchepain, Sister Judde, and Sister Boulanger, where they were met by two Ursulines from Ploërmel, along with with Reverend Father René Tartarin, a Jesuit missionary also bound for Louisiana.[41] Sister Ste. Thérèse Salaon, a native of Ploërmel, whose father was a well-known lawyer, had been a boarding student at the Ursuline convent prior to entering the novitiate. At age twenty-eight, her desire to join the mission in Louisiana was opposed by her brother and by her mother superior, but those obstacles were finally overcome. Her fellow sister, Sister Ste. Michel Marion, also of Ploërmel, was the last of the congregation of Paris to finally receive permission to leave the diocese.[42] All had descended on Hennebont for the voyage to New France. Joining them as the only sister from the congregation of Bordeaux was Sister Ste. Marie Yviguel from the distinguished Ursuline community in Vanne. Two converse nuns, Sister St. Marthe Dain, from Hennebot, and Sister Anne de St. François were the last of the twelve to join the band of sisters in Hennebont prior to leaving for L'Orient.

On New Year Day 1727, the formal inauguration of the New Orleans community took place in the infirmary of the Ursuline convent in Hennebont, less than twelve miles from the port town of L'Orient, the home port of the Company of the Indies, named for the company's trading hubs in the Far East. Prior to leaving for L'Orient, on January 19 Marie was given the holy habit, and on February 22, 1727, the party of twelve Ursulines, the two Jesuit Fathers Doutreleau and Tartarin, and Brother Philippe Crucy boarded the *Gironde* from L'Orient.[43] The events of the treacherous five-month ocean journey were recounted in numerous tales, providing graphic depictions that undoubtedly captivated and entertained readers in France.[44]

In early May they arrived at the port city of Les Cayes in Saint-Domingue (now Haiti) and were graciously welcomed by company officials, Messieurs Cirou and Girard. Several days later Maria wrote that Governor Brache also warmly welcomed the Ursulines into his home. Maria wrote to her father: "The Governor told us that he wanted to have a house of Ursulines in this country. Messieurs Cirou and Girard had the same desire for the education of young Creoles, who are naturally of a happy disposition. It is necessary to send them to France to the Communities for instruction. There is hope that we will someday have a house of our order in this country."[45] The company administrators even attempted to convince the sisters to stay and establish a school.

After a brief stop at Dauphine Island, the sisters arrived at Balize, the southernmost point of the Mississippi River, on July 23, where they were transferred to pirogues for the final, and perhaps most arduous, part of their journey to New Orleans. It was here that they first encountered inhabitants of Louisiana, the Company of the Indies' enslaved African boatmen, who rowed them upstream on the eight-day journey to New Orleans. Along the way they were welcomed by the brother of Claude

Massy (one of the postulants) on his plantation just below New Orleans. Mother Tranchepain noted that "When we were eight or ten leagues from New Orleans, we began to encounter some plantations, they who stopped us vied with each other to make us enter their homes, and everywhere we were received with joy beyond all expression. From all sides they promised us boarding students and some wished already to give them to us."[46] This "joy" at the opportunity to educate their daughters clearly calls into question the stereotypical images of colonial Louisiana as educationally backward and ignorant.

Arriving in New Orleans, Marie had only a brief encounter with the city, as the Ursulines were immediately cloistered, but she described the city as "very beautiful, well constructed and regularly built . . . the streets are very wide and straight; the main one [Decatur today] measures a league in length. The houses are very well constructed in collombage and mortar, whitewashed, paneled and sunlit. The roofs of the houses are covered with little flat plates made of wood cut in the form of slate."[47] The city, which had been designed by the French military engineer Adrien de Pauger, actually was much more reminiscent of Spanish colonial towns characterized by a central plaza, the Place d'Armes (today Jackson Square), overlooked by St. Louis Cathedral, which was flanked by military barracks, as well as government headquarters. A regular grid pattern, made up of fourteen streets, reflected Enlightenment concerns with social control and hierarchy, as well as the separation of public and private.[48]

The Ursulines' provisional quarters, the Kolly house, a two-story residence owned by Bienville, was located on what is today the 300 block of Chartres Street. Though their permanent convent was not yet built and would not be completed until 1734, the sisters wasted no time in preparing their temporary residence on the west end of the city for the arrival of the promised boarding students; they constructed a small building on the property to instruct the day pupils and to house the boarders.[49] Father de Beaubois, who had purchased the land for the newly established Jesuit plantation several blocks away, visited daily to perform mass.

It did not take long for the convent to thrive. Within three months, Marie wrote enthusiastically to her father:

> There are already more than thirty boarders from here and Balize and the surrounding area who insisted on being received. The parents are carried away with joy to see us, saying that they no longer worry that they will return to France since they have here what they need to educate their daughters.
>
> Marie Hachard, October 27, 1727[50]

Despite the many portrayals of New Orleans as corrupt, immoral, and the least desirable of all the global sites of the company, it is clear from Marie's first letter from New Orleans that many of the inhabitants were deeply committed to providing their daughters with a first-class education. The convent school was well-known among the inhabitants of the city. The memoirs of Marc-Antoine Caillot, a company employee in New Orleans between 1729 and 1731, reveals not only the common knowledge inhabitants of the city had of the Ursulines, but the central role that the Ursulines played in shaping this emerging city. He writes, "On Chartres Street there is a convent of Ursuline nuns who are seven in number. There should be twelve more coming from France, and the convent will be at the other end of town, on the quay. They teach the young people without profit or anything else except for what people willingly want to give them. They have some boarders who pay room and board."[51]

Interestingly, Caillot notes that by 1729 there were only seven sisters, not twelve. Not all the sisters adapted as well to the conditions in New Orleans as Marie's glowing accounts might lead one to believe. In fact, two of the sisters (Sr. Ste. Michel Marion, from Ploërmel, and Sr. Ste. Marthe Dain, from Hennebont, one of the two lay sisters) returned to France just three months after their arrival, on November 25, 1727. And as anticipated, the sickly Sr. St Francis Xavier (Madeleine Mahier), from Havre, was not strong enough to fight off fever and died on July 6, 1728. That same year, Sr. Anne de St. Francois left to go back to France and, in 1729, Claude Massy, who had been the other postulate besides Marie Hachard, left the convent to return to the outer world.[52] Thus while some of the sisters were overwhelmed with joy in their missionary activity in New France, it is clear that for some, the challenges of the hot and humid climate, food shortages, epidemics, the frontier conditions, fear of unrest, and the potential economic ruin of the colony, demanded too much of them.

The stress of this reduction in force was exacerbated by the 1729 Natchez revolt in which the Natchez attacked the French settlement of four hundred settlers at Fort Rosalie, 270 miles upriver from New Orleans. Natchez, the perfect location for growing tobacco, was the focus of the company's aspirations for financial success that would rival Chesapeake Bay. But the mounting tensions between the Natchez and the French settlers over Natchez lands were ignored. On November 28, 1729, the Natchez executed their well-planned strategy to rid themselves of the French colonizers. They killed 138 men, 35 women, and 56 children, and they took hostage the remaining women, children, and enslaved Africans. Marc Caillot describes the arrival of French survivors of the revolt at New Orleans in pirogues, recounting that,

When we were quite close enough to be able to distinguish who these new arrivals were, we were very surprised to see some of these people completely naked, others in their drawers maimed. This encounter left us somewhat bewildered, without nevertheless, knowing what it might mean, but alas, how surprised we were to the contrary when we heard these people speak, so pale and disfigured, who told us without any preface that everything was on fire and covered in blood at Natchez, and that they thought they were the only ones who had been able to escape.[53]

Panic and fear spread throughout New Orleans when rumors circulated that the city would be the next target of the revolt and that the enslaved Africans were also planning an insurrection. Ironically, as Emily Clark points out, the Natchez revolt contributed to consolidating and expanding the role of the Ursulines.[54] In the aftermath of the revolt, thirty orphaned girls from Natchez were taken in, as well as several widows. Given the reduced number of sisters, this additional responsibility placed added strain on the remaining sisters. In addition, the revolt ended all aspirations of the company for financial success. They pulled out of the colony, leaving the Ursulines to their own devices to sustain their mission on their own. The looming fear of both enslaved and Indigenous rebellion meant tensions in the colony were at an all-time high.

By 1733, the death of three of the sisters—Mother Tranchepain and Sister Judde (both from Rouen) and Sr. St. Thérèse Salaon (from Ploërmel)—reduced to four the founding generation of Ursuline teachers. While Caillot suggests that twelve new sisters were on their way from France, only three veteran sisters from Normandy arrived in 1732, and two more sisters traveled from Dieppe in 1734. It was these five second-generation sisters, in addition to the remaining four sisters of the founding generation, including Marie, that would make up the core of the teaching/administrative staff of the Ursuline academy during the remainder of the French colonial period. While much attention has been given to the founding generation, less has been written about the period after the Natchez revolt of 1729, and the period after the departure of the Company of the Indies, which for all practical purposes left the colony to its own devices.

The period from 1733 to 1754 (after which the Ursulines entered their second permanent convent, the one that still stands in the French Quarter today) constituted the second generation of Ursulines and is characterized by what I consider the emergence of a creole pedagogy of disorder. This pedagogy of disorder refers to the complex processes of adaptation through creolization that results in the invention of something new. In the case of the Ursulines, disorder was ever present in their mission of providing universal Catholic education to all women and children in the colony regardless of class, race, or ethnicity, as well as being immersed in a plantation slave economy. Colonial frontier conditions challenged the Ursulines in ways they could not have anticipated. In 1727 when the Ursulines arrived, the population of New Orleans and along Bayou St. John was, according to the census, 1,030 residents (781 free whites, 48 indentured servants, 181 enslaved Africans, and 20 Native American slaves).[55] By 1746, the enslaved population of Louisiana had risen to 4,730, far surpassing the free population of French and German colonists, which was estimated to be 3,200. As Gwendolyn Hall has made abundantly clear, Louisiana was thoroughly Africanized during this period of colonization.[56] Convent life differed significantly from France given that they now incorporated enslaved Africans as well as enslaved boarders, enslaved day students, and Indigenous students alongside French girls from all social classes.

The second generation of Ursulines faced numerous challenges they could not have anticipated. First, the focus of their missionary zeal would not be on Indigenous populations as originally intended but would ultimately be enslaved and free Africans. Second, they were thrust into the role of being plantation mistresses, which necessitated a corporate identity. Third, the reach of their missionary activity quickly expanded given the dire social and economic needs of many colonists. Fourth, the fluidity of racial and social hierarchies challenged the conservative nature of the Ursulines, whose goals were initially *not* focused on earthly reform. Lastly, the utopian vision of the Ursulines did not sit well with the male hierarchy in colonial New Orleans, whose vision was focused on earthly wealth. The inclusive Catholic universalism embodied in the common, "public" rituals of the church that were the heart of education contrasted sharply with the rugged individualism that characterized a frontier society. Marie's letters to her father attest to the many challenges the Ursulines faced as they dedicated themselves first and foremost to educating *all* young girls and women in colonial Louisiana. This universal embrace would not only eventually challenge emerging class and racial hierarchies, but would push at the very boundaries of what constituted Enlightenment notions of the public sphere and education.

The Ursuline Academy: Creating a Creole
Counterpublic through Education

> Our little community grows from day to day. We have twenty
> boarders, of whom eight today made their first communion, three
> ladies also board, and three orphans that we took through charity.
> We also have seven slave boarders to instruct for baptism and first
> communion, besides a great number of day students, female blacks
> and female savages who come for two hours a day for instruction.
>
> Marie Hachard, April 24, 1728[57]

Marie Hachard's description of their robust community, nine months after
their arrival, paints a portrait of a thriving educational institution whose
open admission policy welcomed girls and women of all races and social
classes. When the Ursulines began their school in New Orleans, they
brought with them almost two hundred years of experience as educators.[58]
Like the convent schools in France, they would be guided in their educational work by the 1705 *Reglemens des religieuses Ursulines de la congrégation de Paris*, a reprint of the first 1652 edition, which articulated the
Ursuline educational principles and provided a precise methodology. The
New Orleans Ursulines used this as their guiding document in shaping the
school organization, curriculum, and pedagogy of the Ursuline convent.
As Marie indicates in her letter, the school originally replicated the traditional three-tiered Ursuline school organization: boarders (typically for
girls from affluent families), day students (for local girls of modest means),
and afternoon and Sunday catechism (for the enslaved and working poor).
While the curriculum was clearly intended to differentiate girls according
to social class, as a means of social reproduction, the inclusivity of children
from *all* classes had been a revolutionary step in French education (and
education generally) given that it implied that children other than those of
noble birth could benefit from education.[59]

   While the Ursulines had distinguished themselves in France by teaching young girls from all social classes, in New Orleans they faced the additional challenge of educating girls and women from three culturally disparate peoples: French, Indigenous, and West African girls and women.
Unlike French schools, whose boarding students came from wealthy families, at the New Orleans convent boarders included not only girls from
French families, but, as Marie points out, also seven enslaved boarders.
Although the Ursulines had anticipated, and in fact had been motivated
to take up missionary work by the ardent desire to provide instruction to

Native American girls, they now incorporated African girls and women into their afternoon classes, as well as taking in enslaved girls from plantation families along the river as boarders alongside the French girls. Not only does this speak to the racial fluidity of the early colonial period, but, as Marie's matter-of-fact letter suggests, there was a seamless adaptability of the Ursulines to accommodate all in the fold of the convent.

This transatlantic, multilingual, multicultural milieu clearly posed pedagogical challenges they had not faced in France. The Ursulines, however, saw these challenges not as problems (or as students with deficits) but as the very heart of their mission of creating a universal Catholic culture.[60] Their goal was the education of *all* girls, the nobility as well as the poorest children, and of all races. But Ursuline inclusivity sought not only to include all girls, but to actually love them equally. Inspired by Mary, the mother of Jesus, love was understood by the Ursulines as unconditional and without expectation. Angela Merici, the original founder of the Ursulines, wrote:

> Love all of your daughters equally, having no preference for one rather than another, for they are all God's creatures, and you know not what He may choose to make of them. Are you sure that those who seem the most wretched and useless are not called to become the most generous and the most pleasing to His Divine Majesty? . . . Thus, you will ever be cultivating the vineyard entrusted to you, leaning to God to work wonders in His own good time.[61]

For the Ursulines, their pedagogical challenge, then, was not just teaching in multilingual classrooms, with young girls of diverse cultural backgrounds, but doing so without having preferences. Like Mary, the first teacher of Jesus, Ursuline pedagogy strove to love unconditionally as a means to signify their understanding of God's divine nature of compassion.

For the Ursulines, the guiding philosophy that shaped their pedagogy was love. God had created human beings in his image and likeness. God endowed the soul with intellect, with will, and with a strong propensity to love. In the Ursuline theology, human beings were understood as part of a divine cosmology, not separate from it, and for the Ursulines, the role of the educator is first and foremost to help a child perfect this divine resemblance, to develop this divine life.[62] The role of the teacher is to create the conditions in which the child can manifest the divine goodness that is inherently always and already constituted.

Unlike most Protestant theology of the time, in which children are born sinful and only the select are redeemed, the Catholic child, while born sinful, is immediately redeemed through baptism. While humans are bound to sin, in Catholic cosmology, redemption is always available through re-enactments of the rituals of baptism (at Easter, sprinkling of blessed water, sign of the cross), confession, and through communion. Baptism was at this time considered the most important of the Catholic rituals. This was a *public* rite that was a community affair, performed in the presence of an assembly of faithful. The Ursulines' focus on adult conversion of Africans and Natives made adult baptism the norm in the early years of their mission activity.[63] The presence of slave boarders, as noted by Marie, for instruction for baptism and first communion, clearly transgressed the norms of French *class* sensibility. Given the "fluid" nature of race relations in this period, however, taking in slave boarders was a clear indication not only of the Ursulines' commitment to creating a universal Catholic community, but of the early modern French social structure unencumbered by a segregationist and rigid hierarchy regarding race.[64]

While the curriculum of the Ursuline Academy was clearly differentiated among boarding, day or extern students, and catechism classes for the poor and enslaved, the primary focus of instruction was on teaching the rituals that were "common" to all. And while knowledge (math, writing, reading) and skills (stitchery, flower making, etc.) were critical to the practical aspects of women's lives, it was the spiritual life of the young girls that most concerned the nuns. The pedagogy of spirituality was designed to inspire young girls to embody the motherly love of the Virgin Mary. Clearly education in academic, domestic, and religious subjects and a regular regime of personal devotion formed the core of the curriculum. And yet the teaching of religion was more than just imparting "truths" of faith through memorization or recitation. It meant ushering young girls into a way of life. This curriculum was anchored around a specific piety that focused on the Virgin Mary as the embodiment of the new Ursuline spirituality. It was the Virgin's life that young women were to emulate, specifically her central role as mother and teacher. It was implicitly understood that women, particularly mothers, were the primary educators responsible for perpetuating the faith. Ultimately, mothers were the first teachers. Empowering young girls and women to see themselves as active agents in shaping the nature of society through a pedagogy of love transgressed not only emerging gender norms, which suggested that women should devote themselves solely to the "private" sphere, but challenged Protestant pedagogies, which relied on "discipline" rather than caring to instill education.[65]

The "common" pedagogical focus on the public, ritual behaviors of baptism, communion, and confession, as well as the those of marriage, mass, catechism, the rosary, signing of the cross, in addition to oral and visual literacies including singing, music, art, and icons, also functioned to make Ursuline pedagogy accessible to a transatlantic, multilingual, multicultural colonial milieu. Many of these rituals resonated with some Senegambian West African religious practices and did not require literacy or even a common language. Especially among the Bambara, enslaved peoples from the upper Senegal region who were brought in large numbers to Louisiana, the spiritual traditions they brought with them were founded upon belief in a higher being and included ancestor worship, dramatic rituals, music, dance, and art.[66] Each of these elements translated to some degree seamlessly into the veneration of saints, the rituals of mass, and Catholicism's tradition of sacred music, icons, and art.[67] Religious practice, like with the Ursulines, was integrated into all aspects of life. It is highly probable that the Ursuline devotion to the Virgin Mary found parallels to many of the West African female deities who served as protectors. Additionally, the use of sacramentals (blessed objects), such as statues, pictures, candles, incense, holy water, rosaries, vestments, and relics, in Catholic ritual resembled the spiritual piety of West Africans, whose practices included sacred objects that were central to daily conduct to bridge the secular and the sacred.[68] For West Africans, holy days, processions, saints' feast days, and days of fast and abstinence were all recognizable from their experience of sacred days, festivals, and food taboos.

These forms of Catholic religious expression, while clearly imposed on enslaved Africans, were potentially empowering to African women, who eventually entered the Catholic Church in greater numbers than men. Emily Clark and Virginia Gould have theorized that this pattern may be traced to the fact that West African cultures, like Catholicism, revered a maternal figure and empowered women as educators.[69] The Ursuline devotion to the Blessed Virgin offered a particularly rich context for syncretism with the gods of Africa. The prominent role of the Virgin Mary, especially the physical presence of the wooden statue they had brought with them from France in the chapel depicting her, could have signified the feminine spirituality and female agency that was a part of Bambara tradition and may have easily "harmonized with the mother-centered approach of the Ursulines and the Children of Mary (Figure 6)."[70] Undoubtedly, the unusual level of racial inclusion and integration in church rituals, and at the Ursuline convent school, provided opportunities for some enslaved women from West Africa to appropriate Catholic cultural rituals and recreate them as their own.

This process of religious creolization emerged in the second genera-

Figure 6. Our Lady of Victories. Photo Credit: Emilie Gagnet Leumas, PhD, CA, CRM. Courtesy of the Office of Archives and Records, Archdiocese of New Orleans.

tion of Ursulines. The sacraments of both baptism and matrimony, and the tradition of godparenting that the Ursulines enjoined, created cultural structures that strengthened community and recalled familiar African social arrangements.[71] Among the Ursulines' enslaved Africans there was a predominance of nuclear families living under the official blessing of a sacramental marriage. The degree to which Catholicism was imposed on Africans as a means of advancing colonial aims as opposed to giving enslaved Africans space to create and recreate their own unique culture is difficult to ascertain. The introduction of Catholicism functioned in complex and contradictory ways, but the Ursulines themselves interpreted Catholic tradition in ways that extended elements of "humanity" to enslaved persons, albeit within a rigid colonial system based on racial and class hierarchies. Simultaneously, enslaved Africans found within the rituals and sacraments of Catholicism modes of cultural self-expression, agency, literacy, and eventually, in some cases, freedom. We cannot know with certainty how enslaved and free Africans interpreted the sacraments. Their "lived religion" and experience of the sacraments cannot be known. At the same time, the Ursulines' participation in the institution of slavery undoubtedly shaped plantation culture in New Orleans, given the powerful influence they had in colonial society.

Their mission, to convert all members of the colony to Catholicism, was also shown by their sponsorship of the "Children of Mary" confraternity, an association for the laity. Confraternities, led by women, had emerged in early modern France and contributed to the advancement of religious and social goals of the Catholic Church by taking on the task of catechesis not only of their children, but also of their servants.[72] Formed in 1730, the "Children of Mary" represented a range of women from various social standings, offering a different, more egalitarian setting for social relations than was the norm in colonial Louisiana. Generally, laywomen began their educational mission at home, working with their own children as well as sponsoring the conversion of free and enslaved Africans, whom they encountered in their own family circles. By 1744, 30 percent of all individual baptisms of enslaved Africans were sponsored by confraternity members, who either acted as godparents or brought their own enslaved Africans to the font. Confraternity members also included free women of color. They played an especially prominent role in bringing newly enslaved African adults to the baptismal font. In 1731, enslaved Africans or free people of color served as godparents in only two of the 162 baptisms that took place at St. Louis Cathedral, but by 1775, 89 percent of the godparents of the enslaved were of African descent.[73] No other group of affiliated individuals set such a public example of compliance with the Code Noir. This racial inclusivity in the Catholic Church, according to Emily Clark, laid a foundation for a multiracial church that did not know congregational segregation until the era of Jim Crow in the late nineteenth century.[74]

For all practical purposes the Ursuline Academy, as well as the Catholic churches in New Orleans, were racially integrated public spaces that signified the moral equality of all human beings. Racial difference in early colonial Louisiana was not yet the primary category for determining social status, but instead French constructs of social class continued to determine one's social standing. Class structure was reproduced in the Ursuline school through the tradition of denoting students as either boarding students (paying room and board), day students (paying no tuition), or afternoon catechism students (enslaved girls and Indigenous girls paying no tuition). While the religious rituals were the same for all students, signifying a universal church and spiritual equality, a differentiated curriculum was intended to prepare students for their different social stations in life.[75] Local conditions and circumstances, however, soon required adaptations among the second generation of Ursulines whose creole pedagogies loosened and challenged the rigid social boundaries that French colonial administrators sought to maintain.

A Creole Curriculum: The Second Generation

Like in France, boarding students were young girls who came to the live at the convent school for a year or two between the ages of twelve and fourteen, prior to marriage, in preparation for first communion.[76] Marie described with astonishment to her father her first encounter with the boarders:

> The boarders, ranging from twelve to fifteen years of age, have never been to Confession or even to Mass. They were raised in their habitations, five to six leagues from this city, and in consequence without any spiritual succor. They had never heard anyone speak of God. When we tell them the most common things, for them they are oracles that come out of our mouths. We have the consolation to find in them great docility and a strong desire to be instructed. All would like to be nuns, which is not to the liking of Reverend de Beaubois, our very worthy superior. He finds it more proper for them to become Christian mothers who, by their good example, will finally establish religion in the country.[77]

As conveyed in Marie's description, not unlike the African and Indigenous students, the young French girls who came to the convent school were also ignorant about Catholicism. In other words, for all practical purposes, despite class differences, the educational level of these early students upon entering the convent was rudimentary to say the least. The challenges of teaching a multiracial and multilingual study body required adaptation among the teachers of the convent school that necessitated deviations from the protocols they were familiar with in France.

In 1731, three years after their arrival, the sisters, still in their temporary convent at the Kolly House, had managed to establish a thriving school and orphanage despite the reduction of their numbers to six sisters. It was the veteran teachers, forty-four-year-old Sister Angelique (Marie-Anne Boulanger) from Rouen and thirty-five-year-old Sister Ste.

Marie (Renée Yviguel) from Vannes, who took up the role of the first- and second-class mistress (they were the lead coteachers) among the twenty or so boarding students. The school day began every day at 7:00 a.m. with a public mass attended by all students and members of the convent community, followed by a breakfast of sagamité, an Indigenous porridge made of ground corn meal boiled in water with butter or bacon fat.[78] Students then gathered in their classrooms for morning lessons in reading and arithmetic. Among the "profane" subjects, reading was the most important. The beginners' reading was in Latin, the language of the Church. They first learned single letters, then syllables. The mistress would then read a page or two while the students followed the text in their own book. The younger children were then left in the care of the second mistress, or *dizainières*, to practice their reading. Intermediate and senior classes were taught to read in French. To what degree the students left school as fluent readers is difficult to determine. Given that the eighteenth century was still a transition period between an oral and written culture, the opportunities to actually continue reading were limited and often restricted to the upper classes. To what degree writing was taught is undeterminable. While some educators in France argued that reading and writing should be forbidden by women, the Ursulines in New Orleans were far removed from the emerging cultural norms that dictated that women's place was in the domestic sphere. Given that all the Ursuline teachers were well-educated and highly literate, I suspect that the boarding students would have received at least an elementary introduction to writing for the uses of bookkeeping, letter writing, and the signing of documents. Arithmetic was of minor importance. Students were taught simple calculation through the use of *jettons*, or counters.

After the morning classes, students were ushered by Sister Marie and Angelique into the refectory at 11:00 a.m. for their midday meal of bread and broth, which was taken in silence while listening to inspirational readings read by the sisters. It was important to the sisters to dine with the students to make sure that they received the proper nourishment. The health of a child was critical to her overall spiritual well-being and note was taken of each girl's physical strength and wellness. In this regard the sisters paid particular attentions to hygiene in that the girls were to have their hair brushed several times a day and to wash their mouths after each meal. All duties were carried out by the sisters with the utmost maternal care so that students would be encouraged to embrace good habits as a matter of routine. Under no circumstances was a young girl to be punished without special reference to the mistress general. And, the *Reglemens* specifically state that no child should be deprived of her food or exposed to the cold as a form of punishment (clearly these were popular forms of punishment). Love, not physical punishment, was the heart of the Ursuline pedagogy. Like mothers, the class mistresses saw each child as a unique individual who must be unconditionally loved. The role of the teacher was to teach them to overcome their passions and bad inclinations, while helping them to discover their strongest impulses. Teachers often gave students little exercises in the way of virtue and would talk with each student personally from time to time; this was clearly an important part of their system of individual instruction.[79]

Classes for the boarding students resumed at 12:15 p.m. with the afternoon classes focusing on manual work, music, and, most importantly, religious instruction. Next to reading the sisters considered handiwork (embroidery, sewing) to be the most important subject. These skills were essential for young girls who shortly after leaving the convent school would be married and charged with managing a household. Boarders were taught sewing flowers in tapestry, embroidery with gold and silver, lace making, and sewing. All girls were taught to repair clothes, to mend linen, and some dressmaking. Not only were these practical skills, but for the financially strapped Ursulines, handiwork was taken to the professional level in the form of elaborate tapestries that were sold to raise money when they were in financial need. For the boarders, the school day ended with time to study, dinner at 5:00 p.m., and, prior to retiring to the dormitory, attending a final service in the convent chapel at 7:00 p.m.[80]

While Marie, now Sister St. Stanislaus, had originally assisted with teaching the boarding students, she now worked with Sister Marie des Agnes (Cécile Cavalier), the thirty-three-year-old teacher from Elboeuf, in teaching the day, or extern, students. The division of the Ursuline school into boarders and extern (day) students had been written into the original *Reglements* in 1652. This guide specified that they should treat the day girls, those often with lesser means, with as much respect and kindness as they did the boarding students. The *Reglements* clearly stipulated that "The sisters who are destined to the instruction of extern pupils must apply themselves to this task with redoubled affection since, in this occupation, their lives imitate even more closely that of the Son of God who, during his own lifetime, principally sought to instruct the poor and ignorant."[81]

The day students, who arrived at 8 a.m. at the convent school, functioned as a bridge between the spheres of the public and private, between the world outside and the convent space inside of enclosure. The day school operated with great caution in order to uphold the strict rules of enclosure. Instruction for the day students at the convent was conducted in a classroom that had been specially constructed at one end of the temporary residence. Every morning, the students would gather outside an exterior door to the classroom, which was opened for them at 8:00 and immediately locked again behind them. Once they were in and the door was locked, Sisters Marie (Hachard), and Cécile Cavalier would enter by an interior door, itself guarded on the inside by another *soeur portiere*.[82] The classrooms of the day students could be compared to a sort of airlock between inside and outside, secured at either end by heavy, double-locked doors; they enabled the day students to enter the convent while in theory allowing only minimal contact with the outside world. Given the rules of enclosure, this was done so that there would be no other contact between the convent and its day students. Yet, once within the walls, it would be hard to imagine that the sisters did not overhear the gossip of young girls or perhaps even to venture to ask about the going-ons outside the convent walls. In other words, despite the cloistered nature of the convent, there was indeed knowledge of the outside world and the desire to shape the outside world.

In the day classes, the timetable and curriculum were both simplified versions of those provided for the boarders. This was the result of circumstances: boarders had classes all day long; day students came for one and a half hours in the morning and two and a half hours in the afternoon, fitting these sessions around the rest of their working day. For the day students, the cloister provided not only the opportunity for a limited education, but also for interaction with the wide spectrum of classes, races, and ethnicities. There was one factor in which pupils received exactly the same treatment, regardless of whether they were poor or wealthy, enslaved or free: they all benefited from the same lessons in the Catholic doctrine. Embedded within the fabric of devotional life, which was the central organizing feature of the school day, was formal catechesis. The lessons in Catholic doctrine were placed at the climax of the day's instruction, usually from 1:00 to 2:30. The importance of this particular class was signified by the fact that it was taught by the principal herself. In fact, the religious education of wealthy boarders, humbler day pupils, and the enslaved was identical: since the catechism was the axis of the schools, it was taught to all in a uniform manner, culminating in Sunday classes.

Sister St. Jean L'Evangeliste (Marguerite Judde) from Rouen was teaching the catechism classes for Indigenous and African girls and women. Marie, who had previously taught them, had taken up the teaching of the day students from Sr. Ste François Xavier (Madeleine Mahieu), who had died less than a year after arriving in New Orleans. While teaching the catechism classes, Marie wrote to her father:

> We also have a class to instruct the women and girls among the blacks and savages. They come every day from one o'clock in the afternoon until two-thirty.
>
> I cannot express to you the pleasure I find in instructing their little souls and teaching them to know and to love God. I pray the Lord will give me His grace to succeed in this.[83]

Instruction focused specifically on the catechism with the purpose of preparation for the first communion. She wrote:

> What pleases us is the docility of the children, whom one forms as one wants. The blacks are easy to instruct once they learn to speak French. It is not the same for the savages, whom one does not baptize without trembling because of the tendency they have to sin, especially the women, who under a modest air, hide the passions of beasts.[84]

Marie clearly dehumanizes and sexualizes the Indigenous girls, making one wonder how it was possible to embrace her duty to love and teach all. The teaching of catechism classes in New Orleans differed significantly from France because it first required language instruction in French for the Indigenous and African pupils. This was most likely facilitated by the use of symbols (signing of the cross), repetition of prayers, and the rosary, and the singing of hymns and the liturgy. In addition, the Ursulines had brought numerous catechism books with them that would have served as texts, along with religious paintings and carvings.[85] For the Ursulines, this challenge of instructing students whose first language was not French forced them to adapt their pedagogy.

Catechism instruction usually began with the Apostles' Creed, where children learned the orthodox doctrines about God, Jesus Christ, and the mysteries of the Incarnation and the Redemption. Next were the Ten Commandments. The greatest amount of time, however, was spent on the sacraments: children memorized more responses to questions on baptism, confession, and communion than on any other topic. Lastly, children learned prayers in both Latin and French. The lessons learned were not primarily theological. Instead, the pedagogical focus was on routines (prayers, sign of the cross, the rosary) and rituals (going to church, baptism, communion, confession), whose intent was to indoctrinate *all* children into a shared way of public life that was the foundation of the universal Catholic community.

And yet while the catechism classes taught by Marie, and later Marguerite Judde, did consist of memorization, a technique thought to be foundational to all other learning (this predated Rousseau), their curriculum was not limited solely to memorization of text.[86] The question-and-answer method of the catechism was supplemented by music, art, and other rituals (especially the rosary) as well as alms giving and participation in godparenting, confraternities, and charity work. In the Ursuline tradition, as compared to the Jesuit and other religious orders of the time, sacred statues, prayers, liturgical ceremonies, singing of hymns, all were commingled with every element of education. Ursuline education was focused not on mastering a body of knowledge, but on developing a way of life that would be sustained across the lifespan and would provide community continuity. This significant departure from emerging "methods" of education that focused solely on the transmission of knowledge through catechism instruction made Ursuline pedagogy particularly suited to cultural translation and syncretization.

While dominant perceptions of Catholic education focus on the catechism as the heart of pedagogy, one steeped in rote memorization and recitation, this was not strictly the case with the Ursulines. Christian doctrine, however, remained difficult to explain. Between the great mysteries (greatness of God, the Trinity, the Incarnation of the Word, the divine Eucharist, the sacraments, the Commandments of God, etc.) and the complicated, abstract concepts of the catechism, there was an abyss. The simple solution had been memorization, but this "method" was questioned by serious catechists.[87] The compromise was a method that combined memorization with informal questions. The Ursulines chose their catechism carefully. The selection of the Bellarmine catechism, which was specifically designed for children, suggests the Ursulines' emerging understanding of children as unique from adults in their needs, aptitudes, and dispositions. The notion that children were not miniature adults, but were in fact unique was, for this time, a radical notion. In fact, the concept of the child and constructs of childhood, which were central to the emergence of "schooling," were just being invented.[88]

Robert Bellarmine's *Dotrina christiana breve*, first published in Italian in 1597, has the distinction of being the first catechism designed specifically to be memorized in its entirety by children. What was unique about this text, as compared to Canisius's text, is that it begins with an explanation of the sign of the cross, a practice that became universal from this point forward. The Bellarmine catechism also had a new method for teaching the Apostles' Creed using one question-and-answer set for each of the twelve articles. The catechism was designed to be practical, concentrating on the essentials of what children should know, and it specifically emphasized the external aspects of Catholicism since visible practices could be more easily grasped by children. The focus of the catechism was on the sacraments, particularly on those that would be repeated throughout one's life: confession and communion. The catechism was not a set of doctrines to be memorized but was to be a comprehensive set of duties and rituals that constituted a "method" for living a Christian life.

The effectiveness of catechism lessons in conversion or even instilling some given degree of Catholic belief is almost impossible to ascertain. What is significant is that the educational spaces at the Ursuline convent resulted in communal behaviors that signified a shared public culture. Catechism emphasized behavior rather than doctrine, not the other way around. It was the outward and visible elements of Catholicism—the public, ritualistic characteristics of the sacraments—that were stressed in catechism classes. During catechism classes children not only responded to questions, they learned how to sit still in church, pray, respect the church, give confession, take communion, and obey their superiors. As Karen Carter has pointed out, "these societal expectations and behaviors could last a lifetime, even if children eventually forgot the exact words of the catechism itself."[89]

Religious education of children in the early modern period has been overlooked in educational history, with much more attention paid to the laity's involvement through confraternities, missions, the cult of saints, charity, poor relief, and the persistence of popular religious practices. Especially in colonial Louisiana, where *petite écoles* were slow to establish themselves, the primary form of education of children, as well as African and Indigenous adults, was the catechism provided by the Ursulines, and to some extent the Jesuits.[90] And while this type of education or indoctrination has been portrayed as backward by many educational historians, "in the early modern world instruction in religion and morals was indispensable to both individual and community formation."[91] Particularly for Ursulines, the pedagogical focus was not on developing individual beliefs. Alternatively, given the multiracial and multilingual students they encountered, the Ursulines adapted and improvised a creole pedagogy that was focused on creating a Catholic community through shared behaviors, rituals, and public rites.

For the enslaved Africans and Indigenous peoples, the forced participation in these pedagogies and rituals most likely resulted not so much in a commitment to the Catholic Church, but the creation and adoption of a "folk" Catholicism.[92] This included interpretations of the sacraments, especially of baptism and the mass. Acts such as making the sign of the cross and genuflecting, as well as the use of objects such as holy water, blessed candles, palms, ashes, oils, crucifixes, and rosaries, provided avenues through which to appropriate rituals and give them new meanings.[93] The syncretism or creolization constituted part of a complex acculturation process that provided avenues for both individual agency and solidifying group/community identity. Beyond the official dogma and structures of the Catholic Church, a wide range of folk religious practices flourished, drawing upon African influences, medieval Catholicism, Afro-Creole ritual systems, and Indigenous medicinal and belief systems. It is highly likely that enslaved peoples who lived in the Ursuline compound had home altars with saints, statues, candles, and holy water. Their quarters might have been decorated with blessed palms or magnolias in the form of crosses over the doors. The practices of healing, especially among those enslaved who worked at the hospital in the Ursuline compound, might also reflect a folk Catholicism. Later in the chapter we will meet the enslaved African Baptiste, an apothecary in the Ursuline pharmacy who assisted Sister St. Francois Xavier in the laboratory. He might also have used an eclectic mix of prayers, candles, special saints, and charms for his work as a healer. These types of folk religion exemplify the dynamic ways in which Catholic rituals and African rituals exemplified a pedagogy that was grounded in the lived experience and day-to-day practices that made up daily life.

Ursuline pedagogy sought to infuse the individual with a deep, abiding love of God that was woven into the daily fabric of life. In other words, daily life and religion were not separate and distinct. To organize life around devotion and love of God required discipline, ritual, order, and routine as well as inspiration, imagination, contemplation, and compassion. Spirituality was not the result of rote learning or memorization. In fact, learning "knowledge" was secondary in the holistic education that the Ursulines sought to provide. Education was not an epistemological project but was an ontological one. In other words, the purpose of education was to engender a particular way of being in the world, in the case of the Ursulines, one of devout piety and compassion as modeled by the Virgin Mary. For the Ursulines, education as a way of life meant the embodiment of lifelong rituals and practices in young girls that would guide them in their adult lives as Christian mothers. One practice that the second generation of Ursulines (1734–1754) found especially effective in teaching such a diverse student body was the use of music, particularly singing, which united this disparate community into one body.

Music as "Folk" Pedagogy

Undoubtedly, music was a particularly powerful way to transcend the linguistic barriers that Marie and her fellow teachers faced. Given the polyglot linguistic environment of early colonial New Orleans, music functioned to some degree as a universal language. Music was a critical component of the education of the Ursuline students. From classical times through the medieval foundations of the European university, music was understood to be a primary function of education and central to the formation of character, essential both to the salvation of the individual soul and the health of the body politic. Within a few years of moving into the convent, the Ursulines received from France a book of songs, including "parodies": religious and moral texts set to popular music (opera music). Sister St. Pierre, who arrived from Caen in 1732, was praised in the *Lettres Circulaires* as having a "cultivated taste in music and a beautiful voice."[94] Music was integral to their teaching, starting with the most elementary little religious songs and extending to the training of young ladies in the arts that was believed critical to "civilizing" their future families.

According to Ned Sublette, there is no doubt that the West Africans, French, German, and Indigenous peoples had plenty of music, we just "don't know much about it."[95] We do know that the Capuchin priests at St. Louis Cathedral had music at vespers and masses. And in 1725, when the Capuchin brothers opened a school (of short duration) in New Orleans, they hired a choirmaster so that their young boys could learn to sing. Given that the military had a central presence, we also know there was a military band with drummer and a fifer. The singing of the *Te Deum* was also a regular part of many public ceremonies. Music functioned not only as a ritual, but also as a "public" pedagogy that was central to teaching community. We know that music was an integral part of Ursuline convent life given that its use was central to not only mass, but to the regular prayer times of the nuns and to the curriculum of the boarding students, orphans, day students, and most likely the catechism classes, which included the enslaved and Indigenous girls. It is not unlikely that the Lord's Prayer was set to music or that other songs from the Ursuline music manuscript were taught to the students, who at age ten or eleven would have easily picked up a popular tune and simultaneously have learned religious lessons. Song and text, put to music, not only potentially provided a way to teach religious and moral lessons, but at mass it was a *public* ritual engaged in by *all* members of the community.

Marie describes how in the Easter week of April 1728, in addition to a retreat held by Father de Beaubois, in which he gave talks to over two hundred inhabitants, that:

> We had the lessons of *Tenebre* in music, and a *Miserere*, accompanied by instruments every day. Our Mother assistant who is Madame Le Boulenger, distinguished herself on this occasion. On Easter Sunday, during Mass and the benediction of the Blessed Sacrament, we sang motets in four voices, and on the last of the Easter feast days we sang the entire mass with music. The convents in France, with all their fame, do not do as much.[96]

While the rhythm of French baroque music of the Ursulines might have sounded strange to the West Africans and the Indigenous peoples in attendance during the Easter mass, the use of music to signify religious activity would have been familiar to them. Marie's poignant description provides a window into how this disparate community of French, African, and Native girls and women of all classes and backgrounds might be developing a sense of shared community, not necessarily one based in a shared theological understanding, but one in which shared public rituals created spaces of community.

Like Ursuline pedagogy, which relied on communal rituals, West African religious beliefs were carried into action through ritual.[97] Closely interwoven with the ritual experience of the enslaved West African peoples who were transported to Louisiana was the vibrant pattern of music in which musical performance was considered a religious activity, or even a prayer. The chanting of the priests and of the Ursulines, as part of the mystical rituals of the Catholic Church, were to some degree similar to the elaborate procedures and rituals that West African diviners performed to communicate with the African spirits and ancestors.

The baroque music of Ursulines was also mutable enough to be appropriated and creolized by those Africans from the Senegambia region. As noted by Ned Sublette, the Ursulines' music manuscript is characterized by uneven eighth notes, a French practice known as *notes inégales*.[98] Modern jazz artists would recognize this as "swing." There is an uncanny similarity between French New Orleans and Senegambian New Orleans: both played unequal eighth notes. The Ursulines who were teaching and practicing the musical practice of *notes inégales* thus created an environment where, Sublette maintains, "white, free colored and enslaved musicians all crossed paths . . . to hypothesize a continuum between Afro-Baroque New Orleans and the jazz era."[99] Clearly, music at the Ursuline convent provided a site for the mutual recognition of the relationship between music and religion, as well as a space for the syncretization of rituals and pedagogies resulting in creolization.[100]

Music simultaneously allowed for West Africans, as well as the Indigenous, to reinscribe and maintain their own musical cultural traditions. Indigenous peoples appropriation of French liturgical music was common throughout all of New France. Especially among the Illinois, their adoption of sacred music functioned as a primary vehicle for cultural acquiescence and survival. This was most notable when they visited the Ursuline temporary convent in New Orleans in 1730 after the Natchez revolt. Father Le Petit (who replaced Father de Beaubois as the Ursuline confessor from 1729 to 1732) described their visit to the Jesuit plantation in New Orleans: "They had no house but ours during the three weeks they remained in this city; they charmed us by their piety and their edifying life." He then relates that they attended religious services daily, singing the hymns during mass. The nuns sang the first verse, and the Illinois sang the following verses in their language and on the same tone, a form of call and response.

Music was not only taught for its own sake but was also seen as a way to convey theological and moral values through lyrics. In 1754, the Ursulines acquired a manuscript copy of *Nouvelles poésis spirituelles et morales sur les plus beaux airs de la musique françoise et italienne avec la basse* (commonly referred to as the Ursuline music manuscript).[101] The history of the manuscript, however, is much older. Originally part of a tradition of music printers in Paris's Latin Quarter who focused on works of the catechesis, by the 1730s they turned their attention to setting contrafacta-spiritual texts to the music of famous composers. This method of popularizing religious themes through music was especially intended to appeal to nuns and missionaries.[102] Exactly how these songs were used is not known; the archival records leave us no records of the use of specific musical compositions. But use of these songs is especially probable given that several of the Ursuline teachers, including Sister Claude Massy and Sister Ste. Thérèse de Jesus (who arrived in New Orleans at the age of eighteen in 1742 and died in 1752), were gifted and skilled musicians.

Music, perhaps more than any other pedagogy, was the primary teaching tool of the Ursulines, particularly because it functioned to structure daily activities. For the Ursulines, who gathered all members of the convent community, including numerous enslaved Africans, at the chapel for 6:30 mass, the singing was a pedagogy in that it not only signified a communal identity, but it marked a separation of the sacred and the profane as the schoolday/workday began. Beyond acting as a form of prayer, music functioned to embody the pedagogy of the Ursulines. Given that most students (whether French, African, or Indigenous) who came to the convent did not read or write, music and their accompanying lyrics were a primary mode of instruction both in terms of teaching doctrine and morals through the lyrics and in creating an aesthetic, spiritual experience that transcended language. Particularly for the Senegambian girls and women, this communal experience provided a shared space in which they could potentially create a new creole community, as well as perhaps find mechanisms for recreating or reimagining their own belief systems and in essence create an Afro-Creole Catholicism.

The communal, shared public experiences of music but also of mass, catechism, baptism, and communion signified a universal spiritual equality that severely undermined and disordered the goals of male colonial authorities. According to Lawrence Powell, "robed in tradition, this universalist imperative fostered a social inclusiveness that seemed to subvert the very hierarchy the nascent Creole elite were in the process of renovating for their own convenience."[103] Alternatively, their vision was based on shaping a visible, public *community* that endowed *every* soul under the rubric of spiritual universalism. This commitment was a clear counternarrative to emerging Enlightenment notions of subjectivity that increasingly produced the concept of the individual not only through a hierarchy of worth based on material wealth, gender, and race, but through the introduction of schools in which the educated subject was the product of reason. The Ursuline community in New Orleans clearly challenged colonial expectations that focused on earthly gain and that privileged reason over faith. Their success would become increasingly dependent on their ability to negotiate company and colonial demands and to be financially independent in a volatile mercantile economy. As "company women," they faced ongoing economic challenges that would shape their New World lives in profound ways and contribute to expanding their educational mission in ways they had not anticipated.

Company Women: Reluctant "Reformers"

The intention of the commandant and of the principal inhabitants of this city is that we would also take the girls and the women of bad conduct. That is not yet determined on our side, but they let us hear that it would be a great good for the colony.

—Marie Hachard, January 1, 1728[104]

While Marie and her fellow teachers were clear about their mission of education, the Company of the Indies and prominent colonists were more concerned with creating the necessary social order that they saw as critical to economic prosperity. Social order entailed making sure that rogue colonists be reformed to conform to behaviors suited to the demands of hard work, thriftiness, and efficiency.[105] From the standpoint of company officials, the Ursulines were wasting their time educating young girls. Instead, they needed to heal the sick soldiers, reform the wayward, and incarcerate those who were defiant. As suggested in her letter to her father, the Ursulines clearly were not going to be told what to do, but would instead dictate to the company their role in shaping New Orleans.

Ironically, from the beginning, the Ursulines were *not* doing the primary work for which the company had hired them, which was nursing the sick. The hospital where they were to nurse the sick was at the other end of the city from their temporary home. Although the company had cleared the land next to the hospital for the promised convent, and the company engineer Ignace Francois Broutin had drawn up the designs, no progress had been made. After seeing the hospital for the first time, Marie Tranchepain, the first Ursuline mother superior, argued that a stable or cattle shed would be better lodging and that the sisters could not possibly live there until the convent was completed. Despite the insistence of the company that their primary duty was the care of the sick, she argued that the sisters could not possibly walk across town to tend to the sick at the hospital, given their rules of religious enclosure. Holding the company to their contract, the Ursulines avoided hospital responsibilities for the seven years that it took to complete the convent, allowing them to focus solely on their educational mission. Marie wrote to her father in October of 1727:

> We do not expect to take possession of our monastery and the hospital for a year, or perhaps longer, for the workers are not as numerous here as in France, especially since they want to construct it to last; all will be in brick. While waiting, they built us a small lodging area in our residence for extern students and for lodging the boarders. The owner of the house furnished the wood, we the workers. There are already more than thirty boarders from here and Balize and the surrounding area who insisted on being received. The parents are carried away with joy to see us, saying that they no longer worry that they will return to France since they have here what they need to educate their daughters.[106]

The inefficiency of the company provided the Ursulines with the opportunity to take advantage of the parents' enthusiasm and turn their attention to their educational mission. By the time they moved into their first permanent convent in 1734, however, they not only managed a bustling school but were receiving compensation for taking in orphans, housing wayward women, providing an infirmary for widowed and abused women, and running the hospital and pharmacy.

This radical shift in their original reluctance to take up the project of "reform" and focus solely on education was predicated on numerous factors, but it was, in the end, directly tied to the economic necessity of needing to earn income to sustain themselves in light of the colony's economic struggles. The "aggressive entrepreneurship" of the Ursulines was spurred, in part, by the fact that they had been prohibited from transferring their dowries from France to the colonies, but also by the eventual abandonment of the colony by the Company of the Indies, whose hopes of a lucrative tobacco colony ended as "pipe dreams."[107]

While the Ursulines were reluctant reformers, the colonial officials, and in turn the company, assumed they could press the Ursulines into taking up the project of reform, as they were desperate to create a more orderly and productive colonial enterprise. Etienne Périer, the governor and military commander of Louisiana (from 1726 to 1732), and Jacques de La Chaise, the chief financial officer of the company (from 1723 to 1730), were concerned with imposing order, particularly gender order. They wrote on November 2, 1727:

> Directors of the Company of the Indies,
>
> There are many women and girls of bad life here. These wenches become pregnant and afterwards they will not give the name of the fathers of the children so that to-day the Company is obliged to feed five or six nursing children whose fathers are not known. . . . It remains for us to ask you for a house of correction here in order to put in it the women and girls of bad lives who cause a public scandal. They would be put to work either at spinning cotton or at other work but a person from France is needed to direct them.
>
> Your very humble and very obedient servants,
> Périer. De La Chaise.[108]

Not only were these two colonial administrators concerned about harnessing the moral nature of the colony through increased control of its women, but the economic viability and success of the colony was essential to building their own fortunes and key to their future advancement in the company. Urban order and uniformity was increasingly correlated to economic development in Enlightenment thought. The "perfect city" was predicated on rationality expressed through geometric designs that allowed for the ordering of the many functions of the city (economic, legal, military, residential, etc.) as a means of political control.[109] The rogue nature of colonial Louisiana, however, did not lend itself to being tamed. Smuggling, pirating, social intermixing, and disorder was *the* order of the day. But colonial administrators saw social order as essential to economic prosperity. It was imperative that they find ways to cut costs, avoid scandals, and promote the civil conduct and physical and mental health of the colonists, in order that they be productive workers and citizens. Given the questionable status of the colony, the company refused to allocate any further resources to engage yet another order of sisters. They wrote back to Périer and De La Chaise: "put the Ursulines in charge of them. Make a refuge in which to put the women of bad lives."[110]

To take up the work of reform was not what the Ursulines had originally envisioned as their colonial venture. While colonial officials were determined to pursue a policy of *renfermement*, it was clear the Ursulines were reluctant reformers. Their apostolate was directed toward the formation of the young; education, not punishment, was first and foremost the key to moral formation. But circumstances prevailed. After almost a year in the colony it was increasingly apparent that increased revenues would have to be generated to sustain the sisters. By November of 1728 Mother Tranchepain had contracted with the company to house, feed, and maintain orphan girls for the sum of 150 livres a year. By Christmas they had taken in six girls. Commissioner De La Chaise reported that the convent had also fitted a room of correction in which two women were already housed and that a house of correction would be built near the hospital adjoining the convent.[111] He also reported to the company that once the hospital and convent were built, the sisters would oversee orphan boys at the hospital who would eventually be placed as apprentices with workmen at the appropriate age. According to Marie, the community "are going to follow, all at the same time, the functions of four different communities, that of the Ursulines, our first and principal order, that of the hospitalieres, that of St. Josephs and that of the Refuge."[112] Their mission would extend beyond the school doors to include administration of a hospital (and pharmacy), orphanage, and a correctional facility. By 1734, the year that the first permanent convent was completed, the sisters were tending to the spiritual, educational, physical, and mental needs of New Orleanians. For the Ursulines, this expansive social network propelled them not only into administrative roles within the governance of the colony but extended the impact of their community building by providing the majority of social services for the fledgling city.

In contrast to the company's vision of building a prosperous colony based in a tobacco plantation economy, however, the Ursulines envisioned building a community based on a spiritual universalism in which *all* members of society were understood as children of God, not wards of the state. Mother Tranchepain's unrelenting efforts to establish the authority of the Ursulines as agents in determining their own mission had resulted in numerous conflicts with the Company of the Indies and with its spiritual director, Father Raguet.[113] When Father Raguet sought to appoint a clerical superior for the Ursulines whom they did not want, the Ursulines threatened in 1728 to move the entire community to Saint Domingue (now Haiti). Establishing their authority to self-determination was critical to building the community they envisioned: one in which every woman, regardless of social class, race, or ethnicity, would play a role in the propagation of the faith as mothers, the first teachers of children.

The challenges of serving a heavenly vision, not an earthly one, would become apparent as the Ursulines transitioned into their first permanent convent. In colonial Louisiana, where a small group of elite men governed, the Ursulines had not only asserted their influence through the formal institutions they administered, but they had also engaged informal methods that lay outside the formal structures of civil government and politics. In 1734, the Ursulines saw an opportunity to communicate their vision of a "New Eden" by staging a public religious procession at the time of their move from the temporary residence to the first permanent convent eight blocks across town. No doubt this decision was not made lightly by the recently elected mother superior, Sister St. André (Jeanne Melotte), who had been in New Orleans for less than a year before taking over the challenges of directing the convent after the death of Mother Tranchepain in November of 1733. Born in 1694 in Brittany, she had attended the Ursuline boarding school in Caen prior to entering as a novice on November 11, 1713, and she passed her profession on April 27, 1716.[114] At age thirty-six, with sixteen years' experience as a teacher at the Ursuline convent in Caen, one of the largest and most prestigious Ursuline convents in France, she was exceedingly well-prepared for her new administrative position, a task she undertook with "wisdom, cleverness and a virtue as solid as it is high."[115]

Sister St. André, mother superior, in consultation with her eight sisters, clearly saw this move as an opportunity to convey their authority (and perhaps hers) to posit their vision of public life. While the procession across town to the new convent marked the uncontested impact of the Ursulines in seven short years, the challenges they would face in the next thirty years would highlight the increasing tensions surrounding the Ursulines' understanding of their role in civic life as constructors of "public" spaces (churches, schools, hospitals, women's shelters, and confraternities) that signified a universal Catholic culture accessible to all members of society in eighteenth-century New Orleans. The processional from the Ursulines' temporary home to their first permanent convent suggests the degree of this inclusivity and community building, as well as the ruptures that were beginning to form as the Ursuline vision of a universal community contrasted with the emergence of the modern public sphere in which, according to Emily Clark, "the ideology of republican citizenship equated the voting male citizenry with the public and in so doing formally excluded women from the public sphere."[116]

Creating a New Eden: A Radical Epistemology of Disorder and Pedagogical Ruptures

> Then the sky cleared and we carried out the plans in spite of the mud that was so discouraging, especially for a group of some twenty young girls dressed as angels. One young girl representing St. Ursula was clothed in a robe of cloth of silver with a long train of the same material, her hair dressed with ribbons of pearls and diamonds, a small veil flowing from her head and a superb crown. She held in her hand a heart pierced by an arrow. The whole was done with marvelous industry. Eleven young girls clothed in white, holding palms in their hands represented the eleven thousand virgins and accompanied St. Ursula. The little ones were angels.
>
> Sister St. André, Mother Superior, July 17, 1734[117]

By 5:00 p.m. on July 17, 1734, the three-day-long rain had stopped just as the bells rang to signal the procession of the Ursulines through New Orleans to their new convent. While they could have opted to have closed carriages usher them quietly across town, they chose instead "an explicitly public mode of transferring their community, and planned an elaborate procession designed to communicate clearly to the inhabitants of New Orleans . . . the nature and quality of their authority"[118] This authority was clearly evoked in the procession through representing the legendary history of the Ursulines: St. Ursula, the fourth-century martyr, and the eleven young girls dressed in white, who represented the eleven thousand massacred virgins. These symbols clearly conveyed their belief that it was women who were the link between the holy and the profane. This procession no doubt rallied the Catholic faithful. The ritual gestures, the music, the crowd, the sense of exhilaration, all contributed to what Victor Turner would label the "catharsis" of the ritual.[119] This catharsis not only intensified the consciousness of the moment, but helped generate a new sense of Catholic community.

In an age of limited literacy, a public display of authority, like a procession, sent a message to a large public through the use of a nonverbal, symbolic spectacle. The marchers, after arranging themselves in the chapel, sang several verses of the "Pange Lingua," and after the benediction had been given by Father Le Petit, the procession began its march.[120] As recorded in the Book of Deliberations of the council:

> M.de Bienville, Governor of Louisiana, the troops, Swiss as well as French began to file off and ranged themselves in order on both sides of our old house . . . We went out in order, having on our church capes, veil lowered, and each a lighted candle of white wax, our Mother Superior and Assistant near the Blessed Sacrament which was carried under a rich canopy. The little Community composed of nine religious. . . . The troops ranged both sides of the street marching in fine order in file, leaving between them and us a distance of 4 feet. The drums and fifes joining with the songs made an agreeable harmony. The people began the march, our exterior scholars followed, our 30 orphans each with a candle in hand, making a third section, afterwards the ladies of the congregation having each their burning candle, were in the number of more than forty. The Community and the Clergy terminated the march.[121]

This procession with ritual objects, singing, and dignitaries combined to no doubt produce an impressive spectacle of Catholic devotion for the many fledging colonists who lined the muddy streets. This procession, however, would have been markedly different from others they may have witnessed. First, rather than being in the position of honor behind the reserved sacrament, the king's representatives in the colony (the governor and head of the Superior Council) were on the sidelines as spectators. It was the Ursulines who stood in the position of honor behind the canopy that sheltered the blessed sacrament. As Emily Clark suggests, "By excluding the representatives of civil power from their procession, the Ursulines delineated a universe where the power of God was unambiguously superior to worldly authority."[122] Second, among the scholars, orphans, and ladies of the Confraternity of Mary, who marched between the nuns and the inhabitants of the city, were girls of Indigenous and African descent, as well as women of color, poor widows, and destitute orphans who marched right alongside wealthy plantation mistresses. With this display of universalism, they were determined to challenge social and racial distinctions in favor of a hierarchy of pious belief and practices. This would not be without resistance.

The sisters' vision of a "New Eden" was at odds with many in colonial New Orleans. This was subtly alluded to in the sermon that Father Le Petit had delivered at the parish church during the processional to the new convent. Sister Angelique recalled:

> the beautiful sermon given by Rev. Father le Petit of the Company of Jesus, in which he showed our establishment in this country was glorious to God and useful to the Colony. He greatly extoled our Institute for its great good in the education of youth. We have reason to believe that they [the parisheners] were not as much touched by this discourse as they ought to have been, by the little zeal which they show in giving us boarders, having been nearly fifteen months without having more than five or six boarders.[123]

One can only speculate as to why the citizens, who had been so enthusiastic at first, were now lacking in zeal to send their daughters to the Ursulines to be educated. This is certainly in contrast to the enthusiasm of the parents that Marie Hachard described when they received thirty boarders immediately upon their arrival in New Orleans. But, given that at the time of the procession, the convent school consisted of seven enslaved boarders, equal to or more than the number of French girls, one mulatto boarder, and thirty-some orphans, it might be concluded that some colonial families were at best unaccustomed to the fluidity with which the Ursulines formed a community that disrupted social and racial class distinctions.[124] While French colonial New Orleans was marked by racial fluidity, suggesting that racial distinctions were not necessarily fixed, it could very well be the nature of social ruptures within the Ursuline community that were deeply disconcerting. The fact that enslaved, orphans, and French girls all shared the same space deeply violated French social norms based on maintaining class distinctions. This disruption and disorder would continue in the first permanent convent, where orphans and boarding students were housed on the same floor, a clear departure from traditional convent norms. By 1754, when the Ursulines moved into the second permanent convent, they reverted to separating the orphans, who lived on the first floor, from the boarding students, who lived on the third floor, clearly marking class boundaries. This suggests that perhaps the Ursuline attempts at putting into practice universalism in the first convent was not well-received by the French colonists, forcing them to capitulate to expected social norms. Though other scholarship glosses over this early period of the Ursulines, however, this period is critical in illuminating the attempts to create a vision of community based on spiritual equality that, while perhaps thwarted, was critical to shaping the first creole generation of French, African, and Native inhabitants of colonial Louisiana by creating a space accessible to all, in which the spiritual equality of every human was nurtured.

The degree to which the Ursulines promoted a truly "universal" community that unsettled rigid class, racial, and ethnic delineations is much debated and highly contested.[125] The nature of the social organization of the first charter members of colonial Louisiana organized itself around multiple axes that often had conflicting and contradictory visions for the colony. French ministers saw the colony as an experiment in engineering a new society that would reflect burgeoning notions of Enlightenment order, especially regarding class and color. They were particularly keen to limit the influence of the nobility (by not granting new seigneurial titles or allowing the purchase of offices or titles) and the merchant and professional classes, whose increasing political influence in France challenged the absolutism of the monarchy. According to Shannon Dawdy, "With the founding of New Orleans, metropolitan planners attempted to implement their designs for an improved society through urban planning and physical segregation of different sectors of the colonial population."[126]

These attempts at regulation, however, contrasted with the "lived" experience of those on the ground. Ruptures of all kinds—political, economic, and social, especially in regard to the Ursuline convent space—could not be contained. Like the levees' inability to hold the river, manmade structures and designs were unable to contain the human spirit. This was particularly true of the Ursulines, who challenged gender, racial, and social norms through a wide-sweeping project of education. While the Crown hoped to organize and regulate an orderly society through urban planning, census taking, and economic designs, the Ursulines posited a radically different vantage point from which to shape society along their vision. Well in advance (by over a hundred years) of the emergence of "public" common schooling as the vehicle for developing the subject of the "educated" citizen, the Ursulines understood all too well the power of education to shape a common culture, not in the name of the democratic citizen of the nation, but as a universal citizen of the Catholic Church. In this sense, the Ursulines were in many ways the greatest threat to the Crown, given that their "blueprint" for society was *not* directed to ordering earthly power/ treasures and social hierarchies, but was focused instead on challenging the very place of an earthly life in a much larger cosmology. Even more radical was that women, through the education of children, would lead this revolution. The Ursuline convent in this early period exemplifies the ways in which not only the enslaved, but orphans, students, and the nuns themselves "regularly frustrated imperial plans of grand design and exposed the limits of power and control" of absolutism.[127]

In 1734, the Ursulines were fully engaged in their mission to bring *all* women into the fold of the church, regardless of race or social position. Yet their apostolate was also an experiment, given the very different social conditions in France and colonial Louisiana. In regard to social organization, the sisters were accustomed to French social hierarchies limited to the three estates, of which they were traditionally considered part of the nobility. These three classes were barely identifiable in New Orleans. Instead, as Shannon Dawdy has suggested, the principle of social classification was overridden by that of legal status. She maintains that despite the intended blueprint for Louisiana society, according to French policymakers, in New Orleans, social organization:

> Involv[ed] an under-class with origins in three continents representing at least seven different types of legal status—free French subject, freeborn person of color, *affranchit* (freedman), *engagé* (endentured servant), soldier, *forçat* (forced exile or convict labor), and slave. Among themselves, free Frenchmen (and women) experienced a jumbling of the *ancien régime* classes in a new and unsettled order.[128]

And, under the French regime, baptized enslaved (and all Ursuline enslaved were baptized) were both property and protected persons under French law through the Code Noir, meaning they had certain rights.[129] In other words, they had a legal status, unlike slaves in American British colonies.

The social order was anything but clear, especially in regard to slavery.[130] While French colonial policy attempted to use of concepts of race and social hierarchy to impose order in a disorderly society, how the population responded in their everyday lives to this official codification was a different matter.[131] Slavery in urban New Orleans during this early period provided several arenas of slippage between official policy and "street level" deployment. First, enslaved people were highly mobile given the kinds of labor in which they were engaged, which resulted in daily interactions with people from all walks of life. Second, many of the enslaved were skilled laborers (blacksmiths, surgeons, seamstresses, navigators, cooks, nurses), occupations that were in high demand and that gave them a privileged status. Lastly, enslaved people lived in households, and in this case a convent, in which they were involved in intimate relationships with their owners. While a cloistered convent, the space was one which intertwined the lives of French and Indigenous nuns, students of all ethnicities and classes, enslaved Africans, and Indigenous peoples.

When the Ursulines finally moved into the new convent across town in 1734 and took over the management of the hospital, the number of enslaved under their supervision would change dramatically (Figure 7). While they had one enslaved domestic at the old convent, this would be their first experience with managing numerous enslaved Africans who would work both in the convent and the hospital, treating patients (mostly soldiers who were convict labor) and sharing space with soldiers.[132] Income from their plantation, which the 1732 census reveals had sixteen enslaved adults and three enslaved children, would provide income to supplement the king's allowances to run the hospital.[133] The military hospital founded by the Company of the Indies, later known as the King's Hospital, built in 1722, was designed to treat soldiers, sailors, and company workers. In addition, the enslaved working for the company, and after 1731 the king, were also treated, but in segregated facilities.[134] Within the hospital, the medical staff was made up of doctors and surgeons, as well and nurses and domestics.

In 1732, the census records show that there were three enslaved Africans in the service of the King's Hospital.[135] When the Ursulines arrived in July the hospital had twenty-nine patients; by August this number rose to approximately forty-eight. Sister St. Xavier, the recently arrived thirty-one-year-old nun from Bayeux, was installed as chief hospital administrator to assist Dr. Louis Prat, a physician-botanist.[136] The hospital was in deplorable condition, lacking supplies and without an apothecary. While Governor Bienville recommended that the Ursulines provide an apothecary from their ranks, they refused, given that they were already severely understaffed. They hoped to recruit a sister trained as a pharmacist from France, yet had no luck in doing so.[137] Not until 1742 would three more

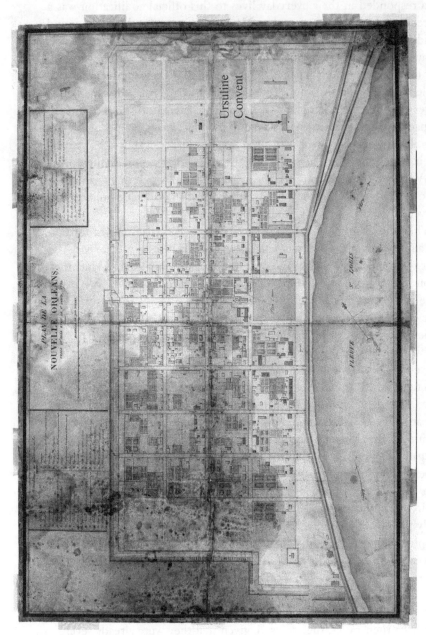

Figure 7. 1732 New Orleans Map, Plan De La Nouvelle Orleans, Telle Qu'elle Etait Le 1er. Janvier 1732, The Historic New Orleans Collection, Acc. no. 1980.175.

sisters arrive to assist the terribly overburdened six sisters who had taken over the hospital and the new convent.

Between 1736 and 1744, the hospital did acquire an apothecary, an enslaved African, Jean-Baptiste, who had been on the king's plantation across the river.[138] It was Jean-Baptiste who would educate Sister St. Xavier in the knowledge of local medicinal plants, mixing drugs, preparing medicines, and *tisanes* (herbal, medicinal teas).[139] Jean-Baptiste and his wife Louison (the hospital cook, a position of high status) would be critical to the management of the hospital. His wife's arrival at the convent in 1744, occurred after a scandal accusing the Ursulines of misappropriation of funds and illegally engaging enslaved Africans from the hospital at the convent. A new contract, *marché*, between the Ursulines and the king was signed to specify how revenues were accounted for and provided seven enslaved Africans from the king's plantation across the river specifically to the Ursulines for use in only the hospital and not the convent.[140] These included Jean-Baptiste's wife Louison (the hospital cook), her five-year-old son Nicholas, Marie Joseph and her two-and-a-half-year-old daughter, and Pierrot and his wife Jeannotoz. It is clear that Jean-Baptiste, since he was not part of this transfer, had at some point been separated from his wife and child, something forbidden by the Code Noir, and had already been working in the pharmacy.[141] His position as apothecary, one with high status, elevated him above other enslaved persons and was signified by his receiving the same ration as that given soldiers. He and Sister St. Xavier would have worked together daily in the pharmacy and laboratory of the hospital, discussing the appropriate remedies for the sick soldiers, preparing teas, tinctures, infusions, and distillates and then working with the sisters who administered the medicines directly to the patients. This required a constant flow of persons between the hospital and convent, which was directly connected to the east side of the convent (Figure 8). Clearly these daily, intimate interactions would have challenged the strict racial and gender boundaries envisioned by the Crown. And, as we will see shortly, this disorder also garnered the attention of the Ursulines' Jesuit superiors.

With the dissolution of the contract with the Company of the Indies in 1731, the Ursulines now came under the direct supervision of the king's representatives in the colony, as well as the direct authority of the Catholic Church. Two years after moving into the first permanent convent, an annual inspection and a written report by the Jesuit superior, Father Le Petit, was conducted. This type of surveillance was not unusual. In fact, an annual inspection of convents had originated in the late seventeenth century. Given that no other known record exists of "annual" inspections, it is

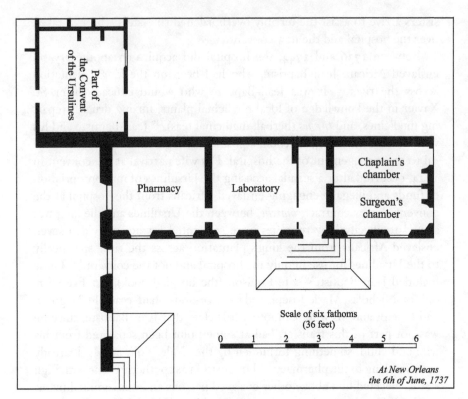

Figure 8. Hospital Wing of Ursuline Convent. Drawn by Mary Lee Eggart based on Samuel Wilson Jr., "An Architectural History of the Royal Hospital and the Ursuline Convent of New Orleans," *Louisiana Historical Quarterly* 29, no. 3 (July 1946), 600.

not totally clear why Father Le Petit chose to conduct one in 1736, but we might speculate that he had concerns about the increasingly "public" role of the cloister in contributing to social disorder. His detailed descriptions of the convent provide rich insights into the daily activities and social relations in the convent. In fact, the 1736 inspection is a one-of-a-kind "street level" description of convent life in New Orleans. It allows us to envision the social relations enacted daily that constituted this fledgling community.

At the time of Father Le Petit's report in 1736, only nine years after their arrival in New Orleans, only four of the original twelve nuns were residing in the new convent. These were Marie Hachard, now Sister St. Stanislaus, who was assigned to teaching the day students; Sister St. Angelique; Sister Ste. Marie (originally from Vanne); and Sister St. Cavalier, who taught day students and catechized enslaved men and women.[142] As mentioned earlier, by this time five more sisters had been recruited from France to help with the increased demands on the nuns: Sister St. André (Jeanne Melotte), who by 1736 had become Mother Superior St. André; Sister St. Pierre (Marguerite Bernard de St. Martin), a gifted teacher and treasurer; Sister St. Francois Xavier (Charlotte Herbert), the pharmacist for the hospital; and the Ramachard sisters, Sister St. François de Paule (Marie Therese de Ramachard) and Sister St. Bernard (Marguerite Antoinette de Ramachard), who had arrived in 1734 to assist with the growing number of students as well as the work in the hospital. These five sisters constitute the second generation of Ursulines, whose dedication over the next twenty years under the most difficult of circumstances resulted in the creolization process that would characterize the first permanent convent.

At the time of the inspection, these nine sisters were fully engaged in teaching boarding students (approximately twenty, of which seven were enslaved), teaching day students, and giving catechism lessons to African and Indigenous students, as well as running the orphanage, which had approximately twenty-seven orphans, tending to the forty-plus patients at the hospital, and managing the pharmacy and the plantation.[143] While the nuns were cloistered, meaning they could not leave the convent, this female space was continually disrupted by male doctors and nurses, male soldiers, sailors, enslaved patients, and the enslaved males. If this was not chaotic enough, we must consider that St. Xavier worked in the hospital treating patients, while several of the other nuns also looked after the religious needs of patients by providing communion and prayer, and lastly, several enslaved females worked in the hospital doing laundry, cooking, and cleaning. These daily human interactions disrupted any semblance of social order, despite the ways in which the buildings had been designed to uphold hierarchical distinctions between the nuns, boarders, day students, orphans, and the enslaved. Quite to the contrary, as we will see in Father Le Petit's report, the hospital and convent were multiethnic spaces composed of people of various class statuses engaged in intimate relationships that blurred class and racial boundaries.

The Ursuline convent property in 1736 comprised four city blocks that included numerous buildings and was totally enclosed by a palisade fence. Four blocks from the parade grounds (now Jackson Square) and closer to the river than the current convent build in 1752, it would have been considered at that time to be on the outskirts of the city. The convent was an impressive three-story brick and timber structure. The first floor included the parlor, refectory (dining room), office for the mother superior, kitchen, pantry, chamber for the servant nuns, and chapel. The nuns occupied the second floor, which included an individual "cell" for each sister, and an infirmary. The third floor held separate sleeping quarters, infirmaries, and day chambers for both the boarders and the orphans, as well as chambers for the mistress of the boarders and the orphans. On the east side of the first floor, connected directly to the convent, was the Royal Hospital, which was made up of a pharmacy, laboratory, the chaplain's chamber (at the time of the inspection Father Doutreleau), surgeon's chamber, and the hall for the sick, which at the time of inspection held forty to fifty sick soldiers. In addition to the convent and attached hospital, the grounds contained a large herb garden for Baptiste and Sister de St. Xavier and a garden for food, both behind the convent. Several other buildings included a kitchen/bakery, henhouse, laundry, store house, cellar, cabins for the enslaved, and classrooms for the extern classes (Figure 9).[144] Although it was a cloistered convent, it is not difficult to imagine that this was a space filled with activity and the comings and goings of Jesuit priests, patients, surgeons, students, and enslaved Africans.

Spatial Relations and Creole Communities

On the morning of November 15, 1736, Father Le Petit, after conducting morning mass, traveled from the Jesuit plantation on the west end of the quarter, down the Rue de Quai (now Decatur).[145] He would have passed the busy morning market on the riverfront, and then on his left the parade grounds where the parish church was on the northern side, flanked on the right by the monastery of the Capuchins and on the left by the prison. On either side of the square were the barracks for the troops. Traveling on after the square in the next block, Father Le Petit would have passed the king's warehouses.[146] After traveling another block along the levee, he would have encountered the high palisade fence that marked the cloistered convent, spanning from the corner of Rue de L'Arsenal (later to be changed to Rue des Ursulines) to Rue Royale (later Royal Street) and on the west Rue du Quarter (now Barracks Street).[147] Following along the fence to the middle of the block, he would have approached the entry to the convent. It is quite likely that he arrived at the same time as the day students scrambled to get to their 8:00 classes in the small wooden building enclosed within the convent walls. His knock most likely roused Pierrot or one of the other three or four male enslaved Africans who would have been stationed in a small reception house at the entrance of the convent.

After being ushered a short distance across the lush gardens filled with

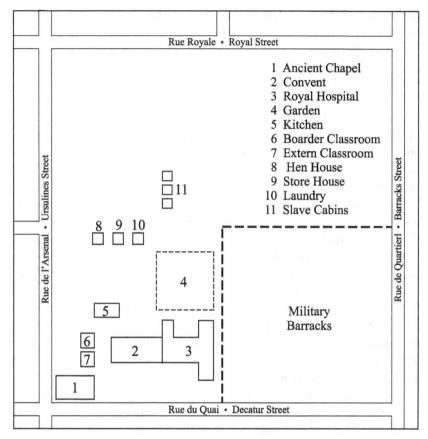

Figure 9. Ursuline Convent Grounds 1734–1752. Drawn by Mary Lee Eggart based on J. Edgar Bruns, *Archbishop Antoine Blanc Memorial: Including New Orleans' Oldest and Most Historic Building* (New Orleans: Roman Catholic Church of the Archdiocese of New Orleans, 1981), 7.

cypress and banana trees, Father Le Petit would have come to the main entrance of the three-story, half-timber convent.[148] After being greeted by the portress, he would have been escorted into the parlor, where the forty-one-year-old mother superior, Sister St. Andre, would have awaited him.[149] Some of the sisters were well acquainted with the father, who had succeeded Father de Beaubois in 1728 as their confessor, and they no doubt remembered his very first visit to their temporary convent in 1729, after the Natchez massacre, when he brought the Yazoo chiefs of Illinois to visit and worship with the Ursulines.[150] With formalities aside, Father Le Petit began his inspection in which he surveyed all the buildings and functions of the convent. Beginning his rounds inside the convent building, he would have toured the ground floor consisting of a small chapel, two parlors, the superior's office, the refectories for the sisters and the students, the community room (the sister's recreation room), the kitchen, scullery (room for the head nurse), and pantry. On the second floor were fifteen cells for the sisters and two infirmaries for sick students. The top floor clearly was an unconventional space because it was shared by *both* the boarders and the orphans. Although each had their own separate dormitories, day rooms, and infirmaries, this mixing of social classes transgressed normative conventions for a French convent, which would require a strict demarcation of social class.

Upon completing his tour of the convent, Father Le Petit continued his inspection of the remaining buildings on the convent grounds. First might have been the hospital and infirmary immediately adjacent to the convent on the east. Beyond the hospital to the back he would have inspected the cabins for the enslaved, sheds for storage, the chicken coop, and the laundry. Glancing behind these buildings, he would have noticed the vegetable gardens, playgrounds, and cemetery. Coming around to the front of the convent property, he would have toured the other outbuildings including the kitchen, which was on the west side of the convent, as well as the academy classrooms for the boarders and the free day school for extern students. Before completing his visit, he would have toured the "Our Lady of Victory" chapel. His detailed report suggests that he spent the day observing the various activities of the nuns, students, and enslaved as they went to mass, ate their meals, and worked in their various jobs in the hospital, laundry room, and kitchen. Two months later, in early January of 1737, he returned to the convent and presented his report to the assembled community.[151] As shall be seen, it reveals a strikingly detailed account of convent life.

Petit's observations suggest a much more fluid nature of the interactions and transactions among the inhabitants than might be expected from a cloistered convent. The convent was right across from the busy Mississippi River port and trading post, and the military barracks were at the end of the block next to the hospital. The daily activities at the hospital and barracks and within the convent, which included the comings and goings of students, patients, and visitors, in addition to deliveries, visitors to the chapel, and weekly meetings of the confraternity "Children of Mary," inevitably resulted in a locus of activity. For all practical purposes, the convent was in many ways a "disorderly" space. In contrast to a peaceful, quiet space, we can imagine a robust community living in relatively close quarters with a great deal of daily activity and a continual flow of exchange with the outside world.

For Father Le Petit, this buzz of activity was far from his understandings of a "cloistered" convent. He recommended that "no one be called, whether child or slave, through the windows, even those facing the inside yard. Sometimes the talking can be so loud in the house that with the windows open, the voices can be heard from afar."[152] Clearly, in his mind, the sisters were being too lax in controlling their community. The majority of his report is preoccupied with the maintenance of strict boundaries between the various social groups, as well as their social interactions. One of his first recommendations is that the "entrance door shall be locked while the carriages are being unloaded, and that a chime be installed in order to announce when it needs to be opened."[153] The inside world of the cloister was obviously not under lock and key. Keys to the outside church, the external students' classroom, and the garden were obviously in the wrong hands, including sisters other than the mother superior and the "gardening negro." In fact, he makes it clear that "the person (sister) in charge of the garden shall not report to the gardening negro and shall check herself whether the garden is under locks."[154] Giving certain responsibilities to enslaved persons violated the social hierarchies designed to maintain authority in a slave society. For Father Le Petit, social control was to be maintained through strict adherence to the rules regulating relationships both within the convent and with outsiders.[155]

Re-establishing the sacred institution of religious cloister was paramount, as evidenced by his recommendation that "None shall enter the house without good reason, for which they may be allowed in the well-regulated communities in France."[156] Clearly, this was not a "well-regulated" house. Father Le Petit stipulated that the sisters adhere strictly to the rule that visitations granted to the sisters should take place only in the parlor, not in the hospital or pharmacy. Based on his sanctions, it was also apparent that the sisters were moving freely between the convent and the outside church, the hospital, and the extern school. Children were also moving about at will, and workers were moving about at their own discretion, even eating in the sisters' kitchen. These ruptures in established boundaries and protocols could not be tolerated. His report highlights that the children were not watched closely enough, nor were the sisters, whom he required to always be accompanied by another sister or older orphan. His report suggests the convent was a less ordered space, one in which boundaries of class, rank, and social status were routinely disrupted. Within the walls of their community, the Ursulines constructed a space in which public and private were racialized and gendered beyond strict eighteenth-century French colonial norms.

This disruption is particularly salient as it pertains to the schooling of the young women in the colony. Transgressions of all kinds were operating in the convent, and while Father Le Petit sought to reinstitute order, boundaries, and control, he simultaneously maintained that "It is appropriate to use the same catechism for all the little girls, may they be external, boarders or orphans; it shall be the same one that is taught in the parish."[157] While Father Le Petit insisted that class distinctions were to be strictly upheld, religious instruction, which was the educational focus of the Ursuline curriculum, was to be the same for every student. The Ursulines took full advantage of the universalist ethic embedded in this mandate to push the boundaries of public and private. In regards to education, the sisters stretched the rules of the *Reglements* to adapt to their new mission. In their zeal to commandeer as many young women as possible, they were reprimanded by Father Le Petit for letting "children aged more or less than what is indicated in the constitutions, even for good reason particular to the missions, be received as boarders or external students, unless they are capable to benefit and they are not an obstacle to the advancement of others."[158] In complying with their mandates, they also took in *all* boarders whose only requirement was that they pay tuition. This is exemplified by the case of the mulatto boarder Marie Charlotte St. Jullien, who entered as a boarding student in June of 1735 and stayed for two years.[159]

Not only were girls of multiple ages and colors being allowed to attend the convent, but Father Le Petit had to remind the sisters that "the orphans need to be trained to work and to the household, more so than writing and even reading; nothing shall be neglected in order to put them in a position to earn a living."[160] Despite suggestions that the orphans were treated as mere servants, it is interesting to note that the care and instruction of the orphans was given to the most experienced and brightest of the sisters, the mother superior, St. Andre, herself a master teacher.[161] And, as suggested by the criticism of Father Le Petit, instruction focused perhaps more on reading and writing than he believed should have been the case. Clearly, they were also taught skills such as sewing, embroidery, housework, and cooking designed to make them desirable housewives. There is no doubt that they received a curriculum different from that of the boarders. But they also shared the public spaces of the second floor of the convent with the boarding students, took meals together in the refectory with all the students, and attended mass together.

Not only were the orphans learning more than they should according to custom, their interactions with the sisters needed to be more closely regulated, as indicated by Father Le Petit's reprimand that "one shall be careful that the orphan who is helping in the kitchen, in order to learn household manners, shall not enter the refectory in order to serve anyone, and shall not be within reach or sight of what happens in the refectory during the meals."[162] He explicitly states that "one must let the person in charge of serving in the refectory perform her duty in accordance with the rules. One shall not rise from the table in order to serve herself or to serve the others."[163] Clearly, the rigid class and social distinctions that had characterized convent life in France were being recast in ways that loosened strict hierarchies.

In regard to the enslaved, Father Le Petit reprimanded the sisters for meeting with them in the classroom of the external students "for personal interviews." They were not to be taught the catechism in the classroom, but were to "be sent back to the parlor." Being reprimanded for teaching the enslaved in "the classroom" suggests a potential rupture in the nature of the education that was being administered to the enslaved. The truth of this "transgression" would not have been unlikely, given that their teacher was Sr. St. Cavalier. Her zeal for teaching the enslaved is evident in her obituary, which notes:

> walking in the steps of St. Peter Claver, she had a boundless zeal for the teaching of the outside poor, and especially the slaves. She delighted herself in their midst, exercising the most fruitful apostolate, removing them from vice, preparing them to receive baptism and other sacraments. Her zeal brought her sometimes beyond the boundaries, but the superiors only had to make a sign to mitigate her activity.[164]

Upon her death in 1742, the community was distraught, but perhaps none so much as the enslaved. Her obituary recounted:

> If she had ever loved the slaves, they proved then how much they appreciated what she did for them. Upon hearing the news of her death, the Negro women were devastated, and to their abundant tears they added considerable sums of money they had collected among themselves in order to have Masses said. They never ceased to repeat that they could never do enough for the one to whom, after God, they owed their salvation.[165]

In the case of Sr. St. Cavalier, the boundaries regarding education of the enslaved Africans were being stretched. While the curriculum was clearly differentiated for boarders, orphans, external students, and the enslaved, the shared public culture of Catholicism, in which all participated in the rituals, rites, and public services of the church, created a common pedagogy and epistemology that functioned at some level to provide a universal public experience despite a deeply stratified social system.[166]

Moving from the convent to the hospital, Father Le Petit would have entered a sealed anteroom chamber that provided a transitional space between the convent and hospital, from which he would have exited to then enter the pharmacy. Several of the pharmacy walls would have been lined with dark glass bottles topped with a cork and labeled with the name of its contents: leaves, seeds, or flowers. A work area would have been visible where Jean-Baptiste or Sister Xavier would be preparing teas or compounds to be administered to the patients. In the next room would have been the laboratory. Upon entering this twenty-by-forty-foot room Father Petit's nostrils would have been filled with the pungent odors of herbs, spices, and other native plants of Louisiana. Most were planted in the garden in the courtyard outside the hospital, where, after being picked, they would have been tied in bundles, covered with netting to protect them from the bugs and dust, and hung from the ceiling and walls to dry. The use of native plants; ginseng, sassafras, sweet gum, tobacco, indigo, mulberry, wax myrtle, oregano for rheumatism, marjoram for convulsions, and dill for insomnia, were good for medicinal purposes. Many of these herbal remedies had been learned about from local Indigenous peoples and recorded by early colonists like Father Du Ru and Antoine-Simon Le Page du Pratz.[167]

Father Le Petit most likely noticed some of the sisters who took on nursing responsibilities chatting amongst themselves, with Jean-Baptiste, or with the patients. His report noted that it was not acceptable for the sister nurses to "dwell there doing nothing, or chatting uselessly, even with the sick."[168] He admonished them that if they were not working, they should retire to a specified room designated for them in the hospital. Clearly the fluid interactions with the patients, most of whom would be considered of a lower class (sailors, soldiers, both French and African) violated the rigid *Ancien Regime* social norms he expected to be upheld. In an emerging plantation society, soldiers, who were for the most part not slaveholders, were positioned on the bottom rungs of the social ladder, which was deeply shaped by class.[169] The Ursulines, who were slaveholders, were expected to uphold their privileged class position. Given Petit's reprimand, however, we know that the sisters working as nurses were crossing both class and race boundaries through intimate relations by chatting with the patients listening to their stories, learning about their travels and exploits and their experiences in the colony. These intimate relationships engendered through the processes of healing between the Ursulines, enslaved Africans of various statuses, and soldiers, sailors, and whites of the working classes created in the eyes of Father Le Petit a disorderly space.

But for Sister St. Xavier and Jean-Baptiste, who worked with the sisters and enslaved persons who were responsible for the laundry, cooking, and cleaning associated with healing the rough and tumble lot of soldiers, this was a cross-cultural space in which orderly relations were not only difficult to maintain but would have impacted the work they were called to do. As a consequence, the everyday practices of ministering to the soldiers who filled the beds of the hospital disrupted dominant perceptions of race, class, and gender among all participants. For Jean-Baptiste and the other enslaved working in the hospital, as well as the soldiers, the authority displayed by Father Le Petit over the Ursulines by his scrutiny of the convent made it apparent that the Ursulines were also subject to mastery. And for the Ursulines, who were forced to tolerate the gaze of Father Le Petit, his harsh report was a clear reminder that women in the church were to be submissive to the patriarchy.

This disorder, in which power relations were transgressed, clearly provided spaces in which subversive activities took place. Foremost among these was the education of orphans in reading and writing, as well as the teaching of the enslaved in the classrooms that should have been reserved for the extern students. Jean-Baptiste, working in the pharmacy, would have been exposed to Sister Xavier's notebooks and books. Jean-Baptiste continued as apothecary until his death and throughout his life he served as godfather in the baptisms of children of African descent in which he signed his name.[170] Whether the Ursulines taught him to write is unknown. It is certainly conceivable, though, that in the community of the enslaved families who lived within the convent walls that he not only taught his own children to write, but that he provided instruction to others as well. As the apothecary, as well as participant in Catholic rituals at the convent, he would have been immersed in a culture of literacy of which he took full advantage. It is hard to imagine that Father Le Petit's reprimands significantly changed the daily interactions between these disparate groups.

While the Ursulines pushed the limits of a universalist ethic, the social order of the colony depended on the maintenance of boundaries of social groups. Father Le Petit reminded the sisters to "ensure that the wall which encloses the hospital yard be so good as to prevent the negroes from going out at night, or from receiving other negroes from the outside to their quarters"[171] By allowing the enslaved the freedom of movement, the Ursulines threatened the stability of colonial society and the social order. The last recommendation of Father Le Petit's report mandates that "the books of the house shall not be lent to the people outside, or to the sick, not even the ones marked to one's usage, except with permission."[172] This transgression of the boundaries of who should have access to books, one of the most significant markers of class distinctions, indicates not only that soldiers or others could read, but that the Ursulines were expanding their mission of education beyond the convent walls. This widening of the circle of education to all members of colonial society through creating spaces that promulgated shared cultural practices was in direct opposition to the goals of the Crown, which relied on strict adherence to a social hierarchy through which they could regulate colonial society.

The portrait that emerges from Father Le Petit's report is one of crossed boundaries, disorder, gossip, and social mixing. It is a newly reconstituted "public and private" space that is messy at best, perhaps chaotic, and that certainly ruptures social norms and sensibilities. What Father Le Petit saw as a lack of order or control was, for the sisters, an ongoing "experiment" in negotiation not only within and against the patriarchal tenets of the Catholic Church, but also the boundaries of what constituted the public and who could participate in it. This reconfiguring of social boundaries in the first permanent convent disrupted not only the relations within the convent walls. By the 1740s the Ursulines were clearly involved in almost every facet of public life, providing social services for most societal ills.[173] This included managing the hospital, orphanage, and shelter for battered women and providing mental health evaluations.[174] In addition, they continued the education of young girls and women of all races at the convent school and through supporting the Confraternity of Mary. And yet, while Ursuline disorder created spaces for agency for the enslaved, soldiers, and even the nuns, at the same time the Ursulines participated in the racialization of New Orleans through their participation in the slave economy. This dual legacy highlights the complex and contradictory power relations in which the Ursulines were complicit in the oppressive systems of slavery as well as being simultaneously oppressed by the patronizing and patriarchal nature of the church and state. In the in-between spaces were the lived practices that shaped everyday life.

Dual Legacy: Unsettling Pedagogies of Ursuline Slavery

It is difficult to ascertain to what degree the Ursulines implemented the recommendations of Father Le Petit. We do know that the Crown continued to scrutinize the Ursulines' work at the hospital. The financial director of the colony in 1744, M. Le Normant, surveyed the hospital's accounts and accused the Ursulines of mismanagement of royal grants.[175] While the Ursulines denied such accusations, the 1744 *marché*, which reduced the number of hospital enslaved from seventeen to six and required them to replace linens, equipment, and furniture and cut food supplies, ultimately placed incredible financial stress on the Ursulines. In May of 1747, after the death of Sister St. André, the new mother superior, St. Pierre, wrote home to the reverent mother superior in Caen to not only provide a detailed report of Sister St. André's death but to describe the poverty of their condition. She wrote, "I find myself at a lack of everything."[176] She requested that they send rosaries and small trinkets for the boarders and orphans, as well as for the day students and enslaved, which were desperately needed for the students religious studies.

Despite these financial hardships the Ursulines continued to provide essential social services to the colony with the expectation that they would be paid. This income never materialized.[177] Consequently, in order to finance their educational mission, they had to become creators of their own material security. For this they would turn to the growing slave economy in which they would buy and sell enslaved Africans. As early as 1734 they had purchased a tract of land (this was in addition to the plantation that the Company of the Indies had given them) with river frontage for two enslaved Africans and five hundred livres in cash.[178] Again in 1736, they purchased a tract of land for three enslaved Africans and five hundred livres from Joseph Larche, who then turned around and mortgaged them to the company in order to pay his debts.[179] What happened to these former Ursuline enslaved is not known. In the period from 1736 to 1752, before they moved into the second permanent convent, they made seven transactions in which enslaved persons were either sold or purchased. They sold three young male slave boys, one of them thirteen-year-old Jacob "for not showing proper respect."[180] They purchased a total of twenty-nine enslaved, of which twenty-four were purchased in 1744, no doubt to shift part of their plantations from the production of staple and subsistence crops to more profitable cash crops.[181] By 1763, the Ursulines had in addition to their plantation enslaved, fourteen enslaved men, women, and children at the convent, in addition to the enslaved they supervised at the hospital.

Throughout this time the Ursulines continued their mission to educate all who came into their fold. First and foremost was their commitment to promoting baptism and marriage. As the central rite of initiation in Christianity, baptism was the gateway to the formal recognition of personhood. No baptismal records have survived from the period from 1727 to 1763 during the time that the Jesuits performed and recorded this sacrament. In the period following the move into the second permanent convent, the sacramental records of New Orleans from 1763 to 1803 reveal the baptism and marriage of nearly two hundred of the Ursulines' enslaved Africans.[182] And while many owners of the enslaved were not as concerned with enforcing the Code Noir as the Ursulines, Jesuits, and Capuchins, the sacramental registries show that two-thirds of those baptized in the early 1730s and 1750s were enslaved Africans.[183] Whether or not the enslaved acquiesced to baptism only to comply with their master's demands, this ritual reinforced not only a "right," but embodied a spiritual universalism through a public display in one of the most powerful institutions in colonial Louisiana. For the enslaved, especially women, this provided them with access to cultural capital, as well as a vehicle to recreate their own traditional religious practices and extend kinship networks.

Baptisms, which required the designation of race in the baptismal record, have increasingly been shown to be central to the creation of race in colonial Louisiana.[184] Yet in addition to the legal and bureaucratic nature of baptism, it was for all practical purposes the ritual that allowed legitimate participation in the public life of the city. It was essential to become married and to serve as a godparent. Jean-Baptiste made the strategic choice to be a godparent, a ritual that allowed him to create fictive kinship groups and have a position of authority.[185] Building community through cultivating, protecting, and defending kinship relations was a practice of freedom, as well as a vehicle to navigate and contest the complex racial boundaries of New Orleans. The important role of godparenting among the enslaved can be attested to by the fact that by 1775, 89 percent of the enslaved who were baptized were sponsored by persons of African descent.[186] Baptism, more than any other sacrament, was the rite that connected the Atlantic world.[187]

The daily encounters in the Ursuline convent from 1736 to 1752, as made visible by Father Le Petit's report, attest to the ways the Ursulines pushed the boundaries of rigid gender and racial conventions in their daily lives. These lived experiences no doubt created shared understandings and tensions, but it was through these interactions that both the Ursulines and the enslaved were inevitably changed. Throughout this time, diversity continued to characterize the convent. In 1740, upon his death, Jean Detharade bequeathed to the Ursulines a young Indigenous woman of the Fox nation.[188] How long she stayed or what role she filled is unknown. It is clear, however, that at least some French colonists understood the Ursuline convent as a space in which Indigenous girls were welcome and most likely would be educated. Not only were free Indigenous girls present at the convent, but in 1744, the Ursulines bought an Indigenous slave for three thousand livres from Francoise Jallot, the widow of Francois Carriere.[189] Again, in what capacity she served is not known. And whether she was still there when Marie Turpin arrived in 1749 from the Illini country, when at least one other Indigenous boarder was present, is unknown. What is clear is that the convent continued to be a multiracial, multiethnic, and multilingual space in which all were exposed to a multitude of social, racial, and gender positionalities. Nothing would have been consistent except the daily rituals of mass and prayer in which all participated as spiritual equals.

In many regards, the Ursuline experiment in universal education can be seen as a failure. By the time the second permanent convent was built in 1754, boarding students and orphans were housed on separate floors, indicating the capitulation of the Ursulines to the emerging class and social norms of the day. In 1763, when the French turned over the colony to the Spanish, the colony would undergo major economic and social changes. The Ursuline convent, now under the jurisdiction of the Spanish Catholic Church with its seat in Cuba, admitted to the convent nine Spanish Creole women whose mode of religious life were at odds with the French Ursuline tradition. The Spanish had an elaborately articulated concept of racial difference and set of social hierarchies that were in direct conflict with the mission of universalism of the Ursulines. By 1797, the acceptance of mulattoes as day school students and half-boarders was opposed by the Spanish Ursuline community, although they could still receive religious instruction. It was agreed, however, that legitimate daughters (those from married couples) who had a white father and a quadroon mother would continue to be received as boarders, as was already the practice.[190] When the Spanish returned the colony to France in 1801, and then to the Americans in 1803, not only had a plantation economy based on a dual racial system developed, but the majority of sisters were no longer of French origin but were New Orleans French Creoles. While they were shaped by Ursuline universalism, they were also shaped by Louisiana's race-based plantation system.

Clearly, Ursuline notions of the class and race were not static but were always dependent on the shifting power relations to which they were subject. While the Ursuline influence and power shifted under Spanish colonial rule beginning in 1763, they had in effect provided every social service in the city for the previous fifty years, as well as educated most girls and women. In fact, literacy rates in colonial French Louisiana were higher than in France, no doubt in part due to the Ursulines. Conditions in early colonial New Orleans were such that the Ursulines established a comprehensive educational program that embodied not only their understanding of spiritual universalism, but also of female agency, which included the incorporation of enslaved Africans as active agents in the Catholic Church. Enslaved Africans in French Louisiana had a strong sense of justice and demanded their rights within the framework of slavery. Thus enslaved Africans took advantage of the pedagogical spaces within the convent, church, hospital, and the confraternity to not only leverage as many rights and freedoms as they could, but also to re-establish and maintain their own African cultural systems. In other words, enslaved persons not only appropriated these spaces; they shaped them.

Catholicism brought New Orleans' residents together under the umbrella of a single church. Likewise, the church also linked European, African, and Indigenous peoples, enslaved and free, into a web of fictive kinship relations that integrated them into one spiritual community. But the emerging institution of plantation slavery and its racialization was shaped just as much or more by economics, demography, and individual ownership than by theology, even among the Ursulines. However flawed or limited their vision might have been, they contributed to establishing a French-Afro-Creole-Catholic educational tradition shaped by concepts of universal rights. At the Ursuline convent Jean-Baptiste, Marie Turpin, and Marie Hachard drew on the universalism of the Catholic Church, as well as the creole pedagogy of disorder, to fashion themselves as active agents in claiming their humanity.

Reverberations

Imagine my surprise when on Sunday night about a year ago I turned on *60 Minutes* and heard the loud cadence of drums blaring from the television. There they were, the famed Marching 100 from St. Augustine's all-Black male Catholic high school in the seventh ward of New Orleans. The school, founded by the Josephite priests in 1951, was ironically born out of the Catholic Church's attempts to avoid desegregation. They were the first African American band to integrate Mardi Gras when they marched in the traditionally all-white Rex parade in 1967. They have played for numerous presidents and the pope. They are in fact the "Best Band in the Land."

While having no direct relation to the Ursulines, it is difficult to imagine an all-Black male Catholic school in any city other than New Orleans. Afro-Catholic culture in New Orleans runs deep and shapes those who do not even consider themselves Catholic. This was certainly the case after Hurricane Katrina in 2005, when the Catholic diocese of New Orleans, under severe financial hardships, decided to close the African American St. Augustine Parish, originally built to accommodate the growing number of Afro-Creole parishioners in the eighteenth century. Built in 1842 by free people of color, the enslaved, and French Creoles as an integrated institution, today it is known as the oldest African American Catholic church in the United States. Not only did the Black Catholic community revolt, but a vast number of non-Catholic lovers of jazz and New Orleans culture understood the significance of the parish as a cultural treasure not only of Tremè, but of the nation. The African American Catholic community drew on the resistance and resilience of their ancestors to fight successfully to keep St. Augustine Church and Parish open.[191]

In 1841, the land for St. Augustine's in Tremè (now the corner of St. Claude Ave. and Governor Nichols) had been donated by the Ursulines under the condition that they name it after their patron saint Augustine of Hippo. When the church opened in October of 1842, free people of color purchased enough pews for their families, as well as purchasing all the pews in the aisles for the enslaved. Whites also rushed to buy their pews, making it the most integrated church in the country at the time. St. Augustine, which embodied the vision of Catholic universalism, is a space, like a text, that has been written on and painted over, but the traces of previous iterations have never fully disappeared. It reveals a multilayered story/history that speaks to the resilience of people over time to name and claim their identity and humanity through spatial acts.

The current site of St. Augustine Catholic Church can be described as a palimpsest. Originally this space, based on archeological excavations, was a portage site and seasonal settlement site for Indigenous peoples who were shuttling trade goods between the Mississippi River to Bayou St. John up to Lake Ponchatrain.[192] After the French colonized this area, the bayou thoroughfare was named the "Chemin au Bayou St. Jean" or Road to Bayou St. John. The Compagnie des Indies developed the land in 1720, building a two-story, brick-between-posts house, as well a brick yard that supplied building materials for the city. After the Company of the Indies departed in 1731, Charles Antoine Morand purchased the property, built a plantation house on the property, and kept it running until 1756.

The plantation passed through various hands until it was passed to Paul Moreau in 1775, and then to his widow Julie Moreau, a manumitted slave, who then became the wife of Claude Tremé. After the influx of Haitian refugees, the Tremés eventually began to sell off lots and eventually sold the brickyard and plantation house to the city, who developed it into the College d'Orléans in 1812. Then in 1834, after the College d'Orléans closed, with the support of the Ursulines, the old college became the interracial St. Claude Catholic school for colored girls, the oldest elementary Catholic school for African American people in the United States. Eventually it became the Sisters of Mt. Carmel school until 1929, which served both white and African American students, including the enslaved. In 1841, the Ursulines divided the property on which St. Claude's stood, giving half the block for the building of St. Augustine's Church.

The hallowed ground/space of St. Augustine represents three centuries of the history of African peoples in New Orleans, whose struggle for self-determination was rooted in the plantations, schools, and churches, institutions they had built as testaments to their agency in fighting for human equality.[193] For the descendants of free people of color, enslaved Africans, and African Americans living in Tremè today, this space is sacred ground, embodying the spirit and soul of a people. It not only symbolizes the rich, multiple roots of Afro-Creole culture in New Orleans, but it embodies the activism of generations of African American men and women in their fight for freedom and social equality. From the Indigenous peoples, who saw this site as critical to their exchange economy, to the current African American parishioners at St. Augustine Catholic Church, this site embodies a palimpsest, a layering of erased pasts that continually re-emerges to structure and privilege diversity. This diversity demands a revisioning of conceptual systems based on linearity, center, and hierarchy and instead reimagines space as multilinear, multitemporal, and as a network of entanglements which weave across different spaces and times.

Consequently, I read the agency of the Ursulines, the enslaved Africans, the free people of color, as spatial acts of disorder that challenged the increasingly rigid racial norms that emerged in colonial and antebellum Louisiana. These educational spaces shed important light on the ways in which ideologies of the public were contested, negotiated, and imagined in the transatlantic pedagogical circuit. Public rights and public spaces were critical to those who sought to have their humanity acknowledged. The stories of the Ursulines, St. Augustine Church, and the Marching 100 are intertwined in the palimpsest of transatlantic history.

THREE

Remapping the "Unthinkable"

*The Haitian Revolution, White Citizenship,
and the Common School Movement*

On a muggy morning in June of 1809, Jean Baptiste Bazanac, originally a refugee from Saint-Domingue, left his home in the French Quarter on Bourbon Street to travel a short distance around the corner to begin his new position as school master and music teacher in his recently opened school. He was not sure how many students would be in attendance given that he had only placed an advertisement in the *Courrier* a few days earlier. His decision to offer his services as a teacher were not of his own making. Arriving just two months earlier from Cuba in May of 1809, Jean Bazanac, like Pierre Roup, whom we met in the introduction to this book, was a free man of color and one of 9,059 refugees originally from the French colony of Saint-Domingue, of whom 3,102 were free people of color, 2,731 were white and 3,226 had been enslaved. Jean had not fled Saint-Domingue in 1791, when enslaved Africans in the northern plain revolted. Most likely he left to escape the warfare that was engulfing the countryside in 1802, when Napoleon sent his army to recapture Saint-Domingue, overthrow the Black General Toussaint Louverture, and reinstate slavery. The fear of losing his freedom due to recolonization by France sent Jean and his family to Santiago, Cuba, a Spanish colony where free men of color had most rights afforded to all Spanish colonists. Most likely arriving in Cuba in 1803, Jean could not have anticipated that his family would once again be uprooted in 1809, when Napoleon invaded Spain. Fear of French aggression in Cuba spurred Spanish colonial officials to eject all French citizens.

Having lost his fortune twice (once when he left Haiti in 1803 and then Cuba in 1809), Jean was fortunate to be a skilled professional whose educational talents were increasingly in high demand in the recently formed United States Louisiana territory. The influx of refugees into New Orleans, of which he had been a part, had doubled the population of the city. Jean and his family were just one of hundreds of refugee families who sought housing, jobs, and schools for their children. Many refugee families, both white and free of people of color, settled on Bourbon and other French Quarter streets that were home to a predominantly Creole, Francophone, Catholic population. While Charters and Royal streets were home to a wealthier demographic—*les grands*—Bourbon, Dauphine, and Burgundy became home to the many middle- and working-class refugees, both white and free people of color, who were educated but had little money.[1]

Without property and having lost his financial means, Jean relied on the fact that he was educated and could offer his services as a teacher. Fortunately, there was a great demand for education and schools not only among the Haitian refugees who expected their sons and daughters to continue their educations in their new homes, but also among large numbers of European exiles and the Americans who were swarming into the city. New Orleans, now a major port city, part of the United States, was on the verge of being transformed from a neglected colonial backwater to becoming one of the richest and most important cities in the nation as well as in the transatlantic hemisphere. While Jean would have to begin again to build a new home, he was optimistic that he and his family would thrive not only economically, but that this new republic would also fulfill its revolutionary promise of full citizenship to men of color. Free men of color in New Orleans at the time were still anticipating that they would acquire full citizenship rights as set forth in the terms of the 1803 treaty of cession, which entitled all inhabitants of the colony to "the enjoyment of all rights, advantages and immunities of citizens of the United States."[2]

Among refugees from Saint-Domingue, Jean was not alone in his quest to establish himself as an educator. He, like many of the other white and free people of color refugees of his generation, both male and female, had taken for granted access to education, as well as the right to education. Before the Code Noir came into effect, when the Spanish colonized Saint-Domingue from 1492 to 1624, the order of Saint Francis of Assisi had provided religious instruction to those who had been forced to convert. In 1503, the Franciscans were asked to teach reading and writing to the Indigenous converts.[3] Queen Isabella of Spain promoted teaching reading, writing, Spanish, and Latin to the children of Indigenous leaders in order that they might hold administrative positions in the colony.[4] When the first enslaved West Africans arrived in 1503, many of whom were Islamic, they had already been well-educated in the major cities of the empire of Mali. When the French took control of Saint-Domingue from the Spanish in 1697, the Code Noir required Catholic instruction. Education among the enslaved was also conducted in secret in private homes or in "forest" schools. These schools must have been prolific given the ordinance signed in 1717 by the mayor of Cape-François, which was directed toward keeping educational development under control by requiring those who did not have the written approval of the parish priest to stop teaching reading, writing, catechism, and other subjects.[5]

Like the rest of New France, education for young girls, both white and those of mixed-race parentage, was seen as invaluable in providing not only good wives for the colonists, but as critical to evangelization. In the 1720s, the Sisters of the Company of Jesus were the first order of nuns in Saint-Domingue who undertook the teaching of reading and writing, but only to white girls. In the 1740s, under the leadership of the Jesuit father Boutin, a boarding school administered by the *La Compagnie des Filles Notre Dame* from Perigueux, France, was established in Le Cap to educate both white and mixed-race girls.[6] Over time, the sisters also took responsibility for the educational and material welfare of poor Black women. This dedication to girls of all races and classes eventually alienated the parents of the white boarders. When in 1780 free girls of color were admitted as boarders, white parents withdrew their students.[7] The boarding school continued until 1790 with 145 free girls of color and somewhere between three and four hundred catechism/day students of color who attended three times a week.[8] In addition to these Catholic efforts, Moreau de Saint-Méry, who produced one of the most in-depth studies of Saint-Domingue before the revolution, chronicles several private schools for girls. Young men of well-to-do planter families, both white and mixed-race, were sent to France for education.

Joseph Bazanac and most refugees from Saint-Domingue were Catholic. Clearly, the concept of racially integrated education was not unknown to the refugees, nor was the idea of public education foreign to those who had been in Saint-Domingue in the prerevolutionary period. By the 1780s Le Cap and Port-au-Prince had experienced an increase in public schools organized by private citizens who saw the economic advantage of educating young boys at home.[9] The secularization of education in France, due to increasing Republican and Enlightenment ideologies, also saw education as critical to the qualifications of citizenship. In fact, a central issue taken up by the French National Assembly after they granted political rights to free people of color in May of 1791 was the need for public education. Members of the French legislative committee were sent to Saint-Domingue in 1792 not only to ensure that free people of color had been given citizenship, but also to require that there were sufficient teachers to teach the children of ex-slaves reading, writing, and arithmetic and to explain the rights and duties of man and citizen. By May of 1794, a public "republican" school had been established in Le Cap for students of all colors. By 1801 Louverture's constitution for Saint-Domingue included plans for establishing a national system of public schools.[10] When Napoleon took power in France in 1801, he ended all support for the development of public schools. What is clear, though, is that Jean Bazanac, as well as other refugees, had experienced a national public education system in which education was understood as critical to citizenship. No doubt this shaped their efforts to create and promote a system of public education they saw as lacking upon their arrival in New Orleans.

New Orleans had appeal to only a few of the earliest Haitian refugees. At the beginning of the revolution, New Orleans was a Spanish city, described by James Pitot, a visiting Frenchman, as a colonial city in a "distressed state," suffering from "stagnant mediocrity."[11] In contrast, the northeastern cities of the newly established republic of the United States: Philadelphia, New York, Baltimore, Norfolk, Charleston, and Savannah were economically and politically much more suitable for rebuilding their lives. Philadelphia, the nation's largest port and city, was intimately bound with Saint-Domingue through its robust trade relations. When the enslaved African laborers of the Northern Provence of Saint-Domingue rose in a mass rebellion in the summer of 1791, setting the whole of the northern island on fire, those who feared for their lives and loss of property set sail for Philadelphia. Wherever the refugees settled, they contributed significantly to the national discourse on race and slavery and to the local culture.[12] This was particularly the case with education.

Throughout the next several years, approximately three thousand refugees, including whites, enslaved Africans, and free people of color resettled in Philadelphia, which became known as the new Cap Français (New Cape). Commerce between Saint-Domingue, the richest of the French colonies, and the United States had expanded tremendously in the 1780s.[13] Merchants in Philadelphia saw the economic benefits of a successful revolution against France that would liberalize trade. Numerous Philadelphians also supported the revolution given their opposition to slavery. Pennsylvania had abolished slavery in 1780 and was the center of the new republic's antislavery movement, headed by the Pennsylvania Abolition Society (PAS), which had been established in 1784.[14] The abolition acts of 1780 and 1788 guaranteed freedom after six months to enslaved persons brought into the state by an owner who established residency. Most refugees, both whites and free people of color, brought enslaved persons that would now be freed. In addition, free of people of color, who having received the rights of full citizenship from France in May of 1791, expected that they would be considered as full citizens in their new country. The radical notion of racial equality, embodied through citizenship to all, prompted lively discussions in the newspapers, markets, coffee houses, taverns, churches, masonic lodges, political circles, and schools regarding what it might mean to fulfill the promises of the age of revolution.

The presence of émigrés from Saint-Domingue, not only in Philadelphia but in the major port cities along the Eastern coastline, galvanized public discourse in the relatively newly established republic regarding the transatlantic revolutionary project of human equality and citizenship. Saint-Domingue refugees, both white and free people of color, went about re-establishing their lives with the full expectation that they would be treated as full citizens in their newly adopted home. This would require the establishment of schools, which were emerging as institutions central to the republican ideals of an educated citizenry. In Philadelphia numerous schools were opened by white refugees that introduced French models and philosophies of education. Since the American Revolution, Jefferson had been studying French educational thought and practice to learn about new educational forms and the role education should play in a democratic and republican state.[15]

This French influence on American education throughout the country, and especially in New Orleans, would continue well into the 1830s.[16] This included Madame Grelaud's Seminary for Girls (1809–1849), as well as the Mantua Academy, where Saint-Domingue native Victor Value (1792–1859) taught and was principal from 1819 to 1835.[17] His friend and coauthor, refugee John Manesca (1778–1838), taught French in New York and authored several books on language instruction and phrenology, as well as coauthoring with Victor Value in 1815 a language instruction book using French literature, which they shared with Thomas Jefferson.[18] In 1837, Manesca was a founder of a society that promoted the beliefs of the utopian socialist thinker and women's rights advocate Charles Fourier, whose ideas influenced the founding of several utopian communities in the United States. These educator activists, while teaching primarily white refugees and free people of color, saw themselves as part of a larger community of transatlantic French revolutionaries who saw education as critical to the republican ideals of liberty, freedom, and equality.

While Philadelphia was the first city to experience a wave of refugees, other U.S. cities were also attractive to refugees given commercial relations, but also due to the presence of communities of Roman Catholics, especially French clergy. Both Baltimore and Savannah had a small but significant presence of Catholics. Maryland, established in 1634, had long been a home for Catholics in the colonial period and became a refuge for French Catholics in the aftermath of the Jesuit suppression (1773–1814) and the French and Haitian Revolutions.[19] Maryland was a slaveholding state and by 1785, one out of every five Catholics in Maryland was Black.[20] Baltimore, the first diocese of the Roman Catholic Church formed in the United States in 1789, provided a logical place for Catholic exiles from Haiti, who began arriving in 1793. Like in other cities, one of their greatest impacts was on education, especially Catholic education. The Catholic teaching order the Sulpician Fathers, refugees from France after the revolution, conducted Sunday catechism classes for the community of about a thousand Black refugees, both free and enslaved, who attended St. Mary's Chapel at the Sulpician seminary. By 1820, Baltimore was known as the "free black capital of America" with over ten thousand free people of color, many of whom formed a discrete Black Catholic community.[21] They created and supported a rich community life of religious, social, and educational institutions that gave birth in 1829 to the Oblate Sisters of Providence, the first permanent Roman Catholic sisterhood of African descent, whose primary goal was education.

The Oblate Sisters of Providence charter members—Elizabeth Clarisse Lange, Maire Balas, Rosine Boegue, and Therese Duchemin—shared a common identity as Catholic, Francophone, free women of color who had emigrated from Saint-Domingue or other parts of the Caribbean. Well-educated and deeply religious, they each desired to "offer" their lives to God by pursuing religious communal life in the Roman Catholic tradition. For free women of color, collective Catholic religious life, with traditional entitlements of respectability, offered a form of social opposition to counter the increasingly racist society that denied Black humanity. Forming a Black sisterhood would, however, require unimaginable tenacity. Lange and Balas began by serving as godmothers, joining several confraternities, and opening a home-based school to address the need for education for colored people. "Miss Lange's School" served the Black Francophone community, "from poor families to those enjoying sufficiently comfortable circumstances to finance their children's education."[22]

With the support of the white Sulpician priest James Joubert, Lange and Balas began the process of forming a religious order. According to the Oblate Rule, the primary purpose of the Oblate Sisters was the Christian education of girls of color. By June of 1828, they had begun their novitiate and started the Oblate School for Colored Girls (with eleven boarding students and nine day students) in a rented residence that served as both school and convent, in close proximity to St. Mary's Seminary.[23] In 1853, the school was renamed St. Frances School for Colored Girls and later was shortened to St. Frances Academy, the name it still goes by today as the oldest continuously operating African American Catholic high school. In Charleston and Savannah, as well, smaller communities of Black Catholics, some whose ancestors had already been converted to Catholicism by the Portuguese in Africa, also established religious communities and schools.[24] These communities of refugees were not insular groups but participated in a pedagogical circuit through regular correspondence, newspapers, Masonic lodges (to be discussed in the next chapter), confraternities, and trade and through a network of Catholic priests and nuns. Refugees from Saint-Domingue drew on the rhetoric of the Catholic Church and its mission of universal education, as well as the age of revolution, to recreate Catholic community and educational institutions. But it was in New Orleans, where the largest number of refugees would arrive in 1809, that education would make its greatest inroads.

For the Haitian refugees in New Orleans arriving from Cuba, teaching, as well as work on plantations as engineers, carpenters, mechanics, and architects, were the two types of employment that were most often sought through newspaper advertisements.[25] Throughout 1808 and 1809, at least fifteen advertisements appeared in New Orleans newspapers in which both white and free men of color originally from Saint-Domingue offered their services as teachers, many of them opening their own schools. While some engaged in education only briefly until they could secure more lucrative employment, many were committed educators who saw education as critical to creating an interracial, democratic public sphere through which human equality would be embodied. This commitment is exemplified by Jean Bazanac's school on Dauphine Street, which welcomed students of all shades. His son, Joseph, would go on to be a renowned music teacher who in the 1840s administered an interracial school in the Faubourg Marigny with Jean Louis Marciacq, a white, exiled Frenchman. These interracial schools mark a dynamic period of experimentation in public education long neglected in traditional narratives of education.

The early part of the nineteenth century in New Orleans has been described by Alisha Johnson as a "liberated" space in which free people of color, while not full citizens, were able to garner respect through their educational attainment.[26] Restrictions on literacy, as well as the curtailment of the "rights" of free people of color and enslaved peoples did not begin until the 1830s, and only intensified in the 1850s, leaving this early period of the nineteenth century a space in which more fluid race relations enabled experimentation in democratic education. These experiments in educational equality emerged from a creole pedagogy in which counterpublic spaces envisioned a universal citizenship not necessarily bound by the nation. Ironically, these experiments in interracial, democratic education came to an end in 1841 with the introduction of the common school movement in which "public schools" were established as "white only," marking the public sphere as a segregated space and constructing African Americans as noncitizens.

Forgotten Atlantic Pasts: Education in Early New Orleans/Louisiana

When Jean Baptiste Bazanac arrived in New Orleans in the early summer of 1809, little did he know that he would become part of a much larger movement of educational initiatives that sought, to varying degrees, to aspire to the lofty ideals of republicanism. These initiatives were as varied as the polyglot, diffuse population that occupied New Orleans. For Bazanac and the nine thousand Saint-Domingue refugees who doubled the population of New Orleans, they revived the city's Francophone culture, boosting the French language, Catholic religion, French newspapers, theater, and education. Prior to their arrival, at the time of the transfer of Louisiana from Spain to France and then to the United States in 1803, New Orleans had a population of about 8,056 (3,948 whites, 2,773 slaves, and 1,335 free people of color). Coming from cosmopolitan Cap Français, Jean Baptiste, as well as all the emigres, would have been dismayed at the provincial nature of the city. There was no theater, no public library, no daily newspaper, and very few schools, things he had taken for granted in Saint-Domingue.[27]

During the Spanish colonial period (1767–1803), the ideas of establishing primary and secondary schools at public expense had been put forward by King Charles III, but they did not have much success. A Spanish school, begun by the bishop in 1772, had received little support from the French and never exceeded thirty students. After the school burned in the city fire of 1788, Don Andrés Almonaster y Rojas provided one of his properties for reopening the school, which was staffed by six Franciscans who had arrived from Spain to serve as teachers. But few students attended.[28] Instead, Governor Miro reported that the French had opened eight private schools, which accommodated four hundred French-speaking students.[29] While these schools have been considered private, they had to be approved by the Spanish director of the royal schools, Don Andrew Lopez de Armesto. This was the case in 1800 when Don Luis Francisco Lefort, a native of France, applied to open a "house of education" for not only the lower grades but the higher grades as well. Given that he was a learned scholar with fifteen years of experience teaching in Maryland, had authored a book of English and French grammar, had been naturalized as a Spanish subject, and was a Catholic, his "license was approved to start a public school."[30]

Refugees would contribute to the rising number of schools in New Orleans upon their arrival, as well as to the tradition among those with means of hiring tutors for private instruction at home. While these "private" schools served primarily young men, young girls would certainly continue the tradition of attending the Ursuline Academy, only blocks from where Jean Baptiste lived. These schools would reinforce French as the primary language of the territory, as well as Catholicism, and their curriculum would in many cases be influenced and shaped by French revolutionary ideals, which saw education as central to republican government. Often overlooked, perhaps, were the many opportunities for apprenticeships, which also often included various types of instruction. Given that many refugees, both white and free people of color, were artisans in trades such as laying bricks or making shoes, cigars, or sails, apprenticeships in these skilled trades provided families valuable opportunities for education.[31]

As a newly established American territory, the city was flooded with Americans pursuing not only economic gains but also political advantage. Americans were still in the midst of determining how a government under the new republic would operate, especially in regard to the issue of citizenship rights for free men of color, the status of Indigenous peoples, and the role of slavery. In contrast, the French and Haitian Revolutions had abolished slavery and granted full citizenship to all people. For the newly arrived free people of color, whose status as citizens was uncertain, they immediately began the work of establishing their right to citizenship. Education was central to this claim. Bazanac most certainly understood the importance of education not only as a pragmatic necessity in an age of increasing print culture, but he understood its impact as a mark of human equality and citizenship. In the aftermath of the American, French, and Haitian Revolutions, slavery was abolished in France (1794) and England,

and the international slave trade was made illegal in the United States in 1800. In the United States as early as 1780, Pennsylvania passed an act for the gradual abolition of slavery, followed by New Hampshire (1783), Connecticut and Rhode Island (1784), New York (1799), and Ohio and New Jersey (1802). This movement to gradually abolish slavery, while far from eliminating notions of white superiority, provided support to those who had fled to the new Louisiana territory and envisioned this as a space in which to realize the fruits of revolution. In 1809 Bazanac, along with many newly arrived emigres and exiles, followed closely the actions of the territorial governor, William Claiborne, as a barometer of the degree to which their vision of full equality might be fulfilled. For the educators among this group, the Governor's Act of 1805 to establish a state system of public education would have been of intense interest. While the act had languished between 1805 and 1809 due to lack of funding, it would be the Haitian refugees who would breathe life back into this act.

Claiborne's First University Act: An Educational Revolution

> The news of the Revolution of St. Domingo and other Places
> has become common among our Blacks . . . the spirit of Revolt
> and Mutyny has Crept in amongst them–a few Days since we
> Discovered a Plan for our destruction.
> —Governor William Claiborne, 1804[32]

1804 marked a turning point in the impact of the Haitian Revolution on the United States. Not only did Haiti become the first independent Black nation, but the initial return of Louisiana by the Spanish to the French sparked the ongoing hopes of Jacobins in the transatlantic world that the revolutionary ideals of Haiti might also manifest themselves in French Louisiana and the larger American South.[33] In 1791, word of the French Revolution had made its way to Spanish colonial Louisiana. *The Declaration of the Rights of Man and Citizen* (1789) circulated throughout the colony, providing the enslaved with a discourse of equality from which to argue for their freedom. Shortly after his arrival in Louisiana in 1791, the Spanish governor of Louisiana, Carondelet, suppressed an uprising of the Mina, a community of African slaves in Point Coupée. Three years later in April of 1793, he again put down a conspiracy when he became aware that several Frenchmen in New Orleans, who were partisans of the new French republic, none from Saint-Domingue, were secretly plotting a revolt. In 1795 a conspiracy to revolt organized by both whites and the enslaved was discovered by the Spanish authorities in Point Coupée, just miles upriver from New Orleans. The origins of this discontent are traced to a Waloon (a French-speaking Belgian) teacher and tailor, Joseph Bouavel, who had read to the slaves from the *Declaration of the Rights of Man.* Although the revolt was not successful, conceptions of freedom and equality were being envisioned and acted on among enslaved Africans, Jacobins, and free people of color. This was not the only reverberation.[34] Tanguy Boisière, a Haitian refugee to Philadelphia, reported in the 1793 edition of his *Journal des révolutions de la partie française de Saint-Domingue* of a plan in Charleston to "promote a system of freedom for Negroes in the Southern American states, to arm them and to give them as leaders free Saint-Domingue mulattoes, and to have them march against Louisiana and the other Spanish possessions."[35]

Given the rumors of the return of Louisiana to France, as well as the increasing number of Haitians thought to be abolitionists, Governor Carondelet believed the Spanish king would proclaim a general emancipation of slaves by the end of 1796. While this did not happen, enslaved Africans in the city of New Orleans, as well as many merchants, carpenters, sailors, masons, coopers, and artisans, were clearly aware of republican sentiments that would benefit their positions as freedmen and as citizens. On the other hand, large planters whose sympathies were allied with the monarchy listened with interest in 1802 to rumors of retrocession to France, which could make Louisiana a meeting place for all French colonists exiled in the United States, in other words, a colony that would replace Saint-Domingue. This was in contrast not only to the French republicans, but other European abolitionists and radicals who sought spaces in which their revolutionary ideals could be materialized. The widespread interracial, cross-class nature of these fomenting revolts not only challenged the institution of slavery but represented to many the "unthinkable": the claim to Black citizenship grounded in the republican ideals of human equality.[36] This influx of refugees from Haiti, particularly to New Orleans, as well as other French, English, Irish, and German exiles—products of the age of revolution—saw Louisiana as a site for enacting their republican visions, including the establishment of public education as a means of forging human equality.

Given this rhetoric of revolution, racial anxiety was heightened in the frontier town of New Orleans. It was feared that racial mixing between slaves, free people of color, sailors, boatmen, and workers in taverns, dance halls, markets, hospitals, and wharfs would result in alliances across class that would contribute to unrest and potential uprisings against the slave-holding elite.[37] The fear of class solidarity across racial lines was well-founded given the nature of a port city in which young soldiers, sailors, and boatmen—a cosmopolitan transatlantic population—equaled as much as a quarter of the permanent population and had a visible presence in the city. The very nature of social relations based in class privilege was being challenged in the age of Atlantic revolutions. Yet slave imports were on the rise due to Louisiana's recent expansion of and demand for sugar and cotton production.[38] This surge, according to Eberhard Faber, "combined with the related rise of the libre population, had created a new, unsettled racial order that many whites experienced as a threatening rise in black unruliness."[39] In the early nineteenth century, New Orleans slaveholders were thinking about the Haitian Revolution precisely because it challenged racism and its corollary trajectories of nation, citizenship, and education. This threat to white superiority, that Blacks could be "citizens" of an independent nation, sent shock waves throughout most of the United States.

While slavery was being abolished in most European countries, as well as in the northeastern states of the republic, New Orleans emerged as a major American metropolis as its enslaved population exploded. From 1803 to 1830, the enslaved constituted one-third of the population of New Orleans.[40] Given the transatlantic, cosmopolitan nature of the city, in which enslaved persons were often given a great degree of mobility to engage in various types of work and exchanges, it has been suggested that they were "citizens of the world."[41] Rapid urbanization in the 1790s had left the city unable to control the movement and lives of the enslaved.[42] For the white Creole elite whose wealth depended on the containment of enslaved as chattel, the increasing sense of racial discord was exacerbated by the increasing number of free people of color, especially those from Saint-Domingue, who were perceived as potential revolutionaries. And while this class has generally been treated as a unique and distinct group from enslaved people, their kinship ties and economic circumstances created some degree of racial solidarity.[43]

The acquisition of Louisiana, it was hoped, would help to hasten a solution to the question of slavery. President Jefferson and Territorial Governor Claiborne, as well as other Democratic Republicans, thought slavery was in a state of decline. By 1804, seven of the original states had either abolished slavery or instituted gradual emancipation schemes. Only South Carolina and Georgia had expanding plantation economies that continued to rely on slavery. Jefferson, in particular, envisioned that with the expansion of the nation westward, settlers would diffuse the enslaved population west and challenge the profitability of large-scale southern plantation agriculture. In tandem with increasing rates of white reproduction, Jefferson and those supporting gradual emancipation, believed that slavery would slowly be extinguished in the early republic.[44]

Much has been written about the political challenges that faced the first territorial governor, William Charles Cole Claiborne, when he took over the administration of the Louisiana territory in October of 1803. Many of Claiborne's contemporaries, including President Jefferson, had painted portraits of Louisiana as backward, ignorant, and unprepared to engage in democratic government.[45] But in 1804, New Orleans had a highly literate population, many of whom spoke and read multiple languages, as evidenced by the numerous bilingual newspapers that were published. Approximately half of the population was literate, able to both read and write.[46] By 1820, it would become the fifth largest city in the United States. Its geographic location was key. At the crossroads of the Mississippi River, the Atlantic Ocean and the Caribbean, New Orleans would provide Americans with the nexus for uniting the commercial interests of U.S. imperial expansion. Louisiana was critical to U.S. geopolitical interests given the "tensions of empire" that continued to manifest themselves in the Americas.[47] Spanish Florida and New Spain flanked the nation, and French desires to reestablish colonies in the Caribbean and ongoing British interests in North America continued to threaten the stability of the new American republic, whose national identity was extremely fragile and still in the making. But nothing threatened the volatile national unity more than the divisive issue of slavery.

Undaunted, Claiborne approached his task of uniting the polyglot population of Louisiana. His pragmatic goal of maintaining a multilingual, multicultural, transatlantic society can best be seen in the educational initiatives that he, as well as the French, American, and Haitian advisors he engaged, set into motion. Little has been written about the University Act and its role in shaping the history of education in Louisiana or about the influence of the Haitian refugees in the successful implementation of this act. While much neglected in the narratives of education in Louisiana and the nation, the University Act provides a window into Louisiana's attempts to create a public system of education well before the common school movement and in a city that was multilingual (French, Spanish, English, Choctaw), multiethnic, and in the dynamic crossroads of the Atlantic.

Within the first month of his administration, Claiborne set about to establish a public school system in the Louisiana territory. "An Act to Institute an University in the territory of New Orleans" was passed by the Legislative Council on April 19, 1805. The act provided for the establishment of a state system of secondary schools, one in each parish, with the College of New Orleans (also known as the College d'Orléans) at the head. Although Claiborne's commitment to instituting a system of public education has often been attributed to his desire to "Americanize" the population of Louisiana, it must be remembered that an "American" identity was still in the making given that "nationhood" as a concept was still in its infancy.[48] More likely than wanting to mold "Americans" was Claiborne's desire to instill a certain allegiance to the American government, given the ongoing potential threats of the French, Spanish, English, and even some Americans to reacquire the territory of Louisiana for their own political ambitions. The notion that Americanization was a "homogeneous process with singular goals" has been problematized, and in fact the establishment of a public education system provides a new lens for understanding the meaning of this process. As Mark Fernandez maintains, "the aims of the Americans and the process of Americanization was something much more fluid and contentious."[49] Claiborne's actual plans for a state system of public education were in fact delegated by the Legislative Council to three lawyers who represented the factional divisions in territorial politics: Edward Livingston (Claiborne's ally at times but eventually his archrival), James Brown (a Kentuckian and critic of Claiborne), and James Workman (Claiborne opponent). While all appointees of Claiborne with positions in the territorial government, their later involvement in the Burr Conspiracy revealed just how contentious American identity was in early America. The conspiracy was aimed at liberating Mexico from Spain in order to create a new state of liberated slaves that would include Mexico, parts of the Louisiana Purchase, and Kentucky.

For James Workman, British-trained lawyer, Irish immigrant, and opponent of slavery, a public system of education was deemed essential to republican ideals. His appointment to the committee to draft the state system of education was fortuitous, and he took full credit for designing the University Act.[50] Workman, who had arrived in the United States in 1799, originally settled in Charleston, South Carolina, where he took up work as a merchant and was associated with the *Courrier*, a Federalist newspaper. In his *Political Essays* (1801) and play, *Liberty in Louisiana*, which premiered in Charleston, he advocated for the American government to seize Spanish Louisiana before the French did, arguing that the imperial pursuits of both Spain and France included the proliferation of slavery. He argued in a November 15, 1801, letter to Thomas Jefferson regarding the dangers of slavery:

Were the United States to take those countries, that danger [of slavery] would not only be forever removed; but the Congress might, in virtue of the right of conquest, make such beneficial regulations respecting the slaves, there and enforce such laws against the perpetuity of slavery, as would in time annihilate that odious condition. This would necessarily lead to similar measures in the adjoining states, and consequently to the total abolition throughout the Empire of an establishment by which it is enfeebled, endangered, contaminated and disgraced. Louisiana and the Floridas would afford abundant choice of districts, suitable in every respect for the settlement of emancipated negroes.[51]

Workman likely saw ample opportunities in Louisiana to shape the future of the young nation along his republican ideals, including the abolition of slavery. In 1804, after becoming a citizen, he moved to New Orleans, where he worked as a lawyer. Within a year, he was appointed as a judge of the territorial county of Orleans and was named a regent of the College d'Orléans.[52] Later that year, as secretary of the territory's Legislative Council, he worked with Edward Livingston, James Brown, Lewis Kerr, and Louis Moreau-Lislet to craft Louisiana's legal system.[53] This group reflected the factional division in territorial politics, revealing the contentious process of Americanization. For Workman, who believed that America should be based on the premise of human equality, the opportunity to design the state system of education was an ideal way to embody his political agenda.

Workman's sound understanding of both French and American law likely contributed to his appointment by Claiborne to draft legislation for a system of public education. In fact, he based the "University Act" on the accepted French tradition designed in 1763 by René de La Chalotais for a secular system of schools in France, as well as Diderot's (1776) plan for a university.[54] Both the university of the State of New York in 1784 and the state of Georgia in 1785 had also drawn on the French model to design their systems of education. The term "university" was used to describe a state system of education for secondary schools and higher education.[55] It provided an academy for boys *and* for girls in each of the twelve parishes, with the College d'Orléans at the head of the system. This was placed under the administration of twenty-four regents, including the governor, various judges, and the mayor and recorder of the city of New Orleans, among others. The regents were empowered to select all officers of their board, including the chancellor, a vice chancellor and secretary-treasurer, and the school masters of such academies as should be established in the parishes of the state.[56] They were also empowered to appoint the president and professors of the College d'Orléans. In addition, the Board of Regents was to establish as many academies for girls as they saw fit, becoming the first state system to mandate education for girls. Finally, the act called for the board to establish a public library in New Orleans and for each county to have a public library. Workman's vision of a "university system" was overwhelmingly supported by the legislature, and the Board of Regents went to work immediately to finance the plan.

At the first meeting of the Board of Regents, held July 5, 1805, the *Louisiana Gazette* reported that Governor Claiborne was elected chancellor and Mayor James Pitot of New Orleans was elected vice chancellor of the university system.[57] Of the remaining ten regents, the majority (6) were French Creoles, three were American, and one, Louis Moreau-Lislet, was a Saint-Domingue refugee. The inclusion of Lislet marks the increasing influence of refugees on matters of education. Moreau, born in Saint-Domingue in 1762 and educated at the Sorbonne during the height of the French Revolution, returned to Cap Français and took up a position as an assistant public prosecutor.[58] Upon his arrival in New Orleans in 1804, his skills as a lawyer were quickly recognized. He and James Brown were chosen to draft a civil code for the territory of New Orleans. He wrote both the Digest of 1808 and the Civil Code of 1825.[59] While a proponent of slavery, he was also the founder of the interracial Masonic lodge, La Parfaite-Union (Perfect Union), which included free men of color.[60]

Advancement toward this public school system came to a complete halt due to a lack of financial support from the legislature. This should not, however, be understood as a lack of support for public education. Although Claiborne sought legislative support for education, the Americans had not yet extended citizenship to Louisianans, suggesting the uncertainty of the future status of the territory and whether, given international politics, Louisiana would remain an American territory at all. This uncertainty among Louisianans was exacerbated by the fact that Louisiana was not granted statehood immediately after it was transferred into the possession of the United States. Many of the inhabitants of Louisiana had been opposed to territorial status, hoping instead for immediate statehood, where they could elect their own officials rather than have officials sent from Washington who did not know their language, customs, or culture. A 1804 petition written by a group of planters, merchants, and other Louisianans, "Mémoir présenté au Congrès des États-Unis Amérique par les Habitants de la Louisiane," was presented to Congress by Pierre Derbingy (a French expatriate), Jean Noël Destrehan, and Pierre Sauve (both French Creoles). It demanded immediate incorporation and admittance to the Union according to the principles of the federal constitution with the full rights of citizens of the United States and the protection of their liberty, property and exercise of their religion, Catholicism. After they met with President Jefferson, though, it was clear that he was unresponsive to their desires to be counted as full citizens and fellow countrymen. Both Derbingy and Destrehan would be appointed by Claiborne to serve on the first Board of Regents of the University of Orleans, appointments that would hopefully serve to garner support for his educational initiatives.

A primary concern of opponents of the Louisiana Purchase had been whether it would be prudent to grant citizenship to the French, Spanish, and free people of color living in New Orleans, as the treaty would dictate. Critics in Congress worried whether these "foreigners," unacquainted with democracy, could or should become citizens. Additionally, the U.S. government had to use English common law to make them citizens to collect taxes. Thus, another reason that Louisianans were opposed to a general tax for public education was that they were not officially citizens. For Claiborne, education might potentially serve as a vehicle for uniting a polyglot population, but for the native Louisianans who were being denied citizenship, this imposition only reinforced their humiliation and the perception that they were "too ignorant" to exercise their right of election. They countered in their "Mémoir présenté au Congrès des Êtas-Unis Amérique par les Habitants de la Louisiane" when they asserted:

> [T]he original settlement of the province was marked by circumstances peculiarly favorable when *science* had attained a great degree of perfection, and from a country in which it flourished; many individuals possessing a property and rank, which suppose a liberal education, were among the first settlers; and perhaps there would be no vanity in asserting that the first establishment of Louisiana might vie with that of any other in America, . . . their descendants now respectfully call for the evidence which proves that they have so far degenerated as to become totally incompetent to the task of legislation.[61]

This view of the inhabitants of Louisiana as unprepared for citizenship and the refusal of the U.S. government to extend to them what they deemed as universal rights resulted in a political animosity in which Claiborne was unable to execute his plan of "public" education for five years due to lack of support from the territorial legislature. The influx of refugees from Haiti would revive his efforts.

The Saint-Domingue refugees, along with the already existing free people of color in New Orleans, would by 1810 result in the population of free people of color making up 29 percent of the population of New Orleans.[62] Whether free or enslaved, they had in Saint-Domingue experienced various forms of education as well as "public" rights. Under French and Spanish colonial law, slaves had enjoyed certain rights, and free people of color were citizens. But these rights were being rolled back by Jeffersonian politics and Louisiana's planter-dominated territorial legislature through the Black Code of 1806 and in the new Louisiana legal system. The Black Code targeted the rights of free persons of color; while they had experienced the full rights of citizenship under the Spanish, they were now denied the right to vote, to seek public office, and to freely assemble. As self-identified "citizens" they were determined to pursue their rights as citizens, including the right to education, which would not only promote their French language, culture, and traditions, but would support their understandings of themselves as full and equal citizens.[63]

The regents, who had been unsuccessful in acquiring funding from the legislature for the "university system" since 1806, faced a radically different legislature in the spring of 1811, one that was shaped by the many Saint-Domingue refugees who were eager to establish education as a means to reinforce their language, culture, and way of life. What was needed was support and funding for the system from the territorial legislature. Lack of funding was partly because without primary schools to function as feeders for the secondary schools, the success of the college and parish academies was seen as limited. As a consequence, on May 2, 1806, the Legislative Council passed "An Act to provide for the establishment of public free schools in the several counties of the Territory." The schools were not academies, but were free "neighborhood" schools. This act provided the primary schools the university act had failed to provide. Responsibility for the schools was directly upon the counties and five school commissioners, who were to be elected by the patrons in mass meetings in the fashion of the New England town meeting.[64]

Another stumbling block to the enactment of this act has commonly been attributed to the unwillingness of the people to submit to a general tax to fund schools.[65] The rejection of taxation as a method of funding public schools, however, should not be equated with a rejection of support for education or even "public" schooling. Given that the former French and Spanish were accustomed to a "tuition" system to support universal

Catholic education, it is not surprising that people did not want to be taxed (essentially twice) to fund new schools. Consequently, Claiborne turned to the U.S. Congress for the funding that would enable,

> The Territorial Legislature to immediately establish seminaries of learning in the several counties, where the children of native Louisianans and the native Americans, the native Frenchmen and the native Spaniards, now inhabiting this Territory, might be instructed in useful knowledge, and the effects of whose early intercourse and friendship would probably be such as to induce the rising generation to consider themselves one people, and no longer to feel that jealousy and want of confidence that exists among their fathers.[66]

It would eventually take the influx of refugees from Saint-Domingue to provide the support for public education.

New Orleans: Teachers as Exiles

Although the College d'Orléans floundered due to a lack of funding, this certainly did not impede zeal for education among newly arrived Haitian and French exiles or the increasing number of Americans who were flooding into New Orleans. But it was the final wave of Haitian refugees, who doubled the population of New Orleans, that would ultimately have the greatest impact on education in the early American period. As Caryn Cossé Bell has maintained, this wave of refugees "reinforced the city's Latin European racial order and *revitalized* Gallic culture and institutions."[67] Schools established by the refugees, as well as the teachers, both white and free people of color, were central to this revitalization and to what many saw as the vital role of education in a republican government. In 1811, at least 25 percent of the teachers listed in the *City Directory* of New Orleans were refugees from Saint-Domingue (Figure 10). This included six white males, one white woman, Madame Duconge, and two who were identified as free men of color: Jean Baptiste Bazanac and Réné Pre Gaignard.[68] A least seventeen percent of all teachers were free people of color and at least twenty-seven percent were women—diversity that was unprecedented in other American cities of the time, where teachers were predominantly white and male.

New Orleans already had at least three teachers who identified as free men of color: Pre. H. Lavocat in the Faubourg Marigny, Jean Baptiste Mayorquin at 22 Dauphine, and Charles Vivant at 11 Toulouse. These

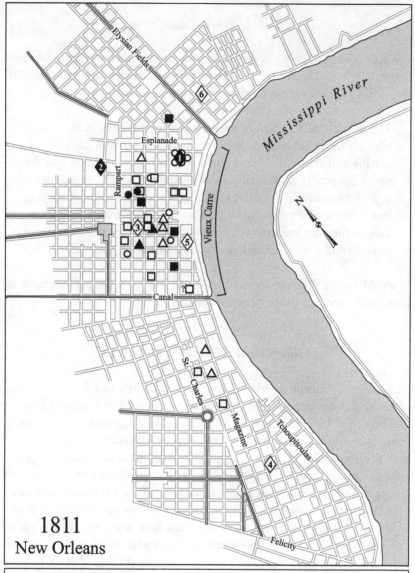

1811
New Orleans

State Funded Schools
❶ Ursuline Academy
❷ College D'Orleans

Non-State Funded Schools
③ Bazanac FPC School
④ Ladies Boarding School
⑤ Ladies Academy
⑥ Dorefeuille School

Teachers
○ Women
● Women/St. Domingue
△ White Male/ St. Domingue
▲ Free Male of Color/St. Domingue
■ Free Male of Color
□ Male Teacher (presumed white)

Figure 10. Map of New Orleans Schools, 1811. Drawn by Mary Lee Eggart based on *Whitney's New Orleans Directory and Louisiana and Mississippi Almanac, 1811* (New Orleans, 1811), microform. Main Branch New Orleans Public Library.

men were not recent immigrants but came from a mixed lineage of French, Spanish, and African families whose ancestry in Louisiana could be traced back several generations. Charles Vivant was not only a teacher but was well-connected within the social network of free people of color who had been engaged in building community institutions, including social, religious, economic, and political entities, since the period of Spanish colonization. Shortly before Charles began his teaching career, on October 4, 1810, he married Iris Lugar, a free woman of color, at St. Louis Cathedral with a host of guests that included militia officers Charles Brulé and Joseph Cabaret, who stood as sentinels.[69] The bride was the daughter of Juan Lugar, a well-to-do free man of color of Spanish descent who lived next door to Joseph Cabaret in the newly developed Tremé neighborhood. When the time came for Iris's wedding, it was only natural that Joseph and his friend Charles Brulé, who was known as the "Captain of the Granadies" for his leadership role in the free Black Spanish militia, would participate in this significant public event.

The presence of these two militia men not only signaled the close personal friendship between neighbors but highlighted the tight webs of kinship that spun powerful networks of free people of color. These threads were woven through personal relationships—godparenting, marriages, economic partnerships, Catholic lay societies—and community institutions that were built from the ground up through schools, Freemasonic lodges, and the militia. Participation in the free Black militia, begun under Governor Galvez in 1779 to aid Spain in the fight against England in the American Revolution, was tantamount to being "awarded virtual equality with white men."[70] In 1804, the free Black militia, numbering three hundred men, addressed Governor Claiborne as "free citizens of Louisiana" in their request to be made full citizens of the United States. While this did not happen, the public presence of the free Black militia symbolized to others the Afro-Creole communities' belief that they were entitled to full citizenship rights. So when Charles and Iris married in the Catholic church, they not only acknowledged their spiritual equality in the public sphere of the Catholic church, but the presence of the free Black militia was a bold statement of their understandings of themselves as full citizens. As Charles entered his one-room classroom in the creole Cottage on Toulouse, these powerful networks bolstered his conviction that he was entitled to full equal rights. This was the lesson he passed on to his students, a powerful curriculum indeed.

Of the six white male teachers from Haiti, two have been identified as having free women of color as wives or lifelong partners, whose mixed-race children we can assume attended the schools in which they taught.[71] We can speculate then that some of these schools were interracial and that some might also have educated both sexes. This rich diversity goes against common perceptions that education was not only almost nonexistent at this time, but that all teachers were white. The fact that Afro-Creole and Haitian-Afro-Creole teachers made up a significant number of educators in 1811 New Orleans not only demands a reconsideration of dominant narratives of educational history, but it suggests that education was clearly important in developing the identity of the community as fully equal and entitled to citizenship. This degree of diversity marked the ongoing fluidity and integration of the races, and this rich mosaic of educators was critical to shaping the educational culture of New Orleans.

Jean Baptiste Bazanac and Réné Pre Gaignard established their schools in the French Quarter, in the "back of town," within blocks of each other. In addition to both being teachers, they were also friends who had social networks not only as educators but also through the Catholic Church. Gaignard, who had originally been a merchant in Port-au-Prince, emigrated as a young man with his wife, Maire Louise Laurent, a free woman of color, also from Port-au-Prince. Shortly after he began teaching in New Orleans, his wife gave birth to a son, Jean Baptiste August Gaignard, in late August 1813. It was Jean Baptiste Bazanac who stood at the baptismal font as godfather, along with Marie Rose Mathieu as godmother, when the young boy was baptized. These networks developed through the Catholic Church, provided spaces in which refugees could not only rebuild their lives, but also take part in and shape the public sphere of their new home.

Pierre Lambert, a white refugee, took out a notice in the September 15, 1809, *Courrier* advertising that he would be offering arithmetic, algebra, geometry, infinitesimal calculus, and navigation every day of the week except Thursday and Sunday, for only sixteen dollars a month.[72] He would go on to teach at the College d'Orléans when it finally opened in 1811. Francois Bocquet, a refugee from Havana, opened a school in the summer of 1809 where he taught children reading, writing, French, Spanish, English, history, arithmetic, and geography.[73] Of particular note in the 1811 *City Directory* is a record of Louis Duhart, whose transatlantic story of education as central to the quest for human dignity extended across three generations and has been exquisitely told by Rebecca Scott and Jean Hébrard in *Freedom Papers*.[74]

Louis Duhart, a Saint-Domingue refugee originally from France, was, like many of his fellow refugees, listed as a teacher. His school at 50 Dauphine Street was only three blocks south of the College d'Orléans, where several fellow refugees taught, and six blocks east of Jean Baptiste Bazanac's school for free children of color. A Freemason from near Fort-Dauphin in Saint-Domingue, Louis had come from southwest France, where his paternal ancestors were part of a lineage of sailors and sea captains who shipped out of Nantes. After his arrival in New Orleans (most likely somewhere between 1805 and 1810), Louis created a household with Marie Francoise Bayot, a Saint–Domingue refugee, and her son, Jacques Tinchant, both free persons of color who had made their way from either Baltimore, Maryland, or Nova Scotia to New Orleans.[75] Jacques's father, Joseph Tinchant, a French colonist from Saint-Domingue who had arrived in Baltimore by 1793 as part of the first wave of refugees to the United States, had brought Marie along with perhaps a sister and one male slave. Exactly when and why Marie and her young son traveled to New Orleans is not clear. Sometime after they arrived, however, Marie and Louis created a lifelong partnership and family that included Jacques and later two more sons: Pierre and Louis Alfred Duhart.

Although a schoolteacher and a Mason with considerable standing, Louis struggled to make a living since New Orleans was full of refugees who were trying to support themselves through teaching. To supplement their income, the couple engaged in the buying and selling of slaves, and eventually Louis unsuccessfully tried to establish himself as a cotton planter. As a cross-racial couple, by the 1820s it was becoming increasingly difficult to conduct business transactions that would protect Marie and the boys' futures, as the 1825 Civil Code forbade those who lived in "open concubinage" from receiving substantial real property from their partners.[76] This code sought to establish a firm color line by deterring unions between white men and free women of color. The increasing legal and social restrictions on free people of color and the rigid racial categories they imposed eventually became intolerable to Louis and Marie, who in the early 1830s decided to emigrate to France, near the Spanish border. Settled in the town of Pau, Louis and Marie were finally able to marry, designate their children as "legitimate," and, most importantly, send their two sons to the local schools that were open to all. In 1840, Jacques Tinchant, Marie's first son, and his wife also arrived in France, having learned from his parents about the prospect of education for their sons. Ultimately, their last son, Édouard Tinchant, returned to Louisiana in 1861 and joined the Union army, which he believed was part of the revolutionary fight for emancipation and equal rights. After the war, like his step-grandfather, Louis Duhart, Édouard took up teaching and became principal of a mixed-race school in the Faubourg

Tremé in New Orleans during that brief interlude when public, integrated schools had been made law in the 1868 constitution.

This transatlantic family story is just one of many that reflect what I call a creole pedagogical circuit that shaped New Orleans educational history. While not necessarily always bound by brick-and-mortar schools, it conveys the restless pursuit to obtain an education as central to acknowledging human equality. Teachers like Louis Duhart, Jean Baptiste Bazanac, and Charles Vivant played a significant role in establishing a culture of universal education that sought to educate all persons regardless of race. It is of course difficult to speculate to what degree other schools were interracial, but given the racial fluidity of this period, it is conceivable that these private schools did have a diversity of students. What stands out as well in this period is the high percentage of women teachers noted in the 1811 *City Directory*. Thirty-one percent of the teachers listed were women. Of a total of twelve women teachers, one was from Saint-Domingue. A Mrs. Martin, a native of London, advertised her school, at 32 Toulouse Street, to open on November 1, 1810, for either boarders or day pupils. Offering Italian and mythology in addition to the subjects usually offered for girls, she clearly sought to attract students from the surrounding areas, as well as young girls seeking a rigorous academic curriculum.[77]

Also of note was the school to be opened by Mr. Visinier, who advertised that he wished to make known to "those young people wishing to learn the English language and to perfect their French and Arithmetic, he will have classes from the hours of 6 to 9" in the evening.[78] A night school was certainly intended for young boys who were engaged in some daytime occupation, perhaps an apprenticeship or family business. What it suggests was the educational opportunities being afforded were not restricted to the well-to-do but cut across class lines. This is particularly evident in the apprenticeship system, which grew dramatically during this early territorial period. Apprenticeship had long offered formally established avenues for education in Louisiana, as attested to by the story of Doucet in the opening of this book. The rapid growth of the New Orleans economy after the Louisiana Purchase necessitated skilled labor, increasing the need for apprenticeships, especially in carpentry, bricklaying, and shoemaking and for tailors, coopers, and blacksmiths. As noted with the case of Doucet, the enslaved boy, instruction in reading and writing was often part of the apprenticeship. Apprenticeships were available for the enslaved, free people of color, and white boys who sought a trade. Those who trained apprentices were also not only white, but also free men of color. Cross-racial interactions such as these created networks that would often extend beyond the time of the apprenticeship. Thus, apprenticeships functioned not only to train one in a skill, but they also facilitated literacy, community networks across the color line, and economic autonomy.[79]

What is recognizable in this early American period is that despite characterizations of New Orleans as backward, educational opportunities across class, gender, and race were prolific. What is remarkable is the degree to which institutions were also interracial. Looking at the spatial layout of these institutions, it is also evident that there was little segregation at this time. Those walking to schools as students or teachers would have passed by a variety of students, teachers, and schools. While there was still no central organizing body for education, what emerged at the street level was a diverse, complex system that was self-organizing. And while these individual efforts were critical, attempts were still being made to create a system of public education through the funding of the College d'Orléans. In no small part, this vision of a more cohesive system of education was supported and finally financed by the support of the last wave of Haitian refugees. Their support, on the heels of the 1811 slave revolt in New Orleans, the largest in U.S. history, cannot be understood without recognizing that many of these refugees understood the temporal nature of the institution of slavery and that the abolishment of slavery would require a program of state education.

The College d'Orléans: A Rogue Curriculum

In the summer of 1812, now Governor Claiborne of the new state of Louisiana appeared before the opening session of the state legislature:

> The regents of the University of Orleans will lay before you, Gentlemen, an interesting view of the College of New Orleans, and of the several county schools under their superintendence. You will notice with great satisfaction the progress of science, nor do I doubt your readiness to contribute by such means as may be in your power, to its further advancement.[80]

After languishing for five years, financial support for the College d'Orléans was finally achieved in the spring of 1811. The third Legislative Council, which met from January to April 1811, unlike the previous two councils, was dominated not by Americans, but by a majority of French Creoles and Frenchmen.[81] On April 9, 1811, the Legislative Council and House of Representatives of the Territory of Orleans convened and passed a supplementary act (titled "An Act to Institute a University in the Territory of Orleans") that provided a total of $39,000, $15,000 of which was to be dedicated to instituting the Collège d'Orléans and $2,000 for an academy in each of the twelve parishes of the territory.[82] The city council, many of whom had supported relief services for the ongoing influx of destitute refugees from Saint-Domingue, also asked the legislature to approve $5,000 per year for free instruction for fifty students from the poorest class, who were to be chosen by the regents of the University.[83] They also stipulated that the College d'Orléans be situated near enough to New Orleans to enable these children of said city and of its suburbs (meaning Tremé and Marigny, where most of the refugees lived), to go there as day scholars. By allocating state money for schools, and specifically for children of lesser economic means (many of whom were probably refugees), the state extended education to the poor, expanding the public sphere. After five years and with a great deal of support from the refugees from Saint-Domingue, The Act for Public Education was finally executed by the Legislative Council.[84] Likewise, when the first Board of Regents was selected by Governor Claiborne, while the majority were French Creoles and Frenchmen, at least one Saint-Domingue exile was appointed.[85] At least initially, the Board of Regents gave preference in admission to the children of Saint-Dominique refugees.[86]

With funding secured, the Collège d'Orléans lacked only a site. The college was to be situated near enough to New Orleans to enable the students from the city and its suburbs to go there as day scholars. In 1810, the city had purchased the Tremé plantation, between St. Claude and Hospital Streets, just adjacent to Congo Square, from Claude Tremé (1759–1829), a French hatmaker who came to New Orleans in 1783, and his wife Julie Moreau (1758–1818), a free woman of color who had originally inherited the land in 1794 from her father.[87] This marked the development of New Orleans's first suburb, the Faubourg Tremé, extending the city along both Esplanade and Bayou Road upland toward the backswamp. Known for its French Afro-Creole and immigrant population, Tremé is described today as America's oldest Black neighborhood, but it was quite racially diverse.[88] In May of 1812, the home and grounds of Claude Tremé were transferred from the Board of Regents to the Collège d'Orléans.[89] The stipulation for the transfer of the property from the city to the regents was that the city would be allowed to send four boarders and ten day students, tuition-free.[90] This, in addition to the previous fifty students who were to be admitted gratis, not only expanded access to the poor, but it unsettled strict class boundaries by allowing boarders from the poorest classes. The school opened in late 1811 with approximately one hundred students, half of them supported by public funds.[91] The college consisted primarily of boarding students, who paid $450 a year, and day students from the city, who paid $8 a month tuition. In addition, all students paid $50 a year for books, paper, pens, and ink. According to the *Organic Regulations of the College of Orleans*, the day students were "required to attend school in becoming dress, but they shall not wear the uniform of boarders" (Figure 11).[92] Nor were they allowed to present at the recreations of the college, or "have any communication with the boarders, except in school, and in the presence of professors."[93] While students of lesser means were admitted to the college, it clearly appears that rigid class distinctions were still enforced. It is unclear, however, whether this also applied to race and ethnicity. Despite class distinctions enforced between the boarding and day students, both received the same curriculum, which consisted of religion, French, English, Spanish, and Latin languages, philology, and philosophy, as well as useful and ornamental arts. One full year was dedicated to each subject, with the exception of philosophy, which was taught for the term of two years.[94]

The college, located in the renovated Moreau plantation family home in order to accommodate boarders, finally opened its doors on Bon Enfants, between St. Claude and Hospitilier, at the end of 1811 (Figure 12). Students were warmly welcomed by the newly appointed president, Jules D'Avezac (1768–1831), a refugee from Aux Cayes, in the southern part of Saint-Domingue. He had fled with his life—several of his brothers were not as fortunate—in 1803, along with his sister-in-law, Marie Rose Geneviève, now a widow, and four of her children, resettling in New Orleans.[95] A practicing lawyer in Saint-Domingue, he may have been recommended for the position of president by fellow refugees who sat on the Board of Regents, including Louis Moreau-Lislet. He had a passion for the humanities, and also taught Latin and French. In addition to D'Avezac, fellow refugees made up three-fifths of the original faculty of the College d'Orléans.[96] This included Pierre Lambert (?–1827), a native of Saint-Domingue, who later moved to Cuba, where he established a coffee plantation and then fled to New Orleans in 1809. He would teach math at the college, own a pharmacy, and practice medicine. Jean Baptiste Augustin (1764–1832), a native of France, fled France during the Reign of Terror, relocating in Saint-Domingue, where he established himself as a coffee planter. In 1803 he fled to Cuba and in 1809 to New Orleans, where he took a position as teacher of Latin at the Collège d'Orléans. In addition to the three teachers from Saint-Domingue, Professor Carr taught English

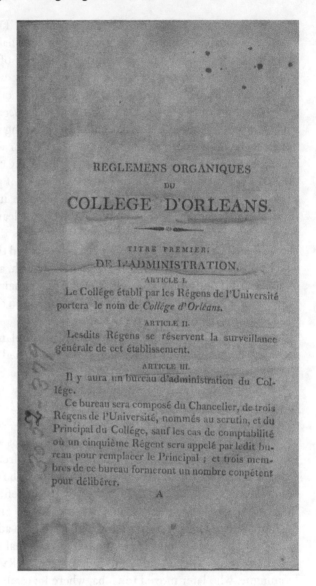

REGLEMENS ORGANIQUES
DU
COLLEGE D'ORLEANS.

TITRE PREMIER.
DE L'ADMINISTRATION.

ARTICLE I.
Le Collége établi par les Régens de l'Université portera le nom de *Collége d'Orléans*.

ARTICLE II.
Lesdits Régens se réservent la surveillance générale de cet établissement.

ARTICLE III.
Il y aura un bureau d'administration du Collége.

Ce bureau sera composé du Chancelier, de trois Régens de l'Université, nommés au scrutin, et du Principal du Collége, sauf les cas de comptabilité où un cinquième Régent sera appelé par ledit bureau pour remplacer le Principal ; et trois membres de ce bureau formeront un nombre conpétent pour délibérer.

A

Figure 11. Organic Regulations of the College of Orleans. The Historic New Orleans Collection, Acc. No. 76–1414-RL.

during a brief absence from the college taken by D'Avezac, and Monsieur Pierre Rochefort, a native of Saint-Domingue and bachelor, took over as principal and taught Latin and literature and gave music lessons.[97] He was also a poet and known for his passion for the histories of Rome, Greece, and France.[98] Within the next few years, several other teachers were hired to complete the prescribed curriculum, including the bachelor Teinturier,

Figure 12. College d'Orléans, 1812. Image from Plan of the City and Suburbs of New Orleans from an actual survey made in 1815 by Jacques Tanesse. New Orleans, 1817.

a professor of mathematics who also provided knowledge of natural history and horticulture and who developed a garden on the grounds, and Mr. B. Selles, also a refugee from Saint-Domingue, who was professor of drawing. By 1814, a second English teacher was hired, a Mr. Beunos, and a Spanish teacher, Don Santyago Acella.[99] In addition to the faculty, a proctor, a cousin of Teinturier, was hired to be in charge of policing, given that the boys were not allowed to leave the college without permission, nor were they to have correspondence with any persons other than their parents.[100] Two house mothers, Mrs. Crestin and Mrs. Lambert, were also engaged to provide the maternal affection young boys would need.

Enthusiasm for the college was immediate, with many of the small private school teachers complaining that they had lost their students to the college.[101] By late October 1811, shortly after the school opened, the college had enrolled approximately one hundred students, of whom twenty-five were admitted tuition free.[102] It is difficult to determine how many of these were boarding students versus day students. What we do know is that boarding students' costs were extremely high. In addition to the $450 a year tuition, boarding students were required to bring a complete wardrobe of clothes with their school uniform, as well as a silver spoon, fork, and goblet, six napkins, and two pair of sheets, all new. This was in addition to their own bed, mattress, bolster, blankets, mosquito netting, and $50 for books, paper, ink, and pens.[103] The total cost clearly limited enrollment of boarding students to the wealthiest of families from New Orleans and the surrounding plantations, who previously had sent their sons abroad or had hired private tutors. Whether any free boys of color attended as boarding students can only be speculation at this point, given that most student records have been lost. What we do know is that within the confines of the school, there were clear transgressions of rigid class norms and, perhaps to a lesser extent, racial boundaries among the day students and those admitted gratis.[104]

We are fortunate to have some accounts and reminiscences of the school by several renowned graduates who attended as boarding students: Charles Gayarré (1805–1895), Adrien Rouquette (1813–1887), and Tullius Saint-Ceran (1800–1855). Saint-Ceran was born to French parents in Jamaica, but due to unrest on the island, they fled for New Orleans in 1805. When the college opened in 1811, Saint-Ceran was most surely one of the first to be enrolled and would have been a classmate of Charles Gayarré. A bright young man gifted in several languages as well as a romantic poet, he went on to become the editor of the French section of the *Gazette de la Louisiane*, a newspaper in which he aired his republican sentiments. His first book of poetry was published in 1836. He continued to publish poetry throughout his life as well as work as a teacher of modern languages in New Orleans.[105]

One of the most well-known graduates of the college was the writer, historian, and slave owner Charles Gayarré (1805–1895), who began attending the school in 1812 and described the college in his memoir and fictional book, *Fernando de Lemos, Truth and Fiction* (1872).[106] Charles Gayarré, a descendant of both Spanish (his great-great-grandfather, Éstevan de Gayarré, was a royal accountant under the first Spanish governor) and French (his grandmother Constance de Grand-Pré, whose father was a Bienville-era pioneer) families, came from one of the most prominent French Creole elite families in New Orleans. His mother, Marie Elizabeth de Boré, was the daughter of Marie d'Estréhan and Jean Étienne de Boré (born in Kaskasia in 1741), known for revolutionizing the sugar cane plantation industry and being the first mayor of New Orleans.

In many respects, the college had been designed to attract Franco-Creole families of privilege like the Gayarrés. Most likely they were not expecting the exposure to a cross-section of society, especially class differences. He wrote,

> There were in the college of Orleans only a few day scholars. They were youths, who generally on account of the poverty of their parents, could not afford to be full boarders. Most were admitted on half pay; others did not pay at all, being sent by the Board of Regents, every member of which had the privilege to select a poor boy, who, on the recommendation of his patron, and on the assurance of his family being in destitute circumstances, was entitled to be educated gratis. Those who were thus selected by the regents, were designated as "charity students" by those who had been more favored by fortune. . . . Among those "charity boys" who composed the *plebs*, and who were treated with lofty disdain by some of the

sons of wealth, was a lad called Treviño. We had frenchified his name, and we pronounced it Trévigne (Roderic, first name). His father was a Spaniard, who lived in a hut on Bayou Road, midway between Bayou St. John and the city."[107]

The presence of students from lesser economic means clearly made an impression on Gayarré, although it might have only reinforced rigid class boundaries. Nonetheless, the college throughout its existence until 1826 continued to sponsor boys of lesser means, making it one of the few public spaces in which young men of quite different social and economic backgrounds would interact. That some of the boys who were state-sponsored might have been the children of Haitian refugees who were free people of color is distinctly possible given not only the location of the college but also the transatlantic, familial ties across the color line that permeated the influx of Haitian refugees (Figure 13). This might also have been the case with Afro-Franco or Afro-Spanish Creole boys like Roderic. It is possible that Roderic Trévigne was the uncle of Paul Trévigne (1825–1908), free man of color and staunch advocate for civil rights who went on to teach at the Catholic Institute for Colored Orphans. Also, the location of the college in Tremé, in close proximity to the Marigny—both interracial neighborhoods with large numbers of Saint-Domingue refugees—indicates the possibility that students of color, especially those of few means who might have been admitted gratis, were attending the college.

Gayarré was deeply impacted by his time at the college, especially through the relationship he built with Monsieur Rochefort, the second president of the school and a lover of Greek and Roman antiquity. They had a lifelong relationship that impressed upon him "the conception of white Francophone exceptionality across the Atlantic world."[108] This exceptionality was deeply embedded in a hierarchical ideology that reinforced Gayarré's belief in white supremacy and led him to idealize French Creole southern antebellum society. His belief that Louisiana should maintain its French cultural roots catapulted him into educational politics in the 1840s, when he became a school board member in the First Municipality (French Quarter) to ensure that French remained the primary language of instruction in the newly formed "public" schools.

The French, transatlantic nature of education, both at the college and at other French educational institutions in the rest of the country, is exemplified by another of the more well-known graduates of the college, Adrien Rouquette (1813–1887), a priest, writer, and missionary among

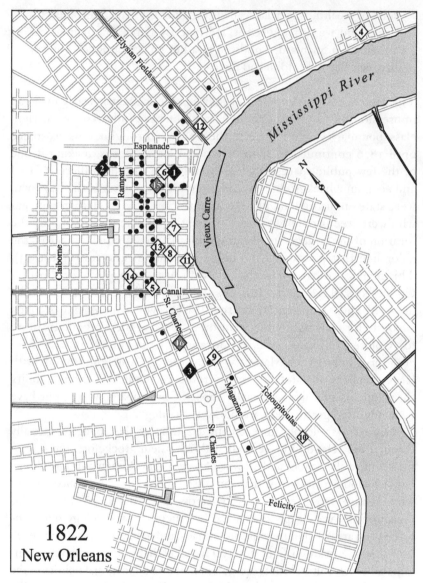

Figure 13. Map of New Orleans Schools, 1822. Drawn by Mary Lee Eggart based on John Adams Paxton, comp., *The New Orleans Directory and Register* (New Orleans, 1822), microform. Main Branch New Orleans Public Library.

- <u>Teachers</u> (93 total)

  <u>State-Funded Schools</u>:

❶ Ursulines (funded until 1824, 5 teachers)

❷ College d'Orléans (6 total teachers)

❸ Poydras Female Orphan Asylum (white only)

<u>Non State-Funded Schools:</u>

④ Academy (Rev. Bertrand Martial, Catholic, 4 teachers)

⑤ Academy (Rev. James F. Hull, Episcopal, 3 teachers)

⑥ Young Ladies' Academy

⑦ Lancaster Academy (Rev. Michel Poitier, Catholic, for boys, 6 teachers)

⑧ Lancaster Academy for Young Ladies

⑨ Lancaster Academy (Francois F. Lafon/ Lafontaine, for boys, 3 teachers)

⑩ Academy (Lefort)

⑪ Academy (Newton)

⑫ Female Academy (Clothilde Bornet, 2 teachers)

⑬ School of Constant Lepouze and John B. George
(free children of color taught there)

⑭ Brainard's School

<u>Non-State-Funded School Specifically Labeled for</u>
<u>Children of Color</u>:

⑮ Lancaster School for Colored Children (Louis Bernard)

⑯ School for Persons of Color (John Marsenat)

the Choctaw. Living on the Bayou St. John and the north shore of Lake Pontchartrain as a child, he began attending the college as a boarding student. While the college had languished, he was fortunate that shortly after he arrived the school would be revitalized by a dynamic new president, Joseph Lakanal, a French exile. Adrien went on to briefly attend Transylvania University in Lexington, Kentucky, founded in 1780, which was a popular school attended by the sons of New Orleans French Creoles. Upon the death of his mother, he joined his brother Dominique, who was studying law in Philadelphia, and attended the Mantua Academy, mentioned at the beginning of the chapter, where Victor Value, a refugee from Haiti, taught. He then traveled often to France, where he studied in Brittney and began his writing career in Paris. Coming of age in the late 1820s, his education reinforced his French Catholic heritage, which ultimately resulted in his having to "wrestle with his multiple identities."[109] Among these identities was his role as a Catholic priest among the Choctaw, with whom he lived as a missionary from 1846 until his death, dedicating his life like his earlier Jesuit brothers to the conversion and education of the Indigenous peoples of Louisiana.[110] This was a pedagogical educational circuit that was in continuous motion in Louisiana since Father Du Ru in 1702. What role the college played in his development can only be speculation, but his French identity was certainly solidified and his penchant for poetry and romanticism (like those of his contemporary Afro-Creole poets, to be introduced in the next chapter) was nurtured in an environment that prided itself in challenging students to achieve the highest intellectual traditions of the humanities.

By 1821, however, there were only twelve students, and the school was in debt. Given the state of decline and threats to close the college, in the spring of 1821 (February 16) the state legislature effected a new administrative plan abolishing the Board of Regents and placing the college under a Board of Administrators consisting of nine persons to be appointed annually by the governor (Thomas B. Robertson, an American) and the Senate.[111] James Workman, back in New Orleans after his own exile due to his supposed involvement in the Burr Conspiracy, was appointed as the first president of the Board of Administrators of the college.[112] It was Edward Livingston who most likely recommended to Workman that he contact Joseph Lakanal (1762–1844), a French exile from the Bourbon restoration living in Kentucky, to fill the position of president of the college.[113] Upon his acceptance of the job he was unanimously elected by the board.

College d'Orléans—1822: The Progress of Science

[N]o talent is too great for the College of Orleans. . . . After having
finished their studies in the College, these students will not retreat
to the cities to idle away their time, . . . : No, they will dispose of
themselves amongst our warehouses, in the country, on the sea,
and the state will have ingenious artists, scientific agriculturalists,
seaman active as intrepid, and worthy of treading in the footsteps
of their fathers.

—Joseph Lakanal, May 30, 1822[114]

On Thursday, May 30, 1822, shortly after six o'clock in the evening, Joseph
Lakanal, the newly appointed president of the College d'Orléans, was presented by James Workman to a distinguished New Orleans audience that
included the Louisiana secretary of state (Pierre Derbingy), the attorney
general (Etienne Mazureau), the mayor (Louis Philippe de Roffignac),
the city council, the judges of the courts, and other prominent citizens.[115]
Workman, the newly appointed president of the Board of Administrators
of the College d'Orléans, an Irish immigrant, lawyer, ardent champion
of republican ideals, and proponent of abolition, had recruited Lakanal,
a French émigré, staunch supporter of the French Revolution, and architect of France's national system of public education.[116] After being introduced, Lakanal addressed the audience in French, promising "that the
College d'Orléans shall resume that rank, which it formerly held."[117] Not
only would he restore the college, but he would prepare a new generation
of young men shaped by Enlightenment notions of science, reason, and
human equality that would set them apart from the idle aristocrats of the
old regime. A staunch supporter of the French Revolution who had served
on the Committee of Public Instruction, Lakanal maintained that public
education was "an indispensable instrument in a great democracy."[118] His
full speech from that evening was printed in both French and English the
next morning in the *Courrier de la Louisiane*, which also devoted several col-
umns of its editorial page to the installation of Lakanal as president.[119] Few
could have foreseen the short-lived tenure, not only of Joseph Lakanal, but
also of the revived college.

Joseph Lakanal was born on July 14, 1762, to a middle-class family in
the small city of Foix in southern France. One of five children, his early
education, after the death of his mother when Lakanal was four years old,
was directed by the local priest. At age eleven he entered the College de

l'Esquile, a collegiate institution attached to the University of Toulouse, after which he began teaching grammar and rhetoric throughout southern France. He pursued theological studies at the Seminary of Saint-Magloire of the Doctrinaires and was ordained a priest, although he later refused to perform the functions of the priesthood. In fact, during the Reign of Terror, he saved his own life by arguing that he had been coerced into becoming a priest while he was suffering under severe illness. In 1782, he was granted the degree of *docteur-ès-arts* at the University of Anger, after which he took a position as professor of rhetoric at Bourges, and in 1785 was appointed professor of philosophy at Moulins.

A strong proponent of revolutionary ideals, he was elected as deputy to the French National Convention in 1792. In his autobiography, *Exposé sommaire es Travaux de Joseph Lakanal*, written in 1838, he describes his work at the convention as a "very special mission that I had assigned myself" based on the conviction that a system of public education was pivotal to upholding the ideals of the Revolution.[120] As part of the legislative assembly tasked with applying the constitution, Lakanal was appointed to the Committee of Public Instruction in the fall of 1793. Committed to establishing a system of education based on the ideals of the new republic, he urged on the floor of the convention that a "national education suitable to the shaping of free men, in place of the present education which is fit only for Capuchin monks" must be implemented.[121] His commitment was shared by others in the legislative assembly, including Nicolas de Condorcet (1743–1794), whose plan for reforming the education system was based on a free and equal public education for all, including women and people of all races. Condorcet was a proponent of women's suffrage, a staunch abolitionist who denounced slavery, and an active member of the Society of the Friends of Blacks. Like other Enlightenment thinkers, including Lakanal, both of them believed that the nation needed enlightened citizens and education needed democracy to become truly public. In other words, unlike Horace Mann's educational philosophy in which public schools were central to producing democracy, for Lakanal, democracy was what enabled public schools. Democracy implied free citizens, and ignorance was the source of servitude. Citizens had to be provided with the necessary knowledge to exercise their freedom and understand the rights and laws that guaranteed their enjoyment. Although education could not eliminate disparities in talent, all citizens, including women, had the right to free education. And while Lakanal and Condorcet shared many radical democratic ideals, they differed significantly in their vision of education. When Condorcet died after being jailed during the Reign of Terror, Lakanal returned to the convention and replaced Condorcet as the president of public instruction. It was at this point that Lakanal would make his most significant contribution in the development of the system of public education in France including the establishment of the École Normale (teacher training), the École polytechnique, the Conservatoire des art et métiers, the Institute of France, and the national library.

Following the Reign of Terror, the Committee of Public Instruction was reorganized with Lakanal once again being chosen as the president. In June of 1793, he presented his report on primary education, in which he advocated for equal education of women with men, insistence on physical education, service-learning projects, and vocational training in manual labors. The following year his report on the Écoles Centrales (secondary schools) advocated that they replace the ancient *collèges*, most of which had been under the management of various teaching orders of the church.[122] These schools, nineteen of which Lakanal established, were institutions of higher training for the teaching of the sciences, letters, and arts. Each school included a public library, a garden and cabinet of natural history, a cabinet of experimental physics, and a collection of machines and models for the arts and trades. He would certainly have been happy to continue administrating the development of his plan for public education were it not for the rise of Napoleon, whose coup d'état, he did not support. With no national position, Lakanal went back to teaching as a professor of ancient languages in the Central Schools. But with the abdication of Napoleon in 1814 and impending restoration of the monarchy under Louis XVIII, Lakanal faced the fear of reprisal for his part in regicide. He quickly made plans to go into exile, setting sail for America with his wife and daughter, Alexandrine, in January 1816. Armed with letters of introduction to Thomas Jefferson, including one from the Marquis de Lafayette and one from the United States consul general in Paris, Lakanal arrived in New York, where he joined many other French exiles.

Ideally, he saw himself as becoming a gentlemen farmer and engaging in writing projects, including a history of the United States. Within the year, Lakanal and his family had settled on the Ohio River in Kentucky, across from the French settlement of Vevay in Indiana. Being a farmer on the American frontier was not quite what he had envisioned, and he turned his energy to making political contacts, wasting no time in writing to Thomas Jefferson and Henry Clay to see what opportunities might arise. He also became embroiled in a conspiracy to help free Napoleon from Saint Helena and make him emperor of South America and to establish Joseph Bonaparte on the throne of Mexico and the Indies.[123] The failure of this plot, as well as Lakanal's desire to once again take up a scholarly position, contributed to his immediate acceptance as president of the College d'Orléans when James Workman, under the advice of Edward Livingston, reached out to him in the March of 1822.[124]

After his arrival in New Orleans and warm reception, Lakanal quickly went to work to reinvigorate the college. On September 16, 1822, the *Gazette de la Louisiane* featured a one-page special publication that announced the opening of the new term for October 1 and listed the courses of studies to be offered (Figure 14). Unlike the previous curriculums that had focused primarily on the classics, Lakanal broadened the curriculum so that it would contribute as well to the practical development of young men as farmers, merchants, and navigators/engineers. Based on his reform work in France, he implemented a curriculum that focused on secular and nationalistic tenets, rather than religion; this was a curriculum that was less classical and religious and more practical and scientific in content.[125] His pedagogy was innovative as well: he discouraged rote learning by not giving students textbooks, he advocated tuition-free instruction, and he was an advocate for women's education.[126] For many of the citizens of New Orleans accustomed to a classical education, this was indeed a "rogue" curriculum.

Above all he emphasized science. He equipped the college with a laboratory for experimental physics, an herbarium of eight thousand plants, a collection of objects of natural history, and two hundred geographical maps. His curriculum would be similar to that of the Écoles Centrales that he had implemented in France, in which he combined the liberal arts, the sciences, and technical studies. While he would take the responsibility for the teaching of scientific and philosophical studies, his faculty was representative of a network of transatlantic educators. Fellow exile Pierre Guillot, a graduate of Grenaoble and former artillery officer in France, was versed in mathematics and ancient literature as well as English and Italian; Chapelin, an Irish lawyer, taught English literature, Greek, and Latin and spoke both French and English; Sullivan, also an Irishman, taught Latin, English, and French; James M'Karaher, an American, the former proprietor and editor of the New Orleans Journal *L'Amis des Lois*, also taught French and English; and lastly there has been mention made of Mr. Gaudin, from Cuba, who also taught French and most likely the classics.[127] In addition, John P. Louis was hired as a professor of painting.[128]

Influenced by Rousseau, Lakanal discouraged rote learning by not giving students textbooks and encouraged a less authoritarian approach with students.[129] This progressive pedagogy anticipated a more "child"

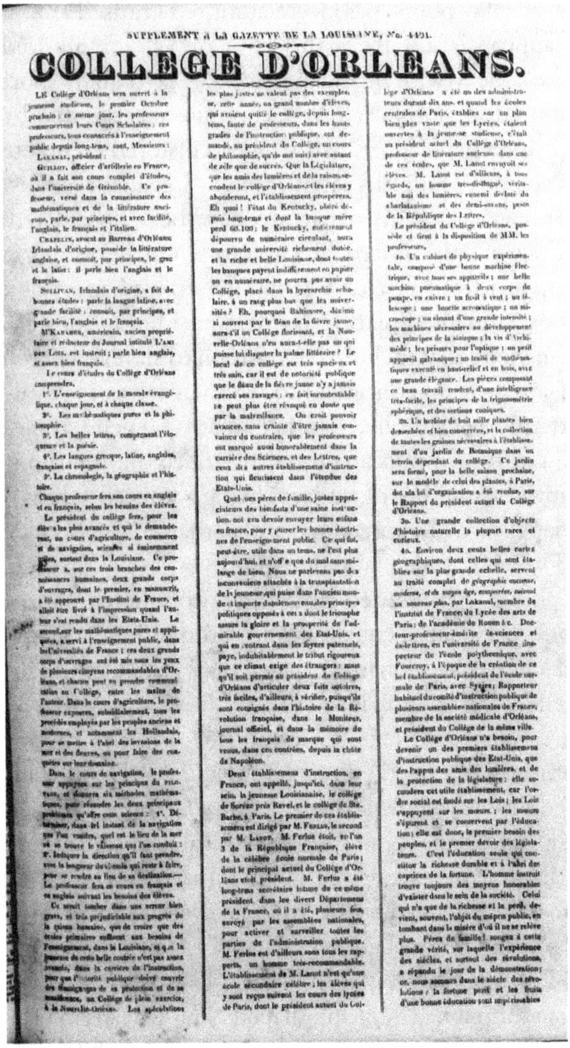
SUPPLEMENT A LA GAZETTE DE LA LOUISIANE, No. 4491.

COLLEGE D'ORLEANS.

Figure 14. Gazette de la Louisiane, Sept. 16, 1822, Courtesy of Louisiana State University Libraries, Special Collections.

centered approach. Lakanal advocated that "A public teacher ought to be a father over his children, possessing all that dignity of character which presents paternal authority, and that gentleness, that patience so necessary with scholars which is calculated to represent maternal tenderness."[130] This modernist vision of education also assumed the capacity of *all* human beings for unlimited intellectual advancement.

By the end of 1822, eighty students were attending the College: forty-four boarding students and thirty-six day pupils; in addition there were two boarders and thirty-five day pupils who were admitted gratis. Tuition, along with an annual appropriation from the state of $5,000, allowed Lakanal to administer the college with financial success. A favorable report of the college was submitted in April 1823 by a committee appointed by the legislature, in which the chairman, Elijah Clark, registered complete support of Lakanal.[131] Not three months later, though, Lakanal resigned his position. Numerous reasons for his departure have been speculated: not relying heavily enough on the Board of Directors, not becoming a U.S. citizen, a lack of support from French Creoles due to his history as a regicide, being an ex-priest, and his affiliation as a Mason. This, in addition to his staunch Republican views that included opposition to slavery, incited many French New Orleanians who continued to see themselves as royalists, proslavery, and certainly as Catholic.[132] In fact, many French Creoles continued to envision a return of Louisiana to France once the Bourbons were on the throne again. The number of students being admitted "gratis," including boarding students, also disrupted class and perhaps racial boundaries in the eyes of the French Creole plantation elite.

Lakanal and his supporters represented all that was considered part of Enlightenment thought: rationality, equality, and brotherhood. While defenders of Lakanal, like James Workman, challenged his critics and advocated for this man of intellect and science, it was to no avail. Knowing that he had lost public support, Lakanal left New Orleans in late 1823 and continued his transatlantic journey by joining the French settlement at Demopolis, Alabama, where he joined the well-known Vine and Olive Colony.[133] Settled by numerous French exiles who had set out from Philadelphia to settle there in 1817, the colony was already in disarray when Lakanal arrived. He settled in Mobile, Alabama, and after the death of his wife, he eventually returned to France in September of 1837, where he was reinstated as a member of the Academy of Moral and Political Sciences. While his role as a transatlantic pedagogue whose activism for public education shaped New Orleans in profound ways, he barely receives a mention in Louisiana's history, while he is revered in France. He died in 1844 in Paris, where a monument was erected to him in the Cemetery Pere-Lachaise (Figure 15).

Lakanal's son-in-law Lucien Chevart was elected to succeed him in 1823 as president of the college.[134] This suggests that despite public opinion, the Board of Administrators, still under Workman, favored the direction Lakanal had taken the school. The College, however, did close its doors in 1826. That same year, a law was passed by the Louisiana state legislature prohibiting anyone who was not an American citizen from teaching in state schools (Lakanal had not been a citizen, a bone of contention). This was certainly meant to keep out "rogue" transatlantic educators like Lakanal.

Figure 15. Joseph Lakanal. Photo taken from John Charles Dawson, *Lakanal the Regicide: A Biographical and Historical Study of the Career of Joseph Lakanal* (University of Alabama Press, 1948).

Although his son-in-law was unsuccessful in maintaining the college, when it closed, the state legislature, on March 31, 1826, authorized the establishment of three schools: one secondary school called the Central School and two primary schools in both the American and French sections of New Orleans.[135] These were to be governed by a board of ten regents who were to select a director to be placed in charge of the schools.[136]

In the 1831 education report to the state, it was noted the new Central School was not much different from the college; they had adopted

Lakanal's curriculum and school organization and were bilingual, teaching French, English, Latin, mathematics, and literature. Most significantly, in each of the schools, like the college, fifty indigent children were to be instructed gratis, creating public access to those who were of lesser means. These schools continued to receive the state funding that had previously gone to the college and thus were considered public schools, but they also charged tuition, at the primary school $2 per month and in the central school $4 per month.[137] The provisions of this act also "created one of the earliest school boards in any city of the United States, if not the earliest."[138] For all practical purposes, these were public schools that educated both girls and boys, were bilingual, and sought to provide access to education for those whose resources did not allow them the luxury to attend private schools.

In March of 1827, the number of teachers in these schools had to be increased, and the number of beneficiary students was also raised to a maximum of 100 for each of the schools. Governor Henry Johnson in his message of January 7, 1829, said, "they are in flourishing condition, and now contain upward of 250 students."[139] In the 1833 report to the state by the Board of Regents, it was noted that the Central School had 46 students, the lower primary schools had 108 and the upper primary school 82 students. While these figures were low, the Board of Regents conveyed to the legislature that the schools served an important purpose especially for students who would not have access to education because of lack of finances. Regular school board inspections of the schools were quite positive, especially in the area of language instruction (French, English, and Spanish), indicating that by 1836, the number of students receiving free tuition had increased to almost half of the students (190 of 440 total students).[140] This clearly indicated an increase in support for public education, at least at the state level.

The schools, however, soon acquired the reputation for being schools for indigents only, with instruction being adapted since students often stayed only a short period of time. Like critiques of the College d'Orléans, the mix of tuition-paying students and those admitted gratis disrupted normative class boundaries. While the intent of these public schools was to make education more accessible, the resistance to the transgressions of class norms resulted in severe criticism of these schools. For those who had envisioned public education as early as 1805—Claiborne, Lakanal, and many of his supporters (James Workman, other French and Haitian exiles, and Irish immigrants)—the struggle over education in 1820s Louisiana was not merely due to ethnic tensions between French Creoles and the Americans, or Catholics and Protestants, as has often been portrayed, but were ongoing tensions over how democracy functioned to create a public, how it was constituted, and, most importantly, whose voices contributed to that conversation. From the ruins of the college, Afro-Creole activists and French women religious claimed this site and transformed it into an interracial educational space that exemplified their vision of public education. The story of the St. Claude School allows us to trace the construction of public education in Louisiana in relation to the shifting racial and gender norms that constructed what constituted the public. Simultaneously, it brings from the shadows of educational history the female Black civil rights activism of Henriette Delille, Juliette Gaudin, and Josephine Charles, in which education was clearly understood as the marker of moral and human equality.

St. Claude School for Colored and White Girls

Leaving her creole cottage house on Burgundy, which she shared with her mother Pouponne Dias and sister Cecil, Henriette Delille crossed the back of the French Quarter on her way to her friend Juliette Gaudin, before the two walked up to the corner of Ursuline and Bon Enfans to the Catholic St. Claude School for free colored and white girls. For young free girls of color like Henriette (1812–1862) and Juliette (1813–1885), whose families were among the well-to-do free persons of color, the educational landscape of New Orleans in the later part of the 1820s was undergoing some unsettling shifts. While the Ursuline Academy, just five blocks down from St. Claude's, had traditionally been a space in which free girls of color looked for Catholic education, growing anti-Catholicism and political Anglo-centrism had led the Ursulines to reluctantly leave the French Quarter in 1824 to relocate their convent school two miles downriver. Before their departure, they sponsored a French religious woman from Lyons, France, Sister Ste. Marthe Fontière, who established St. Claude School for girls of color to ensure that the female activism and inclusive educational of the Ursulines would be maintained.[141] This ended their direct role as sponsors of Black religious education in the French Quarter. The Ursulines did not entirely abandon their influence in the French Quarter, however. The congregation retained control of their original convent property by donating it to the church instead of offering the valuable real estate for sale. The women then drew up a set of stipulations for the use of the property that laid the groundwork for the founding of both the first Black Catholic school (St. Claude) and the first Black Catholic religious order (Sisters of the Holy Family). The act specified that "on all Sundays and feasts an instruction or catechism be given to the Negresses of the district to replace what we give on such days."[142] In this way, the Ursulines obligated the bishop and his successors to continue the universalist educational mission of the sisters.

For Henriette, the ties to the Ursuline convent went back to her great-great-great-grandmother, Nanette, who as an enslaved person had been brought into the fold of the Ursuline community through baptism, catechism, and first communion and eventually taking a role serving in the ladies confraternity.[143] This multigenerational Afro-Creole female activism within the Catholic Church had been nurtured by the Ursulines with considerable success. Henriette had already been inducted into Ursuline tradition, serving numerous times as a godmother at the baptismal font at St. Mary's Chapel. With the departure of the Ursulines, however, St. Claude School struggled, as it lacked a permanent visible teaching order as its sponsor and was vulnerable both financially and due to increasing anti-Catholicism. This instability made it abundantly clear to both Henriette and Juliette that the void the Ursulines left would need to be filled if Black Catholic education would continue to be available to free girls of color and the enslaved.

As the girls approached the school, the porter opened the gates into the lush courtyard, filled with overgrown tropical plants. The two-story former plantation house that served as the St. Claude School had formerly been the College d'Orléans. Juliette was well-acquainted with the school given that her father, Pierre Gaudin, had taught there, along with many of his fellow Haitian refugees from Cuba. The former site of the college provided an ideal space for the Ursulines to continue their role as sponsors of Black religious education in the French Quarter. For Henriette and Juliette, the small St. Claude School on the corner of Rampart and Esplanade Avenue to which they walked each morning for their lessons was a critical space of self-formation for these two young girls. As a Catholic space, this was a site that reinforced the long history of women of color as active participants in creating and recreating Catholic culture in New Orleans. In fact, it was the dominance of women of color in the church that was central to the way New Orleanians understood their faith and practices. Whether a person was white or Black, slave or free, the church was a space that demonstrated a racial fluidity, where Henriette and Juliette took their places kneeling on the stone floor of St. Louis Cathedral side by side with every shade of person.[144] While people might go their separate ways upon leaving the church, there was a brief interlude in which they experienced the practice of equality, at least in a spiritual sense. At the St. Claude School this practice was also embodied, giving Henriette, Juliette, and the many other free girls of color who attended not only access to a formal education, but access to extend and build social networks between the Afro-Franco-Creole community and the Catholic Church.

The Ursuline Academy had historically been where free girls of color had gone to school as both boarders and day students. While Henriette and Juliette still attended mass at St. Mary's chapel at the Ursuline convent, the Ursuline school was no longer available after their move downriver.[145] But the Ursulines supported the work of sister Ste. Marthe Fontière, a former Dames d'Hospitaliére nun from Lyon, France, at the St. Claude School in continuing their apostolate among free people of color and enslaved Africans in the French Quarter. Sister Ste. Marthe had initially entered the novitiate of Les Dames d'Hospitaliére in France in 1806. Finding this work did not suit her, she entered the Ursuline convent in Bordeaux to prepare for missionary work. When Bishop Dubourg arrived in France in 1817 on a recruiting trip at the bequest of the Ursulines, Ste. Marthe, along with eight other nuns, left France for New Orleans. Upon arriving she took charge of the classes for free girls of color, eventually establishing a separate school on St. Claude Street. In 1823, although she had not joined the Ursuline order, she took over their educational mission, dedicating herself to the ministry of the city's people of African descent when the they left the French Quarter for their new convent.[146] Sister Marthe, with donations from free people of color and the enslaved, received permission from Bishop Dubourg to proceed with fundraising to purchase a building for the school. The property at the corner of Rampart and Esplanade, the old college, was purchased to found the St. Claude School for free girls of color.[147] Given the vacuum created by the departure of the Ursulines and the swelling number of free Afro-Creole and Afro-Haitian families settling in the both Tremé and the Marigny, there was an insatiable need for education. The school grew quickly, with eighty students of color by 1824 and three additional teachers: Sister St. Francis de Sales Aliquot, an Ursuline nun, and her two biological sisters, Adèle and Marie Aliquot.[148]

The withdrawal of the Ursulines from the French Quarter was emblematic of the disarray and destabilization of the Catholic Church that happened after Louisiana came under American control. Prior to 1803, under Spanish colonial rule, the whole territory that made up the Louisiana Purchase, as well as most of the Southwest, had been part of the Archdiocese of San Cristobal de la Habana based in Havana, Cuba. Upon transfer to the United States, Archbishop Carroll nominated Louis William Valentine Dubourg, and in August 1812, the Holy See named him bishop of the Diocese of Louisiana and the two Floridas. Born in Saint-Domingue in 1766, Dubourg was educated in France at the Seminary of St. Sulpice in Paris and ordained a priest in 1790. He fled France in 1792 in the aftermath of the revolution, first to Spain, then to Baltimore in 1794, where he founded what came to be known as St. Mary's College and Seminary in 1805, a school primarily for the children of Haitian refugees. A school for girls was opened in 1806 under Mother Elizabeth Seton with his encouragement. The French consul in Baltimore encouraged the development of French schools, especially in Louisiana, since he believed it would counterbalance "the ambition of the Americans [who] would have one believe that all of islands in the Gulf of Mexico belong to them."[149] Clearly the French schools that emerged in the coastal cities of the American transatlantic, as a result of the Haitian Revolution, were central to shaping education in the early republic.

Likewise, when Dubourg became bishop of New Orleans in 1815 he initiated an aggressive campaign to open Catholic schools throughout Louisiana and former French colonial Louisiana. As bishop, he reinvigorated what many Americans believed was and would be a dying institution, the Catholic Church. For Dubourg, however, schools would become central to his plan to revitalize the Catholic faith, as well as the French language in the face of the increasing challenges of Americanization and anticlerical sentiment. Dubourg returned to France in 1817 to begin recruiting female teaching congregations and priests. He was highly successful due to the Catholic restoration's explosion of apostolic missionary fervor in the aftermath of the French Revolution. Dubourg was met with great enthusiasm among several orders who initially envisioned their mission as being primarily among Indigenous peoples. One such order, the Sisters of the Sacred Heart, arrived in New Orleans in 1818 and after a brief stay with the Ursulines made their way up the Mississippi, passing through Kaskaskia, where the Illini received them, to St. Charles, Missouri, where they opened the first tuition-free "public" school for both Indigenous and European girls west of the Mississippi. Some of the sisters returned to Louisiana in 1821 to open a school at Grand Coteau, thus opening the first Catholic school for girls outside of New Orleans. Not long after, the Sisters of Mount Carmel (1838), the Marianites of the Holy Cross (1849), the Sisters of Saint Joseph (1854), and the Daughters of the Cross (1855) arrived in Louisiana to serve rural parishes, providing education for children of all races and classes.[150] This

"French Invasion" provided not only the sole education for many rural communities but it reinforced French, Catholic culture and the notion of universalist education. The spread of both female and male Catholic orders throughout Louisiana in the early American republic, under the leadership of Bishop Dubourg, provided a significant and invaluable source of education prior to the common school movement.

The impact of Dubourg's work was especially fruitful in New Orleans at a time when anti-Catholicism was on the rise. The Americanization of New Orleans brought with it a distinct disdain for Catholic nuns. While President Jefferson wrote personally to the nuns and guaranteed the Ursulines that they could continue their important work, the increased Protestant presence in New Orleans began to vie with the Catholics, especially the Ursulines, challenging their capacity and authority as educators, as well as their status as independent women.[151] In 1804, the opera *Une Folie*, performed at the Theatre St. Philippe, mocked the Ursulines, who responded with a swift rebuke, demanding an apology from the city fathers. In the eyes of the Protestant Church, Catholic female religious communities threatened the exclusive hold men had on the church. For Protestant America, nuns not only belonged to a religion much despised, "but they also were vowed virgins, strange unnatural creatures in the eyes of a society that prized domesticity and held marriage and motherhood to be a woman's highest calling."[152] Growing anti-Catholic hostility in the United States resulted in the 1834 Ursuline riots and burning of the convent outside Boston, Massachusetts.[153]

While violence like this never erupted in New Orleans, shortly after moving to their new site in 1824, the Ursulines once again faced challenges to their authority. While the Ursulines had been the only public institution since 1728 to receive public subsidies for the care and education of female orphans, in 1817 the Female Charitable Society (later known as the Poydras Orphan Asylum), founded by Phoebe Hunter, a Quaker and native of Philadelphia, was launched to support an orphan asylum.[154] The orphanage, which took in only white children, marked the first segregated educational institution New Orleans. The influx of Haitain refugees, as well as other immigrant groups in the early 1800s, combined with the yellow fever epidemics of 1817, 1819, and 1822, had overwhelmed the city's benevolent institutions, which resulted in the proliferation of orphanages.[155] Unlike the long history of the Ursulines, this new form of Protestant female benevolence was grounded in notions of republican motherhood in which women's duties were defined by the domestic/private sphere occupied by virtuous married women. The public sphere was the realm of white men, certainly not unmarried, single women like the Ursulines, whose wealth allowed them the independence to control their own lives and determine their own destiny.

In their new convent downriver, out of sight of the city fathers, the Ursulines were proceeding to educate all within their realm, including the increasing number of orphans in the city. Rumors circulated that the Ursulines were not treating their orphans properly. In October of 1824, the city council launched an investigation into the conditions at the new convent, which concluded that the young girls were treated like mere servants. The damning report not only sealed the fate of the orphans, who were removed to the Poydras Asylum, but signaled the end of "public" support for female Catholic education in the city of New Orleans. This redefinition of the "public" sphere as a Protestant space was not merely a foreshadowing of national anti-Catholic sentiment but signified the coding of the public sphere as a white male space in which they had power and authority over women. For the Ursulines, who had long wielded moral and social authority in New Orleans, this recoding of what constituted the public, and who could hold power in it, was a direct affront to the hundred-year history of the Ursulines as independent agents in administrating educational and benevolent institutions that had served, to the best of their ability, all persons regardless of color. This change in the gendered and racial order of the city was no doubt not lost on women of color like Henriette and Juliette, who saw their sphere of influence being increasingly circumscribed.

The supposed transgressions of the Ursulines did not only pertain to gender roles, but also challenged the racial order of the plantation society of New Orleans in which white superiority required the complete dehumanization of Blacks. Despite increasingly rigid racial boundaries, the Ursulines had continued to admit girls of color as boarders and day students whose social position for all practical purposes was higher than that of the orphans (mostly white). What distressed the men of the city council on their visit to the Ursuline convent was that white orphans who often served the boarders, both white and free girls of color, inverted the racial hierarchy of a plantation society. Class and social standing, not race, had continued to shape the social order of the Ursuline convent and school. For Anglo-Protestants and some French Creoles, this was a "rogue" curriculum, given the rigid racial boundaries that were necessary to a plantation society.

The Ursuline convent and school was increasingly coded as undemocratic, elitist, and "unladylike." Public funding was cut off, and for all practical purposes this space became "private." The expulsion of both the Ursulines and Joseph Lakanal from New Orleans signaled that education as a social space increasingly was used to define the public sphere along racial, gender, and Anglo-Protestant class lines. While both the Ursuline Academy and the College d'Orléans had sought to enlarge the scope of the "public," the new Protestant orphanages functioned as a sorting mechanism for race and class.[156] This reproduction of class distinctions undid what the university system had originally been designed to do. By the 1830s race, class, and gender were being disciplined in new ways to produce and increasingly signify the public sphere, and thus education, as white and male.

And yet there were ruptures. In 1829, David Walker, an antislavery activist born of a white mother and Black father, wrote *Appeal to the Colored Citizens of the World*, in which he was an outspoken advocate of the Haitian Revolution as an example of Black unity in the fight against racial oppression. The pamphlet was distributed all along Black communication networks up and down the Atlantic coast. Blacks in New Orleans were arrested for distributing Walker's pamphlet. While the threat of Black insurrection was always paramount, Walker's appeal to "colored" citizenship undermined the very foundation of democracy in America: white citizenship. Citizenship was a racialized concept in which the space of citizenship effectively made one white. One is a citizen because one is not a slave. As Tocqueville argued in *Democracy in America*, democracy/citizenship and white supremacy/slavery were not contradictory; in fact, they were interdependent. Citizenship is produced in a social space that is racialized as well as gendered; the freedom of some is guaranteed through the subordination of others, and this connection is sealed through citizenship. The spatial, racial geography of Louisiana disrupted these boundaries by making visible the in-between spaces occupied by free people of color.

Between Worlds

The liminal or in-between spaces occupied by free Afro-Creoles in antebellum New Orleans meant that they were neither white nor slave, Black nor free; in other words, their world was made up of "shades of gray."[157] But for women religious like the Ursulines and the fledgling community at St. Claude, they also navigated complex gender norms that emerged as Louisiana became more American and Protestant. As Catholic, unmarried women, they occupied a unique space in which women could act independently as institution builders, teachers, and entrepreneurs. They certainly did not conform to the norms of Republican motherhood. For free women of color who sought to take up the veil of a Catholic woman religious, the gender norms of the antebellum period were complicated even more by the racial norms of Black women's supposed inferiority, immorality, and sexualization.[158] Much of the writing pertaining to the lives of free women of color has emphasized their involvement in quadroon balls or *plaçage*, thus focusing on free women of color's sexual relations with white men. These representations have obscured the history of many free women of color as social activists, economic entrepreneurs, and community build-ers.[159] This activism shaped numerous aspects of antebellum New Orleans, including economic, social, and, in the case of this study, education. Free women of color navigated gender norms in which, on the one hand, white women were understood to represent piety and morality, whereas Black women were cast as sexualized objects incapable of being moral beings. In fact, the construction of whiteness and femaleness depended on this binary. These binary subjectivities were taken up in multiple, complex ways, but rarely has scholarship focused on how women of color took up Catho-lic religious practices, specifically education, to negotiate the in-between spaces of gender norms that relegated Black women to being not only less than human (slave), but also incapable of being virtuous (woman). Hen-riette and her companion's active agency in taking up the practices of the Catholic religion by eventually establishing a religious order, the Sisters of the Holy Family, whose primary aim was the education of free women of color and the enslaved, disrupted this binary. Walking the streets of New Orleans in the habit of a religious woman was a direct way to "talk back" to the gender and racial discourses that were meant to continually reinforce the dehumanization of people of color.

The invisibility of women of color activists, and specifically the Sisters of the Holy Family, can be attributed to the gendered constructs of his-torical scholarship, but particularly to the gendered history of the South and religion. Not only are Catholic women religious a mere footnote, but when their achievements are acknowledged, credit is often given to male clergy (Archbishop Blanc, Father Etienne Rousselon) and free Creole of color men (Francois LaCroix, Thomy Lafon) for initiating the actions of women religious. While credit is due, their role, as well as that of Hen-riette, must be understood as embedded in a long history of educational activism located in a transatlantic, transnational, interracial pedagogical circuit. Henriette Delille was not an aberration but was the product of the long tradition of radical protest by Afro-Creole Catholics who sought to create counterpublic spaces in which their humanity was acknowledged. How a community of Afro-Creole free women of color, French women religious, and French male clergy navigated the patriarchal, racist, slave-holding terrain of antebellum New Orleans to establish educational and humanitarian institutions for people of color—which are still in existence today—is the story to which I now turn.

For Henriette and Juliette, the liminal spaces between free and slave, Black and white, nun and jezebel, French and American, Catholic and Protestant, heightened their awareness of the need for female Afro-Creole control and self-determination in establishing educational institutions. This was especially the case for free girls of color, whose life choices included marriage to free men of color, but also included the system of *plaçage*, an arranged relationship between a white man and a free girl of color on a contractual or quasi-contractual basis.[160] This arrangement, often a source of economic security for women of color, simultaneously threatened the role of legitimate marriage in the Catholic Church among free people of color, whose ties to the church provided them institutional legitimacy. And, as we will see in the next chapter, Black literary figures, like Armand Lanusse, used their poetry to critique what they saw as the exploitive nature of *plaçage* relationships. Alternatively, legitimate marriages were critical to a relational network of support within the Afro-Creole free community, as well as the church, whose sacraments, like marriage, were central to recognizing the moral/spiritual equality of people of color.

Henriette was all too familiar with the system of *plaçage*. Her older sister Cecile had entered such a relationship with a wealthy Austrian Jewish businessman, Samuel Hart, with whom she had four children before his death. At age fifteen Henriette formed a liaison with a Monsieur Bocno, and between 1827 and 1833 bore him two sons, both of whom died, after which Bocno left.[161] At age twenty-one, recovering from numerous tragedies, she sought solace at the chapel of the nearby St. Claude School and Convent. When Sister Ste. Marthe Fontière recognized her aptitude for teaching and her religious devotion, she asked her to help instruct the day students. Not long after, both Henriette and her childhood friend Juliette Gaudin began to help with the catechism classes for enslaved girls and night school for adults.[162] Despite laws and customs forbidding slave literacy, the St. Claude School, most likely under the guise of catechism lessons, taught the enslaved to read and write, thereby strategically resisting the dehumanization of people of color.[163] Juliette (1808–1887), also a free woman of color, was the daughter of Marie Thérèse Lacardonie, a free woman of color born in Haiti, and Pierre Gaudin, who was born in southwest France and then settled in Saint-Domingue, who both fled to Cuba, where Juliette was born in 1808. Although never married, Marie and Pierre maintained a lifelong relationship in which Pierre supported the family through his work as a teacher at a boy's high school, most likely the College d'Orléans.

For Henriette, a slave owner herself, the project of Catholic universalism mandated the conversion of *all*, including those who were enslaved. In fact, for those who adopted a gradualist approach to the abolition of slavery, literacy among the enslaved was understood as a prerequisite for successful emancipation. And for the enslaved, as argued earlier in the book, the relationship between literacy and freedom was abundantly clear. New Orleans, as an urban center, provided numerous possibilities for acquiring literacy given the relative mobility and the nature of everyday activities in which the enslaved were engaged. The proximity of urban slaves to each other provided the conditions under which illiterate people could meet and share knowledge with one another. There they could enjoy relative autonomy as well as exposure to valuable knowledge. Domestic slaves were often expected to perform errands that took them outside of the home, where they walked the streets to the markets, to the river to wash clothes, and to deliver messages. Enslaved women and girls who performed general domestic labor—such as cooking and cleaning—were at times sent on household errands, giving them opportunities to escape the watchful eye of their masters. Likewise, slaves often lived in spaces separate from their owners, where they could share their knowledge among themselves. This semiautonomous existence created not only confusion over an individual's status, but also more opportunities for engaging in illicit activities, including schooling at the St. Claude School.

Within a short time, the St. Claude School was bursting at the seams.[164] With the help of the recently arrived Ursuline Sister Francis de Sales Aliquot (Jean Marie), Sister Ste. Marthe purchased in 1834 the large Claude Tremé property, which had housed the College d'Orléans, from the city for $9,000. Although the actual college had been partially torn down when Ursuline Street was extended in 1827, the original plantation house still survived, as well as the spacious grounds.[165] In their new quarters, under the leadership and philanthropy of Aliquot, this interracial band of Catholic women, including Jean Marie, Marthe, Henriette, and Juliette, created an institutionalized space that was meant to correct the structural injustice of slavery/racism by teaching free girls of color and the enslaved. Under the umbrella of the Catholic Church, they could rely on the fundraising activities of Bishop Dubourg, as well as Bishop Neckere (1830–1833) and Archbishop Blanc (1835–1860), for the recruiting of missionary teaching orders and for the establishment and maintenance of schools like St. Claude. Institutional support for integrated education and interracial initiatives was critical to embodying the universalism of the transatlantic French Catholic Church.[166]

It was this universalist philosophy that propelled Jean Marie Aliquot, whose ardent opposition to slavery had resulted in a tense relationship with the Ursulines, to leave the Ursulines to teach at the St. Claude School, where she eventually took over for Sister Ste. Marthe in 1834. As the school continued to grow, Jean Marie was in desperate need of more teachers. She reached out to the newly appointed Bishop Neckere (1799–1833), a missionary recruit originally from Belgium, whose primary work in New Orleans was focused on expanding Catholic education. He approached the Ursulines at their new convent downriver to request that they send several sisters to help at the St. Claude School. Between 1831 and 1838, several of the Ursuline sisters, including Jean Marie's sister, Felicite Aliquot, were among the eight Ursulines who taught at St. Claude.[167] It was during this time that Henriette and Juliette were also recruited by Jean Marie Aliquot not only to help with the instruction of free girls of color, but to provide evening catechism classes for the enslaved. In these endeavors, this eclectic transatlantic group of teachers (Afro-Creole, Afro-Caribbean-Creole, French, and Franco-Creole) was joined and supported by the thirty-seven-year-old French Jesuit priest Etienne Rousselon, who had been assigned to work as the chaplain at the St. Claude School and Convent. Born in France in 1800 and ordained in 1827, Father Rousselon had been the director of the Grand Seminaire in Lyon prior to his arrival in New Orleans in 1837. At the St. Claude School, he met and was inspired by the work and dedication of Henriette, Juliette, and Jean Marie, as well as the community of free people of color whose vibrant interracial educational missionary work impressed him. Within the year, Father Rousselon and Henriette were serving together as godparents for the young free girls of color at the school, signaling a crucial partnership between the Catholic Church and Afro-Creole women.[168] The importance of St. Claude School in shaping and preserving a universalist, interracial, transnational mission of education has rarely been acknowledged.[169]

For Henriette and Juliette, the universalism of the Catholic Church, which signaled the moral equality of all people, became the scaffold from which they sought to broaden the institutional scope of the church among free people of color, especially women, as a means of developing the critical networks of community building.[170] For Henriette, whose female ancestors had a long history of participation in the Catholic Church, the formation of a lay confraternity would have naturally come to mind. Her great-great-great-grandmother, Nanette, whom we have met in the previous chapter, had been a member of the Children of Mary, the Ursuline interracial confraternity.[171] Harnessing the institutional stamp of the church in organizing themselves into a confraternity dedicated to the education of women of color, the poor, and the enslaved was an important step in institutionalizing their ministry of education To this end, in 1836, Henriette (Afro-Franco-Creole), Juliette (Afro-Caribbean-Franco-Creole), Josephine (Afro-Franco-Germanic-Creole), and Jean Marie Aliquot (French) organized an interracial, transnational group of women into a confraternity named the Congregation of the Sisters of the Presentation of the Blessed Virgin Mary. They established the rules and regulations of the confraternity, which included an elected council, director, officers, and, most importantly, recruiters. With the support of Father Rousselon and Bishop Blanc, they forged ahead to receive official recognition of their integrated religious community. This commitment to practicing the universalism of the Catholic Church was a direct effort by an interracial network of French clergy, Caribbean immigrants, Afro-Creole free people of color, and French immigrants to preserve interracial practices at a time when they were increasingly vulnerable to both forces inside and outside of the Church.

In fact, this was not the first attempt to create an integrated, interracial group of women religious. In 1822, Bishop Dubourg recruited the Daughters of the Cross (Sisters of Loretto) from Kentucky to work in the vicinity of Assumption Church in Plattenville on Bayou Lafourche. Because the sisters only spoke English, Dubourg suggested that they accept French-speaking Afro-Creole women to help them with the language barrier and to instruct the enslaved girls.[172] The thoroughly Americanized Sisters of Loretto refused to accept Afro-Creole postulants. Dubourg's suggestion, however, not only speaks to his desire to maintain and grow a universal church, but it suggests that he was keenly aware of the presence of well-educated women of color in New Orleans who desired to take up religious life and potentially to serve as teachers. While many of the Sisters of Loretto returned to Kentucky, some did stay in Louisiana, learned French, and eventually joined the Sisters of the Sacred Heart, teaching in Grand Coteau and Plattenville to girls of all races.

While the formation of the interracial Sisters of the Presentation was supported by the Catholic Church, the endeavor did not succeed because it violated the state segregation laws.[173] Extremely disheartened by this failure, as well as financial troubles in maintaining the St. Claude School,

Jean Marie accepted the Ursuline sisters' offer to pay the debts owed by the school. Eventually, she sold the house and property to the Ursulines in 1836 for $5,000, under the condition that they promise to continue the school for girls of color and provide free education for at least five girls of color at their downriver convent. Never content to miss an opportunity to expand not only their reach but also their investments, the enterprising Ursulines also bought the land adjacent to the school on the corner of St. Claude and Bayou Road from Pierre Soule for $10,000. Control of the St. Claude School would now pass from the Ursulines to the Sisters of Mt. Carmel, who had recently been recruited by Bishop Dubourg from France with the stipulation that they would provide education for the girls of color in the neighborhood.[174] They would anchor this school until 1929.

Given that St. Louis Cathedral was a good mile from the Faubourg Tremé, many residents of the neighborhood attended mass at St. Claude's chapel, where Father Rousselon preached on Sundays. It was not long before the interracial parishioners to St. Claude's chapel exceeded its capacity and a delegation of free people of color requested a meeting with the bishop regarding the building of a church in Tremé. Father Rousselon, under the leadership of Bishop Blanc, worked to raise funds for a new church among both Franco-Creole families and Afro-Creole families in the neighborhood. For the property-owning Catholic Afro-Creole families, increasingly aware of the growing conservatism among Anglo-American Catholic officials, the establishment of a church in Tremé would reinforce neighborhood relationships, kinship patterns, and business practices among free people of color that were critical to strengthening the networks upon which they relied to protect their rights.[175] The Ursulines eventually donated the land next to St. Claude's for the building of the church (on the corner of Hospital and St. Claude) to Archbishop Blanc with the stipulation that it be dedicated to their patron saint, St. Augustine. Father Rousselon became the first pastor of the St. Augustine Church, completed in September of 1842.

On October 9, 1842, parishioners filled the new church; half of the pews had been rented by Afro-Creole free people, the other half by Franco-Creoles, and enslaved people filled the small pews in the aisles. The first service was marked by great fanfare given that it was seen as a victory for the French Catholics in maintaining local control over the direction of the Catholic Church in New Orleans. The presence of the city's Franco-Catholic clergy—including Father Rousselon, who was not only pastor but vicar-general; Father Maenhaut, a Dubourg recruit from France who had served in Natchez and Pensacola prior to arriving in New

Orleans and who said the first mass; and Father Anduse, another Dubourg recruit from France, the assistant to the cathedral—suggested the ongoing support for interracialism among Catholic clergy in New Orleans. The establishment of this church not only marked the persistence of the Franco-Afro-Catholic community to retain control over their parishes, but it secured a site, which included the St. Claude School and eventually the Bayou School of the Sisters of the Holy Family, in which interracialism was the norm. St. Augustine Church marked a space that exemplified the interracial "layering of economic, educational, and religious activities that would continue to thrive within the parish."[176]

But while St. Louis Cathedral and St. Augustine's continued interracial/ integrated practices within the churches themselves, interracial associations like the Sisters of the Presentation were increasingly scrutinized for suspicious activity in which enslaved and free people of color might be incited against whites. Undeterred, with the support of the larger community and Franco-Catholic clergy, Henriette and a group of free women of color were determined to carve a path to establish a religious order of women of color that would be dedicated to the education of people of color and to the care of the poor and the elderly. Father Rousselon, at the bequest of Henriette, approached Bishop Blanc with the request that the Sisters of the Presentation become affiliated with the Roman Sodality of the Blessed Virgin Mary, which had been founded in 1563 in the College of the Society of Jesus. This formal recognition by the Roman Catholic Church was critical to legitimating this band of women, as well as to providing the necessary protection to form the community of the Souers de Sainte-Famille (Sisters of the Holy Family), which was founded on November 21, 1842. Given the legal restrictions imposed by the Louisiana legislature and the fomenting of anti-Catholic sentiments in New Orleans, Bishop Blanc capitulated to the hardening racial lines and authorized a racially segregated congregation of women of color. In order to erase all suspicion from connections with the interracial Sisters of the Presentation, the name was changed to the Sisters of the Holy Family.[177]

Upon approval by the Vatican in 1842, the Sisters of the Holy Family represented the first Catholic order for Blacks in the Deep South, male or female, and only the second religious order in the nation after the foundation of the Oblate Sisters of Providence in Maryland. The establishment of a racially segregated order was just one of several modifications (the others being eventually building segregated schools and accommodating the slave regime) to the religious ideals of universalism that the Catholic Church, and certainly Bishop Blanc, believed was necessary to function in an oppressive slave regime whose construction depended on maintaining a rigid racial binary. The increasing restrictions by the state legislature of the rights of free people of color had already resulted in the exodus of thousands of Catholic free people of color to countries that had already abolished slavery: France (1848), Mexico (1829), Haiti (1793), Belize (1833), Honduras (1824), Nicaragua (1824), as well as countries that had not abolished slavery but guaranteed rights to free people of color (Cuba) (Figure 16). The population of free people of color went from 19,226 in 1840 to 9,961 in 1850. By 1830, the overall Catholic population was a bare majority of the population due to this exodus and the growing influx of English-speaking Protestant Americans.[178] It is remarkable that the Catholic Church even dared to push for the formation of an order of religious black women. For Henriette, Juliette, and the sisters who would soon join the order, this was indeed not only a revolutionary act of courage, but an indication of the persistent pursuit to build educational institutions.

They established their congregation and school in a home that Father Rousselon rented for them at 72 Bayou Road. This became the base from which they moved out across the city, providing care to aged and poor Afro-Creoles, both men and women, and providing education to adult free people of color and the enslaved. Unlike the Ursulines, they were not a cloistered order. Moving freely around the city, they ministered to the enslaved at different locations around the French Quarter. According to church records, the women appeared regularly at key places of worship: St. Louis Cathedral, St. Mary's Chapel (at the old Ursuline convent), and the new St. Augustine Church.[179] They used these sites to teach catechism classes and sponsor initiates in baptism and marriage. While the sisters were missionaries, intent on increasing the numbers of Catholics, they also recognized the invaluable role of the Catholic Church in providing protection and legitimacy to the most vulnerable and marginalized in their community by making them part of the larger network of a well-established community.

Within the year, Henriette Dellile and Juliette Gaudin were joined by Josephine Charles (1812–1885), all serving as teachers and caregivers to the poor, sick, and the enslaved. While their professed task of teaching the official catechism to the enslaved was legal, the 1830 state law that prohibited teaching slaves to read or write would have put them at risk of imprisonment. Of course, as several historians have established, religious education was often the guise under which freedom workers created spaces for advancing reading and writing.[180] Literacy skills enabled various forms of communication among the enslaved that could then be taught to other

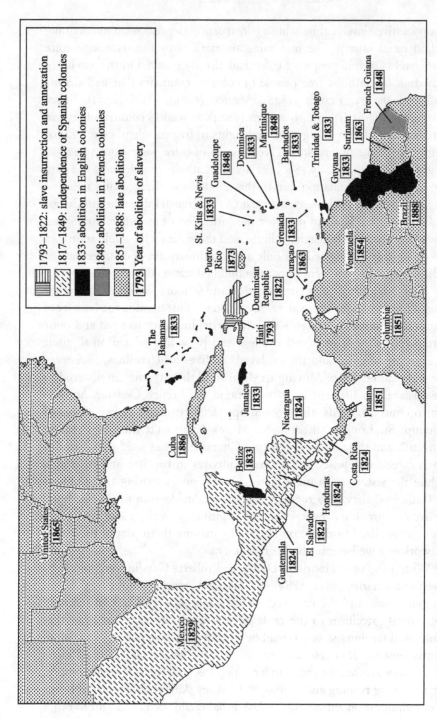

Figure 16. Map of the countries and years in which slavery was abolished in the Caribbean. Drawn by Mary Lee Eggart.

enslaved, enabled enslaved to write passes, and most importantly could be understood as a form of liberation and humanization. Within the context of religious instruction, especially catechism, catechists could also acquire potentially liberating literacies: subversive skills (e.g., reading between the lines, critiquing social practices, principles of Judeo-Christian rhetoric and argument), cultural knowledge (values, tastes, and requirements) and languages (Latin, Greek, French, Spanish, or English), and, as mentioned earlier in the book, various forms of music literacy. Thus, while catechism could certainly be used as an instrument of social control, it is conceivable that the Sisters of the Holy Family used the catechism to further formal literacy but also as a means to highlight the discontinuities between the practices of universal Catholicism and the secular American ideals of race. For Henriette, who took up the "veil" as a form of resistance to the dehumanizing practices of *plaçage*, it is not inconceivable that she saw catechesis as the ideal and safest pedagogy through which to render to the oppressed an understanding of the systems that oppressed them.[181] In this regard we will see in the next chapter that she was part of a larger educational community of free people of color who saw the advantages of the cloak of the Catholic Church to advance liberation struggles.

Associations among free people of color that legally permitted them to gather, hold meetings and raise funds were increasingly seen by whites as sites of agitation for civil rights and antislavery organizing. Restrictions against these types of associations flourished in the state legislature in an attempt to curtail the activism of free people of color and their institution building, including schools.[182] The fledgling community recognized the necessity of becoming legally incorporated after an act was passed by the state legislature in 1847 that required that literary, scientific, or religious association have more than six members to be reincorporated. Given that their initial incorporation consisted of only three persons, they would need to act to retain their congregation. Recognizing that this legislation was intended as a direct threat to their agency as educators, the Sisters of the Holy Family engaged the larger community of free people of color in order to seek ways in which to subvert this law.

To reincorporate their community, the Sisters of the Holy Family relied on a group of free people of color who incorporated an Association of the Holy Family under the new state mandates and then named Henriette as president. Not only did this provide legal recognition in Louisiana, but it was necessary to own property and to raise and avoid taxes. Henriette most certainly had reached out and discussed the matter with her close friend Cecile Edouarde Lacroix, who with her husband, François

Lacroix, formed part of a network of free men and women of color that supported missionary work among the enslaved, poor, orphans, and sick people of color. This network also included Etiènne Cordeviolle (a notable builder, real estate speculator, tailor, and business partner of François Lacroix), Armand Richard Clague (half-brother of the well-known landscape painter Richard Clague), Joseph Lavigne (a teacher at the Catholic School for Indigent Orphans), François Boutin (or Broutin, a close friend of Henriette's), Chazel Thomas (a board member of the Catholic School for Indigent Orphans), and Joseph Dumas (prosperous slaveholder). For all practical purposes the association functioned as a "front" for the Sisters of the Holy Family, but it also expanded the network of those directly involved in the fundraising and financial support for the institutions the Sisters of the Holy Family would build. In fact, it would be Cecile LaCroix who in the following year, acting as president of the association, would purchase property on St. Bernard Street between Marais and LaHarpe Street for the Sisters of the Holy Family, who eventually used this site for a hospice for the elderly.[183] These practices refute dominant narratives that give the French Catholic clergy credit for many of the initiatives of the Sisters of the Holy Family, and they highlight the agency of women of color to work together to enact business practices that would further the social justice work directed to those most marginalized.[184]

It has been noted that the humanitarian activities of free Black activists, like the Sisters of the Holy Family, would not have been possible without the support of Afro-Creole slaveholders, all of whom were Catholic.[185] It is difficult to speculate about why they owned slaves. While never denouncing slavery, most of these wealthy Catholic Afro-Creole slave owners took seriously their obligation to treat the enslaved as part of the universal Catholic Church by acknowledging their moral equality through providing religious instruction, the Catholic sacraments, including slave marriage, mission work, philanthropic work, and even manumissions (made increasingly difficult by new state laws). These efforts to provide education, even if nominal, to the enslaved functioned to mitigate the dehumanizing status of slavery.

These humanizing measures often met with intense opposition not only from American Protestants, but from the American Catholic Church (based in Maryland), which reinforced a racialized, oppressive, dehumanizing form of slavery. Afro-Creole free slaveholders, whose roots were in French Catholicism, were unlike Americans (both Protestant and Catholic) in that many provided Catholic education for the enslaved, often resulting in accusations that they were abolitionist sympathizers. It is impossible to know how free people of color negotiated constructions of slavery, race, gender, social status, and Catholicism. What we do know is that by 1830, many free people of color were among the most successful businessmen and women in the city, in part due to their investments in land and slaves. At this time 735 free persons of color in New Orleans owned 2,351 slaves, many of whom were members of their own families.[186] Cyprian Davis has posited three explanations for why free people of color (both those who were born free and those who were manumitted) were slaveholders: (1) they purchased their children or grandchildren, (2) they purchased slaves in order to improve their condition but did not manumit them because this would require the former slave to leave the state, (3) they purchased and owned slaves for the same reason as white people—to exploit their labor and as a form of speculation in human property.[187] Additionally, owning slaves provided an identification/alliance with white people, which served to protect them from being identified as slave.

Ironically, while Delille has been called a "servant of slaves," she also owned at least one slave, Betsy, whom she had inherited from her mother, and according to her will, Betsy was to be manumitted upon her death.[188] While questions continue to rage around the profound paradoxes of being a Catholic, a free woman of color, a slaveholder, and a missionary, these complex subjectivities were continually shifting given place and space in time. What remained constant over time were Henriette's practices and pedagogies and her ardent desire to educate and catechize enslaved persons, even when this defied the law and threatened her own freedom. What has also often been overlooked is that Henriette consistently identified as a free woman of color. Her family had been listed in the 1830s census as "white," not Negro or mulatto, and for all practical purposes she could have "passed" as white.[189] Regardless of whether she was a quadroon or one-eighth Black, or any shade in between, what is clear is that she consistently chose to identify herself as colored. It is also important to note that while free people of color were often considered privileged due to their lighter skin color and wealth, Henriette and the Sisters of the Holy Family were by no means wealthy. In fact, in order to survive financially, they were compelled to engage in the same types of work done by the enslaved, including house cleaning, taking in laundry, sewing, peddling products (dolls), and doing the housework for the archbishop.[190] The sisters, not the enslaved, did this labor all in addition to running schools, running orphanages, operating a home for the elderly, fund raising, and managing their properties and institutions. This was a life far removed from the stereotypes of privileged quadroons and wealthy free women of color, although these certainly did exist. In fact, without the philanthropy of free men of color, educational institutions for people of color would most likely not have existed.

Afro-Creole people, while constituting the majority of those supporting the missionary work of the Sisters of the Holy Family through the Association of the Holy Family, strove for interracial integration and cooperation.[191] Two white French emigrés, Agathe Mager Collard and her brother Jean Mager, a wealthy landowner in the Faubourg Tremé, were also members of the association and Jean served one term as president. These interracial networks made possible the legal incorporation in 1847 and provided critical support for the survival of the Sisters of the Holy Family in these times of increasingly racial hostilities. Henriette Delille and Juliette Gaudin's activism provided both the legal and financial standing that institutionalized a place and space from which to counteract through education the inhumane and oppressive social and racial order in antebellum Louisiana. This clearly was a counterpublic.

Following incorporation, Henriette and her fellow sisters wasted no time in expanding the reach of their missionary work. First was the establishment of the Hospice de la Société de la Sainte Famille to care for the old and homeless people of color. Working with Cecile LaCroix to collect donations from free people of color and to raise money through a lottery, the hospice was completed on St. Bernard Street in 1849. Clearly, Henriette knew the importance of institution building and the power of property to advance the cause of individuals and communities of free people of color. As restrictions on the civic participation of free people of color hardened during the 1830s and 1840s, property ownership and institution building, especially educational, became a primary way in which free people of color created public spaces and claimed public rights throughout the New Orleans landscape to assert their visibility and legitimate their human dignity. The second property acquisition was a house at 72 Bayou Road that was bought in order to convert it into a convent with dormitories, classrooms, dining facilities, and a chapel.[192] By the end of 1851, Henriette, Juliette, and Josephine moved into the completed convent on Bayou Road to continue teaching catechism to the enslaved, as well as to operate a school that taught both day students and boarders.[193] The school also offered free classes for indigent girls at St. Augustine Church, which was right next door.

The Bayou Road School, similar to that of the Ursulines, was most likely based on the French classical tradition. Based on what we know about the education and backgrounds of Henriette, Juliette, and Josephine, it is likely that courses in religion, grammar, French, Latin, history, bookkeeping, geography, music, sewing, and embroidery were offered. Henriette, who was made first mistress of the novices, was most likely responsible for the preparation of the postulants and novices. Accordingly, she taught religion as well as sewing and nursing skills, which were critical not only for their missionary work but were essential to earning money for the financing of the convent, school, and other philanthropic institutions. Juliette was described by Sister Mary Bernard Deggs as having "a superior intellectual capacity," no doubt because her father Pierre Gaudin had been a professor at the College d'Orléans.[194] A portion of her personal library, found in the book collection of the Holy Family archives, includes mystical works by Teresa of Ávila and St. Francis de Sales, classical French grammar texts, choir music, and Latin versions of the New Testament. Josephine Charles (1812–1885), daughter of a free woman of color, Philomene, and Joseph Charles, a wealthy German entrepreneur, was also exceptionally well-educated, having been privately tutored by Madame Eulalie Peruque, a French tutor.[195] Given their exceptional training and background, these teachers were undoubtedly able to provide a rigorous education to the young girls of color that served to deflect from common antebellum ideologies of racial inferiority, as well as gendered images of free women of color as the tragic mulatto. Obscured in the traditional histories of antebellum New Orleans is the Afro-Creole female schoolteacher, principal, and nun. Practicing these identities, the Sisters of the Holy Family challenged the dehumanizing effects of slavery.

It was not long before boarders began arriving at the Bayou Road School, in addition to a growing number of day and evening scholars. Like the class-based education of the Ursulines, boarding students received a classical French education while day students received basic literacy education as well as marketable skills, primarily sewing, and in the evening, catechism classes were held for enslaved women and girls. At this time, the Sisters of the Holy Family were still considered an association of vowed women living in community. Their desire, though, was to be acknowledged as a religious order. Although under civil law they would not be recognized as religious, Archbishop Blanc arranged for Henriette to undergo a novitiate at Saint Michael's Convent with the all-white Sisters of the Sacred Heart in Grand Coteau. In late 1851, Father Rousselon received "Mother Henriette" and presented Juliette Gaudin and Josephine Charles as novices. In October 1853, at the altar of St. Augustine's, these women recited their vows to the archbishop and Father Rousselon. It would not be until 1869 that the community would receive a formal religious rule, adopt a habit, and take the three vows of poverty, chastity, and obedience.

Prior to her death in 1862, Henriette turned her attention to further institution building as well as recruiting novices to the religious community. Despite the chaos of the Civil War and destitute conditions, the Sisters of the Holy Family worked to continually expand their institutional reach through the hospice for the elderly (St. Bernard Street), the Bayou convent school for free girls of color, the evening school for the enslaved, and the orphanage (Asylum of the Children of the Holy Family). While most new postulates continued to be from well-educated families of Louisiana, the order now also attracted women of color from other states. In 1862, Suzanne Navarre (1820–1887), age forty-two, arrived from Boston to join the community. The 1860 census also lists, in addition to Henriette, Juliette, and Josephine, Josephine Vecque (age fifty-seven), Ann Marie Henriette Fazende (age fifty-seven), and Orfise Romain (age forty-six). In addition to this transatlantic group of teachers, the census also recorded four elderly, formerly enslaved women living next door who were under the care of the sisters.[196] During this time, boarding students also began to arrive from areas outside of New Orleans, including Baton Rouge, Pointe Coupée, and Opeaulousas, where Catholic education for girls of color was not as readily available. Maria Magdelene Alpaugh from Pointe Coupée arrived in 1860 to become a student at St. Mary's School. Eventually she entered the community, becoming mother superior in 1882 until her death in 1890.

In 1870, not long after the Civil War, the first former slave, Chloé Joachim Preval, who had been engaged by Archbishop Odin as a servant, was admitted to the order, creating a rift in the fledgling community. This was a radical departure from the rule of the first motherhouse, which had accepted only women from free and well-known families as postulates.[197] Whether this dispute was over her status as a former slave and her dark skin, or her former working-class position as a housekeeper, the community split over whether she would be admitted. Juliette Gaudin, who opposed her entry, stayed at the Bayou School, while Josephine Charles, with the assistance of Father Gilbert Raymond, opened a second convent and school, St. Mary's, on Chartres Street (between Peace and Esplanade).[198] Shortly after moving, Mother Josephine Charles received two new sisters who "were as dark as the head of a jet pine."[199] In 1883, the two houses were reunited after Josephine Charles had moved the convent and St. Mary's to 717 Orleans Street. At this location, the former Quadroon Ballroom, St. Mary's school educated generations of young women during Jim Crow and through segregation. In 1964, when the sisters numbered 357, they moved to their new motherhouse on the 123 acres in the Gentilly area purchased by Mother Austin Jones in the early twentieth century, where they continue to operate today.

After the death of Henriette Delille in 1862 and the end of the Civil War, the Sisters of the Holy Family continued to persevere in their educational work despite white supremacists' attempts to intimidate the newly freed slave population and to curtail the political, educational, and economic successes of Black activists during radical reconstruction. St. Mary's School, under Mother Josephine's direction, expanded the curriculum and offerings to accommodate the flood of freed slave women and children, whom they could now freely offer an education without fear of retribution. In addition to the evening catechism classes, Mother Josephine offered Latin and music to young women who could not attend day classes.[200] Ironically, the Catholic Church's eventual capitulation to segregation after the Civil War provided opportunities for the Sisters of the Holy Family to expand their mission. Throughout Reconstruction and the Jim Crow era, they went on to establish seven more schools before the end of the century:

1874: St. Joseph's school in Opelousas
1876: The Louisiana Asylum for girls in New Orleans
1885: St. Augustine's school in Donaldsonville
1889: St. Mary's School, later Holy Family Academy, in Baton Rouge
1891: Holy Family Boy's School in New Orleans
1898: Holy Rosary Academy in Galveston and Sacred Heart School in Belize

Eventually, the order expanded as well to Arkansas, Florida, Oklahoma, Texas, Tennessee, and California, as well as internationally to Belize and Nigeria.[201] Educational history's traditional focus on the Freedmen's Bureau and northerners as the primary agents in educating the freed slaves in the aftermath of the Civil War has obscured the role of Black Catholic women in the long history of a transatlantic pedagogical circuit.[202]

The pioneering intervention of the antebellum Sisters of the Holy Family to imagine an interracial sisterhood committed to embodying a universal humanity through education in New Orleans, home to the nation's largest slave market, was indeed radical. The thirty-five-year journey from an informal group of young Afro-Creole girls teaching in their neighborhood school, to an approved religious congregation speaks to the profound power they and their community saw in education as central to acknowledging all people's dignity and humanity. Establishing schools for free people of color and the enslaved, however imperfect, was a radical political act. Given the formation of the Sisters of the Holy Family and the Bayou Road School in 1842, their story compels us to ask why their educational activism has been eclipsed by the dominant narrative of education in New Orleans as beginning with so-called "public" education (white only) in 1841.[203] These two events cannot be seen as separate/parallel histories but must be acknowledged as deeply implicated and intertwined. Elevating "public" education in the history of Louisiana functions to obscure the long history of Afro-Franco-Catholic educational institution building in which the vision of interracialism was the norm. While this goal had to be continually adapted, given the increasingly repressive, racist system of slave apartheid, the Sisters of the Holy Family were able to anchor educational institutions whose influence extended worldwide and still continue today. The untold thousands of students across time and space impacted by this transatlantic Afro-Franco creole vision of universal education speaks to a much longer history of a counterpublic vision of education dating well before 1841. This is a history that was revolutionary in its quest for human equality yet is still in the making.

Counterpublics as Creole Pedagogies

While New Orleans, and Louisiana, have often been characterized as delayed in their development of public education (1841), it is essential to reiterate again that the "public" education that emerged in the 1840s in Louisiana was not public, it was for "whites" only.[204] Prior to 1841, attempts at establishing public education, meaning schools that had open access to all students regardless of class, race, or ethnicity had been ongoing in Louisiana since the Ursulines through to the Sisters of the Holy Family and through Governor Claiborne's early legislative actions, including the College d'Orléans. While the late establishment of "public" education in New Orleans has often been attributed to resistance to Americanization given the large French-Afro-Catholic population, alternatively I suggest that it was American resistance to interracial, universal education that resulted in segregated public education as a mechanism to exclude Black people from the body politic. The creation of public, segregated education sheds light on the larger transatlantic revolutionary world within which education, and its corollary, citizenship, was being racialized in the early eighteenth century. Across the country in Washington D.C., Philadelphia, Boston, Baltimore, New York, and New Haven, Black education came under attack.

Hilary Moss maintains that "The expansion of public schooling and white opposition to black education thus was not coincidental. To the contrary, they were part and parcel of a larger impulse to expel black people from the polity in the early nineteenth century."[205] Ironically, the introduction of exclusively white public schools in New Orleans in 1841 contributed *not* to expanding citizenship and democracy, but instead contributed to reifying social constructions of citizenship as white and race as permanent and scientifically grounded.[206]

Tensions around race, ethnicity, religion, and language had ultimately led in 1836 to key "American" leaders pushing legislative approval to divide New Orleans into three separate municipalities: the first covering the French Quarter; the second the new American sector above Canal Street, and the third downriver from Esplanade Avenue. Each sector operated as a virtually independent city with its own school system and superintendent managed by its own board of directors. Between 1836 and 1841, the municipalities operated independently to develop school systems. The second municipality, under the leadership of Joseph Baldwin, quickly adopted the model of Horace Mann, which included the segregation of schools by race and gender. The first and third municipalities, which were predominantly Catholic and French-speaking, continued to operate bilingual, sex-segregated schools, and often interracial schools.

In February of 1841, the state legislature passed a law that apportioned to the councils of the municipalities shares of the existing state appropriations for public education, on the condition that they match those funds with their own appropriations. For most historians of education, this marks the beginning of "public education" in New Orleans. By 1842, schools in the city, while still demarcated by race and gender, were now primarily divided by whether they were state-sponsored, receiving public funds and thus all white, or non-state-sponsored (Figure 17). The formation of state-run publicly funded schools advocated by social reformers like Horace Mann were also supported by Protestant businessmen who saw schools as critical to economic growth and to stabilizing cities increasingly populated by immigrants, as well as African Americans. Creating cohesion through the common school movement "gave white children from all classes and ethnicities the opportunity to become citizens or, at the very least, to feel a part of the larger society; yet at the same time it also reinforced a conception of citizenship as synonymous with whiteness in which black Americans, enslaved or free, could not participate."[207] Constructing "public" schools or state-sponsored schools functioned to produce citizenship as "whiteness."[208] For Afro-Creole free people of color and the enslaved, this

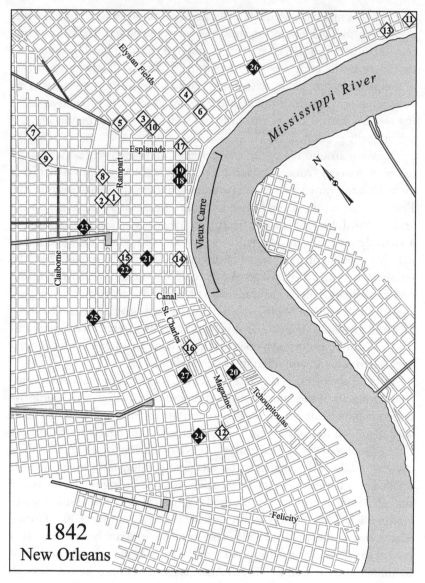

Figure 17. Map of the schools in New Orleans, 1842. Drawn by Mary Lee Eggart based on *New Orleans Directory for 1842* (Pitts and Clarke: New Orleans, 1842) and *The New Orleans City Directory* (New Orleans 1842). Main Branch New Orleans Public Library.

Non State-Funded Schools
(Open Access to FPC and possibly others):

1. Francois D'Herbecourt
   (St. Domingue Refugee)

2. Sainte-Barbe Academy
   (Director Michel Seligny/FMC)

3. Joseph Bazanac (FMC) and Jean Louis Marciacq (Frenchmen)

4. Ludger Boguille & Wife, Grand Hommes School (FPC)

5. Joanni Questy (FMC)

6. Tuhait Lois (FMC)

7. Paul Trevigne (FMC)

8. Sisters of Mount Caramel
   (FPC All Girls School)

9. Bayou Road School, Henriette Delille
   (FPC All Girls School)

10. Catholic Institute for Indigent Orphans (FPC, officially opened 1848)

11. Ursuline Convent School

12. New Orleans Female Orphan Asylum
    (Sisters of Charity)

13. Catholic Male St. Mary's Orphan Asylum

14. Boyer's Academy (G. Boyers, Diago Morphy, Moroy Morozoni Guilpi)

15. Female Academy
    (Clotilde Bornet, since 1822)

16. New Lafayette Academy (J.M. Weymouth, I. Coffin, R. Crawford)

17. G.W. Harby's School
    (in 1841 private school)

State Funded Schools
(WHITE ONLY, commonly referred to as PUBLIC Schools):

18. Central School

19. Lower Primary School

20. Upper Primary School

21. First District (male and female)

22. Second District
    (male and female)

23. Third District (male and female)

24. Third Ward

25. Fourth Ward

26. G.W. Harby, principal

27. Poydras Female Orphan Asylum (established 1817)

constriction of education marked another step toward their exclusion from full citizenship, excluding them from the rights of full and equal membership of a common humanity.

When American leaders outnumbered French Creoles they took control of the Louisiana legislature in 1845, extending the provisions of the 1841 legislation to the state's other parishes and called for free public education for all white children in the constitutional convention. By 1847 the new legislature complied with the new constitutional mandate to fund a state-wide system of "white" only education. While this was the official law, the racial mixing of schools continued, as evidenced by the need for regular inspections of the public schools in the first and third municipality for students who had any trace of African ancestry. Ongoing trespassing of this new "color line" and restrictions to regulate the teaching of the enslaved in private schools run by free people of color eventually required a city resolution, passed in 1852, which made "it a duty of the police to inquire into the condition and character of free negro schools . . . and whether or not slaves were educated in them."[209]

While Afro-Creole free people of color and their Francophone allies were eventually forced to segregate their educational institutions (the focus of the next chapter), it must be remembered that this accommodation to ever-increasing racial hostility occurred only after half a century of robust educational institutional building and experiments, many of which sought to create counterpublic spaces, in which students from all social classes and racial backgrounds could be educated in common spaces. While there is inadequate evidence to ascertain to what degree enslaved people became literate, we do know that by 1850, 91 percent of whites and 60 percent of free Blacks were literate. In comparison, Baltimore, another city with a network of private and Catholic schools for free Blacks, had literacy rates that were lower, reaching only 41 percent.[210] In New Orleans, nearly one-third of school-aged free children of color attended school in 1850, compared to one-sixth in Baltimore. This is a remarkable achievement given the staunch resistance among whites to education for both free people of color and the enslaved.

When we look across the Gulf South, as well as the rest of the state of Louisiana, we see that New Orleans was not an exception in the efforts of free people of color and the enslaved to build educational institutions. While much scholarship has focused on free people of color in New Orleans, rural, farming communities like Point Coupée, Opelousas, and Natchitoches also had significant populations who engaged in educational institution building. Opelousas, which had been established in 1720 as an outpost/fort for French trappers who traded with the Opelousas, list in their 1792 census 20 free people of color. Enslaved Africans who arrived at the post and were freed increased the population to 82 free persons of color in the 1763 census. By 1850, the Attakapas and Opelousas regions had a robust population of free people of color numbering 2,234.[211] In the 1830s, a school for free people of color, the Grimble Bell School, was established in Washington. It was a private school that offered instruction on both the primary and secondary level for the education of children of free people of color, the majority of whom were planters in the area.[212] During the antebellum period the school enrolled an average of 125 students, and the teaching staff consisted of four teachers who used the Lancastrian method of teaching. The monthly tuition was fifteen dollars for board and tuition. The school taught all the usual subjects, including writing, arithmetic, history, accounting, French, English, and Latin. By 1860, however, the anti-free-black St. Landry night riders had forced the school to close. After it closed, many of the students were sent to New Orleans to attend private schools for free people of color. After the Civil War, Emerson Bentley, a young white teacher from Ohio, came to Opelousas and staffed a Freedmen's Bureau school for freed slaves as well as free people of color. In the 1868 election, he enraged whites with his radical Republican activism and was attacked and beaten by a white mob. The "Opelousas Riot," as it was known, resulted in the school's closure. It was not until the Sisters of the Holy Family opened the Academy of St. Joseph in 1874 that education was again available to the African American community.

In northwest Louisiana, the first French settlement founded in 1712, Natchitoches, eventually became the second most important religious center of the state and home to a large community of Catholic free people of color. Descendants of the interracial partnerships of the early eighteenth century settled just south of Natchitoches, in Isle Brevelle, becoming prosperous farmers and traders, with many of them owning enslaved Africans. In 1829, Augustin Metoyer, a free man of color and one of the wealthiest men in the Natchitoches area, constructed a Catholic church in honor of St. Augustine, which is considered one of the oldest Black Catholic churches in the United States. In his last will and testament, he made clear that "outsiders [whites] possessing our holy, catholic, apostolic, and Roman religion will have the right to assist at the divine office in the said chapel."[213] His emphasis on an interracial congregation highlights the reach and extent of

Catholic universalism throughout Louisiana, denoting that New Orleans was not an exception. Free children of color attended not only the Grimble Bell School, but the Ursuline Academy in New Orleans, as well as Catholic colleges in Kentucky, St. Louis, and Georgetown.[214]

In many ways we might say that the early nineteenth century in the Gulf South—not just New Orleans—was a "Golden Age" for educational experimentation in interracial education. Fueled by the legacy of Catholic universalism, the Haitian Revolution, and the vision of human equality, there is a rich legacy of experimentation to establish public education well before 1841. Public, in this sense, did not always mean "state"-funded. What made many of these schools public was a common commitment to educate all students regardless of race, ethnicity, social class, or gender. This was accomplished through a number of different ways: partial state funding, through a "tuition" system, through philanthropic gifts, or through laboring to make ends meet. Undergirding these attempts was a commitment to signifying a common humanity through universal education. This is a dream still deferred.

For many "exiles," including French emigres, refugees from Saint-Domingue, both white and free people of color, and Africans in the revolutionary Atlantic world arriving in New Orleans, education was an important venue for creating counterpublics, providing a site to create institutional alternatives to an increasingly harsh racial order. For those who embraced the republican ideals of the revolutionary era and the universalism of the Catholic Church, "public" spaces—in particular educational spaces—were critical spaces in which to embody the values of universal equality. Joseph Bazanac, Sister Ste. Marthe Fortiére, Joseph Lakanal, James Workman, Jean Aliquot, Henriette Delille, Josephine Charles and Juliette Gaudin represent a transatlantic group of educators whose vision of universal, interracial education provides an alternative trajectory to the well-worn narratives of "public education" that obscures the revolutionary, radical educational vision of "exiles" at home. They brought a unique diasporic, multilingual, multinational, and multiethnic cultural identity to bear on the ways they imagined freedom, citizenship, and democracy, and their corollary, education. The stories of these exiles challenge dominant narratives of educational history by situating New Orleans as part of the vibrant, dynamic, revolutionary transatlantic world. New Orleans provided a space to imagine the role that education might play in shaping a community grounded in the revolutionary ideals of a common humanity.

Reverberations

On August 29, 2005, no one could have anticipated the impact that hurricane Katrina would have on public education in New Orleans: elimination. While 1841 is hailed as a momentous step in the march of democracy in Louisiana, 2005 might be marked as the year public education officially ended. Of course, it could be said that public education has never really existed. From 1841 to 1861, "public" education was "white" only. From 1861 to 1878, the schools were integrated, but most whites refused to attend. After Radical Reconstruction, white supremacists made sure that no Blacks attended public schools. And by 1896, segregation was legalized, and for all practical purposes, public schools were white. Apartheid education became the norm, with Black communities and schools the new Soweto. After *Brown vs. Board of Education*, most whites in New Orleans resisted integration through white flight to private and Catholic schools. By 2005, New Orleans public schools were over 90 percent Black. In other words, the intent of public education has never been fulfilled.

The history of public education is clearly not one of progress. It is certainly not a story of success. It is a story of the complex ways in which education is continually invented and reinvented in order to maintain a human hierarchy of value and worth. The very founding of "public education" as "white only" marked the supposed superiority of one race over another. In the aftermath of Katrina, all New Orleans public schools, which were more than 90 percent Black, were taken over by the state-run Recovery School District (RSD), and all 7,500 New Orleans public school teachers, 75 percent of whom were Black, were fired. The public school system was dismantled and replaced by private entrepreneurs who understand education as part of the marketplace. In many ways this is not unsimilar to the New Orleans "slave market" described by Robert Johnson in his groundbreaking book *Soul by Soul*. In the new market economy of schools, students are reduced to data, in which they are graded, ranked, and valued, disciplined and standardized, then put on the college or career-readiness market. If along the way, they are disobedient or unsuccessful, they are returned to the market, to another school, or to the prison system. This is the complete commodification of human beings, not far removed from antebellum New Orleans.

Perhaps the stories in this chapter of Joseph Bazanac, Sister Ste. Marthe Fortiére, Joseph Lakanal, James Workman, Jean Aliquot, Henriette Delille, Josephine Charles, and Juliette Gaudin remind us that the work of education for humanity is a daily practice. Even within oppressive systems, there are spaces of resistance. Oppressive systems do not work monolithically. Creating counterpublic spaces, whether it be through the hard work of maintaining and building community networks, staying put on sacred ground, or taking up vulnerable identities, is the pedagogical work of claiming one's humanity. The stories in this chapter tell us this. While we will always live in systems of power, this does not oblige us to capitulate. The goal is not to reform education or revolutionize it: this is an impossible dream, one made of grand narratives and final endings. Instead, the work of education is in the practices of the everyday in which we acknowledge the humanity of each person. That is a pedagogical moment.

FOUR

A Curriculum of Imagination

Counterpublic Spaces in the Age of Segregation, 1841–1868

May 27, 1858
To S. Armstrong, Esq.
Attakapas, La.

Dear Brother,

The Catholic Institution, to which I belong has increased its prices two weeks ago and I will tell you the causes thereof. You know yourself, dear brother, that the prejudice against the colored population is very strong in this part of the country. The Legislation used to give every year, for this establishment, fifteen hundred dollars; but this year, when they went to get it, they did not want to give anything at all, and they treated them very bad. Then the Direction (director) of this establishment had a session so as to see what could be done. They saw that they could not go any further. Then they increased the contribution of every scholar, by a few cents. The pupils who have a father and mother, have to pay fifty cents a month, instead of twenty, those who have their mother only, have to pay half price. But the ones who are deprived of both, their father and mother needn't to pay nothing at all. Is this not too bad, my dear brother? The white people have an Institution in every district, and they are all protected very well. But we, who have, but a single one, cannot be protected at all.

Your invariable friend,
Frilot[1]

The sense of despair that A. Frilot, a free teenage boy of color, conveys in his letter reflects the increasing racial discrimination being experienced by students at the L'Institution Catholique des Orphelins dans Indigence (the Catholic Institute), the public school for free people of color in New Orleans. For the young Frilot, he had most likely already experienced the harsh sting of racism. A native of Opelousas, it can be surmised that he was one of several boys who transferred from the Grimble Bell School in Washington, Louisiana, to the Catholic Institute when the Grimble Bell School had been forced to close due to the terrorizing threats of white vigilantes, the St. Landry night riders. The state's withdrawal of funding for the school was one more indignity and injustice that free people of color were forced to endure. As Frilot points out, the schools for whites in every district were being funded, but the withdrawal of funds from the Catholic Institute in 1858 marked the first time since its founding in 1848 that the state had not given it some financial support. While state-supported New Orleans schools had been segregated since 1841, the state had continued to provide some funding for the Catholic Institute, making it for all practical purposes a public institution. But 1858 marked a turning point: Not only would schools continue to be segregated in New Orleans, but only white schools would be financed by the state. For the community of free people of color, who had spent decades building educational institutions to claim a space in the public sphere signifying their full humanity, this was a severe setback to their activist agenda.

The withdrawal of public funds for Black education followed on the heels of the 1857 Supreme Court decision *Dred Scott v. Sandford*.[2] This landmark decision held that the U.S. Constitution was not meant to include American citizenship for Black people, regardless of whether they were enslaved or free, and so the rights and privileges that the Constitution confers upon American citizens could not apply to them. In March of 1857, the Supreme Court had issued a 7-2 decision against Dred Scott, a slave who sued for his freedom on the basis that he had traveled to free soil with his master. The Court ruled that Black people "are not included, and were not intended to be included, under the word 'citizens' in the Constitution, and can therefore claim none of the rights and privileges which that instrument provides for and secures to citizens of the United States." Chief Justice Taney supported his ruling by suggesting that the Constitution's drafting in 1787 was designed with the intent to show that a "perpetual and impassable barrier was intended to be erected between the white race and the one which they had reduced to slavery." Because the Court ruled that Scott was not an American citizen, he was also not a citizen of any state and, accordingly, could never establish citizenship. For young Frilot, and the community of free people of color, the Dred Scott decision foreclosed the long-awaited prospect of recognized citizenship in the United States.

Bearing the brunt of exclusion, Frilot and his fellow classmates and teachers were left to imagine how full freedom and citizenship might yet be achieved. But for the time being they focused on their studies, having already been taught that education and freedom were intimately linked. Several letters written during the week of May 27, 1858, conveyed concerns about the impact of the increased tuition, including whether students would be forced to leave the school and the outrage of parents at rising costs. What made this financial burden more painful was that it brought home the privilege of white children at Black children's expense. Frilot was quite aware that whites had schools that were paid for through public funding, whereas free people of color paid taxes and received no educational assurances in return.

The ongoing indignities suffered by free people of color had already caused many to emigrate to other countries where they would enjoy the full benefits of citizenship. In 1810 the free people of color population made up 29 percent of New Orleans. By 1850, the percent of free people of color had dwindled to 9 percent of the city's population.[3] For many free people of color, the increasing legal restrictions and discrimination were intolerable. While many had moved permanently to France, others chose to stay closer to New Orleans by relocating to Mexico, Haiti, and Cuba rather than endure continued persecution.[4]

For those remaining in New Orleans, the Catholic Institute, as well as other Black institutions including Masonic lodges, literary associations, and benevolent societies created "black counter-publics" as a means of fostering political activities that allowed them to claim their political subjectivity despite their racial subordination.[5] Unlike the institution building prior to 1841 that sought to create interracial spaces, the institutions built after 1841 were out of necessity segregated, in other words, designed to serve the Black community. The ultimate success of these institutions, however, rested on the decades-long activism that created a rich social network, community institutions, economic wealth, and a relational space-based matrix in which the meanings of a place were not ahistorical, but always connected to people, communities, and the past, present, and future.

The Catholic Institute: A Community Assemblage

In 1837, widow Marie Justine Couvent, a free woman of color in New Orleans and devout Catholic, bequeathed to the Catholic Church the money necessary to provide a "free school for orphans of color of the Faubourg Marigny."[6] Marie Couvent was born about 1757 in West Africa, where she was enslaved as a child and in the 1760s sent to Saint-Domingue. She escaped to New Orleans around 1804 during the Haitian Revolution and purchased property in both the French Quarter, on Barracks Street in close proximity to the Ursuline convent, and in the newly developing Faubourg Marigny at the corner of Grand Hommes and Union. It is likely that Couvent worked peddling goods at the market, raising enough money to also buy slaves; by 1812 she owned five.[7] One of these slaves, [Gabriel] Bernard Couvent, a carpenter and former enslaved of the Ursulines, she freed, and in 1812 they married.

Over the course of the next twenty years, Marie and Bernard Couvent were part of a growing network of free people of color who would be considered institution builders. As a carpenter, Bernard would have been connected to other artisans who were working in the growing suburbs of Tremé and Marigny. The Marigny was particularly popular given the affordability and availability of lots. In 1809, Bernard Marigny had marketed 535 lots in what he called the New Marigny. This was prime real estate, and for the free people of color from Saint-Domingue who were builders, this provided ample opportunity to establish businesses. Among the most notable builders that Bernard Couvent would most likely have known were Jean-Louis Dolliole, Joseph Dolliole, Henry Fletcher, Louis Nelson Fouché, and Charles Laveaux. These builders were not only ambitious entrepreneurs; they were well-educated and deeply invested in building a strong Afro-Creole community through developing networks in the Catholic Church, Masonic lodges, and business enterprises. Bernard and Marie were part of this network. Bernard profited from all the construction and amassed a considerable estate, which he left to his wife Marie when he died in 1829 at the age of seventy-one. Networks were also forged through Bernard's son, also a carpenter, and his grandson, whose godparents were Marie and Bernard.

While Marie Couvent could not sign her name, it would have been clear to her that education, along with legal status, property ownership, and marital status, were significant markers for free people of color in securing social standing and respectability in New Orleans. Perhaps most importantly, these markers contributed to securing their independence, which was paramount to retaining the freedoms they still exercised. It would not have gone unnoticed by Couvent, who lived a stone's throw from the Ursuline convent, that schools were springing up almost on every street corner during the decade of the 1820s and early 1830s. Of course, the Ursuline Academy would have been intimately familiar to her, and she was certainly aware that the academy's move downriver in 1824 had left a vacuum in educational institutions for people of color. A young ladies academy had opened a block from her home on Barracks. The Lancaster School for Colored Children also opened only a few blocks away, and the interracial St. Claude School had opened in the former College d'Orléans. These were only the schools directly in her neighborhood. Walking to her property in the Marigny, Couvent would have passed several private schools that served students of all colors. While there was a blossoming of schools, none were specifically designated for orphans of color. In 1832, while suffering from illness, she wrote her will stipulating that funds be used to establish a free school for orphans of color.

There were only three orphanages in New Orleans at the time: The Poydras Asylum for Girls at 153 Julie Street, established by Protestant women in 1817, the orphanage at the Ursuline convent, and the Asylum for Destitute Orphan Boys, opened by Protestant men in 1824. It was not until 1836 that the Catholic Church would open a facility for orphaned girls known as the Female Orphan Asylum, run by the Sisters of Charity. These institutions preceded the establishment of public schools, providing children of the poor and those who had no family their only opportunity for an education. Both of the Protestant orphanages established prior to Couvent's will, however, did not admit children of color.[8] In other words, at the time she wrote her will in 1832, there were few, if any, options for destitute children of color.

Couvent's astute perception of the need for an institution to educate poor children of color, which she laid the groundwork for in her will, far preceded that of other free people of color activists and philanthropists. St. Mary's Academy, started by the Sisters of the Holy Family and which included on orphanage, was not in operation until 1848. The Thomy Lafon Orphan's Home, funded by Thomy Lafon (1810–1893), a wealthy free man of color and philanthropist, housed and educated orphaned boys of color starting in 1893 and was administered by the Sisters of the Holy Family. Madame Couvent clearly saw the need for education among those in most need. In this regard she was a pioneer whom others followed as a model for increasing the opportunities for education for all classes of Black children. Her agency as a former enslaved African and free woman of color with no formal education enlarges our understanding of those who initiated educational institutions across gender and class boundaries within the community of free people of color. While scholars have given credit to Couvent for the financing that made the school possible, credit for actually fulfilling her bequest has been a subject of controversy. The Catholic priest, Father Maenhaut, who was the religious supervisor of her estate, is given credit, as is Henry Fletcher, a free man of color, who was named executor of her will. The fundraising initiative of François LaCroix and Armand Lanusse, which were critical to bringing the school to life, also receive a great deal of attention. These obscure the agency of Couvent as the visionary of the school.

Couvent recovered from her illness in 1832 and lived another five years after writing her will. Upon her death in 1837, Henry Fletcher took over as executor of the estate. Public officials at the time, though, opposed expanding educational opportunities for free people of color and discouraged the formation of the school. After ten years and after aiding in the formation of the Sisters of the Holy Family, Father Maenhaut, along with François LaCroix, Louis Nelson Fouché, Armand Lanusse, Adolphe Duhart, Barthelemy Rey, Emile Brule, and other prominent French-speaking free men of color gathered to carrying out widow Couvent's will.[9] This mix of native New Orleanian free men of color (Dollioles, Decoudreau, and Fletcher) and descendants of Saint-Domingue refugees (LaCroix, Fouché, Duhart, Rey, and Brule) represented the bonds of brotherhood that had been forged over several decades with the goal of establishing educational infrastructures that made education accessible to as many people as possible.[10] These men formed the "Catholic Society for the Instruction of Indigent Orphans," which was chartered in Baton Rouge in 1847. In 1848, the society was able to execute the terms of the Couvent will and Armand Lanusse (1812–1867), a leading intellectual in the community, took leadership of establishing the school, designing the curriculum, and hiring the faculty.

While the school remained under the auspices of the Catholic Church (which functioned to legitimate and protect the school), the institution admitted children of any religious denomination, French-and English-speaking students, rich and poor children, as well as boys and girls, who were housed on separate floors. At various times, the board of directors had heated discussions about whether the school should educate enslaved children, but given the severe penalties for educating slaves, the directors decided that slave owners themselves should direct the Catholic education of their slaves.[11] According to the school's prospectus, every child, *both* girls and boys, would receive a practical, moral, and religious education, regardless of economic status or future profession. The curriculum was designed to offer "invaluable advantage" to children of the poorest classes who might only be able to attend a few months or at most a year.[12] Orphan children were educated for free, while the remaining students paid tuition.[13] According to Mary Mitchell, "the Catholic Institute was the cornerstone of the Afro-Creoles' political work. One in which they developed a radical agenda aimed at attaining civil and political rights for people of color in the Americas."[14]

The status of the Catholic Institute as either a "public" or "private" space has long been contested. While some have characterized it as "the most famous Negro private school," evidence suggests that the directors and the free people of color considered the school a public one.[15] Donations and such sent to the Catholic Institute were often addressed to the "Public School for Indigent Orphans of the Third District" (l'Ecole Publique des Orphelins indigents du Troiseme District). The school had received funds from the state legislature from 1848 until 1858. The directors justified their request for state funding by saying that Black property owners had to pay taxes for "white" public schools their children could not attend. This blatant exclusion from the public sphere fueled the activism of Afro-Creoles, who, according to Rebecca Scott, saw "public" rights as reflecting "an even deeper and more radical insistence on the moral equality of all human beings" than political or civic rights.[16] Directors of the school did manage to convince the state legislature and the New Orleans city council to appropriate money to the school for the care of its indigent and orphaned pupils. These grants may well have constituted the first governmental subsidy for Black education in the South.[17] The school's board of directors also agreed to follow the disciplinary rules of the public schools. By mimicking the public schools, as well as providing a rigorous education to *all* free children of color regardless of class or gender, the Catholic Institute sought to position itself as part of the public sphere.

Classes operated on the basis of the pupil's aptitude and progress, meaning classes were composed of multiple ages, and only at the turn of the century was the regular grade system adopted. In 1850, 1,008 free children of color were attending schools in New Orleans, many at the Catholic Institute.[18] It is estimated that in 1850 almost 80 percent of the city's free people of color were literate.[19] In 1852 there were 165 students enrolled at the Catholic Institute, the number of boys and girls being equal. In the following year there were 240 students, 25 percent of the free children of color attending school in New Orleans. The school provided pupils with six years of instruction, and classes were taught in French. English was taught as a second language. In addition to the traditional subjects, the school's curriculum included drawing, music, and logic, as well as bookkeeping and geometry for use in carpentry and machine building. Boys and girls from across the city attended.

With a cadre of Afro-Creole men and women teachers, Armand Lanusse developed a curriculum that challenged emerging theories of scientific racism that posited Blacks as intellectually inferior. The curriculum was designed to counteract American conceptions of race that were based in a dual conception in which one was either white or Black. Throughout the 1850s this color line was increasingly legislated to construct and maintain racial boundaries that segregated the races.[20] This legislation not only disregarded the unique identity and culture of free people of color, but it was designed to establish white supremacy. Challenging these dominant stereotypes, the Catholic Institute had to work within the increasingly severe restrictions placed on Blacks in antebellum New Orleans to protect their culture, language, and quest for full citizenship. The Catholic Institute was designed as a counterpublic space to provide a rigorous curriculum in which students were to become activists who imagined what freedom and full citizenship in a democratic society based on human equality might look like.

The school opened in 1848 with Félicie Callioux, a free woman of color and the wife of André, a cigar maker, as principal. André Callioux, who would become the first Black hero of the Civil War, is perhaps more well-known.[21] Overshadowed by her husband, Félicie Callioux's remarkable journey from enslaved to free woman of color to school administrator reflects the long-neglected role of female agency in the educational activism of free people of color. She was born Félicie Coulon in 1818 on Grand Isle to Antoine Coulon a slave, and Feliciana, a slave of Valentin Encalada. Félicie's mother was freed by Encalada in New Orleans in 1835. After raising enough money, Feliciana purchased her slave daughter, Félicie, from Encalada in 1841, and freed her through the manumission process in 1846.[22] In June of 1847, Félicie married the former slave André Callioux. Afterwards, the couple purchased property and a slave, André's mother. The Calliouxes settled in the faubourg Lafayette on a racially and economically diverse block from which André traveled each morning to his cigar shop on Union and Royal, two blocks downriver from the French Quarter and one block from the Catholic Institute. Félicie was described as "exceedingly intelligent, highly respected and a devout Catholic.[23] We can only speculate as to how she became educated. Since she was not freed until the age of twenty-one, it is most likely that she received her education while she was the slave of Valentia Encalada.

The Catholic Institute hired five teachers: Joseph Bazanac (son of Jean Baptiste, introduced in chapter 3), Ludger B. Boguille, Joseph Vigneaux-Lavigne, Madame Joseph Bazanac, and Adolphe Duhart. All were experienced teachers—many had taught at private schools—who brought a wealth of experience with them. Joseph Bazanac, whose father had opened a school in the French Quarter in 1811, was teaching at an interracial school he and French exile Jean Louis Marciacq were operating right across the street from what would become the Catholic Institute. Ludger B. Boguille had begun a private academy in 1840 at 37 Great Men Street, which enrolled about forty children, girls and boys.[24] In addition he gave private lessons to the enslaved in their homes. After beginning his teaching at the Catholic Institute, his school on Great Men Street remained open and was run by his "wife," Mary Ann Taff, a white northerner who was an English teacher who had come from New York to work in the free colored community. Together they lived at 198 Esplanade Street, where they raised Boguille's four children from his first marriage whose mother had died, two orphaned children whose relatives were from Saint-Domingue, and eventually their own two children. Boguille was also a member of the Société d'Economie et d'Assitance Mutuelle (the Economy and Mutual Aid Association), founded in 1836 as a social and benevolent society. It is yet another example of the institution building among Afro-Creoles of color that functioned as a counterpublic space in which men who were denied their full equality and citizenship in the public sphere could create their own worlds in which they could aid others and, in the process, assert their humanity. The society's mission was "to help one another and teach one another while holding out a protective hand to suffering humanity."[25] Clearly, education is seen as lifelong endeavor through which one can come to understand the human condition.

By 1852, the school had grown tremendously, which required the addition of faculty and staff. Armand Lanusse, who became principal at this time, recruited his teachers from the intelligentsia and literary artists who had burgeoned in New Orleans in the preceding decades. Over the next twenty years, the faculty included Constant Reynès, Joseph Vigneaux-Lavigne, Joanni Questy, Francois Escoffie, Noel J. Bacchus, Basile Crokere, Samuel Snaier, Louis Lainez, J. Manuel Camps, William F. Vigers, Louis Nelson Fouché, Nathalie Populus Mello, Paul Trévigne, Armand and Adolphe Duhart, Henry Louis Rey, Aristide Mary, Rodolphe Lucien Desdunes, Eugene Luscy, and Louis A. Martinet.[26] The Catholic Institute had a wellspring of highly educated Afro-Creole activists from which to draw on in staffing their school. This was no doubt due the quality of education available to Afro-Creole children, as well as a rich literary tradition of Afro-Creole Francophone writing and publishing that had flourished in the early part of the nineteenth century.

This flowering of Afro-Creole literature in the 1830s and 1840s was a direct response to the increasing Americanization of Louisiana in which the unique identity of free people of color was being threatened by the imposition of a binary racial social organization.[27] Fighting to retain their language, culture, identity, and rights, they were also shaped by the French Romantic movement, which emphasized not only the expression of self, but also of the marginalized and the oppressed. The assertion by French Romantic writers and poets, like Victor Hugo and Lamartine, that one could embrace both individuality (a unique identity) and universality (being part of a common culture/democracy) offered a "transatlantic reimagining" to Afro-Creoles throughout the Atlantic world in which they could envision a political community around republican ideals of *libertié*, *égalité*, and *fraternité* without sacrificing the specificity of their Afro-Creole culture.[28]

While much has been written about this literature, the connections between this literary movement and education has received less attention. The first Black literary publication in the United States, *L'Album littéraire: journal des jeunes gens, amateurs de littérature*, was launched in 1843 by Armand Lanusse (1812–1868) and Joanni Questy (1817–1869). It published the works of both French Creoles and Creoles of color. Although only six issues were published, it was bold for its time and place. Both Lannuse and Questy would serve as principals at the Catholic Institute, Lanusse from 1852 to 1868, during which time Questy was assistant principal, and upon Lanusse's death Questy was principal from 1868 to 1869, when he died unexpectedly. In addition, Questy taught French and Spanish at the school and influenced two generations of students. He later went on to write for the newspaper *La Tribune* (the focus of chapter 5) and in 1867 published a novella, *Monsieur Paul*, a highly politicized work of fiction set in the Civil War which critiques the United States through highlighting the revolutionary universalism of Haiti. Adolphe Duhart (1830–1908), a prolific poet who contributed numerous poems to *Les Cenelles*, used his writing to highlight the hypocrisy of racial ideologies in a country that maintained it was a democracy. Also a beloved teacher at the Catholic Institute, he took over as principal after the death of Questy. His father Louis-Adolphe Duhart, who had roots in Saint-Domingue, served on the board of directors that incorporated the Catholic Institute. His brother Armand served on the school's board of directors, and his mother Françoise Palmyre Brouard, originally from Saint-Domingue, was also a teacher at the school.

Two years after the publication of the journal in 1845, Armand Lanusse edited *Les Cenelles: choix de poésies indigènes* (The Mayhaws: Selected Indigenous Poetry), a collection of eighty poems by seventeen Afro-Creole writers, considered the first anthology of African American literature published in the United States.[29] Both *L'Album littéraire* and *Les Cenelles* provided a venue to develop a discourse of protest by Afro-Creoles to challenge the eroding civil liberties for people of color. In contesting racism, they addressed not only the plight of free people of color, but also the enslaved. Critical to their work was situating their struggle for full equality within the larger context of the revolutionary transatlantic. The transnational nature of the exchange of ideas was part of a global network that linked Afro-Creoles both to France and the Caribbean and Mexico. These relationships allowed Afro-Creoles to expand their community networks by developing a sense of allegiance to other free people of color in other transatlantic nations and imagining their lives outside of the confines of American racism. The teachers at the Catholic Institute brought this expansive vision of racial equality, set in a global context, to the students through a rigorous curriculum grounded in the humanities, arts, and literature. Armand Lanusse was one of the most well-respected intellectuals and writers in their community.

"I Am a Man": The Writer's Life

A need for learning is being felt everywhere. We are beginning to understand that no matter what situation fate has placed us in, a good education is a shield against the spiteful and calumnious arrows shot at us.[30]

The "shield" to which Armand Lanusse, a New Orleans Afro-Creole free man of color born to Haitian refugee parents, refers to is education. Lanusse's introduction to *Les Cenelles* (1845), declared that a "good education" was the shield that would protect young men and women of color from the "spiteful" arrows of racial discrimination. While Lanusse has received much scholarly attention for his literary work, his life and work as a radical educator has generally been ignored. As part of a larger community of free persons of color whose Afro-Franco-Catholic traditions can be traced to at least the beginnings of the French colonial period, Lanusse was part of an Afro-Creole protest tradition shaped by a multilingual, transcultural, transatlantic process of creolization that was critical to his unique theorizing of the relationship between identity, education, freedom, and citizenship. Citizenship was not understood as a static political or civic right (which ultimately always essentializes), but as situated in the ongoing tensions between a vision of the equality of all human beings and the possibilities of given historical circumstances.

Lanusse was part of the emergence of a class of educated persons of color, proficient in multiple languages, the classics, music, theater, and drama that challenged the increasingly insidious images of Black inferiority perpetuated in the emerging constructs of "scientific racism." By 1830, legislation was passed making it a crime to write anything that might cause "discontent among free people of color or insubordination among the slaves," the penalty being life imprisonment at hard labor or death. By 1855, a revision of the Code Noir of 1806 by the state legislature placed restrictions on the manumission of slaves. Other laws restricted freedom of assembly and curtailed the freedom of movement of free persons of color by requiring free people of color to carry passes certifying their status. The assaults on their rights made it imperative to men like Lanusse that education was even more important than ever to empower youth with a sense of self-confidence and agency.

Armand Lanusse, unlike many other free men of color, was not sent to Paris to receive his education, but most likely attended one of the small private schools in the French Quarter. He would have been educated by a tutor in the classics, French, and Latin, and introduced to the great French Romantic writers such as Alexandre Dumas, Victor Hugo (who set one of his novels during the Haitian Revolution), Alphonse de Lamartine (an advocate of universal suffrage), and Pierre-Jean de Béranger (an advocate of social reform). This group of French Romantic writers had an abiding faith in the ideals of the French Revolution. No doubt these writers, among others, had a deep impact on Lanusse as he imagined a society in which all men would be treated as full human beings. In fact, Lanusse was part of a larger network of transnational intellectuals whose political radicalism was, according to Caryn Cosseé Bell, based in the egalitarianism of the age of democratic revolution, a Catholic universalist ethic, and Romantic philosophy that saw education as central to liberation.[31] Shaped by the ideals of the Haitian and French Revolutions, as well as the revolutionary fervor of French émigrés to New Orleans, Lanusse's vision of an egalitarian society came to fruition in a unique interracial intellectual tradition that saw "public" education as critical to humanization and the democratic ideals of equality.

As a young man in his early thirties, Lanusse saw education not only as a means to maintain a vibrant Afro-Creole culture, but as a means to counter the racial degradation implicit in a plantation/slavery society. Free people of color were determined to challenge the increasingly harsh nature of race relations through developing counterpublic spaces as a response to the exclusions they suffered in dominant public spaces.[32] Afro-Creoles had focused much of their activism on crafting a body of literature that offered opposing interpretations of the identities attributed to them in the public sphere.[33] The development of educational institutions and schools, as seen in the previous chapter, had contributed immensely to shaping a public sphere based on egalitarian principles. State-sanctioned segregation established through "public" education in 1841, however, necessitated novel responses to this new variant of racism.

Despite these setbacks, Afro-Creoles like Lanusse redirected their activism to the establishment of literary and educational institutions through which they could contest images of racial inferiority. But the Afro-Creoles' political activism was severely repressed. Lanusse's writing did not directly address political issues (given that this was a crime), but his writing and publications sought to combat ignorance of racial prejudice by highlighting the contributions of Creoles of color to the intellectual and cultural life of New Orleans. In *L'Album littéraire: journal des jeunes gens, amateurs de littérature*, Lanusse published "Un Marriage de conscience," a story that criticized *plaçage*, a practice in which a young Creole woman of color would be "placed" with a rich white man in exchange for financial security and support. This practice demeaned women as property (a parallel to slavery) and often left them destitute. This critique of gender relations (and perhaps also mirroring race relations) was also a critique of the Catholic Church, which Lanusse suggested closed their eyes to the practice.

In *Les Cenelles*, he published a second piece critiquing *plaçage* entitled "Epigram." A mother of a young Creole woman of color is in the confessional ready to be absolved of all her sins when she asks the priest "Before grace sparks my soul, tell me I can. . . . Set up my daughter with a rich white man!" With these final lines the poem ends, the complicity of the priest a critique not only of the Catholic Church, but of institutionalized white (sexual) supremacy.[34] *Plaçage* was not only a severe blow to the manhood of free men of color, but it reinforced perceptions of free women of color as mere property, a clear dehumanization of both sexes.[35] Based on Lanusse's beliefs, it is not surprising that despite the norms of Catholic education, which had always been segregated by sex, that the Catholic Institute chose to educate both boys and girls in the same school (although on separate floors). Like Henriette Delille's Bayou School, the Catholic Institute believed that providing education for girls was one way to deter them from entering *plaçage* relationships. At the same time, educating boys and girls together provided a common space where girls could be encouraged to marry within their group rather than entering relationships where they would be exploited by white men.

Dubbed "the nursery for revolution," the Catholic Institute provides a unique space in which to examine Lanusse's role as principal and to examine the curriculum, in which education was not only critical to liberation, but in which notions of "public" education redefined the relationship between citizenship, nation, and identity.[36] For Lanusse and his fellow teachers, it was becoming abundantly clear that their hopes for full citizenship were further from their reach than ever before. The next generation, their students, would require the development not only of resilience, but creativity in imagining counterpublic spaces where they could claim their rights as full human beings, including citizenship. While the pedagogy of the Catholic Institute provided a rigorous academic curriculum, it also provided spaces for a curriculum of imagination. One example was in the school's English classes, where English was taught as a second language. In this course students learned the English language through engaging in real-world writing—letter writing—at the time a dominant genre of communication. Students in the class were asked to write letters to "friends" in which they imagined what their political, economic, and social futures might hold given the increasingly repressive state of the country. These student letters from 1858 to 1865, written as an English exercise, have survived. Not only do they speak of the school, their classmates, the curriculum, and their principal Armand Lanusse, but the exercises in writing fictive letters provided students an opportunity to construct alternative identities and imagine worlds in which freedom was a reality.

Reimagining Citizenship: The Transatlantic, Imaginative Spaces of Letter Writing

May 8th, 1857

Dear Friend,

I write you this short letter in order to let you know that I desire tolerance in this country. Tell me what you think of Mexico if I should be well there with my family.

Your devoted friend,
Armand Nicolas[37]

Fourteen-year-old Armand Nicolas, writing to a fictive friend in Pueblo, Mexico, is trying to imagine what it might be like to emigrate to a country that is free of racial discrimination. Although barely a teenager, it is obvious that Armand has experienced the increasing restrictions on free people of color preceding the Civil War. Despite these racial prejudices, Armand sees himself as clearly entitled to the full benefits of citizenship. His keen sense of social justice has been nurtured by the radical pedagogy of his principal and teachers who empowered these young men to envision their lives as active agents despite the harsh realities of racial oppression. The curriculum of imagination of the Catholic Institute was infused with a global, transatlantic sense of identity in which connections to France, Haiti, Cuba, and Mexico not only allowed them to conceptualize freedom, but also underscored a sense of global citizenship (as opposed to being a citizen of a nation) with those in other countries and their struggles for equality. For the students at the Catholic Institute, democratic revolution would require a radical reimagining of the public sphere in which citizenship was conceptualized within the transatlantic, imaginative spaces of freedom.

For Armand and his approximately 240 classmates, the school provided a rich liberal arts, humanities education including instruction in French and English (eventually the school also offered Spanish), grammar, composition, mathematics (arithmetic, algebra, and geometry), rhetoric, geography, catechism, history, logic, basic accounting, and personal hygiene.[38] The curriculum of the Catholic Institute (which went from first to eighth grade) stressed the importance of learning a trade as well as creating a community network in order to succeed economically. Many of the children were expected to enter an apprenticeship with an artisan or tradesman, most likely as a tailor, cigar maker, grocer, or shoemaker, professions that had long been the monopoly of free people of color. Encouraged to engage their imaginations, students were given the space to ponder different futures and to envision themselves as active agents in shaping a society where the ideals of democratic revolution and universal brotherhood would come to fruition. Nowhere was this more apparent than in the letters students were asked to write in which they could imagine alternative constructs of their lives as free men and full citizens. In November of 1856, Armand had written to his imaginary friend in Grand Lake, Louisiana.

> My mother is very well now, she is going off for Marseilles, and then to Paris to see her brother who lives in the city, and she will go and see your wife. I think in the course of the next month I will write you more than I do now because I have not this month left my plantation. Present my best to your wife, and all your family.

> Your faithful friend,
> Armand Nicholas[39]

The young boys write convincingly about their travels throughout the world, including visits to Spain, France, Mexico, and Haiti, as well as various cities throughout the United States, such as Boston, St. Louis, and Cincinnati. The letter above captures the transatlantic nature of domestic life among some families of free people of color. It is clear from the letter that students were aware that emigration to other countries was a distinct option should circumstances become untenable in New Orleans. According to the letter, some family members had already left Louisiana to make their permanent home in France. Students envisioned family members spread throughout the globe engaging in business ventures, leisure, travel, and commerce. These assignments allowed the boys to imagine positions of wealth and authority that were denied them given the political situation in the South. As well as economic rights, students were encouraged to visualize the prospects of full citizenship with equal political rights.

A few days later, on November 28, Armand's classmate William Green wrote to his brother in Monterez, Mexico:

> You inform me that after you have settled in Mexico (where you are making a good business) that you have the intention to leave for Nicaragua where you expect to succeed.[40]

In the 1850s, under the increasing racial repression preceding the Civil War, the Catholic Institute's teachers encouraged students to forecast lives for themselves in places outside the United States, countries that might offer them freedom and equality. It is clear in the letters that these migrations and success in a foreign country were dependent on being well-educated and engaging in a profession. William Greene wrote in February of 1857 to his friend in Grand Lake, Louisiana:

> Oh! What a prize it is to me who has a good hand, and more especially to one who is about to enter the commercial line. My intention is not to inhabit this country forever, a country that offers so little advantage as this. And I am about to prepare seriously to leave by studying, to bid an eternal adieu to my native home.[41]

William imagines that he, like his brother, will settle in Mexico or Nicaragua after he has completed his studies and learned a trade. He clearly envisions his life elsewhere given that the United States offers so little. Throughout the letters, the boys make connections between Marseilles, Paris, Mexico, and Nicaragua, intertwining commerce with transatlantic relationships. Mary Mitchell has highlighted that the focus on emigration in the letter writing of the students did two important things: "first, it strengthened the ideological and historical ties that existed between free blacks in the U.S. and other settlements of free blacks in the Diaspora. Second, the prospect of emigration created an ideological and geographic space in which free blacks could envision and articulate the kind of freedom they hoped to achieve in a society without slavery."[42] The challenge inherent in these pedagogical moments was for these young men to negotiate these tensions between "freedom" and "slavery," as well as their own space in between.

Given these contradictory spaces, a curriculum of imagination was not only a powerful antidote to the increasing racial discrimination that these young men were experiencing but situates the students as active agents in negotiating the complex terrain of race, identity, and power relations in which they are simultaneously privileged and oppressed. In these early letters, the boys' understanding of freedom is located within countries in which slavery has already been declared illegal (France, Mexico, and Haiti). According to Mary Mitchell, "the students at the Catholic Institution constructed their own moral geography; that is, they mapped their prospects about freedom, testing ideas about a future in other nations outside of their own."[43]

While we might read this migration as a form of escape from oppression, these letters envision a Black Atlantic community that transcended boundaries of individual nations and, in the minds of the students, perhaps transcended racial oppression as well. This curriculum of imagination was one that the institute hoped would ignite a revolutionary zeal among the students to construct freedom for all people of color, uniting them in a transatlantic citizenship extending beyond national boundaries. This transgression of the dominant discourses of citizenship as transnational was intimately connected to the ways in which rights discourse was emerging in relation to conceptions of public and private. Nowhere was this discussion more relevant than in relation to the Catholic Institute. The directors, teachers, and students were actively engaged in contesting dominant notions of what constituted the public by reinscribing the term with their own understandings. First and foremost was their absolute right to complete participation in the "public" sphere as equals, especially as it pertained to education.

In this regard, the Catholic Institute created a culture in which the students were given every opportunity to understand themselves as highly capable and gifted students. Drawing on the rich history of the cultural, artistic, scientific, and literary successes of the community, students were expected to excel and were being prepared to participate as equals in what they undoubtedly saw as the eventual revolution through which they would attain full equality. Consequently, the curriculum included "public" performances where students could showcase their talents and accomplishments. Leon Dupart wrote:

> April 30, 1858
> Leonard Santos Esq.
> Terrebonne, LA
>
> Dear Friends,
>
> I think it a great pleasure of giving you an idea of the examinations that took place here a few days ago; for they were very beautiful . . . we read, made dictation, conjugated verbs, and made grammatical exercises. For the pieces of poetry, the school was so full of people that we could not get a place to sit down. The recitation began at three in the afternoon and finished at half past nine. There was a little girl that had two pieces she recited so well, that they threw two bouquets at her, and one cake to my friend Isidore.
>
> Yours,
> Leon Dupart[44]

His letter reflects not only a deep sense of pride in his classmates' intellectual prowess, but suggests that community performances such as these were popular literary events designed to pay tribute to the emerging talents of young Afro-Creole poets, artists, and scholars.

While students were acutely aware of the ways in which they were discriminated against, they were not oblivious to the prejudice experienced by other groups. Most of the students at the Catholic Institute lived in the Marigny, in close proximity to the growing number of German, Irish, and Italian immigrants who were moving into the neighborhood after fleeing political oppression in Europe. While the Germans desired to retain their language and attended separate churches and schools, both Afro-Creoles and Germans wanted the rights to full citizenship. Early civic organizations like the Masons made attempts to be interracial (to be discussed later in the chapter), but language barriers prohibited long-term alliances. The day-to-day activities of the neighborhood, however, made clear to many of the students that the quest for full equality would require a transnational, interracial collaboration.

The young student S. A. Claiborne was acutely aware of the growing nativist, anti-Catholic sentiment that had garnered enough political support to establish the Know-Nothing Party. In the 1856 presidential election, the incumbent Millard Fillmore ran as a Know-Nothing candidate against James Buchanan, the proslavery Democrat, and John Fremont, the Republican who favored abolition. Young Claiborne writes about what he experienced on election day as he went to the market about six in the evening:

New Orleans, November 24th, 1856
To A John Macmurdo Esq.,
Montgomery, Alabama

I saw fifteen men disguised as Indians who were riding on horse-back, each having a knife in his hand and two revolvers in his girdle. They have frightened all the Irishmen who were in the streets, and all the Sicilians who were selling fruit in the market. I saw a German who came to vote. As he had no right to do so, a young American, that is to say, a Know-Nothing, gave him a cuff; he took off a revolver from his pocket, and shot the Know-Nothing, in his arm; another Know-Nothing came in his turn, shot the German in his head. He fell down a corpse. This is all that I have seen. Adieu, give my best wishes to all your family and to my old friend Peter Parley. Be assured that I will always be

Your most affectionate friend,
S. A. Claiborne

In seeing that racial prejudice and hatred was not reserved for Afro-Creoles alone but was also directed at the Irish, Italians, and Germans, Claiborne recognized that oppression is widespread and systematic. For the students at the Catholic Institute, democratic revolution would require building alliances across races and ethnicities in order to reimagine citizenship as a "public right" inclusive of all male members of society.[45] Unfortunately, Afro-Creoles did not connect their struggle for equality to the movement for women's rights. When the Civil War broke out in 1861, Armand Lanusse and the students at the Catholic Institute believed this would be the democratic revolution they had been waiting for. Central to this revolution would be a society in which the human dignity of all persons would be signified in the public sphere through free, integrated schools. The revolutionary fervor of the time was also shared by others, especially the new immigrant groups from Germany, Ireland, and Italy. Yet their arrival would tear at the fabric of racial integration given that they, like French Creoles and Afro-Creoles, also sought to maintain their language and culture.

The "French Invasion:" The Second Wave of Catholic Missionaries

The Catholic Church would play a large role in helping to maintain both the French and German language through its expansion of new parishes and educational institutions. This growth of Catholic institutions by the French was part of a revival of missionary activity throughout the world given the resurgence of the Catholic Church during the Bourbon Restoration. This nineteenth-century missionary movement was part of a much larger religious revival in France directed at all nations that were not Catholic; these areas received renewed missionary attention from the French Society for the Propagation of the Faith, who especially saw the frontier regions of the United States as spaces ripe for missionary activity among "lapsed Catholics, heretical Protestants, miserable slaves, and indigenous peoples."[46] By the 1840s, Catholic educational institutions were growing throughout the Gulf South and the Mississippi Valley, serving to reinforce both the French language and culture and providing for educational institutions for new German immigrants.[47] The reconstituted Diocese of New Orleans in 1830, which encompassed present-day Louisiana and Mississippi, allowed for targeted growth in the area and recruitment of numerous new teaching orders among women religious, as well as the expansion of the existing orders.[48]

The influence of the Catholic Church grew in New Orleans and also extended well beyond the city throughout the whole Gulf South and into Texas and the Southwest. These educational missions continued the apostolic work of providing religious education to the enslaved as well as Indigenous peoples at a time when access to education, especially in the rural areas of Louisiana, was almost nonexistent.[49]

The rapid expansion of Catholic institutions suggests the desire among vast swaths of the population to retain the French language and religious culture, and it was designed to provide a counterpublic to the "white-only" public schools that eventually expanded in the 1840s. The return of

French Catholic Women Religious Congregations and Schools 1818–1866

Ursulines	Sisters of the Sacred Heart
1727, New Orleans, LA	1818, St. Charles, MO
1847, Galveston, TX	1819, Florissant, MO
1851, San Antonio, TX	1821, Grand Coteau, LA
1868, Laredo, TX	1825, St. Michael, LA
1874, Dallas, TX	1827, St. Louis, MO
1892, Puebla, Mexico	1828 La Fourche, LA
1900, Bryan, TX	1841, Sugar Creek, MO
1930, Pecos, TX	1847, Natchitoches, LA
	1852, St. Joseph, MO

Sisters of the Incarnate Word & Blessed Sacrament	Sisters of Mt. Carmel
1853, Brownsville, TX	
1867, Victoria, TX	1838, New Orleans, LA
1871, Corpus Christi, TX	1846, Lafayette, LA
1873, Houston, TX	
1879, Shiner, TX	

Sisters of Notre Dame	
1882, Halletsville, TX	
1856, New Orleans, LA	

Sisters of Divine Providence	Marianites of the Holy Cross
1866, Austin, TX	1849, New Orleans, LA
1868, Corpus Christi and Castrovill, TX	1856, Opelousas, LA
1895, San Antonio, TX	

Sisters of St. Joseph	Daughters of the Cross
1854, Bay St. Louis, MS	1855, Cocoville, LA
1858, New Orleans, LA	1857, Ile Brevelle, LA
1868, Baton Rouge, LA	1858, Alexandria, LA

the Jesuits in 1837 to both the New Orleans and St. Louis dioceses, also contributed to the growth of educational missions. While the majority of Jesuit recruits were French, between 1837and 1861 the Jesuit ministry to the increasing number of Irish and German immigrants also attracted a number of Irish and German Jesuits, who eventually expanded Catholic schools among these immigrants.[50] The 1840 Catholic Almanac provides a snapshot of the educational institutions in the state, excluding parish-based evening and Sunday schools for catechism.

Male Academies
Ecclesiastical Seminary of St. Vincent de Paul, Assumption Parish, Louisiana, Lazarists, 1835, 7 seminarians.

St. Charles College, Grand Coteau, Louisiana, Jesuit, founded 1837, 100 boarders.[51]

Female Academies

Ursuline Academy, New Orleans, 26 sisters, 125 pupils, 25 orphans (founded 1727).

Mount Carmel Convent Boarding School for Free Girls of Color, New Orleans, 8 sisters, 25 boarders, 65 extern students (founded 1836).

Academy of the Sacred Heart, Grand Coteau, 21 sisters, 100 boarders (founded 1821).

Academy of the Ladies of the Sacred Heart at St. Michaels, Acadia, 38 Religious, 230 boarders, 31 orphans.

Female Religious Institutions

Catholic Male Orphan Asylum, at New Orleans, contains 55 orphans.

St. Patrick's Female Orphan Asylum, New Orleans, under the care of the Sisters of Charity, Sister Francis Regis, 82 orphans and 26 externs.

Charity Hospital, New Orleans, under the care of 15 Sisters of Charity. Sister Regina Smith. Number of patients varies from 175 to 360.

Despite increasing anti-Catholicism and the pressures of Americanization, Catholic teaching orders and religious institutions continued to proliferate, providing a counterculture to the emerging "all-white" common school movement, challenging constructs of what constituted "public" universal education. The role of French clerics and women religious in the expansion of schools also contributed to the institutional legitimacy and support for the educational initiatives of the Sisters of the Holy Family and the Catholic Institute. For Afro-Creoles the founding of educational institutions was a direct challenge to the emerging "public" sphere of education for "whites" only, which was the complete antithesis of their understanding of the public sphere as an interracial space which signified the common humanity of all people.

This "French Invasion" of religious orders also resulted in the founding of several institutions of higher education in the Gulf South and Mississippi Valley that provided access to postsecondary education in the region for the first time.

St. Mary's of the Barrens Seminary, Perryville, Missouri, Vincentians, 1818.

St. Mary's Seminary and St. Joseph College, Bardstown, Kentucky, founded 1819, Jesuits, 1848.

Spring Hill College, Mobile, Alabama, Jesuit, 1847.

College of the Immaculate Conception (became Loyola), New Orleans, Louisiana, Jesuit, 1848.

College of Sts. Peter and Paul, Baton Rouge, Louisiana, Jesuit, 1849.

Jefferson College, Convent, Louisiana, became St. Mary's College in 1864 under the Marist fathers.

While a full discussion of Catholic higher education is beyond the scope of this research, it is important to note that all these institutions, particularly those of the Jesuits, relied on the labor of enslaved peoples. When the Jesuits emerged from their decades-long suppression (1763–1814), coerced labor from enslaved communities allowed them to expand their missionary and educational presence. The Jesuit entanglement with slavery in the nineteenth century does not get the attention it deserves, with most histories being silent on the topic.[52] In fact, Jesuit slaveholding was by no means exceptional but was deeply embedded in the local, regional, and globally connected economies that the Jesuits operated throughout the South. The enslaved supplied the profits and labor that sustained Jesuit schools, churches, and missions.

That people enslaved to Catholics experienced a more benign form of slavery is of course a myth that is increasingly being challenged.[53] While the brutality of slavery was experienced, those enslaved by the Jesuits also asserted their agency by forging community, appropriating the Catholic faith for their own purposes, and practicing resistance in a variety of ways. Enslaved people took advantage of the Catholic recognition of the universalism of the sacraments and sacramental sponsorships to expand, strengthen, and protect their kinship networks and bring new kin into their networks through the witnesses they chose for godparenting and marriage. The expansion of slavery within the missionary arm of the Catholic Church contributed to contradictory notions of modern education, freedom, and citizenship. Education, whether the common school movement, the Catholic educational missions, or Protestant private institutions, contributed to coding the nation and citizenship as white through exclusion. For Afro-Creole free people of color, as well as newly arrived German and Italian immigrants to Louisiana, this designation of the "public" sphere of education as for "whites" only was the complete antithesis of their understanding of a democratic republic in which the public sphere was an interracial space that signified the equality of all people. In the face of this racialized citizenship, Afro-Creoles and newly arrived German and Italian immigrants created counterpublic spaces in which they formed "nations" of their own making through fraternal organizations, religious brotherhoods, public associations, and educational institutions like the Catholic Institute. These spaces were public displays of political landscapes that challenged the constructs of citizenship grounded in race and ethnicity by positing alternatives to the nation-state as defined by national constitutions and state codes that defined more noncitizens than citizens.

Building Counterpublic Spaces through *Bildung*: German Immigration and Education

Free people of color were not the only group that sought to be acknowledged as full citizens in the antebellum period. The 1840s and 1850s would see a massive influx of Irish, Italian, and German immigrants to New Orleans. Many German immigrants continued from New Orleans up the Mississippi to the Midwest or west to Texas, while many remained in Louisiana, especially New Orleans. While Haitian refugees had been the first major group of immigrants to Louisiana, by 1830, 7,000 Germans had arrived and within a few years made up about 12 percent of the population of New Orleans. By 1850, German immigrants made up 20 percent of the population. While the Irish also arrived in significant numbers (by 1850, 2,200 lived in New Orleans), that they spoke English and were Catholic facilitated the process of cultural assimilation to a greater degree than the Germans. Given that they were cheap labor, however, the overwhelming majority of the Irish would eventually take many of the jobs the enslaved formerly held, working in the most undesirable occupations the city had to offer.[54] The Germans, who made up the majority of European immigrants in this period, were a diverse group made up of Protestants, Catholics, and Jews; members of the working and professional classes; and political exiles. They were by no means a monolithic ethnic group. Some sought assimilation, while others were staunch German nationalists who nonetheless held steadfast to the liberal ideals of democracy in which diverse cultures would be united in an international brotherhood. Their arrival in the city added to the complex politics surrounding the emergence of "public" education, in which the tensions between assimilation and maintaining cultural identity and language resulted in the production of multiple alternative counterpublic spaces.

The very first Germans had been recruited by John Law's Company of the Indies to settle Louisiana in the 1720s; they established farms about twenty-five miles upriver from New Orleans in what became known as the Côte des Allemands (German Coast). These farms provided produce to feed the still-struggling colony of New Orleans. Over time many of the Germans were integrated into French-speaking Creole society and later with Acadians through intermarriage. The second wave of German immigrants, arriving after the displacement of German peasant farmers due to the Napoleonic wars, were "redemptionists," or indentured servants. The indentured servant became important in the South when Congress forbade the further importation of slaves after 1807. The price of slaves then rose so high that hiring indentured servants became much more economical. The practice of recruiting destitute peasants for this purpose arose in the Rhineland, which had suffered the hardships of war resulting from the French Revolution.[55] For minors, the period of indenture ended in the eighteenth year for females and the twenty-first year for males. Adults were required to serve up to seven years. Legally, masters were to provide some education, especially in terms of training in a trade. The law considered indentured runaways to be the same as runaway slaves, and indentured servants could be legally punished for making the attempt. That some of the servants found their circumstances intolerable enough to attempt escape is shown by advertisements describing runaway Germans from the years 1807, 1818, and 1820.[56]

By the 1830s, German as well as Irish immigration swelled in New Orleans, resulting in the Black population losing its numerical majority for the first time since the 1730s. Immigrant servants and laborers replaced many of the urban enslaved Africans. The Germans were dispersed through the city, with some settling in Lafayette and Carrollton, but most settled in the third municipality, where rent was cheap and working-class jobs were abundant. In later years, the Marigny was referred to as "Little Saxony" given the number of Germans and their influence in the neighborhood.[57] These early Germans quickly became involved in creating a community network by establishing German print and literary outlets. As early as 1830, German immigrant Emil Johns had opened a bookstore at 113 Chartres between Conti and St. Charles. The first German-language newspaper, *Der Deutsche*, was published in November of 1839 in both English and German.[58] A second paper, the *Deutsche Courier*, started publication in January of 1842, and in 1848, Joseph Kohn, a German Jew, established the *Deutsche Zeitung* and opened a German bookstore in Jackson Square. To provide aid and guidance for Germans arriving in New Orleans, Kohn founded in 1843 the Deutsche Geselleschaft zum Schuz der Einwanderer.

This organization was invaluable to Germans in navigating their temporary stays in New Orleans in transit to the Midwest or West.

Those settling in the Faubourg Marigny contributed to the rich diversity of the community and bolstered the mostly Catholic community. As the number of Germans who sought a role in the public sphere increased, however, they became embroiled in the political tensions between French-Creole, Afro-Creole, and American factions, particularly in regards to language, religion, and education. While German Protestants established a congregation in 1828 on Clio Street between St. Charles and Carondelet, German Catholics worshipped at either Saint Patrick's Cathedral on Camp Street or Saint Louis Cathedral, both of which held services only in French, not German. It was not until 1844 that Saint Mary's Assumption Church, in the Lower Garden District, opened and became the first German Catholic Church in Louisiana. Not long after, in 1847, German Catholics in the Marigny were able to worship in German at church services in the newly built Holy Trinity Catholic Church.

While French Creoles had hoped to maintain the dominance of the French language through its use in the Catholic churches, Bishop Blanc saw the benefit of diversifying languages in the Catholic churches in New Orleans as a way to maintain the strength of the Catholic Church in light of the increasing number of Protestants. Bishop Blanc, like Catholic clergy in other cities with large Catholic populations, saw that the increasing number of Catholic immigrants allowed them to develop new churches, hospitals, and schools not only in New Orleans, but throughout the state.[59] While St. Louis Cathedral was the city's only parish until 1833, under the leadership of Bishop Blanc, four new parishes were established by 1847: St. Patrick's 1833 (to serve the Irish), St. Augustine in 1842 (to serve the Afro-Creole population), St. Joseph's in 1846 (to serve the Italians), and Holy Trinity in 1847 (to serve the Germans). The creation of these new parishes required recruitment from a variety of orders of priests who spoke English, German, and Italian, as well as orders of teaching sisters who could educate the children in their native tongue.[60]

This growth in Catholic schools for immigrants during the 1840s was a direct challenge to the Anglo-Protestant white only "public" education movement that was being launched. Not only was the Catholic diocese in New Orleans providing support for the Catholic schools that educated free people of color (Sisters of the Holy Family Bayou School and the Catholic Institute), but they were also extending their reach to immigrant groups. While "public" education at this time was still in its infancy, the private Catholic and Protestant churches that were providing education and literacy for the newly arrived Europeans, in effect undermined the public schools. In fact, all German religious institutions, whether Protestant, Catholic, or Jewish, provided schools associated with their places of worship.[61] As early as 1842, two years after St. Paul's Lutheran Church was established, the pastor Christian Sans organized two schools for the children of the fourteen thousand Germans living in New Orleans. One was in the Second Municipality (Race and Constance Streets) and the second was in the Third Municipality on Moreau Street. The three hundred students were taught a complete curriculum after the Pestalozzian and Prussian systems.[62]

While the Catholic Church sought to increase its influence by accommodating the waves of immigrants, one unintended consequence was the reinforcement of emerging segregation in New Orleans along lines of nationality, language, and race/ethnicity. The divisions created by the Catholic Church through the establishment of new parishes occurred at the same time as the 1841 division of New Orleans into three municipalities. This division created power struggles among the American, Franco-Creole, and Afro-Creole communities. The First Municipality (the French Quarter) was primarily in the hands of Franco-Creoles who sought to maintain a Latin, French, and Catholic culture. The Third Municipality (Faubourg Marigny) was by far the most ethnically and racially diverse, with a strong presence and history of Afro-Creoles. Alexander Dimitry, an Afro-Creole passing as white, became superintendent of the Third Municipality, home to the first "public" school opened in the city. Throughout the 1850s, private schools for free people of color, Catholic schools for free people of color (which could be considered public since no child was turned away), and Catholic and private schools for Germans dominated the landscape of the Marigny (refer to figure 18, map of 1842). The Second Municipality (the American sector, what is now the central business district), under the leadership of John Angier Shaw, a reformed slaveholder from Massachusetts, opened a "public" school in January 1842. He recruited teachers from New England who taught in English only, initiated schools that educated both genders, and recruited women teachers, who were paid significantly less than men.[63] For French-Creole Catholics, these supposed revolutionary "innovations" conflicted with long-held French Catholic traditions regarding the separation of genders and their staunch adherence to French as their primary language. The German and Irish immigrant communities were drawn into this struggle. Although the German and Irish shared a common Catholic heritage with both Creole communities, it has been suggested that they sided with the Americans (those representing the Second Municipality) because they did not want to speak French.[64] By aligning with the Americans, those German politicians seeking a role in civic life clearly alienated the French, signaling their allegiance not only to their newly adopted country but also to its racial norms of white superiority.

By 1843, the First Municipal Council, which had been under the control of Franco-Creoles, was dominated by the Americans with the help of the German voters. One of the first items on their agenda was to reorganize the school board to rid it of the French Creoles and replace them with American and Germans. Christian Roselius (1803–1873), a German immigrant, was appointed head of the school board and immediately began holding meetings in English. At the time of his appointment to the school board, he was serving as the state's attorney general. Roselius had left Bremen, Germany, in 1820, securing his passage by an indenture, which he served in New Orleans at a printing office. After his attempt to start a literary journal, *The Halcyon*, failed, he joined his friend Alexander Dimitry in studying law in the offices of Auguste Davezac and James Workman from 1826 to 1828. James Workman, the prominent Irishman who had spearheaded the recruitment of Joseph Lakanal at the College d'Orleans, and August Davezac (D'Avezac), a refugee from Saint-Domingue and brother of Jules D'Avezac, first president of the College d'Orleans, represented the transatlantic, multicultural influence that was shaping New Orleans politics. Yet for the Americans, the multiracial, fluid nature of New Orleans was unnatural. They sought to impose a strict biracial logic. Several court cases in the 1850s made it abundantly clear that racial purity was being increasingly policed.[65] The newly arrived, unaccustomed to these notions of racial identity, quickly learned the stakes, including participation in public education, of not capitulating to the newly imagined constructs of pure bloodlines. This was the case with Alexander Dimitry, superintendent of the Third Municipality, whose family came under suspicion of having mixed blood.

Alexander Dimitry (1805–1883), from a prominent Afro-Creole family (his father, Andrea, was from Greece and his mother, Marianne Celeste Dragon, was a free women of color but was listed as white in the marriage record), typifies Afro-Creole families that Shirley Elizabeth Thompson has termed as "seeking shelter under white skin."[66] His nephew George Pandelly, accused of being a "man of color" in the 1853 court case *Pandelly v. Wiltz*, was defended by Christian Roselius, who argued that it was Indian, not African blood that resulted in features that were not typically Caucasian. Wiltz (another prominent German) claimed that he had no objection to Pandelly "passing" "as long as they were in ordinary [private] business . . . but whenever they pretended to get into public employment, then he was determined to put them down."[67] Evidence submitted by Roselius drew on ethnological theory, a recent "science" that ranked the physical characteristics and mental capacities of races. In the end, the Pandelly case revolved around demarcating the public sphere as "white" and constructing whiteness as a biological category that could be scientifically read. Given the recent invention of "public" schooling as white only, this court case contributed to solidifying the public sphere as a "white space." This was one more microstep toward complete racial segregation.

Immigrants—Germans, Italians (who were also considered colored), and Irish (who had been considered inferior to the English)—were cognizant of the fragility of the color line. These immigrants had arrived in New Orleans at a time when racial lines were being ever more tightly defined and slaves were indiscriminately sold at the market on Chartres and Esplanade in the French Quarter, a stone's throw from the Marigny. One day one could be "white" (free/citizen), and the next day a person of color (slave/noncitizen). For recent immigrants to New Orleans, the consequences of racial identification were abundantly clear given the numerous stories circulating throughout the city. The cautionary tale of Salome Müller, a German immigrant and indentured servant, who had been orphaned and then enslaved for twenty years, sent a clear message to volatile immigrants whose own identities as Americans were in flux.[68] The tenuous nature of racial identity would be mitigated in part through participating in and supporting public schools because this space would mark them as "white."

This disciplining of the public spaces through educational segregation during the 1840s became critical to constructing and maintaining whiteness through reinforcing white supremacy and white citizenship despite the rhetoric of public education as central to shaping the ideals of democracy. The establishment of German schools, independent of the public school system, suggests that this segregation impacted not only people of color, but also newly arrived German immigrants. As Catholics and foreign-language speakers, German immigrant children did not conform to the Anglo-Protestant requirements for "public" education. By 1852, only 184 German children were attending the public schools in School District Two (the former First Municipality).[69]

German support helped the Anglo-Americans wrest control of the Louisiana legislature from the French-Creoles in 1845. That same year the first constitutional convention since 1812 was held: the rewritten document mandated free public education for white children throughout the state and created the office of superintendent for public education, to be appointed by the governor. Alexander Dimitry, who had been superintendent of the Third Municipality, was chosen by Governor Isaac Johnson to serve two terms as superintendent from 1847 to 1852. Between 1843 and 1852, control of the school board in the First Municipality alternated between the French-Creole and Anglo-American factions until 1852, when the city dispensed with separate municipal governments. This reunification, according to Walter Stern, "concentrated political power in the hands of Anglo-American officials who had long sought to eliminate New Orleans's blurred racial lines."[70]

The hardening of racial binaries continued with the passage of state legislation in 1855 that banned all charitable, scientific, or literary societies. According to Caryn Cossé Bell, this legislation was designed to suppress the spread of free Black institutions like the Bayou Road School of the Sisters of the Holy Family and the Catholic Institute, who had received public funds through the societies that had supported them.[71] With no more state recognition or public funding, these educational institutions would have to rely on the philanthropy of the free people of color and the Catholic Church. Public education now functioned as a proxy for racism, limiting public funds to public schools for whites only. Yet free people of color and their allies continually challenged the construct of the public sphere as white only. While schools continued to be sorting mechanisms for race, ethnicity, and class, some German immigrants and free people of color turned to other avenues for shaping counterpublic spaces where they could imagine a more inclusive and democratic space of universal brotherhood. This was particularly the case with the third generation of Germans who came to Louisiana.

The Forty-Eighters

The third generation of German immigrants, known as the Forty-Eighters, were political refugees from the European revolutions of 1848. Beginning in the early nineteenth century, new social and political movements across Europe started advocating for republican forms of government. In Germany, leaders of this movement varied from moderate liberals whose views were heavily influenced by the Enlightenment to radical democrats whose ideas became formative for later socialist movements. This movement gained momentum in the 1830s and 1840s, culminating in March 1848, when political unrest spilled over from France and sparked the March

Revolution, which was suppressed by the summer of 1849. Systematic persecution and prosecution of those involved in the revolution followed, with many being sentenced to long prison terms and some condemned to death. For some, sentences were commuted on condition that they agreed to depart for America. New Orleans was a primary destination for many of these political exiles.

This new wave of immigrants arrived when regional tensions over slavery were on the rise, anti-immigrant nativism was gaining ground, and New Orleans politics was more contentious than ever. German immigration to New Orleans peaked in 1853, and the majority of these immigrants settled in the Faubourg Maringy, doubling its population by 1851. Most Germans who settled in the Maringy were working-class grocers, carpenters, shoemakers, coffeehouse owners, beer brewers, and draymen. Germans settled among the working-class free people of color who made up the majority of the city's masons, carpenters, and cigar makers. For the newly arrived Germans who spoke no English, sending their children to "public" schools was not an option. Their lack of knowledge of English, as well as a desire to maintain their own German identity, meant that students living in the Marigny in the 1850s attended German church-affiliated schools at either the Catholic church (Holy Trinity), the Evangelical-Lutheran church (St. Paul on Burgundy and Port) or the Methodist church.[72] Other private schools were also available, including the well-known school of Jacob and John Ueber, who had originally been principals at the Lutheran School but in the mid-1850s started their own school at 2718 Rampart (between Port and Saint Ferdinand Streets), which was in operation until 1901. During the Civil War, the school attendance was counted at 279.[73] All these schools continued to be vibrant institutions throughout the Civil War, the turbulent years of Reconstruction, and even well into the turn of the century. In 1886, Holy Trinity had a total of 320 students, St. Paul's had 165 students, and the Ueber School (now at 658–660 N. Rampart) had 75 students. German Catholic schools throughout New Orleans educated by far the most students (1,831 students in 1886) of those who attended German church schools.[74]

Unique among the German endeavors in education was the Turn Schule, a school that was operated by the Turngemeinde, an organization that sought to educate men physically, ethically, intellectually, and culturally. An outgrowth of the "Bildung" tradition, an educational movement in nineteenth-century Germany, the Turn Schule sought to inspire self-cultivation both on a personal and cultural level. Education in the Bildung tradition focused on holistic growth, with the self-realization of the individual being attained through acquiring a sense of entirety, freedom, and self-understanding as well as social responsibility. Turngemeinde saw themselves as vital in the sphere of education for engaging boys and men in developing culture, freedom, and good citizenship. In addition to providing formal education, they also had libraries, singing societies, debating clubs, lectures, gymnasiums, and dramatic performances. Most attractive to young German boys were the "Turncours" or gymnastic classes that were offered to boys age six to sixteen.[75]

Turner Societies had emerged at the beginning of the nineteenth century in the German states during the time of the Napoleonic occupation, with the goal to strengthen physical and moral powers through the practice of gymnastics. The movement became more politicized during the 1830s, and Turner Societies became important vehicles of political organization during the revolutions in Germany. The emergence of Turner Societies in the United States coincided with the Forty-Eighters' arrival. The first American Turner Society was founded in 1848, followed by an explosion in their number, especially after 1854, when the Forty-Eighters revived their political engagement. Historians agree that the Forty-Eighters were directly involved in founding many societies and turning them into highly political organizations.[76] The 1855 Turner Societies (Turnerbund) national convention in Buffalo, New York, articulated a clear abolitionist platform by 1855.[77] This resulted in many southern Turner clubs like those of Mobile, Savannah, Augusta, and Charleston withdrawing their membership from the national organization.[78] While New Orleans did not withdraw, their members were divided regarding abolition. The April 19, 1861, *New Orleans Bee* praised the Turners for preparing to fight with the Confederacy. Yet a splinter group of twenty-two Turners, allied with the Vorwaerts, declared their loyalty to the Union in April of 1862, when Union forces occupied the city.[79] The Turners would frequently form bodyguards for antislavery activists during public speeches, and in 1860 they made up Lincoln's bodyguards at his inauguration. During the Civil War, Turner Societies would often enlist in the Union Army, forming so-called "Turner Regiments."

In 1853, German immigration reached its highest level when 35,965 Germans landed in New Orleans. While many continued to St. Louis, Louisville, Cincinnati, Mobile, and Galveston, at least 2,000 were struck dead by the yellow fever epidemic that ravaged the city that year. While a total of 8,000 New Orleanians died, the impact on immigrants was especially severe since they had no immunity to the disease. By 1854, approximately 36,700 Germans lived in the city.[80] The Forty-Eighters immediately became involved in social and political clubs including the Turn Verein (turners were gymnasts, or tumblers) or Turners' Associations, an organization that sought to *educate* members and "enable them to fulfill their duties as men and as fit and useful citizens."[81] Chartered in 1851, the Turner Society immediately became engaged in educating its members on the status of the revolution in Germany. In January of 1852, Gottfried Kinkel (1815–1882), a German poet, art and cultural historian, and survivor of the failed 1848 revolution, was welcomed by Dr. Maas, president of the Turners, as a "freedom martyr."[82] Speaking at the St. Louis Hotel, he drew an audience of Americans, Germans, French, Spanish, and Italians, uniting the various ethnic groups of the city and asking them to support the success of the liberation and democratic revolution in Germany.[83] German support for republican government extended not only to the motherland, but to the German population in New Orleans. The German newspapers urged Germans to register so they could vote. Civic clubs promoting citizenship, like the German Society of the Third Municipality (Faubourg Marigny), organized in 1851.[84] By 1854, these societies had merged to establish a central organization known from then on as the German Society.[85] They met each first Tuesday to discuss topics of general interest of both national and foreign politics.[86] The most pressing topic centered around slavery, a question around which Germans were divided.

The egalitarian and prorepublican convictions of the Forty-Eighters mapped closely to the political struggles that were emerging in the years leading up to the Civil War. During the first few years after their arrival, the Forty-Eighters' political convictions lay dormant as their lives were dominated by the practical necessities of earning a livelihood in their new home. This changed when the Kansas-Nebraska Act of 1854 blew the lid off the sectional political conflict around slavery.[87] The act repealed the Missouri Compromise, which had prohibited slavery in the North. This resulted in the formation of the Republican Party and the subsequent disintegration of the Whig Party. This led the Forty-Eighters to revive the spirit of the failed struggle for liberty in the fight against slavery. By the time this conflict culminated in the Civil War, the Forty-Eighters had become influential campaigners against slavery and mobilizers of Union Army volunteers.[88] The Forty-Eighters' strongly held convictions of republicanism, liberty, and equality in Europe would map into the political struggles in the United States a decade later. This is important because the same ideals the Forty-Eighters had fought for in Europe now found a natural (and measurable) continuation in the United States. Forty-Eighters became pivotal in articulating rational arguments for emancipation by tying the slavery issue into a broader debate on liberty and equality. An editorial by Friedrich Kapp in the *New York Abendzeitung* illustrates this: "The problem of slavery is not the problem of the Negro. It is the eternal conflict between a small, privileged class and the great mass of the non-privileged, the eternal struggle between aristocracy and democracy." Such arguments resonated far more with most Americans than the previously dominant moralistic arguments presented by Puritan abolitionists on the back of the Second Great Awakening. The Forty-Eighters thus contributed to the spread of a wide-ranging culture of anti-slavery activism in the middle of the 1850s. They were mostly middle-class, well-educated, aspiring professionals. Above all, they hoped to persevere their revolutionary goals both in their newly adopted country as well as in Germany.

The Forty-Eighters were also instrumental in swaying the immigrant vote, particularly the German American vote, for the Republican Party in the 1860 election. This was important because German Americans had traditionally supported the Democratic Party and had been put off by the Republican Party when after 1857 it absorbed large numbers of anti-immigrant Know-Nothings. The Forty-Eighters demanded a formal repudiation of nativism by the Republican Party at its Chicago convention in May 1860, effectively "forcing the party to choose between Eastern nativists and the German vote in the West."[89] This repudiation became known as the "Dutch plank" in the Republican Party platform. As a result, the German American vote swung Republican, while the nativists "were absorbed into a party which made no concessions to them."[90]

In New Orleans the Forty-Eighters engaged in four educational practices through which they sought to not only abolish slavery, but to work across political, racial, and ethnic divides to achieve their republican ideals. First, like earlier German immigrants, they founded and contributed to local newspapers; second, they founded and were involved in local social and political clubs, especially the Turner Societies (Turnvereine); third, they became involved in politics; and lastly and most importantly they initially sought to work across the color line through their participation in and establishment of Masonic lodges. Masonic lodges, benevolent societies, were counterpublics where those who were excluded from the public sphere could create alternative spaces of citizenship. Masonic lodges had a long history in New Orleans, but the 1840s and 1850s saw renewed activity with the influx of immigrants who sought to develop an interracial brotherhood. These spaces were critical to imagining a public sphere that was truly democratic.

Masonic lodges in the first half of nineteenth-century New Orleans are rarely treated by historians as institutions of learning and are even less likely to be credited with contributing to a counterpublic where working-class and other disfranchised persons could claim a measure of political subjectivity, allowing them to function as full citizens in an imagined brotherhood. Yet the flourishing of Freemasonry in New Orleans with the arrival of refugees from Saint-Domingue beginning in the 1790s, and the arrival of German immigrants during the early 1840s, strongly influenced the intellectual life of New Orleans.[91] Both contributed to an interracial, international movement that sought to create a cosmopolitan "brother-hood of man" as a political ideal that imagined citizenship not linked solely to the nation through a set of "rights," but to an international, universal brotherhood.

Stephen Kantrowitz argues that Black activists' "vision of belonging" encompassed not simply a set of specific rights, but recognition by white Americans as "brothers and equals," including the establishment of "bonds of trust and even love across the color line."[92] Only when all Americans embraced "the fraternal unity of man" would the country fully leave behind the legacy of slavery. In pursuit of this goal, I would argue that free people of color in New Orleans, many of them Haitian refugees, and newly arrived immigrants from Germany created their own educational institutions "a world apart" in which they could imagine a community whose time had not yet come. While segregated lodges flourished from the late 1840s onward, Freemasonry allowed people excluded from most forms of partisan political life to vote, hold office, and establish bonds of affiliation across great distances. Both before and after the Civil War, white Free-masonry's nominal commitment to universalism and cosmopolitanism did offer activists a forum to argue that racial exclusion violated basic Masonic principles in which all men were understood as created equal. Interracial lodges had existed in New Orleans since the arrival of refugees from Saint-Domingue, including the Freemason Pierre Roup.

Masonic Lodges as Counterpublic Educational Spaces of Citizenship

Pierre Roup, whom we met in the introduction, like other free men of color, was an active and successful builder in the well-established Faubourg Tremé, and he owned property both on Esplanade Avenue and North Rampart. The building trade had been a traditional occupation among free people of color. Major developers and builders in Faubourg Tremé between 1820 and 1855 included Myrtile Courcelle and the Soulié brothers. Norbert Soulié's office was only eight blocks down from Pierre's on 200 North Rampart, and his brothers Albin and Bernard, who were active Tremé real estate agents, divided their time between living in Paris and their homes on Tremé Street. A stone's throw from Pierre's cottage on Bayou Road lived Jean Louis Dolliole, another free man of color and noted builder who constructed scores of houses in the area and would help establish the Catholic Institute.[93] Pierre Olivier and François Muro, living east of Esplanade, were also active builders of the hundreds of edifices that were constructed in this burgeoning suburb of New Orleans during the early nineteenth century.

While occupation united these men, their common heritage as Haitian/Saint-Domingue refugees (or children of) also connected them to a transnational, transatlantic, multilingual network of political activity and thought that crisscrossed the Caribbean, Mexico, France, and the United States. For Pierre Roup, central to this political activity was the work of building networks of solidarity among New Orleanians, other Haitian refugees, and other free people of color and émigrés from France who would advance Masonic efforts to create a "brotherhood of man." We know this because as a young man Pierre played a leading role in the interracial Persévérance Masonic lodge No. 4 in New Orleans (Figure 18).[94] For Pierre and other free men of color, whose rights were increasingly vulnerable, Freemasonry provided an enclave of self-governance in which to engage political networks and, perhaps just as importantly, a space in which to imagine what equal citizenship could be.[95]

Pierre Roup was part of a diasporan racial collectivity of the wider Atlantic world in which Freemasonry circulated. He had most likely been exposed to the rich tradition of Freemasonry in Haiti, where it had flourished among men of color in the early 1790s. While the Afro-Franco aspects of this transatlantic circulation of political ideologies has been well-documented, the inclusion of German immigrants to New Orleans in the 1830s in Persévérance lodge has been neglected. But this interracial confraternity was key to developing a political ideology in which Masonic lodges allowed men to "function as full citizens of an imagined brotherhood in which all men were emphatically created equal."[96]

The interracial Persévérance Lodge No. 4, of which Roup was an active member and leader, and its offshoot, the Germania Lodge No.46, a predominantly German lodge, engaged in abolitionist thought in achieving their desired vision of a "universal brotherhood." While both lodges were composed mostly of white Europeans, the intertwined histories of these lodges signals a brief period in the 1830s and 1840s of interracial activ-

PERSEVERANCE LODGE.

Figure 18. Persévérance Masonic Lodge No. 4. The Historic New Orleans Collection Acc. No. 1974.25.3.280i.

ity.[97] Masonic lodges in the antebellum period, both French and German, viewed Masonry as a secular religion compatible with the republican ideals in which all people belonged to the family of mankind and shared the same rights.[98] This cosmopolitan vision of a perfect human society constituted through a "brotherhood of man" added new dimensions to the political ideal of equal citizenship. As Stephen Kantrowitz has argued, while this ideal was never achieved, it allowed for members (including African Americans, Germans, French, Cubans) to imagine a cosmopolitan universal brotherhood.[99] As proposed by Benedict Anderson, an "imagined community" is one where members will never know most of their fellow members, yet in the minds of each lives the image of their communion. This community was produced through the various activities (libraries, correspondence, meetings, publications, rituals, and lectures) of the two aforementioned Masonic lodges through a creole pedagogy of the imagination.

Imagined Brotherhood

Pierre Roup, an émigré from Haiti, was the son of Pierre Roup and Hélène Lesseige, both of Saint-Domingue.[100] While there is no conclusive evidence of when he arrived in New Orleans, it can be surmised that he might have

been part of the group of refugees who originally left Haiti in 1803 after
the Napoleonic invasion and reinstitution of slavery for Cuba. In 1809, the
expulsion from Cuba of French colonials who had originally sought asylum
there included Pierre, who arrived in New Orleans circa 1809. As a young
man, he was part of the largest wave of Haitians to reach New Orleans,
which included 2,731 whites, 3,102 free people of color, and 3,226 slaves.[101]
This large influx of free people of color arrived at a time when the territorial government under Governor Claiborne was increasingly worried
about the cosmopolitan and faction-ridden population of Louisiana, which
for the most part did not see themselves as Americans. While partisans of
Napoleon, England, and Spain still vied for power, a primary concern for
Claiborne was also the internal security of the territory given the ongoing
revolutionary fervor throughout the region among free people of color and
the enslaved for full emancipation and citizenship. This fear of radicalized
elements seeking republican ideals resulted in legislation in June of 1806
that forbade free men of color above the age of fifteen from Hispaniola and
other French islands from settling in the territory of Orleans. Less than a
year later, this legislation was extended to all free persons of color regardless of origin. In 1809, when Pierre Roup, at age ten, most likely arrived,
Governor Claiborne was unable to enforce the ban on the admittance of
free of people of color, and by January 1810 the mayor of New Orleans
reported to Claiborne that 428 free men of color had taken up residence in
the city. Pierre was one of these.

As Shirley Thompson maintains, "in a nation that precariously bal-
anced the ideals of freedom and equality with the practice of slavery, the
events in Saint Domingue would continue to point to the inconsistencies
in the national creed."[102] In the eyes of many Americans, enslaved and free
people of color from Haiti and Saint-Domingue were potential carriers of
rebellion and discontent. A number of slave rebellions and plots could be
directly or indirectly traced to Haitian influence, including the 1795 Pointe
Coupée rebellion, the 1812 Aponte Conspiracy in Spanish Cuba, and the
slave Gabriel's plot in 1800 in Virginia. In 1811, shortly after Pierre Roup
arrived, the largest slave revolt in U.S. history took place upriver from New
Orleans, apparently through a plot instigated by enslaved people, fugitive
maroons, free people of color, and privateers. In 1813, Joseph Savry, a free
man of color, along with other refugees from Haiti and Saint-Domingue,
raised a regiment to support the republican revolutions in Mexico.

While we cannot know with certainty the sympathies of Pierre Roup, it
is clear that he was part of what Rebecca Scott has called the "regional variant of the long nineteenth century" in which the circulation of revolution-

ary ideas in the Atlantic and Caribbean circuits were produced and mobilized by free people of color and enslaved Africans to imagine freedom.[103] Masonic lodges, like Persévérance Lodge No. 4, were the product of an Atlantic and Caribbean rights-consciousness that Rebecca Scott maintains contributed to a vernacular ideology in which shared public space and public culture were the measure of social equality. And while Masonic lodges were secret societies and as such have been understood as private, historian Craig Wilder posits that for Blacks in early national America, Freemasonry was a primary venue through which they not only pursued their collective welfare, but also enacted a claim to public, civil society.[104]

Pierre Roup, as well as many of his fellow pioneering entrepreneurs, contributed not only to the rapid growth of the New Orleans suburbs, but they were part of a social and political network of free men of color whose interests transcended economic advancement to include the pursuit of the rights of full citizenship in the new American nation. Jean Dolliole, a fellow builder who had served in the Spanish militia, was part of a larger contingent of free men of color who had extended their military services to the newly arrived American Governor Claiborne in 1804 with the expressed confidence that the new government would assure their "personal and political" freedom.[105] When Andrew Jackson called on the free Afro-Creole militia to fight against the British in 1812, he appealed to free men of color as "sons of freedom" and "fellow citizens."[106] Dolliole and others clearly expected that their participation in defending American national rights would garner their right to full citizenship and equal status. But this was not to be the case: no political recognition was extended to the Afro-Creole community after the Battle of New Orleans.

While military service served as a significant vehicle for advancement for free men of color under both the French and Spanish colonial regimes, the new American government was determined to impose a dual racial order on the new Louisiana territory. This new order required that the fluid and dynamic racial order that had characterized both French and Spanish Louisiana be harnessed to conform to an ideology of white supremacy. Given increasingly limited public spaces from which to enact their agency, free men of color engaged with Freemasonry as a means to embody their human dignity as part of a universal brotherhood. Having been denied American citizenship, free men of color turned to the development of what Joanna Brooks calls "black counter-publics" as a means of fostering political activities that allowed them to reclaim their political subjectivity despite their racial subordination.[107] One of these avenues was participation in Masonic activity. While secret and private, Freemasonry ironically provided free people of color a space to act as citizens of a brotherhood even though they were denied legal and political rights.[108]

Pierre Roup, while only ten years old when he came to Louisiana, most likely experienced his father or other Haitians in Cuba participating as members in the lodges of Freemasons. Persévérance Lodge No. 113, originally a Scottish Rite Lodge, was organized in 1806 in Jeremy, Haiti/Saint Domingue, then re-established in Cuba, and in 1812 it was one of the five lodges that constituted the present Grand Lodge of the State of Louisiana and was given the designation of No. 4.[109] As a young man, Roup, a well-connected member of the Saint-Domingue émigré community, was nominated to join the lodge.[110] Along with white Saint Domingue immigrants, Roup served as a high-ranking officer of the lodge. While the Persévérance Masons had originally convened their meetings in the interracial Etoile Polaire Lodge, in 1810 they received their own charter, and in 1819 they purchased a site to build their own lodge.[111] In 1820, as an officer of the lodge, Roup signed the contract to build the complex that was to house Persévérance Lodge No. 4.[112]

When Pierre Roup died in 1836, the Persévérance Lodge No. 4 served as a thriving center for the building and maintenance of community among an interracial, multilingual, transnational group of men. Men could join the lodge with the unanimous consent of its members, after which they passed through Masonry's three degrees (apprentice, fellow craft, and master) by taking part in elaborately scripted rites of passage that instructed them in the mythic stories and bound them to secrecy and confraternity. Monthly meetings of the lodge functioned as social gatherings to not only reaffirm the brotherly bonds of fictive kinship through numerous rituals, but to reinforce a collective history that traced its lineage to the fundamental truths of wise men and priests of the Egyptian and Ethiopian dynasties.[113] While Masons were in theory forbidden to discuss controversial matters of religion or politics, it is hard to imagine that issues of the day were not part of conversations before, during, and after lodge meetings. And while discussion of politics was considered taboo, the lodges for all practical purposes were sites that functioned as gathering places and training grounds for citizenship, not of the nation, but of a universal community.

While members of the lodge who were free men of color were restricted from full participation in the civic life of Louisiana, the lodge functioned as a counterpublic educational space on two levels: One, it was a space in which practical political skills were learned, and two, it was a space where men could imagine an interracial society based on universal brotherhood, not one in which racial subordination structured public spaces as well as citizenship. Within the confines of the lodge men participated in the discussion and writing of bylaws and annual election of officers and were able to develop leadership skills. The writing of bylaws required discussion of the provisions for consensus and power sharing. Principles of civil debate and equal time were established. At the monthly meetings, no one was to speak more than twice on the same topic, and men were to speak, listen, and address one another respectfully. As an institution, Persévérance Lodge functioned as an educational space in which men, particularly free men of color, claimed and engaged in the civil rights and political practices from which they were excluded in the public sphere due to the racial privilege that was assumed to be the natural provenance of whites. Free men of color forged political subjectivities and organizational expertise and became leaders at the local, state, and national level of their lodge. But on another level, for men like Pierre Roup these political processes were not the ends, but the means to connect the lodge to a "millenia-old project to perfect human society—a cosmopolitan project that welcomed men 'of all nations, tongues, kindreds, and languages.'"[114] For all practical purposes, they developed their own political ideals in which a universalist cosmopolitanism challenged white supremacy by reimagining "rights" and "citizenship" beyond race and the nation.

It should be no surprise then that when a wave of German immigrants arrived in New Orleans after the disruptions of the Napoleonic Wars in the 1830s, many of whom settled in the Tremé/Marginy neighborhood, they were invited to join the lodge. By 1844 the number of German immigrants in New Orleans who spoke only German raised concerns that potential members might be excluded given that Persévérance Lodge No. 4 was a French-speaking institution.[115] On March 24, 1844, thirteen German brethren met in the hall of Persévérance Lodge No. 4 for the purpose of forming a German Masonic lodge.[116] Gustave Martel, J. U. Haussner, and L. Rose were elected as the chief officers, C. Dannaples was elected secretary, and J. D. Kamper was elected treasurer. On April 16, 1844, they met again at Persévérance Lodge No. 4 after a charter was granted by the Grand Lodge under the name and number of Germania Lodge No 46, F. & A.M. (Figure 19). At this meeting it was decided that the minutes would be trilingual, with Secretary Dannaples writing them in German, French, and English (this was done from 1844 to 1850), reflecting the transnational nature of Freemasons.[117] While they initially met in the home lodge, in 1845 they purchased three lots and a two-story building on St. Louis Street.[118] While Persévérance Lodge No. 4 was always considered the mother lodge of Germania, there was now for the first time a German-speaking offspring of a French

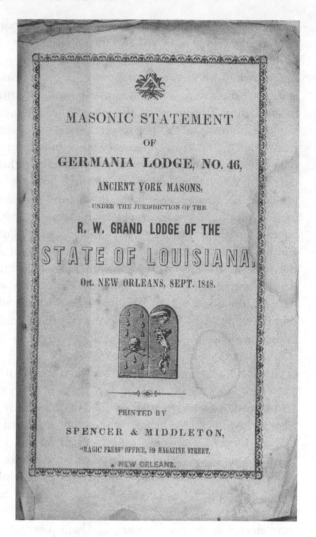

Figure 19. Masonic Statement of Germania Lodge No. 46, September 1848. Courtesy of Germania Lodge No. 46, Inc., The Historic New Orleans Collection Acc.no. EL2.2001.

lodge. For the first year Germania met on the second and fourth Sundays at 9:00 a.m.; after that meetings were moved to 4:00 p.m.

Germania Lodge No. 46, like its mother lodge, saw itself as a political and educational institution committed to promoting a universal brotherhood. Their movement sought to unite men of different religions, political views, and nationalities to create a more perfect society.[119] Two officers of the Germania Lodge No. 46, J. D. Kamper and J. U. Haussner, were also members of the German Society of New Orleans, which was originally organized to provide relief for thousands of German immigrants during the 1840s and 1850s.[120] Like the lodge, the German Society was dedicated to providing aid to newly arrived German immigrants, many of whom were of moderate means and some who were destitute.[121] At a meeting to organize the German Society led by Christian Roselius on May 5, 1847, at the Conti Street Hotel, J. D. Kamper was elected as treasurer of the German Society. J. U. Haussner, another officer of the Germania Lodge, was not only a member of the German Society, but was hired by them in 1847 as an agent and collector. Roselius, a German immigrant who had arrived in New Orleans in 1820, was a well-respected lawyer who was active politically with other German immigrants, many of them exiles from the 1848 revolution. He was also an antislavery proponent.[122] While Roselius was not a member of the Germania Lodge, the participation of two of the lodge members in the German Society reveals a network of relationships whose goal was pushing Masonry's ideals of universal fraternity to full expression.

The political commitments of the Germania Lodge No. 46 can be gleaned from the extensive library housed there. The lodge's library housed 168 books including German-French dictionaries, works on history, politics, and religion (including six books on Judaism). The complete works of Johann Wolfgang von Goethe and Heinrich Heine as well as Alexandre Dumas's *Der Graf von Monte Christo* were available to lodge members. Dumas, a leading Romantic writer born in France in 1802, was the son of a mulatto father born in Haiti to an enslaved African, whose French father had brought him to France at age fourteen to be educated. As a writer who combined literary and political themes, his work appealed not only to the German Masons, but influenced the literature of free men of color like Armand Lanusse, Victor Sejour, and Joanni Questy, who like the Freemasons were committed to a vision of an egalitarian society. This vision was one that necessitated the work of the abolition of slavery. And while there is no direct evidence linking Kamper and Haussner to the abolitionist movement, the works of British novelist and antislavery proponent Laurence Stern were also part of the Germania Lodge.[123] They were clearly part of a larger community of German activists including Roselius, who, like the Freemasons, held a well-developed philosophy of political radicalism rooted in the egalitarianism of the age of democratic revolution. Like the meetings of the Persévérance Lodge No. 4 from which they were descended, members of the Germania Lodge No. 46, newly arrived immigrants, learned the political skills of running elections, voting, taking minutes, effective leadership, and democratic dialogue. These were attributes of democratic citizenship few of these men had access to in Germany. Most significantly, though, they were part of a vibrant cosmopolitan, multilingual, transnational community that sought to transcend differences of religion, class, and race in the hopes of creating a universal brotherhood.

The minute books of the Germania Lodge No. 46 from 1844 to 1850 suggest a flurry of activity including invited lectures; a host of visitors from various countries, representing numerous religions (Jewish, Lutheran) and a variety of occupations; and visits from other lodges including, in December 1848, a list of representatives from nine other lodges in New Orleans, including Etoile Polaire, La Parfaite No. 1, and Friends of Harmony Lodge. By 1848 there were approximately sixty-seven members, with regular attendance of about sixteen to thirty members and often as many as fifteen visitors. These visitors often were from around the country including Fond du Lac, Wisconsin; Reading, Pennsylvania; New York City; Charleston, South Carolina (Washington Lodge); Augusta, Georgia; Detroit, Michigan; New York state (Henry Clay 277); Minnesota; Mississippi; Arkansas; St. Louis, Missouri; Brunswick, Maine; Baltimore, Maryland; Brooklyn, New York; Memphis, Tennessee; Mobile, Alabama; Providence, Rhode Island; and Donaldsonville, Louisiana.[124] The building of these networks contributed to establishing solidarity across lines of geography and forums for deliberation. Visitors and practices crossed not only the line between free states and slave states, but also the boundaries of nation and empire, contributing to a circulation of ideas about civil and political rights, as well as abolition.

This dynamic, cosmopolitan space of Germania Lodge No. 46 functioned as a site of civic and political education for newly arrived working-class Germans, much like Persévérance Lodge No. 4 had done for newly arrived Haitian immigrants several decades prior. Throughout the antebellum period, these lodges continued to provide counterpublic spaces where members participated in political organization, rituals, study, lectures, and political and intellectual dialogue. And while the direct intersections of these lodges were brief, they continued to share a common network and bond that provided both groups a sense of agency through self-governance and collective solidarity through Freemasonry's philosophy of "universal brotherhood" in which all men were equal. Although the activism of Freemasons, including that of Pierre Roup, J. D. Kamper, and J. U. Haussner, failed to transform the American republic, the order served as a pedagogical space, a counterpublic, that nurtured expansive ideas and extensive networks of leadership. It did much more than that, however. It imagined a "universal brotherhood" beyond "rights" and "citizenship" that displaced the nation-state as the site of the production of the "educated subject." Little did they know that the "nation" they so hoped to democratize would be radically altered with the coming of the Civil War.

The Revolution Is at Hand: Universal Equality and The Civil War

[Segregated schools] perpetuate from childhood the infatuation
of the white, and prompt the black to retaliate by enmity or envy,
[and] . . . draws a line between the two elements of one and the
same people, from the cradle itself up to the time of manhood and
throughout life.

Armand Lanusse, *New Orleans Tribune*, February 17, 1865[125]

When the Civil War began, Armand Lanusse and the students at the Catholic Institute believed this was the democratic revolution they had been waiting for. Central to this revolution would be a society in which the human dignity of all persons would be signified in the public sphere through free, integrated schools. Once again, a curriculum of imagination played a powerful role in envisioning a new America. Teachers at the Catholic Institute, including Lannuse and Paul Trévigne, along with the students, engaged in real-world activism by writing editorials and poems to the *L'Union* (which became the *Tribune* two years later), the French-language biweekly newspaper founded in 1862 by Afro-Creole leaders. Cofounded with Dr. Louis Charles Roudanez and his brother Jean-Baptiste Roudanez and edited by Jean-Charles Houzeau, a Belgian activist who passed for "colored," the *Tribune* published editorials, essays, and literary works that set the Civil War within the context of an ongoing age of revolution.

Franco-Afro-Creole writers, as well as the students, drew on their radical literary traditions to address the possibilities and circumstances of the Civil War and Reconstruction, using the medium of the newspaper to imagine with readers a nation of composite citizenry, an unprecedented United States. For Afro-Creole activists, the Civil War was far more than a struggle to preserve the Union. It was a necessary step toward the fulfillment of republican ideals. The *Tribune* noted that when France had emancipated all remaining slaves in her possession in 1848, they also were granted universal male suffrage. The objective was clear: achieving the full rights of citizenship for all people of color in the United States. How this would be achieved was the task that lay before them.

Expectations that the students would participate in constituting the public sphere were also clearly conveyed to students. Student activism was not limited to the practices of a curriculum of imagination by writing letters within the confines of the schoolhouse. Student letters to the newspaper reflect how the outbreak of the Civil War challenged them in new ways to negotiate the meanings of freedom and citizenship. When

Lanusse took a stand with the Confederacy in 1862, the Union had not made any commitment to the abolition of slavery. President Lincoln was resolved to preserve the Union without freeing the slaves. The Emancipation Proclamation would not be declared until January 1, 1863, and slavery was not abolished in Louisiana until May 11, 1864. And while slavery came to an end, the question of citizenship and full equality were still very much disputed in the United States. Abolishing slavery was one thing, but complete racial equality was quite another. For the teachers and students at the Catholic Institute, equality would not be complete without integrated public education.

A student letter from April 1861 describes the large assembly held in the schoolyard at which Lanusse, "a brave Creole of our glorious Louisiana," roused Creoles of color to enlist in the Confederacy. Lanusse was quoted as saying:

> So my dear friends, it is not for liberty that we are about to spill our blood in struggling; but our right and "our right we shall have or die on the fields of battle."

Invoking the language of "rights," Lanusse is referencing a long-held tradition going back to the American Revolution and the War of 1812 of free men of color participating in the military with the hopes of gaining citizenship. But defending Louisiana, their homes, their property, and their families cannot be conflated with support for the Confederacy. Lanusse's decision to initially join the Confederacy suggests the complex, contextual, and situated meanings of public rights. Within seven months, he declared in an October 1862 editorial in *L'Union* that although he did not want to fight against fellow Louisianans, he could not cooperate in the preservation of prejudice.[126]

On December 6, 1862, an article signed "A student of the Catholic Institute" (no doubt it would have been potentially dangerous for the writer to sign their name) criticizes an article in the *L'Abeille* (*The Bee*, another New Orleans newspaper), for misrepresenting the actions of the school's director, Armand Lanusse. The incident referred to by the student was Lanusse's refusal to fly the Union flag as ordered by General Benjamin F. Butler after the surrender of New Orleans. The student's scathing critique of *L'Abeille* suggests that the paper purposely misrepresented the incident to cast suspicion on the school. The student warns that readers of newspapers must have a critical eye in order to "leave aside everything that is only there to tease partisan hatred." The student describes the majority of newspaper readers as "those old geezers stuck in the groove of a routine and who for all their life have not missed reading the digest after sipping on a half cup of coffee, still believe blindly the news found in the papers; or maybe the pure-bred secessionist, the kind that does not exist in Europe, that was engendered by the Southern States' rebellion." The curriculum of the school clearly resulted not only in critical readers of the news, but in students who were empowered to write in real-world spaces to expose the social injustices they experienced.

Shortly after General Butler occupied New Orleans in 1862, he turned his attention to education. By early September, the school system was unified, a single course of instruction was prescribed for all municipal districts, and instruction could only be given in English. No provisions were made for the education of the enslaved or free people of color. The newly freed slaves, however, had already begun to self-organize, creating an educational movement that was deeply rooted in their own understanding of the relationship between freedom and literacy. Small private schools were established between 1860 and 1862 called "native schools" in which "self-teaching" was practiced.[127] While the newly freed slaves accepted help from northern missionary societies and the Freedmen's Bureau, it was their self-determination and action that resulted in schooling for their children. By 1865, when the Freedmen's Bureau took control of the Louisiana school system, the freedmen's educational movement had resulted in 126 schools, 19,000 pupils, and 100 teachers.[128] Freed people, formerly freed people, and their white allies saw education as central to the economic and political future of all people of color. Their efforts were among the first to campaign for universal public education. These schools, however, were faced by fierce opposition because they threatened white supremacy and a permanent uneducated Black labor force.

After the Emancipation Proclamation was enunciated, Butler appointed Lt. George Hanks, the superintendent of free labor, to address the issue of the education of Blacks. By October 1863, seven schools for Blacks were in existence, with an approximate enrollment of 1,700. In 1864, the commanding general, Nathaniel Banks, set up a separate Board of Education to direct an educational program for Black Louisianans. When the school board temporarily halted the 5 percent school tax, which meant that schools for freed children would be closed, Maj. Gen. E. R. S. Canby received a petition with the signatures of ten thousand freed people asking that the tax be reinstated.[129] The freedmen's program, however, was completely distinct from the white public school system that had been reinstituted by the Unionist government in 1864. The continued segregation of public schools and education by the Union signaled to those like Lanusse that the revolution was far from complete.

Not only did Afro-Creoles and white radicals want public integrated education, they expected to achieve universal suffrage when the legislature met in 1864 for the constitutional convention. Voting rights for newly freed slaves were denied, with limited black suffrage for free people of color sometime in the future. An 1866 editorial in the *Tribune* wrote:

> Our future is indissolubly bound up with that of the negro, and we have resolved . . . to rise or fall with them. We have no rights which we can reckon safe while the same are denied to the fieldhands on the sugar plantations.[130]

Only complete universal suffrage would be accepted. Without the enslaved also getting the right to vote, no rights would be secured. The strategic political use of race distinguished *Tribune* writers as radical thinkers of the time. Given that the prevailing theories of race were biological, to construct race as political or as the result of historical circumstances was radical. Radicals banded together in 1865 to form the Friends of Universal Suffrage, whose goal was the equality before the law for all Black Louisianans.

When the failed 1864 constitutional convention was reconvened at the Mechanics Institute in July of 1866, tensions between former Confederates and radical Republicans erupted into a riot later known as the Massacre of 1866 that resulted in the death of forty-four Blacks.[131] One anonymous poet (perhaps Lanusse) wrote shortly after the Massacre of 1866,

> Whatever happens, my lute cannot vibrate with rage,
> It calls for peace and fraternity;
> To the oppressed, it says: brothers, arise and have courage,
> The hour is near, rescue liberty!

The *Tribune* poets used the literary and political heritage of Romanticism to imagine how they might overcome hatred and join in universal brotherhood. The political premises of Reconstruction were revolutionary, and *imagining* a nation of equality was necessary to carry people's spirits through the violence and hardships that lay ahead. Throughout the Civil War, the teachers and students contributed poems, editorials, and articles to New Orleans newspapers, where they sought to articulate a vision of the "public" that was not merely rights-based but was revolutionary in imagining a transatlantic brotherhood in which citizenship transcended the nation.[132] Imagination, not just the rational discourse of rights, was seen as essential to creating a "public" where the equality of all human beings would be honored. Shortly before his death in 1867, Lanusse, while still principal, published a poem in *L'Union*:

And since among us the ills of slavery
will cease, let us forget our suffering of yesterday;
Let us honor our martyrs and forgive the outrage
This is how a proud and free people avenges itself!![133]

While the ideal of complete freedom had yet to be reached, the activism of both the teachers and students of the Catholic Institute cannot be underestimated. After the Civil War, the former students and teachers were among the leaders in creating an integrated public school system open to every child in Louisiana. The Louisiana constitution of 1868 not only mandated the establishment of a state-funded system of public education, but it forbade segregation. According to Caryn Cossé Bell, the 1868 state constitution was by far the most radical blueprint for change in the Reconstruction South. Although Lanusse died in the year preceding the writing of the constitution, it embodied his vision of a truly "public" sphere that honored the dignity of all humans. For Lanusse, civil or political rights could never bestow equality if unequal social relations (like segregation) were sanctioned by the law. It was in the public sphere, not in individual civic rights, that the roots of true "brotherhood" took shape. For Afro-Creoles, the constitution of 1868 fulfilled this radical revolutionary vision. "Public" integrated schools (the first in the nation) in New Orleans lasted only through Radical Reconstruction, giving way to the segregation that increasingly marked the "Jim Crow" South. The ideology of "public rights" as central to equality continued to inform an Afro-Creole protest tradition that would become the impetus for *Plessy v. Ferguson* and the modern civil rights era.

While the national narratives of history have located the origins of public education in a Northern, Anglo-Protestant, common school narrative, the Afro-Creole protest tradition, the Catholic Institute, the interracial Masonic lodges, and interracial *Tribune* disrupt this narrative by situating Louisiana as part of a complex transnational, Atlantic world that developed "vernacular concepts of equality" grounded in the principle of universal public rights. The Afro-Creole protest tradition sought to articulate a radical vision of freedom, education, and citizenship rooted *not* in notions of the nation-state, but of a global, transatlantic cosmopolitan citizenship in which boundaries of identity were disrupted and dispersed to embrace a "worldliness" where equality was not a product of the "state," but the consequence of the humanizing effects of education.

Reverberations

> I have a different idea of a universal. It is of a universal rich with all that is particular, rich with all the particulars there are, the deepening of each particular, the coexistence of them all.
>
> —Aimé Césaire

The reverberations of transatlantic pedagogies of the imagination continue to circulate. In July of 2020, protesters drawing attention to the ongoing legacy of colonialisms' racial injustice in Fort-de-France, Martinique, tore down the statue of Napoleon's wife, the Empress Josephine, as well as the statue of Pierre Bélain d'Esnambuc, the French trader introduced in the beginning of this book, who in 1635 established France's first permanent Caribbean colony on Martinique. This current protest is part of a long legacy of postcolonial activism in Martinique, including that of Aimé Césaire (1913–2008), who, like the many activists in this chapter, drew on the concept of universalism. The *universal* that Aimé Césaire, the postcolonial Francophone theorist, poet, and politician from Martinique, embraces transgresses the borderlands of modernity signified through and in a linear conception of history. *Universal* is not synonymous with *sameness*, which always has as its precondition some normative measure. For Césaire, the founder of the négritude movement, the normative spaces in constructs of "universal" derived from Enlightenment philosophy valued above all "freedom" as the highest and universal political value. Paradoxically, freedom as a concept was only possible with its antithesis, slavery. The political philosophy of "universal" rights of freedom, liberty, and equality that birthed modernity, as well as global capitalism and the nation-state, were predicated on the enslavement of non-Europeans as a labor force in the colonies. It is the paradox between the discourse of freedom and the practice of slavery that Césaire illuminates in his unique idea of the universal. His critique is a remapping of the very practice of history to secure a critical space *elsewhere* from modernity from which to think history differently. This is a history grounded in particulars, one that acknowledges the spatial confrontations between different concepts of history.

Césaire's négritude movement was based on a pan-African understanding of history that critiqued colonialism's inevitable construction of identity as either free/colonizer, subject/citizen, slave/colonized, object/noncitizen. By grounding history in the African diaspora and a Black consciousness, which rejected these dualisms, the négritude movement disrupted the linchpin of modernity, the nation-state, with its corollary construct of "white" citizenship. Deflecting the nation, new subjectivities based in the "universal as particular" continue to be imagined. Like the imagined brotherhoods of transnational Freemasonry, or the imagined communities around universalist ideals of the students at the Catholic Institute, counterpublic spaces continue to reverberate.

FIVE

The *New Orleans Tribune* and the *Crusader*

Interracial Community-Based Texts

It [prejudice] closes the eye of reason. . . . And our enlightened
neighbors, in the enlightened and progressive age, ought to cease
fostering and fomenting the prejudices which enslave them or warp
their judgments, and to listen to the voice of reason.[1]

This quotation from the January 24, 1869, edition of *La Tribune de la
Nouvelle-Orléans/The New Orleans Tribune* (1862–64, 1869–70), the first
Black-owned daily newspaper in the United States, speaks to the newspaper's mission to differentiate its rhetoric of equal rights from other newspapers of its time and locale by becoming the "voice of reason." This mission
would challenge America's increasing reliance on scientific racism to justify
White supremacy and racial segregation in the aftermath of slavery.[2] At
the heart of this argument, the *Tribune* and later the *Crusader* maintained
that human equality was ultimately signified through "public rights," not
solely through civil or political rights. Public, integrated education would
not only counteract the illogical tenets of the budding eugenics movement,
but it also would exemplify a public space that acknowledged the humanity of all persons as a means to form one, united American nation. The
Tribune was confident that rational men would not only see the economic
and social benefits of "one people" united under one nation, but also would
ultimately see a different future in which the nation could finally fulfill the
revolutionary potential of the American ideals of freedom and equality.
For the *Tribune*, this necessitated a public space that was first and foremost

to be forged in free, public, and integrated schools. The *Tribune's* vision for public, integrated education was in contrast to that of other liberal Republican newspapers and nontext entities that sought to influence Black education during Reconstruction. These papers, while arguing for Black education, did not support integrated education, and most articulated a different curriculum for Blacks based on a hierarchy of intelligence and human worth rooted in scientific racism. The *Tribune*, on the other hand, not only rejected any form of segregation as antithetical to America's desire for restoring democracy, it was also unique in its rhetorical argument that segregation was unenlightened and irrational. Likewise, the *Crusader*, which modeled itself on the *Tribune*, echoed these same arguments in the 1890s in response to the Separate Car Act. For both newspapers, segregation would always be a mark of inferiority and would create a caste system that was antithetical to the "public rights" they saw as critical to the equality promised in American democracy. These interracial, community-based newspapers were neither Black nor white spaces but liminal spaces, thresholds between what was and what could be in a true democracy based on public rights. A creole pedagogy of liminality disrupts hierarchical notions of binaries and dichotomies by embracing ambiguity, in-between spaces, and the ongoing potential of transformation. For the transnational, interracial radicals in the post-Reconstruction era, liminality signified the contradictions of separating races on the basis of color.

The *Tribune* as Advocate for Public Integrated Education

While a few Republican newspapers in the North, such as William Lloyd Garrison's *Liberator* and *Frederick Douglass' Paper*, shared news coverage of the integration of schools in Boston's *Roberts* case in 1849, most members of the early Black and Southern Republican presses stopped short of arguing for public, integrated education. They demanded "far more and better educational opportunities" for Black children, which initially advocated private schools, and later public schools, but never public, integrated schools.[3] Likewise, Northern benevolent societies like the National Freedmen's Relief Association, religious organizations such as the Catholic Church and African Methodist Episcopal Church, and the Freedmen's Bureau each had a unique reason for sponsoring Black education, but, according to the *Tribune*, they all suffered from the same limitation: Northern philanthropy, religious instruction, and collusion with the government supported segregated education for Blacks. "The *New Orleans Tribune* [and the city's

Afro-Creole community of which it was a part] took the most advanced or radical position" in its "equal rights proposals" for universal suffrage, equal accommodation laws, and particularly public, integrated education.[4]

The *Tribune* was the singular text in the public South during Reconstruction to staunchly advocate for public, integrated education. In this way, The *Tribune* anticipated the ruling of *Brown v. Board of Education* and argued that separate education would always be synonymous with unequal education and would reinforce the mark of inferiority already placed upon Blacks by slavery. The *Tribune* grounded its argument against segregated education in its own logic and rationality that focused specifically on combating the dominant discourse of white supremacy and Black inferiority embedded in the emerging ideology of scientific racism. The *Tribune*'s logos-centered rhetoric forced its audience—all too familiar with the "scientific" claims of the emerging eugenics movement—to question whose rationality represented "good sense and sound reason."[5] Therefore, the staff of the *Tribune* carefully crafted a counterdiscourse that "[used] the same categories [of the dominant discourse] by which it was . . . disqualified" to defend against the divisive rhetoric of scientific racism, instead posing public, integrated education as a necessary prerequisite to rebuilding a nation destroyed by the Civil War.[6]

More specifically, French-speaking Afro-Creole contributors to the *Tribune*, like Paul Trévigne, reasoned that public, integrated education was essential if laws promising equal citizenship and universal suffrage, which they assumed (unlike their contemporaries) emancipation would entail, were to be enforced. They recognized that since the dominant discourse, scientific racism, had penetrated the public sphere, law alone could not remedy racial oppression. Instead, they saw schoolrooms as the new battleground for American democracy, deeming the social interaction promised by integrated education as the best weapon to change the public's thinking. Whereas scientific racism used presumed biological differences among races to provide a rationale for separate education, the *Tribune* reasoned that changing individuals' thinking necessitated an integrated common education that would unite the nation. The goal of such an education was not assimilation or acculturation but rather creation of a united brotherhood that would serve to heal the deep divisions of the Civil War and fulfill the promises of American democracy. Taking up the northern call for the New England model of "common schools," the editors of the *Tribune* maintained that "[i]n order to have only one nation and one people, we must educate all children in the same public schools."[7]

The *Tribune*'s rhetoric provides an invaluable perspective into the unique vision of self-determination that reasoned that free, public, integrated education for *all* citizens was essential to creating a public sphere that acknowledged the humanity of all persons. This revolutionary vision of public, integrated education as central to an egalitarian society was taken up by the newspaper through two distinct arguments: (1) that scientific racism was illogical and unfounded and (2) that public, integrated education was the next rational step in fostering a collective national identity based on public rights.

Newspapers as Community-Based Texts: Situating the *Tribune*

"This journal is the organ of the oppressed, whether black, yellow, or white."[8] Most existing histories have identified the post–Civil War educational mission in Louisiana with northern philanthropy, religious instruction, and governmental sponsorship, whether in the figure of the Yankee schoolmarm or the Freedmen's Bureau. These histories "have focused on what happened *to* black communities, not what transpired *within* them."[9] Alternatively, the *Tribune* provides a window into the self-advocacy and agency of Afro-Creoles as they engaged other people of color, including Anglicized Blacks and white Europeans, as fellow activists.[10] While scholars like James D. Anderson, Christopher Span, and Heather Andrea Williams have focused on Black agency, this research extends the notion of agency to encompass community-based texts, like the *Tribune*, as sites for public conversations that focused on the relationship between race, education, and republican government.

The role of the southern Black press, especially in regards to Blacks' struggle for self-determination during Reconstruction, has been omitted from this conversation. Richard H. Abbott, historian of Republican newspapers in the Reconstruction South, emphasizes the scholarly marginalization of the dozen Black papers that existed in the South between 1826 and 1867, the date of the First Reconstruction Act: "The few characterizations of Southern Republican journalists as a whole are generally unfavorable," dismissed as "carpetbagger" or "vicious, wholly self-seeking journals, that cared not to make the South a truly integrated part of the nation."[11] Penelope Bullock, historian of the Black press, goes one step further to erroneously claim that "none of the periodicals initiated before 1865 were still in existence when the Civil War ended, and the publishing of black periodicals did not begin again until the decade of the 1880s." Bullock attributes this "hiatus" to "the optimism that pervaded the black population":

"Negroes anticipated that legal measures taken by the federal government would guarantee first-class citizenship and place them in the mainstream of American life. Thus the periodical, as an agent for the vindication of equal rights, was no longer needed."[12] Claims like Bullock's make the existence of the *Tribune* an impossibility due to its publication dates (1864–1870), but also serve as examples of the ways in which Black periodical studies have unfortunately often ignored southern newspapers.[13] Afro-Creole New Orleanians and émigré radicals, who owned and edited the newspaper, did envision the Civil War as the culmination of a long struggle for democratic equality that would result in a "republican millennium of racial justice and harmony."[14] But their optimism did not eliminate the need for a fighting press, especially in the South and in New Orleans, home to "the bloodiest riot of the entire Reconstruction era."[15] Unfortunately, Bullock's oversight is representative of many histories of the Black press, which either ignore or inaccurately narrate the founding of the *Tribune*.[16]

Finally, while some Louisiana historians mention the *Tribune* within their texts, William P. Connor, one of the few authors to critically write about the newspaper, concludes, "The *Tribune* has been mentioned often as the first black daily newspaper in the United States. The real importance of the newspaper lies not in this fact, but in its intellectual content."[17] Unfortunately, previous scholars have paid scant attention to the newspaper's "intellectual content." Caryn Cossé Bell, who has perhaps done the most work on the *Tribune*, mentions the newspaper's advocacy of integration, but mostly in terms of public conveyances (streetcars) and Freemasonry lodges, and Mary Niall Mitchell, while arguing that the *Tribune* "framed the question of separate schools in Louisiana—indeed, the segregation of black and white children for generations—in terms of nation rather than region," portrays the *Tribune*'s main opposition as the "sexualizing of integrated schoolrooms' and whites'" fears of miscegenation.[18] Most recently, Clint Bruce has collected the poems printed in the newspaper by twenty Afro-Creole activist authors whose prose highlights their contributions to the fight for civil rights.[19] None of these sources, however, place the *Tribune* in direct conversation with the dominant discourse of scientific racism to uncover how and why its editors used logos to appeal to its various audiences. A rhetorical analysis illuminates not only *what* the *Tribune* signifies but *how* its contributors signify: "How [did] African Americans during this period [use] language and to what ends, to whom [were they] arguing and how [did] that [shape] their discourse, and what factors influenced their persuasive strategies," particularly in relation to public, integrated education.[20]

The "Afro-Creole Protest Tradition" and Founding of the *Tribune*[21]

> That education is desirable we acknowledge from the fact that we
> have never failed to advocate education at the proper time and on
> the proper occasion.[22]

While the *Tribune's* staff argued for public, integrated education in direct
opposition to the dominant discourse of scientific racism, they also recognized and inserted themselves into an Afro-Creole protest tradition, which
had "never failed to advocate education." The *Tribune* itself described the
tripartite racial structure, which existed in New Orleans dating back to its
origin as a French colony, as follows: "Louisiana is in a very peculiar situation. Here, the colored population has a twofold origin. There is an old
population, with a history and mementos of their own, warmed by patriotism and partaking of the feelings and education of the white. The only
social condition known to these men is that of freedom. . . . There is, on
the other hand, a population of freedmen, but recently liberated from the
shackles of bondage. All is to be done yet for them."[23] Many members of
the former group considered themselves Creoles, native-born Louisianans
of African and Latin European descent. New Orleans Afro-Creoles, the
nation's largest and "most politicized and articulate free black community
in the South," "advocated education as a means to counteract the damaging
effects of an increasingly oppressive social and political order."[24] Before and
during the Civil War and Reconstruction, Afro-Creoles in New Orleans
like Armand Lanusse (introduced in the previous chapter) had used literary
works like *L'Album littéraire* and *Les Cenelles* to "recall the unfulfilled promise of the age of democratic revolution" as a means to simultaneously contest images of racial inferiority (as these texts proved that many Blacks were
not just literate, but also classically educated) and advocate for access to
public education.[25] This Afro-Creole literary and textual tradition "served
as a springboard to other forms of social and political activism," including
the Catholic Institute and then the *Tribune* and *Crusader*.[26]

By 1860, the literary production of Afro-Creoles shifted to rely primarily on the Black press. Driven by a universalist ethic grounded in the
French colonial Catholic Church as well as the French and Haitian revolutionary traditions, New Orleans Afro-Creoles were poised for a social and
political revolution on the eve of the Civil War. When Union forces swept
into the city in the spring of 1862, Afro-Creole leaders met with Gen. Benjamin F. Butler to place their troops at his disposal. In the fall of that year,
Paul Trévigne, language teacher at the Catholic Institute for more than

forty years, began editing the first Black newspaper in the South, *L'Union: Mémorial politique, littéraire et progressiste* (The Union: Political, Literary, and Progressive Record), a French-language biweekly that sought to mobilize support for emancipation of the slaves, the involvement of Black troops in the war effort, and the legal recognition of racial equality. Cofounded with Paris-educated, Afro-Creole Dr. Louis Charles Roudanez and his brother Jean-Baptiste Roudanez on September 27, 1862, *L'Union* "published editorials, essays, and literary works that set the Civil War within the context of an ongoing age of revolution."[27] Like the previously discussed texts, it carried the poems of local Afro-Creole poets and showed that the editors and correspondents drew from French Romanticism—having read Pascal, Voltaire, Rousseau, Montesquieu, Balzac, Commettant, Gregoire, Plato, and other writers—as well as the "republican idealism" of the French and Haitian Revolutions.[28] Trévigne wasted no time in setting out the goals of radical Afro-Creoles: "We inaugurate today a new era in the South. We proclaim the Declaration of Independence as the basis of our platform. . . . You who desire to establish true republicanism, democracy without shackles, gather around us."[29] A few weeks later, he wrote of "a new sun, similar to that of 1789 . . . is on our horizon."[30] For Afro-Creole activists, education, and specifically public education, was a prerequisite to the "democracy without shackles" that they foresaw as the result of the Civil War. *L'Union* pointed out that slavery reduced a man to the "level of a farm animal" because it "prohibited the slave from cultivating his intelligence."[31] When *L'Union* failed, Trévigne became coeditor of the *Tribune*.

On July 21, 1864, Roudanez reconstituted *L'Union* as the *New Orleans Tribune*, which ran until 1870.[32] Roudanez was born in St. James Parish, Louisiana, on June 12, 1823, the son of a French merchant and a free woman of color. He went to school in New Orleans, where he eventually accumulated a small fortune through his investment in bonds. He then traveled to France at the age of twenty-one to study medicine under Phillipe Ricord at the University of Paris's Faculty of Medicine. While in Paris, Roudanez was an active participant in defense of working people during the democratic, socialist revolution of 1848. Upon graduating with honors in 1853, Roudanez returned to the United States to earn a second medical degree from Dartmouth College. He established a successful medical practice, serving both Blacks and whites, when he eventually returned to New Orleans in 1857. Jean-Baptiste Roudanez, the older brother of Dr. Louis Charles Roudanez, was often listed as the *Tribune*'s publisher. While the paper clearly served to make Afro-Creoles visible to Union occupiers who may not have been familiar with the fluid racial makeup of Louisiana, it also sought to work across racial and cultural barriers by including English-speaking Blacks and reaching out to national Black American leaders.

Louis Charles Roudanez and Paul Trévigne made significant changes to build cross-racial coalitions with Anglicized Blacks and white unionists. They decided to publish the *Tribune* as an English-French bilingual paper and to make it a daily paper. In November 1864, they hired white radicals Belgium-born Jean-Charles Houzeau and French-born Michel Vidal as editors.[33] Houzeau later recalled that his mission was "to prepare for the future, by immediately making it [the *Tribune*] the organ of five million black and brown-skinned men of the United States" and "to transform a local newspaper into a newspaper of national importance."[34] The *Tribune* also hired both Afro-Creole and English-speaking Anglicized Black editors.[35] In working to create a broad coalition, the *Tribune* sought to become the mouthpiece of various political organizations, including the National Union Brotherhood Association started by Anglicized Black ministers, the National Equal Rights League formed by James Ingraham to advocate for the abolition of slavery and for Black suffrage, and the Friends of Universal Suffrage, an interracial organization led by Thomas D. Durant, Lieutenant Governor Oscar J. Dunn, and Catholic Institute teacher Firmin Christophe. Creating interlacing networks among these diverse groups to promote equal rights would function not only to disrupt the rigid color line but would elevate to a national level the vision of equal citizenship that the *Tribune* advocated.

The *Tribune* was first issued from 21 Conti Street between Chartres and Levee, where it was published three days a week.[36] The owners dedicated themselves to the success of the paper: "Convinced that a newspaper, under the present circumstances, representing the principles and interest which we propose to defend and advocate was much needed in New Orleans, we shall spare no means at our command to render the *Tribune* worthy of public confidence and respect, and these were the reasons which prompted us to its publication."[37] The *Tribune* became the first Black daily on October 4, 1864, when its staff "receive[d] a new press and a complete assortment of material from New York."[38] The *Tribune* was published in both French and English, and its editors associated the newspaper with the Republican Party of Louisiana to aid their goal of elevating all Blacks politically. The *Tribune* received its designation in 1867 as an "Official Organ of the United States Government" and was distributed to congressmen, chief northern newspapers, and many European subscribers in addition to the Black community. The newspaper itself claimed that "there is not a single colored man who does not feel that the *Tribune* is the rostrum from which the oppressed and the down-trodden may be heard by the American nation," and twentieth-century historians such as Ficklen, DuBois, Litwack, and McFeely continued to recognize the *Tribune* as "the most important Negro newspaper of the Civil War era."[39]

Texts like *L'Album Littéraire* and *Les Cenelles* and Afro-Creole leaders such as Trévigne and Lanusse clearly laid the ideological groundwork for the *Tribune*'s passionate commitment to public, integrated education. Trévigne and his fellow staff members at the *Tribune* used the printed word to make an argument for public, integrated schooling, which Blacks would sponsor themselves through their payment of taxes:

> We hold that the question of the schools will only be settled when all children, without discrimination on account of race or color, will be admitted to sit together on the same benches and receive from the same teachers the light of knowledge. At that time there will only be one set of schools and all the energies of the State, all the talent of the teachers, will be directed to one end and one aim—the promotion of public education for the greatest good of all. Being one nation, we want to see the young generation raised as one people, and we want the State to take care of educating all her children.[40]

The *Tribune* uniquely engaged in an interracial and intraracial dialogue that advocated for public, integrated education and contributed to shaping Louisiana's 1868 constitution, which was, according to Caryn Cossé Bell, "the Reconstruction South's most radical blueprint for change . . . enabl[ing] black Louisianans to join society as equal participants."[41] Unlike other state constitutions, it specifically required equal treatment in public places, and it forbade segregation in public schools. As a result, New Orleans's public schools underwent racial desegregation in the 1870s, an experience that Louis Harlan suggests was "shared by no other southern community until after 1954 and by few northern communities at the time."[42]

The Afro-Creole protest tradition's (and the *Tribune*'s) commitment to creating one unified nation has often been obscured, and some scholars have seen New Orleans's free Black population as "aristocrats of color" rather than "bearers of republican ideals."[43] The *Tribune*, however, used the same logic to defend itself against claims of classism as it did to oppose scientific racism: by staunchly subverting any arguments that presumed biological differences among men as a rationale for justifying unequal treatment. Sharing a vision of human rights grounded in the French and

Haitian Revolutions, New Orleans's Afro-Creoles, along with the newspaper, argued that it would be "easier to demand the freedom of all in the name of the Laws of Nature than the elevation of a handful of men of varying lighter shades in the name of expediency. It was necessary to invoke justice, and justice is the same for all men, whatever the shade of their skin."[44]

Therefore, the *New Orleans Tribune*'s self-identified mission was to unite all the city's Black population—those free and enslaved before the war—as well as the Black and white communities. The newspaper declared that it was "the organ of the oppressed, whether black, yellow or white,"[45] and on December 23, 1868, the staff wrote, "We are the organ of the whole colored population. The *Tribune* has always defended the interest of every colored man, without regard as to whether he was free before or since the war." As quoted above, the *Tribune* sought equal education for "all children, without discrimination on account of race or color." Reconstruction offered a rare opportunity for this vision to come to fruition and to renegotiate the unique tripartite racial structure that existed in nineteenth-century New Orleans. Through a close reading of the *Tribune*, it is evident that this periodical as text became an active shaper of the African American and larger national cultures' understanding of the role of public education in uniting the nation for democracy. Critical to this vision of public, integrated education was the *Tribune*'s rhetoric of logic and reason to refute the dominant discourse's use of scientific racism as the justification for segregated schools.

The Illogical Enemy of Scientific Racism

> He is a true man who conquers prejudice, or who, despite of lingering feelings which he condemns but cannot quite overcome, compels his conduct to conform to *reason* and right.[46]

Not surprisingly, the *Tribune* met with much opposition when it came to the issue of school integration. But it named its greatest obstacle: prejudice rooted in scientific racism. New Orleans Afro-Creoles and their white allies began protesting segregated schools as early as 1865, when the House of Representatives legislated that "white and colored children shall not be taught in the same school." Hoping to expose the Democratic legislature's faulty reasoning, the staff of the *Tribune* pointed out that according to these Democrats, "free and freed persons of color are not . . . real and complete men, made in the image of their Creator. They are held as a kind of bastard race, half-way between man and ape, a race that the law has to protect in some form, but that men of Caucasian, and particularly of Anglo-Saxon descent, can only look upon with disdain." The *Tribune* went on to say, "If we have done [away] with slavery, not so with the aristocracy of color."[47] The newspaper concluded that such evidence of scientific racism was "nothing like sound sense or calm reasoning," but instead "all is whim, prejudice and mania."[48] According to the *Tribune*, the bill, which mandated separate schools, was "marked by a kind of repulsion or fear of colored children, in the same manner that the denizens of infested cities feared, during the Middle Ages, the unfortunate leper."[49] This construction of Black children as other, as inferior, reflected the emergent scientific racism that classified humans into discrete species characterized as either superior or inferior. Louis Agassiz placed Blacks at the bottom level of his racial hierarchy, and physicians such as Dr. John H. van Evrie and Dr. Samuel Cartwright (who was a native of Louisiana) described the brains of Blacks as underdeveloped and small.[50]

The writings of Samuel Aldophus Cartwright particularly garnered a great deal of attention in New Orleans in regard to his claims of the racial inferiority of Blacks. A surgeon, born in Virginia in 1793, he attended medical school at the University of Pennsylvania before moving his practice to New Orleans in 1858. He used his scientific and medical training to ground his arguments for slavery in the inherent differences between the races, arguments that he shared in the form of articles in the *New Orleans Medical and Surgical Journal* throughout the 1850s and as lectures such as "Ethnology of the Negro or Prognathous Race" delivered before the New Orleans Academy of Science on November 30, 1857.[51] What distinguished Cartwright's argument was his "scientific" claim that these differences were immutable. He wrote in 1860, "The ethnology of the prognathous race does not stop at proving that subordination to the white race is its normal condition. It goes further, and proves that social and political equality is abnormal to it whether educated or not."[52]

Cartwright's use of "science" to advance his argument of inherent racial inferiority was in direct opposition to *Tribune* editor Jean-Charles Houzeau's belief that science proved that environment was more important than heredity in shaping all human capacities. In this regard, Houzeau broke with most of his contemporaries and denied the basic tenets of the emerging eugenics movement. He held steadfastly that environment was the most critical factor in development. This led him to his belief in the importance of education as the great equalizer in combating racist beliefs that undermined a truly revolutionary, democratic government. These beliefs permeated his efforts at the *Tribune* and were critical to informing the stance the paper took in regard to the importance of public, integrated education. "But this matter of 'instinct,' this innate 'sense of superiority' is not conceded by us to have its foundation in fact. That there are varieties in the different branches of the human family, natural and super-induced, is true. . . . No one race combines in itself all the separate excellencies of the rest. Differences are also very largely the result of circumstances, and will in time vanish or be materially modified."[53] The *Tribune*, like Houzeau, refused to accept scientific racism or biological determinism as justification for segregated schooling.

Houzeau's scientific background and understanding of evolution were critical to the newspaper's challenge of scientific racism and segregated schools. When Houzeau took over the newspaper's editorship on November 14, 1864, Trévigne continued as associate editor.[54] Unlike Trévigne, who was a member of the city's free Black community, Houzeau was an outsider. He was a Belgian scientist and utopian socialist born on October 7, 1820, in Mons, Belgium, to an aristocratic family. After attending the College of Mons and the University of Brussels, Houzeau failed his university exams and decided to tour Europe from 1840 to 1845.[55] He visited Paris during the lead-up to the French revolution of 1848 and found its ideologies and support of republican government influential on his own worldview and future work. He was appointed assistant astronomer of the Royal Observatory when he returned to Brussels but was eventually removed from his position because of his membership in the Phalange, a secret society dedicated to democratic principles.[56] After traveling to New Orleans in 1857, he settled in Texas, where he helped Blacks and white abolitionists flee to Mexico. Houzeau, eventually forced to leave Texas himself, then moved to Philadelphia, by way of New Orleans, and began writing articles for *L'Union* under the pseudonyms "Cham" and "Northern Correspondent."[57] After completing a 220-page book of abolitionist arguments, *Question de L'Esclavage*, Houzeau accepted Roudanez's plea to return to New Orleans and to serve as editor of the *Tribune* under the pen name "Dalloz."[58]

Houzeau began his writing career not as a journalist, but within the discipline of science. He had begun work on a book exploring the mental faculties of men and animals before beginning his post at the *Tribune*. His scientific writings were heavily influenced by Alexander von Humboldt, who wrote, "Whilst we maintain the unity of the human species, we at the same time repel the depressing assumption of superior and inferior races of men. . . . All are in like degree designed for freedom."[59] In *Études sur les facultés mentales des animaux comparées à celles de l'homme*, which was finally published in 1872, Houzeau argued that "humanity progresses without interruption." He voiced his opposition to eugenicists like Sir Francis Galton, who claimed that intellectual capacities were influenced primarily by heredity; Galton created a hierarchy of races in *Hereditary Genius* in 1869: ancient Greeks first; Anglo-Saxons and other Europeans second; Africans third; and Australian aborigines last.[60] On the other hand, Houzeau wrote, "But if one wants to speak of dynasties of intelligence, succession is not from father to son; it passes from master to disciple. It is not by genealogies but by schools that knowledge is transmitted." His own experiences as a teacher in Jamaican schools only confirmed his fundamental belief that he could "see nothing—at least nothing clearly and unmistakably discernible—that can be referred to as the differences of race."[61] Houzeau gained much attention, albeit critical, from Alfred R. Wallace, Charles Darwin's colleague. Wallace criticized Houzeau for challenging Galton, but Darwin cited Houzeau several times in *The Descent of Man* and sent him a personal copy of his text, *The Expression of the Emotions in Man and Animals.*[62]

On December 9, 1865, the *Tribune* critiqued its contemporary, the *Times*, a popular newspaper in New Orleans, precisely for its use of the rhetoric of scientific racism. Four days earlier, the latter explained its justification for segregated schools: "Though the negro has been freed, God has set a mark of inferiority upon him which has always been regarded as well by blacks as whites as an unmistakable sign of inferiority. Only when puffed up by demagogues and fanatical humanitarians does the negro pretend to be white man's equal, and though our people entertain no deep-seated prejudices on the subject, yet the two races can never stand on the same social level, either practically or theoretically, and different schools will have to be provided for their children and their children's children for all time to come." The *Tribune* responded, "If there is anybody who did not learn . . . it is, we believe, the editor who utters such a language."[63]

William Watkins points out the importance of scientific racism within segregationist discourse: "Perhaps the most damaging aspect of the eugenic views on African Americans was its application to segregation. So-called scientific data provided a rationale for containment and segregation. The notion of human difference undergirded the segregationist argument. The differences were beyond skin color; they were about mental characteristics."[64] The *Tribune*, however, sought to undercut this argument with its own appeals to reason and logic in its advocacy for integrated schooling, "proof that the system of Jim Crow that eventually claimed the South was far from inevitable."[65] The *Tribune* emphasized, "He is a true man who conquers prejudice, or who, despite of lingering feelings which he condemns but cannot quite overcome, compels his conduct to conform to *reason* and right."[66] For the writers of the *Tribune*, public, integrated spaces, like schools, were the logical place to eliminate the racial prejudice that stood in the way of building one nation and creating one people in pursuit of a truly republican government.

The *Tribune* clearly functioned to broadcast a succinct message of equal rights in all spheres—political, educational, economic, and social—based on their ardent belief "that the ideal of an enlightened rational public sphere might be achieved by the 'courteous combat' of reasoned, progressive discussion."[67] Yet those involved in the *Tribune* did not stop with mere rhetoric. In 1865, Thomas J. Durant, an attorney and politician, organized the Radical Republican Club in the *Salle d'Economie* to focus on obtaining the rights they had been promised in the Thirteenth, Fourteenth, and Fifteenth Amendments.[68] Their strategy was to focus their efforts not at the local level, where efforts were already underway to deprive Blacks of their new freedoms, but on Congress. The leaders of the party were a group of longtime activists, educators, and supporters of the *Tribune*, including Dr. Louis Roudanez, J. B. Roudanez, Oscar J. Dunn, Arnold Bertonneau, Aristide Mary, Thomy Lafon, Victor Macarty, Laurent Auguste, Antoine Dubuclet, J. P. Lanna, Paul Trévigne, and Formidor Desmaziliére.[69] The right that was of most importance to them was that of public, integrated education, a vision they extended to the whole nation, not just Louisiana. In speaking to the nation, they also spoke to the various diasporic communities in which they were embedded—Haiti, Cuba, Mexico, Nicaragua, France, Belgium—thereby envisioning a liminal space not bound by the nation-state in which they could unite all men in a universal brotherhood.

One People and One Nation: Advocacy for Public, Integrated Education

> The integrity of a nation is her first interest for it is key to her preservation. Let the nation be ONE, so that she could live and be perpetuated. The result of rebellion was an attempt to [dissolve] the unity of our country. Where had that rebellion been taught? In the white schools of the South. . . . As long as we do not touch these schools, we allow the same spirit to be perpetuated among the rising generation.[70]

Drawing on the rhetoric of nation building, the writers of the *Tribune* sought to promote the union of races as critical to the patriotism that was required for a strong and powerful nation. The call for all to be united as "Americans" was a radical departure from the pre–Civil War era in which white Creoles and Afro-Creoles resisted Americanization, given their fierce pride in maintaining the French language and their unique cultural history and identity. For Afro-Creoles, the call to unite under "one nation" as "one people" articulated a political ideology and policy critical to establishing their political leadership, but it also embodied a vision of citizenship as neither Black or white, French or English, South or North. They maintained, "Do not make any longer white and black citizens; let us have but Americans."[71] For the Afro-Creole writers of the *Tribune*, public, integrated education was "an essential part of their campaign for racial equality after the Civil War."[72] Given that supposed white racial superiority was increasingly legitimized through scientific racism, which argued that there were inherent biological differences that distinguished the intellectual capacities of the races, public, integrated education was seen by Afro-Creoles as the primary way to combat the professed superiority of the White race. The argument that uniting all Americans was necessary to creating a democratic nation was yet another logos-centered rhetorical strategy that the *Tribune* used to undermine the white racial supremacy inherent in scientific racism. Public, integrated education was the rational means to securing the reconciliation of the nation and to ending racism.

Taking up the mantle of "common schools," Afro-Creole activists sought to situate their argument squarely in a national conversation. While public education had made inroads in New Orleans prior to the Civil War, it was limited to white children. According to Mitchell, "the debate over the education of black children in Louisiana officially began with a session of the Louisiana legislature called by Maj. Gen. N. P. Banks in Union-occupied New Orleans in 1864."[73] Public schooling for Blacks in the city was legislatively mandated by Louisiana's 1864 constitution.[74] Article 141, "the first constitutional provision ever made for the education of Negroes in Louisiana," stated, "The Legislature shall provide for the education of all children of the State, between the ages of six and eighteen years, by maintenance of free public schools by taxation and otherwise." The constitutional convention's education committee, however, called for a dual, segregated system. General Banks charged a sixteen-member board of directors with the administration of these public schools; a subordinate five-man citizens' advisory board was set up in each of the nineteen newly drawn school zones to give voice to the special concerns of the city's ethnic neighborhoods. By the end of 1865, 14,000 Black students were attending 150 such schools.[75] These schools, however, were soon subsumed under the control of the Freedmen's Bureau.[76]

Unfortunately, the Freedmen's Bureau was not originally given a budget but was instead to operate solely on the funds raised from the rents of abandoned lands, which were drastically curtailed by President Johnson's later pardon of ex-Confederates in 1865.[77] Therefore, on December 27, 1865, bureau officials closed all Black schools in New Orleans under their charge per Circular No. 34, resulting in the transformation of former bureau schools once again into local, private schools run by the Black community.[78] On January 30, 1866, the *Tribune* observed, "Some schools have been shut up: others have exacted a fee, and a rather heavy one ($1.50 per month) from the pupils." As a consequence, more Black students attended private schools than bureau schools in the Crescent City; in January 1867, 2,967 students attended sixty-five private schools, whereas only 2,527 students attended fifty-six bureau schools.[79] The *Tribune* extended its critique of the financially insolvent Freedmen's Bureau to the bureau's failure to integrate its schools: "It automatically segregated the black from the white, and second, the system of tutorage automatically kept the freedmen in a dependency state."[80]

As the solution to the bureau's financial crisis, the bureau's general superintendent, O. O. Howard, recommended that a 5 percent tax, in addition to the state school tax already in place, be paid by Blacks laboring on the plantations and that property taxes "already paid by most of the colored property-owners, but flatly refused by the whites (whose schools are sustained by all property holders, without distinction of color)," be more strictly enforced.[81] Conversely, the *Tribune* posed integration as the answer. The newspaper responded, "Let the Freedmen's Bureau go down," for despite these additional revenues "still many (the great number colored) teachers have not received their pay for a long time, and the people of color are called upon to sustain part if not all of their schools."[82] The *Tribune* joined forces with *True Delta* editor T. W. C. in opposition to legislation that "separates the races in the process of education, and obliges each race to bear its own burdens" because Blacks had paid taxes that only supported White schools: "This is, in a degree, worse than formerly; for in the dismal days of slavery, the colored people were taxed with the whites for the support of the sort of schools of those times. If the money paid by these people at *that* time, to educate those who are now fighting against the Union, were returned to them, they would be well able to bear this burden."[83]

Additionally, in "Talking and Acting" on October 29, 1867, the *Tribune* critiqued the *Picayune* for saying that Blacks "should recollect that it is quite enough for them to have their children educated at the expense of the white people." The *Tribune* pointed out its contemporary's ignorance by reminding its readership of the facts: "The fact is that up to the year of our Lord, 1867, the white had their children educated at the expense of the colored people. For over thirty years, the colored residents of New Orleans have paid taxes upon fifteen millions of assessed property; they have paid the school tax among others, and never was this tax used but to the exclusive benefit of white children."[84] The newspaper called the public's attention to the double standard that Blacks had paid taxes to support white schools, so why should whites not pay taxes to support Black schools?

The *Tribune* advocated for common schools: "Let us all pay an equitable school tax, in common with all other citizens in the State, according to a common basis; and let the money be managed in the ordinary way, and be spent for the benefit of all." It continued, "Should the present State school tax of $1.50 per thousand be not sufficient, let it be made one-half per cent, which would be more than three times larger; and then carry out a system of general schools, like those of Massachusetts." In contrast to Maj. B. Rush Plumly's suggestion that the then-present system of separate schools be continued but without the maladministration of the bureau and instead under the private control of an all-Black board, the *Tribune* responded, "For us, the question is not how to sustain and conduct separate schools, but how to bring about a fusion of schools."[85] The attitudes taught by segregated schooling had "draw[n] a line between the two elements of one and the same people" and had fostered a civil war: "[Segregated schools] perpetuate from childhood the infatuation of the white, and prompt the black to retaliate by enmity or envy, [and] . . . draws a line between the two elements of one and the same people, from the cradle itself up to the time of manhood and throughout life."[86] In contrast, integrated schooling would change this way of thinking, would prevent history from repeating itself in yet another civil war, and would heal these divisions to create one unified, American nation.

Integration was the only way to ensure that all Americans, both Blacks and whites, had access to an equal education. The newspaper anticipated the separate but equal ruling of *Plessy v. Ferguson* and contested its rationality by citing evidence to the contrary:

> But it is said that separate colored schools may be made as available, as efficient, as the white ones. This is in no way evident. The white schools, that are of long standing, are provided with ample material,

and with experienced teachers. As long as they will remain affected to the children of a privileged class they will be privileged schools, and as such they will be better cared for and better conducted than any other set of schools devoted to what is called an "inferior race." There is no guaranty and no probability that "star schools" be, for a long period of time, the object of a solicitude equal to that bestowed upon the schools of the old citizens. But should the "star schools" be even a real equivalent, and remain so, we still question the right of the civil authority to appropriate such schools to the education of colored children; for these children are intitled [*sic*] not to an equivalent of the public school, but to the public schools themselves.[87]

Another argument that bolstered the irrationality of separate schools was the challenge posed by rural areas. The *Tribune* questioned, "And how are separate schools to be maintained in the parishes, where the population is often sparse, and there are not children enough for two schools in a neighborhood?"[88]

The *Tribune*'s ultimate solution to the Freedmen's Bureau's inability to financially support Black schools was public, integrated education. The editors of the *Tribune* drew on the vision of "common schools" to argue for integrated schools in 1867 when the Reconstruction Acts in Congress stipulated a new state constitution.[89] They had declared, "We want that they [Black children] shall be received in the common schools, as it is done in Massachusetts. We want to see our children seated on the same benches with the white girls and boys, so that every prejudice of color may disappear from childhood, and the next generation be aroused to a sentiment of fraternity."[90]

The *Tribune* refused to accept that "it is too soon" to integrate schooling: "This has for four years been the language of those who acted, as far as our interests were concerned, with our bitterest enemies. . . . We need no 'too soon men' at this time. We need men of action, boldness and sincerity."[91] After making the case for common schools on January 18, 1868—"As to the right of children of African descent to receive education, there is, and there can be no doubt. No sensible man refuses them to-day the privilege of schools. . . . But the question is, 'What schools will they have?'"—the *Tribune* once again drew on logic and precedents of integrated education in other Black communities to affirm its argument. For example, Roberts (the plaintiff in *Roberts v. Boston*, the first case to contest segregated schools in the United States in 1849) successfully took his argument for integrated education to the Massachusetts legislature after his appeal failed in the state's Supreme Court. Unfortunately, the *Tribune* conflated the two, but drew on the spirit and eventual success of Roberts before the legislature to show that a precedent existed for integrated education. In 1855, Massachusetts became the first state to pass a law prohibiting segregated schools.

> Now, from the point of view of their rights, we answer, that the colored children are entitled to be admitted in the common public schools of the State, as well as any other children. So was it decided by the Supreme Court of Massachusetts, some thirty years ago, upon an argument of Chas. Sumner, the most important part of which we recently reprinted. So is it pointed out by good sense and sound reason; for our cardinal principle is that rights are independent of color. Therefore, in accordance with that principle, the trustees, directors of schools or teachers have no authority whatever to inquire into the origin and race of pupils, and these pupils have to be admitted into any public school they choose to attend.[92]

The *Tribune* referenced *Roberts* once again in "Separate, or Mixed Schools" on January 22, 1869: "Twenty-five years ago the good city of Boston began to be excited over the question whether colored children should be admitted into its public schools without distinction. There were at that time two colored schools. . . . The controversy went on in this way till the year 1849, when it reached the highest tribunal in the State, the Supreme Court, where it was finally settled on the principle, which now governs the action of Boston as to her public schools, that no discrimination on account of color or race could be made."

"Good sense and sound reason" demanded that Black students be granted access to the public schools in New Orleans just as they had been in Boston. The *Tribune* quoted Sumner's argument to the Supreme Court, "*The whites themselves are injured by the separation.* Who can doubt this? With the law as their monitor, they are taught to regard a portion of the human family, children of God, created in his image, coequals in his love, as a separate and degraded class—they are taught practically to deny the grand revelation of Christianity—THE BROTHERHOOD OF MANKIND." The newspaper drew its own conclusion, "There must be agitation and irritation so long as we attempt to build on prejudice, policy, caste, and not on principle."[93] Integration was not only based on sound logical principles, as opposed to the prejudice of scientific racism, but was in the best interest of Blacks and whites and the entire nation. States, which made up one nation, should share educational practices, starting with the integration of public schools. The newspaper agreed with Sumner that "the rights of colored children to education in common schools" was "paramount" to "the national interest."[94]

The *Tribune* advocated, "There is, in fact, nothing more important, more conducive to the general welfare and the national progress and grandeur than the imparting of a solid education and sound principles to the rising generation."[95] Education, and specifically public, integrated education, was a prerequisite to the rebuilding of a nation, left divided after the devastation of the Civil War. In his history of the Black press, Frederick Detweiler writes, "Instead of merely reflecting 'life,' the newspapers, in setting themes for discussion and suggesting the foci of attention, help powerfully to create that life."[96] And the *Tribune* helped to "create that life," as its campaign for public, integrated schooling met with success in the form of Louisiana's 1868 constitution, "the first biracially written constitution in the history of Louisiana."[97]

Half of the ninety-eight delegates who met on September 27, 1867, to draft the document were Black.[98] Article 135 related specifically to the integration of education: "All children of this State between the ages of six (6) and twenty-one (21) shall be admitted to the public schools or other institutions of learning sustained or established by the State in common without distinction of race, color, or previous condition." Sharing his support of James Ingraham, who proposed the article, Victor Lange wrote, "Gentlemen, please allow me a small space in your official journal to record my vote on the adoption of the constitution as a whole. I vote yes, and shall give my reason why: Title I, Bill of Rights . . . follows the free school system, secures to my child and to all children throughout the state their education which their forefathers have been deprived of for two hundred and fifty years, and I shall sign the Constitution without any hesitation."[99]

While delegates to the constitutional convention of 1868 discussed public education, they also shaped a Bill of Rights designed to include the concept of public rights as essential to the concept of universal equality. The concept of public rights can be traced to multiple trajectories, including Catholic universalism and the egalitarian ideals of the American, French, and Haitian Revolutions. Rebecca Scott notes that public rights were defined as "the absence of castes which place one portion of the members of the State into orders or classes from which they cannot exit."[100] Afro-Creoles, the formerly enslaved, and Anglicized English-speaking Blacks had all experienced various degrees of racial prejudice based on white privilege. To secure full racial equality for all people of African descent, in all spheres of life, the concept of "public rights," as opposed to legal rights, was seen as essential. The *New Orleans Tribune* argued, "When one or a few colored men are excluded from certain public rights enjoyed by *all* white men, not the few alone but the entire colored population are wronged."[101]

On December 2, 1867, Robert I. Cromwell, an Anglicized Black representative, first presented this new series of clauses for the Bill of Rights. His proposed article 1 states,

> We hold these truths to be self-evident that all men are created equal, endowed with certain inalienable rights, and therefore the law should afford equal protection to all in the exercise of their civil, *public*, political and religious rights, and insure [*sic*] perfect equality under the law.[102]

He then proposed an article, "There shall be no discrimination in the public, political, civil or religious rights or immunities among the citizens of this State on account of race or color or previous condition of involuntary servitude."[103] The next day, Caesar C. Antoine offered more clauses for the Bill of Rights, including one that stated,

> All persons born or naturalized in the United States, and subject to the jurisdiction thereof, are citizens of the United States, of the States in which they reside, and shall be protected in their civil and political rights and public privileges.[104]

Some white conservative delegates adamantly rejected the term "public rights," suggesting that it was being promoted to achieve "social equality," which would debase whites and ultimately result in Negro supremacy. Despite white resistance, "public rights" language remained in the constitution. Along with Article 13 of the Bill of Rights and Article 135 on public education, the Afro-Creoles, Anglicized Blacks, and white radicals enacted the most radical Reconstruction constitution in the South.

In addition to supporting integrated schooling, Article 142 of the 1868 constitution established an integrated university in New Orleans. This university was to contain "a law, a medical, and a collegiate department, each with appropriate facilities," and would be maintained by the state as long as "all departments of this institution of learning shall be open in common to all students capable of matriculating." The constitution was ratified on April 16 and 17, 1868.[105] It returned Louisiana to its place within the Union, and its commitment to public rights sought to finally enact the promise of full equality and citizenship to all men. During Reconstruction, Afro-Creoles succeeded in desegregating about one-third of the city's public schools. Some approximate that between five hundred and one thousand students attended integrated schools in New Orleans during Reconstruction.[106]

This integration of public schools would allow all children the opportunity to engage in the public sphere as equals, For Afro-Creoles, integration would embody the liminal spaces of creolization—being neither fully white nor fully Black and being both Creoles and Americans; the erasure of the color line would create spaces for the formerly enslaved, Anglicized English-speaking Blacks, white Creoles, Americans, French, Germans, and Italians to create a new public sphere, one that embodied human equality. White resistance grounded in theories of white supremacy, scientific racism, and white capitalism would eventually defer to this vision. If only for a short time, New Orleans public education exemplified the *Tribune*'s vision of a democratic nation in which integrated schools created a public sphere that signified equality and brotherhood. The integrated schools ultimately ceased, not because teachers or administrators opposed integration, but because of federal withdrawal of troops and the return of Democrats to power in 1877. The White Redeemers who took over the reins of state power were determined to undo the radical advances of Reconstruction.[107]

The Return to Battle: 1877–1896

[P]ersonal observation and universal testimony concur to establish the fact that public education has greatly deteriorated since colored and white children were admitted indiscriminately into the same schools.[108]

New Orleans School Board, 1877

Little did the writers of the *Tribune* know that Louisiana's 1868 constitution would be but a momentary success in a much longer struggle for racial equality. The national presence of the *Tribune* came to an end when its owner, Roudanez, refused to support the Republican Party's gubernatorial candidate, Henry Clay Warmoth, in 1868. *Tribune* contemporary and Warmoth mouthpiece the *New Orleans Republican* "support[ed] the city's segregated school system and disavow[ed] the party's pledge to 'enforce the opening of all schools . . . to all children.'" By 1877, the radical Republican agenda had increasingly lost support on the national level. With the removal of federal troops in 1877 and the compromise that put Republican Rutherford B. Hayes in the White House, the Democratic Redeemers at the state and local level were determined to roll back the reforms in public education during Reconstruction. A new school board was appointed that reinstated the pre–Civil War superintendent, William O. Rogers, who was resolved to segregate schools by race and sex once and for all.[109] Robert Lusher, an outspoken racist and pre–Civil War school board member, was appointed state superintendent and reinforced support for segregation by suggesting that Louisiana should abandon the "fanaticism" of integration given that even northern cities like New York, Philadelphia, and Cincinnati had long been segregated. He advocated separate schools with equal facilities and advantages for both races.

On July 3, 1877, at the New Orleans school board meeting, a crowd of Afro-Creoles and Anglican Blacks, led by Aristide Mary, presented a petition against reinstituting segregation. Aristide, one of the wealthiest Afro-Creole men in New Orleans, prominent philanthropist, and activist, had a long history as an advocate of public education, beginning with his support of the institutional growth of the Catholic Institute. He most certainly made an impression as he entered the board meeting wearing his white gloves, neatly dressed in his wide-standing collar and wide-brimmed plug hat, with his mustache waxed and natty cane swinging.[110] The board, composed of eighteen members (four African American and fourteen European Americans), listened impatiently to Aristide and proceeded to pass an earlier resolution:

> Whereas: This board, in the performance of its paramount duty; which is to give the best education possible with the means at its disposal to the whole population, without regard to race, color or previous condition, is assured that this end can be best attained by educating the different races in separate schools.[111]

The resolution passed by a vote of fifteen to three. Of the four African American men serving on the board—Louis A. Martinet, Joseph A. Craig, George H. Fayerweather, and Pascal M. Tourne—it was Craig who choose to break with his colleagues and vote for the resolution. Like other accommodationists, he believed that the best way to work with the Democrats and hold off White supremacists was to support segregation in hopes that this would "protect other civil rights, bring social peace, and perhaps even promote some advancement in black public education."[112] These differences in tactics—accommodation versus protest—among African American activists would continue to shape the political battles around civil rights throughout the Jim Crow era.

But it was Afro-Creole activists, schooled in the long history of the protest tradition, who launched the most assertive resistance to segregation in the United States. Their goal was single-minded: full equality in the public sphere and political rights as guaranteed by the 1868 constitution.[113] They believed that any nod to legalized segregation would promote the subordination of all colored citizens in all spheres of life. This was already evident in the segregation of trolley cars, train cars, and riverboats in Louisiana. Since the 1820s, the street railroad companies, who operated the mule-drawn carts, had operated separate cars. Resistance to segregation began as early as 1833, when a group of African Americans on their way to Lake Pontchartrain were denied entry to a car, and although they stormed the car, they were beaten back.

While periodic protests occurred, it was not until the Civil War that protests were carried out on a mass scale and were reported and discussed by the Black press. The *Tribune* had been campaigning against the "star" cars (segregated carts for Blacks designated by a star) since 1865 when they wrote "our exclusion from 'white cars' is a brand put upon us, and a relic of slavery that ought not to be tolerated."[114] With the help of the *Tribune*, the streetcar issue received noticeable coverage, resulting in enough pressure that General Banks issued an order in 1865 that "the attempt to enforce police laws or regulations that discriminate against the negroes by reason of color, or their former condition of slavery . . . will not be permitted."[115] Not always enforced, in May of 1867, the attack on segregated "star" cars heightened when a crowd of more than five hundred people gathered at Congo Square to demonstrate against them. The protest mounted enough pressure on the Republican mayor and the companies, who feared loss of profits due to the disruptions, that they capitulated and instructed their drivers to permit travelers of all colors to ride the cars.[116] A few weeks later, the stars formerly designating Negro cars were painted over.[117]

The Afro-Creole fight against racial segregation now pivoted to the public schools, where three legal challenges were filed to block the segregation of public schools in New Orleans. Paul Trévigne, Arnold Bertonneau, and August Dellande, all seasoned activists and members of the Radical Republican Party, knew that their best chances of enforcing both the state and federal constitutions was through the courts.[118] These cases were not random, but were launched as a coordinated effort among Afro-Creole Republican activists and their white allies.[119] This fight was an interracial effort between lawyers and community activists focused on the third district (the interracial, Francophone Marginy) to forge a legal strategy that would undermine segregation in order to fulfill the promises of integrated public education.

Their efforts focused on the Fillmore school (a Grammar A school), four blocks from the Catholic Institute on the corner of St. Claude and Bagatelle, which sat in the heart of the Marginy.[120] Initially established as a whites-only school in 1850, it became integrated after 1871 and became one of the most popular racially mixed schools.[121] This was in no small part because Fillmore had hired teachers of African descent, including Charles P. Guichard, the first assistant teacher and brother of Creole house representative Leopold Guichard, and second assistant teacher Antonia Hart.[122] By 1877, however, the school was once again designated as white only. Resegregation of Fillmore as a whites-only school created major setbacks for Creole children. First, they had fewer school options. In the third school district, where Fillmore was located, only five out of sixteen schools served African Americans. Villere and LaHarpe Schools, the closest Black schools, church-based and much smaller, reported multiple problems such as poor facilities, not enough qualified teachers, and lack of school supplies including textbooks. Second, neither school was categorized as a Grammar A school, and thus graduates were ineligible to apply for high schools.[123] Given the success of the Fillmore school during integration, it was chosen as the best site from which to launch a challenge.

The first of the cases was filed by Paul Trévigne, who, after serving as editor of the *Tribune*, had returned to teaching at the Catholic Institute, as well as serving a year on the Orleans parish school board until the Redeemer Democrats replaced almost all the Republicans with White Leaguers in 1877. In September of that year, Trévigne engaged two white Republican lawyers—Samuel Belden, who had served as the state attorney general from 1868 to 1871, and Guy Duplantier (a native of Louisiana)—in his suit to enjoin the school board's segregation plan of July 1877, which would prevent Trévigne's son, also called Paul, from attending the Fillmore school, which he had attended during integration. Trévigne and his lawyers submitted a brief to the state district court that claimed that segregation violated Trévigne's privileges under the Fourteenth Amendment as a citizen of the United States and of the state. Segregation by law, they argued in the petition, "tends to and does degrade . . . petitioner and his son Paul Trévigne and the entire colored population of this city."[124] They argued that the separation of schools by race was unconstitutional because "a distinction thus made detracts from their status as citizens and consigns them to the contempt of their fellow man and citizens of this community and elsewhere."[125]

Sixth District judge Nicholas H. Rightor, a white Leaguer who had initially issued a temporary injunction that stopped the resegregation of schools, later dismissed the entire suit on the grounds that Trévigne failed to prove any personal injury and that he had filed too late after the segregation resolution had already passed and the board had begun resegregating the schools. In effect, the judge evaded the constitutional issue of the Fourteenth Amendment by quibbling over technical questions, saying that Trévigne had no case because his son had not been excluded (school had not started yet) and dismissing the national and state constitutional rights issues. Trévigne then appealed to the state supreme court, which delayed the case, during which time the petition to segregate was passed. On January 20, 1879, Justice Alicibiades De Blanc stated in an opinion that because Trévigne had filed his suit too late, given that segregation was now an accomplished fact, an injunction restraining the board from refusing to admit his son was no longer the appropriate action. In the aftermath of the case, the *New Orleans Democrat* termed Trévigne's suit an effort to gain "cheap notoriety" by a "haughty descendant of Ham," whose attempt to substitute "African supremacy" for "civilization and Christianity" endangered any white support for the education of "African ignorance and savagery."[126] This threat to cut off support for Black education furthered accommodationists' fears of radicals pushing for complete integration. Better to have some funding for schools than none at all.

On November 9, 1877, Ursin Dellande, with the help of Trévigne's attorney, Samuel Belden, sued the school board in the Sixth District Court of New Orleans, explaining that his two children, Arnold Joseph, age fourteen, and Francis Clement, age eleven, had been forced out of Fillmore. Dellande sought a court order mandating that the principal accept his children. According to the city register, Dellande was a cigar manufacturer, and he and his family lived less than a block away from Fillmore. In his briefs, Belden referred to the same provisions of the 1868 constitution as he had in Trévigne's, but this time he invoked the Fourteenth Amendment generally rather than specifying the Privileges and Immunity Clause. Citing two Louisiana and one U.S. Supreme Court public accommodations cases that had ruled separate but equal unlawful, Belden again grounded his case on the confluence of state and federal constitutional provisions.[127]

In his May 20, 1887, district opinion, Judge Rightor declared that Article 135 had never been intended to be executed but was a "mere general declaration addressed to the legislative department, unenforceable by the judiciary."[128] He went on to say that integration "upsets the whole order of society, tramples on the usages of centuries and contains the germs of social war."[129] The societal "order," and thus personal rights as God intended, was predicated on the separation of the races. In other words, he rested his case on natural rights constitutional theory: No law is necessary to affect a constitutional declaration of a personal right or liberty. For Rightor, the races might have equal political and civil rights, but they would never be social equals.

On appeal, the Supreme Court delayed its decision on the Dellande case for three years. During that time, the 1879 constitutional convention expunged articles 2, 13, and 135 from the constitution. Without legal grounding, Afro-Creoles and Anglicized Blacks were left to the mercies of Democratic legislators and administrators. When Supreme Court justice Felix Poché finally ruled on the Dellande case, he declared that the Radicals had never intended to prohibit segregation, nor had they even intended to establish separate but equal. According to his interpretation, they only wanted to ban "public schools for the exclusive benefit of any race," which would "*entirely* deprive other races of school facilities or privileges."[130] Justice Poché could not conceive of a world in which there was not a hierarchy of value, worth, and intelligence. This was the new world of Jim Crow.

Arnold Bertonneau (1834–1912), a wine merchant and one of the first participants in Louisiana's Reconstruction period, lived on Rampart Street just a few blocks from Fillmore. On behalf of free men of color, he, along with Dr. Louis Charles Roudanez and his brother Jean Baptist, had led the suffrage petition in 1864 that met with President Lincoln to advocate that Black men who were free before the Civil War obtain suffrage. As a delegate at the constitutional convention of 1867, he had drawn up Article 135, which declared that "there shall be no separate school or institution of learning established exclusively for any race by the State of Louisiana." He was ready to put this to the test. On November 13, 1877, Bertonneau walked three blocks from his residence at 367 Rampart to the all-white Fillmore school, the closest public school to his house, where he attempted to register his sons John, age nine, and Henry, age seven. George H. Gordon, the principal of the school, refused to admit the two boys on the grounds that they were of African descent.

Bertonneau engaged the white Radical Republican John Ray as his lawyer in the case. Ray, a former state senator who had supported the 1868 state constitution integration laws, was also a member of the "Louisiana

Club," a largely Black social and political group, and was a staunch integrationist and supporter of racial equality. Ray argued that Bertonneau's sons had been denied nationally guaranteed privileges or immunities, as well as the equal protection of the laws. He based his case not only on the Fourteenth Amendment, but also on article 135 of the 1868 state constitution that gave Bertonneau the right as a state citizen to a nonsegregated school. To deny that right was an abrogation of his Fourteenth Amendment right to the equal protection of state laws, even if integration was not guaranteed by the Fourteenth Amendment.

The case landed in the federal district court of William B. Woods, a Democrat from Ohio.[131] Woods ignored the argument that excluding a person from a public school because of his race degraded him and denied him the "equal benefit" of the laws guaranteed in the national 1866 civil rights act.[132] Instead, Woods argued that under segregation, "Both races are treated precisely alike. White children and colored children are compelled to attend different schools. That is all. The state while conceding equal privileges and advantages to both races, has the right to manage schools in the manner which, in its judgment, will best promote the interest of all."[133] While cases in Michigan and Iowa had ruled segregation unlawful, Woods chose to ignore these and instead drew on the Supreme Court case *Hall v. Decuir* to assert that "any classification which preserves substantially equal school advantages does not impair any rights and is not prohibited by the constitution of the United States. Equality of rights does not necessarily imply identity of rights."[134] His use of the term "substantially equal school advantage" set the precedent for arguments that "separate" is legal as long as it is equal. While Woods was criticized for not going far enough and ruling that the Fourteenth Amendment could not be used to regulate state education, his use of the term "substantially equal school advantage" gave Democrats the ability to slash expenditures for the education of Blacks and poor whites with no fear of retribution.

For Paul Trévigne, Arnold Bertonneau, Ursin Dellande, Samuel Bellende, and John Ray, the loss of these cases was more than a devasting setback for equal rights. For all practical purposes, these cases had solidified "separate but equal" in public education. The hard lesson learned was that constitutions are what the judges say they are. The promise that the 1868 constitution would usher in an era of public rights and human equality was shattered. How could this brief moment of victory have slipped through their hands? The sense of defeat after decades of activism was devasting not only to these individuals, but also to their families and community who had their hopes dashed. This defeat took a personal toll as well. Both Bertonneau and Dellande withdrew from political activity; only Paul Trévigne continued his political activism.[135] He would eventually participate in the work of the Citizens' Committee to protest the Separate Car Act of 1890, which led to the *Plessy v. Ferguson* Supreme Court case.

The resegregation of schools created complete chaos for both white and Black families, especially in the Third District. Many white families continued to send their children to schools closest to their homes, even if they were all-Black. At the same time, many people of color continued to push for admission to their formerly desegregated schools. Some Afro-Creoles, many of whom were clearly exhausted, went so far as to cross the color line.[136] This included the children of Arnold Bertonneau and Ursin Dellande, who enrolled their children at the now all-white Fillmore. Their children and other children of color attended Fillmore, making it clear that in "everyday practice," segregation did not have a totalizing impact. Thus, while legal routes to integration were closed for the immediate future, on the street level, parents of every race made decisions based on their local histories, experiences, political goals, and practical needs. For generations of families who had lived in the interracial Marigny neighborhood, integration was a way of life that always defined their community. Their resistance to segregation reveals the lengths to which white supremacists had to go to impose not only the separation of the races but the prejudice required to do so.[137] In other words, white supremacy had to be constructed, learned, and institutionalized. In New Orleans, there was little "natural" about it.

In the immediate aftermath of the new state constitution of 1879 that eradicated state-mandated desegregation, Afro-Creoles and Anglicized Blacks turned their attention to re-establishing and creating "all-Black schools." Louis Nelson Fouché, Rodolphe Desdunes, and Armand Duhart, longtime supporters of the Catholic Institute, turned their energies to reviving it. Many of the students and teachers had left the school to support the integration of public schools during Radical Reconstruction, some of whom now returned, including Paul Trévigne. Arthur Estéves, a Haitian-born sail maker who had immigrated as a young boy, joined the Catholic Institute's board in 1884, when the school was almost in ruins, and went on to serve as president until 1902. Given that the school was no longer receiving any state funding, it counted on the ongoing financial contributions from members of the Afro-Creole community, including Thomy Lafon and Aristide Mary, who both designated money in their wills at their deaths in 1893 to help maintain the institution.[138]

For many Afro-Creole families, the "Black" public schools were unacceptable, given that they were underfunded, overcrowded, understaffed, and clearly not "equal" to the white schools. Even the white schools suffered, given the lack of public funding and general ambivalence about public education among the planters and merchants who now dominated state politics. Many families within the large Catholic and Lutheran populations sent their children to the sixty or so parochial schools that had been established by the 1880s.[139] In 1881, when all persons of color were removed from the school board, the board eliminated all classes after the sixth grade for colored children. During Reconstruction, textbooks had been free; now students were required to pay for their own books. Many poor white and Black students attended school without the books for their daily lessons. By 1881, the eleven Black elementary schools in New Orleans were no longer required to follow the prescribed curriculum, given that students had no books. And while the schools were considered segregated, only nineteen of the seventy-three teachers in Black schools were Black men or women due to the lack of certified Black teachers.[140] In 1883, public education was totally shut down due to lack of funding. By 1885, 16,400 students were enrolled in private schools and 24,331 in public schools. The poor conditions in Black schools caused many families to send their children to private schools, in essence paying a "double" tax: their state taxes and tuition for private education.

The desire for quality education, long associated with liberation, galvanized the community of Afro-Creole, formerly enslaved, and Anglicized Black parents to establish alternatives to the inadequate public schools. In addition to the revived Catholic Institute, small private Catholic institutions (prior to African American parochial schools) existed throughout New Orleans and along the Gulf Coast. One example was the school operated by Médard Nelson (1850–1933), an Afro-Creole Catholic educator who, while first pursuing the priesthood, instead saw the desperate need for Catholic education in the post-Reconstruction era.[141] He began teaching in 1872, and in 1887 he purchased a home at 1218 Burgundy that would serve as his home and a school for forty-six years. His school was open to all: the formerly enslaved, Black and white, immigrants and native-born, rich and poor. Classes covered ten years of schooling, from grammar to high school, with instruction in both French and English. Eventually, graduation exercises were held at Economy Hall, of which he was a member. While Catholic education was also provided by the Ursulines, Carmelites, and Religious of the Sacred Heart, the Sisters of the Holy Family were the only religious group to provide exclusive instruction for African American children. Small, private, secular schools like those that had proliferated in the 1840s and 1850s also emerged to meet the needs of parents seeking quality education for their students. In regard to higher education, the Freedmen's Bureau and several Northern Aid societies had focused their attention on Black higher education in Louisiana, resulting in the establishment of three predominantly Black private institutions: Leland University, New Orleans University, and Straight University. In 1881, Southern University became the first public Black university. All four of these universities also initially provided primary and secondary education for African American children. While educational institutions were forged by African Americans throughout the city for African American children, it was not the public integrated schools for which radical Republicans had fought. Throughout the 1880s, escalating white suppression, violence, and unrest increasingly necessitated the acceptance of separate schools. However, in 1890, the Separate Car Act provided one more opportunity to fight for equal rights.

"Citizenship Has No Color": The Last Stand

> The colored people must be given a chance to develop, to rise, and the hands of oppression must be stayed from them, and they must be taught properly—they must be taught, not only to read, write and pray, but also that to combat wrong and injustice, to resist oppression and tyranny, is the highest virtue of the citizens.
>
> —Louis Martinet, 1893[142]

Afro-Creole radical activists like Armand Lanusse, Marie Couvent, Paul Trévigne, Dr. Charles Roudanez, and countless others continued to fight for legal acknowledgment that education was a public right critical not only to book learning, but also to the recognition of the full humanity of each person and to their preparation for the rights and responsibilities of full citizenship. As the forty-four-year-old Martinet (1849–1917) penned these words to his friend and white ally Albion Tourgée (1835–1905), the *Plessy v. Ferguson* case was pending at the United States Supreme Court (Figure 20). Martinet, a New Orleans lawyer and editor of the *Crusader*, had played a leading role in bringing this case to the highest court in the land. He had recruited Tourgée as the lead lawyer to coordinate the strategy of the case. The legal road to challenging "separate but equal" in the Supreme Court was plagued by challenges and setbacks. Martinet was not only exhausted but despaired that the case would not succeed, possibly making matters worse by hardening the lines of segregation. Yet Martinet,

Figure 20. Albion Tourgée. Charles Roussève Papers, Amistad Research Center, New Orleans, LA.

who lived with the unbearable consequences of discrimination, was deter-mined that no one should have to endure that constant indignity.

Working together with other Afro-Creoles, Martinet had established the *Crusader* in 1889, a newspaper in the radical tradition of the *Tribune*, whose national distribution sought to place the injustice of segregation on the national stage. Published in both French and English, it became a daily in 1894, its office at 122 Exchange Alley in the French Quarter serving as a hub for Afro-Creole activists, Anglicized Black leaders, and white supporters.[143] Tourgée, the renowned writer-jurist-activist, was the country's best known white advocate for equal civil rights. He was an ardent critic of white racism and white Christianity, campaigning for antilynching legislation and refuting the ideology of segregation. He would become a close friend to Martinet and primary legal counsel in the *Plessy* case. While cross-racial collaborations from this era are often critiqued as paternalistic, the alliances and networks built throughout the *Plessy* case purposefully sought to embody the very racial equality for which they were fighting.[144] It was Martinet who initiated this crucial relationship, while all the time recognizing that no matter how well-intentioned Tourgée might be, he could never know the experience of being a person of color who lived under continual threat from white supremacy.

Together they built a national network through the National Citizens' Rights Association (NCRA), the interracial civil rights organization Tourgée founded in October 1891 to agitate for equal citizenship. The *Crusader*, as well as other African American newspapers across the country, played a central role in publicizing the NCRA and soliciting members from among three main membership groups: Black southerners, Black northerners, and white northerners. Tourgée focused on developing grass-roots activism by encouraging members to enlist new recruits, and he used the NCRA as a conduit for reporting local atrocities against Blacks. Both Tourgée and Martinet hoped that by elevating the issues of racial injustice as a betrayal of America's democratic commitment to equality, public opinion would sway the Supreme Court's ruling in *Plessy*. Although this was not to be, this interracial activism, like that during the period of Reconstruction and the *Tribune*, highlights not only the long history of the protest tradition, but suggests the ongoing struggle for public rights through which human equality is signified.

"A slap in the face of every member of the black race": Betrayed Again

Louis André Martinet, like Arnold Bertonneau and countless other Afro-Creoles, could have passed for white. Born a free person of color in St. Martin's parish to a Belgian carpenter, Hippolite Martinet, and Marie Benoit, a Louisiana free women of color, he was raised a French-speaking Catholic. During Radical Reconstruction, when the state's capital was in

New Orleans (meeting at the Mechanics Institute), he served as a state representative to the Louisiana legislature from 1872 until 1875. During that time, he attended the newly opened law school at Straight University. Straight, founded in 1868 by the American Missionary Association for newly freed Blacks, opened its law school in 1873. Committed to maintaining an integrated racial learning environment, the charter specifically stated that "men and women, irrespective of color or race," were to be admitted. The Board of Trustees was interracial as well.[145] Louis A. Bell, an African American from Massachusetts and graduate of Howard University Law School, was named the first dean of the law school. Upon his death in 1874, he was followed by Afro-Creole Robert Isabelle, who worked to create an interracial faculty. His first faculty appointment was his ally, Rufus Waples (1825–1902), a white radical, esteemed constitutional lawyer, and survivor of the Mechanics Institute massacre. Originally from Delaware, he graduated from the University of Louisiana's New Orleans Law School (which became Tulane) in 1852 and in 1863 was appointed United States attorney for the Eastern District of Louisiana by President Lincoln. Isabelle also recruited to the faculty his fellow Radical Republicans Henry C. Dibble and A. T. Belden, both of whom had worked on the public school desegregation cases mentioned earlier in the chapter with Paul Trévigne, Arnold Bertonneau, and Ursin Dellande.[146] Last, he hired James C. Walker, who would become the attorney that would defend Homer Plessy.

Under this interracial group of radical law professors, all ardent defenders of racial equality, Louis Martinet received his training in law. After two years of study, he was one of eight students in a graduating class that was one-third white. The law department went on to graduate several legal scholars and attorneys who would, like Martinet, go on to become members of the Citizens' Committee, including Rodolphe Desdunes. Their foundation in law, as well as the integrated racial learning environment at Straight, would shape the legal framework for the challenge to racial segregation that would culminate in the *Plessy* case.[147]

Like most Afro-Creoles who lived in the Faubourg Tremé or Maringy, Martinet settled on Burgundy Street in Tremé. Starting his career as a lawyer, he established himself as a notary, setting up shop at 117 Exchange Alley. Although working full time, his political activism continued to be woven into his daily life. After a brief stint on the Orleans Parish School Board in 1877, in which he opposed the efforts to resegregate public schools, he (like other Afro-Creole activists) returned his attention to the Catholic Institute as a primary site for Black education. He initially served as legal counsel to the Board of Directors and later became a full member of the board leadership, as well as serving on the Board of Trustees of the newly constituted Southern University in New Orleans from 1889 to 1897.

While the legal segregation of schools was complete by 1877, other areas in the public sphere remained integrated, including streetcars, churches, railways, and hotels. While whites in other states across the South had passed Jim Crow segregation laws to solidify white-supremacist ideology, Louisiana resisted until 1890. Throughout the 1880s, however, growing religious and social reform movements started to incorporate supremacist and separatist ideologies into their campaigns.[148] While New Orleans had always been racially fluid, white racist ideologies required a hard-and-fast color line that would be the mark of Black inferiority. Segregationist ideology was also critical to the rural planters' plans; they, in reconstituting the sugar industry after the Civil War, exploited the formerly enslaved through a sharecropping system in which their meager pay was issued in scrip, not cash. After the war, freedmen seeking fair wages had organized in racially integrated unions like the Knights of Labor, culminating in a three-week strike in November 1887 known as the "Thibodaux Massacre," in which at least thirty Black sugar workers were slain.[149] For the Democrats of Louisiana, Blacks were to remain labor, not workers with a civic, political identity. Segregation served the purpose of thwarting any potential alliances between Black and white labor that would undermine the white economic power structure. Segregation as a spatial tactic, as well as voter suppression, lack of funding for schools, and constant threat of retaliation by white supremacists, were the mechanisms used to enforce the color line.

Shortly after the Supreme Court upheld Mississippi's separate car act, Louisiana's legislators introduced House Bill No. 42, the Separate Car Act, in May of 1890. It stated that "railway companies in this state [Louisiana] shall provide equal but separate accommodations for the white and colored races. . . . No person or persons shall be permitted to occupy seats in coaches other than the ones assigned to them on account of the race they belong to." Section 2 declared that the officers of the train were required to assign each passenger to their compartment based on their race. Those refusing to comply were fined $25 or twenty days in jail. The bill was justified by its authors because it would "act to promote the comfort of passengers on railways."[150]

The burden of this act fell on the railway officers who would be charged with determining the correct "race" of each passenger. Like the argument they made against the segregation of schools, Afro-Creole activists stressed the arbitrary nature of determining a person's race, given the complex interracial makeup of the state. In essence, they continued to point out the absurdity of basing a law on a color line that did not exist. Outraged by this act, Afro-Creoles immediately formed the American Citizen's Equal Rights Association (ACERA), led by Martinet, which advocated for a new movement focused on dismantling the tyranny of segregation. Martinet was joined by Rodolphe Desdunes (1849–1928), his fellow student at Straight law school, who had also worked with Martinet, Paul Trévigne, and Arthur Estéves to reopen the Catholic Institute. In addition to working as an activist, Desdunes worked at the customs office and as a teacher at the Catholic Institute. Incensed by the Separate Car Act, he responded by writing one of his many editorials on Independence Day in the *Crusader*, the newspaper begun in the tradition of the *Tribune* by Martinet. Desdunes's indignation is clear: "Among the many schemes devised by Southern Statesmen to divide the races none is so audacious and insulting as the one which provides separate cars for black and white people on the railways running through the State. It is like a "slap in the face of every member of the black race, whether he has the full measure or only one-eighth of the blood."[151]

While some members of the House protested the bill, given that it would codify "Jim Crow," it moved to the Senate, where it lay dormant. Following the bill closely, Martinet was galvanizing the Afro-Creole activists, white allies, and the public through the *Crusader*. On May 24, 1890, joined by members of the ACERA, which included local white leaders and Black Protestant ministers, the group traveled to Baton Rouge to deliver a petition to the legislature. It decried the bill as "unconstitutional, un-American, unjust, dangerous and against sound public policy."[152] Reiterating their long-held ideals of universal human equality, they proclaimed that "Citizenship is national and has no color."[153] The potential insult, humiliation, and mistreatment to people of color that would result from this bill was a clear rebuke of public rights. The bill fell three votes short of passing in the Senate. White supremacists turned to their newspapers, insisting that "the two races shall live separate and distinct from each other in all things, with separate schools, separate hotels, and separate cars."[154] The goal of the white supremacists was clear and simple: prevent the doctrine of social equality from taking shape in any way or form. Without the separation of races, the danger from interracial alliances—in the labor movement, in schools, in politics, and in religion—would undermine the power of the Democrats and their agenda of white supremacy. The spatial construct of race, codified as Black and white, would now delineate the space of the public sphere in order to signify the mark of Black inferiority. On July 10, the bill was taken up again and passed. Despite Martinet sending a telegram to Governor Nicholls asking him to veto the bill, he signed it that evening. The next day, Martinet wrote in the *Crusader*, "We'll make a case, a test case, and bring it before the Federal Courts." This was the official beginning of the legal case of *Plessy v. Ferguson*, a case that among Afro-Creoles would hopefully be the final step in the long struggle for public rights for all people of color.

The Beginning of the End of Public Rights

Because the *Plessy* case is one of the most well-known Supreme Court cases, its story so familiar, we might assume that it was a simple, straight-forward legal case. Nothing could be further from the truth. This was not a simple case of Black vs. white separatists; rather, this was a case that would challenge U.S. law to denounce white supremacy by fully acknowledging persons of all colors as full and equal citizens. The vision was driven by the ideology of universalism, the ideals of the revolutionary Atlantic, and the promise of a universal brotherhood. This was a radical vision. The case would require careful and strategic legal maneuvering to succeed in reaching the Supreme Court. This was essential: the case must be settled at the national level, establishing once and for all that human dignity, equality, and citizenship were guaranteed through public rights.

The ACERA, under the leadership of P. B. S. Pinchback, made an unsuccessful plea to the state legislature against the separate car bill. Unable to raise funds and lacking any specific strategy to bring the case to court, Martinet also believed that what was needed at the time was not a Blacks-only organization, but a national multiracial campaign against racial violence and segregation.[155] Frustrated with the lack of effective resistance, Louis Martinet, Laurent Auguste, Rodolphe Lucien Desdunes, and Aristide Mary called for a meeting at the *Crusader*'s office on September 5, 1891. Those attending formed the Comité de Citoyens, also known as the Citizens' Committee to Test the Constitutionality of the Separate Car Law. Arthur Estéves served as president, C. C. Antoine as vice president, Firmin Christophe as secretary, George G. Johnson as assistant secretary, and Paul Bonseigneur as treasurer. In addition, there were eighteen other members, including Louis Martinet, Rodolphe Desdunes, and several Anglicized Blacks. The immediate priority was to raise funds to arrange for legal counsel that had experience in constitutional law. Not only the *Crusader*, but other Black newspapers, including the *Southwestern Christian Advocate*, called for action and financial aid in organizing a legal challenge.

In November of 1891, the *Southwestern* admonished, "Let every self-respecting colored man, contribute his means, and let every friend of public right and justice unite with their help and sympathy in the movement. Contributions will be received and credited to the cause at this office."[156]

Calls from the newspapers resulted in galvanizing a community-wide response that rippled through the networks of Afro-Creole organizations. These included, among others, the Justice, Protective, Social and Educational Club; La Société des Artisans; Les Dames Inseparables; La Société des Demoiselles Unies; La Société des Francs Amis; Ida Club; and Straight University's Sumner Literary Debating Club.[157] Many of these organizations had members who also served on the Citizens' Committee. Myrtil Piron, an organizing member who was also an active member of Economy Hall, informed the hall of the new challenge they were mounting to segregation. The Economy Hall members agreed to each pay an extra fee so that they could make a twenty-dollar donation to the Citizens' Committee.[158] The outrage against this bill was also felt by the people of color in other parishes beyond New Orleans, who responded with donations from St. Martinsville to Shreveport. Calls for support also rallied donations from numerous cities, including San Antonio, Chicago, San Francisco, and Washington D.C. A far cry from being a local, Afro-Creole battle, a central strategy of the Citizen's Committee was to garner interracial grassroots support at the national level.

The committee moved quickly to begin planning a legal strategy by determining the court cases that would be necessary to have the case reach the Supreme Court. For this they needed to assemble an interracial team whose legal experience spanned state to federal law. Martinet's first move was to reach out to Albion W. Tourgée, who was now living in New York. Tourgée had been increasingly active in national politics, warning the American public about the increasing repression of African Americans in the South. He believed "education was the most effective counterweight to white dominion and black inequality."[159] His "master key" to combat white supremacy was the creation of a national education fund to send money directly to towns and schools, bypassing Democratic state governments, with the goal of wiping out illiteracy and protecting people of color from white exploitation.[160] An avid reader of the colored press, Tourgée was well acquainted with the *Crusader*, which he characterized as a "new beacon of bravery in a landscape dominated by timidity."[161] He often drew on the paper to craft his column "A Bystander's Notes," published from 1888 to 1898 in the *Chicago Daily Inter Ocean*, a Republican-supported newspaper. His column, syndicated in numerous other papers, was the mouthpiece of his crusade for social reform and justice, bringing national attention to the issues of lynching, segregation, disfranchisement, white supremacy, and white racism.

Tourgée was the Citizens' Committee immediate choice for lead lawyer on the case and he did not hesitate to accept. To support the efforts of the Citizens' Committee, Tourgée used his *Bystander* column to issue a nationwide call for the establishment of the National Citizens' Rights Association (NCRA) to help promote and inform people of the organized movement to test Jim Crow laws in the South. In the fall of 1891, the column published a subscription blank promising a "certificate of membership" to anyone who sent a two-cent stamp and pledged to uphold the NCRA's aims. Thousands of whites and Blacks from around the country sent applications, and clubs formed in Chicago and Mississippi. Ida B. Wells joined and began correspondence with Tourgée, urging him to write on behalf of an antilynching bill.[162] She continued to promote the organization among the network of contacts she cultivated as she began lecturing against lynching. Tourgée's vision of the NCRA drew on the abolitionist movement as well as his work during Reconstruction in North Carolina framing a democratic constitution. He also served as a state superior court judge, where he convicted Ku Klux Klan terrorists. The outpouring of support was immediate, and within a year the NCRA claimed 100,000 members, ultimately reaching 250,000. This number equals that of the American Anti-Slavery Society's in the 1830s and exceeded that of the NAACP in the 1910s.[163]

These large numbers were no doubt the result of active canvassing among Blacks in the South. Most of the NCRA's Black southern members were rural and less literate, often using word of mouth to spread the news of the NCRA. Those who worked to increase membership were often under surveillance and vulnerable to the threat of white supremacist reprisals, including the ever-present threat of a lynch mob. The December 17, 1892, issue of the *Crusader* relayed the story of a young African American, a member of the NCRA, who was circulating applications and was accused of inciting a group of laborers to leave their jobs; he was promptly arrested. He was tried and convicted, then sent to a "contract" farm to work out his fine. After four months, a white man wrote to Tourgée, who hired a lawyer and paid the fine to release this young man. Many who joined the NCRA did not sign their names in fear of retaliation and used only their membership certificate numbers. This interracial organization, often eclipsed in our history by the NAACP, and receiving only passing mention by historians of civil rights, positioned the case against the Separate Car Act as a national one, with the goal of educating and holding the nation accountable for delivering on the promise of equal rights for all persons.[164]

Because Tourgée worked from New York, the Citizens' Committee also hired James C. Walker, a white criminal law specialist and local Republican judge from New Orleans. Martinet and other committee members had studied at Straight while Walker was a professor there and knew he would be a trusted ally. The rich correspondence between Martinet and Tourgée suggests that every detail of strategy and argument in the case was thoroughly discussed between them.[165] The Citizens' Committee and its commitment to social justice had inspired the formation of the NCRA. Through this organization, Tourgée and Martinet worked to forge a national interracial coalition that would collect and disseminate information about the violations of citizens' rights and would shape public opinion, electoral politics, and judicial decisions. Yet the significance of the NCRA has often been overlooked, not only as the precursor to the NAACP, but also as a critical interracial civil rights organization.[166] This omission has to do with the misperception that the Citizens' Committee was serving only the interests of Afro-Creoles. Clearly, Afro-Creoles were focused on affirming their unique identity, yet they also saw this as a strategy to undermine the racial dichotomy that made segregation possible and seemingly natural. They were living in a political climate in which the Black/white color line would not only negate their identity/history/culture but, just as important, would give white supremacists the justification for relegating all people of color to a position of inferiority. The Citizens' Committee and their white allies envisioned another reality, one in which there was not a Black and white America, but a liminal space with no color line.[167]

From Public Rights to Civil Rights

Now that the legal team was assembled, they planned two cases, one to argue the constitutionality of the separate car act at the interstate level, and the other to challenge the constitutionality of segregation within the state. Prior to determining the specific plaintiffs in the cases, Tourgée and Martinet discussed the issue of "color." Tourgée argued that they needed a light-colored litigant to make sure that the client would succeed in purchasing a ticket designated for whites. Martinet was not convinced. He was deeply concerned about alienating the African American community in New Orleans, believing they would see this as Afro-Creoles' desire to pass as white. A central argument that would be used in both cases, however, was the arbitrary nature of determining racial classification, given that no legal definition of race had been provided in the separate car act. They planned to pursue the legal argument that it was too difficult to determine a passenger's race given the fluidity of race in Louisiana. Essentially, they were arguing that because there was no color line, binary racial categories could not exist. Martinet eventually agreed with Tourgée, resulting in the committee choosing Daniel Desdunes and Homer Plessy, both young men who could have passed for white.

The twenty-two-year-old teacher and musician Daniel Desdunes, son of Rodolphe, became the defendant in the first case to test the constitutionality of the state's Separate Car Act for interstate travel. In February of 1892, he boarded the Louisville & Nashville Railroad train from New Orleans to Mobile on Canal Street sitting in the all white car. Two miles down the track, as planned, private detectives hired by the Citizens' Committee arrested him for violating the Separate Car Act. But the case never came to trial. While awaiting a court date, the Louisiana Supreme Court, referencing the recent *Abbott v. Hicks* case, decided that the Separate Car Act could not be enforced against interstate passengers.[168] The Desdunes case was no longer relevant to the cause.

The committee now was pressed to find a new defendant to test the constitutionality of the statute as it pertained to intrastate train travel. It was either Arthur Estéves, president of the Citizens' Committee, or L. J. Joubert, a member of the Citizens' Committee, who most likely suggested Homer Plessy (1863–1925) as the next defendant, given their common work with the Justice, Protective, Social and Educational Club. Homer, in his early twenties, started serving as vice president of the club in 1887 and Estéves was treasurer. Organized in 1886, the charter, published in both French and English, declared itself

> an organization for the purpose of uniting and protecting ourselves, both socially and morally, and protecting our intellectual welfare, thereby inculcating a true sense of the importance of education, and uniting ourselves politically that our support and influence may be brought to bear where our interest and welfare can be advanced and our rights as citizens of this State and of the United States protected and respected.[169]

Plessy and his fellow members clearly saw the need for educational reform, given the negative impact of school segregation on large numbers of children. At the time, only nineteen of seventy-three teachers in Black Schools were Black, and there were only eighteen public schools in New Orleans for 5,306 Black children and 19,555 white children.[170] Just as important, the club continued to stress the relationship between education and citizenship, which had underpinned the Afro-Franco-Creole protest tradition for generations. In their 1887 pamphlet, "To All Who May Be Concerned," they cried out, "Our young men and women will grow up in ignorance and immorality, thereby crumbling our societies, and prove themselves unworthy citizens of the State and the United States of America."[171] Their plan of action included, among other things, obtaining a library, receiving their share of public education funds, good teachers, full terms, and maintenance of schools.

Homer Plessy was not officially on the Citizens' Committee, but he was well-connected to many of the eighteen members through the various social organizations to which he belonged, thus establishing him within the important social networks among Afro-Creoles.[172] Plessy had been ushered into the community networks of Afro-Creoles by his stepfather, Victor M. Dupart, whose family activism could be traced back several generations. He came from a family of free people of color who traced their freedom to his great-grandmother in 1779. His maternal grandfather had fought with Andrew Jackson in 1814 with the expectation of full citizenship for his service, and in 1864, he signed the petition to President Lincoln demanding equal rights. Homer Plessy is often depicted first and foremost as a shoemaker who challenged racial segregation by riding in a "white only" train car on June 7, 1892. But this focus on his occupation has served to obscure and diminish the decades of political activism that preceded his well-known train trip. He was part of the much larger struggle for public rights in which education and citizenship were intertwined in the campaign to be acknowledged as full human beings.

The rest of the story of Homer Plessy is well-known. After boarding a "whites-only" East Louisiana Railway Company train going from New Orleans to Covington, he was arrested as arranged, charged, and released on $500 bond for trial in criminal court. On October 28, he entered the courtroom of Judge John Ferguson, a Massachusetts native, accompanied by his lawyer James C. Walker, Rodolphe Desdunes, and Louis Martinet. While Tourgée was not present, months of correspondence between Walker, Martinet, and Tourgée had been exchanged to develop the legal arguments that were presented in Walker's brief. The first was that the Separate Car Act conferred upon the conductor the power to determine the question of a person's race. According to Walker, the state had no power to authorize any person to determine the race of another person. Second, the act established an "invidious distinction and discrimination based on race, which is obnoxious to the fundamental principles of national citizen-

ship" rights already secured by the Thirteenth and Fourteenth Amendments.[173] District Attorney Lionel Adams supported the right of the states
to determine their own guidelines regarding race relations. On November
18, Judge Ferguson overruled Plessy's plea for jurisdiction.

The legal team was elated; the case could move forward and be appealed
to the Louisiana Supreme Court. In December 1892, the five-judge court,
headed by Justice Charles Erastus Fenner, gave short shrift to the arguments presented. The court based most of their arguments on the simple
fact that it did not matter whether Plessy was white or colored because the
Separate Car Act "applies to the two races with such perfect fairness and
equality."[174] Whites could be arrested for entering colored cars, coloreds
could be arrested for entering white cars. The court did not accept that
the law had been targeted at people of color. Once again, they received the
unanimous decision they had anticipated. On January 5, 1893, Tourgée
and Walker filed a brief for a hearing before the Supreme Court.

While the case was in limbo until 1896, the Citizens' Committee continued their work. Privately, Louis Martinet was questioning not only the
viability of overturning the act; he worried about the danger to activists
given the widespread repression and violence that was sweeping the South.
Ida B. Wells had reported 118 lynchings that year, 18 of them in Louisiana,
making it third in the nation. Tourgée and Martinet were also concerned
about the recent appointments to the Supreme Court that gave them serious doubts about the success of the case. They counted only one judge
in their corner, Justice John Marshall Harlan, a Kentuckian born into a
slaveholding family. A Republican, he had a strong history of supporting
civil rights. It did not look good for their case. Martinet despaired that they
were fighting a hopeless battle. Desdunes wrote, "There is nothing forlorn
about our 'battle,' nothing about which we may be shaken in our faith. Our
cause is grounded in law, reason, and humanity, and we feel as strong in our
convictions of right as we are confident of ultimate success" (Figure 21).[175]
Martinet and the Citizens' Committee threw themselves into making a final
stand against segregation the best way they knew how: using print. They
made the *Crusader* a daily paper, the only African American daily in the
country at the time, using it as a trumpet to sound their call for equal rights.

At the same time, Louisiana began to enact even more restrictive laws
that cemented segregation. The *Crusader* took up each new law that threatened equal rights for all citizens. They knew from long experience that
separate would never be equal. In 1894, interracial marriage was made
illegal. In July of 1894, the state mandated separate waiting rooms in railroad stations. The *Crusader* also challenged Whites-only juries. And, per-

Figure 21. Rodolphe Desdunes. Charles Roussève Papers, Amistad Research Center, New Orleans, LA.

haps most disheartening, was the impending segregation of the Catholic Church. Archbishop Janssens (1843–1897), from Holland, moved the church away from its French distinctiveness into the Catholic American mainstream. Addressing the needs of immigrants, he established separate Italian parishes. Joining with Mother Katherine Drexel, founder of the Sisters of the Blessed Sacrament, he also established a separate church, St.

Katherine's, the first Black national parish, on Tulane Ave., with the belief
that it would facilitate Black leadership. Desdunes took to the *Crusader*
on February 28, 1895, to announce his displeasure with Drexel: "Mother's benevolence is being used to destroy that fundamental principle of
our religion. If men are divided by, or in the Church, where can they be
united in the bonds of faith and love of truth and justice?"[176] Desdunes, a
descendant of generations of Afro-Creole Catholics, invoked the principle
of universalism under which French Creoles, Afro-Creoles, and enslaved
Africans had worshipped together in interracial churches since the founding of the city of New Orleans in 1718. Black Catholics resisted the segregation of churches, seeing it as the final step in establishing a caste system
in America.[177]

In the fall of 1896, the Supreme Court was composed of nine white
men, all northerners except for John Marshall Harlan. Ironically, he would
be the only dissenting vote. On April 13, 1896, Tourgée made his way to the
Supreme Court. Martinet and Walker remained in Louisiana, exhausted
and skeptical. Tourgée had consulted with both and worked endlessly on
polishing his brief. He did not, however, anchor his arguments in precedents; instead, he pushed the court to see the amendments differently. The
underlying premise of his argument was that race was a kind of property.[178]
He pushed the justices to consider if they would choose to be Black.[179] If
the answer was no, then wouldn't it be possible to conclude that the reputation of being white was indeed property. If you were white, it enhanced not
only your reputation but your economic value. Consequently, the separation of the races in the Separate Car Act reinforced notions of difference
and dominance, beliefs that had been central to slavery. The Thirteenth
Amendment was meant to extinguish the caste system that had legitimated
slavery. The Separate Car Act reimposed a caste system, he argued. Likewise, the Fourteenth Amendment called for equal protection under the
law, challenging the justices to determine how there could be a law that
made it a crime to sit in a wrong car.

Justice Henry Brown wrote the majority opinion, which focused on the
Fourteenth Amendment. He wrote:

> A statute which implies merely a legal distinction between the white
> and colored races—a distinction which is founded in the color of
> the two races, and which must always exist so long as white men
> are distinguished from the other race by color—has no tendency to
> destroy the legal equality of the two races, or reestablish a state of
> involuntary servitude.

For Brown, the "distinction" in which the "white" man is distinguished from the other race reflected the deep hold that scientific racism had taken on American culture and ideology. Social equality was inconceivable given the now accepted "natural" difference that Samuel Cartwright had articulated; "The negro is not a white man painted black" but "a different being, of a different nature. . . . Nature has ordained that the negro shall serve the white man, and the white man shall take care of the negro."[180] While Afro-Creoles sought to argue the irrationality of race, the Supreme Court ruled that the Constitution of the United States was powerless "to eradicate racial instincts."[181] Brown wrote regarding the equal protection clause of the Fourteenth Amendment:

> The object of the amendment was undoubtedly to enforce the absolute equality of the two races before the law, but, in the nature of things, it could not have been intended to abolish distinctions based upon color, or to enforce social, as distinguished from political, equality, or a commingling of the two races upon terms unsatisfactory to either.[182]

The court's interpretation of the Separate Car Act was that a distinction between the white and colored races "has no tendency to destroy the legal equality of the two races or reestablish a state of involuntary servitude."[183] The justices argued that the law was intended to establish the equality of the races before the law but was not intended to enforce social equality.

Justice Brown used as a precedent for this argument the long history of segregated schools. He cited his own state of Massachusetts as among the earliest to sanction public school segregation, followed by California, Indiana, Kentucky, Louisiana, Ohio, Missouri, and New York. Even the District of Columbia provided racially separate schools approved by Congress. Brown argued that "Laws permitting, and even requiring . . . separation in places where they are liable to be brought into contact do not necessarily imply the inferiority of either race to the other, and have been generally, if not universally, recognized as within the competency of the state legislatures in the exercise of their police power."[184] His reliance on the precedent of segregated public schools as a place where the "races" had historically been separated highlights the strategic role that education has played in producing, legitimating, and constructing race and racism.

Harlan's dissent was forceful. He predicted that "the judgement this day rendered will, in time, prove to be quite as pernicious as the decision made by this tribunal in the Dred Scott Case."[185] He clearly understood that "separate but equal" laws would place "the brand of servitude and degradation upon a large class of our fellow citizens, our equals before the law."[186] In fact, he predicted that such laws would keep "permanent peace impossible" and keep alive a conflict of the races.[187] The *Plessy* decision became the bedrock of segregation. Governor Murphy Foster, after the passage of the new Louisiana constitution of 1898, heralded "the White supremacy for which we have so long struggled . . . is now crystallized into the constitution."[188] The new 1898 state constitution implemented literacy tests and a grandfather clause that eliminated more than 120,000 mostly African American voters from the rolls. In 1902, New Orleans resegregated streetcars; in 1908 it mandated separate water fountains. The long battle for equality grounded in the revolutionary transatlantic concept of "public rights" would give way to the next civil rights struggle whose rhetoric would be "legal rights."

After *Plessy*, Jim Crow was imposed on every aspect of American life. Black activism centered on the polarizing struggle between accommodation to Jim Crow led by Booker T. Washington and the political radicals under W. E. B. Dubois. The activism of Afro-Creoles was obscured by what Desdunes attributed to the difference between the "Latin Negro" and the Anglo-Saxon one. In his pamphlet, "A Few Words to Dr. Dubois: 'With Malice Toward None,'" he wrote, "The Latin Negro differs radically from the Anglo-Saxon in aspiration and method. One hopes, the other doubts. . . . One aspires to equality, the other to identity. One will forget that he is a Negro in order to think that he is a man; the other will forget that he is a man in order to think that he is a Negro. . . . One is a philosophical Negro, the other practical."[189] Desdunes hoped that a hybridity of these predispositions would create a liminal space in which race, identity, and language would not be reduced to binaries but reinvented in the ongoing processes of transatlantic creolization.

Much of the nation paid little attention to the *Plessy* ruling at the time. Homer Plessy returned to court with James Walker (who died later that year), pleaded guilty, and paid his twenty-five-dollar fine. He and his wife Louis and their children went on with their lives until Homer passed away on March 1, 1925. The Citizens' Committee issued a formal report stating that despite their loss, they believed they had pursued the right path toward justice. The presses stopped rolling at the *Crusader*. Given the increasingly oppressive conditions, Desdunes wrote in *Nos Hommes et Notre Histoire* that given the tyranny of our oppressors, "the continuation of the *Crusader* would not only be fruitless but decidedly dangerous."[190] When he completed his book in 1908, no American press would publish it. In 1911, L. Martin of Montreal published the manuscript in the largest French-speaking city in the Americas.

Desdunes passed in 1928 visiting his son, Daniel, in Nebraska; thirty-six years prior, it was Daniel who had initiated the *Plessy* case. Martinet, exhausted and discouraged, left the political arena to practice medicine. He died at his home in New Orleans in 1917. In 1957, a group of African American lawyers founded the Louis A. Martinet Legal Society, dedicated to ending racial segregation.[191] Tourgée was devastated. In return for supporting William McKinley in the 1896 presidential election, he was given an appointment in the U.S. consulate in Bordeaux, France. Before leaving for France, he wrote:

> The power of the Supreme Court for good, as well as for evil, can scarcely be exaggerated. . . . It can by its judgments strengthen our institutions in the confidence and affection of the people, or, more easily than any other department of the government, it can undermine the foundations of our government systems.[192]

He died in France on May 21, 1905. Little did he realize that the *Plessy* case would stand and legally undermine the equal rights of citizens for the next half century. In that time, a new generation of activists would emerge who would not rely on public rights for social justice but would turn to legal rights to craft the arguments necessary to overturn *Plessy* in *Brown v. Board of Education*. Yet *Brown* did not argue against segregation based on the pathology of white supremacy or the racism inherent in the law.[193] Instead, it argued that Black inferiority, the result of the psychological harm of segregation, was the reason to overturn *Plessy*. The Brown decision never addressed the systematic racism inherent in American democracy. Once again, the hope of "public rights" as critical to human equality was deferred. The implementation of *Brown* was met with massive white resistance, the consequences of which are apartheid schooling.[194] The struggle for real democracy and full citizenship, to be understood as fully human, is still ongoing.

Reverberations

The *Tribune* and *Crusader* were critical to the articulation of an argument that "public" rights were more important than civil or legal rights in establishing a culture of human equality. In this regard, integrated, public education was essential to creating a public sphere in which "one nation" could be cultivated to achieve the ideals of republican government. The *Tribune's* vision of "one nation and one people" persisted, despite the dissolution of the *Tribune*, and it continues in New Orleans today as a critical voice informing dialogues regarding some of the most sweeping educational reforms this country has seen, perhaps not unlike the vast changes that confronted the shapers of a new culture after the Civil War. Even today, the newspaper and the Afro-Creole protest tradition of which it is a part continues, molding disparate time periods into a history of shared struggle, for we can trace the legacy of the *New Orleans Tribune* to a monthly paper of the same name started in 1985 by Dr. Dwight McKenna and Beverly Stanton McKenna. The modern-day *Tribune* describes itself as "part of a publishing legacy that began 146 years ago, when Roudanez published the first black daily newspaper in the United States. Then, as now, the *Tribune* was dedicated to social justice and civil rights for all Louisiana citizens."[195] Like the men of the 1864 *Tribune*, the McKennas hope that "through an accurate portrayal of the African–American community, their publications have the power to open windows of greater appreciation for working relationships between the races and diverse cultural groups in our city, our state, and our nation."[196]

Henry Louis Gates Jr. describes Black periodicals as containing "a remarkable account of information about the world's impact every day upon African Americans, and their impact upon the world, [which] can be scrutinized by scholars, thus filling in lacunae that even the most subtle intellectual history cannot otherwise address."[197] There is much work that remains to be done to unearth the rhetorical strategies and historical accomplishments of the Black press as a shaper of educational culture, especially in the South. Periodicals can create a lasting influence despite the ephemeral quality of newspapers, which are "date-stamped" and often thrown away before their subsequent edition is printed.[198] Perhaps the *Tribune* and *Crusader* will draw increased scholarly attention to periodicals as unique spaces for historically oppressed populations to enter public discourse, for "those qualities of fluidity and openness to the future which characterize serial forms do make them attractive to the powerless."[199] As scholars, however, we must rethink the ways we study periodicals. Lyn Pykett describes a shift from studying periodicals as reflective of a culture, meaning that these texts must be mined to gain insight about that same culture, to their investigation as contributors to culture: "Periodicals can no longer be regarded in any simply reflective way as 'evidence' (either primary or secondary), as transparent records which give access to, and provide the means of recovering, the culture which they 'mirror'. . . . the periodicals have come to be seen as a central component of that culture—'an active and integral part', and they can only be read and understood as part of that culture and society, and in the context of other knowledges about them."[200]

The story of the *Tribune* and *Crusader* as community texts that advocated for the fulfillment of "true republicanism, democracy without shackles" is a poignant reminder that history does not always follow a process of small incremental changes that eventually lead to progress. Instead, the *Tribune* is a reminder that history takes unexpected twists and turns that follow no rational trajectory. Like the paper, advocates for democratic education must continually be engaged in creating a public dialogue that challenges the ideologies and institutions that do not serve to fulfill the vision of a democratic nation. While the *Tribune* did not ultimately succeed in achieving lasting, free, public, integrated schools in Louisiana, it did contribute to shaping a culture in which alternative futures were possible. These futures were not based on paternalism or subordination; instead they assumed the fundamental equality of all human beings. Given that the trends in American educational reform, such as the increase of charter and magnet schools and corporate-funded curriculums, are resegregating schools (leading to "apartheid schooling," according to Jonathan Kozol's *The Shame of the Nation*), there is perhaps much we can learn today from the rhetorical practices of the *Tribune*.[201] As exemplified by the *Tribune*, the Black press in the South was a "fighting press . . . and an important segment of American social history," and its legacy should continue to be studied as a rhetorical tool and to inform our understanding of the purpose of and vision for education.[202]

Epilogue

Democracy is hard to love.
—Iris Marion Young, 2002[1]

The relationship between democracy and public education is a dominant narrative in American history. Not only has public education traditionally been seen as the great equalizer, but public schools have been understood as critical sites for the production of the educated citizen. The stories told in this book remind me that democracy is "hard to love." In fact, democracy can be cruel, hateful, and exclusionary. Yet at the same time it holds the promise of a universalism in which the full humanity, including all the particulars, of each individual will be honored. It was this promise of democracy that galvanized the many actors in this book. Despite their exclusion and dehumanization, they continued to create spaces in which their humanity would be acknowledged. As democracy seems once again to be under attack, these are stories that remind us that democracy is always in the making. We are all part of an unfinished project.

The counterstory in this book maintains that constructs of public education and democratic citizenship in the struggle to constitute a U.S. national identity are inseparable from the simultaneous emergence of transatlantic constructs of the educated citizen along transnational and transracial networks. By illuminating a well-established cosmopolitan tradition of transatlantic, anticaste activism that shaped a transnationalized idea of democratic citizenship, the monumental narratives of the common school movement are dislodged, creating spaces for alternative readings

338

of the relationship between citizenship, education, and democracy. The mobilizing of racism, as central to nation building and the very essence of citizenship, was consistently challenged by transatlantic activists, who grounded citizenship in a universalist ethic of human dignity cultivated through a socially conscious transatlantic order expressed in shared public spaces. By challenging definitions of citizenship through grounding them in the concept of "public rights" (both a psychic and social space) as opposed to "civil/political" rights (a legal space) transatlantic activists maintained that equal standing in the public sphere, especially in schools, was essential to challenging white supremacy.

The creole pedagogies of transcultural translation, disorder, counterpublic spaces, imagination, and liminality are not those we associate with education for citizenship. Quite to the contrary, the educated citizen is one grounded in rationality, knowledge, and objectivity and above all is subject to the nation. These constructs, clearly gendered and racialized, have long made citizenship, a sense of belonging, elusive and slippery. In fact, the construct of the educated citizen has been used to exclude, marginalize, and oppress. The stories told in this book remind us that full citizenship for *all* has always been and continues to be in the making/unmaking. Current attempts to limit voting rights, deport immigrants, and restrict personal liberties signal a reconfiguring of the boundaries of citizenship. These are the liminal spaces, much like those navigated by the interracial activists Louis Martinet, Albion Tourgée, Rodolphe Desdune, and Homer Plessy, in which the fundamental desire to be acknowledged as fully human and equal is continually deferred. How does one make sense of that irrationality?

The stories told here provide windows into the struggles to be recognized as fully human, as educable, as citizens. They remind us that we can reimagine what constitutes a citizen, we are not chained to historical constructs of citizenship grounded in exclusion. Imagining freedom, like the boys at the Catholic Institute, is a subversive pedagogy because it transcends the limitations imposed by others by disregarding their truth and claiming one's own. A creole pedagogy of imagination rejects knowledge as the only source of truth. When truth (the Supreme Court, the Code Noir, the Superior Council) corrupts, a creole pedagogy of imagination is the space of reclaiming one's own understanding of self and community.

Marie Turpin, Jean Baptiste, Joseph Bazanac, Henriette Delille, Pierre Roup, Marie Couvent, Joseph Lakanal, Armand Lanussee, Louis Charles Roudanez, and Homer Plessy used their imaginations to create (the process of creolization) counterpublic spaces in which they could place themselves as members of communities of their choosing. For Henriette and the Sisters of the Holy Family, their radical subversion of racial and gendered norms of nineteenth century New Orleans through creating a Black sisterhood resituates citizenship from the purview of the state to one in which self-determination within a spiritual universalism holds one accountable to nurturing not equality, an impossible and perhaps undesirable concept, but the humanity of each person.

It is often theorized that public education in the United States has functioned to reproduce social hierarchies. The assumption is that schools were formed and the unintended consequence was the reproduction of race and social class. But when we situate the history of education within the pedagogical circuits of the transatlantic in relation to the Haitian and French Revolutions, the revolts of the enslaved, and the Afro-Creole protest tradition we see that schools were the intervention to impede notions of equality and universal citizenship. Schools do not function to reproduce class and race, they were designed to produce race and class. I am not sure where this leaves us in regard to the national myth that schools are the great equalizer and essential to producing the democratic citizen.

The radical agency of the teachers and students at the Catholic Institute have remained unintelligible given that the normative tropes of educational history continue to be wedded to an Anglo-Protestant–northern common school narrative. Like the recent work of Daniel Tröhler, the deployment of history must interrogate the methodological roots that are at the base of Anglo-American historical studies of the modern school, disrupt the borders and boundaries that constitute national studies of curriculum history, and historicize the "languages" of education that have naturalized a science of education that is devoid of history.[2] Unleashing curriculum history from the tropes of monumental narratives, the nation-state, and the dominant languages of education will require a re-envisioning of educational history that takes seriously the powerful and essential role of imagination in creating the public sphere.

While schools, and many American institutions (the Supreme Court, the legal system, etc.) have functioned to maintain white supremacy, the narratives in this book present a parallel educational culture, one born in the counterpublic spaces of necessity. These spaces—Masonic clubs, benevolent societies, schools like the Catholic Institute and St. Mary's, Turnvereins and the print culture of the *Tribune*—have provided spaces in which the disenfranchised, the marginalized, and the oppressed could claim a political subjectivity despite racial subordination. These spaces created a counterculture that signified the dignity of each person by engaging them as full human beings capable of democratic organization, education, and moral responsibility to one another. While these lofty ideals were perhaps not always met, it was understood that true democracy required a vision of universalism grounded in public rights that allowed for both a unique identity and a common culture. The concept of universal public rights seems utopian in this age of fervent nationalism, an idea that seems misguided given the deep divisions that divide nations and people. Yet perhaps we have reached the limits of the nation-state as the trope for citizenship. It is my hope that the histories in this book provide spaces from which to reimagine the educated citizen.

Notes

Introduction

1. Records of the Superior Council of Louisiana (RSC), August 9, 1741 (hereafter RSC), in the *Louisiana History Quarterly*, vol. 11, no. 1, January 1928, 131, documents the petition to cancel an apprenticeship. Madame Marie Anne Hoffman, widow of Jean Barbier, now wife of André Hoffman, sued to recover her young Negro slave who had been left in Mr. Dupare's charge as an apprentice even though he had neglected to fulfill his contract of teaching the enslaved boy to read and write.

2. RSC, *Louisiana History Quarterly*, vol. 10, no. 4, October, 1927, 567, documents at least four runaways earlier in 1741. On January 16, Pierrot, age thirty, of the Biefada nation, was prosecuted for marooning. He ran away because he was put in irons and wrongly accused of stealing. He and another runaway lived on wild cats and rats of the wood. He had run away once before, discontented with his wife. Also on January 16, the court examined five runaway slaves; Denny of the Samba nation, aged fifty, slave of Chapron's; Sans peur, thirty years old, Bambara nation; La Richer, twenty-five years old, Bambara nation; L'Eveillé, aged thirty years old, Samba nation; and Bambara, twenty-seven years old, Samba nation. Not only slaves ran away, but wives did as well. On April 28 that same year, a report was recorded (p. 582) by Jean Baptiste Turpin of Kaskaskia, regarding the disappearance of his wife. She had left him twice, the first time to take up with an Outaoua mate named Pintaloir and the second time with a Huron. No further word was heard from her.

3. RSC, August 9, 1741, translation mine.

4. Stuart G. Noble and Arthur G. Nuhrah, "Education in Colonial Louisiana." *Louisiana Historical Quarterly* 32 (1949), 762–63, report that in 1727 a locksmith, Laurent Chevirty, agreed to teach his trade to a slave apprentice who was owned by the Company of the Indies. Length of the apprenticeship was one to five years depending on the trade. Boys, orphans, and Negro slaves were apprenticed.

343

5. RSC, August 1741. There are several recorded cases where the contracts stipulated that the trade master was to teach the boy reading and writing in addition to a trade. Such an agreement was entered into by Guillaume Lemoine and Paul Moreau. Lemoine was bound to the service of Moreau for a period of three years to learn the trade of shoemaker. Moreau was, in addition, to teach Lemoine to read and give him examples of good writing.

6. See Noble and Nuhrah, "Education in Colonial Louisiana, 762–63.

7. In this regard, the British colonies similarly advocated some forms of literacy, particularly the teaching of reading in order that slaves could read the Bible. See Jared Ross Hardesty, *Unfreedom: Slavery and Dependence in Eighteenth-Century Boston* (New York: New York University Press, 2016), for a further discussion of literacy in the British Colonies.

8. See Lawrence Powell, *The Accidental City: Improvising New Orleans* (Cambridge, MA: Harvard University Press, 2012), chap. 4, for a detailed discussion of the economy and labor in early colonial New Orleans. Also see Daniel Usner, "From African Captivity to American Slavery: The Introduction of Black Laborers to Colonial Louisiana," *Louisiana History: The Journal of the Louisiana Historical Association* 20, no. 1 (Winter 1979), 25–48, for a description of the use of apprenticeships by the Company of the Indies for training enslaved Africans.

9. See Sophie White, *Voices of the Enslaved: Love, Labor and Longing in French Louisiana* (Chapel Hill: University of North Carolina Press, 2019), for a detailed discussion of the judicial system in French colonial New Orleans.

10. Article 24 of the 1724 code allowed slaves to act as witnesses in civil and criminal cases when it was a matter of necessity, meaning that no other witnesses were available, and only in default of white people; but in no case were they be permitted to serve as witnesses either for or against their masters.

11. White, *Voices of the Enslaved*, 28.

12. Rebecca Scott and Jean M. Hébrard, *Freedom Papers: An Atlantic Odyssey in the Age of Emancipation.* (Cambridge, MA: Harvard University Press, 2012).

13. Michel de Certeau, *The Practice of Everyday Life* (Berkeley: University of California Press, 1984).

14. Scott and Hébrard, *Freedom Papers*, specifically looks at the spaces of literacy that enslaved and free people of color garnered in order to achieve and maintain their emancipation.

15. See Cécile Vidal, ed., *Louisiana: Crossroads of the Atlantic* (Philadelphia: University of Pennsylvania Press, 2014), for a further discussion of the place of Louisiana in the Atlantic world.

16. See Sophie White, *Wild Frenchmen and Frenchified Indians: Material Culture and Race in Colonial Louisiana* (Philadelphia: University of Pennsylvania Press, 2012), for a fuller discussion of Marie's story.

17. White, *Wild Frenchman and Frenchified Indians*.

18. See Christopher Bilodeau, "'They honor our lord among themselves in their own way': Colonial Christianity and the Illinois Indians," *American Indian Quarterly* 25, no. 3 (2001): 352–77.

19. For more details on the Jesuit mission in Kaskaskia see Roger Baudier, *The Catholic Church in Louisiana* (New Orleans: Hyaytt, 1939); White, *Wild Frenchmen and Frenchified Indians*.

20. Kathleen DuVal, "Interconnectedness and Diversity in 'French Louisiana,'" In *Powhatan's Mantle: Indians in the Colonial Southeast*, ed. Gregory A. Waselkov, Peter H. Wood, and Tom Hatley (Lincoln: University of Nebraska Press, 1989), 133–62.

21. Charles E. Nolan and Dorenda Dupont, eds., *Sacramental Records of the Roman Catholic Church of the Archdiocese of New Orleans, Volume 18, 1828–1829* (New Orleans, 2003), 352. Catherine Coralie Roup was the natural daughter of Pierre Lafitte and Marie Louisie Villard, a free woman of color.

22. The house built between 1816 and 1823 was one of the earliest urban-style creole cottages built in the Fauborg Tremé. See Roulhac Toledano and Mary Louise Christovich, *Fauborg Tremé and the Bayou Road* (Gretna, LA: Pelican Publishing, 2003).

23. Toledano and Christovich, *Fauborg Tremé and the Bayou Road*, 102.

24. Carl Brasseaux and Glenn R. Conrad, eds. *The Road to Louisiana: The Saint-Domingue Refugees 1792–1809* (Lafayette: University of Louisiana At Lafayette Press, 1992), 247.

25. Brasseaux and Conrad, *The Road to Louisiana*, 258.

26. Peter Linebaugh and Marcus Rediker, *The Many-Headed Hydra: Sailors, Slaves, Commoners and the Revolutionary Atlantic* (Boston: Beacon Press, 2000).

27. Rebecca Scott, "The Atlantic World and the Road to *Plessy v. Ferguson*," *Journal of American History* (Dec. 2007), 726.

28. Caryn Cossé Bell, *Revolution, Romanticism and the Afro-Creole Protest Tradition in Louisiana, 1718–1868* (Baton Rouge: Louisiana State University Press, 1997), 55.

29. Bell, *Revolution, Romanticism*, 54.

30. Joanna Brooks, "The Early American Public Sphere and the Emergence of a Black Print Counterpublic," *William and Mary Quarterly* 62, no. 1 (Jan. 2005): 70. While Brooks refers to "black" persons with a small "b," I will follow the July 2020 style change of the New York Times to capitalize "Black" given that the designation refers to people of African ancestry who have a shared cultural identity. Likewise, I will follow the style used by the New York Times and use lowercase when using the term "white."

31. Brooks, "The Early American Public Sphere," 73.

32. Stephan Kantrowitz, "'Intended for the Better government of Man': The Political History of African American Freemasonry in the Era of Emancipation." *Journal of American History* (2010), 1001–26.

33. I borrow the term "practicing" history both from de Certeau, *The Practice of Everyday Life*, and Gabrielle M. Spiegel, *Practicing History: New Directions in Historical Writing After the Linguistic Turn* (New York: Routledge, 2005).

34. See William Boelhower, *Atlantic Studies: Perspectives and Challenges* (Baton Rouge: Louisiana State University Press, 2019), for a more detailed discussion of the critique of this binary.

35. See Guillaume Aubert, "'To establish one law and definite rules': Race, Religion, and the Transatlantic Origins of the Louisiana Code Noir," in *Louisiana: Crossroads of the Atlantic*, ed. Cécile Vidal (Philadelphia: University of Pennsylvania Press, 2014), 44–67, for a further discussion of the interpretation of the Louisiana Code Noir in relation to rights.

36. I use the term "creolization" to describe a process of creative adaptation, an inventive, improvisational aesthetic that characterized the intersections of peoples in the transatlantic world. For further illumination of this use of the term see Shannon Dawdy, *Building the Devil's Empire* (Chicago: University of Chicago Press, 2008); Nicholas Spitzer, "Monde Créole: The Cultural World of French Louisiana Creoles and the Creolization of World Cultures," *Journal of American Folklore* 116, no. 459 (2003): 57–72; Doris Garraway, *The Libertine Colony: Creolization in the Early French Caribbean* (Durham: Duke University Press, 2005); Robyn Anderman, "Brewed Awakening: Re-Imagining Education in Three Nineteenth Century New Orleans Coffee Houses" (PhD. thesis, Louisiana State University, 2018). The term "Creole" has also been used in Louisiana to mean "native born" meaning that Louisiana Creoles in the French colonial period could be Black or white, free or enslaved, or any mixture. Later in the nineteenth century the term changed to describe white descendants of French origin or the mixed-race descendants of free people of color. For further discussion of these uses of the term see Joseph G. Tregle Jr., "On That Word 'Creole' Again: A Note," *Louisiana History* 23 (1982): 193–98. More recently, the term "Creole" has been commercialized to describe products, food, and music from Louisiana. While I use the term Afro-Creole in later chapters to describe free people of color in the eighteenth century, I primarily use the term as a process, not a noun.

37. See Bernard Bailyn, *Education in the Forming of American Society* (Chapel Hill: University of North Carolina Press, 1960); Ellwood P. Cubberly, *Public Education in the United States* (Boston: Houghton Mifflin Company, 1919); Lawrence Cremin, *The Transformation of the American School* (New York: Alfred A. Knopf, 1961).

38. Cubberly, *Public Education in the United States*, viii.

39. Emile Durkheim, *The Elementary Forms of Religious Life*, trans. K. Fields (New York: The Free Press, 1912/1995). Also see David Trohler, *The Languages of Education: Protestant Legacies, National Identities, and Global Aspirations*. (New York: Routledge, 2011).

40. Max Weber, *The Protestant Ethic and the Spirit of Capitalism* (New York: Charles Scribner's Sons, 1904).

41. See Bernard Bailyn, *Atlantic History: Concept and Contours* (Cambridge, MA: Harvard University Press, 2005); Paul Gilroy, *The Black Atlantic: Modernity and Double Consciousness* (Cambridge, MA: Harvard University Press, 1993); Cécile Vidal, *Caribbean New Orleans: Empire, Race and the Making of a Slave Society* (Chapel Hill: University of North Carolina Press, 2019).

42. See Petra Munro Hendry, *Engendering Curriculum History* (New York: Routledge, 2011).

43. See Jerome Bruner, *The Culture of Education* (Boston: Harvard University Press, 1997).

44. Linebaugh and Rediker, *The Many-Headed Hydra*, 332–33.

45. See Michel Foucault, *Discipline and Punish: The Birth of the Prison* (New York: Vintage Books, 1975); Steven Selden, *Inheriting Shame: The Story of Eugenics and Racism in America* (New York: Teachers College Press, 1999); Ann Winfield, *Eugenics and Education* (New York: Peter Lang, 2007).

46. See Boelhower, *Atlantic Studies*, for a fuller discussion.

47. See Brent Davis, *Inventions of Teaching: A Genealogy* (New York: Routledge, 2004).

48. Foucault, *Discipline and Punish*.

49. See Bernadette Baker, *In Perpetual Motion* (New York: Peter Lang, 2001), for a thorough discussion of the history of the emergence of the category of child.

50. Dawdy, *Building the Devil's Empire*, 20.

51. Susan Buck-Morss, *Hegel, Haiti and Universal History* (Pittsburgh: University of Pittsburgh Press, 2009), 111.

52. David Scott, *Conscripts of Modernity* (Durham, NC: Duke University Press, 2009).

53. Buck-Morss, *Hegel, Haiti and Universal History*, 114

54. Édouard Glissant, *Poetics of Relation*, trans. Betsy Wing (Ann Arbor: University of Michigan Press, 1997).

55. Gilroy, *The Black Atlantic*, 4.

56. Laurent Dubois and Julius Scott, *Origins of the Black Atlantic* (New York: Routledge, 2010), 1.

57. Jane Landers, *Atlantic Creoles in the Age of Revolutions* (Cambridge: MA: Harvard University Press, 2010).

58. Scott, "The Atlantic World and the Road to *Plessy v. Ferguson*, 726–33.

59. Laurent Dubois, *A Colony of Citizens: Revolution and Slave Emancipation in the French Caribbean, 1787–1804* (Chapel Hill: University of North Carolina Press, 2004), 7.

60. C. L. R. James, *The Black Jacobins* (New York, Vintage Books, 1989), 25.

61. Benedict Anderson, *Imagined Communities* (London: Verso, 1983), 141

62. William F. Pinar, *Educational Experience as Lived: Knowledge, History, Alterity* (New York: Routledge, 2015), 193.

63. Anderson, *Imagined Communities*, 4.

64. de Certeau, *The Practice of Everyday Life*, 97.

65. de Certeau, *The Practice of Everyday Life* 102.

66. de Certeau, *The Practice of Everyday Life*, 93.

67. de Certeau, *The Practice of Everyday Life*, xviii

68. This introduction does not allow for a full discussion of these concepts, but this work has been undertaken by Brian Casemore, *The Autobiographical Demand of Place: Curriculum Inquiry in the South* (New York: Peter Lang, 2008); Ugena Whitlock, *This Corner of Canaan: Curriculum Studies of Place and the Reconstruction of the South* (New York: Peter Lang, 2007); William F. Pinar and Joe Kincheloe, *Curriculum as Social Psychoanalysis: The Significance of Place* (New York: State University of New York Press, 1991); Rob Helfenbein, *Critical Geographies of Education: Space, Place and Curriculum Inquiry* (New York: Routledge, 2021); Sue Middleton, *Henri Lefebvre and Education: Space, History, Theory* (New York: Routledge, 2013).

69. Henri Lefebvre, *The Production of Space*, trans. Donald Nicholson-Smith (Malden, MA: Blackwell Publishing, 1974).

70. Lefebvre, *The Production of Space*, 26.

71. Lefebvre, *The Production of Space*, 13.

72. David Harvey, *The Limits of Capital* (London; Verso, 2006), 124.

73. Shirley E. Thompson, *Exiles at Home: The Struggle to Become American in Creole New Orleans* (Cambridge, MA: Harvard University Press, 2009).

74. Michel-Rolph Trouillot, *Silencing the Past: Power and the Production of History*, (Boston: Beacon Press, 1995), xii.

75. Lefebvre, *The Production of Space*, 116.

76. Trouillot, *Silencing the Past*, 15.

77. Shannon Dawdy, *Patina: A Profane Archaeology* (Chicago: University of Chicago Press, 2016).

78. Dawdy, *Building the Devil's Empire*, 6. See also Robert Baron and Ana C. Cara. "Introduction: Creolization as Cultural Creativity." In *Creolization as Cultural Creativity*, edited by Robert and Ana C. Cara Baron (Jackson: University of Mississippi Press, 2011); and Anderman, "Brewed Awakening," for detailed discussions of the history of the term "Creole," as well as the process of creolization.

79. Édouard Glissant, *Europe and the Antilles: An Interview with Edouard Glissant/Interviewer: A. S. Hiepko*. Rethinking Europe: Electronic Media, Orality, and Identity (Durham, NC: Duke University Press, 1998).

Chapter 1

1. Guillaume Aubert, "'To establish one law and definite rules': Race, Religion, and the Origin of the Louisiana Code Noir," in *Louisiana: Crossroads of the Atlantic World*, ed. Cécile Vidal (Philadelphia: University of Pennsylvania Press, 2014), 26.

2. See Vernon Valentine Palmer, *The Origins and Authors of the Code Noir*, 56 *La. L. Rev.* (1996), for a fuller discussion of the legal precedents that shaped the code.

3. The Capuchins were not alone among Catholic missionaries in their assault on slavery. The second archbishop of Mexico (1551–1572), the Dominican Alonso de Montúfar, wrote to the Spanish king in 1560 protesting the importation of Africans and questioning the "justness" of enslaving them. Tomás de Mercado, a Dominican theologian and economist at the School of Salamanca (Spain), had lived in Mexico and in 1571 had written his *Summa de Tratos y Contratos* ("Manual of Deals and Contracts"), which was a scathing critique of the morality of the enslavement of Africans by Europeans.

4. See Cécile Fromont, *The Art of Conversion: Christian Visual Culture in the Kingdom of Kongo* (Omohundro Institute Book Publication Program with the University of North Carolina Press, 2014); and David Thornton, *Africa and Africans in the Making of the Atlantic World, 1480–1680* (Cambridge: Cambridge University Press, 2012), for specific discussions of the intertwined history of Angola and Catholicism.

5. Aubert, "To establish one law and definite rules," 28.

6. See David Eltis and David Richardson, *Atlas of the Transatlantic Slave Trade* (New Haven, CT: Yale University Press, 2010), for a detailed discussion of the slave trade and emergence of global economy.

7. Philip P. Boucher, *France and the American Tropics to 1700; Tropics of Discontent* (Baltimore: John Hopkins University Press, 2008).

8. The French had begun colonizing in the Caribbean in the early 1620s. In 1625, they established the colony of St. Kitts, followed by Guadaloupe and Martinique in 1635, St. Lucia in 1650, and lastly Saint-Domingue in 1664. See Stephan Lenik, "Mission Plantations, Space, and Social Control: Jesuits as Planters in

French Caribbean Colonies and Frontiers," *Journal of Social Archeology* 12, no. 1 (2011): 51–71, for a detailed discussion of the Jesuit plantation system.

9. Mathé Allain, "Slave Policies in French Louisiana," *Louisiana History* 21 (1980): 127–38.

10. See Caryn Cossé Bell, *Revolution, Romanticism, and the Afro-Creole Protest Tradition in Louisiana 1718–1868* (Baton Rouge: Louisiana State University, 1997) for detailed discussion of this assimilation.

11. Jurgen Habermas, *The Structural Transformation of the Public Sphere: An Inquiry into a Category of Bourgeois Society*, trans. Thomas Burger (Cambridge, MA: The MIT Press, 1998).

12. This re/mapping or tracing of freedom, rights, and citizenship within the Atlantic world has recently been given a great deal of attention by various scholars: Rebecca Scott, *Degrees of Freedom: Louisiana and Cuba after Slavery* (Cambridge, MA: Harvard University Press, 2005); Paul Gilroy, *The Black Atlantic* (Cambridge, MA: Harvard University Press, 1988); Laurent Dubois and Julius S. Scott, eds., *Origins of the Black Atlantic* (New York: Routledge, 2010); Peter Linebaugh and Marcus Rediker, *The Many-Headed Hydra: Sailors, Slaves and Commoners, and the Hidden History of the Revolutionary Atlantic* (Boston: Beacon Press, 2000).

13. Tracy Neal Leavelle, *The Catholic Calumet: Colonial Conversions in French and Indian North America* (Philadelphia: University of Pennsylvania Press, 2012).

14. Robbie Ethridge, *From Chicaza to Chicksaws: The European Invasion and the Transformation of the Mississippian World, 1540–1715* (Chapel Hill: University of North Carolina Press, 2010), 2.

15. See Joel Spring, *The Universal Right to Education* (Mahwah, NJ: Lawrence Erlbaum Associates, 2000), for a lengthy discussion of the concept of universal education.

16. In his 1987 analysis of the Code Noir's significance, Louis Sala-Molins claimed that its two primary objectives were to assert French sovereignty in her colonies and to secure the future of the cane sugar plantation economy. Central to these political and economic goals was control of the slave trade. The code aimed to provide a legal framework for slavery, to establish protocols governing the conditions of colonial inhabitants, and to end the illegal slave trade. Louis Sala-Molins, *Le code noir* (Paris: Presses Universitaires de France, 1987); and Louis Sala-Molins, *Dark Side of the Light: Slavery and the French Enlightenment*, trans. John Conteh-Morgan (Minneapolis: University of Minnesota Press, 2006).

17. Isabel Wilkerson, *Caste: The Origins of Our Discontents* (New York: Random House, 2020), traces this now hidden caste system based on rigid racial, class, and other hierarchies of human ranking.

18. Karen E. Carter, *Creating Catholics: Catechism and Primary Education in Early Modern France* (Notre Dame, IN: University of Notre Dame Press, 2011). For a detailed history of catechism, see Berard L. Marthaler, *The Catechism Yesterday and Today: The Evolution of a Genre* (Collegeville, MN: Liturgical Press, 1995).

19. Brad Petitfils, *Parallels and Responses to Curricular Innovation: The Possibilities of Posthumanist Education* (New York: Routledge, 2015).

20. See Allan P. Farell, *The Jesuit Code of Liberal Education: Development and Scope of the Ratio Studiorum* (Milwaukee: Bruce, 1938); Aldo Scaglione, *The Liberal Arts and the Jesuit College System* (Amsterdam: John Benjamins Publishing Com-

pany, 1986); and John W. Donohue, *Jesuit Education: An Essay on the Foundations of Its Idea* (New York: Fordham University Press, 1963).

21. For detailed discussion of Renaissance humanism, see Paul F. Grendler, *Schooling in Renaissance Italy: Literacy and Learning, 1300–1600* (Baltimore: Johns Hopkins University Press, 1989); and Albert Rabil Jr., ed., *Renaissance Humanism: Foundations, Forms, and Legacy*, 3 vols. (Philadelphia: University of Pennsylvania Press, 1998).

22. *La Règle de Saint Augustin et Constitutions pour les religieuses de Sainte-Ursule, 1643* (Bibliothèque National), De la Fin Principale de l'institut des Religieuses de Saint Ursula; Marie-Andree Jegou, *Les Ursulines du Faubourg St-Jacques à Paris 1607–1662* (Paris: Presses Universitaires De France, 1981).

23. Elizabeth Rapley, *The Dévotées: Women and Church in Seventeenth Century France* (Montreal: McGill-Queen's University Press, 1990).

24. Thus anticipating Rousseau by a good hundred years. See Brent Davis, *Inventions of Teaching* (New York: Routledge, 2004), for a further discussion of the genealogical differences between the concepts of "filling up" and "drawing out."

25. Michel Foucault, *Discipline and Punish* (New York: Vintage Books: 1975); see part III, chap. 1 for detailed discussion of this shift in power.

26. Foucault, *Discipline and Punish*, 160.

27. Foucault, *Discipline and Punish*, 176.

28. James E. McClellan III, *Colonialism and Science: Saint Domingue in the Old Regime* (Baltimore: John Hopkins University Press, 1992).

29. Charlotte de Castelnau-l'Estoile, "Jesuit Anthropology: Studying 'Living Books,'" in *The Oxford Handbook of the Jesuits* (Oxford: Oxford University Press, 2019).

30. Susan Juster and Linda Gregerson elaborate on these connections in their edited collection *Empires of God: Religious Encounters in the Early Modern Atlantic* (Philadelphia: University of Pennsylvania Press, 2011); see also William Simmon, "Cultural Bias in the New England Puritans' Perception of Indians," *William and Mary Quarterly* 38, no. 1 (1981): 56–72; G. E. Thomas, "Puritans, Indians, and the Concept of Race," *New England Quarterly* 48, no. 1 (1975): 3–27; Alfred A. Cave, "New England Misperceptions of Native American Shamanism," *International Social Science Review* 67, no. 1 (1992): 15–27.

31. See Daniel Tohler, *The Language of Education* (New York: Routledge, 2011); and Doug McKnight, *Schooling, the Puritan Imperative, and the Molding of an American National Identity: Education's "Errand in the Wilderness"* (Mahwah, NJ: Lawrence Earlbaum Associates, 2003), for a detailed discussion of the ideologies of Protestantism and relationship to constructs of education.

32. Juster and Gregerson, *Empires of God*, suggest that the Indian Library of the Puritan evangelist John Eliot (including an Algonquian-language Bible, the first vernacular Bible printed in the Americas) was a monumental achievement of literary translation (p. 7).

33. Thomas Peace, "Borderlands, Primary Sources, and the Longue Durée: Contextualizing Colonial Schooling at Odanak, Lorette, and Kahnawake, 1600–1850," *Historical Studies in Education/Revue d'histoire de l'éducation* 29 no. 1 (2017): 8–31. For further insights into the relationship between orality and literacy, see Lisa Brooks, *The Common Pot: The Recovery of Native Space in the Northeast* (Minne-

apolis: University of Minnesota Press, 2008); and Germaine Warkentin, "In Search of 'The Word of the Other': Aboriginal Sign Systems and the History of the Book in Canada," *Book History* 2, no. 1 (1999): 1–27.

34. This is exemplified by Roger Williams and Anne Hutchinson, who were exiled by the Puritan community in part due to their advocacy for Native Americans as equals. See Petra Munro Hendry, *Engendering Curriculum*, (New York: Routledge, 2011), for further discussion.

35. Dominique Deslandres, "Dreams Clash: The War over Authorized Interpretation in Seventeenth-Century French Missions," in *Empires of God: Religious Encounters in the Early Modern Atlantic*, ed. Susan Juster and Linda Gregerson (Philadelphia: University of Pennsylvania Press, 2011): 142–53.

36. Deslandres, "Dreams Clash," 145.

37. See Marc Lescarbot, *History of New France*, ed. and trans. I. Grant (Santa Barbara, CA: Praeger, 1969), for a detailed discussion of intermarriage in the French colonies. Also see Guillaume Aubert, "'The Blood of France': Race and Purity of Blood in the French Atlantic World," *William and Mary Quarterly* (Third Series) 61, no. 3 (2001): 439–78.

38. See Lawrence Venuti, *Translator's Invisibility: A History of Translation* (New York: Routledge, 2008), for an articulation of cultural translation that challenges the traditional view that a translation's quality lies in its closeness or faithfulness to the original text.

39. Dwayne Trevor Donald, "Fort, Curriculum, and Indigenous Métissage: Imagining Decolonization of Aboriginal-Canadian Relations in Educational Contexts," *First Nations Perspectives* 2, no. 1 (2009): 1024.

40. Cynthia Chambers, Erika Hasebe-Ludt, Dwayne Donald, Wanda Hurren, Carl Leggo, and Antoinette Oberg, "Métissage: A Research Praxis," in *Handbook of the Arts in Qualitative Research: Perspectives, Methodologies, Examples, and Issues*, ed. J. Gary Knowles and Ardra L. Cole (Thousand Oaks, CA: Sage), 141–53.

41. See Allan Greer, "A Wandering Jesuit in Europe and America," in *Empires of God: Religious Encounters in the Early Modern Atlantic*, ed. Susan Juster and Linda Gregerson (Philadelphia: University of Pennsylvania, 2011), 106–22, for a further discussion of Jesuit influence and identity in the New World. Also see Allan Greer, ed., *The Jesuit Relations: Natives and Missionaries in Seventeenth-Century North America* (Boston: Bedford/St. Martin's, 2000); Luke Clossey, *Salvation and Globalization in the Early Jesuit Missions* (New York: Cambridge University Press, 2008); C. J. McNapsy, *Conquest or Inculturation: Ways of Ministry in the Early Jesuit Missions* (Regina: Campoin College, University of Regina, 1979).

42. Anya Mali, *Mystic in the New World* (Leiden: E. J. Brill, 1999): 108.

43. Greer, "A Wandering Jesuit," 107.

44. For a history of early Jesuit missionary work see Carole Blackburn, *Harvest of Souls: The Jesuit Missions and Colonialism in North America 1632–1650* (Montreal: McGill-Queen's University Press, 2000); Raymond A. Schroth, *The American Jesuits: A History* (New York: New York University Press, 2007).

45. Nicholas Ng-A-Fook, Patrick Phillips, Mark T. Currie, and Jackson Pind, *Purposes of Education: Unsettling Historical Accounts of Settler Colonial Public Education.* (In Press).

46. Blackburn, *Harvest of Souls*, 4.

47. See Micah True, *Masters and Students: Jesuit Mission Ethnography in Seventeenth-Century New France* (Montreal: McGill-Queen's University Press, 2015).

48. The *Relations* have been criticized for their portrayals of success, given that the Jesuits were cognizant of their audience, who were potential donors to the missions.

49. The *Relations* were written before the European Enlightenment, before the emphasis on science and reason, and the link between them and the notion of progress; before the secularization that displaced the sovereignty of the church and the dominant religious interpretations of humankind's place in the world; and before Darwin and evolutionary theories that encouraged interpretations of colonized people as close to animals (in other words, primitive or savage) in ways that were quite different from those advanced by the Jesuits. See Allan Greenblatt, *Marvelous Possessions: The Wonder of the New World* (Chicago: University of Chicago Press, 1991), 36, for a detailed discussion of these differences.

50. R. G. Thwaites, ed., *The Jesuit Relations and Allied Documents: Travels and Explorations of the Jesuit Missionaries in New France 1610–1791*, 73 vols. (Cleveland: The Burrows Brothers, 1896), vol. 5.

51. R. G. Thwaites, ed., *The Jesuit Relations and Allied Documents: Travels and Explorations of the Jesuit Missionaries in New France 1610–1791*, 73 vols. (Cleveland: The Burrows Brothers, 1896), 5:31. Hereafter *Jesuit Relations*.

52. *Jesuit Relations*, 5:16.

53. See Roger Magnunson, *Education in New France* (Montreal: McGill-Queen's University Press, 1992), for a complete history of Jesuit education in New France.

54. See Brett Rushforth, *Bonds of Alliance: Indigenous and Atlantic Slaveries in New France* (Chapel Hill: University of North Carolina Press, 2013); Afua Cooper, "Unsilencing the Past: Memorializing Four Hundred Years of African Canadian History," In *Multiple Lenses: Voices from the Diaspora Located in Canada*, ed. David Divine (Newcastle upon Tyne: Cambridge Scholars, 2007), 11–22, for further information on slavery in Canada.

55. University of New Orleans Archives (UNOA), Marcus Christion Collection, MSS011, Series XI; *Jesuit Relations*, V:63.

56. *Jesuit Relations*, 16:183–85.

57. Peter A. Dorsey, "Going to School with Savages: Authorship and Authority among the Jesuits of New France," *William and Mary Quarterly* 55, no. 3 (1998): 399–420.

58. *Jesuit Relations*, ed. Thwaites, 10:91.

59. Anya Mali, *Mystic in the New World* (Leiden: E. J. Brill, 1999), i.

60. Peace, "Borderlands, Primary Sources, and the Longue Durée," 14.

61. Peace, "Borderlands, Primary Sources, and the Longue Durée," 15.

62. Peace, "Borderlands, Primary Sources, and the Longue Durée," 16.

63. See Kathryn Labelle, *Dispersed but Not Destroyed: A History of the Seventeenth-Century Wendat People* (Vancouver: University of British Columbia Press, 2012).

64. See Peace, "Borderlands, Primary Sources, and the Longue Durée," for a detailed discussion of the long-term impact of Jesuit and Ursuline pedagogies on Indigenous agency in regard to education.

65. See Greer, *The Jesuit Relations*, for a fuller discussion of Laval's educational accomplishments.

66. In 1759, during the Seven Years' War, Quebec fell to the English, and New France was under British control. The English barred the immigration of more Jesuits to New France. By 1763, there were only twenty-one Jesuits stationed in New France. By 1773, only eleven Jesuits remained. During the same year, the English crown laid claim to New France and declared that the Society of Jesus in New France was dissolved.

67. Like Vincent de Paul, Marie's utopian visions were a response to what many saw as the chaos and decline of the Catholic Church. See Natalie Zemon Davis, *Women on the Margins: Three Seventeenth-Century Lives* (Cambridge, MA: Harvard University Press, 1995), for a more detailed discussion.

68. Claude Martin, *La Vie de la vénérable Mère Marie de l'Incarnation, Première supérieure des Ursulines de la Nouvelle France: Tirée de ses Lettres et de ses Ecrits* (Paris: Louis Billaine, 1677; facsimile editions Solesmes: Abbaye de Saint-Pierre, 1981).

69. Mary Dunn, "When 'Wolves Became Lambs': Hybridity and the 'Savage' in the Letters of Marie del'Incarnation," *Seventeenth Century* 27, no. 1 (2012): 104–20.

70. Martin, *La Vie de la vénérable Mère Marie de l'Incarnation*. This citation for the autobiography of Marie of the Incarnation, compiled and published by her son in 1677 from letters written to him, and a revised version of her *La Relation de 1654*, is taken from Davis, *Women on the Margins*. Her translation of this quote appears on page 79.

71. See Dom Guy-Marie Oury, *Madame de la Peltrie et ses fondations Canadienes* (Quebec: Presses Université de Laval), for a detailed discussion of her role in New France.

72. Martin, *La Vie de la vénérable Mère Marie de l'Incarnation*, 169, as cited by Davis, *Women on the Margins*, 74.

73. The common period of the emergence of teaching as women's true profession is the mid-nineteenth century with the work of Catherine Beecher to legitimate the public work of women in the common school movement. See Nancy Hoffman, *Women's True Profession: Voices for the History of Teaching* (New York: McGraw Hill, 1981), for a fuller discussion of the gendered construction of teaching. See also Petra Munro, *Subject to Fiction: Women Teachers' Life History Narratives and the Cultural Politics of Resistance* (Buckingham, UK: Open University Press, 1998).

74. See Davis, *Women on the Margins*, and Guillaume Postel, *De orbis terrae concordia* (Concerning the Agreement [in Doctrines] of the World, in Latin), 1544.

75. Mitchell Greenberg, *Baroque Bodies: Psychoanalysis and the Culture of French Absolutism* (Ithaca, NY: Cornell University Press, 2001), 52.

76. John Sullivan, trans., *The Autobiography of Vénérable Marie of Incarnation, O.S.U. Mystic and Missionary* (Chicago: Loyola University Press, 1964), 172.

77. Martin, *La Vie de la Vénérable Mère Marie de l'Incarnation*, 401.

78. Martin, *La Vie de la Vénérable Mère Marie de l'Incarnation*, 63.

79. Renée Descartes, *Discourse on the Method*, 1637. New York: Macmillan, 1986.

80. See Davis, *Inventions of Teaching*, 25–83, for a detailed discussion of these differences.

81. Mali, *Mystic in the New World*, 73.

82. Mali, *Mystic in the New World*, 74.

83. See Marie-Florine Bruneau, *Women Mystics Confront the Modern World* (New

York: State University of New York Press, 1998); Davis, *Women on the Margins*; and Dunn, "When 'Wolves Became Lambs.'"

84. Her son was also to become the editor of his mother's writings. He published two spiritual relations and countless letters after her death in 1672. In addition, he revised the original texts of the relations, one from her time in the convent in Tours and the other from her time in Canada. *Lettres de la vénérable Mère Marie de l'Incarnation, première supérieure des Ursulines de la Nouvelle-France: divisées en deux parties*, ed. Claude Martin (Paris, 1681). See Katherine Ibbett, "Reconfiguring Martyrdom in the Colonial Context: Marie de l'Incarnation," in *Empires of God: Religious Encounters in the Early Modern Atlantic*, ed. Susan Juster and Linda Gregerson (Philadelphia: University of Pennsylvania, 2011), 175–90; Mitchell Greenberg, *Baroque Bodies: Psychoanalysis and the Culture of French Absolutism* (Ithaca, NY: Cornell University Press, 2001); and Bruneau, *Women Mystics Confront the New World*, for a fuller analysis of this editing.

85. Jérôme Lalemant (1593–1673), a Jesuit brother, was assigned in 1638 as Jesuit superior of the Huron Mission. He had been a teacher in France from 1615 to 1638 and had brought with him a wealth of experience in education. After running the Huron Mission from 1639 to 1649, he was assigned as the Jesuit superior in Quebec.

86. Ibbett, "Reconfiguring Martyrdom in the Colonial Context," 178.

87. Between 1642 and 1649, eight Jesuit priests were martyred in French Canada.

88. Ibbett, "Reconfiguring Martyrdom in the Colonial Context," 186.

89. See Bruneau, *Women Mystics Confront the New World*, for a full discussion of the shifts in female mystical tradition. Shifts in Christian mysticism have been discussed by Michel de Certeau, *The Mystic Fable*, trans. Michael B. Smith (Chicago: University of Chicago Press, 1992); Hendry, *Engendering Curriculum History*.

90. Bruneau, *Women Mystics Confront the Modern World*, 3.

91. We see this in the Salem witch trials in Boston.

92. See Leslie Choquette, "'Ces Amazones du Grand Dieu': Women and Mission in Seventeenth-Century Canada," *French Historical Studies* 17, no. 3 (1992): 627–55.

93. *Jesuit Relations*.

94. See Sophie White, *Wild Frenchman and Frenchified Indians: Material Culture and Race in Colonial Louisiana* (Philadelphia: University of Pennsylvania Press, 2012), 6.

95. See Luke Clossey, "Faith in Empire: Religious Sources of Legitimacy for Expansionist Early-Modern States," in *Politics and Reformations: Communities, Polities, Nations and Empires*, ed. Christopher Ocker, Michael Printy, Peter Starenko, and Peter Wallace (Leiden: Brill, 2007): 571–87; Saliha Belmessous, *Assimilation and Empire, Uniformity in French and British Colonies, 1541–1954* (Oxford: Oxford University Press, 2013); Mairi Cowan, "Education, Francisation, and Shifting Colonial Priorities at the Ursuline Convent in Seventeenth-Century Quebec," *Canadian Historical Review* 99, no. 1 (2018): 1–29.

96. Peace, "Borderlands, Primary Sources, and the Longue Durée."

97. Davis, *Women on the Margins*, 120.

98. Cowan, "Education, Francisation and Shifting Colonial Priorities," 7.

99. Allan Greer, *Mohawk Saint: Catherine Tekawitha and the Jesuits* (New York: Oxford University Press, 2005), 102.

100. Cowan, "Education, Francisation and Shifting Colonial Priorities," 11.

101. Cowan, "Education, Francisation and Shifting Colonial Priorities," 20.

102. This cultural syncretization was common throughout the Jesuit missions as well. At Notre-Dame-de-Lorette, the Jesuit mission for the Wendat, a devotional wampum belt with the inscription "Vigini pariturae votum huronum" was sent to Notre-Dame de Chartres, where it is still conserved. In exchange, a silver reliquary prepared containing a number of relics of the saints was received by the Wendat in 1680. The type of gift exchange so common in building alliances among Indigenous peoples clearly was adapted to the new transatlantic relations of which they were a part.

103. Bruneau, *Women Mystics Confront the New World*.

104. Nicholas P. Cushner, in *Why Have You Come Here? The Jesuits and the First Evangelization of Native America* (Oxford: Oxford University Press, 2006), cautions that missionary writing was often constructed to create a favorable impression in the minds of financial supporters and to present a positive view of missionary work in order to gain the support of critics.

105. Davis, *Women on the Margins*, 97.

106. Davis, *Women on the Margins*, 98.

107. Greenberg, *Baroque Bodies*, 169.

108. Bruneau, *Women Mystics Confront the New World*, 101.

109. Bruneau, *Women Mystics Confront the New World*, 102–103.

110. It should be noted that the Wendat of Lorette sent a postulatory letter to Pius IX in the autumn of 1875. In recognition of the services that Marie de l'Incarnation had lavished upon their fathers, they requested for her the honors of beatification.

111. As quoted in Davis, *Women on the Margins*, 109.

112. In addition to the Ursulines, two other orders of cloistered nuns established themselves in Canada in the seventeenth century: the Chanoinesses hospitalières de Saint-Augustin (1639) and the Hospitalières de Saint-Joseph. By the time of the British conquest (1763), there were 204 nuns living in Canada. In addition there were laywomen, like Mme. de La Peltrie and Mlle. Jeanne Mance (1606–1673), who committed themselves to missionary work in the form of establishing hospitals whose primary goal was to aid the poor and Indigenous groups. In 1643, Mance built a hospital, the Hotel Dieu, at the foot of Mount Royal. This work required the development of administrative skills and managerial skills that furthered women's independence from ecclesiastical authorities and allowed them an agency not available in France. Jeanne Mance was known as the "noble heroine of charity." See J. H. Schlarman, *From Quebec to New Orleans: The Story of the French in America* (Belleville, IL: Buechler Publishing Co., 1929).

113. Rapley, *The Dévotées*, 92.

114. Jacques Marquette, "Of the First Voyage Made by Father Marquette Toward New Mexico, and How the Idea Thereof was Conceived," *Jesuit Relations*, 59:115.

115. See Ian W. Brown, "The Calumet Ceremony in the Southeast and its Archaeological Manifestations," *American Antiquity* 54, no. 2 (1989): 311–31, for a full discussion of the history of the Calumet ceremony.

116. Jacob F. Lee, *Masters of the Middle Waters: Indian Nations and Colonial Ambitions along the Mississippi* (Cambridge, MA: Harvard University Press, 2019), 40.

117. This process of frenchification is discussed in more detail in Lee, *Masters of the Middle Water.*

118. John Hogan, *History of the Jesuits in Colonial French Louisiana* (Loyola University Archives, New Orleans [LUANO], 1907).

119. The term "middle ground" is borrowed from Lee, *Masters of the Middle Water.*

120. Robert Michael Morrissey, *Empire by Collaboration: Indians, Colonists, and Governments in Colonial Illinois Country* (Philadelphia: University of Pennsylvania Press, 2015), 45.

121. Lee, *Masters of the Middle Waters,* 6.

122. Robert Englebert, "Making Indians in the American Backcountry: Récits de voyage, Cultural Mobility, and Imagining Empire in the Age of Revolutions," in *French Connections: Cultural Mobility in North America and the Atlantic World, 1600–1875,* ed. Robert Englebert and Andrew N. Wegmann (Baton Rouge: Louisiana State University Press, 2020), 197.

123. Morrissey, *Empire by Collaboration,* 7–8.

124. For more information on intermarriage between colonists and Indigenous peoples, see Kathleen DuVal, "Indian Intermarriage and Métissage in Colonial Louisiana," *William and Mary Quarterly* 65 (April 2008): 267–304; Lucy Eldersveld Murphy, *A Gathering of Rivers: Indians, Métis, and the Mining in the Western Great Lakes, 1737–1832* (Lincoln: University of Nebraska Press, 2000); Sylvia Van Kirk, *Many Tender Ties: Women in Fur-Trade Society, 1670–1870* (Winnipeg: Watson and Dwyer, 1999).

125. See Susan Sleeper-Smith, *Indian Women and French Men: Rethinking Cultural Encounter in the Western Great Lakes* (Amherst: University of Massachusetts Press, 2001), for a detailed discussion of the way in which Indigenous women appropriated and resisted the encounter with the French and the meanings they gave to them.

126. Aubert, "The Blood of France."

127. Father Julien Binneteau (1653–1699), Father Gabriel Marest (1662–1714), Father Jean Mermet, Father Jean Baptiste Le Boullenger, Father Sebastien Rasles, Father Jacque Largillier, and Father Pierre-Francois Pinert. Father Binneteau arrived as a missionary from France in 1691 and served in Michilimackinac, after which he went to Kaskaskia in 1696. Father Marest arrived in Canada in 1694, and in 1698 was appointed to Kaskaskia, where in addition to teaching catechism, he taught various trades and crafts.

128. Gravier's dictionary was not edited and published until 2002, but the work has contributed to the Miami Tribe of Oklahoma's language revitalization project with Miami University in Oxford, Ohio.

129. See Leavelle, *The Catholic Calumet,* for a detailed description of the struggles of the Jesuits to maintain the purity of Christian concepts in translation and the ways they adapted translations to incorprate Illini concepts. This was especially difficult with concepts like the incarnation, the Holy Trinity,

130. Richard White, *The Middle Ground: Indians, Empires, and Republics in the Great Lakes Regions, 1650–1815* (Cambridge: Cambridge University Press, 2011), 67.

131. Leavelle, *Catholic Calumet*, 123.

132. Hogan, *History of the Jesuits*, 63.

133. Caryne A. Eskridge, "Illinois Culture, Christianity and Intermarriage: Gender in Illinois Country, 1650–1763" (undergraduate honors thesis, College of William and Mary, 2010), Paper 674.

134. *Jesuit Relations*, 65:66, as cited in Morrissey, *Empire by Collaboration*, 74.

135. See White, *Wild Frenchmen and Frenchified Indians*, 89–94 ,for a detailed discussion of the gender dynamics among the Illini in the later seventeenth century.

136. For a more detailed discussion of why Indigenous women took up Catholicism, see Sleeper-Smith, *Indian Women and French Men*; Greer, *Mohawk Saint*; Leavelle, *The Catholic Calumet*.

137. For a full account of the life of Marie Rouensa regarding Catholic conversion, intermarriage, and the process of Frenchification, see White, *Wild Frenchmen and Frenchified Indians*, chap. 2.

138. *Jesuit Relations*, Gravier to "My Reverend Father," February 15, 1694, 64: 181–223.

139. The use of social network analysis by Robert Morrissey has been critical to illuminating the rich network of relationships created through godparenting. He examined baptismal records from 1694 to 1718 that show that twenty-five interracial families of Kaskaskia gave birth to at least thirty-six children. By using arrows to indicate the action of godparenting to the mother or the father of the baptized child, he linked eighty-five men and women together in a large, dense, and continuous network, rather than several small networks. In other words, godparenting resulted in connecting people together in a shared Catholic community through the diffusion of educational responsibilities, making them community-based.

140. See Anne F. Hyde, *Empires, Nations, and Families: A New History of the North American West 1800–1860* (Lincoln: University of Nebraska Press, 2011).

141. Ste. Geneviève was not founded until the early 1750s and St. Louis not until 1764.

142. Lee, *Masters of the Middle Waters*, 81.

143. Admitted to the Society of Jesus on October 29, 1706, Nicolas-Ignace de Beaubois made his novitiate in Paris. After two years, he remained in Paris to add to the philosophical studies he had begun before entering the order. He then went to Rennes to teach in the fall school term of 1710; for three years, he moved up a grade with the same group of boys, as was the custom. After another year of teaching, this time in Alençon, he began his preordination theological studies at La Flèche. Ordained in 1717, he remained at La Flèche for the usual fourth year of theology.

144. For a full description of the visit see Richard N. Ellis & Charlie R. Steen, "An Indian Delegation to France, 1725." *Journal of the Illinois State Historical Society*, 67, no. 1 (1974): 385–405.

145. The opera was last recorded in 2019. The fourth entrée, The Savages, was the last of four love stories in exotic locales that made up the opera. In it, Adario, a Native American, is in love with Zima, daughter of a Native chief, but he fears the rivalry of the Spaniard Don Alvar and the Frenchman Damon (Air: *Rivaux des mes exploits, rivaux des mes amours*). The Europeans plead with Zima for her love, but she says Damon is too fickle and Alvar is too jealous; she prefers the natural love shown by Adario (Air: *Sur nos bords l'amour vole*) and the couple vow to marry

(Duet: *Hymen, viens nous unir d'une chaîne éternelle*). The act ends with the Europeans joining the Natives in the ceremony of peace (Chorus: *Forêts paisibles*).

146. Enslaved Indigenous peoples were acquired through trade with, or as gifts from, Indigenous peoples.

147. Kelly L. Schmidt, Ayan Ali, and Jeff Harrison, "Jesuit Slaveholding in Colonial Era Kaskaskia" (Slavery, History, Memory, and Reconciliation Project, online, 2020). From 1720 to 1763, the Jesuits in Kaskaskia were the largest slaveholders in Illinois. According to White, *Wild Frenchman and Frenchified Indians*, by 1752, enslaved Africans made up 32.2 percent of the population in Illinois. In 1763, when the order was suppressed, the Jesuits claimed ownership over sixty-eight enslaved people.

148. Erin Greenwald, *Marc-Antoine Caillot and the Company of the Indies in Louisiana: Trade in the French Atlantic World* (Baton Rouge: Louisiana State University Press, 2016), reminds us that African labor in Louisiana was not limited to landbound slaves. Twenty-four percent of the company's slaves were classified as sailors. In fact, the frontier economy of Louisiana relied on these boaters to transport supplies. See also W. Jeffrey Bolster, *Black Jacks: African American Seaman in the Age of Sail* (Cambridge, MA: Harvard University Press, 1997).

149. Cécile Vidal, "Antoine Bienvenu, Illinois Planter and Mississippi Trader: The Structure of Exchange between Lower and Upper Louisiana." In *French Colonial Louisiana and the Atlantic World*, ed. Bradley Bond (Baton Rouge: Louisiana State University Press, 2005), 115.

150. Francois Philibert Watrin, S.J. "Banishment of the Jesuits from Louisiana," *The Jesuit Relations* and Allied Documents (Paris, Sept 3, 1764): LXX, 265.

151. Pierre Le Moyne, Sieur d'Iberville, *Iberville's Gulf Journals*, ed. Richebourg Gaillard Mc Williams (Tuscaloosa: University of Alabama Press, 1991 translation of 1700 journal), 60.

152. Richard Campanella, *Bienville's Dilemma: A Historical Geography of New Orleans* (Lafayette: Center for Louisiana Studies, University of Louisiana at Lafayette, 2008), 101.

153. M. Cavelier de la Salle, "Memoir of M. Cavelier de la Salle," in *On the Discovery of the Mississippi*, ed. Thomas Falconer (London, 1844 translation of the 1680s original): app. 3–4, 24–27.

154. See Marcel Giraud, *A History of French Louisiana*, vol. I (Baton Rouge: Louisiana State University Press, 1974), for a detailed discussion of the events leading up to the choice of the Jesuits for the mission field in Louisiana.

155. See Germain Joseph Bienvenu, "Another America, Another Literature: Narratives from Louisiana's Colonial Experience" (PhD diss., Louisiana State University, 1995), for a discussion of other Louisiana colonial writers whose works make up a rich literary culture that is often marginalized.

156. Paul Du Ru, *Journal of Paul Du Ru: Missionary Priest to Louisiana*, ed. Ruth Lapham Butler (Chicago: The Caxton Club, 1934), 8.

157. This is surmised by Ruth Lapham Butler, whose translation, introduction, and notes provide the first English translation of Du Ru's journal.

158. Although "schooling" was a recent invention in Europe, the term only being introduced in the seventeenth century, Father Du Ru was heir to a much longer liberal arts tradition of education begun by the Society of Jesus in 1540. For

a more detailed discussion of the history of "schooling," see Davis, *Inventions of Teaching*; Hendry, *Engendering Curriculum History*.

159. These interactions resulted not only in enhancing local relations, but they contributed to a network of communications and flow of information that radiated throughout the Mississippi Valley, which Daniel Usner, in *American Indians in Early New Orleans: From Calumet to Raquette* (Baton Rouge: Louisiana State University Press, 2018), has described as part of "frontier exchange economy."

160. Du Ru, *Journal of Paul Du Ru*, 12.

161. See the following for a detailed history of the Indigenous peoples in the southeast United States: Gregory A. Waselkov, Peter H. Wood, and Tom Hatley, *Powhatan's Mantle: Indians in the Colonial Southeast* (Lincoln: University of Nebraska Press, 2006); Fred B. Kniffen, Hiram F. Gregory, and George A. Stokes, *The Historic Indian Tribes of Louisiana* (Baton Rouge: Louisiana State University Press, 1987); Daniel H. Usner, *Indians, Settlers, & Slaves in a Frontier Exchange Economy: The Lower Mississippi Valley Before 1783* (Chapel Hill: University of North Carolina Press, 1992).

162. Several historians of early Catholicism now advocate a "global" approach to the history of early modern missions. See, for example, the work of Simon Ditchfield, most recently, "Catholic Reformation and Renewal," in *The Illustrated History of the Reformation*, ed. Peter Marshall (Oxford: Oxford University Press, 2015), 152–85. See also Ditchfield, "Carlo Borromeo in the Construction of Roman Catholicism as a World Religion," *Studia Borromaica* 25 (2011): 3–23; Clossey, *Salvation and Globalization in the Early Jesuit Missions*; Ditchfield, "Of Dancing Cardinals and Mestizo Madonnas: Reconfiguring the History of Roman Catholicism in the Early Modern Period," *Journal of Early Modern History* 8, no. 3–4 (2004): 386–408; R. Po-chia Hsia, *The World of Catholic Renewal, 1540–1770* (Cambridge: Cambridge University Press, 1998). For an illustration of the Society of Jesus's global reach, see the broad geographical range of essays in John O'Malley, S.J., Gauvin Alexander Bailey, Steven J. Harris, and T. Frank Kennedy, S.J, eds., *The Jesuits: Cultures, Sciences and the Arts, 1540–1773*, 2 vols. (Toronto: University of Toronto Press, 1999–2006).

163. Blackburn, *Harvest of Souls*; Cushner, *Why Have You Come Here?*

164. See, for example, Tzvetan Todorov, *The Conquest of America: The Question of the Other* (Norman: University of Oklahoma Press, 1984); White, *The Middle Ground*; Morrissey, *Empire by Collaboration*.

165. I borrow the use of this term from Michael Pasquier, *Fathers on the Frontier: French Missionaries and the Roman Catholic Priesthood in the United States 1789–1870* (Oxford: Oxford University Press, 2010).

166. See Antje Flüchter and Giula Nardini, "Threefold Translation of the Body of Christ: Concepts of the Eucharist and the Body Translated in the Early Modern Missionary Context," *Humanities and Social Sciences Communications* 7 (2020): 86. https://doi.org/10.1057/s41599-020-00566-z

167. Du Ru, *Journal of Paul Du Ru*, 19.

168. Du Ru, *Journal of Paul Du Ru*, 19–20.

169. See Brown, "The Calumet in the Southeast," 311–31, for a full discussion of the calumet ceremony.

170. See William Brown, "Mask of the Colonizer: French Men, Native Passions,

and the Culture of Diplomacy in New France," in *French Connections: Cultural Mobility in North America and the Atlantic World, 1600–1875*, ed. Robert Englebert and Andrew N. Wegmann (Baton Rouge: Louisiana State University Press, 2020), for a detailed discussion of the ways in which understandings of early modern performance and public life shaped French approaches to Indigenous peoples.

171. Du Ru, *Journal of Paul Du Ru*, 22.

172. See Jon L. Gibson, "Navels of the Earth: Sedentism in Early Mound-Building Cultures in the Lower Mississippi Valley," *World Archaeology* 39, no. 2 (2006): 311–29, for a detailed discussion of mound-building.

173. See George I. Quimby, "The Bayou Goula Site Iberville Parish Louisiana," *Fieldiana: Anthropology* 47, no. 2 (Chicago Natural History Museum, 1957), for a detailed discussion of what we know about the Bayagoula mounds based on archaeological evidence.

174. See Bronwen McShea, *Apostles of Empire: The Jesuits and New France* (Lincoln: University of Nebraska Press, 2019).

175. Du Ru, *Journal of Paul Du Ru*, 29.

176. This process of accommodation was central also to the early Christians, who incorporated European pagan rituals and beliefs to promote conversion.

177. Du Ru, *Journal of Paul Du Ru*, 23.

178. See, for example, Erik R. Seeman, *The Huron-Wendat Feast of the Dead: Indian-European Encounters in Early North America* (Baltimore: Johns Hopkins University Press, 2011); Greer, *Mohawk Saint*; Allan Greer and Jodi Bilinkoff, eds., *Colonial Saints: Discovering the Holy in the Americas, 1500–1800* (New York: Routledge, 2003); Allan Greer, "Conversion and Identity: Iroquois Christianity in Seventeenth-Century New France," in *Conversion: Old Worlds and New*, ed. Kenneth Mills and Anthony Grafton (New York: University of Rochester Press, 2003).

179. Du Ru, *Journal of Paul Du Ru*, 38.

180. Du Ru, *Journal of Paul Du Ru*, 38.

181. Du Ru, *Journal of Paul Du Ru*, 37.

182. Du Ru, *Journal of Paul Du Ru*, 27.

183. Du Ru also continued to be a student of Indigenous knowledges, particularly those associated with healing. He lauded the healing practices and medicinal knowledge of the Bayagoula. He observed Indigenous healing practices, recording in detail the plants, application processes, and results of the wounded and sick who were treated.

184. Du Ru, *Journal of Paul Du Ru*.

185. See Linda Carol Jones, *The Shattered Cross: French Catholic Missionaries on the Mississippi River, 1698–1725* (Baton Rouge: Louisiana State University Press, 2020), for a detailed description of these differences.

186. Iberville makes no mention of his sponsorship in his own journal. Pierre Le Moyne, Sieur d'Iberville, *Iberville's Gulf Journals*.

187. In addition to rituals as signifiers of bonds of relationships, the exchange of gifts (physical objects) also signified friendships. The ritual of the calumet, a greeting ceremony, included not only the smoking of the pipe, but also the exchange of gifts.

188. Du Ru, *Journal of Paul Du Ru*, 117–18. The reference to offering work suggests not only labor exchanges that extended through the whole Mississippi Valley,

but also suggests that paid labor, which took many forms, coexisted with the forced labor of enslavement of Native Americans.

189. See Mark L. Thompson, "Locating the Isle of Orleans: Atlantic and American Historiographical Perspectives," *Atlantic Studies* 5, no. 3 (2008): 305–33, for a further discussion of a "continental" approach. In addition, see Vidal, "Antoine Bienvenu; and Marcel Giraud, *Historie de la Louisiana Française*, 4 vols. (Paris: Presses Universitaires de France, 1953–1991).

190. Du Ru, *Journal of Paul Du Ru*, 48–49.

191. Unfortunately, within several years of Father Du Ru's visit, epidemics decimated the Bayagoula, and warfare between the Bayagoula and Mugulasha further dwindled the population. In 1706, tensions with the Taensa, who had moved in with the Bayagoula, resulted in a massacre that killed half of the Bayagoula; the church was destroyed in this raid. In 1715, the French counted 200 Bayagoula who then joined the Houma. A historical marker commemorates this site in the current city of Bayou Goula. It reads "Mugulasha Indian village captured by Bayagoulas. In 1699, Bienville here found Tonti's letter of 1686 to La Salle. Father Paul Du Ru built the first chapel in Louisiana near the village in 1700." The current town of Bayou Goula has 442 residents, with 91.9 percent being African American.

192. Du Ru, *Journal of Paul Du Ru*, 7.

193. Usner, *Indians, Settlers and Slaves in a Frontier Exchange Economy*, 278.

194. Du Ru, *Journal of Paul Du Ru*, 71.

195. See Timothy James Lockley, *Maroon Communities in South Carolina* (Columbia: University of South Carolina Press, 2009) for a detailed discussion of maroon communities.

196. This "old Mobile site," about twenty-five miles from current-day Mobile, was the original capital of French Louisiana from 1702 to 1711 and was governed by Iberville; upon his death, governorship was passed to his brother. In 1711, the capital and fort were moved to Mobile, where Fort Condé was built. A replica of this fort stands in downtown Mobile today.

197. Hogan, *History of the Jesuits in Colonial French Louisiana*.

198. In response, the company formulated a plan to divide the colony into three spiritual jurisdictions, each under the care of a religious order, which they would support with annual supplies. The Seminary Priests from Quebec would remain at Mobile. The Capuchins were selected to minister to the French colonists and Indigenous peoples in New Orleans and the surrounding area, including Les Allemands (the German Coast), La Balize, Point Coupee, Natchez, Mobile, and Apalacha Village. The Jesuits would establish missions in the Mississippi Valley.

199. See Archives des Colonies, Archives Nationales des France, Paris, C01/02 F5a/3 Canada et Louisiane: Eglise et Missionaires 1667–1782 for the correspondence between L'abbe Raguet, the ecclesiastical officer of the Company of the Indies, and Father Beaubois, which illuminates the ongoing tensions between the interests of the company and those of Beaubois.

200. Michael Pasquier, "Missionaries, Martyrdom, and Warfare in French Colonial Louisiana, 1699–1764," *Catholic Historical Review* 105, no. 2 (2019): 314. See also Jean Delanglez, *The French Jesuits in Lower Louisiana 1700–1763* (Washington, DC: Catholic University of America, 1935); and Charles Edward O'Neil, *Church and State in French Colonial Louisiana: Policy and Politics to 1732* (New Haven, CT: Yale University Press, 1966).

201. Father Baudoin, assigned initially to the Chickasaws and then for eighteen years to the Choctaw mission until becoming superior in 1749, died in New Orleans in 1768; Father de Guyenne, initially assigned to the Alibamons, in what is now central Alabama, went in 1743 to the Illinois mission until his death in 1762; Father du Poisson, assigned to the Quapaws nation in Arkansas, died during the Natchez Revolt in 1729; Father Souel, along with his enslaved African, was assigned to the Yazoo; both died in the Natchez Revolt in 1729; Father Dumas, assigned to the Illinois mission, returned to France in 1740; and Father Le Petit, the first Jesuit assigned to the Choctaw, would later become superior of the Louisiana Mission until his death in 1739. Two years after this initial group, two more Jesuits, Fathers Doutreleau and Tàrtarin, arrived with the twelve Ursuline sisters. Father Doutreleau was assigned to the Wabash mission in the Illinois country and stayed there until recalled to France in 1747. Father Tàrtarin was also assigned to the Illinois mission, where he died in 1741.

202. To reduce operational expenses during the Choctaw wars in the 1740s, Maurepas, the minister of the marine, closed all the Jesuit missions except in New Orleans, Illinois, and among the Choctaw. This began the eventual reduction of Jesuit Missions until 1763, when the Jesuits were expelled.

203. Ursuline Convent Archives, New Orleans (hereafter UCANO) at the Historic New Orleans Collection, Des Negres et Negresses qui sont venus au Convent sur notre habitation le 2 Octobre 1824 (People of Color at Ursuline convent 1752–1894), documents all births, deaths, baptisms, and marriages of the enslaved Africans. The 1731 census records 16 adult slaves and three children living on the Ursuline plantation, none at the New Orleans convent. By 1770, the census records 61 enslaved people living on the Ursuline plantation, putting them in the top 4 percent of plantations owning between 50 and 99 slaves. The Jesuit plantation numbered 130 enslaved Africans, putting them in the top 2 percent of plantations owning more than 100 slaves.

204. Samuel Wilson Jr., *The Capuchin School in New Orleans, 1725* (New Orleans: Archdiocesan School Board, 1961), 9–10.

205. See Roger Baudier, *The Catholic Church in Louisiana* (New Orleans: Hyatt, 1939): 108–9.

206. Hogan, *History of the Jesuits in Colonial French Louisiana*; Albert Hubert Biever, S.J., *The Jesuits in New Orleans and the Mississippi Valley* (New Orleans, 1924), 11.

207. See Jean Delanglez, *The French Jesuits in Lower Louisiana 1700–1763* (New York: AMS Press, 1935), for detailed descriptions of these scientists. Laval was said to have built an "observatory" with a mast on a little mound, a pulley, and ropes to raise or lower his eighteen-foot-long telescope, considered to be the first Jesuit astronomical observatory in the United States. Laval's book was dedicated to the members of the Royal Academy of Sciences and is composed of several scientific treatises. The part dealing directly with the voyage to Louisiana (304 pages with twenty-one maps and plans) forms half the book. Also see Baudier, *The Catholic Church in Louisiana*, 49–50.

208. Carl A. Brasseaux, "The Administration of Slave Regulations in French Louisiana, 1724–1766," *Louisiana History: The Journal of Louisiana History Association* 21, no. 2 (Spring 1980): 139–52.

209. At this time, the enslaved Africans from the Jesuit plantation were sold at a public auction. Following the Code Noir, all nuclear families were maintained.

210. Hogan, *History of the Jesuits in Colonial French Louisiana*, 62.

211. The first Jesuit college, the College of the Immaculate Conception, was opened in New Orleans in 1849. It would eventually become Loyola College in 1904 and Loyola University in 1912. See Bernard A. Cook, *Founded on Faith: A History of Loyola University New Orleans* (New Orleans: Loyola University Press, 2012), for a detailed discussion of the history of the university.

212. See Peter H. Wood, "The Changing Population of the Colonial South: An Overview by Race and Region 1685–1790," in *Powhatan's Mantle: Indians in the Colonial Southwest*, ed. Gregory A. Waselkov, Peter H. Wood, and Tom Hatley (Lincoln: University of Nebraska Press, 1989), for specific details as to the decline in population. Also, Usner, *Indians, Settlers & Slaves in a Frontier Economy*, has a detailed discussion of the urban trade and ongoing diplomatic relations in New Orleans.

213. Father Raphael to Abbé Raguet, May 15, 1725, Mississippi Provincial Archives: French Dominion, volume 2: 486.

214 . James Taylor Carson, "Sacred Circles and Dangerous People: Native American Cosmology and the French Settlement of Louisiana," in *French Colonial Louisiana and the Atlantic World*, ed. Bradley Bond (Baton Rouge: Louisiana State University Press, 2005), 65–82, 78.

215. Joan-Pau Rubiés, "Ethnography and Cultural Translation in the Early Modern Missions," *Studies in Church History* 53 (June 2017), 272–310.

216. Monique Verdin, *Return to Yaknichitto: Houma Migrations* (New Orleans: University of New Orleans Press: The Neighborhood Story Project, 2019), 3.

217. Verdin, *Return to Yaknichitto*, 6.

218. According to Heather Stone (private correspondence), who is completing an oral history of the Point-au-Chien Tribe, the Baptist mission built a school on the Island in the 1940s. The teacher, Jeanette LeBoef, was transported from the mainland every morning and afternoon in Chief Antoine's pirogue.

219. See Nicholas Ng-A-Fook, *An Indigenous Curriculum of Place: The United Houma Nation's Contentious Relationship with Louisiana's Educational Institutions* (New York: Peter Lang, 2008), for a detailed narrative of the history of Houma education.

220. Ng-A-Fook, Philips, Currie, and Pind, *Purposes of Education*.

Chapter 2

1. Emily Clark, ed., *Voices from an Early American Convent* (Baton Rouge: Louisiana State University, 2007), 38.

2. Shannon Dawdy, *Building the Devil's Empire: French Colonial New Orleans* (Chicago: University of Chicago Press, 2008).

3. Desiderius Erasmus, *In Praise of Folly* (New York: Hendricks, 1959).

4. Emily Clark, *Masterless Mistresses: The New Orleans Ursulines and the Development of a New World Society, 1727–1834* (Chapel Hill: University of North Carolina Press, 2007), 33.

5. Michel de Certeau, *The Possession at Loudun*, trans. Michael B. Smith (Chicago: University of Chicago Press, 1996), 6.

6. According to Jane Heaney, *A Century of Pioneering: A History of the Ursuline*

Nuns in New Orleans, 1727–1827 (New Orleans: Ursuline Sisters of New Orleans, 1993), three of her relatives were Capuchin priests and a cousin was mother vicar of the Religious of St. Francis. One brother was a religious and another was preparing for the priesthood. Of her four sisters, the eldest was a Franciscan, her sister Elizabeth would also enter the same order, and her sister Louise had been admitted to the Val-de-Grace.

7. "Letters circulaires," Archives of the Ursuline Nuns of the Parish of New Orleans, 99–1-L (hereafter AUNPO), Historic New Orleans Collection (hereafter HNOC). Sister Marie of St. Therese of Jesus, the mother superior of the Ursuline convent in New Orleans where Marie died in 1760, surmised in Marie's obituary that "God, who had taken possession of her heart wanted her in holy orders."

8. During the last half of the seventeenth century, a cadre of Jesuit and Ursuline archivists constructed and circulated Ursuline histories that linked L'Incarnation to a lineage of Catholic reformers and martyrs. Some closely connected the Ursulines to the tradition of classical Greek Amazon warriors and biblical heroines, and others associated the founding of the Jesuits to the founding of the Ursulines in 1534. In 1656, for example, a compilation of such texts titled *The Glory of St. Ursula* was published and disseminated to solidify the place of the Ursulines in Catholic missionary history. Its contents included Paul de Barry (Jesuit), *Devotion to the Glorious St. Ursula, the Most loved Mother of the Ursulines* (1645); Herman Crombach, (Jesuit), *The Life and Martyrdom of St. Ursula and the Society of Eleven Thousand Virgins* (1647); Jean Hugue-Quarr' (Oratorian), *The Life of Blessed Angela Merici* (1648); and *Book Three of the Religious Ursulines of Canada or New France* (1656) by an unknown author. This latter text, for instance, praised one of the Ursulines of Quebec, "a Canadian Amazon," who became like a warrior, raising her "daughters" in the ways of fighting in the "militia of Jesus Christ."

9. Jean Hugue-Quarr' (Oratorian), *La Vie de la B. Mère Angèle de Bresse*, 1648 in *La Gloire de S. Ursule* (Valen[c]iennes: L'Impr. De L. Boucher, 1656), 99.

10. Marie-Augustine de Pommereu, *Les Chroniques de L'Ordre des Ursulines recuielles pour l'usage des religieuses du mÂme ordre.* 1 ère et 2nde parties. (Paris: J. Henault, 1673), preface, 379, 493.

11. See Gayle K. Brunelle, *The New World Merchants of Rouen 1559–1630* (Kirksville, MO: Sixteenth Century Journal Publishers, 1991).

12. See Ibrahima Seck, "The Relationships between St. Louis of Senegal, Its Hinterlands, and Colonial Louisiana," trans. Joanne E. Burnett, in *French Colonial Louisiana and the Atlantic World*, ed. Bradley G. Bond (Baton Rouge: Louisiana State University Press, 2005), 270. Also see Gwedolyn Mildo Hall, *Africans in Colonial Louisiana: The Develoopment of Afro-Creole Culture in the Eighteenth Century* (Baton Rouge: Louisiana State University Press, 1992).

13. Ibrahima Seck, "The Relationships between St. Louis of Senegal."

14. See Robert A. Houston, *Literacy in Early Modern Europe: Culture and Education 1500–1800* (New York: Routledge, 2002), for a detailed discussion of these shifts.

15. The Jesuit presence unmistakeably shaped the ideas and interests of future generations of Rouennais including not only Cavalier de La Salle, but the Jesuit missionaries and martyrs Jean de Brébeuf (1593–1649) and Antoine Daniel (1601–1648), who went to New France.

16. Jean de Brébeuf, born in Caen in Normandy and a student at the Jesuit

College in Rouen, was among the first Jesuits to land in Quebec in 1625. He lived among the Wendat near Lake Huron, learning their customs and language. He wrote a dictionary of the Wendat language and is known as Canada's first real ethnographer. De Brébeuf returned briefly to France before returning to Canada in 1632, where he returned to the mission of St. Mary among the Wendat in 1644. Soon, however, the Haudenosaunee began to win their war against the Wendat. They seized Brébeuf and his fellow Jesuit Gabriel Lallemont and tortured them—by scalping, mock baptism with boiling water—until they died.

17. See Houston, *Literacy in Early Modern Europe*, for a further discussion.

18. Houston, *Literacy in Early Modern Europe*, 6.

19. See H. C. Bernard, *Girls at School Under the Ancien Regime* (London: Burnes and Oates, 1954); and Gwynne Lewis, *France 1715–1804: Power and the People* (London: Longman, 2004).

20. François Furet and Jacques Ozouf, *Reading and Writing: Literacy from Calvin to Jules Ferry* (Cambridge: Cambridge University Press, 1977).

21. See Carolyn C. Lougee, "Noblesse, Domesticity, and Social Reform: The Education of Girls by Fénelon and Saint-Cyr*," *History of Education Quarterly* 14, no. 1 (1974): 87–113.

22. Merry E. Weiner, Women and Gender in Early Modern Europe (Cambridge: U.K., 1993), R. Po-Chia Hsia, *The World of Catholic Renewal, 1540–1770* (Cambridge, U.K., 1998), Barbara B. Diefendorf, "Contradiction of the Century of Saints: Aristocratic Patronage and the Convents of Counter-Reformation Paris," *French Historical Studies* 24, no. 3 (Summer 2001): 469–99.

23. See Dena Goodman, *The Republic of Letters: A Cultural History of the French Enlightenment* (Ithaca, NY: Cornell University Press, 1994), for a discussion of the gendered construction of public and private in eighteenth century France.

24. See M. Choudhury, "Despotic Habits: The Critique of Power and Its Abuses in an Eighteenth-Century Convent," *French Historical Studies* 23, no. 1 (2000): 33–65; de Certeau, *The Possession at Loudin*, for a further discussion of the increasing suspicions and critiques of female monastics as a mechanism for curbing female power.

25. Choudhury, "Despotic Habits," 47.

26. See Joan B. Landes, *Women and the Public Sphere in the Age of the French Revolution* (Ithaca, NY: Cornell University Press, 1988), for a detailed discussion of these revolutionary shifts.

27. Natalie Zemon Davis, *Society and Culture in Early Modern France: Eight Essays* (Stanford, CA: Stanford University Press, 1975).

28. Heidi Keller-Lapp "Floating Cloisters and Heroic Women: French Ursuline Missionaries, 1639–1744," *World History Connected* 4, no. 3 (2013).

29. Natasha Gill, *Educational Philosophy in the French Enlightenment: From Nature to Second Nature* (New York: Routledge, 2010).

30. Elizabeth Rapley, *The Dévotées: Women and Church in Seventeenth-Century France* (Montreal: McGill-Queen's University Press, 1990), 199.

31. See Clark, *Masterless Mistresses*, 41–49, for a detailed discussion of the company's initial plan for the role of women religious in New Orleans.

32. See Roger Baudier, *The Catholic Church in Louisiana* (New Orleans: Hyatt, 1939), for a detailed account of the Ursuline arrival in New Orleans.

33. Clark, *Voices from an Early American Convent*, 21.

34. While there is no evidence at this time of their direct knowledge of one another, it can be speculated that Father de Beaubois and Father Boulanger were in Illinois simultaneously.

35. See Heloise Crozat, "The Ursulines of Louisiana," *Louisiana Historical Quarterly* 2, no. 1 (1919): 5–7, for a fully translated copy of the treaty.

36. Clark, *Voices From an Early American Convent*, 117. The obituary written for Marie Madeleine Hachard by the reverend mother, Sister Marie of St. Therese of Jesus, on August 9, 1760, recounted that the Ursuline sisters in Rouen did not take lightly the decision to admit her given the immense undertaking of mission work in New France. After three months, however, she was received with inexpressible joy.

37. Clark, *Voices from an Early American Convent*, 22.

38. Clark, *Voices from an Early American Convent*, 25.

39. The books brought from France to New Orleans by the Ursulines, including numerous volumes of religious and philosophical texts, made up one of the first private libraries in New Orleans. The original books are part of the collection of the Historic New Orleans Collection (HNOC).

40. Father Doutreleau (1693–?) served among the Illini on the Wabash as a teacher for twenty years before returning to France in 1747. He served briefly as the chaplain at the hospital in New Orleans, but requested to be returned to work with the Illini.

41. Father René Tartarin was born in France on January 22, 1695; he entered the Jesuit Order on August 20, 1712. He came to Louisiana in 1727, one of the seven missionaries brought back from France by Father Beaubois. Father Tartarin was active at Kaskaskia from 1727 to 1730, and again in 1741. He died in the Louisiana missions on September 24, 1745.

42. These sisters had also been thwarted in their attempts to engage in missionary activity, with some of the bishops declining to grant the necessary permits to leave the dioceses, which required that Cardinal Fleury intervene. See Heaney, *A Century of Pioneering*, for further accounts.

43. It was named L'Orient because the Company of the Indies primary trade was with countries in the "orient."

44. See Marie Tranchepain de St. Augustin, *Relation du Voyage Des premières Ursulines à la Nouvelle Orleáns et de leur éstalissment en cette ville* (New York, 1859); and Marion Ware, "An Adventurous Voyage to French Colonial Louisiana: The Narrative of Mother Tranchepain, 1727," *Louisiana History: The Journal of the Louisiana Historical Association* 1 no. 3 (1960): 212–29.

45. Clark, *Voices from an Early American Convent*, 57.

46. While no complete English translation of Mother Tranchepain's account has been found, an unpublished English translation by Olivia Blanchard was made in 1940 under the Work Projects Administration. This translation is reproduced in Ware, "An Adventurous Voyage to French Colonial Louisiana, .227.

47. Clark, *Voices from an Early American Convent*, 77. For a further firsthand description of the city of New Orleans and its architecture, see Erin M. Greenwald, *A Company Man, The Remarkable French-Atlantic Voyage of a Clerk for the Company of the Indies* (New Orleans: The Historic New Orleans Collection, 2013), 79–81.

48. See Dawdy, *Building the Devil's Empire*, specifically chapter 2, for a full description of the relationship between urban planning, imperialism, and the Enlightenment in colonial New Orleans.

49. See Heloise Crozat, "The Ursulines of Louisiana," *Louisiana Historical Quarterly* 2, no. 1 (1919), for a fully translated copy of the treaty, 9.

50. Crozat, "The Ursulines of Louisiana," 71.

51. See Greenwald, *A Company Man*, 79–80.

52. Given that her brother lived on a plantation downriver, we might speculate that she at least initially went to live with him.

53. Greenwald, *A Company Man*, 124.

54. Clark, *Masterless Mistresses*, 75.

55. See Greenwald, *A Company Man*, 80.

56. Hall, *Africans in Colonial Louisiana*, 9.

57. Clark, *Voices from an Early American Convent*, 82.

58. Their educational tradition had flourished in France, producing some of the most educated women in Europe. The Ursulines, especially the convent school in Paris at the monastery Rue St. Jacques, were well-known for excellent education. Madame de Maintenon, who opened the Maison Royale de St Cyr in 1686, was educated at the Ursuline St. Jacques school. While she credited the nuns for her education, she and Louis XIV were fearful of too much responsibility for the education of girls being given to religious orders. Their concern was that young girls would not receive enough practical formation for motherhood and their domestic duties. The influence of the Ursulines was not only throughout France but included young girls from Ireland, who were placed in the *pensionnat* at Rue St. Jacques in the seventeenth century. For a more detailed description of Ursuline educational philosophy, see Peter M. Waters, *The Ursuline Achievement: A Philosophy of Education for Women* (North Carlton, VIC: Colonna Publishers, 1994); M. Marie De Saint-Jean Martin, *L'Éducation des Ursulines*. (Rome: Maison Généralice De L'Union Des Ursulines, 1944); Sister M. Monica, *Angela Merici and her Teaching Idea (1474–1540)* (New York: Longmans, Green and Co., 1927).

59. See Roger Magnuson, *Education in New France* (Montreal: McGill-Queen's University Press, 1992), for a further discussion of educational history in France.

60. Current educational discourses construct "multicultural" education as a problem to be solved through a variety of interventions in which multiple cultures will become fluent or appreciative of diverse cultures. Culturally relevant pedagogy is designed to address "difference." Cultures not part of the dominant culture are seen as "deficient." Ironically, these discourses function to reify a hierarchy of cultures.

61. Saint Angela, *Eighth Souvenir*, in Marie de Saint Jean Marti, *Ursuline Method of Education* (Rathway: Quinn & Boden Company, 1946), 18.

62. See M. Marie De Saint-Jean Martin, *L'Éducation des Ursulines* (Rome: Maison Généralice De L'Union Des Ursulines, 1944); M. Monica, *Angela Merici and Her Teaching Idea*; and Waters, *The Ursuline Achievement*.

63. Among the Creole or second generation of Louisiana's Catholics, adult baptism decreased, and first communion would become an important step in the life of children. Baptism occurred shortly after birth and godparents were chosen to accept the responsibility of the child's education, which included making sure they attended catechism classes as a young adult with the goal of first communion.

64. See Hall, *Africans in Colonial Louisiana*, 155; Guillaume Aubert, "'The Blood of France': Race and Purity of Blood in the French Atlantic World," *William and Mary Quarterly* 61, no. 3 (July 2004), 439–78.

65. I would also suggest the Ursuline pedagogy of love can be traced to contemporary educational philosophers like Nel Noddings, Sara Ruddick, and Carol Gilligan, who theorize "caring" and "maternal thinking" as central to pedagogies that critique overly technocratic, utilitarian views of curriculum.

66. See Hall, *Africans in Colonial Louisiana*.

67. For a more detailed discussion of the syncretism between Senegambian and Catholic religious rituals, beliefs, and customs see Claude F. Jacobs and Andrew J. Kaslow, *The Spiritual Churches of New Orleans: Origins, Beliefs, and Rituals of an African-American Religion* (Knoxville: University of Tennessee Press, 1991); Margaret Cormack, *Saints and Their Cults in the Atlantic World* (Columbia: University of South Carolina Press, 2007).

68. This was in distinct contrast to Puritan America, where such objects were held as idolatrous. As Albert J. Raboteau, *Slave Religion* (Oxford: Oxford University Press, 2004), has maintained, "Protestantism, with its emphasis on biblical preaching, inward conversion, and credible accounts of the signs of grace, was not as conducive to syncretism with African theology and ritual" (88).

69. Emily Clark and Virginia Meacham Gould, "The Feminine Face of Afro-Catholicism in New Orleans, 1727–1852," *William and Mary Quarterly* 59 (April 2002), 409–48.

70. Clark and Gould, "The Feminine Face of Afro-Catholicism in New Orleans."

71. See Clark and Gould, "The Feminine Face of Afro-Catholicism in New Orleans."

72. See Joseph Bergin, *Church, Society and Religious Change in France 1580–1730* (New Haven, CT: Yale University Press, 2009); and Emily Clark, "'By All the Conduct of Their Lives': A Laywomen's Confraternity in New Orleans, 1730–1744," *William and Mary Quarterly*, 3d Series, LIV, no. 4 (October 1997), 769–94.

73. Clark, *Masterless Mistresses*, 185.

74. Clark, *Masterless Mistresses*, 187.

75. The distinction between the boarding and day students was primarily economic. In keeping with the "open access" policy of the Ursulines, schooling was in theory free for all pupils. Boarders, however, were charged for room and board, as well as for extra classes or supplies. Few parents in this period could afford full educational fees. According to Roger Magnuson, in order to keep the boarding school open to young girls from all social classes, the Ursulines had a sliding scale and also provided scholarships (Magnuson, *Education in New France*, 15).

76. As was the custom of the Ursulines, they took in boarding students whose room and board, as well as tuition, was an important source of income that not only helped to support them, but which allowed them to take in day students (or extern students) and to provide catechism instruction for Indigenous and enslaved African girls.

77. Clark, *Voices from an Early American Convent*.

78. Mary Austin Cauvin, "The French Ursulines in Colonial Louisiana 1727–1824" (MA thesis, Louisiana State University, 1939).

79. M. Monica, *Angela Merici and Her Teaching Idea*, 371.

80. The boarding students were also allowed to play in the garden and to play games such as battledore, shuttlecock, bowls, or chess. Pupils were free to visit their

parents and friends in the salon and could go home occasionally for a wedding or christening or some other family event, though rarely overnight.

81. *Reglements des religieuses de la congregation de Paris, divises en trios livres* (Paris, 1751), part 2, 158.

82. See Laurence Lux-Sterritt, *Redefining Female Religious Life: French Ursulines and English Ladies in Seventeenth-Century Catholicism* (Hants, UK: Ashgate, 2005), 143, for a further discussion of day students.

83. Clark, *Masterless Mistresses*, 74.

84. Clark, *Masterless Mistresses*, 78.

85. HNOC, Ursuline book collection.

86. As suggested by Karen Carter, *Creating Catholics: Catechism and Primary Education in Early Modern France*, (Notre Dame, IN: University of Notre Dame Press, 2011), catechism as an important form of education in the seventeenth and eighteenth centuries has been neglected because it is thought to be an ineffective method of instruction focused merely on memorization and repeated recitation.

87. See Carter, *Creating Catholics*, for a further discussion.

88. Bernadette Baker, *In Perpetual Motion: Theories of Power, History and the Child* (New York: Peter Lang, 2001).

89. Carter, *Creating Catholics*, 5.

90. *Petite écoles* were primary schools that emerged in France during the Counter Reformation era in which religious instruction and schooling were to be merged as a means to educate the lower social classes and those in rural areas. See Bergin, *Church, Society and Religious Change in France*.

91. Karen E. Carter, *Creating Catholics*, 14.

92. Folk Catholicism is the syncretism between Catholic and non-Catholic or non-Christian beliefs such as Haitian Vodou and Cuban Santeria.

93. See Jacobs and Kaslow, *The Spiritual Churches of New Orleans*, for a further discussion of folk Catholicism.

94. Susan Vandiver Nicassio, "Opera and New Orleans: Spectacle, Race and Religion," unpublished manuscript.

95. Ned Sublette, *The World that Made New Orleans: From Spanish Silver to Congo Square* (Chicago: Lawrence Hill Books, 2009), 69.

96. Clark, *Voices from an Early American Convent*, 81–82.

97. See Raboteau, *Slave Religion*, for a further discussion of these synchronicities.

98. Sublette, *The World that Made New Orleans*, 72.

99. Sublette, *The World that Made New Orleans*, 72.

100. For further insights into the creolization of culture, especially music in Louisiana, see Nicholas Spitzer, "Monde Créole: The Cultural World of French Louisiana Creoles and the Creolization of World Cultures," *Journal of American Folklore* vol 116, no. 459 (2003): 57–72; Jason Berry, "African Cultural Memory in New Orleans Music," *Black Music Research Journal* vol 8, no. 1 (1988), 3–12.

101. Alfred E. Lemmon, *French Baroque Music of New Orleans: Spiritual Songs from the Ursuline Convent (1736)* (New Orleans: Historic New Orleans Collection, 2014), viii. Although the details of how exactly they acquired the manuscript are murky, it is believed that it was sent to the Ursulines by a "Mr Nicollet," possibly Gabriel-François Nicollet, "a poet and lyricist of several spiritual parodies who strongly encouraged nuns and missionaries to embrace devotion to the Scared Heart of Jesus."

102. The success of these songs is clearly attested to by the fact that the printers completed several volumes of songs that soon were out of print. In 1736 a young woman, known only as "C.D.," copied the first four volumes of the collection, after which it came into the hands of Mr. Nicollet and eventually made its way to New Orleans.

103. Lawrence Powell, *The Accidental City* (Cambridge, MA: Harvard University Press, 2012), 125.

104. Clark, *Voices from an Early American Convent*, 74.

105. See Dawdy, *Building the Devil's Empire*, for a detailed discussion of the French colonial policy of creating Enlightenment order.

106. Emily Clark, *Voices from an Early American Convent*, 71.

107. For more about the entrepreneurship of the Ursulines, see Lawrence Powell, *The Accidental City* (Cambridge, MA: Harvard University Press, 2012), 126. Also see Clark, *Masterless Mistresses*.

108. Ministry of the Colonies, Series C 13, General Correspondence of Louisiana, Vol X, pages 184–200. English translation by Rowland and Sanders, *Mississippi Provincial Archives*, 1701–1729, II, 546–60.

109. See Dawdy, *Building the Devil's Empire*, for a more complete discussion of the relationship between urban planning, imperialism, and New Orleans.

110. Ministry of the Colonies, Series C 13, General Correspondence of Louisiana, Vol X, pages 184–200. English translation by Rowland and Sanders, *Mississippi Provincial Archives*, 1701–1729, II, 559.

111. Ministry of the Colonies, Series C 13, General Correspondence of Louisiana, Vol X, pages 184–200. English translation by Rowland and Sanders, *Mississippi Provincial Archives*, 1701–1729, II, 601–2.

112. Clark, *Voices of an Early American Convent*, p. 75

113. See Heaney, *Century of Pioneering*, 72–91, and Clark, *Masterless Mistresses*, for detailed accounts of the conflicts.

114. Convent Obituaries, Ursuline Convent Archives, Caen, France (hereafter UCAC).

115. Letter from Mother Sister St. Pierre to the reverent mother superior of the Reverent Ursulines of Caen, May 9, 1747, UCAC.

116. Clark, *Masterless Mistresses*, 119.

117. "Book of Deliberations of the Council," UCANO, 252–55. Samuel Wilson, "An Architectural History of the Royal Hospital and the Ursuline Convent of New Orleans," *Louisiana Historical Quarterly*, 29 no. 3 (1946): 591.

118. Clark, *Voices of an Early American Convent*, 123.

119. Keith P. Luira, "Rituals of Conversion," in *Culture and Identity in Early Modern Europe (1500–1800)*, ed. B. B. Diefendorf and C. Hesse (Ann Arbor: University of Michigan Press, 1993), 71.

120. A hymn written by St. Thomas Aquinas (1225–1274) for the Feast of Corpus Christi. It is also sung on Maundy Thursday, during the procession from the church to the place where the Blessed Sacrament is kept until Good Friday. The last two stanzas, called separately Tantum Ergo, are sung at Benediction of the Blessed Sacrament. The hymn expresses the doctrine that the bread and wine are changed into the body and blood of Christ during the celebration of the Eucharist.

121. Wilson, "An Architectural History of the Royal Hospital," 591–92.

122. Clark, *Masterless Mistresses*, 62.

123. Wilson, "An Architectural History of the Royal Hospital," 592. The exact number of boarders in 1734 is difficult to ascertain given that no account records exist from this time. Martin L. Riley, "The Development of Education in Louisiana Prior to Statehood," *Louisiana Historical Quarterly* XIX, no. 3 (1936): 606, maintains that on the day the nuns moved into the new convent in 1734 they had twenty boarders, three parlor boarders, three orphans, and seven slave boarders. While the number of slave boarders is consistent with other accounts, the number of French boarders differs from the accounts given in Father Le Petit's sermon. Regardless of the numbers, the admonishment given to the public in Le Petit's sermon is suggestive that the colonists were neglecting their duties to educate their daughters.

124. The accounting for seven slave boarders comes from Alcée Fortier, *Louisiana Studies: Literature, Customs and Dialects, History and Education, Vol. 1* (New Orleans, 1894), 245–46.

125. While Emily Clark argues that the Ursulines never contested slavery, she argues that the Ursulines were the central figures in bringing enslaved persons into the fold of the Catholic Church, thus providing spaces in which enslaved persons could establish a degree of agency. It can also be argued, however, that the Ursulines contributed to the establishment of a slave culture through complicity in the institution.

126. Dawdy, *Building the Devil's Empire*, 143.

127. Robert Englebert and Andrew N. Wegmann, eds., *French Connections: Cultural Mobility in North America and the Atlantic World, 1600–1875* (Baton Rouge: Louisiana State University Press, 2020), 1. The far-reaching vision of the French imperial state was begun under Jean-Baptiste Colbert. The vision of the colonies' functioning within the strictures of a closed mercantilist policy turned out to be mere fantasy.

128. Dawdy, *Building the Devil's Empire*, 143. Dawdy also suggests that "if we add the dimensions of gender and age for women and minors, then we can count at least twenty-one different types of legal person populating French colonial New Orleans, with frequent visitors and visiting Native Americans expanding the possibilities further" (144).

129. Sophie White, *Voices of the Enslaved: Love, Labor, and Longing in French Louisiana* (Chapel Hill: University of North Carolina Press, 2019), examines French judicial slave testimony as a means to illuminate the historical voices and life stories of the enslaved in Louisiana.

130. See Hall, *Africans in Colonial Louisiana*; Clark, *Masterless Mistresses*; Dawdy, *Building the Devil's Empire*; Daniel Usner, *Indians, Slaves and Colonists in a Frontier Exchange Economy: The Lower Mississippi Valley Before 1783* (Chapel Hill: University of North Carolina Press, 1992); Jennifer Spear, *Race, Sex and Social Order in Early New Orleans* (Baltimore: John Hopkins University Press, 2009), as examples of those historians who characterize race as fluid during the French colonial period. In contrast, there are those historians who argue that in a slave society race determines all social relations: Thomas N. Ingersoll, *Mammon and Manon in Early New Orleans: The First Slave Society in the Deep South, 1718–1819* (Knoxville: University of Tennessee Press, 1999).

131. Spears, *Race, Sex and Social Order in Early New Orleans*; Englebert and Wegmann, *French Connections*.

132. Glenn R. Conrad, *The First Families of Louisiana, Volume II* (Baton Rouge, LA: Claitor's Publishing Division, 1970), 68.

133. Clark, *Masterless Mistresses*, 169. This number puts the Ursulines in the top 30 percent of slaveowners in the Lower Mississippi Valley. By 1770, there were sixty-eight enslaved people, which put them in the top 6 percent of slaveholders.

134. Cécile Vidal, *Caribbean New Orleans: Empire, Race and the Making of Slave Society* (Chapel Hill: University of North Carolina Press, 2019), 215.

135. Conrad, *The First Families of Louisiana*, 68.

136. Ursuline Collection, Folder 1, Archives du Calvados (ADC), details the formation of the Ursuline convent in Bayeaux, Normandy, in 1604; this was a large and prestigious convent that flourished at the time Charlotte Hebert entered in the early 1700s. Born in 1698, Charlotte was well read, and it has been speculated that her father was a doctor from whom she learned some of her medical knowledge.

137. Heaney, *A Century of Pioneering*, 120.

138. There is evidence to suggest that Jean-Baptiste might have been a free person of color at one time. According to the "Records of the Superior Council of Louisiana," Jean-Baptiste was charged with stealing expensive wearing apparel from his employers. He was "reduced to slavery for the benefit of the Hospital of the City." Cruzat, trans., "Records of the Superior Council of Louisiana," *Louisiana Historical Quarterly* IX (October 1928), 649–51. See Donald E. Everett, "Free Persons of Color in Colonial Louisiana," *Louisiana History: The Journal of the Louisiana Historical Association* 7, no.1 (Winter 1966), 21–50, for more examples of free people of color being re-enslaved.

139. There is evidence of other African physicians. Daniel Usner, in "From African Captivity to American Slavery: The Introduction of Black Laborers to Colonial Louisiana," *Louisiana History* 20, no.1 (Winter 1979) 25–48, reports that "Antoine Le Page, manager of the Company of the Indies plantation, wrote that he was taught by an African physician his secret cures for yaws and scurvy. For yaws he prescribed an ointment consisting of powdered iron rust and citron juice and warned against the mercurial medicine used by surgeons, which proved fatal to their patients. He applied an ointment made from scurvy grass, ground ivy, and water-cresses to the infected gums of scurvied patients. Le Page wrote, 'The negro who taught me these remedies, observing the great care I took of both the negro men and women, taught me likewise that cure of all the distempers to which the women are subject; for the negro women are as liable to diseases as the white women'" (33).

140. Financial problems plagued the Ursulines at the new convent. The Crown had allocated five thousand livres for the yearly maintenance of the hospital in addition, they provided pensions for the orphans, and the Ursulines collected tuition from the boarding students. The Crown believed that this was more than sufficient to cover their expenses at the hospital, which included medicines, food, beds, linens, and other equipment for the hospital. In 1744, M. Le Normant, newly appointed general commissioner of the marine and financial director of the colony organized a *marché*, or contract, which delineated the specific financial responsibilities of the nuns at the hospital and those the Crown would undertake in order to resolve disputes over finances. For a description of the *marché* and further details regarding the financial state of the Ursulines and accusations of misconduct, see Karen Greene, "The Ursuline Mission in Colonial Louisiana," 86–91; and Heaney,

A Century of Pioneering, in which she cites Jean-Baptiste Le Moyne Bienville and Edmé Gatien Salmon to the minister of the navy, May 12, 1733, C13A 16, fols. 89v-91.

141. Karen Denise Greene, "The Ursuline Mission in Colonial Louisiana" (MA thesis, Louisiana State University, 1982), app. B, is a translation of the *marché* (contract) between the Ursulines and the French Crown regulating hospital procedures and responsibilities that was concluded on December 1, 1744. Article Eleven states, "His majesty also allows the nuns to use the Negro Baptiste, who will continue to work in the pharmacy."

142. Of the eight other nuns, four had died, including within the first year Sister St. Francis Xavier (from LeHavre, she taught day pupils, but had wanted to teach the slaves); in 1731 Sister St. Jean L'Evangéliste, assistant superior (from Rouen, she had taught the Indigenous and enslaved); in 1733 Sister St. Therese (from Ploërmel, who had taken up various duties in the house); and then in 1733 Mother St. Augustin. The remaining four nuns returned to France, unable to tolerate the conditions in New Orleans.

143. Riley, "The Development of Education in Louisiana Prior to Statehood," 606.

144. See Wilson "An Architectural History of the Royal Hospital and the Ursuline Convent of New Orleans," 559–602, for a detailed description of both the convent and hospital.

145. Father Mathurin Le Petit, of the Province of France, was born at Vannes, February 6, 1690, and entered the Society, September 14, 1712. He came to New Orleans in 1726, with several other fathers, and was sent as a pioneer missionary to the Choctaw Indians, where he remained until appointed, in 1728, to succeed Father de Beaubois as superior of the Louisiana mission. He held this office until his death on October 13, 1739.

146. Detailed descriptions of New Orleans are taken from Jean-François-Benjamin Dumont de Montigny, *The Memoir of Lieutenant Dumont, 1715–1747: A Sojourner in the French Atlantic*, trans. Gordon M. Sayre (Chapel Hill: University of North Carolina Press, 2012).

147. Descriptions of the convent during this time were taken from R. Baudier, *Through Portals of the Past: A Story of the Old Ursuline Convent in New Orleans* (New Orleans: Catholic Archdiocese Archives, 1955).

148. The convent, while taking seven years to build, was constructed with the approval and input of the sisters. Marie Hachard wrote in January 1728, "the engineer came yesterday to show us the plan of it, we could desire nothing more than to see ourselves in this house." In April of 1728, she wrote again on the progress of the convent: "we often see the plan, it will be all of brick and sufficient to house a large community, there will be all the rooms we could wish for, very regularly built, well paneled, with large windows and with glass in the sash, but it scarcely advances." Wilson, "An Architectural History of the Royal Hospital and the Ursuline Convent of New Orleans," 575.

149. Sr. St. André was the second mother superior of the Ursulines. She was elected in November of 1733, right after the death of Mother Superior St. Augustine, the founding mother of the New Orleans mission, and right before the move to the new convent. The new Mother Superior St. Andre, born in 1694 in Brittany,

had attended the Ursuline boarding school in Caen prior to entering as a novice on November 11, 1713, and taking the cloth on April 27, 1716. She arrived in New Orleans in 1732 at age thirty-six, with sixteen years' experience as a teacher in one of the largest and most prestigious Ursuline convents in France. Sister Andre was to remain mother superior until September of 1737, when her colleague from Caen, Sister St. Pierre, was elected as superior, a post in which she served until November of 1745.

150. In 1729, after the Natchez Massacre, Father Le Petit wrote of the visit of the Illinois chiefs who came to console the French. He wrote, "the Yazoos they came here to weep for the Black Robes and the French and offer the services of their nation." While in New Orleans they stayed with the Jesuits on their plantation, and attended religious services daily. When singing hymns, the Ursulines sang the first verse and the Illinois sang the following verses in their language and on the same tone. On their visit to the Ursuline Convent, they were surprised that the nuns were not simply recluses working for their own advantage." Heloise Cruzat, "The Ursulines of Louisiana," *The Louisiana Historical Quarterly* 2, no. 2 (1919): 5–23.

151. "Deliberations du counseil, 1727–1902" (Reel 1). Williams Research Center, Historic New Orleans Collections (HNOC), Archive of the Ursuline Nuns of the Parish of Orleans, 99–1-L (AUNPO).

152. "Recommandations faites par le Rev. Pere Petit a la communaute des Ursulines, après sa I visite 10 Janvier 1737." HNOC, AUNPO, reel 19.

153. "Recommandations faites par le Rev. Pere Petit a la communaute des Ursulines, après sa I visite 10 Janvier 1737." HNOC, AUNPO, reel 19.

154. "Recommandations faites par le Rev. Pere Petit a la communaute des Ursulines, après sa I visite 10 Janvier 1737." HNOC, AUNPO, reel 19.

155. Father Le Petit also comments that the sisters shall not receive visitors in the hospital or in the pharmacy. All visitors had to meet with sisters in the area specifically designated for visitations, the parlors.

156. "Recommandations faites par le Rev. Pere Petit a la communaute des Ursulines, après sa I visite 10 Janvier 1737." HNOC, AUNPO, reel 19.

157. "Recommandations faites par le Rev. Pere Petit a la communaute des Ursulines, après sa I visite 10 Janvier 1737." HNOC, AUNPO, reel 19.

158. "Recommandations faites par le Rev. Pere Petit a la communaute des Ursulines, après sa I visite 10 Janvier 1737." HNOC, AUNPO, reel 19.

159. Records of the Superior Council of Louisiana, XXX. In *Louisiana Historical Quarterly* 9, no. 2 (April 1926): 310–11. In July of 1737, Mother Superior Andre petitioned Sr. de Salmon for payment of board for a mulatress, named Marie Charlotte, who had been placed under their care in June 1735. Her total for room and board for two years amounting to 449 livres; 10 sols was owed by the deceased St. Jullien, who had her listed in his inventory of goods. The claim was upheld and the debt order paid.

160. "Recommandations faites par le Rev. Pere Petit a la communaute des Ursulines, après sa I visite 10 Janvier 1737." HNOC, AUNPO, reel 19.

161. Karen Greene, *The Ursuline Mission in Colonial Louisiana*, suggests that the orphans were, at times, used as workers both within the convent and the plantation, which suggests they were treated or used more as servants.

162. "Recommandations faites par le Rev. Pere Petit a la communaute des Ursulines, après sa I visite 10 Janvier 1737." HNOC, AUNPO, reel 19.

163. "Recommandations faites par le Rev. Pere Petit a la communaute des Ursulines, après sa I visite 10 Janvier 1737." HNOC, AUNPO, reel 19.

164. "Lettres Circulaires depuis 1727 jusqu'en 1835," HNOC, AUNPO.

165. "Lettres Circulaires depuis 1727 jusqu'en 1835," HNOC, AUNPO.

166. According to Eugene Genovese, *From Rebellion to Revolution: Afro-American Slave Revolts and the Making of the Modern World* (Baton Rouge: Louisiana State University Press, 1979), 16, while the slaves' conversion to Christianity has been characterized as submission and "Uncle Tomish," he suggests that ultimately Christianity "also drove deep into his soul [the enslaved] an awareness of the moral limits of submission, for it placed a master above his own master and thereby dissolved the moral and ideological ground on which the very principle of absolute human lordship must rest."

167. Father Du Ru in his 1702 journal remarked on the medicinal plants used by the Indigenous peoples. Antione Simon La Page du Pratz (1699–1775) in his *Historie de le Louisiane* catalogued more than three hundred herbs (simples), to which he gave a name, detail of their virtues, and the manner of their use, many of which he had learned about while living among the Natchez. After taking over the king's plantation he developed a botanical garden for the Company. This was most likely the place where Baptiste learned his knowledge of medicinal plants. The training of enslaved Africans as surgeons and apothecaries during this time was common. See also Karol K. Weaver, *Medicinal Revolutionaries: The Enslaved Healers of Eighteenth-Century Saint-Domingue* (Urbana: University of Illinois Press, 2006).

168. "Recommandations faites par le Rev. Pere Petit a la communaute des Ursulines, après sa I visite 10 Janvier 1737." HNOC, AUNPO, reel 19.

169. For a detailed description of the status of soldiers in colonial society in relation to class and race, see Cécile Vidal, "The Streets, the Barracks, and the Hospital: Public Space, Social Control, and Cross-Racial Interactions among Soldiers and Slaves in French New Orleans," in *New Orleans, Louisiana, and Saint-Louis, Senegal: Mirror Cities in the Atlantic World, 1659–2000s*, ed. Emily Clark, Ibrahima Thioub, and Cécile Vidal (Baton Rouge: Louisiana State University Press, 2019), 75–102.

170. Vidal, *Caribbean New Orleans*, 220.

171. "Recommandations faites par le Rev. Pere Petit a la communaute des Ursulines, après sa I visite 10 Janvier 1737." HNOC, AUNPO, reel 19.

172. "Recommandations faites par le Rev. Pere Petit a la communaute des Ursulines, après sa I visite 10 Janvier 1737." HNOC, AUNPO, reel 19. For all practical purposes, we might also assume that the Ursulines provided the first library in New Orleans. They had brought with them at least thirty books from France, which undoubtedly were the ones they were lending.

173. See Clark, *Masterless Mistresses*, for a fuller discussion of the broad range of social services that the Ursulines undertook.

174. In 1728 they had taken in Madame Louise Jousset La Loire, who had lodged complaints against her husband for violent cruelty, *Louisiana Historical Quarterly* 4, no. 1 (January 1921). The case regarding mental health is revealed by an August 11, 1741, letter written by Mother Superior St. Pierre to Mr. Moyan, asking that

he send for his Negro girl Charlotte, who does not need to stay any longer at the convent to furnish evidence of her insanity, *Louisiana Historical Quarterly* 11, no. 1 (January 1928): 131.

175. Le Normant accused them of using the money and supplies they received for the patients for their own needs. Specifically, he accused them of selling the yearly ration of jugs of wine for the patients given that the jugs were gone before the patients could have possibly consumed them. He charged the nuns with trafficking a number of other hospital items. See Greene, *The Ursuline Mission in Colonial Louisiana*, 88–91.

176. Mother Superior St. Pierre to the Reverent Mother, May 9, 1747, UCAC.

177. See Emily Clark, "Patrimony without Pater: The New Orleans Ursuline Community and the Creation of Material Culture." In *French Colonial Louisiana and the Atlantic World*, ed. Bradley G. Bond (Baton Rouge: Louisiana State University Press, 2005): 95–109.

178. Greene, *The Ursuline Mission in Colonial Louisiana*, 169.

179. Records of the Superior Council of Louisiana, Feb 8, 1736, *The Louisiana Historical Quarterly* 5, no. 1 (January 1922): 379.

180. Greene, *The Ursuline Mission in Colonial Louisiana*, 171.

181. It was not until the last decades of the eighteenth century that Louisiana's economy shifted from a frontier exchange economy and slaveowning society to a slave society based in plantation agriculture.

182. Clark, *Masterless Mistresses*, 168.

183. Spear, *Race, Sex and Social Order in Early New Orleans*, 71. While baptisms were conducted among the enslaved, the requirement that slaves marry was not followed as diligently.

184. Rebbeca Ann Goetz, *Baptism of Early Virginia: How Christianity Created Race* (Baltimore: John Hopkins University Press, 2012); Stuart B. Schwartz, *All Can Be Saved: Religious Toleration and Salvation in the Iberian Atlantic World* (New Haven, CT: Yale University Press, 2008); and Ben Groth, "'Sacred Legalities'; The Indelible and Interconnected Relationship Between Baptism and Race in Spanish New Orleans" (MA thesis, Tulane University, 2021).

185. See Clark, *Masterless Mistresses*, 176–87, for a detailed discussion of the frequency and role of godparenting among the Ursuline enslaved in the later half of the eighteenth century.

186. Clark, *Masterless Mistresses*.

187. Jessica Marie Johnson, *Wicked Flesh: Black Women, Intimacy, and Freedom in the Atlantic World* (Philadelphia: University of Pennsylvania Press, 2020).

188. Cruzat, Records of the Superior Council of Louisiana, XXXIV, LHQ, 10, no. 2 (1927), 255.

189. Cruzat, LHQ, 12, no.4 (1929), 667.

190. Discussed in Cyprian Davis, *Henriette Delille: Servant of Slaves, Witness to the Poor* (New Orleans: Archdiocese of New Orleans, 2004).

191. See Rev. Jerome G. LeDoux, *War of the Pews: A Personal Account of St. Augustine Church in New Orleans* (Donaldsonville, LA: Margaret Media, Inc., 2011), for a full account of this struggle.

192. Lauren Zych, "Low-fired Earthenwares and Intercultural Relations in New Orleans, 1718–1763: Preliminary Results from Three Sites in the French Quarter," *Louisiana Archaeology* 39 (In Press).

193. See LeDoux, *War of the Pews*, for his narrative and historical accounting of the place of St. Augustine in the history of New Orleans.

Chapter 3

1. According to Richard Campanella, *Bourbon Street: A History* (Baton Rouge, Louisiana State University Press, 2014), in 1820, Burgundy Street had 37.6 percent of free people of color, Dauphine had 29.3 percent, and Bourbon had 21.7 percent.

2. "Address from the Free People of Color," January 1804, in Clarence Edward Carter, ed., *Territorial Papers*, IX, 174–75. Also see Caryn Cossé Bell, *Revolution, Romanticism, and the Afro-Creole Protest Tradition in Louisiana, 1718–1868* (Baton Rouge: Louisiana State University Press, 1997), for a further discussion of the rights free people of color expected.

3. Madeleine G. S. Bouchereau, *Education des Femmes en Haiti* (Port-au-Prince: Imprimerie de L'Etat, 1944).

4. Job B. Clément, "History of Education in Haiti: 1804–1915." *Revista de Historia de América* 87 (1979): 141–81.

5. Clément, "History of Education in Haiti: 1804–1915," 155.

6. Gabriel Debien, "Une maison d'education a Saint-Domingue: les religieuses du Cap, 1731–1802," *Revue d'histoire de l'Amérique française* 2, no. 4 (1949): 565.

7. Debien, "Une maison d'education a Saint-Domingue," 155.

8. J. C. Dorsainvil, *Manuel d'Histoire d'Haiti* (Port-au-Prince, privately printed, 1934), 383, as cited in Clément, "History of Education in Haiti: 1804–1915."

9. Erica Robin Johnson, "The Revolution From Within: Abolitionists and the Revolution in Saint-Domingue" (PhD diss., Florida State University, 2012).

10. Johnson, *The Revolution from Within*, 79. Also see Clément, "History of Education in Haiti: 1804–1915," 157.

11. James Pitot, *Observations of the Colony of Louisiana from 1796 to 1802*, trans. Henry C. Pitot (Paris, 1802).

12. For a full discussion of the impact of the Haitian Revolution on the United States, see David P. Geggus, *The Impact of the Haitian Revolution in the Atlantic World* (Columbia: University of South Carolina Press, 2001); Eugene Genovese, *From Rebellion to Revolution: Afro-American Slave Revolts and the Making of the Modern World*. (Baton Rouge: Louisiana State University Press, 1979); Alfred N. Hunt, *Haiti's Influence on Antebellum America: Slumbering Volcano in the Caribbean* (Baton Rouge: Louisiana State University Press, 1988); Gary B. Nash, "Reverberations of Haiti in the American North: Black Saint-Dominguans in Philadelphia," *Exploration in Early American Culture Pennsylvania History* 65 (1998): 44–73; Ashli White, *Encountering Revolution: Haiti and the Making of the Early Republic* (Baltimore: John Hopkins University Press: 2010).

13. By 1790, the value of American exports to Saint-Domingue alone was greater than all other West Indian islands combined. Specifically in Philadelphia, between August 1789 and 1793, ships arriving from Saint-Domingue made up between 18 and 25 percent of all vessels arriving to Philadelphia from foreign ports. See Garvey F. Lundy, "Early Saint Dominguan Migration to America and the Attraction of Philadelphia," *Journal of Haitian History* 12, no. 1 (2006): 83.

14. For a detailed discussion of the abolition movement in Philadelphia and the impact of the Haitian Revolution, see Emily Clark, *The Strange History of the*

American Quadroon: Free Women of Color in the Revolutionary Atlantic World (Chapel Hill: University of North Carolina Press, 2013); Lundy, "Early Saint Dominguan Migration," 76–94; Gary Nash, *Forging Freedom: The Formation of Philadelphia's Black Community, 1720–1840* (Cambridge, MA: Harvard University Press, 1988); Gary B. Nash and Jean R. Soderland, *Freedom by Degrees: Emancipation in Pennsylvania and its Aftermath* (New York: Oxford University Press, 1991)

15. Jefferson, much like the French in the aftermath of the French revolution, was skeptical of a traditional, classical curriculum, instead focusing on developing a scientific, practical, and vocational curriculum.

16. See Roland G. Paulston, "French Influence in American Institutions of Higher Learning, 1784–1825," *History of Education Quarterly* 8, no. 2 (1968): 229–45; and Malone Dumas, *Correspondence between Thomas Jefferson and Pierre Samuel DuPont de Nemours, 1798–1817* (New York: Houghton Mifflin Company, 1930), for more detailed discussion of both the French influence on Thomas Jefferson and on the United States.

17. In addition, other St. Dominguan refugees, including Anne Marie Sigoigne, opened a French school, as did Charles and Marie Picot.

18. The book which Jefferson received was titled *Historiettes Nouvelles, a l'Usage de la Jeunesse des Deux sexes et des Ecoles* (Philadelphia, 1815). His other book was *An Oral System of Teaching Living Languages: Illustrated By a Practical Course of Lessons, in the French, through the Medium of English,* 1839.

19. Anticlericalism in France after the Revolution resulted in nine Sulpician priests and seven seminarians arriving in Baltimore between 1791 and 1793. Their first order of business was to establish St. Mary's College as a preparatory institution and St. Mary's Seminary to educate priests. This is yet another example of the French influence on American education.

20. Cyprian Davis, *The History of Black Catholics in the United States* (New York: Crossroad, 1990).

21. Dianne Batts Morrow, *Persons of Color and Religious at the Same Time: The Oblate Sisters of Providence, 1828–1860* (Chapel Hill: University of North Carolina Press, 2002), 6.

22. Morrow, *Persons of Color and Religious at the Same Time,* 15.

23. It should be noted that in the early 1800s, various Protestant organizations in Baltimore such as Sharp Street Methodist Episcopal Church's Free African School (1802), Daniel Coker's Bethel Charity School (c. 1812), St. James Protestant Episcopal Day School (1824), and William Lively's Union Seminary (1825) created schools for African American students. While providing a valuable service, they could not meet the demands of Baltimore's growing free African American population. There were no free public schools for children of color in Baltimore until 1866.

24. Suzanne Krebsbach, "Black Catholics in Antebellum Charleston," *South Carolina Historical Magazine* 108, no. 2 (2007). Also see Davis, *The History of Black Catholics in the United States.*

25. Carl A. Brasseaux and Glenn R. Conrad, *The Road to Louisiana: The Saint-Domingue Refugees 1792–1809* (Lafayette: University of Louisiana at Lafayette Press, 1992), 271.

26. Alisha Johnson, "Respectable from their Intelligence: The Education of

Louisiana's Gens de Couleur Libres, 1800–1860" (PhD diss., University of Illinois, 2017), 25.

27. Roger P. McCutcheon, *Louisiana Historical Quarterly* "Libraries in New Orleans, 1771–1833," XX (1937): 152–58, provides a detailed history of the evolution of libraries in New Orleans.

28. Mary Bernardine Hill, "The Influence of James Hubert Blenk on Catholic Education in the Archdiocese of New Orleans, 1885–1917" (PhD diss., Louisiana State University, 1964), 10.

29. M. A. Carroll, "Education in New Orleans in Spanish Colonial Days," *American Catholic Quarterly Review* XII, no. 46 (1887): 257. Alma H. Peterson, "The Administration of Public Schools in New Orleans, 1841–1861." (PhD diss., Louisiana State University, 1964), 22.

30. Henry P. Dart, "Public Education in New Orleans in 1800," *Louisiana Historical Quarterly* 11, no. 2 (1928): 243.

31. Johnson, "Respectable From Their Intelligence," 88–90.

32. Hunt, *Haiti's Influence on Antebellum America*, 114.

33. Eberhard L. Faber, *Building the Land of Dreams: New Orleans and the Transformation of Early American* (Princeton, NJ: Princeton University Press, 2016).

34. In 1760, 1,500 enslaved men and women organized a revolt in British Jamaica. Known as Tacky's Revolt, this was the largest antislavery revolt in the Americas to that point. The first incident that linked the revolutionary ideals of Saint-Domingue to the United States was in Virginia in 1793. John Randolph discovered two enslaved persons whom he overheard plotting to kill the whites just as the "blacks had killed the whites in the French Islands and took it." In Hunt, *Haiti's Influence on Antebellum America*, 116.

35. Beginning with an issue dated February 1, 1794, Claude Corentin Tanguy de la Boissière, a refugee from Saint-Domingue, published a triweekly newspaper in Philadelphia called the *American Star, or, Historical, Political, Critical, and Moral Journal*. Published in both English and French, it carried an alternative title of *L'Étoile Américaine, ou Journal Historique, Politique, Critique et Moral*. Publication was suspended after May 3, 1794.

36. Michel-Rolph Trouillot writes in *Silencing the Past* that the Haitian Revolution "entered history with the peculiar characteristic of being unthinkable even as it happened," 73.

37. See Robyn Andermann, "Brewed Awakening: Re-imagining Education in Three Nineteenth-Century New Orleans Coffee Houses" (PhD., diss., Louisiana State University, 2018), for a more detailed discussion of the cross-class and interracial mixing in taverns and coffee houses.

38. See Rashauna Johnson, *Slavery's Metropolis: Unfree Labor in New Orleans during the Age of Revolution* (Cambridge: Cambridge University Press, 2016); Walter Johnson, *Soul by Soul: Life Inside the Antebellum Slave Market* (Cambridge, MA: Harvard University Press, 1999).

39. Faber, *Building the Land of Dreams*, 79.

40. See Johnson, *Slavery's Metropolis*, 2.

41. Johnson, *Slavery's Metropolis*, 5.

42. Faber, *Building the Land of Dreams*, 69.

43. Faber, *Building the Land of Dreams*, 70.

44. See Thomas Jefferson, *Notes on the State of Virginia*, ed. Frank Shuffleton (New York: Penguin Books, 1999 [originally published in 1785]), 9.

45. Thomas Jefferson Papers, Louisiana Boundaries, 1804, January 14, University of Virginia Archives (UVA).

46. Martin Luther Riley, "The Development of Education in Louisiana Prior to Statehood," *Louisiana Historical Quarterly* XIX, no. 3 (1936): 625.

47. Frederick Cooper and Ann Laura Stoler, eds., *Tensions of Empire: Colonial Cultures in a Bourgeois World* (Berkeley: University of California Press, 1997).

48. See Peter J. Kastor, "'They are all Frenchmen': Background and Nation in an Age of Transformation," in *Empires of the Imagination: Transatlantic Histories of the Louisiana Purchase*, ed. Peter J. Kastor and François Weil (Charlottesville: University of Virginia Press, 2009), 239–67, for a detailed discussion of the troublesome concept of nationalism during the territorial period.

49. Mark Fernandez, "Edward Livingston, American and France: Making Law." In *Empires of the Imagination: Transatlantic Histories of the Louisiana Purchase*, ed. Peter J. Kastor and François Weil (Charlottesville: University of Virginia Press, 2009), 268–300.

50. *Louisiana Gazette*, April 10, 1807.

51. "To Thomas Jefferson from James Workman, 15 November 1801," *Papers of Thomas Jefferson*, vol. 35, *1 August–30 November 1801*, ed. Barbara B. Oberg. (Princeton, NJ: Princeton University Press, 2008), 669–71.

52. Charles S. Watson, "A Denunciation on the State of Spanish Rule: James Workman's Liberty in Louisiana," *Louisiana History: The Journal of the Louisiana Historical Association* 11, no. 3 (1904): 245–58.

53. See Fernandez, "Edward Livingston, America and France: Making Law," 268–300, for further discussion.

54. The fifth oldest public high school in the United States is the Academy of Richmond County, established in Augusta, Georgia, in 1783, also drew on the French model to design their system of education.

55. Stuart Grayson Noble, "Governor Claiborne and the Public School System of the Territorial Government of Louisiana," *Louisiana Historical Quarterly* 11 (1928): 535–52.

56. On April 10, 1805, the territorial legislature organized twelve parishes/counties (starting from the southeast corner moving west and north): Orleans County, LaFourche County, German Coast, Acadia County, Iberville County, Attakapas County, Pointe Coupée County, Opelousas County, Rapides County, Concordia County, Natchitoches County, and Ouachita County.

57. *Louisiana Gazette*, July 19, 1805.

58. There is some indication that he served as the personal secretary to Toussaint l'Ouverture, given his fluency in French, Spanish, English, and Latin.

59. The Digest of 1808 was the first European-style code to be enacted in the Americas, but it was also the first code to incorporate slave law. Moreau-Lislet, like most of the French Creoles, was committed to the institution of slavery, but he was also committed to the code of enlightenment and reason embodied in the French and American Revolutions. Consequently, the digest was the embodiment of two contradictory ideologies in which the principles of equality embodied in republicanism were in direct opposition to those of an emerging plantation, slaveholding society.

60. "Freemason Lodges in Louisiana, 1807–1995," LaRC/Manuscripts Collection 895. Howard-Tilton Memorial Library (hereafter HTML), Louisiana Research Collection, Tulane University.

61. John Charles Dawson, *Lakanal the Regicide: A Biographical and Historical Study of the Career of Joseph Lakanal* (Tuscaloosa: University of Alabama Press, 1948), 126.

62. Walter Stern, *Race and Education in New Orleans: Creating the Segregated City, 1764–1960* (Baton Rouge: Louisiana State University Press, 2019), 29.

63. Stern, *Race and Education*, 29.

64. According to Noble, "Governor Claiborne and the Public School System," the previous act was repealed in January of 1808 and included the omission of "tuition money," making the public schools truly free. In January of 1809, two schools had opened in the parish of Pointe Coupée.

65. Noble, "Governor Claiborne and the Public School System," 535–52.

66. Letter to the secretary of the treasury January 17, 1810 (quoted in Charles Gayarré, *Historie de la Louisiane* [New Orleans: Imprimé par Magne & Weisse, 1846], 224).

67. Bell, *Revolution, Romanticism, and the Afro-Creole Protest Tradition in Louisiana*, 38.

68. *New Orleans City Directory*, 1811.

69. See Clark, *The Strange History of the American Quadroon*, for a discussion of the role of marriage among free people of color in New Orleans, 84–85.

70. Lawrence Powell, *The Accidental City: Improvising New Orleans* (Cambridge, MA: Harvard University Press, 2012), 302.

71. *New Orleans City Directory*, 1811.

72. *Louisiana Courier*, September 15, 1809.

73. *Louisiana Courier*, June 23, 1809.

74. Rebecca J. Scott and Jean M. Hébrard, *Freedom Papers: An Atlantic Odyssey in the Age of Emancipation* (Cambridge, MA: Harvard University Press, 2012).

75. The story of the Duhart/Bayot/Tinchant family is chronicled in detail in Rebecca J. Scott & Jean M. Hébrard, *Freedom Papers*.

76. Rebecca J. Scott & Jean M. Hébrard, *Freedom Papers*, 75.

77. *Louisiana Courier*, October 15, 1810, p. 2, col. 3.

78. *Moniteur de la Louisiane*, April 30, 1803.

79. See Alisha Johnson, "Respectable from Their Intelligence," for a detailed description of the apprenticeship system in the antebellum period and its impact on literacy rates of free men of color.

80. W.C.C. Claiborne, *Official Letter Books, 1801–1816*, Vol 1, ed. Dunbar Rowland (Jackson, MI: State Department of Archives and History), 143.

81. See Marietta Marie Lebreton, *A History of the Territory of Orleans, 1803–1812*, parts I and II (Baton Rouge: Louisiana State University Press, 1969), for a complete history of the three legislative councils during the territorial period.

82. Acts Passed at the Second Session of the Third Legislative Session of the Territory of Orleans (Begun and held in the city of New-Orleans on Monday the twenty-third of January in the year of our Lord One Thousand Eight Hundred and Eleven). Printed by Thierry, Printer of the Territorial Laws, 1811, 64–65. By 1825, the state was appropriating approximately $150,000 a year toward the support of

schools. The academy movement had made some strides throughout Louisiana in the early part of the century. These were for the most part private institutions, many developed on plantations, where a tutor was hired for the white children of one or several plantations. Between 1817 and 1833, academies were established in the parishes of Rapides, Natchitoches, East Baton Rouge, Ouachita, and St. Tammany, all of which received some appropriations from the state under the legislative acts of 1817 that had also supported the College d'Orléans. Between 1833 and 1842, while nineteen more academies came into existence, many were plagued by problems, mostly financial, making their long-term success difficult. By 1842, all state aid had been withdrawn from the academies.

83. Acts Passed at the Second Session of the Third Legislative Session of the Territory of Orleans (Begun and held in the city of New-Orleans on Monday the twenty-third of January in the year of our Lord One Thousand Eight Hundred and Eleven). Printed by Thierry, Printer of the Territorial Laws, 1811, 66.

84. Dawson, *Lakanal the Regicide*.

85. Several Haitians, Louis Moreau-Lislet among them, supported the college, and when Claiborne finally received funding for the College d'Orléans, he appointed several Haitians as regents. The regents were James Mather, Charles Trudeau, Noël Drestrehan, Paul Lanusse, Pierre Derbigny, Joseph Saul, Dr. Joseph Montegut, Evan Jones, Louis Moreau Lislet, Elizius Fromentin, and F. Duplessis.

86. *Common Routes: St. Domingue-Louisiana* (New Orleans: Historic New Orleans Collection, 2006), 89.

87. Ned Sublette, *The World That Made New Orleans: From Spanish Silver to Congo Square* (Chicago: Lawrence Hill Books, 2009). This property, on which Saint Augustine Catholic Church now stands, was part of a plantation estate, tilery, and brickyard headquarters built in 1720. It was part of the province of New Orleans's supervisor, the Company of the Indies, and was an economic stimulus for the province. In 1731 the Company of the Indies left, and the plantation was sold to the Moreau family, eventually coming into the possession of Julie Moreau, a manumitted slave, in 1775. Soon after, Frenchman Claude Tremé married Moreau and took title to the property. The couple subdivided the estate and sold off many lots on a first-come first-serve basis to free people of color and others, including Haitian immigrants fleeing the 1791 Haitian revolution. After selling thirty-five lots, the Tremés left their plantation home in 1810.

88. Richard Campanella, *Bienville's Dilemma: A Historical Geography of New Orleans* (Lafayette: University of Louisiana at Lafayette Press, 2008), 28.

89. At this time the regents were James Mather, Charles Trudeau, Noël Drestrehan, Paul Lanusse, Pierre Derbigny, Joseph Saul, Dr. Joseph Montegut, Evan Jones, Louis Moreau Lislet, Elizius Fromentin, and F. Duplessis.

90. *Organic Regulations of the College of Orleans*, 1811, 28 HNOC.

91. Dawson, *Lakanal the Regicide*, 128.

92. *Organic Regulations of the College of Orleans*, 1811, 28 HNOC.

93. *Organic Regulations of the College of Orleans*, 1811, 28 HNOC.

94. *Organic Regulations of the College of Orleans*, 1811, 21 HNOC.

95. His sister-in-law had been married to his brother Jean-Pierre-Valentin Joseph (1756–1803). She brought with her four remaining children: Louis Auguste (1781–1851), Marie Louise Magdeleine Valentine (1783–1860) who married

Edward Livingston in 1805, a son Jean Francois Gaston (1788–1853), and Aglaé
Pauline Robertine (1793–1835).

96. From Brausseaux and Conrad, *The Road to Louisiana*, 272.

97. The Louisiana Collection, Lambert Family Papers (1798–1862), 244, box
1, folder, 23, *L'Ami Des Lois*, October, 27, 1813, HTML.

98. Charles Gayarré, *Fernando Lemos, Truth and Fiction. A Novel* (New York: G.
W. Carleton, 1872).

99. The Louisiana Collection, Lambert Family Papers (1798–1862), 244, box
1, folder, 23, *L'Ami Des Lois*, October, 27, 1814, HTML.

100. *Organic Regulations of the College of Orleans*, 1811, 27, HNOC.

101. The Louisiana Collection, Lambert Family Papers (1798–1862), Mr. Henry
P. Nugent in October 22, 1811, newspaper, HTML.

102. Dawson, *Lakanal the Regicide*, 128.

103. *Organic Regulations of the College of Orleans*, 1811, 18–19, HNOC.

104. There is no proof that colored students attended the college; student
records are not available. The only indication that suggests a boy of color attended
is by Charles Gayarré in his book, *Fernando de Lemos*, 1872. He writes, "There were
in the college of Orleans only a few day scholars. They were youths, who generally on account of the poverty of their parents, could not afford to be full boarders.
Most were admitted on half pay; others did not pay at all, being sent by the Board
of Regents, every member of which had the privilege to select a poor boy, who,
on the recommendation of his patron, and on the assurance of his family being
in destitute circumstances, was entitled to be educated gratis. Those who were
thus selected by the regents, were designated as 'charity students' by those who
had been more favored by fortune. Among those 'charity boys' who composed the
plebs, and who were treated with lofty disdain by some of the sons of wealth, was a
lad called Treviño. We had frenchified his name, and we pronounced it Trévigne
(Roderic, first name). His father was a Spaniard, who lived in a hut on Bayou Road,
midway between Bayou St. John and the city." (30). Also, the location of the college in Tremé and near the Marigny, which were interracial neighborhoods with
large numbers of Saint-Domingue refugees, indicates the possibility that students
of color, especially those of few means who might have been admitted gratis, were
attending the college. It is possible that Roderic Trévigne was the uncle of Paul
Trévigne (1825–1908), a free man of color, who went on to teach at the Catholic
Institute for Colored Orphans.

105. For further information regarding his contributions to Francophone poetry
and literature see Alcée Fortier, "French Literature of Louisiana," *Transactions and
Procedures of the Modern Language Association of American* 2 (1886): 31–60.

106. For an extended conversation on his contributions see Rien Fertel, *Imagining the Creole City: The Rise of Literary Culture in Nineteenth-Century New Orleans*
(Baton Rouge: Louisiana State University Press, 2014).

107. Gayarré, *Fernando de Lemos*, 30.

108. Fertel, *Imagining the Creole City*, 23.

109. Fertel, *Imagining the Creole City*, 34.

110. Daniel Usner, *American Indians in New Orleans: From Calumet to Raquette*
(Baton Rouge: Louisiana State University Press, 2018), maintains that "Father
Adrien Rouquette's interviews and writings comprise the most comprehensive
documentation about Choctaws living near New Orleans," 108.

111. Acts Passed at the First Session of the Fifth Legislature of the State of Louisiana, 1821, *An Act to Extend and Improve the System of Public Education in the State of Louisiana* (New Orleans: J. C. De St. Roman, State Printer, 1821), 62–88.

112. During his exile he was in Philadelphia and maintained a robust correspondence with Livingston and D'Avezac, as evidenced by his letter of September 15, 1816, to Arsène Lacarrière Latour. Arsène Lacarrière Latour Archive, 1814–1817 (HNOC). For more information on the French adventurer, soldier, and architect see Jean Garrigoux, *A Visionary Adventurer: Arsène Lacarrière Latour 1778–1837, the Unusual Travels of a Frenchman in the Americas*, trans. Gordon S. Brown (Lafeyette: University of Louisiana Press, 2017).

113. Louisiana Research Collection, M 177, Essay 1841. The reference to Livingston is made in the essay titled "The Old College of Orleans as it is, and as it was; its last president Lakanal," written by Louise Augustin Fortier. His father, Jean Augustin Fortier, was a professor of Latin in the Collège d'Orléans, HTML.

114. Dawson, *Lakanal the Regicide*, 132.

115. Derbingy (French royalist, exiled in 1791), Mazureau (French exile under Bonaparte), and Roffignac (French royalist arrived in Louisiana in the early 1800s) represent the diversity of French exiles/émigres in New Orleans during this time. At the time the governor was Thomas B. Robertson, a Virginian. The period 1822–1825 is marked by extreme factional discord between established French Creole citizens, French exiles, and newly arriving American settlers. This resulted in a political crisis in New Orleans.

116. James Workman, *Essays and Letters on Various Political Subjects* (New York: I. Riley, 1809), 145–46.

117. Dawson, *Lakanal the Regicide*, 130.

118. In a letter from Lakanal to J. G. Birney, President of the University of Alabama. Cited in Dawson, *Lakanal the Regicide*.

119. *Courrier de la Louisiane*, May 23, 1822.

120. Dawson, *Lakanal the Regicide*, 5.

121. Dawson, *Lakanal the Regicide*, 11

122. These schools would later be renamed Lycées under Napoleon.

123. This conspiracy was organized by General Lallemand and General Raoul, both exiles who were original members of the Vine and Olive Colony of Alabama.

124. See Dawson, *Lakanal the Regicide*, 129–30, for a copy of the letter and discussion of Lakanal's appointment as president.

125. Lee Nelson Gregory, "Joseph Lakanal and French Educational Reform, 1793–1796" (MA thesis, Tulane University, 1970), 89.

126. Gregory, "Joseph Lakanal," 31–34.

127. Mr. Gaudin, originally from France, was the father of Juliette Gaudin, one of the founders of the Sisters of the Holy Family. In Sister Mary Bernard Deggs, *No Cross, No Crown: Black Nuns in Nineteenth-Century New Orleans*, ed. Virginia Meacham Gould and Charles E. Nolan (Bloomington: Indiana University Press, 2001), it is suggested that "he had been a professor at one of the principal young men's schools in the French part of New Orleans." 18. Given the limited number of high schools during this time, it can be speculated that he was teaching at the College d'Orléans.

128. The city directory of 1822 also lists M. M. Nicolas as a professor of Latin

and French, and two overseers, Ursain Durel and V. Duval. In addition, a Pierre Gaudin, the father of Juliette Gaudin, cofounder of the Sisters of the Holy Family, is listed in the 1822 city directory as a teacher and is referenced as being a professor at one of the "principal young men's highs schools in the French part of New Orleans." In Deggs, *No Cross, No Crown,* 18.

129. Deggs, *No Cross, No Crown,* 31–34.

130. *Courrier de la Louisiane,* May 31, 1822.

131. In fact, the reports were so favorable that the legislature in 1823 added to its annual appropriation to the college revenue from the licensing of gambling houses, clearly another way in which the state supported schools through public government funding. See Sarah L. Hyde, *Schooling in the Antebellum South: The Rise of Public and Private Education in Louisiana, Mississippi, and Alabama* (Baton Rouge: Louisiana State University Press, 2016), for a more detailed discussion of state funding.

132. Much has been written about the expulsion of Lakanal and the controversy surrounding his leaving. See, Donald E. Devore and Joseph Logsdon, *Crescent City Schools: Public Education in New Orleans, 1841–1991* (Lafayette, LA: Center for Louisiana Studies, 1991), 9.

133. During his twenty-two years in America, he spent at least part of his time engaged in selecting a suitable site on which the refugees from France might establish a colony. The American Congress had granted these men a tract of land on which they might settle and which they were to select in the locality they preferred. For further discussion see Dawson, *Lakanal the Regicide,* or Charlotte H. Boatner, "Certain Unpublished Letters from French Scientists of the Revolutionary Period Taken from the Files of Joseph Lakanal," *Osiris: Studies on the History and Philosophy of Science, and on the History of Learning and Culture,* vol. I (Bruges, Belgium: Saint Catherine Press, 1936), 175.

134. Lucien Chevart, a native of New Orleans, had married Lakanal's daughter, Alexandrine, and they had two children, Alexandrine and Lucien. They resided at 31 Bayou Road. He was president of the college and teacher of mathematics from 1824 to 1826. In Cohn's *New Orleans Directory for 1855* a Lucien Chevart (his son?) is listed an an attorney living at Charters, C. Customhouse d.102 Orleans, and prior to the Civil War Lucien was one of the public school directors. Alexandrine eventually married Henri Germain, the French consul in New Orleans, after the death of her first husband, and they returned to France during the Civil War, where they died. Lucien married Amire Monnier (died June 10, 1882, at forty-two years old) on January 7, 1866. They had one child, Adele Alexandrine, who died on May 29, 1887, at twenty years of age. Lucien, her father, died on November 20, 1878, at fifty-two years of age (see Dawson, *Lakanal the Regicide,* 162–63).

135. Acts Passed at the Second Session of the Seventh Legislature of the State of Louisiana, 1826, "An Act establishing two Primary Schools and one Central School in the City of New Orleans, and for other purposes" (New Orleans: James M. Bradford, State Printer, 1826), 146–54.

136. There seems to be no available record of the name of the first director of the schools, but in 1830 J. S. Moreau was director and was serving in this capacity as late June 1841. Journal of Deliberations of the Council of the First Municipality of the City of New Orleans, 1841–1845, June 7, 1841, 43–44.

137. William A. Payne, "Studies Relating to Free Public Education in New Orleans Prior to the Civil War" (MA thesis, Tulane University, 1930), 7.

138. Albert Paul Subat, "The Superintendency of the Public Schools of Orleans Parish, 1862–1910" (MA thesis, Tulane University, 1947), 8.

139. Edwin Whitfield Fay, *The History of Education in Louisiana* (Washington, DC: Government Printing Office. 1898), 44.

140. Hyde, *Schooling in the Antebellum South*, 71.

141. Baudier Historical Collection, Volume 12, Louisiana Religious Orders of Women; Charles Nolan, *Bayou Carmel: The Sisters of Mount Carmel of Louisiana (1833–1903)*. Archdiocese of New Orleans Archives, 1977 (AANO).

142. Jane Heaney, *A Century of Pioneering: A History of the Ursuline Nuns in New Orleans, 1727–1827* (New Orleans: Ursuline sisters of New Orleans), 392.

143. See Emily Clark, *Masterless Mistresses: The New Orleans Ursulines and the Development of a New World Society, 1727–1834* (Chapel Hill: University of North Carolina Press, 2007), for a detailed discussion of Nanette.

144. For firsthand accounts of the diversity of the Catholic Church in the early nineteenth century, see Thomas Hamilton, *Men and Manners in America* (Philadelphia: Carey, Lea and Blanchard, 1833), Harriet Martineau, *Retrospect of Western Travel* (London: Saunders and Otley, 1838).

145. Roger Baudier, *Catholic Church in Louisiana* (New Orleans: Hyatt, 1939), 293. When they left the French Quarter, the property of the Ursulines was deeded to the bishop under the condition that the education of free girls of color continue.

146. During the 1820s, the city was rapidly expanding to the east, which necessitated more direct thoroughfares. The city planned to construct a public road to extend Condé Street right through their French Quarter convent grounds. The increasing frictions between the Ursulines and the city's authorities—whose male leaders they had challenged on several occasions—resulted in the relocation of the Ursuline convent.

147. Davis, *The History of Black Catholics*.

148. Deggs, *No Cross, No Crown*, xxx.

149. D. M. Quynn, "Dangers of Subversion in American Education: A French View," *Catholic Historical Review* XXXIX (1953).

150. See Petra M. Hendry, "Sisters on the Frontier: French Catholic Women Educators and the Shaping of the Early American Republic in the Gulf Coast Southwest," *Catholic Southwest: Journal of History and Culture*, no. 31 (2020), 39–66.

151. Louisiana State Museum, Letter from Thomas Jefferson to Sr. Maire Thérèse Farjon of St. Xavier, May 15, 1804, from the online exhibition One Nation Under God: The Church, the State, and the Louisiana Purchase, http://lsm.crt.sta te.la.us/1nation/ursuline_letter.jpg

152. Elizabeth Rapley, *The Lord as Their Portion: The Story of the Religious Orders and How They Shaped Our World* (Grand Rapids, MI: William B. Eerdmans Publishing Company, 2011), 300. Also see Nancy Cott, *The Bonds of Womanhood: "Woman's Sphere" in New England, 1780–1835* (New Haven, CT: Yale University Press, 1977), for a detailed discussion of the "cult of domesticity" and how it shaped notions of the public/private sphere.

153. See Nancy Lusigan Schultz, *Fire and Roses: The Burning of the Charlestown Convent, 1834* (New York: The Free Press, 2000), for a detailed account of that event.

154. In addition to the Poydras Asylum for Girls, in 1824 they opened the Asylum for Destitute Boys and in 1835 the Catholics opened the St. Mary's Orphan Boy's Asylum. Given that there was no public education or public welfare at the time, these private institutions provided the only education for poor children at the time. See Priscilla F. Clement, "Children and Charity: Orphanages in New Orleans, 1817–1914," *Louisiana History: The Journal of the Louisiana Historical Association* 27, no. 4 (Autumn 1986): 337–51; and David J. Rothman, *The Discovery of the Asylum: Social Order and Disorder in the New Republic* (Boston: Little, Brown, 1971), for more detailed discussion of the role of orphanages in constructing the educable child.

155. See Pamela Tyler, *New Orleans Women and the Poydras Home: More Durable than Marble* (Baton Rouge: Louisiana State University Press, 2016).

156. Tyler, *New Orleans Women and the Poydras Home*, 7.

157. I borrow this term from Anne Ulentin, "Shades of Grey: Slaveholding Free Women of Color in Antebellum New Orleans, 1800–1840" (PhD diss., Louisiana State University, 2014).

158. Clark, *The Strange History of the American Quadroon*.

159. Lyle Saxon, *Fabulous New Orleans* (Gretna, LA: Pelican Publishing Company 1988 [Originally published in 1928]); George Washington Cable, *The Grandissimes: A Story of Creole Life* (New York: Sagamore Press, 1957 [Originally published in 1880]).

160. Such a partnership was usually brokered by the girl's mother or parents. The terms of the arrangement usually included a house and support for any children born of the relationship. These relationships usually ended when the white man entered marriage with a white woman. See Clark, *The Strange History of the American Quadroon*, for a full discussion.

161. Virginia Meachum Gould, *Henriette Delille* (Strasbourg, France: Éditions du Signe, 2012), 41.

162. Davis, *The History of Black Catholics in the United States*, 105.

163. Section 3 in "An Act to Punish the Crimes Therein Mentioned, and for Other Purposes," March 16, 1830, Louisiana Acts, 96–97 (reading, "That all persons who shall teach, or permit or cause to be taught, any slave in this state, to read or write, shall, on conviction thereof, before any court of competent jurisdiction be imprisoned not less than one month nor more than twelve months.")

164. Bishop England of South Carolina also attempted to open a school for free people of color, but it was not successful given the staunch opposition of white Catholics. Davis, *The History of Black Catholics in the United States*, 46.

165. Much of the property had been subdivided and developed by Félix Pinson, Evariste Blanc, and Bazile Raphael Crocker (a free man of color).

166. Caryn Cossé Bell, "French Religious Culture in Afro-Creole New Orleans, 1718–1877." *U.S. Catholic Historian* 17, no. 2 (Spring 1999): 1–16.

167. The other sisters included M. Gougir of St. Aloysisus; Marguerite Aucoin of St. Anne Josephine Blin of St. Arsene (who would go on in 1847 to found the Ursuline convent school in Galveston); Renee Renon of St. Catherine; Marie Morin of St. Stephen Angelique Marcon of St. Helena; and Elizabeth Calmet of St. Theresa.

168. According to Emily Clark and Virginia Meacham Gould, "The Feminine Face of Afro-Catholicism in New Orleans, 1727–1852," *William and Mary Quar-*

terly 59 (April 2002): 409–48, Henriette had sponsored more than a dozen slaves and Afro-Creoles through catechism and godparenting by 1838.

169. See John Bernard Alberts, "Origins of Black Catholic Parishes in the Archdiocese of New Orleans, 1718–1920" (PhD diss., Louisiana State University, 1998), for a detailed discussion of the efforts to maintain the universalism of the Catholic Church in New Orleans.

170. Frank Tannenbaum, *Slave and Citizen: The Negro in the Americas* (New York: Knopf, 1947) argues that the Catholic religious doctrine that recognized the moral personality of the slave contributed to constructs of emancipation. While this has been disputed, the recognition of spiritual and moral equality clearly contributed to a sense of agency among Catholics of color and provided leverage for their expectations of equality.

171. Henriette was part of a century-old mission to instruct and educate girls and women of African descent, which resulted in a female Afro-Catholic tradition in New Orleans. See Clark and Gould, "The Feminine Face of Afro-Catholicism in New Orleans, 1727–1852"; Virginia Meacham Gould, "Afro-Creole Women, Freedom, and Property-Holding in New Orleans," in *Coastal Encounters: The Transformation of Gulf South in the Eighteenth Century*, ed. Richmond F. Brown (Lincoln: University of Nebraska Press, 2007), 151–66; Pierre Force, "The House on Bayou Road: Atlantic Creole Networks in the Eighteenth and Nineteenth Centuries," *The Journal of American History* (June, 2013), 21–45.

172. See Anna C. Minogue, *Loretto Annals of the Century* (New York: The America Press, 1912), 80–81.

173. Davis, *The History of Black Catholics in the United States*, 106.

174. The Sisters of Mt. Carmel were recruited by Bishop Dubourg for the dedicated purpose of educating the girls of every color, the poor, the enslaved, and the orphaned. After two years teaching in Platteville, where their efforts were thwarted, they returned to New Orleans and took over the St. Claude school, which by 1839 had twenty-five boarders and sixty-five day students. By November of 1840, the Sisters of Mt. Carmel (or Carmelites) had purchased the property from the Ursulines. The Claude Tremé plantation house, which had served as the St. Claude School, was converted into their convent as well as the school for white students. The promise to continue teaching girls of color was also carried out in a small school on the grounds. The Metropolitan Catholic directory of 1848 reports that there were eight religious, as well as two distinct schools, one for the white and the other for colored girls. With increased growth, in 1859 a new school, the Mount Carmel Academy, was built on the corner of Bayou Road and North Liberty Street on the property of the recently built St. Augustine Church. The names of girls of color are entered in the ledgers under a separate heading from the white girls. It is clear, however, that despite Louisiana law, which forbade white people and people of color from living, socializing, or working in the same space, that the Sisters of Mt. Carmel were finding ways to subvert these laws. The Carmelite Sisters would remain in the Tremé neighborhood until 1929, eventually fully capitulating to the laws of segregation by maintaining two distinct and separate schools, the Mt. Carmel Academy for white girls at their new location on the lakefront, completed in 1929, and from 1926–1933 the former St. Claude School for colored girls was referred to as the St. Augustine Parochial School. Despite the challenges of ante-

bellum racism, the Civil War, Jim Crow, and *Plessy v. Ferguson*, from 1824 to 1933 there was continuous education for girls and children of color in the Tremé neighborhood block that had first housed the College d'Orléans, then the St. Claude School, the Mt. Carmel Academy, and today contains St. Augustine Church. This story of one hundred plus years of educational agency by an interracial, transatlantic network of relationships reveals the complex context that transnational interests played, and continue to play, in the history of Louisiana's education. Mt. Carmel Academy continues to operate in New Orleans presently.

175. See Alexandra T. Havrylyshyn, "Free for the Moment in France: How Enslaved Women and Girls Claimed Liberty in the Courts of New Orleans, 1835–1857" (PhD diss, University of California Berkeley, 2018), for a detailed discussion of how church networks among Afro-Creole persons also contributed to developing legal networks.

176. Shirley Elizabeth Thompson, *Exiles at Home: The Struggle to Become American in Creole New Orleans* (Cambridge, MA: Harvard University Press, 2009), 135.

177. Bell, *Revolution, Romanticism, and the Afro-Creole Protest Tradition*, 131; Davis, *The History of Black Catholics in the United States*, 106.

178. Alberts, "Origins of Black Catholic Parishes in the Archdiocese of New Orleans, 74.

179. Petra Munro Hendry and Donna Porche-Frilot, "'Whatever Diversity of Shade May Appear': Catholic Women Religious Educators in Louisiana, 1727–1862." *Catholic Southwest*, no. 21 (2010): 49.

180. See Janet Cornelius, *"When I Can Read My Title Clear": Literacy, Slavery and Religion in the Antebellum South.* (Columbia, SC: University of South Carolina Press, 1991); Janet Cornelius, "We Slipped and Learned to Read: Slave Accounts of the Literacy Process, 1830–1865," *Phylon* 44, no. 3 (1983).

181. See further discussion of the subversive use of the catechism in teaching enslaved persons in Donna Marie Porche-Frilot, "Propelled by Faith: Henriette Delille and the Literacy Practices of Black Women Religious in Antebellum New Orleans" (PhD diss., Louisiana State University, 2005).

182. For a list of legislative acts restricting FPC rights, see Bill Quigley and Maha Zaki, "The Significance of Race: Legislative Racial Discrimination in Louisiana, 1803–1865." *Southern University Law Review* 24, no. 2 (Spring 1997): 145–206.

183. Printed act of incorporation, also purchase agreement from September 18, 1848, for the property on St. Bernard Street, Archives of the Sisters of the Holy Family New Orleans (hereafter ASHFNO).

184. Owning property not only rooted Afro-Creoles in the city as institution builders, but property rights and wealth were used to protect and expand legal rights (with property being a critical legal right). See Loren Schweniger, "Black Property Owners in the South, 1790–1915" (PhD diss., University of Illinois, 1990), and Mary Gehman, *The Free People of Color of New Orleans* (New Orleans: Margaret Media, 1994), for further information on the role of property ownership in developing institutions.

185. Bell, *Revolution, Romanticism, and the Afro-Creole Protest Tradition*, 134.

186. Tracy Fessenden, "The Sisters of the Holy Family and the Veil of Race." *Religion and American Culture: A Journal of Interpretation* 10, no. 2 (2000): 187–224.

187. Cyprian Davis, "Henriette Delille: Servant of Slaves, Witness to the Poor."

In *Uncommon Faithfulness: The Black Catholic Experience*, ed. Mary Shawn Copeland, LaReine-Marie Mosely, & Albert J. Reboteau (Maryknoll, NY: Orbis Books, 2009).

188. See Davis, "Henriette Delille: Servant of Slaves and Witness to the Poor," for a detailed discussion of Henriette's three wills and the provisions regarding Betsy.

189. See Joseph H. Fichter, "A Saintly Person of Color," *America* 166 (February 29, 1992): 156–67.

190. Sister Mary Bernard Deggs, *No Cross, No Crown*, recounts in her narrative how Mother Josephine "polished the knives for the whole house, washed the glasses and tea towels, and ground the coffee every day before the children were ready for their prayers and catechism. Then she often went out to beg for something for the next day for the sisters" (31). Deggs continued "everyday when dear mother came home from the market, she took for her duty to dust the house from the top to the last step to remove all disorder that she found" (31). Sister Navarre "worked faithfully . . . with her needle she made many thousands of dolls. She was called the queen of the needle" (100). Sister Deggs also recalled, "For many years, we took in washing and ironing for the church and also for thirty-five or forty persons. Every day, there were five or six masses with altar boys' clothing also. That was more than half again the rest of the washing of the priests in the house. [We] carried from ten to twelve baskets of clothing through the streets of a city like New Orleans two days in every week" (41).

191. See Thompson, *Exiles at Home*, 245–47, for a detailed discussion regarding the interracial institutional networks built by free people of color.

192. New Orleans Notarial Archives (NONA), Felix de Armas, notary, December 12, 1850, and June 13, 1853. Delille purchased the property for $1,400 from Aristide Polene in 1850. Of that amount, $1,091.25 was cash and a one-year note was signed for the outstanding $308.75. Jeanne Marie Aliquot loaned her $700 for the down payment and guaranteed the note.

193. ASHFNO records of the school and its students do not begin until 1880. While there are financial and legal papers, no documentation survives regarding day-to-day activities, curriculum, or rosters of students. By 1880 the congregation's flagship school was renamed St. Mary's Academy and had relocated to the French Quarter, directly behind St. Louis Cathedral, and became one of the first female college preparatory institutions for blacks in New Orleans. The following sources in the archives were consulted for any oral histories of the foundational years at the Bayou Road School. Sister M. David Young, "History of the Development of Catholic Education for Negroes in Louisiana" (MA thesis, Louisiana State University, 1944); Mother Mary Francis Borgia Hart, "Violets in the King's Garden: A History of the Sisters of the Holy Family of New Orleans" (original unpublished manuscript, 1931); Sister Mary Francis Borgia, "A History of the Congregation of the Sisters of the Holy Family of New Orleans" (PhD diss., Xavier College, 1931).

194. Deggs, *No Cross, No Crown*, 14. Sister Deggs (1846–1896) joined the Sisters of the Holy Family in 1874 at age twenty-six and began writing her narrative of the history of the Sisters of the Holy Family in 1894. It is the first written history of the order. Sisters Deggs entered the order well after Henriette Delille's death and relies on oral traditions to piece together the story of the early years of the order.

195. Deggs, *No Cross, No Crown*, 23.

196. Davis, "Henriette Delille: Servant of Slaves, Witness to the Poor."

197. The Oblate Sisters of Providence, the first successful Roman Catholic order of black nuns, are the only nonslaveholding U.S. order of sisters in the United States. Unlike their white counterparts and the Sisters of the Holy Family in New Orleans, the Oblates never employed any admission restrictions based on race, color, class, ethnicity, or previous status. Prior to the Civil War, the Oblates admitted at least ten formerly enslaved women into their ranks. In the case of the Sisters of the Holy Family, the order owned one slave and although they educated enslaved children, they educated them on a segregated basis from free Afro-Creole children. The Holy Family sisters also briefly split apart after the admission of the order's first formerly enslaved member in 1867, with the majority of the Afro-Creole sisters voting against her entry.

198. See Hart, "Violets in the King's Garden," for further details and interpretations regarding the entry of Preval.

199. Hart, *"Violets in the King's Garden,"* 29.

200. Hart, *"Violets in the King's Garden,"* 46.

201. Edward T. Brett, *The New Orleans Sisters of the Holy Family: African American Missionaries to the Garifuna of Belize* (Notre Dame, IN: University of Notre Dame Press, 2012).

202. See James Anderson, *Education of Blacks in the South 1860–1935* (Chapel Hill: University of North Carolina Press, 1988), for a full discussion of the lack of recognition of Blacks as agents in developing their own educational institutions.

203. C. W. Hilton, Donald E. Shipp, and J. Berton Gremillion, "Historical Background of Public Education in Louisiana," in *The Louisiana Purchase Bicentennial Series in Louisiana History, Education in Louisiana*, vol. XVIII, ed. Michael G. Wade (Lafayette: Center for Louisiana Studies University of Southwestern Louisiana, 1999).

204. See Raleigh Suarez, "Chronicle of Failure: Public Education in Antebellum Louisiana," in *The Louisiana Purchase Bicentennial Series in Louisiana History*, vol. XVIII, ed. Michael G. Wade (Lafayette: Center for Louisiana Studies University of Southwestern Louisiana, 1999), 65–74.

205. Hilary Moss, *Schooling Citizens: The Struggle for African American Education in Antebellum America* (Chicago: University of Chicago Press, 2009), 13.

206. Acts Passed at the First Session of the Fifteenth Legislature of the State of Louisiana, 1841, An Act to Authorize the Municipalities of the City of New Orleans to Establish Public Schools therein (New Orleans: A. C. Bullitt, State Printer, 1841), 21.

207. Moss, *Schooling Citizens*, 9.

208. For more detailed discussions of the racial and gendered constructions of citizenship, see Judith K. Sklar, *American Citizenship: The Quest for Inclusion* (Cambridge, MA: Harvard University Press, 1991); Mark Stuart Weiner, *Americans Without Laws: The Racial Boundaries of Citizenship* (New York: New York University Press, 2006); Evelyn Nakano Glenn, *Unequal Freedom: How Race and Gender Shaped American Citizenship and Labor* (Cambridge, MA: Harvard University Press, 2002).

209. Marcus Christian Papers, Negro Education, University of New Orleans Archives (hereafter UNOA); Devore and Logsdon, *Crescent City Schools*, 39.

210. Stern, *Race and Education in New Orleans*, 34.

211. Based on the 1850 census, see Carl A. Brasseaux, Keith P. Fontenot, and Claude F. Oubre, *Creoles of Color in the Bayou Country* (Jackson: University of Mississippi Press, 1994), 70.

212. H. E. Sterkx, *The Free Negro in Ante-bellum Louisiana* (Rutherford, NJ: Fairleigh Dickinson University Press, 1972).

213. Gary B. Mills, *The Forgotten People: Cane River's Creoles of Color* (Baton Rouge: Louisiana State University Press, 1977), 153.

214. Cammie Henry Archives (CHA), Northwestern University, Natchitoches.

Chapter 4

1. Catholic Indigent Orphan Asylum [Couvent School]: Student Composition Books, 1856–1863 AR/00635. Archdiocese of New Orleans Archives (AANO).

2. *Scott v. Sandford*, 19 Howard 393 (1857). See Kenneth Stamp, *America in 1857: A Nation on the Brink* (New York: Oxford University Press, 1990); Don E. Fehrenbacher, *Slavery, Law, and Politics: The Dred Scott Case in Historical Perspective* (New York: Oxford University Press, 1981).

3. Walter Stern, *Race and Education in New Orleans: Creating the Segregated City, 1764–1960* (Baton Rouge: Louisiana State University Press, 2019), 29.

4. Charles Roussève, *The Negro in Louisiana* (New Orleans: Xavier University Press: 1937), 48.

5. Joanna Brooks, "The Early American Public Sphere and the Emergence of a Black Print Counter-public," *William and Mary Quarterly* 62, no. 1 (Jan. 2005): 70.

6. Elizabeth Niedenbach, "The Life and Legacy of Marie Couvent: Property Ownership, Social Networks, and the Making of Free People of Color Community in New Orleans," (PhD diss., College of William and Mary, 2015). See chapter 2 for a detailed description of the will and a discussion of the multiple names that Widow Couvent engaged.

7. Niedenbach, "The Life and Legacy of Marie Couvent." See chapter 5 for a detailed discussion of Couvent's ownership of slaves. Over the course of her life in New Orleans, Couvent bought and sold twenty-five slaves.

8. Priscilla Ferguson Clement, "Children and Charity: Orphanages in New Orleans 1817–1914." *Louisiana History: The Journal of the Louisiana Historical Society* 27, no. 4 (1986): 337–51.

9. M. E. Gallaher, A History of Saint Louis School of Holy Redeemer Parish formerly known as the Catholic Institute for Indigent Orphans founded April 20, 1847. Sister of the Holy Ghost (S.H.G.). AANO.

10. Elizabeth C. Neidenbach, "Articulating a Vision: Free Black Social Networks, Property Ownership, and the Founding of L'Insitution Catholique des Orphelins Indigents in New Orleans." Paper presented at the Louisiana Historical Association, 2018.

11. Roger Baudier, "The Story of St. Louis of Holy Redeemer Parish New Orleans, LA. Formerly St. Louis or the Colored." AANO; also, Donald Devore and Joseph Logsdon suggest that a few of the teachers "dared to teach slaves to read and even to advocate racial equality," 42. As the conditions became increasingly hostile for free people of color prior to the Civil War, it became more and more difficult to challenge the unjust racial system. Given that it was a crime to teach

any slave to read, any efforts to teach the enslaved would have been covert. Donald Devore and Joseph Logsdon, *Crescent City Schools: Public Education in New Orleans 1841–1991* (Lafayette: The Center for Louisiana Studies, 1991).

12. Mary Niall Mitchell, *Raising Freedom's Child: Black Children and Visions of the Future after Slavery* (New York: New York University Press, 2008), 19.

13. Rodolphe Desdunes, *Nos Hommes et Notre Histoire: Notices Biographiques Accompagnées de Réflexions et de Souvenirs Personnels* (Montreal, Canada: Arbour and Dupont, 1911), 104.

14. Mitchell, *Raising Freedom's Child*, 18.

15. John Blassingame, *Black New Orleans 1860–1880* (Chicago: University of Chicago Press, 1973), terms it a private school, whereas Mitchell, *Raising Freedom's Child*, discusses the community's description of it as public.

16. Rebecca Scott, *Degrees of Freedom: Louisiana and Cuba after Slavery* (Cambridge, MA: Harvard University Press, 2005).

17. Devore and Logsdon, *Crescent City School*.

18. Stephan Ochs, "A Patriot, a Priest and a Prelate: Black Catholic Activism in Civil War New Orleans," *U.S. Catholic Historian* 12, no. 1 (1994): 56.

19. Finnian P. Leavens, "*L'Union* and the New Orleans *Tribune* and Louisiana Reconstruction" (MA thesis, Louisiana State University, 1966), 3–4.

20. This began with the municipal law of 1816 that mandated designated sections for racial groups in the theater. In 1840 a municipal law was passed under which neither whites nor slaves could attend a ball designated for free people of color; street cars, with "star" cars for blacks, were segregated by race starting in the 1840s; and an 1852 law was passed that forbade gambling at saloons with persons of another race. See R. A. Fischer, "Racial Segregation in Antebellum New Orleans," *American Historical Review* 74, no. 3 (1969): 926–37; and Ira Berlin, *Slaves without Masters: The Free Negro in the Antebellum South* (New York: Pantheon, 1974), gives a detailed discussion of the construction racial segregation.

21. Ochs, "A Patriot, a Priest and a Prelate."

22. Ochs, "A Patriot, a Priest and a Prelate, 59."

23. Fatima Shaik, *Economy Hall: The Hidden History of a Free Black Brotherhood* (New Orleans: The Historic New Orleans Collection, 2021), 125.

24. See Shaik, *Economy Hall*, for a detailed discussion of Boguille's life as a teacher, as well as how his work as an educator was connected through Economy Hall to a support network of Afro-Creole men of color who were committed to institution building as a mechanism not only for economic security, but also for asserting their rights to full citizenship.

25. Shaik, *Economy Hall*, 22.

26. Caryn Cossé Bell, *Romanticism, Revolution and the Afro-Creole Protest Tradition in Louisiana, 1718–1868* (Baton Rouge: Louisiana State University Press, 1997), 125.

27. For a detailed discussion of the Afro-Creole literary movement, see Michael Faber, "The New Orleans Press and French-Language Literature by Creoles of Color," in *Multilingual America: Transnationalism, Ethnicity, and the Language of American Literature*, ed. William Sollors (New York: New York University Press, 1998), 20–49: Norman R. Shapiro, trans., *Creole Echoes: The Francophone Poetry of Nineteenth-Century Louisiana* (Urbana: University of Illinois Press, 2004); Clint

Bruce, *Afro-Creole Poetry in French from Louisiana's Radical Civil War-Era Newspapers* (New Orleans: The Historic New Orleans Collection, 2020).

28. Bruce, *Afro-Creole Poetry in French*, 12. This literary flowering was a transatlantic movement in which ideas and books were circulated between France, Haiti, and Martinique.

29. Henry Louis Gates Jr. *Loose Canons: Notes on the Culture Wars* (Oxford: Oxford University Press, 1993), considered the work to be "the first attempt to define a black canon," 24.

30. Armand Lanusse, ed., *Les Cenelles: A Collection of Poems by Creole Writers of the Early Nineteenth Century*. Translated and with a preface by Règine Latortue and Gleason R. W. Adams (Boston: G. K. Hall & Co., 1845), xxxvii.

31. Bell, *Revolution, Romanticism and the Afro-Creole Protest Tradition*.

32. See Nancy Fraser, "Rethinking the Public Sphere: A Contribution to the Critique of Actually Existing Democracy," in *Habermas and the Public Sphere*, ed. Craig J. Calhoun (Cambridge, MA: MIT Press, 1992), for a full discussion of counterpublic spaces.

33. See Shapiro, *Creole Echoes*; Lanusse, *Les Cenelles*.

34. Shapiro, *Creole Echoes*, 95.

35. See Emily Clark, *The Strange History of the American Quadroon: Free Women of Color in the Revolutionary Atlantic World* (Chapel Hill: University of North Carolina Press, 2013), 155–59, for a detailed discussion of Lanusse's two poems dealing with *plaçage*. His poems critiquing *plaçage* also function as a prescriptive tale for young girls regarding their propriety and chastity. This patriarchal tone runs through the poems in *Les Cenelles* as well as those of the *Tribune*.

36. Devore and Logsdon, *Crescent City Schools*, 42.

37. Catholic Indigent Orphan Asylum [Couvent School]: Student Composition Books, 1856–1863 AR/00635, AANO.

38. Roussève, *The Negro in Louisiana*.

39. Catholic Indigent Orphan Asylum [Couvent School]: Student Composition Books, 1856–1863 AR/00635, AANO.

40. Catholic Indigent Orphan Asylum [Couvent School]: Student Composition Books, 1856–1863 AR/00635, AANO.

41. Catholic Indigent Orphan Asylum [Couvent School]: Student Composition Books, 1856–1863 AR/00635, AANO.

42. Mitchell, *Raising Freedom's Child*, 26.

43. Mitchell, *Raising Freedom's Child*, 16.

44. Catholic Indigent Orphan Asylum [Couvent School]: Student Composition Books, 1856–1863 AR/00635, AANO.

45. The concept of the "public," and specifically "public rights," in defining citizenship has recently been illuminated by Rebecca Scott in relation to an Atlantic and Caribbean worldview. Specifically, she highlights how "vernacular concepts of equality" in Louisiana were the result of social networks that spanned place (Africa, Europe, and the Caribbean), historical events including the Haitian and French Revolutions, and the constant flow of peoples throughout the Atlantic, who brought a "strong tradition of claiming equal rights for themselves." See Rebecca Scott, "The Atlantic World and the Road to *Plessy v. Ferguson*." *Journal of American History* (December 2007), 727.

46. See Michael Pasquier, *Fathers on the Frontier: French Missionaries and the Roman Catholic Priesthood in the United States 1789–1870* (Oxford: Oxford University Press, 2010), 5, for a detailed discussion of this missionary movement from 1789 to 1870.

47. "The Metropolitan Catholic Almanac and Laity's Directory for the Year of our Lord 1840" (Baltimore: Published by Fielding Lucas Jr.), AANO.

48. These divisions included the 1825 establishment of the Diocese of Mobile, which included Alabama and the Floridas, as well as the 1826 division of Upper and Lower Louisiana, the Diocese of St. Louis, and the Diocese of New Orleans. See Sylvie Dubois, Emilie Gagnet Leumas, and Malcolm Richardson, *Speaking French in Louisiana 1720–1955: Linguistic Practices of the Catholic Church* (Baton Rouge: Louisiana State University Press, 2018), for a detailed discussion of these changes.

49. See Petra Munro Hendry, "Sisters on the Frontier: French Catholic Women Educators and the Shaping of the Early American Republic in the Gulf Coast Southwest." *Catholic Southwest: Journal of History and Culture*, no. 31 (2020): 39–66.

50. For exact numbers regarding the national origins of the Jesuits, see Thomas H. Clancy, "The Antebellum Jesuits of the New Orleans Province, 1837–1861." *Louisiana History: The Journal of the Louisiana Historical Association* 34, no. 3 (1993): 327–43.

51. The Sisters of the Sacred Heart urged the Jesuits to come to Grand Coteau because they needed priests to conduct mass. The land for the Jesuit St. Charles College was donated by the sisters and was built using 200,000 slave-made bricks. Both schools were financed in part by the enslaved labor on the plantation run by the sisters at Grand Coteau. Enslaved persons were often traded to the religious to pay off tuition. In 2016, the United States and Canadian province of the Society of the Sacred Heart convened a Committee on Slavery, Accountability and Reconciliation, which gave the sisters a two-year mandate to recover the story of slavery at Grand Coteau and determine avenues for committing to truth, healing, and reconciliation. The sisters have been engaged in tracking down the descendants of the enslaved and erecting headstones in the cemetery, and in September of 2018 descendants organized a "We Speak Your Names" memorial in which the name of every enslaved person was read.

52. John O'Malley, *The First Jesuits* (Cambridge, MA: Harvard University Press, 1993); John McGreevy, *American Jesuits and the World: How an Embattled Religious Order Made Modern Catholicism Global* (Princeton, NJ: Princeton University Press, 2016), are two examples of Jesuit histories that give scant attention to the role of Jesuits as slaveholders.

53. Kelly Schmidt, "We Heard Sometimes Their Ernest Desire to be Free in a Free Country: Enslaved People, Jesuit Masters, and Negotiations for Freedom on American Borderlands." (PhD. diss., Loyola University of Chicago, 2021).

54. Elizabeth Fussell, "Constructing New Orleans, Constructing Race: A Population History of New Orleans," *Journal of American History* 94 (Dec. 2007), 846–55. The Irish were hired as cheap labor to dig the New Basin Canal because slaves were considered too valuable to be exposed to disease and death. It is believed that six thousand Irish died in the process of construction.

55. J. Hanno Deiler, "The System of Redemption in the State of Louisiana,"

trans. Louis Voss, *Louisiana Historical Quarterly* 12, no. 3 (July 1920): 446; Stanley Joe McCord, "A Historical and Linguistic Study of the German Settlement at Roberts Cove, Louisiana" (PhD diss., Louisiana State University, 1969).

56. J. Hanno Deiler, *Geschichte der New Orleanser Deutschen Presse*, trans. William Black (New Orleans: Paul J. Sendker, 1901), 8–12.

57. See Deiler, *Geschichte der New Orleanser Deutschen Presse.* Also see Scott S. Ellis, *The Faubourg Marigny of New Orleans: A History* (Baton Rouge: Louisiana State University Press, 2018), 72. Hanno Deiler, who came to New Orleans in 1872 to teach at St. Boniface German School, eventually taught German at the University of Louisiana (now Tulane), popularized the term "Little Saxony." Prior to his often idealist depictions of German immigrants to the city, this term was not in common usage.

58. J. Hanno Deiler Papers (MSS 395), HNOC.

59. For a fuller discussion of the impact of immigration on the Catholic Church and the French language, see Dubois, Leumas, and Richardson, *Speaking French in Louisiana 1720–1955.*

60. The Sisters of Notre Dame were the first women religious to provide instruction in German.

61. See J. Hanno Deiler, *Zur Geschichte die Deutschen Kirchengemeinden im Staate Louisiana (Inktank Publishing, 2018)*; also John Frederick Nau, *The German People of New Orleans, 1850–1900* (Leiden: E. J. Brill, 1958).

62. *Lafayette City Adviser*, January 29, 1842.

63. According to Devore and Logsdon in *Crescent City Schools*, by 1844 Shaw had opened nine elementary schools and enrolled more than 1,500 students, almost two-thirds of the children between the ages of six and sixteen in the second municipality. He also distributed free textbooks, created evening schools for working children and adults, and set up a free public library, 18–22.

64. Devore and Logsdon, *Crescent City Schools*, 26.

65. See Shirley Thompson, *Exiles at Home: The Struggle to Become American in Creole New Orleans* (Cambridge, MA: Harvard University Press, 2009), chapter 2, for a detailed discussion of legal cases regarding the struggle to establish white identity.

66. Thompson, *Exiles at Home*, devotes a whole chapter of her book to the nephew of Dimitry, George Pandelly, a member of the New Orleans Board of Assistant Alderman, who was accused of being a man of color instead of a free white person.

67. Thompson, *Exiles at Home*, 42.

68. Thompson, *Exiles at Home*, 82–84.

69. Thompson, *Exiles at Home*, 29.

70. Stern, *Race and Education in New Orleans*, 38.

71. Bell, *Revolution, Romanticism, and the Afro-Creole Protest Tradition*, 126.

72. According to Ellis, *The Faubourg Marigny of New Orleans*, the Lutheran Church had established a school on Charters Street in 1840 even before the church was built.

73. Nau, *The German People of New Orleans*, 88.

74. J. Hanno Deiler, *A History of the German Churches in Louisiana (1823–1893)*, trans. Marie Stella Condon (Lafeyette: Center for Louisiana Studies, University of Southwestern Louisiana, 2014).

75. See *Die Deutsche Zeitung*, January 14, 1852, for a full ad posted by a Mr. Schneider announcing a new course.

76. Carl Frederick Wittke, *Refugees of Revolution: The German Forty-Eighters in America* (Westport, CT: Greenwood Press, 1970).

77. Carl Frederick Wittke, *The German Language Press in America* (Ardent Media, 1973).

78. About one third of all Turners nationally owned slaves.

79. Eugen Miller, "Turner Regiments of the South," *American Turner* (1990): 11.

80. Hanno Deiler Papers, Hanno Deiler, Germany's Contribution to the Present Population of New Orleans with a Census of German Schools, *Louisiana Journal of Education*, May 1886, 3, HNOC.

81. Sally Reeves, The LEH's Home at Turner's Hall, *LEH Magazine*, https://64parishes.org/turners-hall

82. *Die Deutsche Zeitung*, January 11, 1852.

83. Robert T. Clark, "The German Liberals in New Orleans (1840–1860)," *Louisiana Historical Quarterly* 20 (1937).

84. Nau, *The German People of New Orleans*, 31.

85. Louis Voss, *History of the German Society of New Orleans* (Published by the German Society on the Occasion of its Eightieth Anniversary), 1927. HNOC.

86. J. K. Laguaites, "The German Element in New Orleans, 1820–1860" (MA. thesis, Tulane University, 1940).

87. Eric Foner, *Free Soil, Free Labor, Free Men: The Ideology of the Republican Party Before the Civil War* (New York: Oxford University Press, 1970).

88. Christian Dippel and Stephan Heblich, *Leadership and Social Movements: The Forty-Eighters in the Civil War* (Cambridge, MA: National Bureau of Economic Research, 2018), working paper 24656, http://www.nber.org/papers/w24656.

89. Wittke, *The German Language Press in America*, 213.

90. Lincoln himself understood the importance of the Forty-Eighters. Lincoln had set his mind on the Republican presidential nomination by early 1859, and in pursuit of that he had taken a secret ownership stake in the German-language *Illinois Staatszeitung* for that purpose.

91. The first Black Freemasonry lodge, African Lodge No. 459, was formed in Boston by the former slave Prince Hall and fourteen other black Bostonians in the 1770s.

92. Stephen Kantrowitz, "'Intended for the better government of man': The Political History of African American Freemasonry in the Era of Emancipation." *Journal of American History* (March 2010): 1004.

93. Jean Louis Dolliole was the natural child of Louis Dolliole, a white Frenchman from La Sene en Provence who had immigrated to New Orleans at the end of the Spanish colonial period and become a prominent builder. He was Catholic but never married, and he formed a permanent *plaçage* with Geneviève (also known as Mammie). He had four natural children: Jean Louis, Madeleine, Joseph, and Pierre. He recognized them, and in his will dated November 18, 1815, left them everything except four hundred piasters that he willed to his brother, and the silver, furniture, and utensils that he left his common-law wife Geneviève.

94. Bell, *Revolution, Romanticism, and the Afro-Creole Protest Tradition in Louisiana*, 182.

95. Kantrowitz, "Intended for the better government of man," 1004.

96. Kantrowitz, "Intended for the better government of man," 1003.

97. The development of two separate lodges in 1844, resulting in the formation of Germania Lodge No. 46, was most likely the consequence of two factors. One, the increased immigration of Germans necessitated a lodge where German was the primary language. Second, the increased regulation of racial activity imposed on antebellum New Orleans necessitated alternative strategies and organizations.

98. See Bell, *Revolution, Romanticism, and the Afro-Creole Protest Tradition in Louisiana*; and Glenn Lee Greene, *Masonry in Louisiana*, (New York: Exposition Press, 1962), for a further discussion of the ideology of Masonic lodges.

99. Kantrowitz, "Intended for the better government of man," 1004.

100. Roulhac Toledano and Mary Louise Christovich (2003). *Faubourg Tremé and the Bayou Road* (Gretna, LA: Pelican Publishing, 2003), 102.

101. Carl Brasseaux and Glenn R. Conrad, eds., *The Road to Louisiana: The Saint-Domingue Refugees 1792–1809.* (Lafayette: University of Louisiana at Lafayette 1992), 247.

102. Thompson, *Exiles at Home*, 75.

103. Scott, "The Atlantic World and the Road to *Plessy v. Ferguson*," 726.

104. Craig Walker, *In the Company of Black Men: The African Influence on Africa American Culture in New York City* (New York: New York University Press, 2011).

105. Bell, *Revolution, Romanticism and the Afro-Creole Protest Tradition*, 55.

106. Bell, *Revolution, Romanticism and the Afro-Creole Protest Tradition*, 54.

107. Brooks, "The Early American Public Sphere," 70.

108. See also Stephen Bullock, *Revolutionary Brotherhood: Freemasonry and the Transformation of the American Social Order, 1730–1840* (Chapel Hill: University of North Carolina Press, 1996); Marshal Ganz, *What a Mighty Power We Can Be: African-American Fraternal Groups and the Struggle for Racial Equality* (Princeton, NJ: Princeton University Press, 2006).

109. Freemason lodges in Louisiana, 1807–1995, LaRC/Manuscripts Collection 895, Series 1: Perseverance Lodge, volumes 1–12, Minutes of Persévérance Lodge. The lodge was originally chartered as No. 113 under a charter issued by the Grand Lodge of Pennsylvania. During the Haitian Revolution, the lodge emigrated to Cuba and was there during 1807–1808. In the latter part of 1808, the lodge established itself in New Orleans, Louisiana, and in 1810 it obtained a new charter from the Grand Lodge of Pennsylvania under No. 118. In 1812 it was redesignated as No. 4. HTML, Louisiana Research Collection.

110. Freemason lodges in Louisiana, 1807–1995, LaRC/Manuscripts Collection 895, Series 1: Perseverance Lodge, volume 32. HTML, Louisiana Research Collection.

111. Persévérance Lodge originally met in the temple of Etoile Polaire Lodge. On May 25, 1819, it acquired from the City of New Orleans a property at St. Claude and Dumaine Streets. The building was completed April 1, 1820, with no modifications except the addition of some outbuildings and a change of fences. The building was still in use for its original purpose until it was sold to the City of New Orleans on November 10, 1970, where a civic center and park would be built. For many years the Grand Lodge of Louisiana used this temple for its meetings. It is the oldest Masonic temple in existence in Louisiana.

112. Toledano and Christovich, *Faubourg Tremé and the Bayou Road*, 68.

113. See Robert Levine, ed., *Martin R. Delany: A Documentary Reader* (Chapel Hill: University of North Carolina Press, 2003), for further discussion of this identification with African origins and traditions.

114. Kantrowitz, "Intended for the better government of man," 1002.

115. In 1844 there were ten Masonic lodges in the city, nine of these using the French and one the Spanish language.

116. This was one of only nineteen lodges that worked the Scottish Rite craft degree rituals. It was constituted and granted a charter by the Grand Lodge of the State of Louisiana.

117. Archive of the Germania Lodge 46, 1844-1973, box 16 (loose misc.). Minutes were written in German until 1937; afterwards, they were written in English. HNOC, EL2.2001.

118. Archive of the Germania Lodge No. 46, 1844–1973, Pam HS539.N42G472 2004, 150th year anniversary: Germania Lodge No 46, free and accepted Masons—(New Orleans, LA: The Lodge, 2004). The lodge moved its meetings from the Persévérance Lodge to 513 St. Louis Street, where they resided for eighty-three years before relocating to 4415 Bienville Street, where they currently reside. HNOC, EL2.2001.

119. See Bell, *Revolution, Romanticism and the Afro-Creole Protest Tradition*, 145–87, for a detailed discussion of the role of Freemasonry in Louisiana.

120. Louis Voss, *History of the German Society of New Orleans* (New Orleans: Sendker Printing Service, Inc., 1927).

121. The Germania Lodge dedicated themselves to giving aid to those in need, especially those who were members. The lodge helped with purchasing burial plots, funeral expenses and providing a small insurance for the kin of deceased members. See Nau, *The German People of New Orleans*, for a further discussion.

122. See Clark, "The German Liberals in New Orleans. Also see Historic New Orleans Collection, MSS395 Hanno Deiler Papers, PN 4899.n31 G5 1901 Geschichte der New Orleaner Deutschen Presse.

123. Archive of the Germania Lodge 46, 1844–1973 (174 items), box 4b. Laurence Stern, *The Works of Laurence Stern* (Philadelphia, 1843). Stern (1713–1768) was a British preacher and then novelist whose writing went on to influence the abolitionist movement. HNOC, EL2.2001.

124. Archive of the Germania Lodge 46, 1844–1973 (174 items), HNOC, EL2.2001.

125. J. M. McPherson, *The Negro's Civil War: How American Blacks Felt and Acted during the War for the Union* (New York: Vintage Books, 1965), 289.

126. Bell, *Revolution, Romanticism and the African-American Protest Tradition*, 238.

127. James D. Anderson, *The Education of Blacks in the South, 1860–1935* (Chapel Hill: University of North Carolina Press, 1988), 6.

128. Anderson, *The Education of Blacks in the South*, 9.

129. Mitchell, *Raising Freedom's Child*, 198.

130. C. Senter, "Creole Poets on the Verge of Nation," in *Creole*, ed. S. Klein (Baton Rouge: Louisiana State University Press, 2000).

131. For further information regarding the Massacre of 1866, see James Keith Hogue, *Uncivil War: Five New Orleans Street Battles and the Rise and Fall of Radi-*

cal Reconstruction (Baton Rouge: Louisiana State University Press, 2006); Melinda Meek Hennessey, "Race and Violence in Reconstruction New Orleans: The 1868 Riot," *Louisiana History* 20, no. 1 (Winter 1979): 77–91.

132. See Whitney Nell Stewart and John Garrison Marks, eds., *Race and Nation in the Age of Emancipations* (Athens: University of Georgia Press, 2018), for a comprehensive discussion of the various ways in which people of color transformed the concept of the nation in the Atlantic world.

133. *L'Union*, December 2, 1866.

Chapter 5

1. *New Orleans Tribune*, January 24, 1869.

2. Although the *Tribune* used "black," I will continue to use "Black," "African American," or Afro-Creole to refer to men and women of African descent.

3. Frankie Hutton, *The Early Black Press in America, 1827–1860* (Westport, CT: Greenwood, 1993), 141.

4. Richard H. Abbott, *For Free Press and Equal Rights: Republican Newspapers in the Reconstruction South* (Athens: University of Georgia Press, 2004), 119–20.

5. *New Orleans Tribune*, January 18, 1868.

6. Michel Foucault, *The History of Sexuality: An Introduction*, trans. Robert Hurley (New York: Vintage, 1990), 101.

7. *New Orleans Tribune*, July 31, 1867.

8. *New Orleans Tribune*, December 6, 1864.

9. Gary B. Nash, *Forging Freedom: The Formation of Philadelphia's Black Community, 1720–1840* (Cambridge, MA: Harvard University Press, 1988), 7.

10. For examples of histories that credit missionary teachers or the government with educating Blacks during Reconstruction, hence eliminating the agency of Blacks themselves, see Henry Lee Swint, *The Northern Teacher in the South, 1862–1870* (New York: Octagon, 1967); Robert C. Morris, *Reading, 'Riting, and Reconstruction: The Education of Freedmen in the South, 1861–1870* (Chicago: University of Chicago Press, 1981); and Ronald E. Butchart, *Northern Schools, Southern Blacks, and Reconstruction: Freedmen's Education, 1862–1875* (Westport, CT: Greenwood, 1980). On the other hand, for examples of texts that credit Blacks' educational agency, see James D. Anderson, *The Education of Blacks in the South, 1860–1935* (Chapel Hill: University of North Carolina Press, 1988); Heather Andrea Williams, *Self-Taught: African American Education in Slavery and Freedom* (Chapel Hill: University of North Carolina Press, 2005); and Christopher Span, *From Cotton Field to School House: African American Education in Mississippi, 1862–1875* (Chapel Hill: University of North Carolina Press, 2009).

11. Abbott, *For Free Press*, 4.

12. Penelope Bullock, *The Afro-American Periodical Press, 1838–1909* (Baton Rouge: Louisiana State University Press, 1981), 64.

13. Anthony Williams, Hayward Farrar, and Jacqueline Bacon are the few who have devoted book-length texts to the histories and analyses of particular Black newspapers: the *Christian Recorder*, the newspaper of the African Methodist Episcopal Church; the *Baltimore Afro-American*; and *Freedom's Journal*, the first Black newspaper in the United States. These three periodicals, once again, were all begun either before or well after the Civil War and were published in the North.

14. Caryn Cossé Bell, "French Religious Culture in Afro-Creole New Orleans, 1718–1877," *U.S. Catholic Historian* 17, no. 2 (1999): 1–16.

15. David C. Rankin, "The Origins of Black Leadership in New Orleans during Reconstruction," *Journal of Southern History* 40, no. 3 (1974): 434.

16. For example, the *Tribune* is not mentioned in I. Garland Penn's *The Afro-American Press and Its Editors*, which incorrectly cites Georgia's *Colored American* (1865) as the first Black newspaper in the South rather than *L'Union*, the *Tribune*'s predecessor, and describes Illinois's *Cairo Gazette* (1882) as the first African American daily. Frederick Detweiler also ignores the *Tribune* in *The Negro Press in the United States* and makes the same mistakes as Penn. Armistead S. Pride and Clint C. Wilson's *A History of the Black Press* is one of the rare overviews of the black press that even includes the *Tribune*. Unfortunately, however, its description contains errors, claiming that the paper appeared daily except for Sundays rather than Mondays and naming J. B. Roudanez as the son, not the brother, of Dr. Louis Charles Roudanez, the *Tribune*'s proprietor. Roland E. Wolseley's *The Black Press, U.S.A.* also only briefly mentions the *Tribune* and mistakenly cites 1896 as its last year of publication.

17. William P. Connor, "Reconstruction Rebels: The *New Orleans Tribune* in Post-War Louisiana," in *Reconstructing Louisiana*, The Louisiana Purchase Bicentennial Series in Louisiana History (Lafayette: University of Louisiana at Lafayette, 2001), 458.

18. Caryn Cossé Bell, *Revolution, Romanticism, and the Afro-Creole Protest Tradition in Louisiana, 1718–1868* (Baton Rouge: Louisiana State University Press, 1997); Mary Niall Mitchell, *Raising Freedom's Child: Black Children and Visions of the Future after Slavery* (New York: New York University Press, 2008).

19. Clint Bruce, *Afro-Creole Poetry in French Louisiana's Radical Civil War-Era Newspapers* (New Orleans, LA: Historic New Orleans Collection, 2020).

20. Jacqueline Bacon, *The First African-American Newspaper: Freedom's Journal* (New York: Lexington, 2007), 8.

21. Bell, *Revolution, Romanticism, and the Afro-Creole Protest Tradition*.

22. *New Orleans Tribune*, January 12, 1866.

23. *New Orleans Tribune*, December 27, 1864. Although the *Tribune* prioritized differences among Blacks' antebellum legal status, Logsdon and Bell warn that "neither group had emerged from the Civil War either all slave or all free." Joseph Logsdon and Caryn Cossé Bell, "The Americanization of Black New Orleans, 1850–1900," in *Creole New Orleans: Race and Americanization*, ed. Arnold R. Hirsch and Joseph Logsdon (Baton Rouge: Louisiana State University Press, 1992), 203.

24. Bell, *Revolution, Romanticism, and the Afro-Creole Protest Tradition*, 4, 2, 133.

25. Bell, *Revolution, Romanticism, and the Afro-Creole Protest Tradition*, 6.

26. Catholic Indigent Orphan Asylum [Couvent School]: Directors Notebooks, (AANO); Bell, *Revolution, Romanticism, and the Afro-Creole Protest Tradition*, 7.

27. Bell, *Revolution, Romanticism, and the Afro-Creole Protest Tradition*, 2.

28. See Bruce, *Afro-Creole Poetry*; and John W. Blassingame, *Black New Orleans, 1860–1880* (Chicago: University of Chicago Press, 1973), for further discussion of these influences.

29. *L'Union*, September 27, 1862, translated in James McPherson, *The Negro's Civil War: How American Blacks Felt and Acted during the War for the Union* (New York: Vintage, 1965), 276.

30. *L'Union*, October 18, 1862.

31. *L'Union*, September 27, 1862.

32. David C. Rankin, introduction to *My Passage at the* New Orleans Tribune: *A Memoir of the Civil War Era*, by Jean-Charles Houzeau, trans. Gerard F. Denault (Baton Rouge: Louisiana State University Press, 1984); Finnian Patrick Leavens, "*L'Union* and the *New Orleans Tribune* and Louisiana Reconstruction" (MA thesis, Louisiana State University, 1966).

33. Houzeau, *My Passage at the* New Orleans Tribune, 78, 144.

34. Houzeau, *My Passage at the* New Orleans Tribune, 79.

35. Charles Dallas, an Anglicized Black unionist from Texas, was hired as an editor.

36. In November 1866, the *Tribune*'s office moved to No. 122 and 124 Exchange Alley between Conti and St. Louis Streets. Rankin, introduction to *My Passage at the* New Orleans Tribune, 31.

37. *New Orleans Tribune*, July 21, 1864.

38. *New Orleans Tribune*, July 21, 1864.

39. *New Orleans Tribune*, February 1, 1866; Rankin, introduction to *My Passage at the* New Orleans Tribune, 58.

40. *New Orleans Tribune*, January 30, 1866.

41. Bell, *Revolution, Romanticism, and the Afro-Creole Protest Tradition*, 1.

42. Louis Harlan, "Desegregation in New Orleans Public Schools during Reconstruction," *American Historical Review* 67, no. 3 (1962): 663.

43. Bell, *Revolution, Romanticism, and the Afro-Creole Protest Tradition*, 4.

44. Houzeau, *My Passage at the* New Orleans Tribune, 82.

45. *New Orleans Tribune*, December 6, 1864.

46. *New Orleans Tribune*, January 10, 1869.

47. *New Orleans Tribune*, February 17, 1865.

48. *New Orleans Tribune*, October 29, 1867.

49. *New Orleans Tribune*, February 17, 1865, quoted in Mitchell, *Raising Freedom's Child*, 208.

50. William H. Watkins, *The White Architects of Black Education: Ideology and Power in America, 1865–1954* (New York: Teachers College Press, 2001), 29, 31.

51. See Samuel A. Cartwright and family papers, 1826–1864. Lower Louisiana and Mississippi Valley Collection, Hill Memorial Library, Louisiana State University.

52. Samuel Cartwright, "On the Caucasians and the Africans," in *Cotton Is King and Pro-Slavery Arguments*, ed. E. Elliott (Augusta, GA: Pritchard, Abbott & Loomis, 1860), 691–706.

53. *New Orleans Tribune*, February 10, 1869.

54. Connor, "Reconstruction Rebels," 448.

55. Rankin, introduction to *My Passage at the* New Orleans Tribune, 2–4.

56. Rankin, introduction to *My Passage at the* New Orleans Tribune, 6.

57. Connor, "Reconstruction Rebels," 447; Rankin, introduction to *My Passage at the* New Orleans Tribune, 22.

58. Leavens, "*L'Union* and the *New Orleans Tribune*," 22–26. "Dalloz" may have referenced an incorrect pronunciation of the editor's own last name, a French publishing house then in existence, or the nineteenth-century French Dalloz family of

progressive lawyers, journalists, and politicians. Houzeau, *My Passage at the* New Orleans Tribune, 69.

59. Alexander von Humboldt, *Cosmos: A Sketch of a Physical Description of the Universe*, trans. E. C. Otté (New York, 1850), quoted in Rankin, introduction to *My Passage at the* New Orleans Tribune, 12–14.

60. Watkins, *White Architects*, 36.

61. Jean-Charles Houzeau, *Études sur les facultés mentales des animaux comparées à celles de l'homme* (Mons, 1872) quoted in Rankin, introduction to *My Passage at the* New Orleans Tribune, 12.

62. Rankin, introduction to *My Passage at the* New Orleans Tribune, 13–14.

63. *New Orleans Tribune*, December 9, 1865.

64. Watkins, *White Architects*, 39.

65. Mitchell, *Raising Freedom's Child*, 193.

66. *New Orleans Tribune*, January 10, 1869.

67. Shirley Thompson, *Exiles at Home: The Struggle to Become American in Creole New Orleans* (Cambridge: MA: Harvard University Press, 2009), 220.

68. According to Bruce (in *Afro-Creole Poetry* [151]), Durant (1817–1882) came from Pennsylvania to New Orleans as a child. During the Civil War, he was an antislavery supporter and a follower of Charles Fourier, a French social theorist who advocated utopian socialist reform.

69. Rodolphe L. Desdunes, *Nos Hommes et Notre Histoire: Notices Biographiques Accompagnées de Réflexions et de Souvenirs Personnels* (Montreal, Canada: Arbour and Dupont, 1911).

70. *New Orleans Tribune*, January 18, 1868.

71. *New Orleans Tribune*, July 31, 1867.

72. Mitchell, *Raising Freedom's Child*, 190.

73. Mitchell, *Raising Freedom's Child*, 194.

74. Leavens, "*L'Union* and the *New Orleans Tribune*," 56.

75. Mitchell, *Raising Freedom's Child*, 189.

76. In 1865, President Lincoln created the Bureau of Refugees, Freedmen and Abandoned Lands under the authority of the War Department and the leadership of General O. O. Howard. The Freedmen's Bureau was to manage "all abandoned land, and the control of all subjects relating to refugees and freedmen from rebel states . . . under such rules and regulations as may be prescribed by the head of the bureau and approved by the President." Although the bureau's role within education remained unmentioned in the law, a revision that budgeted half a million dollars for the "repair and rental" of school property survived President Andrew Johnson's veto in 1866. Howard agreed that education was the "talisman of power" for the freedmen and eventually spent five million dollars of the bureau's budget on the raw materials for constructing school buildings for the freedmen and for the transportation of northern teachers to the South. Paul A. Cimbala and Randall M. Miller, eds., *The Freedmen's Bureau and Reconstruction: Reconsiderations* (New York: Fordham University Press, 1999), xv, xxvii.

77. Butchart, *Northern Schools, Southern Blacks*, 99.

78. Anderson, *Education of Blacks in the South*, 9–10.

79. Anderson, *Education of Blacks in the South*, 9–10.

80. Ann V. Nugent, "The Attitude of the *New Orleans Tribune* Towards the

Freedmen's Bureau in Louisiana: 1865–1866" (MA thesis, Western Washington State College, 1970), 24.

81. *New Orleans Tribune*, January 30, 1866.

82. *New Orleans Tribune*, December 14, 1865; *New Orleans Tribune*, January 30, 1866.

83. *New Orleans Tribune*, December 28, 1864. Presumably, T. W. C. is Thomas Wharton Collens (1812–1879), New Orleans lawyer, judge, professor, and abolitionist.

84. *New Orleans Tribune*, October 29, 1867.

85. *New Orleans Tribune*, January 30, 1866.

86. *New Orleans Tribune*, February 17, 1865, quoted by McPherson, *The Negro's Civil War*, 289.

87. *New Orleans Tribune*, January 18, 1868.

88. *New Orleans Tribune*, January 22, 1869.

89. The first municipality continued the tradition of predominantly private and Catholic education, as well as segregated (girls and boys) and bilingual education (French and English).

90. *New Orleans Tribune*, March 5, 1865.

91. *New Orleans Tribune*, April 26, 1867.

92. *New Orleans Tribune*, January 18, 1868.

93. *New Orleans Tribune*, January 24, 1869.

94. *New Orleans Tribune*, January 24, 1869.

95. *New Orleans Tribune*, January 10, 1866.

96. Frederick G. Detweiler, *The Negro Press in the United States* (College Park, MD: McGrath, 1968), 268.

97. Charles M. Vincent, "Black Constitution Makers: The Constitution of 1868," in *In Search of Fundamental Law: Louisiana's Constitutions, 1812–1974*, ed. Warren M. Billings and Edward F. Hass (Lafayette: Center for Louisiana Studies, University of Southwestern Louisiana, 1993), 76.

98. Germaine A. Memelo, "The Development of State Laws Concerning the Negro in Louisiana (1864–1900)" (MA thesis, Louisiana State University, 1956), 43.

99. *Official Journal of the Proceedings of the Convention for Framing a Constitution for the State of Louisiana* (New Orleans, 1868), 289, quoted in Vincent, "Black Constitution Makers," 78–79.

100. Denis Serrigny, *Traité du Droit Public des Français Précéde d'une Introduction sur les Fondements des Sociétés Politiques* (Paris: 1846), 287–88, quoted in Rebecca Scott, "Public Rights, Social Equality, and the Conceptual Roots of the *Plessy* Challenge," *Michigan Law Review* 106, no. 5: 777, 785.

101. "Not a Few But All," *New Orleans Tribune*, February 14, 1869.

102. *Official Journal of the Proceedings of the Convention*, 21.

103. *Official Journal of the Proceedings of the Convention*, 21.

104. *Official Journal of the Proceedings of the Convention*, 36.

105. Vincent, "Black Constitution Makers," 130.

106. Mitchell, *Raising Freedom's Child*, 222; Blassingame, *Black New Orleans*, 121.

107. See Donald E. Devore and Joseph Logsdon, *Crescent City Schools: Public Education in New Orleans 1841–1991*. (University of Southwestern Louisiana: The

Center for Louisiana Studies, 1991), 65–76, for a detailed discussion of the successes of integrated public education in New Orleans.

108. Orleans Parish School Board Meeting Minutes, April 4, 1877. Hereafter OPSB Minutes.

109. See Devore and Logsdon, *Crescent City Schools*, 89–91, for a detailed discussion of Rogers's belief in the subordination of women and the lasting impact of sexual segregation on the disruption of schools.

110. This description of his dress comes from a death notice in the *Vicksburg Evening Post*, May 16, 1893, vol XL, no. 116.

111. OPSB Minutes, July 3, 1877.

112. Devore and Logsdon, *Crescent City Schools*, 87.

113. The school board, thinking that Afro-Creoles did not want to go to schools with former slaves and dark-skinned freedmen, had offered to establish a tripartite system of segregation in which Afro-Creoles would have their own school. This was a grotesque misreading of the political vision of Afro-Creoles, who sought the elimination of any kind of caste system in pursuit of full equality of all men.

114. *New Orleans Tribune*, February, 1865.

115. *New Orleans Tribune*, August 20, 1865.

116. *New Orleans Tribune*, May 7, 1867.

117. Roger A. Fischer, "A Pioneer Protest: The New Orleans Street-Car Controversy of 1867," *Journal of Negro History* 53, no. 3 (1968): 219–33.

118. Prior to these three cases, a case had been filed two weeks after the ratification of the Radical state constitution. This case might be considered the first integration case. Alderman Blanc Joubert entered his daughter Cecile into a private school for White girls at the convent of the Sacred Heart in the French Quarter. The school expelled her on the grounds that she was colored. Joubert's lawyer, Alexander P. Fields, a White Unionist politician, charged that as a publicly licensed corporation, the school could not discriminate on the basis of race. The defendants claimed that the three teachers at the school had no legal affiliation with the convent. The Sixth district judge, Guy Duplantier, a native White Republican, accepted the teachers' contention and dismissed the suit. It was not appealed, primarily because under the new constitution and a friendly administration, there was little need for suits between 1870 and 1876. See J. Morgan Kousser, "Before *Plessy*, Before *Brown*: The Development of Racial Integration in Louisiana and Kansas," in *Toward a Usable Past: An Examination of the Origins and Implications of State Protections of Liberty*, ed. Paul Finkleman and Stephen E. Gottlieb (Athens: University of Georgia Press, 1991).

119. See Mishio Yamanaka, "Erasing the Color Line: The Racial Formation of Creoles of Color and the Public School Integration Movement in New Orleans, 1867–1880" (PhD diss., University of North Carolina, 2013), for an excellent accounting of the activism among Afro-Creoles in resisting school segregation.

120. See Mishio Yamanaka, "The Fillmore Boys School in 1877: Racial Integration, Creoles of Color, and the End of Reconstruction in New Orleans," web.unc.edu

121. Blassingame, *Black New Orleans, 1860–1880*, 120.

122. Yamanaka, "Erasing the Color Line," 165.

123. Yamanaka, "Erasing the Color Line," 162.

124. *Trévigne v. Board of Education of Orleans Parish* (unpublished) case #9545, in Orleans Parish Public Library.

125. Mitchell, *Raising Freedom's Child*, 224.

126. *New Orleans Democrat*, Sept. 28, 1877, 4.

127. The three cases were *Josephine Decuir v. John G. Benson*, 27 La. Ann. 1 (1875); *C. S. Sauvinet v. Joseph A. Walker*, 27 La. Ann. 14 (1875); *Washington, Alexandri, & Georgetown Railroad Co. v. Brown*, 17 How. 445 (1873).

128. Kousser, Before *Plessy*, Before *Brown*, 10.

129. Kousser, Before *Plessy*, Before *Brown*, 10.

130. Kousser, Before *Plessy*, Before *Brown*, 10.

131. Bertonneau v. New Orleans, 3 Fed.Cas.294 (1878).

132. Kousser, "Before *Plessy*, Before *Brown*," 11.

133. Bertonneau v. New Orleans, 3 Fed.Cas.296 (1878).

134. Kousser, "Before *Plessy*, Before *Brown*," 11.

135. See Yamanaka for a detailed discussion of the aftermath of "resegregation" on the community and individual activists. Arnold Bertonneau and his family moved uptown and eventually to California in 1901, where they reinvented themselves as White, clearly a tactic used to avoid further denigration and prejudice.

136. See Yamanaka, "Erasing the Color Line," 172–80.

137. See Walter Stern, *Race and Education in New Orleans: Creating the Segregated City, 1764–1960* (Baton Rouge: Louisiana State University Press, 2019).

138. *A History of Saint Louis School of Holy Redeemer Parish formerly known as Catholic Institute for Indigent Orphans founded April 20, 1847*. Sister Mary Eugenius Gallaher, S.H.G. (April 11, 1976). Sisters of the Holy Ghost, AANO.

139. OPSB Minutes, June 22, 1877. As cited in Devore and Logsdon, *Crescent City Schools*, 91.

140. Devore and Logsdon, *Crescent City Schools*, 103.

141. See Jari Honora, "A 'Catholic' Vocation: Médard Hilaire Nelson's Contribution to Education in Post-Reconstruction New Orleans," presented during the "Creoles, Catholics, and the Classrooms: Investigating Black Catholic Education in New Orleans" symposium at the Southern Historical Society (Elizabeth Neidenbach, Chair), New Orleans, LA, Nov., 2021.

142. Steve Luxenberg, *Separate: The Story of Plessy v. Ferguson and America's Journey from Slavery to Segregation* (New York: W. W. Norton & Company, 2019), 449.

143. See Yamanaka, "Erasing the Color Line," 199–200, for a detailed description of the interracial makeup of the *Crusader*.

144. See Carolyn L. Karcher, "Albion W. Tourgée and Louis A. Martinet: The Cross-Racial Friendship behind 'Plessy v. Ferguson,' *Melus* 38, no. 1 (2013): 9–29, for a detailed discussion of the relationship between Tourgée and Martinet.

145. Two of the Blacks named to the board were Oscar Dunn and Aristide Mary. See Shawn Comminey, "The Origin, Organization, and Progression of Straight University, 1869–1880," *Louisiana History: The Journal of the Louisiana Historical Association* 51, no. 4 (2010): 404–41.

146. Amistad Research Center, Tulane University (from now on ARCTU), Dent Family Papers (116), box 7. Joe M. Richardson, "The American Missionary Association and Black Education in Louisiana," 212.

147. Dana Hart, "Toward an Ideal of Moral and Democratic Education: Afro-

Creoles and Straight University in Reconstruction New Orleans, 1862–1896" (PhD diss., Louisiana State University, 2014).

148. See Hilary McLaughlin-Stonham, *From Slavery to Civil Rights: On the Street-cars of New Orleans 1830s–Present* (Liverpool: Liverpool University Press, 2020).

149. See John C. Rodrigue, *Reconstruction in the Cane Fields* (Baton Rouge: Louisiana State University, 2001), and Rebecca J. Scott, *Degrees of Freedom: Louisiana and Cuba after Slavery* (Cambridge, MA: Harvard University Press, 2005), for a detailed discussion of the suppression of an integrated labor force.

150. Luxenberg, *Separate*, 392.

151. *The Crusader*, July 4, 1891.

152. Luxenberg, *Separate*, 393.

153. Luxenberg, *Separate*, 393.

154. Luxenberg, *Separate*, 393.

155. Keith Weldon Medley, *We as Freemen: Plessy v. Ferguson* (Gretna, LA: Pelican Publishing Company, 2003).

156. "Travel in the South, for Colored People Is Getting to Be More and More Intolerable," *Southwestern Christian Advocate*, New Orleans, November 19, 1891.

157. "Report on the proceedings for the Annulment of Act 111 of 1890" (box 1, folder 13), Charles B. Roussève Collection (from now on CRC), ARCTU.

158. Fatima Shaik, *Economy Hall: The Hidden History of a Free Black Brotherhood* (New Orleans: Historic New Orleans Collection, 2021).

159. Luxenberg, *Separate*, 336.

160. While he recommended this plan of action to President Garfield, Garfield was reluctant to expand federal authority and the plan was never put forward.

161. Luxenberg, *Separate*, 408.

162. See Carolyn Karcher, "The White 'Bystander' and the Black Journalist 'Abroad': Albion W. Tourgée and Ida B. Wells as Allies against Lynching," *Prospect* 29 (October, 2005): 5–19, https://doi.org/10.1017/S0361233300001708. And for a more detailed discussion of Ida. B. Wells's antilynching campaign, see Margaret Smith Crocco, Petra Munro, and Kathleen Weiler, *Pedagogies of Resistance: Women Educator Activists 1880–1960* (New York: Teachers College Press, 1999).

163. Carolyn L. Karcher, "The National Citizen's Rights Association: Precursor to the NAACP," *Elon Law Review* 2 (July 2013): 107–69. \\jciprod01\productn\E\ELO\5-1\ELO107.txt

164. See Karcher, "National Citizen's Rights Association," for a much more detailed discussion of the NCRA's role in the civil rights movement and historians' neglect in written accounts of this movement as an interracial, national organization.

165. See Hart, *Toward the Ideal of Moral and Democratic Education*.

166. Historians like James M. McPherson, *The Abolitionist Legacy: From Reconstruction to the NAACP* (Princeton, NJ: Princeton University Press, 1975), give the NCRA only a passing mention.

167. See Medley, *We as Freemen*, 125, and Thomas J. Davis, *Plessy v. Ferguson* (Santa Barbara, CA: Greenwood Press, 2012): 152–53, for detailed discussion of the positionality/identity politics of Afro-Creoles.

168. This case had been organized by the Pullman Palace Company of Chicago,

in which a Pullman conductor refused to eject an African American from a lone sleeping car as it traveled through Louisiana. The company argued that they had done nothing wrong since the Separate Car Act was limited to travel within the state and this passenger was traveling from Louisiana to Texas.

169. "History of the Catholic Institute Indigent Orphan Institute" (box 1, folder 20), CRC, ARCTU.

170. Devore and Logsdon, *Crescent City Schools*, 105–12.

171. Devore and Logsdon, *Crescent City Schools*, 15.

172. He also belonged to the Société des Franc Amis (Society of French Friends), Cosmopolitan Mutual Aid Society, Scottish Rites Mason, L'Union Louisianais, Young Friends of Charity B.M.A.A., the baseball club, and the gymnastics club. See Medley, *We as Freemen*, chapter 1, for a detailed biography of Homer Plessy.

173. Medley, *We as Freemen*, 162.

174. Davis, *Plessy v. Ferguson*, 159.

175. CRP. "Forlorn Hope and Noble Despair" (box 2, folder 1, Saturday, August 15, 1891), ARCTU.

176. "Mother Katherine Drexel and the Color Line," *Daily Crusader*, February 28, 1895, Desdunes Collection, Xavier University Archives.

177. James B. Bennett, *Religion and the Rise of Jim Crow in New Orleans* (Princeton, NJ: Princeton University Press, 2015).

178. This concept is central to Critical Race Theory; see Derrick Bell, *Race and Racism in American Law* (New York: Aspen Law and Business, 1992); Kimberly Crenshaw, "Race, Reform and Retrenchment: Transformation and Legitimation in Antidiscrimination Law," *Harvard Law Review* 101, no. 7 (1988): 1331–87; Gloria Ladson-Billings, *Critical Race Theory in Education: A Scholar's Journey* (New York: Teachers College Press, 2021).

179. Luxenberg, *Separate*, 468.

180. Fatima Shaik, *Economy Hall*, 145.

181. Davis, *Plessy v. Ferguson*, 169.

182. Shaik, *Economy Hall*, 196–97.

183. Shaik, *Economy Hall*, 478.

184. Davis, *Plessy v. Ferguson*, 167–68.

185. Davis, *Plessy v. Ferguson*, 170.

186. Luxenberg, *Separate*, 484.

187. Luxenberg, *Separate*, 486.

188. Davis, *Plessy v. Ferguson*, 171.

189. Thompson, *Exiles at Home*, 272–73.

190. Desdunes, *Our People*, 147.

191. Greater New Orleans Louis A. Martinet Legal Society Records, ARCTU.

192. Luxenberg, *Separate*, 493.

193. See Ladson-Billings, *Critical Race Theory in Education*, chapter 6, for a detailed analysis of the *Brown* case.

194. For a detailed discussion of the ongoing segregation of schools, see Jonathon Kozol, *Savage Inequalities: Children in America's Schools* (New York: Harper Perennial, 1991); Adam Fairclough, *Race and Democracy: The Civil Rights Struggle in Louisiana 1915–1972* (Athens: University of Georgia Press, 1995); Carl L. Bankston

III and Stephen J. Caldas, *A Troubled Dream: The Promise and Failure of School Desegregation in Louisiana* (Nashville, TN: Vanderbilt University Press, 2002).

195. McKenna, "About Us," *New Orleans Tribune* http://www.theneworleansTribune.com/main/about-us.

196. McKenna, "Our Team," *New Orleans Tribune*, http://www.theneworleansTribune.com/main/our-team.

197. Henry Louis Gates Jr., foreword to *African-American Newspapers and Periodicals: A National Bibliography*, by James P. Danky and Maureen E. Hady (Cambridge, MA: Harvard University Press, 1998), x.

198. Margaret Beetham, "Towards a Theory of the Periodical as Publishing Genre," in *Investigating Victorian Journalism*, ed. Laurel Brake, Aled Jones, and Lionel Madden (Basingstoke, UK: MacMillan, 1990), 21.

199. Margaret Beetham, *A Magazine of Her Own? Domesticity and Desire in the Woman's Magazine, 1800–1914* (New York: Routledge, 1996), 13–14.

200. Lyn Pykett, "Reading the Periodical Press: Text and Context," *Victorian Periodicals Review* 22, no. 3 (1989): 102.

201. Jonathan Kozol, *The Shame of the Nation: The Restoration of Apartheid Schooling in America* (New York: Three Rivers Press, 2005).

202. Henry Lewis Suggs, preface and introduction to *The Black Press in the South, 1865–1979*, ed. Henry Lewis Suggs (Westport, CT: Greenwood, 1983), x–xi.

Epilogue

1. Iris Marion Young, *Inclusion and Democracy* (Oxford: Oxford University Press, 2002).

2. Daniel Trohler, *The Languages of Education: Protestant Legacies, National Identities, and Global Aspirations* (New York: Routledge, 2011).

Bibliography

Manuscript Primary Sources

Archives of the Archdiocese of New Orleans, New Orleans, LA
    Archives of St. Augustine's Church, 1841–1899
    Catholic Directories
    Records of l'Institution Catholique des Orphelins Indigents
    Roger Baudier Historical Collection
    United States Catholic Almanacs
Archives de Colonies, Archives Nationales de France, Paris, France
    Series, B43, C1, C2, C13A, D2, D10, F5A
Archives du Calvados, Caen, France
    Ursuline Collection
Amistad Research Center, Tulane University, New Orleans, LA
    Dent Family Papers (MSS 116)
    Charles B. Roussève Collection
Archives of the Sisters of the Holy Family, New Orleans, LA
    Account Books
    Journal of Sister Mary Bernard Deggs
Cammie Henry Archives, Northwestern University, Nachitoches, LA
    DeBlieux Collection
    Melrose Collection
City Archives, New Orleans Public Library, New Orleans, LA
    New Orleans City Directories, 1811, 1823, 1832, and 1842
    New Orleans Annual and Commercial Register, 1846
Hill Memorial Library, Louisiana State University, Baton Rouge, LA
    John Christian Buhler and Family Papers (MSS 1192)
    Turnbull-Allain Family Papers (MSS 4261)
    Samuel A. Cartwright and Family Papers, 1826–1864

Historic New Orleans Collection, New Orleans, LA
   Archive of the Germania Lodge No. 46, 1844–1973
   Archive of the Ursuline Nuns of the Parish of New Orleans
   Deutsches Haus Archive (MSS 609)
   Etoile Polaire Lodge No.1 Masonic Records
   J. Hanno Deiler Papers, (MSS 395)
Howard-Tilton Memorial Library, Tulane University, New Orleans, LA
   Freemason Lodges in Louisiana, 1807–1995, Louisiana Research Manuscripts
      Collection, 895
   Lambert Family Papers, 1798–1862
Louisiana and Special Collections Department, Earl K. Long Library, University
   of New Orleans, New Orleans, LA
   Marcus Christian Collection (MSS 011)
   Orleans Parish School Board Collection (MSS 147)
Loyola University Archives, New Orleans, LA
   Jesuit documents from the National Archives, Paris, France
Ursuline Convent Archives, Caen, France
   Convent Letters
   Convent Obituaries
University of Virginia Archives, Charlottesville, VA
   Thomas Jefferson Papers

Published Primary Sources

Newspapers

Courrier de la Louisiane (New Orleans, LA)
Daily Crusader (New Orleans, LA)
Die Deutsche Zeitung (New Orleans, LA)
Lafayette City Adviser (Lafayette, LA)
Louisiana Courier (New Orleans, LA)
Louisiana Gazette (New Orleans, LA)
L'Union (New Orleans, LA)
New Orleans Democrat (New Orleans, LA)
New Orleans Tribune (New Orleans, LA)
Southwestern Christian Advocate (New Orleans, LA)
Vicksburg Evening Post (Vicksburg, MS)

Books and Pamphlets

Acts Passed at the First Session of the Fifteenth Legislature of the State of Louisiana, 1841, An Act to Authorize the Municipalities of the City of New Orleans to Establish Public Schools therein. New Orleans: A.C. Bullitt, State Printer, 1841.
"Address from the Free People of Color." January 1804, in Clarence Edwin Carter, ed., *The Territorial Papers of the United States*, volume IX, Washington, DC: Government Printing Offices, 1940.

Baudier, Roger. *The Catholic Church in Louisiana*. New Orleans, LA: Hyatt, 1939.

Biever, Albert Huber. *The Jesuits in New Orleans and the Mississippi Valley*. New Orleans, 1924.

Boatner, Charlotte H. "Certain Unpublished Letters from French Scientists of the Revolutionary Period Taken from the Files of Joseph Lakanal." *Osiris: Studies on the History and Philosophy of Science, and on the History of Learning and Culture*, I. Bruges, Belgium: The Saint Catherine Press, 1936.

Bouchereau, Madeleine G. S. *Education des Femmes en Haiti*. Port-au-Prince: Imprimerie de L'Etat, 1944.

Carroll, M. A. "Education in New Orleans in Spanish Colonial Days." *American Catholic Quarterly Review* XII, no. 46 (1887).

Cartwright, Samuel. "On the Caucasians and the Africans." In *Cotton Is King and Pro-Slavery Arguments*, edited by E. Elliott. Augusta, GA: Pritchard, Abbott & Loomis, 1860.

Claiborne, W. C. C. *Official Letter Books, 1801–1816*, Vol 1. Edited by Dunbar Rowland. Jackson, MI: State Department of Archives and History.

Clark, Robert T. "The German Liberals in New Orleans (1840–1860)." *The Louisiana Historical Quarterly* 20 (1937).

Cubberly, Ellwood P. *Public Education in the United States*. Boston: Houghton Mifflin Company, 1919.

Crombach, Herman. *The Life and Martyrdom of St. Ursula and the Society of Eleven Thousand Virgins*, 1647.

Crozat, Heloise. "The Ursulines of Louisiana." *Louisiana Historical Quarterly* 2, no. 1 (1919).

Dart, Henry P. "Public Education in New Orleans in 1800." *Louisiana Historical Quarterly* 11, no. 2 (1928).

Dawson, John Charles. *Lakanal the Regicide: A Biographical and Historical Study of the Career of Joseph Lakanal*. University of Alabama Press, 1948.

Debien, Gabriel. "Une maison d'education a Saint-Domingue: les religieuses du Cap, 1731–1802." *Revue d'histoire de l'Amérique française* 2, no. 4 (1949).

de Barry, Paul. *Devotion to the Glorious St. Ursula, the Most Loved Mother of the Ursulines*, 1645.

Deiler, J. Hanno. "Germany's Contribution to the Present Population of New Orleans with a Census of German Schools." *Louisiana Journal of Education* (May 1886).

Deiler, J. Hanno. *Geschichte der New Orleanser Deutschen Presse*. Translated by William Black. New Orleans: Paul J. Sendker, 1901.

Deiler, J. Hanno. *A History of the German Churches in Louisiana (1823–1893)*. Translated by Marie Stella Condon. Lafeyette: Center for Louisiana Studies, University of Southwestern Louisiana, 2014.

Deiler, J. Hanno. "The System of Redemption in the State of Louisiana." Translated by Louis Voss. *Louisiana Historical Quarterly* 12, no. 3 (July 1920): 446.

Deiler, J. Hanno. *Zur Geschichte die Deutschen Kirchengemeinden im Staate Louisiana*. Inktank Publishing, 2018.

Delanglez, Jean. *The French Jesuits in Lower Louisiana 1700–1763*. New York: AMS Press, 1935.

Delanglez, Jean. *The French Jesuits in Lower Louisiana 1700–1763*. Washington, DC: Catholic University of America, 1935.

de La Salle, M. Cavelier. "Memoir of M. Cavelier de la Salle." In *On the Discovery of the Mississippi*, edited by Thomas Falconer (London, 1844, translation of the 1680s original).

de Pommereu, Marie-Augustine. *Les Chroniques de L'Ordre des Ursulines recuielles pour l'usage des religieuses du même ordre*. 1 ère et 2nde parties. Paris: J. Henault, 1673.

de Saint-Jean Martin, M. Marie. *L'Éducation des Ursulines*. Rome: Maison Généralice De L'Union Des Ursulines, 1944.

Descartes, Renée. *Discourse on the Method*, 1637. New York: Macmillan, 1986.

Desdunes, Rodolphe L. *Nos Hommes et Notre Histoire: Notices Biographiques Accompagnées de Réflexions et de Souvenirs Personnels*. Montreal: Arbour and Dupont, 1911.

de St. Augustin, Marie Tranchepain. *Relation du Voyage Des premières Ursulines à la Nouvelle Orleáns et de leur éstalissment en cette ville*. New York, 1859.

Dorsainvil, J. C. *Manuel d'Histoire d'Haiti*. Port-au-Prince, privately printed, 1934.

Dumas, Malone. *Correspondence between Thomas Jefferson and Pierre Samuel DuPont de Nemours, 1798–1817*. New York: Houghton Mifflin Company, 1930.

Durkheim, Emile. *The Elementary Forms of Religious Life*. Translated by K. Fields. New York: The Free Press, 1912/1995.

Du Ru, Paul. *Journal of Paul Du Ru: Missionary Priest to Louisiana*. Edited by Ruth Lapham Butler. Chicago: Caxton Club, 1934.

Erasmus, Desiderius. *In Praise of Folly*. New York: Hendricks, 1959.

Farell, Allan P. *The Jesuit Code of Liberal Education: Development and Scope of the Ratio Studiorum*. Milwaukee: Bruce, 1938.

Fay, Edwin Whitfield. *The History of Education in Louisiana*. Washington, DC: Government Printing Office, 1898.

Fortier, Alcée. "French Literature of Louisiana." *Transactions and Procedures of the Modern Language Association of American* 2 (1886): 31–60.

Fortier, Alcée. *Louisiana Studies: Literature, Customs and Dialects, History and Education, Vol. 1*. New Orleans, 1894.

Gayarré, Charles. *Fernando Lemos, Truth and Fiction. A Novel*. New York: G.W. Carleton, 1872.

Gayarré, Charles. *Historie de la Louisiane*. New Orleans: Imprimé par Magne & Weisse, 1846.

Hamilton, Thomas. *Men and Manners in America*. Philadelphia: Carey, Lea and Blanchard, 1833.

Hart, Mother Mary Francis Borgia. *Violets in the King's Garden: A History of the Sisters of the Holy Family of New Orleans*. Original manuscript,1931.

Houzeau, Jean-Charles. *Études sur les facultés mentales des animaux comparées à celles de l'homme*. Mons, 1872.

Houzeau, Jean-Charles. *My Passage at the* New Orleans Tribune: *A Memoir of the Civil War Era.* Translated by Gerard F. Denault. Baton Rouge: Louisiana State University Press, 1984.

Hugue-Quarr', Jean. *La Vie de la B. Mère Angèle de Bresse*, 1648. In *La Gloire de S. Ursule.* Valenciennes: L'Impr: De L. Boucher, 1656.

Hugue-Quarr', Jean. *The Life of Blessed Angela Merici.* 1648.

Jefferson, Thomas. *Notes on the State of Virginia.* Edited by Frank Shuffleton. New York: Penguin Books, 1999 [originally published in 1785].

Lanusse, Armand, ed. *Les Cenelles: A Collection of Poems by Creole Writers of the Early Nineteenth Century.* Translated and with a preface by Règine Latortue and Gleason R. W. Adams, xxxvii. Boston: G. K. Hall & Co., 1845.

La Règle de Saint Augustin et Constitutions pour les religieuses de Sainte-Ursule, 1643 (Bibliothèque National). De la Fin Principale de l'institut des Religieuses de Saint Ursula.

Le Moyne, Pierre. Sieur d'Iberville. *Iberville's Gulf Journals.* Edited by Richebourg Gaillard McWilliams. Translation of 1700 journal. Tuscaloosa: University of Alabama Press 1991.

Lettres de la vénérable Mère Marie de l'Incarnation, première supérieure des Ursulines de la Nouvelle-France: divisées en deux parties, ed. Claude Martin. Paris, 1681.

Martin, Claude. *La Vie de la vénérable Mère Marie de l'Incarnation, Première supérieure des Ursulines de la Nouvelle France: Tirée de ses Lettres et de ses Ecrits* Paris: Louis Billaine, 1677. Facsimile editions Solesmes: Abbaye de Saint-Pierre, 1981.

Martin, M. Marie De Saint-Jean. *L'Éducation des Ursulines.* Rome: Maison Généralice De L'Union Des Ursulines, 1944.

Martineau, Harriet. *Retrospect of Western Travel.* London: Saunders and Otley, 1838.

McCutcheon, Roger P. *Louisiana Historical Quarterly* "Libraries in New Orleans, 1771–1833." XX (1937): 152–58.

The Metropolitan Catholic Almanac and Laity's Directory for the Year of our Lord 1840. Baltimore: Fielding Lucas Jr.

Minogue, Anna C. *Loretto Annals of the Century.* New York: The America Press, 1912.

Mobley, James William. "The Academy Movement." *Louisiana Historical Quarterly*, no. 3 (1947): 2–21.

Monica, Sister M. *Angela Merici and Her Teaching Idea (1474–1540).* New York: Longmans, Green and Co., 1927.

Noble, Stuart Grayson. "Governor Claiborne and the Public School System of the Territorial Government of Louisiana." *Louisiana Historical Quarterly* 11 (1928): 535–52.

Noble, Stuart G. and Arthur G. Nuhrah. "Education in Colonial Louisiana." *Louisiana Historical Quarterly* 32 (1949): 762–63.

Pitot, James. *Observations of the Colony of Louisiana from 1796 to 1802.* Translated by Henry C. Pitot. Paris, 1802.

Postel, Guillaume. *De orbis terrae concordia* (Concerning the Agreement [in Doctrines] of the World). In Latin, 1544.

Reglements des religieuses de la congregation de Paris, divises en trios livres. Paris, 1751.

Riley, Martin L. "The Development of Education in Louisiana Prior to Statehood" *Louisiana Historical Quarterly* XIX, no. 3. (1936): 595–634.

Roussève, Charles. *The Negro in Louisiana.* New Orleans: The Xavier University Press, 1937.

Saint Jean Marti, Marie de, *Ursuline Method of Education.* Rathway: Quinn & Boden Company, 1946.

Saxon, Lyle. *Fabulous New Orleans.* Gretna, LA: Pelican Publishing Company. 1988. Originally published in 1928.

Schlarman, J. H. *From Quebec to New Orleans: The Story of the French in America.* Belleville, IL: Buechler Publishing Co., 1929.

Serrigny, Denis. *Traité du Droit Public des Français Précéde d'une Introduction sur les Fondements des Sociétés Politiques.* Paris, 1846.

Stern, Laurence. *The Works of Laurence Stern.* Philadelphia, 1843.

Thwaites, R. G., ed. *The* Jesuit Relations *and Allied Documents: Travels and Explorations of the Jesuit Missionaries in New France 1610–1791*, 73 vols. Cleveland: The Burrows Brothers, 1896.

von Humboldt, Alexander. *Cosmos: A Sketch of a Physical Description of the Universe.* Translated by E. C. Otté. New York, 1850.

Voss, Louis. *History of the German Society of New Orleans.* New Orleans: Published by the German Society on the Occasion of its Eightieth Anniversary, 1927.

Watrin, Francois Philibert. "Banishment of the Jesuits from Louisiana." *The Jesuit Relations* and Allied Documents (Paris, Sept. 3, 1764), (Cleveland, 1900): LXX, 265.

Watson, Charles S. "A Denunciation on the State of Spanish Rule: James Workman's Liberty in Louisiana." *Louisiana History: The Journal of the Louisiana Historical Association* 11, no. 3 (1904): 245–58.

Weber, Max. *The Protestant Ethic and the Spirit of Capitalism.* New York: Charles Scribner's Sons, 1904.

Wilson, Samuel, Jr. "An Architectural History of the Royal Hospital and the Ursuline Convent of New Orleans." *The Louisiana Historical Quarterly* 29, no. 3. (1946): 559–650.

Workman, James. *Essays and Letters on Various Political Subjects.* New York: I. Riley, 1809.

Secondary Sources

Books, Articles, and Chapters in Edited Collections

Abbott, Richard H. *For Free Press and Equal Rights: Republican Newspapers in the Reconstruction South.* Athens: University of Georgia Press, 2004.

Allain, Mathé. "Slave Policies in French Louisiana." *Louisiana History* 21 (1980): 127–38.

Anderson, Benedict. *Imagined Communities.* London: Verso, 1983.

Anderson, James D. *The Education of Blacks in the South, 1860–1935.* Chapel Hill: University of North Carolina Press, 1988.

Aubert, Guillaume. "'The Blood of France': Race and Purity of Blood in the French Atlantic World." *William and Mary Quarterly* (Third Series) 61, no. 3 (2004): 439–78.

Aubert, Guillaume. "'To Establish One Law and Definite Rules': Race, Religion, and the Origin of the Louisiana Code Noir." In *Louisiana: Crossroads of the Atlantic World*, edited by Cécile Vidal. Philadelphia: University of Pennsylvania Press, 2014.

Bacon, Jacqueline. *The First African-American Newspaper: Freedom's Journal.* New York: Lexington, 2007.

Bailyn, Bernard. *Atlantic History: Concept and Contours.* Cambridge, MA: Harvard University Press, 2005.

Bailyn, Bernard. *Education in the Forming of American Society.* Chapel Hill: University of North Carolina Press, 1960.

Baker, Bernadette. *In Perpetual Motion.* New York: Peter Lang, 2001.

Bankston Carl L., III, and Stephen J. Caldas. *A Troubled Dream: The Promise and Failure of School Desegregation in Louisiana.* Nashville, TN: Vanderbilt University Press, 2002.

Baron, Robert, and Ana C. Cara. "Introduction: Creolization as Cultural Creativity." In *Creolization as Cultural Creativity*, edited by Robert and Ana C. Cara Baron. Jackson: University of Mississippi Press, 2011.

Baudier, R. *Through Portals of the Past: A Story of the Old Ursuline Convent in New Orleans.* New Orleans: Catholic Archdiocese Archives, 1955.

Beetham, Margaret. *A Magazine of Her Own? Domesticity and Desire in the Woman's Magazine, 1800–1914.* New York: Routledge, 1996.

Beetham, Margaret. *Towards a Theory of the Periodical as Publishing Genre, in Investigating Victorian Journalism.* Edited by Laurel Brake, Aled Jones, and Lionel Madden. Basingstoke, UK: MacMillan, 1990.

Bell, Caryn Cossé. "French Religious Culture in Afro-Creole New Orleans, 1718–1877." *U.S. Catholic Historian* 17, no. 2 (1999): 1–16.

Bell, Caryn Cossé. *Revolution, Romanticism, and the Afro-Creole Protest Tradition in Louisiana, 1718–1868.* Baton Rouge: Louisiana State University Press, 1997.

Bell, Derrick. *Race and Racism in American Law.* New York: Aspen Law and Business, 1992.

Belmessous, Saliha. *Assimilation and Empire, Uniformity in French and British Colonies, 1541–1954.* Oxford: Oxford University Press, 2013.

Bennett, James B. *Religion and the Rise of Jim Crow in New Orleans.* Princeton, NJ: Princeton University Press, 2015.

Bergin, Joseph. *Church, Society and Religious Change in France 1580–1730.* New Haven, CT: Yale University Press, 2009.

Berlin, Ira. *Slaves without Masters: The Free Negro in the Antebellum South.* New York: Pantheon, 1974.

Bernard, H. C. *Girls at School Under the Ancien Regime*. London: Burnes and Oates, 1954.

Berry, Jason. "African Cultural Memory in New Orleans Music." *Black Music Research Journal* 8, no. 1 (1988): 3–12.

Bilodeau, Christopher. "'They honor our lord among themselves in their own way': Colonial Christianity and the Illinois Indians." *American Indian Quarterly* 25, no. 3 (2001): 352–77.

Blackburn, Carole. *Harvest of Souls: The Jesuit Missions and Colonialism in North America 1632–1650*. Montreal: McGill-Queen's University Press, 2000.

Blassingame, John. *Black New Orleans 1860–1880*. Chicago: The University of Chicago Press, 1973.

Boelhower, William. *Atlantic Studies: Perspectives and Challenges*. Baton Rouge: Louisiana State University Press, 2019.

Bolster, W. Jeffrey. *Black Jacks: African American Seaman in the Age of Sail*. Cambridge, MA: Harvard University Press, 1997.

Boucher, Philip P. *France and the American Tropics to 1700: Tropics of Discontent*. Baltimore: John Hopkins University Press, 2008.

Brasseaux, Carl A. "The Administration of Slave Regulations in French Louisiana, 1724–1766," *Louisiana History: The Journal of Louisiana History Association* 21, no. 2 (Spring 1980): 139–52.

Brasseaux, Carl, and Glenn R. Conrad, eds. *The Road to Louisiana: The Saint-Domingue Refugees 1792–1809*. Lafayette: University of Louisiana at Lafayette Press, 1992.

Brasseaux, Carl A., Keith P. Fontenot, and Claude F. Oubre. *Creoles of Color in the Bayou Country*. Jackson: University of Mississippi Press, 1994.

Brett, Edward T. *The New Orleans Sisters of the Holy Family: African American Missionaries to the Garifuna of Belize*. Notre Dame: University of Notre Dame Press, 2012.

Brooks, Joanna "The Early American Public Sphere and the Emergence of a Black Print Counterpublic." *William and Mary Quarterly* 62, no. 1 (Jan. 2005): 67–92.

Brooks, Lisa. *The Common Pot: The Recovery of Native Space in the Northeast*. Minneapolis: University of Minnesota Press, 2008.

Brown, Ian W. "The Calumet Ceremony in the Southeast and its Archaeological Manifestations." *American Antiquity* 54, no. 2 (1989): 311–31.

Brown, William. "Mask of the Colonizer: French Men, Native Passions, and the Culture of Diplomacy in New France." In *French Connections: Cultural Mobility in North America and the Atlantic World, 1600–1875*, edited by Robert Englebert and Andrew N. Wegmann. Baton Rouge: Louisiana State University Press, 2020.

Bruce, Clint. *Afro-Creole Poetry in French from Louisiana's Radical Civil War-Era Newspapers*. New Orleans: The Historic New Orleans Collection, 2020.

Bruneau, Marie-Florine. *Women Mystics Confront the Modern World*. New York: State University of New York Press, 1998.

Brunelle, Gayle K. *The New World Merchants of Rouen 1559–1630*. Kirksville, MO: Sixteenth Century Journal Publishers, 1991.

Bruner, Jerome. *The Culture of Education*. Boston: Harvard University Press, 1997.

Buck-Morss, Susan. *Hegel, Haiti and Universal History*. Pittsburgh, PA: University of Pittsburgh Press, 2009.

Bullock, Penelope. *The Afro-American Periodical Press, 1838–1909*. Baton Rouge: Louisiana State University Press, 1981.

Bullock, Stephen. *Revolutionary Brotherhood: Freemasonry and the Transformation of the American Social Order, 1730–1840*. Chapel Hill: University of North Carolina Press, 1996.

Butchart, Ronald E. *Northern Schools, Southern Blacks, and Reconstruction: Freedmen's Education, 1862–1875*. Westport, CT: Greenwood, 1980.

Cable, George Washington. *The Grandissimes: A Story of Creole Life*. New York: Sagamore Press, 1957. Originally published in 1880.

Campanella, Richard. *Bienville's Dilemma: A Historical Geography of New Orleans*. Lafayette: Center for Louisiana Studies, University of Louisiana at Lafayette, 2008.

Campanella, Richard. *Bourbon Street: A History*. Baton Rouge: Louisiana State University Press, 2014.

Carson, James Taylor. "Sacred Circles and Dangerous People: Native American Cosmology and the French Settlement of Louisiana." In *French Colonial Louisiana and the Atlantic World*, edited by Bradley Bond, 65–82, 78, Baton Rouge: Louisiana State University Press, 2005.

Carter, Karen E. *Creating Catholics: Catechism and Primary Education in Early Modern France*. Notre Dame: University of Notre Dame Press, 2011.

Casemore, Brian. *The Autobiographical Demand of Place: Curriculum Inquiry in the South*. New York: Peter Lang, 2008.

Cave, Alfred A. "New England Misperceptions of Native American Shamanism." *International Social Science Review* 67, no. 1 (1992): 15–27.

Chambers, Cynthia, Erika Hasebe-Ludt, Dwayne Donald, Wanda Hurren, Carl Leggo, and Antoinette Oberg. "Métissage: A Research Praxis." In *Handbook of the Arts in Qualitative Research: Perspectives, Methodologies, Examples, and Issues*, edited by J. Gary Knowles and Ardra L. Cole. Thousand Oaks, CA: Sage.

Choquette, Leslie. "'Ces Amazones du Grand Dieu': Women and Mission in Seventeenth-Century Canada." *French Historical Studies* 17, no. 3 (1992): 627–55.

Choudhury, M. "Despotic Habits: The Critique of Power and its Abuses in an Eighteenth-Century Convent." *French Historical Studies* 23, no. 1 (2000): 33–65.

Cimbala, Paul A., and Randall M. Miller, eds. *The Freedmen's Bureau and Reconstruction: Reconsiderations*. New York: Fordham University Press, 1999.

Clancy, Thomas H. "The Antebellum Jesuits of the New Orleans Province, 1837–1861." *Louisiana History: The Journal of the Louisiana Historical Association* 34, no. 3 (1993): 327–43.

Clark, Emily. "'By All the Conduct of Their Lives': A Laywomen's Confraternity in New Orleans, 1730–1744." *William and Mary Quarterly*, 3d Series, LIV, no. 4 (October 1997): 769–94.

Clark, Emily. *Masterless Mistresses: The New Orleans Ursulines and the Development of a New World Society, 1727–1834*. Chapel Hill: University of North Carolina Press, 2007.

Clark, Emily. "Patrimony without Pater: The New Orleans Ursuline Community and the Creation of Material Culture." In *French Colonial Louisiana and the Atlantic World*. Edited by Bradley G. Bond, 95–109. Baton Rouge: Louisiana State University Press, 2005.

Clark, Emily. *The Strange History of the American Quadroon: Free Women of Color in the Revolutionary Atlantic World*. Chapel Hill: University of North Carolina Press, 2013.

Clark, Emily. *Voices from an Early American Convent*. Baton Rouge: Louisiana State University Press, 2007.

Clark, Emily, and Virginia Meacham Gould. "The Feminine Face of Afro-Catholicism in New Orleans, 1727–1852." *William and Mary Quarterly* 59 (Apr. 2002): 409–48.

Clark, Robert T. "The German Liberals in New Orleans (1840–1860)." *Louisiana Historical Quarterly* 20 (1937).

Clément, Job B. "History of Education in Haiti: 1804–1915." *Revista de Historia de América* 87 (1979): 141–81.

Clement, Priscilla F. "Children and Charity: Orphanages in New Orleans 1817–1914." *Louisiana History: The Journal of the Louisiana Historical Society* 27, no. 4 (1986): 337–51.

Clossey, Luke. "Faith in Empire: Religious Sources of Legitimacy for Expansionist Early-Modern States." in *Politics and Reformations: Communities, Polities, Nations and Empires*, edited by by Christopher Ocker, Michael Printy, Peter Starenko, and Peter Wallace. Leiden: Brill, 2007.

Clossey, Luke. *Salvation and Globalization in the Early Jesuit Missions*. New York: Cambridge University Press, 2008.

Comminey, Shawn. "The Origin, Organization, and Progression of Straight University, 1869–1880." *Louisiana History: The Journal of the Louisiana Historical Association* 51, no. 4 (2010): 404–41.

Common Routes: St. Domingue-Louisiana. New Orleans: The Historic New Orleans Collection, 2006.

Connor, William P. "Reconstruction Rebels: The *New Orleans Tribune* in Post-War Louisiana." In *Reconstructing Louisiana*, The Louisiana Purchase Bicentennial Series in Louisiana History. Lafayette, LA: University of Louisiana at Lafayette, 2001.

Conrad, Glenn R. *The First Families of Louisiana, Volume II*. Baton Rouge, LA: Claitor's Publishing Division, 1970.

Cook, Bernard A. *Founded on Faith: A History of Loyola University New Orleans*. New Orleans: Loyola University, 2012.

Cooper, Afua. "Unsilencing the Past: Memorializing Four Hundred Years of African Canadian History." In *Multiple Lenses: Voices from the Diaspora Located in Canada*, edited by David Divine, 11–22. Newcastle upon Tyne: Cambridge Scholars, 2007.

Cooper, Frederick, and Ann Laura Stoler, eds. *Tensions of Empire: Colonial Cultures in a Bourgeois World*. Berkeley: University of California Press, 1997.

Cormack, Margaret. *Saints and Their Cults in the Atlantic World*. Columbia: University of South Carolina Press, 2007.

Cornelius, Janet. "We Slipped and Learned to Read: Slave Accounts of the Literacy Process, 1830–1865." *Phylon* 44, no. 3 (1983): 171–86.

Cornelius, Janet. *When I Can Read My Title Clear: Literacy, Slavery and Religion in the Antebellum South*. Columbia: University of South Carolina Press, 1991.

Cott, Nancy. *The Bonds of Womanhood: "Woman's Sphere" in New England, 1780–1835*. New Haven, CT: Yale University Press, 1977.

Cowan, Mairi. "Education, Francisation, and Shifting Colonial Priorities at the Ursuline Convent in Seventeenth-Century Quebec." *Canadian Historical Review* 99, no. 1 (2018): 1–29.

Cremin, Lawrence. *The Transformation of the American School*. New York: Alfred A. Knopf, 1961.

Crenshaw, Kimberly. "Race, Reform and Retrenchment: Transformation and Legitimation in Antidiscrimination Law." *Harvard Law Review* 101, no. 7 (1988): 1331–87.

Crocco, Margaret Smith, Petra Munro, and Kathleen Weiler. *Pedagogies of Resistance: Women Educator Activists 1880–1960*. New York: Teachers College Press, 1999.

Cushner, Nicholas P. *Why Have You Come Here? The Jesuits and the First Evangelization of Native America*. Oxford: Oxford University Press, 2006.

Davis, Brent. *Inventions of Teaching*. New York: Routledge, 2004.

Davis, Cyprian. *Henriette Delille: Servant of Slaves, Witness to the Poor*. New Orleans: Archdiocese of New Orleans, 2004.

Davis, Cyprian. "Henriette Delille: Servant of Slaves, Witness to the Poor." In *Uncommon Faithfulness: The Black Catholic Experience*, edited by Mary Shawn Copeland, LaReine-Marie Mosely, and Albert J. Reboteau, 47–62. Maryknoll, NY: Orbis Books.

Davis, Cyprian. *The History of Black Catholics in the United States*. New York: Crossroad, 1990.

Davis, Natalie Zemon. *Society and Culture in Early Modern France: Eight Essays*. Stanford, CA: Stanford University Press, 1975.

Davis, Natalie Zemon. *Women on the Margins: Three Seventeenth-Century Lives*. Cambridge, MA: Harvard University Press, 1995.

Davis, Thomas J. Davis. *Plessy v. Ferguson*. Santa Barbara, CA: Greenwood Press, 2012: 152–53.

Dawdy, Shannon. *Building the Devil's Empire: French Colonial New Orleans*. Chicago: University of Chicago Press, 2008.

Dawdy, Shannon. *Patina: A Profane Archaeology*. Chicago: University of Chicago Press, 2016.

de Castelnau-l'Estoile, Charlotte. "Jesuit Anthropology: Studying 'Living Books.'" In *The Oxford Handbook of the Jesuits*. Oxford: Oxford University Press, 2019.

de Certeau, Michel. *The Practice of Everyday Life*. Berkeley: University of California Press, 1984.

de Certeau, Michel. *The Mystic Fable*. Translated by Michael B. Smith. Chicago: University of Chicago Press, 1992.

de Certeau, Michel. *The Possession at Loudin*. Translated by Michael B. Smith. Chicago: University of Chicago Press, 1996.

Deggs, Mary Bernard. *No Cross, No Crown: Black Nuns in Nineteenth-Century New Orleans*. Edited by Virginia Meacham Gould and Charles Nolan. Bloomington: Indiana University Press, 2001.

Deiler, J. Hanno. *A History of the German Churches in Louisiana (1823–1893)*. Translated by Marie Stella Condon. Lafayette, LA: Center for Louisiana Studies University of Southwestern Louisiana, 1983.

Deslandres, Dominique. "Dreams Clash: The War over Authorized Interpretation in Seventeenth-Century French Missions." In *Empires of God: Religious Encounters in the Early Modern Atlantic*, edited by Susan Juster and Linda Gregerson. Philadelphia: University of Pennsylvania Press, 2011.

Detweiler, Frederick G. *The Negro Press in the United States*. College Park, MD: McGrath, 1968.

Devore, Donald E., and Joseph Logsdon. *Crescent City Schools: Public Education in New Orleans, 1841–1991*. Lafayette: The Center for Louisiana Studies, 1991.

Diefendorf, Barbara B. "Contradiction of the Century of Saints: Aristocratic Patronage and the Convents of Counter-Reformation Paris." *French Historical Studies* 24, no. 3 (Summer 2001): 469–99.

Dippel, Christian, and Stephan Heblich. *Leadership and Social Movements: The Forty-Eighters in the Civil War*. Cambridge, MA: National Bureau of Economic Research, 2018. Working Paper 24656. http://www.nber.org/papers/w24656

Ditchfield, Simon. "Carlo Borromeo in the Construction of Roman Catholicism as a World Religion." *Studia Borromaica* 2 (2011): 3–23.

Ditchfield, Simon. "Catholic Reformation and Renewal" In *The Illustrated History of the Reformation*, edited by Peter Marshall, 152–85. Oxford: Oxford University Press, 2015.

Ditchfield, Simon. "Of Dancing Cardinals and Mestizo Madonnas: Reconfiguring the History of Roman Catholicism in the Early Modern Period." *Journal of Early Modern History* 8, no. 3–4 (2004): 386–408.

Divine, David, ed. *Multiple Lenses: Voices from the Diaspora Located in Canada*. Newcastle upon Tyne: Cambridge Scholars, 2007.

Donald, Dwayne Trevor. "Fort, Curriculum, and Indigenous Métissage: Imagining Decolonization of Aboriginal-Canadian Relations in Educational Contexts." *First Nations Perspectives* 2, no. 1 (2009): 1–24.

Donohue, John W. *Jesuit Education: An Essay on the Foundations of Its Idea*. New York: Fordham University Press, 1963.

Dorsey, Peter A. "Going to School with Savages: Authorship and Authority among the Jesuits of New France." *William and Mary Quarterly* 55, no. 3 (1998): 399–420.

Dubois, Laurent. *A Colony of Citizens: Revolution and Slave Emancipation in the French Caribbean, 1787–1804*. Chapel Hill: University of North Carolina Press, 2004.

Dubois, Laurent, and Julius S. Scott, eds. *Origins of the Black Atlantic*. New York: Routledge, 2010.

Dubois, Sylvie, Emilie Gagnet Leumas, and Malcom Richardson. *Speaking French in Louisiana 1720–1955: Linguistic Practices of the Catholic Church*. Baton Rouge: Louisiana State University Press, 2018.

Dumont de Montigny, Jean-François-Benjamin. *The Memoir of Lieutenant Dumont, 1715–1747: A Sojourner in the French Atlantic*. Translated by Gordon M. Sayre. Chapel Hill: University of North Carolina Press, 2012.

Dunn, Mary. "When 'Wolves Became Lambs': Hybridity and the 'Savage' in the Letters of Marie de l'Incarnation." *Seventeenth Century* 27, no. 1 (2012): 104–20.

DuVal, Kathleen. "Indian Intermarriage and Métissage in Colonial Louisiana." *William and Mary Quarterly*, no. 65 (April 2008): 267–304.

DuVal, Kathleen. "Interconnectedness and Diversity in '"French Louisiana.'" In *Powhatan's Mantle: Indians in the Colonial Southeast*, edited by Gregory A. Waselkov, Peter H. Wood, and Tom Hatley (Lincoln: University of Nebraska Press, 1989), 133–62.

Ellis, Richard N., and Charlie R. Steen. "An Indian Delegation to France, 1725." *Journal of the Illinois State Historical Society* 67, no. 1 (1974): 385–405.

Ellis, Scott S. *The Faubourg Marigny of New Orleans: A History*. Baton Rouge: Louisiana State University Press, 2018.

Eltis, David, and David Richardson. *Atlas of the Transatlantic Slave Trade*. New Haven, CT: Yale University Press, 2010.

Englebert, Robert. "Making Indians in the American Backcountry: Récits de voyage, Cultural Mobility, and Imagining Empire in the Age of Revolutions." In *French Connections: Cultural Mobility in North America and the Atlantic World, 1600–1875*, edited by Robert Englebert and Andrew N. Wegmann. Baton Rouge: Louisiana State University Press, 2020.

Englebert, Robert, and Andrew N. Wegmann, eds. *French Connections: Cultural Mobility in North America and the Atlantic World, 1600–1875*. Baton Rouge: Louisiana State University Press, 2020.

Ethridge, Robbie. *From Chicaza to Chicksaws: The European Invasion and the Transformation of the Mississippian World, 1540–1715*. Chapel Hill: University of North Carolina Press, 2010.

Everett, Donald E. "Free Persons of Color in Colonial Louisiana," *Louisiana History: The Journal of the Louisiana Historical Association* 7, no.1 (Winter 1966), 21–50.

Faber, Eberhard L. *Building the Land of Dreams: New Orleans and the Transformation of Early American*. Princeton, NJ: Princeton University Press, 2016.

Faber, Michael. "The New Orleans Press and French-Language Literature by Creoles of Color." In *Multilingual America: Transnationalism, Ethnicity, and the Language of American Literature*, edited by William Sollors. New York: New York University Press, 1998.

Fairclough, Adam. *Race and Democracy: The Civil Rights Struggle in Louisiana 1915–1972*. Athens: University of Georgia Press, 1995.

Fehrenbacher, Don E. *Slavery, Law, and Politics: The Dred Scott Case in Historical Perspective*. New York: Oxford University Press, 1981.

Fernandez, Mark. "Edward Livingston, American and France: Making Law." In *Empires of the Imagination: Transatlantic Histories of the Louisiana Purchase*, edited by Peter J. Kastor and François Weil. Charlottesville: University of Virginia Press, 2009.

Fertel, Rien. *Imagining the Creole City: The Rise of Literary Culture in Nineteenth-Century New Orleans*. Baton Rouge: Louisiana State University Press, 2014.

Fessenden, Tracy. "The Sisters of the Holy Family and the Veil of Race." *Religion and American Culture: A Journal of Interpretation* 10, no. 2 (2000): 187–224.

Fichter, Joseph H. "A Saintly Person of Color." *America* 166 (February 1992): 156–167.

Fischer, Roger A. "A Pioneer Protest: The New Orleans Street-Car Controversy of 1867." *The Journal of Negro History* 53, no. 3 (1968): 219–33.

Fischer, Roger A. "Racial Segregation in Antebellum New Orleans." *American Historical Review* 74, no. 3 (1969), 926–37.

Flüchter, Antje, and Giula Nardini. "Threefold Translation of the Body of Christ: Concepts of the Eucharist and the Body Translated in the Early Modern Missionary Context." *Humanities and Social Sciences Communications* 7 (2020): 86. https://doi.org/10.1057/s41599-020-00566-z

Foner, Eric. *Free Soil, Free Labor, Free Men: The Ideology of the Republican Party Before the Civil War*. New York: Oxford University Press, 1970.

Force, Pierre. "The House on Bayou Road: Atlantic Creole Networks in the Eighteenth and Nineteenth Centuries." *The Journal of American History* (June, 2013): 21–45.

Foucault, Michel. *Discipline and Punish: The Birth of the Prison*. New York: Vintage Books, 1975.

Foucault, Michel. *The History of Sexuality: An Introduction*. Translated by Robert Hurley. New York: Vintage, 1990.

Fraser, Nancy. "Rethinking the Public Sphere: A Contribution to the Critique of Actually Existing Democracy." In *Habermas and the Public Sphere*, edited by Craig J. Calhoun. Cambridge, MA: MIT Press, 1992.

Fromont, Cécile. *The Art of Conversion: Christian Visual Culture in the Kingdom of Kongo*. Omohundro Institute Book Publication Program with the University of North Carolina Press, 2014.

Furet, François, and Jacques Ozouf, *Reading and Writing: Literacy from Calvin to Jules Ferry*. Cambridge: Cambridge University Press, 1977.

Fussell, Elizabeth. "Constructing New Orleans, Constructing Race: A Population History of New Orleans." *Journal of American History*, no. 94. (Dec. 2007): 846–55.

Ganz, Marshal. *What a Mighty Power We Can Be: African-American Fraternal Groups and the Struggle for Racial Equality*. Princeton, NJ: Princeton University Press, 2006.

Garraway, Doris. *The Libertine Colony: Creolization in the Early French Caribbean*. Durham: Duke University Press, 2005.

Gates, Henry Louis, Jr. Foreword to *African-American Newspapers and Periodicals: A National Bibliography*, by James P. Danky and Maureen E. Hady. Cambridge, MA: Harvard University Press, 1998.

Gates, Henry Louis, Jr. *Loose Canons: Notes on the Culture Wars*. Oxford: Oxford University Press, 1993.

Geggus, David P. *The Impact of the Haitian Revolution in the Atlantic World*. Columbia: University of South Carolina Press, 2001.

Gehman, Mary. *The Free People of Color of New Orleans*. New Orleans: Margaret Media, 1994.

Genovese, Eugene. *From Rebellion to Revolution: Afro-American Slave Revolts and the Making of the Modern World*. Baton Rouge: Louisiana State University Press, 1979.

Gibson, Jon L. "Navels of the Earth: Sedentism in Early Mound-Building Cultures in the Lower Mississippi Valley." *World Archaeology* 39, no. 2 (2006): 311–29.

Gill, Natasha. *Educational Philosophy in the French Enlightenment: From Nature to Second Nature*. New York: Routledge, 2010.

Gilroy, Paul. *The Black Atlantic: Modernity and Double Consciousness*. Cambridge, MA: Harvard University Press, 1993.

Giraud, Marcel. *Historie de la Louisiana Française*, 4 vols. Paris: Presses Universitaires de France, 1953–1991.

Giraud, Marcel. *A History of French Louisiana*, vol. I. Baton Rouge: Louisiana State University Press, 1974.

Glenn, Evelyn Nakano. *Unequal Freedom: How Race and Gender Shaped American Citizenship and Labor*. Cambridge, MA: Harvard University Press, 2002.

Glissant, Édouard. *Europe and the Antilles: An Interview with Edouard Glissant*, by A. S. Hiepko. Rethinking Europe: Electronic Media, Orality, and Identity. Durham, NC: Duke University Press, 1998.

Glissant, Édouard. *Poetics of Relation*. Translated by Betsy Wing. Ann Arbor: University of Michigan Press, 1997.

Goodman, Dena. *The Republic of Letters: A Cultural History of the French Enlightenment*. Ithaca, NY: Cornell University Press, 1994.

Gould, Virginia Meacham. "Afro-Creole Women, Freedom, and Property-Holding in New Orleans." In *Coastal Encounters: The Transformation of Gulf South in the Eighteenth Century*, edited by Richmond F. Brown, 151–66. Lincoln: University of Nebraska Press, 2007.

Gould, Virginia Meachum. *Henriette Delille*. Strasbourg, France: Éditions du Signe, 2012.

Greenberg, Mitchell. *Baroque Bodies: Psychoanalysis and the Culture of French Absolutism*. Ithaca, NY: Cornell University Press, 2001.

Greenblatt, Allan. *Marvelous Possessions: The Wonder of the New World*. Chicago: University of Chicago Press, 1991.

Greene, Glenn Lee. *Masonry in Louisiana*. New York: Exposition Press, 1962.

Greenwald, Erin. *A Company Man, The Remarkable French-Atlantic Voyage of a Clerk for the Company of the Indies*. New Orleans: The Historic New Orleans Collection, 2013.

Greenwald, Erin. *Marc-Antoine Caillot and the Company of the Indies in Louisiana: Trade in the French Atlantic World*. Baton Rouge: Louisiana State University Press, 2016.

Greer, Allan. "Conversion and Identity: Iroquois Christianity in Seventeenth-Century New France." In *Conversion: Old Worlds and New*, edited by Kenneth Mills and Anthony Grafton. New York: University of Rochester Press, 2003.

Greer, Allan. *The Jesuit Relations: Natives and Missionaries in Seventeenth-Century North America*. Boston: Bedford/St. Martin's, 2000.

Greer, Allan. *Mohawk Saint: Catherine Tekawitha and the Jesuits*. New York: Oxford University Press, 2005.

Greer, Allan. "A Wandering Jesuit in Europe and America." In *Empires of God: Religious Encounters in the Early Modern Atlantic*, edited by Susan Juster and Linda Gregerson, 106–22. Philadelphia: University of Pennsylvania, 2011.

Greer, Allan, and Jodi Bilinkoff, eds. *Colonial Saints: Discovering the Holy in the Americas, 1500–1800*. New York: Routledge, 2003.

Grendler, Paul F. *Schooling in Renaissance Italy: Literacy and Learning, 1300–1600*. Baltimore: Johns Hopkins University Press, 1989.

Habermas, Jurgen. *The Structural Transformation of the Public Sphere: An Inquiry into a Category of Bourgeois Society*. Translated by Thomas Burger. Cambridge, MA: The MIT Press, 1998.

Hall, Gwendolyn Mildo. *Africans in Colonial Louisiana: The Development of Afro-Creole Culture in the Eighteenth Century*. Baton Rouge: Louisiana State University Press, 1992.

Harlan, Louis. "Desegregation in New Orleans Public Schools during Reconstruction," *The American Historical Review* 67, no. 3 (1962): 663–75.

Hardesty, Jared Ross. *Unfreedom: Slavery and Dependence in Eighteenth-Century Boston* (New York: New York University Press, 2016.Harvey, David. *The Limits of Capital*. London: Verso, 2006.

Helfenbein, Rob. *Critical Geographies of Education: Space, Place and Curriculum Inquiry*. New York: Routledge, 2021.

Heaney, Jane. *A Century of Pioneering: A History of the Ursuline Nuns in New Orleans, 1727–1827*. New Orleans: Ursuline Sisters of New Orleans, 1993.

Hendry, Petra Munro. *Engendering Curriculum History*. New York: Routledge, 2011.

Hendry, Petra Munro. "Sisters on the Frontier: French Catholic Women Educators and the Shaping of the Early American Republic in the Gulf Coast Southwest." *Catholic Southwest: Journal of History and Culture*, no. 31 (2020): 39–66.

Hendry, Petra Munro, and Donna Porche-Frilot. "Whatever Diversity of Shade May Appear": Catholic Women Religious Educators in Louisiana, 1727–1862." *Catholic Southwest*, no. 21 (2010): 34–61.

Hennessey, Melinda Meek. "Race and Violence in Reconstruction New Orleans: The 1868 Riot." *Louisiana History* 20, no. 1 (Winter 1979): 77–91.

Hilton, C. W., Donald E. Shipp, and J. Berton Gremillion, "Historical Background of Public Education in Louisiana." In *The Louisiana Purchase Bicentennial Series in Louisiana History, Education in Louisiana*, vol. XVIII. Edited by. Michael G. Wade. Lafayette: Center for Louisiana Studies University of Southwestern Louisiana, 1999.

Hoffman, Nancy. *Women's True Profession: Voices for the History of Teaching*. New York: McGraw Hill, 1981.

Hogue, James Keith. *Uncivil War: Five New Orleans Street Battles and the Rise and Fall of Radical Reconstruction*. Baton Rouge: Louisiana State University Press, 2006.

Houston, Robert A. *Literacy in Early Modern Europe: Culture and Education 1500–1800*. New York: Routledge, 2002.

Hsia, R. Po-chia. *The World of Catholic Renewal, 1540–1770*. Cambridge: Cambridge University Press, 1998.

Hunt, Alfred N. *Haiti's Influence on Antebellum America: Slumbering Volcano in the Caribbean*. Baton Rouge: Louisiana State University Press, 1988.

Hutton, Frankie. *The Early Black Press in America, 1827–1860*. Westport, CT: Greenwood, 1993.

Hyde, Anne F. *Empires, Nations, and Families: A New History of the North American West 1800–1860*. Lincoln: University of Nebraska Press, 2011.

Hyde, Sarah L. *Schooling in the Antebellum South: The Rise of Public and Private Education in Louisiana, Mississippi, and Alabama*. Baton Rouge: Louisiana State University Press, 2016.

Ibbett, Katherine. "Reconfiguring Martyrdom in the Colonial Context: Marie de l'Incarnation." In *Empires of God: Religious Encounters in the Early Modern Atlantic*, edited by Susan Juster and Linda Gregerson. Philadelphia: University of Pennsylvania Press, 2011.

Ingersoll, Thomas N. *Mammon and Manon in Early New Orleans: The First Slave Society in the Deep South, 1718–1819*. Knoxville: University of Tennessee Press, 1999.

Jacobs, Claude F., and Andrew J. Kaslow. *The Spiritual Churches of New Orleans:*

Origins, Beliefs, and Rituals of an African-American Religion. Knoxville: University of Tennessee Press, 1991.

James, C. L. R. *The Black Jacobins.* New York, Vintage Books, 1989.

Jegou, Marie-Andree. *Les Ursulines du Faubourg St-Jacques à Paris 1607–1662.* Paris: Presses Universitaires De France, 1981.

Johnson, Jessica Marie. *Wicked Flesh: Black Women, Intimacy, and Freedom in the Atlantic World.* Philadelphia: University of Pennsylvania Press, 2020.

Johnson, Walter. *Soul by Soul: Life Inside the Antebellum Slave Market.* Cambridge, MA: Harvard University Press, 1999.

Johnson, Rashauna. *Slavery's Metropolis: Unfree Labor in New Orleans during the Age of Revolutions.* Cambridge: Cambridge University Press. 2016.

Johnson, Walter. *Soul by Soul: Life Inside the Antebellum Slave Market.* Cambridge, MA: Harvard University Press, 1999.

Jones, Linda Carol. *The Shattered Cross: French Catholic Missionaries on the Mississippi River, 1698–1725.* Baton Rouge: Louisiana State University Press, 2020.

Juster, Susan, and Linda Gregerson. *Empires of God: Religious Encounters in the Early Modern Atlantic.* Philadelphia: University of Pennsylvania Press, 2011.

Kantrowitz, Stephan. "'Intended for the better government of man': The Political History of African American Freemasonry in the Era of Emancipation." *Journal of American History* (March 2010): 1001–26.

Karcher, Carolyn L. "Albion W. Tourgée and Louis A. Martinet: The Cross-Racial Friendship behind 'Plessy v. Ferguson.'" *Melus* 38, no. 1 (2013): 9–29.

Karcher, Carolyn L. "The National Citizen's Rights Association: Precursor to the NAACP." *Elon Law Review* 2 (July 2013): 107–69. https://eloncdn.blob.core.wi ndows.net/eu3/sites/996/2019/07/Elon_Law_Review_V5_No1_Karcher.pdf

Karcher, Carolyn. "The White 'Bystander' and the Black Journalist 'Abroad' Albion W. Tourgée and Ida B. Wells as Allies against Lynching." *Prospect* 29 (October 2005): 5–19. https://doi.org/10.1017/S0361233300001708

Kastor, Peter J. "'They are all Frenchmen': Background and Nation in a Age of Transformation." In *Empires of the Imagination: Transatlantic Histories of the Louisiana Purchase,* edited by Peter J. Kastor and François Weil. Charlottesville: University of Virginia Press, 2009.

Keller-Lapp, Heidi. "Floating Cloisters and Heroic Women: French Ursuline Missionaries, 1639–1744." *World History Connected* 4, no. 3 (2013).

Kniffen, Fred B., Hiram F. Gregory, and George A. Stokes. *The Historic Indian Tribes of Louisiana.* Baton Rouge: Louisiana State University Press, 1987.

Kousser, J. Morgan. "Before *Plessy,* Before *Brown*: The Development of Racial Integration in Louisiana and Kansas." In *Toward a Usable Past: An Examination of the Origins and Implications of State Protections of Liberty,* edited by Paul Finkleman and Stephen E. Gottlieb. Athens: University of Georgia Press, 1991.

Kozol, Jonathan. *Savage Inequalities: Children in America's Schools.* New York: Harper Perennial, 1991.

Kozol, Jonathan. *The Shame of the Nation: The Restoration of Apartheid Schooling in America*. New York: Three Rivers Press, 2005.

Krebsbach, Suzanne. "Black Catholics in Antebellum Charleston." *South Carolina Historical Magazine* 108, no. 2 (2007): 143–59.

Labelle, Kathryn. *Dispersed But Not Destroyed: A History of the Seventeenth-Century Wendat People*. Vancouver: University of British Columbia Press, 2012.

Ladson-Billings, Gloria. *Critical Race Theory in Education: A Scholar's Journey*. New York: Teachers College Press, 2021.

Landers, Jane. *Atlantic Creoles in the Age of Revolutions*. Cambridge: MA: Harvard University Press, 2010.

Landes, Joan B. *Women and the Public Sphere in the Age of the French Revolution*. Ithaca, NY: Cornell University Press, 1988.

Leavelle, Tracy Neal. *The Catholic Calumet: Colonial Conversions in French and Indian North America*. Philadelphia: University of Pennsylvania Press, 2012.

Lebreton, Marietta Marie. *A History of the Territory of Orleans, 1803–1812*, Parts I & II. Baton Rouge: Louisiana State University Press, 1969.

LeDoux, Rev. Jerome G. *War of the Pews: A Personal Account of St. Augustine Church in New Orleans*. Donaldsonville, LA: Margaret Media, Inc., 2011.

Lee, Jacob F. *Masters of the Middle Waters: Indian Nations and Colonial Ambitions along the Mississippi*. Cambridge, MA: Harvard University Press, 2019.

Lefebvre, Henri. *The Production of Space*. Translated by Donald Nicholson-Smith. Malden, MA: Blackwell Publishing, 1974.

Lemmon, Alfred E. *French Baroque Music of New Orleans: Spiritual Songs from the Ursuline Convent (1736)*. New Orleans: Historic New Orleans Collection, 2014.

Lenik, Stephan. "Mission Plantations, Space, and Social Control: Jesuits as Planters in French Caribbean Colonies and Frontiers." *Journal of Social Archeology* 12, no. 1 (2011): 51–71.

Lescarbot, Marc. *History of New France*. Edited and translated by I. Grant. Santa Barbara, CA: Praeger, 1969.

Levine, Robert, ed. *Martin R. Delany: A Documentary Reader*. Chapel Hill: University of North Carolina Press, 2003.

Lewis, Gwynne. *France 1715–1804: Power and the People*. London: Longman, 2004.

Linebaugh, Peter, and Marcus Rediker. *The Many-Headed Hydra: Sailors, Slaves, Commoners and the Hidden History of the Revolutionary Atlantic*. Boston: Beacon Press, 2000.

Lockley, Timothy James. *Maroon Communities in South Carolina*. Columbia: University of South Carolina, 2009.

Logsdon, Joseph, and Caryn Cossé Bell. "The Americanization of Black New Orleans, 1850–1900." In *Creole New Orleans: Race and Americanization*, edited by Arnold R. Hirsch and Joseph Logsdon. Baton Rouge: Louisiana State University Press, 1992.

Lougee, Carolyn C. "Noblesse, Domesticity, and Social Reform: The Education of Girls by Fénelonand Saint-Cyr." *History of Education Quarterly* 14, no. 1 (1974): 87–113.

Luira, Keith P. "Rituals of Conversion." In *Culture and Identity in Early Modern Europe (1500–1800)*, edited by B. B. Diefendorf and C. Hesse, 71. Ann Arbor: University of Michigan Press, 1993.

Lundy, Garvey F. "Early Saint Dominguan Migration to America and the Attraction of Philadelphia." *Journal of Haitian History* 12, no. 1 (2006): 76–94.

Luxenberg, Steve, *Separate: The Story of Plessy v. Ferguson and America's Journey from Slavery to Segregation*. New York: W. W. Norton & Company, 2019.

Lux-Sterritt, Laurence. *Redefining Female Religious Life: French Ursulines and English Ladies in Seventeenth-Century Catholicism*. Hants, England: Ashgate, 2005.

Magnuson, Roger. *Education in New France*. Montreal: McGill-Queen's University Press, 1992.

Mali, Anya. *Mystic in the New World*. Leiden: E. J. Brill, 1996.

Marthaler, Berard L. *The Catechism Yesterday and Today: The Evolution of a Genre*. Collegeville, MN: Liturgical Press, 1995.

McClellan, James E., III. *Colonialism and Science: Saint Domingue in the Old Regime*. Baltimore: John Hopkins University Press, 1992.

McGreevy, John. *American Jesuits and the World: How an Embattled Religious Order Made Modern Catholicism Global*. Princeton, NJ: Princeton University Press, 2016.

McKenna, "About Us." *New Orleans Tribune*. http://www.theneworleansTribune.com/main/about-us/

McKenna, "Our Team," *New Orleans Tribune*. http://www.theneworleansTribune.com/main/our-team/

McKnight, Doug. *Schooling, the Puritan Imperative, and the Molding of an American National Identity: Education's "Errand in the Wilderness."* Mahwah, NJ: Lawrence Earlbaum Associates, 2003.

McLaughlin-Stonham, Hilary. *From Slavery to Civil Rights: On the Streetcars of New Orleans 1830s–Present*. Liverpool: Liverpool University Press, 2020.

McNapsy, C. J. *Conquest or Inculturation: Ways of Ministry in the Early Jesuit Missions*. Regina: Campoin College, University of Regina Press, 1979.

McPherson, J. M. *The Abolitionist Legacy: From Reconstruction to the NAACP*. Princeton, NJ: Princeton University Press, 1975.

McPherson, J. M. *The Negro's Civil War: How American Blacks Felt and Acted during the War for the Union*. New York: Vintage Books, 1965.

McShea, Bronwen. *Apostles of Empire: The Jesuits and New France*. Lincoln: University of Nebraska Press, 2019.

Medley, Keith Weldon. *We as Freemen: Plessy v. Ferguson*. Gretna, LA: Pelican Publishing, 2003.

Melancon, K., and P. M. Hendry. "'Listen to the Voice of Reason': *The New Orleans Tribune* as Advocate for Public Integrated Education 1864–1870." *History of Education* 44, no. 3 (2015): 293–315.

Middleton, Sue. *Henri Lefebvre and Education: Space, History, Theory*. New York: Routledge, 2013.

Miller, Eugene. "Turner Regiments of the South." *American Turner* (1990).

Mills, Gary B. *The Forgotten People: Cane River's Creoles of Color*. Baton Rouge: Louisiana State University Press, 1977.

Mitchell, Mary Niall. *Raising Freedom's Child: Black Children and Visions of the Future after Slavery*. New York: New York University Press, 2008.

Morris, Robert C. *Reading, 'Riting, and Reconstruction: The Education of Freedmen in the South, 1861–1870*. Chicago: University of Chicago Press, 1981.

Morrissey, Robert Michael. *Empire by Collaboration: Indians, Colonists, and Governments in Colonial Illinois Country*. Philadelphia: University of Pennsylvania Press, 2015.

Morrow, Dianne Batts. *Persons of Color and Religious at the Same Time: The Oblate Sisters of Providence, 1828–1860*. Chapel Hill: University of North Carolina Press, 2002.

Moss, Hilary. *Schooling Citizens: The Struggle for African American Education in Antebellum America*. Chicago: University of Chicago Press, 2009.

Munro, Petra. *Subject to Fiction: Women Teachers' Life History Narratives and the Cultural Politics of Resistance*. Buckingham, UK: Open University Press, 1998.

Murphy, Lucy Eldersveld. *A Gathering of Rivers: Indians, Métis, and the Mining in the Western Great Lakes, 1737–1832*. Lincoln: University of Nebraska Press, 2000.

Nash, Gary B. *Forging Freedom: The Formation of Philadelphia's Black Community, 1720–1840*. Cambridge, MA: Harvard University Press, 1988.

Nash, Gary B. "Reverberations of Haiti in the American North: Black Saint-Dominguans in Philadelphia." *Exploration in Early American Culture Pennsylvania History* 65 (1998): 44–73.

Nash, Gary B., and Jean R. Soderland. *Freedom by Degrees: Emancipation in Pennsylvania and its Aftermath*. New York: Oxford University Press, 1991.

Nau, John Frederick. *The German People of New Orleans, 1850–1900*. Leiden: E. J. Brill, 1958.

Ng-A-Fook, Nicholas. *An Indigenous Curriculum of Place: The United Houma Nation's Contentious Relationship with Louisiana's Educational Institutions*. New York: Peter Lang, 2008.

Ng-A-Fook, Nicholas, Patrick Phillips, Mark T. Currie, and Jackson Pind. *Purposes of Education: Unsettling Historical Accounts of Settler Colonial Public Education*. In Press.

Nolan, Charles E., and Dorenda Dupont, eds., *Sacramental Records of the Roman Catholic Church of the Archdiocese of New Orleans, Volume 18, 1828–1829*. New Orleans, 2003.

Ochs, Stephan. "A Patriot, a Priest and a Prelate: Black Catholic Activism in Civil War New Orleans." *U.S. Catholic Historian* 12, no. 1 (1994): 49–75.

O'Malley, John., S.J. *The First Jesuits*. Cambridge, MA: Harvard University Press, 1993.

O'Malley, John, S.J., Gauvin Alexander Bailey, Steven J. Harris, and T. Frank Kennedy, S.J., eds. *The Jesuits: Cultures, Sciences and the Arts, 1540–1773*, 2 vols. Toronto: University of Toronto Press, 1999–2006.

O'Neil, Charles Edward. *Church and State in French Colonial Louisiana: Policy and Politics to 1732*. New Haven, CT: Yale University Press, 1966.

Oury, Guy-Marie. *Madame de la Peltrie et ses fondations Canadienes*. Quebec: Presses Université de Laval, 1973.

Palmer, Vernon Valentine. *The Origins and Authors of the Code Noir*. Louisiana Law Review 56, no. 2 (1996).

Pasquier, Michael. *Fathers on the Frontier: French Missionaries and the Roman Catholic Priesthood in the United States 1789–1870*. Oxford: Oxford University Press, 2010.

Pasquier, Michael. "Missionaries, Martyrdom, and Warfare in French Colonial Louisiana, 1699–1764." *Catholic Historical Review* 105, no. 2 (2019): 304–26.

Paulston, Roland G. "French Influence in American Institutions of Higher Learning, 1784–1825." *History of Education Quarterly* 8, no. 2 (1968): 229–45.

Peace, Thomas. "Borderlands, Primary Sources, and the Longue Durée: Contextualizing Colonial Schooling at Odanak, Lorette, and Kahnawake, 1600–1850." *Historical Studies in Education/Revue d'histoire de l'éducation* 29, no. 1 (2017): 8–31.

Petitfils, Brad. *Parallels and Responses to Curricular Innovation: The Possibilities of Posthumanist Education*. New York: Routledge, 2015.

Pinar, William F. *Educational Experience as Lived: Knowledge, History, Alterity*. New York: Routledge, 2015.

Pinar, William F., and Joe Kincheloe. *Curriculum as Social Psychoanalysis: The Significance of Place*. New York: State University of New York Press, 1991.

Powell, Lawrence. *The Accidental City: Improvising New Orleans*. Cambridge, MA: Harvard University Press, 2012.

Pykett, Lyn. "Reading the Periodical Press: Text and Context." *Victorian Periodicals Review* 22, no. 3 (1989): 100–108.

Quigley, Bill, and Maha Zaki. "The Significance of Race: Legislative Racial Discrimination in Louisiana, 1803–1865." *Southern University Law Review* 24, issue 2 (Spring 1997): 145–206.

Quimby, George I. "The Bayou Goula Site Iberville Parish Louisiana." *Fieldiana: Anthropology* 47, no. 2. Chicago Natural History Museum (1957): 89–170.

Quynn, D. M. "Dangers of Subversion in American Education: A French View." *Catholic Historical Review*, XXXIX (1953).

Rabil, Albert, Jr., ed. *Renaissance Humanism: Foundations, Forms, and Legacy*, 3 vols. Philadelphia: University of Pennsylvania Press, 1998.

Raboteau, Albert J. *Slave Religion*. Oxford: Oxford University Press, 2004.

Rankin, David C. "The Origins of Black Leadership in New Orleans during Reconstruction." *Journal of Southern History* 40, no. 3 (1974): 417–40.

Rankin, David C. Introduction to *My Passage at the New Orleans Tribune: A Memoir of the Civil War Era*, by Jean-Charles Houzeau. Translated by Gerard F. Denault. Baton Rouge: Louisiana State University Press, 1984.

Rapley, Elizabeth. *The Dévotées: Women and Church in Seventeenth Century France*. Montreal and Kingston: McGill-Queen's University Press, 1990.

Rapley, Elizabeth. *The Lord as Their Portion: The Story of the Religious Orders and*

How They Shaped Our World. Grand Rapids, MI: William B. Eerdmans Publishing Company, 2011.

Reeves, Sally. "The LEH's Home at Turner's Hall." *LEH Magazine*. https://64par ishes.org/turners-hall

Rodrigue, John C. *Reconstruction in the Cane Fields*. Baton Rouge: Louisiana State University Press, 2001.

Rothman, David J. *The Discovery of the Asylum: Social Order and Disorder in the New Republic*. Boston: Little, Brown, 1971.

Rubiés, Joan-Pau. "Ethnography and Cultural Translation in the Early Modern Missions." *Studies in Church History*, no. 53. (June 2017): 272–310.

Rushforth, Brett. *Bonds of Alliance: Indigenous and Atlantic Slaveries in New France*. Chapel Hill: University of North Carolina Press, 2013.

Sala-Molins, Louis. *Dark Side of the Light: Slavery and the French Enlightenment*. Translated by John Conteh-Morgan. Minneapolis: University of Minnesota Press, 2006.

Sala-Molins, Louis. *Le code noir*. Paris: Presses Universitaires de France, 1987.

Scaglione, Aldo. *The Liberal Arts and the Jesuit College System*. Amsterdam: John Benjamins Publishing Company, 1986.

Schroth, Raymond A. *The American Jesuits: A History*. New York: New York University Press, 2007.

Schultz, Nancy Lusigan. *Fire and Roses: The Burning of the Charlestown Convent, 1834*. New York: The Free Press, 2000.

Scott, David. *Conscripts of Modernity*. Durham, NC: Duke University Press, 2009.

Scott, Rebecca. "The Atlantic World and the Road to *Plessy V. Ferguson*." *Journal of American History* (December 2007): 726–333.

Scott, Rebecca. *Degrees of Freedom: Louisiana and Cuba after Slavery*. Cambridge, MA: Harvard University Press, 2005.

Scott, Rebecca. "Public Rights, Social Equality, and the Conceptual Roots of the *Plessy* Challenge." *Michigan Law Review* 106, no. 5 (2008): 777–804.

Scott, Rebecca J., and Jean M. Hébrard, *Freedom Papers: An Atlantic Odyssey in the Age of Emancipation*. Cambridge, MA: Harvard University Press, 2012.

Seck, Ibrahima. "The Relationships between St. Louis of Senegal, Its Hinterlands, and Colonial Louisiana." Translated by Joanne E. Burnett. In *French Colonial Louisiana and the Atlantic World*, edited by Bradley G. Bond, 270. Baton Rouge: Louisiana State University Press, 2005.

Seeman, Erik R. *The Huron-Wendat Feast of the Dead: Indian-European Encounters in Early North America*. Baltimore: Johns Hopkins University Press, 2011.

Selden, Steven. *Inheriting Shame: The Story of Eugenics and Racism in America*. New York: Teachers College Press, 1999.

Senter, C. "Creole Poets on the Verge of Nation" In *Creole*, edited by S. Klein. Baton Rouge: Louisiana State University Press, 2000.

Shaik, Fatima. *Economy Hall: The Hidden History of a Free Black Brotherhood*. New Orleans: Historic New Orleans Collection, 2021.

Shapiro, Norman R., trans. *Creole Echoes: The Francophone Poetry of Nineteenth-Century Louisiana*. Urbana: University of Illinois Press, 2004.

Simmon, William. "Cultural Bias in the New England Puritans' Perception of Indians." *William and Mary Quarterly* 38, no. 1 (1981): 56–72.

Sklar, Judith K. *American Citizenship: The Quest for Inclusion*. Cambridge, MA: Harvard University Press, 1991.

Sleeper-Smith, Susan. *Indian Women and French Men: Rethinking Cultural Encounter in the Western Great Lakes*. Amherst: University of Massachusetts Press, 2001.

Span, Christopher. *From Cotton Field to School House: African American Education in Mississippi, 1862–1875*. Chapel Hill: University of North Carolina Press, 2009.

Spear, Jennifer. *Race, Sex and Social Order in Early New Orleans*. Baltimore: John Hopkins University Press, 2009.

Spiegel, Gabrielle, ed. *Practicing History: New Directions in Historical Writing After the Linguistic Turn*. New York: Routledge, 2005.

Spitzer, Nicholas. "Monde Créole: The Cultural World of French Louisiana Creoles and the Creolization of World Cultures." *Journal of American Folklore* 116, no. 459 (2003): 57–72.

Spring, Joel. *The Universal Right to Education*. Mahwah, NJ: Lawrence Erlbaum Associates, 2000.

Stamp, Kenneth. *America in 1857: A Nation on the Brink*. New York: Oxford University Press, 1990.

Sterkx, H. E. *The Free Negro in Ante-bellum Louisiana*. Rutherford, NJ: Fairleigh Dickinson University Press, 1972.

Stern, Walter. *Race and Education in New Orleans: Creating the Segregated City, 1764–1960*. Baton Rouge: Louisiana State University Press, 2019.

Stewart, Whitney Nell, and John Garrison Marks, eds. *Race and Nation in the Age of Emancipations*. Athens: University of Georgia Press, 2018.

Suarez, Raleigh. "Chronicle of Failure: Public Education in Antebellum Louisiana." In *The Louisiana Purchase Bicentennial Series in Louisiana History*, volume XVIII. Lafayette: Center for Louisiana Studies, University of Southwestern Louisiana, 1999.

Sublette, Ned. *The World That Made New Orleans: From Spanish Silver to Congo Square*. Chicago: Lawrence Hill Books, 2009.

Suggs, Henry Lewis. Preface and introduction to *The Black Press in the South, 1865–1979*, edited by Henry Lewis Suggs. Westport, CT: Greenwood, 1983.

Sullivan, John, trans. *Autobiography of Vénérable Marie of Incarnation, O.S.U. Mystic and Missionary*. Chicago: Loyola University Press, 1964.

Swint, Henry Lee. *The Northern Teacher in the South, 1862–1870*. New York: Octagon, 1967.

Tannenbaum, Frank. *Slave and Citizen: The Negro in the Americas*. New York: Knopf, 1947.

Thomas, G. E. "Puritans, Indians, and the Concept of Race." *New England Quarterly* 48, no. 1 (1975): 3–27.

Thompson, Mark L. "Locating the Isle of Orleans: Atlantic and American Historiographical Perspectives." *Atlantic Studies* 5, no. 3 (2008): 305–33.

Thompson, Shirley Elizabeth. *Exiles at Home: The Struggle to Become American in Creole New Orleans*. Cambridge, MA: Harvard University Press, 2009.

Thornton, David. *Africa and Africans in the Making of the Atlantic World, 1480–1680*. Cambridge: Cambridge University Press, 2012.

Todorov, Tzvetan. *The Conquest of America: The Question of the Other*. Norman: University of Oklahoma Press, 1984.

Tohler, Daniel. *The Language of Education*. New York: Routledge, 2011.

Trouillot, Michel-Rolph. *Silencing the Past: Power and the Production of History*, Boston: Beacon Press, 1995.

Toledano, Roulhac, and Mary Louise Christovish. *Fauborg Tremé and the Bayou Road*. Gretna, LA: Pelican Publishing, 2003.

Tregle, Joseph G., Jr., "On That Word 'Creole' Again: A Note." *Louisiana History* 23 (1982): 193–98.

Trohler, Daniel. *The Languages of Education: Protestant Legacies, National Identities, and Global Aspirations*. New York: Routledge, 2011.

True, Micah. *Masters and Students: Jesuit Mission Ethnography in Seventeenth-Century New France*. Montreal: McGill-Queen's University Press, 2015.

Tyler, Pamela. *New Orleans Women and the Poydras Home: More Durable than Marble*. Baton Rouge: Louisiana State University Press, 2016.

Usner, Daniel. *American Indians in Early New Orleans: From Calumet to Raquette*. Baton Rouge: Louisiana State University Press, 2018.

Usner, Daniel. "From African Captivity to American Slavery: The Introduction of Black Laborers to Colonial Louisiana." *Louisiana History: The Journal of the Louisiana Historical Association* 20, no. 1 (Winter 1979): 25–48.

Usner, Daniel. *Indians, Settlers and Slaves in a Frontier Exchange Economy: The Lower Mississippi Valley Before 1783*. Chapel Hill: University of North Carolina Press, 1992.

Van Kirk, Sylvia. *Many Tender Ties: Women in Fur-Trade Society, 1670–1870*. Winnipeg: Watson and Dwyer, 1999.

Venuti, Lawrence. *Translator's Invisibility: A History of Translation*. New York: Routledge, 2008.

Verdin, Monique. *Return to Yaknichitto: Houma Migrations*. New Orleans: University of New Orleans Press: The Neighborhood Story Project, 2019.

Vidal, Cécile. "Antoine Bienvenu, Illinois Planter and Mississippi Trader: The Structure of Exchange between Lower and Upper Louisiana." In *French Colonial Louisiana and the Atlantic World*, edited by Bradley Bond. Baton Rouge: Louisiana State University Press, 2005.

Vidal, Cécile. *Caribbean New Orleans: Empire, Race and the Making of a Slave Society*. Chapel Hill: University of North Carolina Press, 2019.

Vidal, Cécile. *Louisiana: Crossroads of the Atlantic*. Philadelphia: University of Pennsylvania Press, 2014.

Vidal, Cécile. "The Streets, the Barracks, and the Hospital: Public Space, Social Control, and Cross-Racial Interactions among Soldiers and Slaves in French New Orleans." In *New Orleans, Louisiana, and Saint-Louis, Senegal: Mirror Cities in the Atlantic World, 1659–2000s*, ed. Emily Clark, Ibrahima Thioub, and Cécile Vidal (Baton Rouge: Louisiana State University Press, 2019), 75–102.

Vincent, Charles M. "Black Constitution Makers: The Constitution of 1868." In *In Search of Fundamental Law: Louisiana's Constitutions, 1812–1974*, edited by Warren M. Billings and Edward F. Hass. Lafayette: Center for Louisiana Studies, University of Southwestern Louisiana, 1993.

Voss, Louis. *History of the German Society of New Orleans*. New Orleans: Sendker Printing Service, 1927.

Walker, Craig. *In the Company of Black Men: The African Influence on Africa American Culture in New York City*. New York: New York University Press, 2011.

Ware, Marion. "An Adventurous Voyage to French Colonial Louisiana: The Narrative of Mother Tranchepain, 1727." *Louisiana History: The Journal of the Louisiana Historical Association* 1, no. 3 (1960): 212–29.

Warkentin, Germaine. "In Search of 'The Word of the Other': Aboriginal Sign Systems and the History of the Book in Canada." *Book History* 2, no. 1 (1999): 1–27.

Waselkov, Gregory A., Peter H. Wood, and Tom Hatley, *Powhatan's Mantle: Indians in the Colonial Southeast*. Lincoln: University of Nebraska Press, 2006.

Waters, Peter M. *The Ursuline Achievement: A Philosophy of Education for Women*. North Carlton, Victoria, Australia: Colonna Publishers, 1994.

Watkins, William H. *The White Architects of Black Education: Ideology and Power in America, 1865–1954*. New York: Teachers College Press, 2001.

Weaver, Karol K. *Medicinal Revolutionaries: The Enslaved Healers of Eighteenth-Century Saint-Domingue*. Urbana: University of Illinois Press, 2006.

Weiner, Mark Stuart. *Americans Without Laws: The Racial Boundaries of Citizenship*. New York: New York University Press, 2006.

Weiner, Merry E. *Women and Gender in Early Modern Europe*. Cambridge: U.K., 1993.

White, Ashli. *Encountering Revolution: Haiti and the Making of the Early Republic*. Baltimore: John Hopkins University Press, 2010.

White, Richard. *The Middle Ground: Indians, Empires, and Republics in the Great Lakes Regions, 1650–1815*. Cambridge: Cambridge University Press, 2010.

White, Sophie. *Voices of the Enslaved: Love, Labor and Longing in French Louisiana*. Chapel Hill: University of North Carolina Press, 2019.

White, Sophie. *Wild Frenchmen and Frenchified Indians: Material Culture and Race in Colonial Louisiana*. Philadelphia: University of Pennsylvania Press, 2012.

Whitlock, Reta. *This Corner of Canaan: Curriculum Studies of Place and the Reconstruction of the South*. New York: Peter Lang, 2007.

Wilkerson, Isabel. *Caste: The Origins of Our Discontents*. New York: Random House, 2020.

Williams, Heather Andrea. *Self-Taught: African American Education in Slavery and Freedom*. Chapel Hill: University of North Carolina Press, 2005.

Wilson, Samuel, Jr. *The Capuchin School in New Orleans, 1725*. New Orleans: Archdiocesan School Board, 1961.

Winfield, Ann. *Eugenics and Education*. New York: Peter Lang, 2007.

Wittke, Carl Frederick. *The German Language Press in America*. Ardent Media, 1973.

Wittke, Carl Frederick. *Refugees of Revolution: The German Forty-Eighters in America*. Westport, CT: Greenwood Press, 1970.

Wood, Peter H. "The Changing Population of the Colonial South: An Overview by Race and Region 1685–1790." In *Powhatan's Mantle: Indians in the Colonial Southwest*, edited by Gregory A. Waselkov, Peter H. Wood, and Tom Hatley. Lincoln: University of Nebraska Press, 1989.

Young, Iris Marion Young, *Inclusion and Democracy* (Oxford: Oxford University Press, 2002.

Zych, Lauren. "Low-Fired Earthenwares and Intercultural Relations in New Orleans, 1718–1763: 'Preliminary Results from Three Sites in the French Quarter.'" *Louisiana Archaeology* 39. In Press.

Dissertations, Theses, and Unpublished Material

Alberts, John Bernard. "Origins of Black Catholic Parishes in the Archdiocese of New Orleans, 1718–1920." PhD dissertation, Louisiana State University, 1998.

Anderman, Robyn. "Brewed Awakening: Re-imagining Education in Three Nineteenth-Century New Orleans Coffee Houses." PhD dissertation, Louisiana State University, 2018.

Bienvenu, Germain Joseph. "Another America, Another Literature: Narratives from Louisiana's Colonial Experience." PhD dissertation, Louisiana State University, 1995.

Borgia, Sister Mary Francis. "A History of the Congregation of the Sisters of the Holy Family of New Orleans." PhD dissertation, Xavier College New Orleans, 1931.

Cauvin, Mary Austin. "The French Ursulines in Colonial Louisiana 1727–1824." MA thesis, Louisiana State University, 1939.

Eskridge, Caryne A. "Illinois Culture, Christianity and Intermarriage: Gender in Illinois Country, 1650–1763." Undergraduate honors thesis, College of William and Mary, 2010.

Greene, Karin D. "Ursuline Mission in Colonial Louisiana." MA thesis, Louisiana State University, 1982.

Gregory, Lee Nelson. "Joseph Lakanal and French Educational Reform, 1793–1796." MA thesis, Tulane University, 1970.

Groth, Ben. "'Sacred Legalities'; The Indelible and Interconnected Relationship Between Baptism and Race in Spanish New Orleans." MA thesis, Tulane University, 2021.

Hart, Dana. "Toward an Ideal of Moral and Democratic Education: Afro-Creoles and Straight University in Reconstruction New Orleans, 1862–1896." PhD dissertation, Louisiana State University, 2014.

Havrylyshyn, Alexandra T. "Free for the Moment in France: How Enslaved Women and Girls Claimed Liberty in the Courts of New Orleans, 1835–1857." PhD dissertation, University of California Berkeley, 2018.

Hill, Mary Bernardine. "The Influence of James Hubert Blenk on Catholic Education in the Archdiocese of New Orleans, 1885–1917." PhD dissertation, Louisiana State University, 1964.

Hogan, John. "History of the Jesuits in Colonial French Louisiana." New Orleans: Loyola History Archive.

Honora, Jari. "A 'Catholic' Vocation: Médard Hilaire Nelson's Contribution to Education in Post-Reconstruction New Orleans." Presented during the "Creoles, Catholics, and the Classrooms: Investigating Black Catholic Education in New Orleans" symposium at the Southern Historical Society (Elizabeth Neidenbach, Chair), New Orleans, LA, Nov. 2021.

Johnson, Alisha. "Respectable from Their Intelligence: The Education of Louisiana's Gens de Couleur Libres, 1800–1860." PhD dissertation, University of Illinois, 2017.

Johnson, Erica Robin. "The Revolution From Within: Abolitionists and the Revolution in Saint-Domingue." PhD dissertation, Florida State University, 2012.

Laguaites, J. K. "The German Element in New Orleans, 1820–1860." MA thesis, Tulane University, 1940.

Leavens, Finnian Patrick. "*L'Union* and the *New Orleans Tribune* and Louisiana Reconstruction." MA thesis, Louisiana State University, 1966.

McCord, Stanley Joe. "A Historical and Linguistic Study of the German Settlement at Roberts Cove, Louisiana." PhD dissertation, Louisiana State University, 1969.

Memelo, Germaine A. "The Development of State Laws Concerning the Negro in Louisiana (1864–1900)." MA thesis, Louisiana State University, 1956.

Nicassio, Susan Vandiver. "Opera and New Orleans: Spectacle, Race and Religion." Unpublished manuscript.

Niedenbach, Elizabeth. "Articulating a Vision: Free Black Social Networks, Property Ownership, and the Founding of L'Institution Catholique des Orphelins Indigents in New Orleans." Paper presented at the Louisiana Historical Association, 2018.

Niedenbach, Elizabeth. "The Life and Legacy of Marie Couvent: Property Ownership, Social Networks, and the Making of Free People of Color Community in New Orleans." PhD dissertation, College of William and Mary, 2015.

Nugent, Ann V. "The Attitude of the *New Orleans Tribune* towards the Freedmen's Bureau in Louisiana: 1865–1866." MA thesis, Western Washington State College, 1970.

Payne, William A. "Studies Relating to Free Public Education in New Orleans Prior to the Civil War." MA thesis, Tulane University, 1930.

Peterson, Alma H. "The Administration of Public Schools in New Orleans, 1841–1861." PhD dissertation, Louisiana State University, 1964.

Porche-Frilot, Donna Marie. "Propelled by Faith: Henriette Delille and the Literacy Practices of Black Women Religious in Antebellum New Orleans." PhD dissertation, Louisiana State University, 2005.

Schmidt, Kelly. "We Heard Sometimes Their Ernest Desire to be Free in a Free Country: Enslaved People, Jesuit Masters, and Negotiations for Freedom on American Borderlands." PhD dissertation, Loyola University of Chicago, 2021.

Schmidt, Kelly L., Ayan Ali, and Jeff Harrison. "Jesuit Slaveholding in Colonial Era Kaskaskia." Slavery, History, Memory, and Reconciliation Project, online, 2020.

Schweniger, Loren. "Black Property Owners in the South, 1790–1915" PhD dissertation, University of Illinois, 1990.

Subat, Albert Paul. "The Superintendency of the Public Schools of Orleans Parish, 1862–1910." MA thesis, Tulane University, 1947.

Ulentin, Anne. "Shades of Grey: Slaveholding Free Women of Color in Antebellum New Orleans, 1800–1840." PhD dissertation, Louisiana State University, 2014.

Yamanaka, Mishio. "Erasing the Color Line: The Racial Formation of Creoles of Color and the Public School Integration Movement in New Orleans, 1867–1880." PhD dissertation, University of North Carolina, 2013.

Yamanaka, Mishio. "The Fillmore Boys School in 1877: Racial Integration, Creoles of Color, and the End of Reconstruction in New Orleans." web.unc.edu.

Young, Sister M. David. "History of the Development of Catholic Education for Negroes in Louisiana." MA thesis, Louisiana State University, 1944.

Index

Abbey of St. Ouen, 102
Abbott, Richard H., 291
Abbott v. Hicks (1892), 328, 407n168
L'Abeille/The Bee (newspaper), 268, 282–83
absolute space, 25
Acadia, 42–43. *See also* Canada
Acarie (Carmelite nun), 54
Accault, Michel, 70
accommodation: in Catholic Church, 41, 360n176; *versus* protest, 310–11, 313, 334, 375n166
Acella, Santyago, 191
Act for Public Education (1806), 180–81, 188
Adams, Lionel, 330
Africans, 1–4, 11, 15, 20–21, 29–34, 85–94, 101, 111–19, 140, 358nn147–48, 361n191, 362n201, 362n203, 372n139; African-Americans, 160–63; Africanization, 115; African Lodge No. 459, 397n91; African Methodist Episcopal Church, 289, 400n13; Bambara, 119; Code Noir of 1685 (revised 1724, 1855), 3–4, 15, 30–34, 46, 73–74, 92, 121, 142, 145, 158, 164–65, 248, 344n10, 349n16, 363n209; religious music, role of, 61,
130–33, 221, 374n150. *See also* Haitian Revolution; slavery
Africans, enslaved, 73–75, 91–92, 161–66, 170–73, 186–87, 216, 233, 279, 375n166; St. Claude School for Colored and White Girls, 162, 205–12, 213–15, 216–17, 218, 241, 386nn145–46, 388n174; at Ursuline schools, 115–21, 129, 140–48, 154–56. *See also* catechism classes; formerly enslaved people; slavery
Afro-Creoles, 29, 161, 162, 183, 346n36, 405n113; Catholicism, 133, 161; female activism, 206; literature, 245–47, 248–50, 279, 293, 394nn28–29; militia, 12, 183, 275; protest tradition, 293–97, 309–18, 334, 336, 340; as slaveholders, 222–23, 240, 392n7. *See also* newspapers
Agassiz, Louis, 298
agency, 3, 5, 13, 16, 19–20, 209–10, 212, 222, 340, 371n125, 388n170; in early Jesuit missions, 37, 50, 56–57, 67–69, 78, 86; during Segregation, 241–42, 248, 259, 283; in Ursuline schools, 94, 109, 118, 120–21, 129, 137, 156, 160, 162. *See also* La Tribune
L'Album littéraire (Black literary publication), 246, 249, 293, 296

Aliquot, Adèle and Marie, 207
Aliquot, Felicite, 215
Aliquot, Jean Marie (Sister St. Francis
  de Sales), 207, 214–15, 216, 217, 234,
  235–36, 390n192
Allouez (Catholic priest), 65
Almonaster y Rojas, Andrés, 170–71
Alpaugh, Maria Magdelene, 226
alterity, 39, 61; subalternity, 20–21, 25
Amazons, 100, 364n8
American Anti-Slavery Society, 326
American Citizen's Equal Rights Asso-
  ciation (ACERA), 323, 324
Americanization, 176–77, 209, 228–29,
  246, 258, 302
American Missionary Association, 321
American Revolution, 22, 167, 183, 282,
  380n59
Americans, 171–72, 178, 384n115. See
  also United States
L'Amis des Lois (journal), 200
Ancien Regime, 142, 154
Anderson, Benedict, 23, 273
Anderson, James D., 291
Anduse (Catholic priest), 218
Anglicized Blacks, 291, 295, 308, 314,
  316–17, 320, 324, 402n35
Anishabe (Algonquin/Algonquian), 7,
  42, 44–45, 53, 58, 59, 60, 66, 350n32
Anne de St. François (Ursuline nun),
  111, 113
anti-Catholic sentiment, 205–6, 209–10,
  218, 255, 258
anti-slavery, 166–67, 171–77, 187,
  202, 211, 214, 219–20, 253, 268–70,
  279–80, 295, 299, 348n3, 391n197,
  403n68; Abolition Acts (1780, 1788),
  167; American Anti-Slavery Society,
  326; in Catholic Church, 30–32;
  Pennsylvania Abolition Society (PAS),
  167; Society of the Friends of Blacks,
  198
Antoine, Caesar C., 308, 324
apartheid schooling, 235, 335, 337
Aponte Conspiracy of 1812, 11, 274
Appeal to the Colored Citizens of the World
  (Walker), 211
apprenticeships, 1–4, 171, 186–87, 251,
  343n1, 343n4, 344n5

Aquinas, Saint Thomas, 46, 370n120
Archbishop Antoine Blanc Memorial:
  Including New Orleans' Oldest and Most
  Historic Building (Bruns), 149
Arkansas (Indigenous peoples), 88
Association of the Holy Family, 221–22,
  224
Asylum for Destitute Orphan Boys, 241,
  387n154
Asylum of the Children of the Holy
  Family, 226
Auger, Edmund, 35
Auguste, Laurent, 301, 324
Augustin, Jean Baptiste, 189
Augustine of Hippo, 161
Augustinians, 102

Balas, Maire, 168–69
Baldwin, Joseph, 229
Baltimore, Maryland, 168, 185, 208,
  232, 378n19, 378n23, 400n13
Bambara, 119
Banks, Nathaniel P., 283, 302–3, 311
baptism, 68, 70–71, 83–84, 118, 158,
  219, 365n16, 367n63, 376n183
Barré, Charlotte, 57
Battle of New Orleans, 12, 275
Bayagoulas, 77–81, 83–85, 93, 360n183,
  361n191
Bayot, Marie Francoise, 185
Bayou Road School, 218, 224–25, 226,
  228, 249, 390n193
Bazanac (wife of Joseph), 244
Bazanac, Jean Baptiste, 163–64, 166,
  169, 170, 171, 172, 181, 184, 186
Bazanac, Joseph, 165, 169, 234, 235–36,
  244–45, 339–40
Beaubois, Nicolas Ignace de, 71–72,
  87–93, 106–8, 110, 112, 122, 131, 149,
  357n143, 361n199, 366n34, 366n41,
  373n145
Belaire, Jerome Perinne Elizabeth de
  (Sister Ste. Thèrése of Jesus), 132
Belden, A. T., 321
Belden, Samuel, 312–14
Bell, Caryn Cossé, 181, 248, 266, 285,
  292, 296, 401n23
Bell, Louis A., 321
Bellarmine, Robert, 127–28

Benoit, Marie, 320
Bentley, Emerson, 233
Bernard de St. Martin, Marguerite (Sister St. Pierre), 130, 147, 157, 374n149, 375n174
Bertonneau, Arnold, 301, 311–12, 314–16, 406n135
Bertonneau, Henry, 314–15, 316
Bertonneau, John, 314–15, 316
Betsy (enslaved woman), 223
Beunos (English teacher), 191
Bienneteau (Catholic priest), 68
Bienville, Jean-Baptiste Le Moyne, 73, 76, 86–87, 89, 92, 106–7, 112, 139, 143, 361n191, 361n196
Bildung, 267–68
Bill of Rights (Louisiana), 307–9
Black Catholic religious. *See* Sisters of the Holy Family
Black Code (1806), 180
Black counterpublics, 12–13, 16, 239, 275–76, 345n30, 397n91. *See also* counterpublic spaces: in the age of Segregation; Freemasonry
Black female civil rights activism, 205
Black Indies of the interior, 40
The Black Jacobins (James), 23
Black militia, 12, 183, 275
Blacks, Anglicized, 291, 295, 308, 314, 316–17, 320, 324, 402n35
Black schools, 95, 160–61, 283–84, 316–18
Black teachers, lack of, 317, 328
Blanc (Archbishop), 214–15, 216, 217, 218–19, 225, 262
boarding students, 5–9, 57–59, 165, 169, 186, 188–96, 201–2, 210, 224–26, 368n80, 368nn75–76, 371n123, 372n140, 374n159; tuition system, 180–81, 188–91, 202, 204, 233–34, 242–43, 303, 317, 381n64; at Ursuline schools, 112–13, 116, 121–24, 140–41, 150–52, 159
Board of Education (State of Louisiana), 283
Bocno (liaison of Henriette Delille), 213
Bocquet, Francois, 184
Boegue, Rosine, 168
Boguille, Ludger B., 244–45, 393n24

Bonaparte, Joseph, 199–200, 384n123
Bonaparte, Napoleon, 10, 166, 199–200, 261, 268, 274, 277, 384nn122–23
Bonseigneur, Paul, 324
Bouavel, Joseph, 173
Boulanger (Catholic priest), 108, 366n34
Boulanger, Marie-Anne (Sister St. Angelique), 7, 108, 110, 122–23, 131, 140, 146–47
Boulanger/Boullenger, Antoine-Robert Le, 7
Boutin (Catholic priest), 165
Boutin/Broutin, François, 222
Brache (Governor of Saint-Domingue), 111
Brébeuf, Jean de, 43, 46–47, 102, 364n15, 364n16
Brooks, Joanna, 12, 275–76, 345n30
brotherhood, imagined, 13, 16, 242, 271, 272, 273–80, 284–85, 301–9. *See also* Freemasonry
Brouard, Françoise Palmyre, 246
Broutin, Ignace Francois, 134
Brown, Henry, 332–33
Brown, James, 176, 177, 178
Brown v. Board of Education (1954), 235, 290, 335
Bruce, Clint, 292
Brulé, Charles, 183
Brule, Emile, 242
Bruneau, Maria-Florine, 60, 61
Bruns, J. Edgar, 149
Bruscoly (Ursuline nun), 108, 110
Buchanan, James, 255
Buck-Morss, Susan, 20
Bullock, Penelope, 291–92
Burr Conspiracy, 176, 196
Butler, Benjamin F., 282–83, 293

Cabaret, Joseph, 183
Caddos at Natchitoches, 88
Caen, Hyacinthe de, 30, 31
Cahokia mission, 66, 71
Caillot, Marc-Antoine, 113–14
Callioux, André, 244
Callioux, Félicie (Coulon), 244
calumet ceremony, 63–64, 67, 73, 79, 84, 360n187
Canada, 34, 43–49, 66, 87, 97, 106–7

Canadoises, 100

Canby, E. R. S., 283

Canisius, Saint Peter, 127–28

capitalism, 17, 95, 105, 286

Capuchins, 30–31, 40, 87, 91, 130, 148, 158, 198, 348n3, 361n198, 364n6

Carmelites, 54, 102, 162, 208, 217, 257, 258, 317, 388n174

Carondelet (Governor), 172–73

Carr (Professor), 189–90

Carriere, Francois, 159

Carroll (Archbishop), 208

Carson, James Taylor, 93

Cartas annuas (Jesuits), 41–42

Carter, Karen, 128, 369n86

Cartesian rationality, 37, 53

Cartwright, Samuel Aldophus, 298, 333

catechism, 35, 60–61, 67, 78, 83, 94, 388n168

catechism classes, 5, 45–46, 68, 146–47, 168, 219, 221, 224–27, 367n63, 368n76, 369n86; at Ursuline schools, 116, 121, 125–28, 130, 146, 147, 153–54

Catholic Church, 15, 17, 183, 193, 196, 289, 404n87; American, 222–23; anti-Catholic sentiment, 205–6, 209–10, 218, 255, 258; anti-slavery in, 30–32; Augustinians, 102; beatification, 54, 355n110; Capuchins, 30–31, 40, 87, 91, 130, 148, 158, 198, 348n3, 361n198, 364n6; Carmelites, 54, 102, 208, 258, 317, 388n174; catechism, 35, 60–61, 67, 78, 83, 94, 388n168; Catholic Almanac (1840), 257–58; Catholic colleges, 234; Catholic diocese of New Orleans, 161; Catholic Male Orphan Asylum, 258; Catholic School for Indigent Orphans, 222; Catholic Society for the Instruction of Indigent Orphans, 242; celibacy, 69, 70, 104–5; Code Noir, 3–4, 15, 30–34, 46, 73–74, 92, 121, 142, 145, 158, 164–65, 248, 344n10, 349n16, 363n209; conversion, 35, 41, 44–47, 51–59, 62–71, 85, 92, 118, 164, 214, 360n176, 375n166; Counter Reformation, 18, 40, 50, 51, 52, 54, 101–2, 369n90; Daughters of Charity, 107;

Dominicans, 102; folk Catholicism, 129, 130–33, 369n92; Franciscans, 102, 164, 171, 364n6; Holy See, 208; Josephites, 160; Lazarists, 257; Marianites of the Holy Cross, 208, 257; Marist fathers, 259; martyrdom, 54–55, 102, 139, 364n8, 364n15; second wave of French Catholic missionaries, 256–60; segregation of, 331–32; Sisters of Charity, 241, 358; Sisters of Divine Providence, 257; Sisters of Loretto, 208, 216, 257; Sisters of Notre Dame, 257, 396n60; Sisters of St. Joseph, 208, 257; Sisters of the Blessed Sacrament, 331–32; Sisters of the Company of Jesus, 165; Sisters of the Incarnate Word & Blessed Sacrament, 257; Sisters of the Presentation, 218; Sisters of the Sacred Heart, 208, 216, 225, 227, 257–58, 317, 395n51, 405n118; universalism, 286–87, 290, 301–9, 332, 341; Vincentians, 51, 259, 353n67. *See also* catechism classes; global spiritual universalism; Jesuits; Sisters of the Holy Family; Ursulines

The Catholic Institute (L'Institution Catholique des Orphelins dans Indigence), 193, 237–38, 239–47, 249–50, 258, 281–86, 293–94, 316, 321–23, 339, 340, 383n104, 392n111; letter writing, as student activism, 250–56

Cavalier, Cécile (Sister Marie des Agnes), 109, 110, 124, 125, 146, 153–54

Cécile de St. Croix (Ursuline nun), 57

celibacy, 69, 70, 104–5

Cemetery Pere-Lachaise, 202

Les Cenelles (The Mayhaws, poetry compilation), 246–47, 249, 293, 296, 394n29

Central School (New Orleans), 203–4

Césaire, Aimé, 286–87

Chapelin (Irish lawyer), 200

Charles, Joseph, 225

Charles, Josephine, 205, 216, 219, 224, 225, 226–27, 390n190

Charles, Philomene, 225

Charles III, 170

charter and magnet schools, 337

Chauvin, Marianne, 5, 7
Chevart, Lucien, 202–3, 385n134
Chicago Daily Inter Ocean (newspaper),
  325–26
Chicagou (Chief), 72
Chickasaws, 8, 78, 85, 95, 362n201
children, 127–28, 260; child-centered
  approach to schooling, 200–201;
  student activism, 250–56, 281–86.
  See also The Catholic Institute; girls,
  education of; Ursuline Academy in
  New Orleans
Children of Mary confraternity, 121,
  140, 150, 156, 216
Chitimachas, 89, 93, 96
Choctaws, 8, 78, 88–89, 93, 96, 196,
  362n201, 362n202, 373n145, 383n110
choir nuns, 4–5, 8
Christophe, Firmin, 295, 324
Circular No. 34, 303
Citizens' Committee to Test the Constitutionality of the Separate Car Law,
  316, 321, 324–27, 328–35
City Directory (New Orleans), 181, 182,
  184, 186, 230, 384n128, 385n134
civic clubs, 269
civic virtue, 23
Civil Code of 1825, 178, 185–86
civilité (orderly political life), 80
civil rights, 205; from public rights to,
  327–35, 339–41
Civil War, 29, 226–27, 244, 255–56,
  267–70, 281–86, 294, 311. *See also La
  Tribune*
Clague, Armand Richard, 222
Claiborne, S. A., 255
Claiborne, William Charles Cole,
  10–11, 12, 183, 187–88, 228, 274,
  275, 382n85; University Act of 1805
  (supplement 1811), 172–81, 188,
  381n64
Clark, Elijah, 202
Clark, Emily, 114, 119, 121, 138, 140,
  371n125
class, 4–5, 15, 57, 115–18, 164, 186–89,
  192–93, 202, 204–5, 225, 270; Ancien
  Regime, 142, 154; classism, 296–97;
  class solidarity, 173–74, 368n75,
  369n90; social order, 134–38, 140–43,

151–53, 154–56, 210, 314; at Ursuline
  schools, 115, 116, 118, 121–22, 150,
  159
Clay, Henry, 199
cloister (clausura), 57, 60–62, 105–6,
  108, 112, 125, 147, 151, 355n112,
  366n42
Code Noir of 1685 (revised 1724, 1855),
  3–4, 15, 30–34, 46, 73–74, 92, 121,
  142, 145, 158, 164–65, 248, 344n10,
  349n16, 363n209
Colapissas, 77, 82, 93
Collard, Agathe Mager, 224
College d'Orléans (College of New
  Orleans), 162, 184, 187–96, 206, 214,
  225, 228, 382n82, 382n85, 383n104;
  Board of Administrators, 196, 197,
  202; Board of Directors, 202, 321–
  22; Board of Regents, 177–78, 179,
  187–88, 189, 192, 196, 204, 382n85,
  383n104; progress of science, 197–
  205, 385n131; University Act of 1805
  (supplement 1811), 172–81, 188,
  381n64
College of the Immaculate Conception
  (became Loyola), 259, 363n211
College of the Society of Jesus (Collège
  des Jésuites), 48, 218
collèges, ancient, 199
Collens, Thomas Wharton "T. W. C.,"
  303
colonization, 13–14, 22, 26, 39–41, 93,
  115; postcolonial activism, 286–87;
  reverberations of, 95–97; rogue
  colonialism, 19–20. *See also* imperialism; race
colonization, British, 8, 11, 42, 95, 171–
  72, 344n7, 353n66, 355n112; Jamaica,
  379n34; South Carolina, 2, 86, 174
colonization, French, 58, 70, 76, 171–72,
  180, 219; francization (Frenchification), 58, 59, 69, 71; Guadaloupe,
  31, 348n8; Martinique, 31, 106, 286,
  348n8; Saint Domingue (now Haiti),
  10–13, 137, 163–64, 348n8, 377n13.
  See also Haiti; Haitian Revolution;
  Haitian Revolution: refugees from;
  Louisiana; Ursulines
colonization, German, 8

colonization, Portuguese, 169
colonization, Spanish, 54, 159–60, 164,
　170–71, 172–73, 180, 207, 275; Cuba,
　10–13, 159, 163–64, 219, 274, 369n92;
　Florida, 2
color line, 232, 244, 271, 295, 316, 322–
　23; colored, passing as, 281; white
　passing, 263, 264–65, 320, 327–28,
　396n66, 406n135
Committee of Public Instruction
　(France), 197, 198, 199
common school movement, 14–15, 18,
　20, 23, 29, 34, 142, 170, 209, 229,
　258, 290, 302–7, 353n73
communion, 122, 126
community identity, 129, 132–33, 139
La Compagnie des Filles Notre Dame,
　165
Company of New France, 57
Company of the Indies, 73, 87, 261,
　343n4, 361nn198–99, 366n43,
　372n139, 375n167, 382n87; Ursulines
　and, 99, 101, 107–9, 111, 114, 133–38,
　143, 145, 161
Conception mission, 45
Condorcet, Nicolas de, 198–99
confraternities, 168, 169, 206; Children
　of Mary, 121, 140, 150, 156, 216;
　Congregation of the Sisters of the
　Presentation of the Blessed Virgin
　Mary, 216–17. *See also* Freemasonry
Congregation of the Sisters of the
　Presentation of the Blessed Virgin
　Mary, 216
Congress (US), 178–79, 181, 301, 305,
　333, 385n133
Connor, William P., 292
Conservatoire des art et métiers, 199
Constitution (Louisiana): 1864, 265–66,
　302; 1868, 186, 284–85, 296, 307–9,
　311, 313–14, 315, 405n118; 1879,
　314, 316–17; 1898, 334
Constitution (US), 238–39, 265–66, 301,
　312–13, 315, 329–30, 332–33
converse nuns, 4–5, 9, 57, 111
conversion, 35, 41, 44–47, 51–59, 62–
　71, 85, 92, 118, 164, 214, 360n176,
　375n166
Cook, Bernard A., 90

Coralie, Catherine, 10
Cordeviolle, Etiènne, 222
cosmologies, shifting, 81, 93, 103
Coulon, Antoine and Feliciana, 244
counterpublic spaces, creole pedagogy
　of, 29, 163–236, 339–41; at Col-
　lege d'Orléans, 162, 184, 187–96,
　206, 214, 225, 228, 382n82, 382n85,
　383n104; creole counterpublic, 116–
　22; education in early New Orleans/
　Louisiana, 170–72; St. Claude School
　for Colored and White Girls, 162,
　205–12, 213–15, 216–17, 218, 241,
　386nn145–46, 388n174; Teachers
　as exiles in New Orleans, 181–87;
　University Act of 1805 (supplement
　1811), 172–81, 188, 381n64. *See also*
　Black counterpublics; free women of
　color: liminality of; Haitian Revolu-
　tion: refugees from
counterpublic spaces, in the age of
　Segregation, 29, 237–87; The Forty-
　Eighters, 266–71, 397n90; Lanusse,
　Armand, 213, 242–50, 255–56, 279–
　85, 293, 296, 394n35; reverberations
　of, 286–87; second wave of French
　Catholic missionaries, 256–60; student
　activism, 250–56, 281–86; universal
　equality and The Civil War, 281–
　86. *See also* The Catholic Institute;
　Freemasonry; German immigration
　and education; imagination, creole
　pedagogy of
Counter Reformation, 18, 40, 50, 51, 52,
　54, 369n90
Courcelle, Myrtile, 272
coureurs de bois (illicit traders), 66,
　68–69
Courrier de la Louisiane (Federalist news-
　paper), 163, 176, 184, 197
Coushatta tribe, 96
Couvent, Bernard, 240
Couvent, Marie Justine, 239–42, 339–
　40, 392n7
Craig, Joseph A., 310
creole pedagogies: creole pedagogical
　circuit, 186–87, 340–41; defining,
　15–16, 18, 20–24, 29, 339–41. *See
　also* counterpublic spaces; disorder;

imagination; liminality; transcultural translation

Creoles, 111, 293; creole cottages, 10, 183, 205, 345n22; creole counterpublic, 116–22; creole mysticism, 52–58; French, 161, 178, 187, 192–93, 196, 202, 384n115; Spanish Creole women, 159. *See also* Afro-Creoles

creolization, 3, 14, 20–24, 28–29, 247–48, 334, 339–41, 346n36, 355n102; in Catholic Church, 40–42, 59–62, 73, 94, 115, 119–20, 129, 131–32, 141, 147. *See also* hybridity; syncretism

Crestin (house mother), 191

Cromwell, Robert I., 308

Crucy, Philippe, 110, 111

Crusader (newspaper), 29, 288, 289, 318–20, 323, 324; *Plessy v. Ferguson*, from public to civil rights, 327–35; *Plessy v. Ferguson*, legal preparation for, 324–27; reverberations of, 335–37. *See also* Separate Car Act

Cuba, 10–13, 159, 163–64, 219, 274, 369n92

Cubberly, Ellwood P., 16

cult of family, 105

cultural osmosis, 85

Currie, Mark T. S., 97

Daigleville school, 96–97

Dain, Marie-Anne (Sister St. Marthe), 111, 113

Les Dames d'Hospitaliére, 207

Daniel, Antoine, 102, 364n15

Danis, Charles, 7

Danis, Marie Ann, 5, 7

Dannaples, C., 277

Darwin, Charles, 300

Daughters of Charity, 107

Daughters of the Cross (Sisters of Loretto), 208, 216, 257

D'Avezac, Jules, 189–90, 264, 382n95, 384n112

Davezac/D'Avezac, Auguste, 264

Davis, Cyprian, 223

Davis, Natalie Zemon, 105

Dawdy, Shannon, 19–20, 141, 142, 371n128

Dawson, John Charles, 203

day students, 169, 186, 188–93, 201–2, 210, 224–25, 368nn75–76, 383n104; at Ursuline schools, 116, 121, 124–25, 146–47, 159

De Blanc, Alicibiades, 313

de Boré, Jean Étienne, 192

de Boré, Marie Elizabeth, 192

de Castelnau-l'Estoile, Charlotte, 38–39

de Certeau, Michel, 4, 24, 56

Declaration of Independence, 294

The Declaration of the Rights of Man and Citizen (1789), 172, 173

deculturization, resistance to, 45

deficit pedagogy, 39, 44, 117

Deggs, Mary Bernard, 225, 384n127, 390n190, 390n194

dehumanization, 19–20, 126, 210, 213, 221, 222, 249

de La Chaise, Jacques, 135–36

de La Peltrie, Madeleine, 51, 57, 355n112

Delille, Cecile, 213

Delille, Henriette, 205–7, 210, 212–16, 218–27, 234–36, 249, 339–40, 388n168, 388n171, 390n192, 390n194

de Limoges, Joseph, 86, 87

Dellande, Arnold Joseph, 313–14, 316

Dellande, August, 311–12

Dellande, Francis Clement, 313–14, 316

Dellande, Ursin, 313–14, 315–16

democracy, 18, 22, 167, 179, 197–98, 204–5, 211, 248, 265, 338–41

Democratic Party, 255, 270, 297–98, 309; Redeemer Democrats, 309–10, 312

Democratic Republicans, 174

de Pauger, Adrien, 112

Derbingy, Pierre, 178–79, 197, 384n115

Der Deutsche (newspaper), 261

The Descent of Man (Darwin), 300

Desdunes, Daniel, 328, 335

Desdunes, Rodolphe Lucien, 245, 316, 321, 323–24, 328–32, 334–35, 339

desegregation, 296, 309

Deslandres, Dominique, 39–40

d'Esnambuc, Pierre Bélain, 286

Destrehan, Jean Noël, 179

d'Estréhan, Marie, 192

Detharade, Jean, 158–59

Detweiler, Frederick, 307, 401n16
Deutsche Courier (newspaper), 261
Deutsche Geselleschaft zum Schuz der
    Einwanderer, 261–62
Deutsche Zeitung (newspaper), 261
Dias, Cecil, 205
Dias, Pouponne, 205
Dibble, Henry C., 321
Diderot, Denis, 177
Digest of 1808, 178, 380n58n59
Dimitry, Alexander, 263, 264, 266
Dimitry, Andrea, 264
Diocese of New Orleans, 256, 395n48
disorder, creole pedagogy of, 29, 114–
    15, 138–48, 162, 339–41; spatial
    relations of, 148–56. *See also* Ursuline
    Academy in New Orleans
dizainières (second mistress), 123
Dolliole, Jean Louis, 12, 240, 272, 275,
    397n93
Dominicans, 102
Donald, Dwayne, 40–41
Donge, Pierre, 86, 87
Dotrina christiana breve (Bellarmine),
    127–28
double pedagogy, 82
double settings, 39–40, 41–42
Doucet (young enslaved African male),
    1–4, 186, 343n1
Doutreleau, Étienne, 110, 111, 148, 362,
    366n40
Dragon, Marianne Celeste, 264
Dred Scott v. Sandford (1857), 238–39,
    333
Drexel, Katherine, 331–32
DuBois, Laurent, 22
DuBois, W. E. B., 334
Dubourg, Louis William Valentine, 207,
    208–9, 214–15, 216, 217, 388n174
Duchemin, Therese, 168
Duconge (white woman teacher), 181
Duhart, Adolphe, 242, 244–45, 246
Duhart, Armand, 245, 246, 316
Duhart, Louis, 184–85, 186
Duhart, Louis-Adolphe, 246
Duhart, Louis Alfred, 185
Duhart, Pierre, 185
Dumas, Alexandre, 248, 279
Dumas, Joseph, 222

Dunn, Mary, 50
Dunn, Oscar J., 295
Dupart, Leon, 254
Dupart, Victor M., 329
Dupart/Dupare, Pierrer Delisle de, 1–4,
    343n1
Duplantier, Guy, 312–13
Durant, Thomas D., 295
Durant, Thomas J., 301, 403n68
Durkheim, Emile, 17
Du Ru, Paul, 34, 76–86, 154, 196,
    358nn157–58, 360n183, 361n191,
    375n167
Dutch plank, 270
Duval, Kathleen, 8

École au-Chien French Immersion
    school, 96
École Normale (teacher training), 199
École polytechnique, 199
Écoles Centrales (secondary schools),
    199, 200
Economy Hall *(Salle d'Economie)*, 301,
    317, 325, 393n24
educational history, reimagining narra-
    tive of, 14–15, 16–19
Eggart, Mary Lee, 6, 72, 74, 88, 90, 146,
    149, 182, 194, 220, 230
Emancipation Proclamation, 282, 283
emigration, from the United States,
    185–86, 202, 208, 239, 247, 250–56
Encalada, Valentin, 244
encounter narrative, 61
engages (indentured servants), 66. *See
    also* indentured servants
English common law, 179
Enlightenment ideologies, 17–19, 29,
    32, 55, 91, 94, 98–99, 106, 133, 136,
    141, 165–66, 266, 286; at College
    d'Orléans, 197–205
"Epigram" (Lanusse), 249
Erasmus, 98
Estéves, Arthur, 316, 324, 328
Etoile Polaire Lodge, 276, 280, 398n111
*Études sur les facultés mentales des ani-
    maux comparées à celles de l'homme*
    (Houzeau), 300
*Exposé sommaire es Travaux de Joseph
    Lakanal* (Lakanal), 198

The Expression of the Emotions in Man and Animals (Darwin), 300

Faber, Eberhard, 174
Faubourg Marigny, 169, 181–82, 240, 262–63, 269
Faubourg Tremé, 10, 188–89, 217, 224, 271–72, 321
Fayerweather, George H., 310
Fazende, Ann Marie Henriette, 226
Female Charitable Society (Poydras Orphan Asylum), 209–10, 241, 387n154
femaleness, 212
Female Orphan Asylum, 241
Fénelon, Francois, 104, 105
Fenner, Charles Erastus, 330
Ferguson, John, 329–30
Fernandez, Mark, 176
Fernando de Lemos, Truth and Fiction (Gayarré), 192–93, 383n104
Ferrer, Vincent, 51
"A Few Words to Dr. Dubois: 'With Malice Toward None,'" (Desdunes), 334
fictive kinship, 64, 66–67, 68, 83–84, 160, 360n187; godparenting, 70–71, 83, 120, 155, 158, 168, 184, 215, 240, 259, 357n139, 367n63, 388n168
Filles de la Charité (Daughters of Charity), 107
Fillmore, Millard, 255
Fillmore school, 312–16
First Municipal Council, 264
First Reconstruction Act (1867), 291
Fletcher, Henry, 240, 242
Florida, 2
folk Catholicism, 129, 130–33, 369n92
Fontière, Marthe, 205, 207, 213, 214–15, 234, 235–36
forest schools, 165
formerly enslaved people, 226–27, 244, 283–86, 391n197
Fort Chartres mission, 71
Fort Louis de La Louisiane, 86
Fort Maurepas, 76, 77, 86
Fort Rosalie, 113–14
The Forty-Eighters, 266–71, 397n90
Foster, Murphy, 334

Foucault, Michel, 18, 37–38
Fouché, Louis Nelson, 240, 242, 245, 316
Founded on Faith: A History of Loyola University New Orleans (Cook), 90
Fourier, Charles, 167, 403n68
Fox nation, 71, 159
Franciscans, 102, 164, 171, 364n6
Francis de Sales, Saint, 225
francization (Frenchification), 58, 59, 69, 71
Frederick Douglass' Paper (Douglass), 289
Freedmen's Bureau, 227, 233, 283–84, 289, 291, 303, 305, 318, 403n76
freedom, 11–12, 22, 66, 82, 158, 211, 214, 239, 251–53, 283, 286; freedom martyr, 269
Freedom Papers (Scott and Hébrard), 184
Freemasonry, 12–13, 20–21, 29, 169, 185, 202, 254, 270–71, 292, 397n91, 399nn115–16; Etoile Polaire Lodge, 276, 280, 398n111; Germania Lodge No. 46, 13, 272–73, 277–80, 398n97, 399n121, 399n123, 399nn117–18; Grand Lodge of Louisiana, 276, 398n111, 399n116; Grand Lodge of Pennsylvania, 398n109; imagined brotherhood in, 273–80; Masonic Lodges as counterpublic educational spaces of citizenship, 271–73; La Parfaite-Union (Perfect Union) No. 1, 178, 280; Persévérance Lodge No. 4 (formerly No. 113), 13, 272–73, 275–77, 398n109, 398n111, 399n118; Scottish Rite Lodges, 276, 399n116, 408n172
free people of color, 10–13, 73, 161–68, 170–79, 180–87, 193, 232–33, 345n21, 372n138, 377n1, 378n23, 382n87, 387n164; Black militia, 12, 183, 275; free-soil principle, 31; legislation limiting (1806), 11; liminality of, 211–28; St. Claude School for Colored and White Girls, 162, 205–12, 213–15, 216–17, 218, 241, 386nn145–46, 388n174. *See also* The Catholic Institute; counterpublic spaces, in the age of Segregation; Haitian Revolution, refugees from; *La Tribune*

free women of color, liminality of, 121, 165, 168–69, 183–85, 188, 239–42, 244, 264, 294; Congregation of the Sisters of the Presentation of the Blessed Virgin Mary, 216; plaçage, 212, 213, 221, 249, 387n160, 394n35, 397n93. *See also* Sisters of the Holy Family
Fremont, John, 255
French Creoles, 161, 178, 187, 192–93, 196, 202, 384n115
French National Assembly, 166
French National Convention, 198
French Revolution, 22, 172, 178, 197, 208, 248, 261, 378n15, 378n19, 380n59
French Romantic movement, 246, 248, 279, 284, 294
French (Abstract) School of Mysticism, 54
French Society for the Propagation of the Faith, 256
Friends of Harmony Lodge, 280
Friends of Universal Suffrage, 284, 295
Frilot, A., 237–39
fur trade, 57, 66, 68–69, 70

Gabriel's Plot (1800), 11, 274
Gaignard, Jean Baptiste August, 184
Gaignard, Réné Pre, 181, 184
Galton, Francis, 300
Galvez (Governor), 183
Garrison, William Lloyd, 289
Gates, Henry Louis, Jr., 336
Gaudin, Jean Francois, 200, 206, 384n127
Gaudin, Juliette, 205–7, 210, 213–16, 219, 224–26, 234–36, 384n127, 385n128
Gaudin, Pierre, 213–14, 225, 385n128
Gayarré, Charles, 192–93, 383n104
Gayarré, Éstevan de, 192
Gazette de la Louisiane (newspaper), 192, 200, 201
gender, 80, 135–36, 211–12, 339; femaleness, 212; imagined brotherhood, 13, 16, 242, 271, 272, 273–80, 284–85, 301–9; norms of public/private binary, 106, 118, 151–52, 209–11;

patriarchy, 155, 156, 210, 394n35; plaçage, 212, 213, 221, 249, 387n160, 394n35, 397n93; segregation, 229, 249, 263, 404n87; shifting roles, 104–6, 109; universal male suffrage, 281, 284, 290, 295, 314. *See also* Freemasonry; girls, education of; whiteness, white men; women
Geneviève, Marie Rose, 189, 382n95
Georgia, 174, 177, 380n54
German immigration and education, 254–55, 256–57, 260–71, 277–80; Bildung, 267–68; The Forty-Eighters, 266–71, 397n90; Germania Lodge No. 46, 13, 272–73, 277–80, 398n97, 399n121, 399n123, 399nn117–18; German schools, 265, 267, 396n57; German Society, 269, 278–79; Turner Societies (Turnvereine), 267–69, 270, 397n78; Vorwaerts, 268. *See also* Freemasonry
Gilroy, Paul, 21, 22
girls, education of, 186, 224; Bayou Road School, 218, 224–25, 226, 228, 249, 390n193; The Louisiana Asylum for girls in New Orleans, 227; Madame Grelaud's Seminary for Girls, 167; Poydras Orphan Asylum for Girls, 209–10, 241, 387n154; St. Claude School for Colored and White Girls, 162, 205–12, 213–15, 216–17, 218, 241, 386nn145–46, 388n174; St. Frances School for Colored Girls (St. Frances Academy), 169; St. Patrick's Female Orphan Asylum, 258. *See also* Ursulines; women
Glissant, Édouard, 21
global citizenship, 251, 253
global spiritual universalism, 33–43, 49–51, 57–58, 62–67, 76, 84, 94, 97, 214–16, 233–34, 359n162, 388n170; at Ursuline schools, 115–17, 133, 137, 140–42, 158–60
godparenting, 70–71, 83, 120, 155, 158, 168, 184, 215, 240, 259, 357n139, 367n63, 388n168
Gordon, George H., 314
Gould, Virginia, 119
Der Graf von Monte Christo (Dumas), 279

Grammar A schools, 312
Grand Coteau, Louisiana, 208–9, 216, 225, 257–58, 395n51
grandfather clause, 334
Grand Lodge of Louisiana, 276, 398n111, 399n116
Grand Lodge of Pennsylvania, 398n109
Grand-Pré, Constance de, 192
grand renfermement, 63
Gravier, Jacques, 65, 67–68, 69, 70, 88, 356n128
great forgetting, 97
Great Nanhoulou, 84–85
Green, William, 252
Greenberg, Mitchell, 51–52
Greer, Allan, 41–42
Grey Nuns, 107
Grimble Bell School, 233, 234, 238
Guadeloupe, 31, 348n8
Guichard, Charles P., 312
Guichard, Leopold, 312
Guillot, Pierre, 200
Guyart, Marie. *See* Marie de l'Incarnation

Hachard, Jacques, 98–99, 101, 126, 134
Hachard, Marie Madeleine (Sister St. Stanislaus), 98–117, 122, 124, 125–27, 131, 133–34, 140, 146, 160, 364nn6–7, 366n36, 373n148; early life and culture surrounding, 99–107; life with the Ursuline mission to Louisiana, 98, 107–15
Haiti, 219, 246, 279, 369n92
Haitian Revolution, refugees from, 10–13, 22–23, 29, 95, 162–70, 211, 234, 240, 248, 294, 378n17, 379n36; education in early New Orleans/Louisiana, role in, 170–72; in Masonic Lodges, 271–73; Persévérance Lodge No. 4 (formerly No. 113), 13, 272–73, 275–77, 398n109, 398n111, 399n118. *See also* counterpublic spaces, creole pedagogy of; Freemasonry; Saint Domingue (now Haiti)
The Halcyon (literary journal), 264
Hall, Gwendolyn, 115
Hall v. Decuir (1878), 315
Hanks, George, 283

Harlan, John Marshall, 330, 332, 333–34
Harlan, Louis, 296
Hart, Antonia, 312
Hart, Samuel, 213
Harvard College, 91
Harvard University, 45
Haudenosaunee (Iroquois), 45, 53, 56–60, 62, 66, 102, 365n16
Haussner, J. U., 277, 278–79, 280
Hayes, Rutherford B., 310
healing practices, 81, 129, 154, 225, 360n183, 375n167; hospitals, 107–9, 134–37, 143–48, 150, 154–57, 258, 372n138, 372n140, 373n141, 376n175
Hébrard, Jean, 184
Hegel, Haiti and Universal History (Buck-Morss), 20
Herbert, Charlotte (Sister St. Francois Xavier), 126, 129, 143, 145, 147, 148, 154–55, 373n142
Hereditary Genius (Galton), 300
Historie de le Louisiane (Page du Pratz), 375n167
history, as everyday spatial relations, 24–29
Hoffman, Marie Ann, 1–4, 343n1
Holy Family archives, 225
Holy Family Boy's School in New Orleans, 227
Holy Rosary Academy in Galveston, 227
Holy See, 208
Holy Trinity Catholic Church, 262, 267
Honduras, 219
hospices, 222, 224, 226
hospitals, 107–9, 134–37, 143–48, 150, 154–57, 258, 372n138, 372n140, 373n141, 376n175
Hôtel-de-Dieu-de-la-Madeleine, 102, 355n112
Houmas, 77–78, 85–86, 89, 93, 95, 96–97, 361n191
Houppeville, Father de, 99
House of Representatives (Louisiana), 187–88, 323
House of Representatives (US), 297
Houzeau, Jean-Charles ("Dalloz"), 281, 295, 298–300, 402n58
Howard, O. O., 303, 403n76
Howard University Law School, 321

Hugo, Victor, 246, 248
Huguenots, 106
humanism, 36, 39, 42
Humboldt, Alexander von, 299–300
Hundred Years War, 100
Hunter, Phoebe, 209
Hurricane Ida, 96
Hurricane Katrina, 161, 235
hybridity, 56–57, 94, 103, 334. *See also* creolization; syncretism

Ibbett, Katherine, 54–55
Iberville, Pierre Le Moyne, 75–76, 78, 79, 83, 84, 86–87, 360n186, 361n196
identity, 5, 53, 58–59, 69–71, 176, 184, 196, 223, 265, 291; community, 129, 132–33, 139. *See also* color line
Illinois (Illiniwek Confederation), 4–10, 21, 27, 84, 87–89, 94, 132, 149, 362n201, 366n40, 374n150. *See also* Turpin, Marie (Sister St. Marthe); Upper Louisiana Territory, early Jesuit missionary activity in
imaginary spaces, 16
imagination, creole pedagogy of, 29, 237–87, 339–41; The Forty-Eighters, 266–71, 397n90; Lanusse, Armand, 213, 242–50, 255–56, 279–85, 293, 296, 394n35; reverberations of, 286–87; second wave of French Catholic missionaries, 256–60; student activism, 250–56, 281–86; universal equality and The Civil War, 281–86. *See also* The Catholic Institute; Freemasonry; German immigration and education
imagined brotherhood, 13, 16, 242, 271, 272, 273–80, 284–85, 301–9. *See also* Freemasonry
Imagined Communities (Anderson), 23
Immaculate Conception (mission), 7
Immaculate Conception Church, 73–74
imperialism, 33, 42, 63, 67, 175, 371n127. *See also* colonization
indentured servants, 14, 20, 22, 66, 115, 261, 264, 265
Les Indes galantes (Rameau), 73, 357n145
Indigenous peoples, 29–31, 39–41, 44, 54, 61–62, 129, 154, 161–65, 171, 208,

343n2, 375n167; Alibamons, 362n201; Anishabe (Algonquin/Algonquian), 7, 42, 44–45, 53, 58, 59, 60, 66, 350n32; Apalachee, 94; Arkansas, 88; Bayagoulas, 77–81, 83–85, 93, 360n183, 361n191; Caddos, 88; calumet ceremony, 63–64, 67, 73, 79, 84, 360n187; Chickasaws, 8, 78, 85, 95, 362n201; Chitimachas, 89, 93, 96; Choctaws, 8, 78, 88–89, 93, 96, 196, 362n201, 362n202, 373n145, 383n110; Colapissas, 77, 82, 93; Coushatta tribe, 96; early Jesuit missionary activity in Canada, 34, 43–49; enslaved, 115, 361n188; Fox nation, 71, 159; Haudenosaunee (Iroquois), 45, 53, 56–60, 62, 66, 102, 365n16; Houmas, 77–78, 85–86, 89, 93, 95, 96–97, 361n191; Innu (Montagnais), 44–45, 58; languages and local customs, study and use of, 38–39, 41–48, 55, 58–63, 67, 77–79, 350n32, 356n128; Miami Tribe of Oklahoma, 356n128; Michigamea, 71; Mougoulachas, 93; Mugulasha, 361n191; Oneota, 66; Onquilousas, 83; Pascagoulas, 76; Pawnee, 45; Point-au-Chien Tribe, 96, 363n218; Quapaws nation, 362n201; Quinipissas, 84; religious education, effects of, 95–97; religious music, role of, 61, 130–33, 221, 374n150; sovereignty of, 8, 71, 79, 95; Taensas, 77, 82, 93, 361n191; Tamarouas, 84; Tunicas, 88, 96; Upper Creeks, 88; Wendat (Huron), 43–47, 53, 56–58, 60, 62, 94, 102, 354n85, 355n102, 355n110, 365n16; Yazoos, 88, 149, 362, 374n150. *See also* catechism classes; Illinois (Illiniwek Confederation); Natchez
Indigenous women, 50–51, 56–57, 59–60, 62, 66, 68–71, 73, 116–17, 140, 159. *See also* catechism classes; Turpin, Marie
individualism, 37–38, 115, 133
industrial school at Saint Joachim, 49
Ingraham, James, 295, 307
Innu (Montagnais), 44–45, 58
Institute of France, 199
integration, Post-Civil War. *See* public schools, integrated

intermarriage, 7, 66–67, 68–71, 92, 185–86, 261, 330; plaçage, 212, 213, 221, 249, 387n160, 394n35, 397n93

Irish immigrants, 173, 176, 197, 200, 254–55, 257, 262, 265, 395n55

Isabella, Queen of Spain, 164–65

Isabelle, Robert, 321

Islam, 165

Italian immigrants, 254–55, 259–60, 262, 265

Jackson, Andrew, 12, 275, 329

Jacob (enslaved boy), 157

Jacobins, 172, 173

Jallot, Francoise, 159

James, C. L. R., 23

Janssens (Archbishop), 331–32

Jean-Baptiste "Baptiste" (apothecary), 129, 145, 148, 154–55, 158, 160, 339–40, 372n138, 373n141, 375n167

Jeannotoz (enslaved woman), 145

Jefferson, Thomas, 167, 174–75, 176–77, 179, 180, 199, 209, 378n15, 378n18

Jefferson College (became St. Mary's College), 259

Jemmy (enslaved person), 2

Jesuits, 7, 29–33, 56, 61–63, 107, 128, 132, 158, 257–58, 355n104, 364n8, 364n15, 365n16, 366nn40–41; "anthropology," 38–39, 41, 42–43, 44–45, 46–48; early missionary activity in Canada, 34, 43–49, 353n66; expulsion of (1763), 92–93, 95, 259, 362n202; global educational reform movement of, 34–43; Jesuit College (Collège de Bourbon), 102; in New Orleans and Lower Louisiana, 87–94; Paul Du Ru, first Jesuit missionary in Louisiana, 34, 76–86; *Relations* (annual reports), 42–44, 47, 54, 57, 60, 70, 77, 80–81, 100, 102–3, 352nn48–49; slavery, role in, 73–75, 89–92, 259–60, 358n147, 395n51; suppression of (1773–1814), 168. *See also* Petit, Mathurin Le; transcultural translation, creole pedagogy of; Upper Louisiana Territory, early Jesuit missionary activity in

Jesus, Christ, 36

jettons (counters), 123

Jim Crow, 29, 121, 227, 285, 301, 311, 323, 334–35. *See also Plessy v. Ferguson; La Tribune*

Johns, Emil, 261

Johnson, Alisha, 170

Johnson, Andrew, 303, 403n76

Johnson, George G., 324

Johnson, Henry, 204

Johnson, Isaac, 266

Johnson, Robert, 235

Jolliet (Catholic priest), 64, 75

Jones, Austin, 227

Joseph, Marie, 145

Josephine, Empress, 286

Josephites, 160

Joubert, James, 169

Joubert, L. J., 328

Judaism, 32, 213, 261–62, 279

Judde, Marguerite (Sister St. Jean L'Evangeliste), 108, 110, 114, 125–26, 127, 373n142

juries, whites-only, 330

Justice, Protective, Social and Educational Club, 325, 328

Kamper, J. D., 277, 278–79, 280

Kansas-Nebraska Act (1854), 269–70

Kantrowitz, Stephen, 13, 271, 273

Kapp, Friedrich, 270

Kaskaskia, 4–5, 7, 34, 65, 66–75, 88–89, 108, 343n2, 356n127, 366n41

Keller-Lapp, Heidi, 106

Kerr, Lewis, 177

Kinkel, Gottfried, 269

kinship, 183. *See also* fictive kinship; marriage

Knights of Labor, 322

knowledge transmission pedagogy, 27, 36, 37, 127

Know-Nothing Party, 255, 270

Kohn, Joseph, 261–62

Kolly House, 112, 122–23

Kongo, 30

Kozol, Jonathan, 337

Ku Klux Klan, 326

Lacardonie, Marie Thérèse, 213

La Chalotais, René de, 177

LaCroix, Cecile Edouarde, 221–22, 224

LaCroix, François, 221, 242
Lafayette, Marquis de, 199
Lafon, Thomy, 241, 301, 316
LaHarpe school, 312
Lakanal, Alexandrine, 199, 385n134
Lakanal, Joseph, 196–203, 211, 234, 235–36, 339–40, 384n123, 385nn133–34
Lalemant, Charles, 43
Lalemant, Jérôme, 43, 54, 354n85
Lalemont (Catholic priest), 46
Lamartine, Alphonse de, 246, 248
Lambert (house mother), 191
Lambert, Pierre, 184, 189
Lancastrian method of teaching, 233, 241
Lange, Elizabeth Clarisse, 168–69
Lange, Victor, 307
languages and local customs, study and use of, 38–39, 41–48, 55, 58–63, 67, 77–79, 350n32, 356n128. *See also* literacy
Lanusse, Armand, 213, 242–50, 255–56, 279–85, 293, 296, 394n35
Larche, Joseph, 157
La Salle, René-Robert Cavelier de, 75, 76, 361n191, 364n15
Laurent, Maire Louise, 184
Laval, Antoine Jean de, 91, 362n207
Laval, François de Montmorency de, 48–49, 65
Lavigne, Joseph, 222
Lavocat, Pre. H., 181, 183
Laws of Nature, 297
Lazarists, 257
Leavelle, Tracy Neal, 33, 68
Lefebvre, Henri, 25
Lefort, Luis Francisco, 171
legal status, 142–43, 371n128, 389n184. *See also* civil rights
Legislative Council, 176–77, 180, 187–88
Le Jeune, Paul, 43–46, 57
Le Maire, François, 91
Le Moyne brothers. *See* Bienville, Jean-Baptiste Le Moyne; Iberville, Pierre Le Moyne
Le Normant (financial director), 157, 372n140, 376n175

Lesseige, Hélène, 10, 273
letter writing, 250–56
Lettres Circulaires (Ursulines), 130
Leumas, Emilie Gagnet, 120
Liberator (newspaper), 289
Liberty in Louisiana (Workman), 176
libraries, 178, 182, 199, 201, 279, 375n172, 396n63
liminality, 289; of free people of color, 211–28. *See also* free women of color, liminality of
liminality, creole pedagogy of, 29, 288–337, 339–41. *See also Crusader; La Tribune*
Lincoln, Abraham, 268, 282, 314, 321, 329, 397n90, 403n76
Lindbaugh, Peter, 17
literacy, 35, 47–53, 70, 170, 175, 187, 225, 243, 263, 283, 326; among enslaved people, 1–4, 46, 213–14, 219, 221, 232, 242, 343n1, 343n4, 344n5, 344n7, 344n14, 387n163, 392n11; literacy tests, 334; in Ursuline schools, 101–3, 119, 123, 139, 155, 160. *See also* languages and local customs, study and use of
living books, 39
Livingston, Edward, 176, 177, 196, 200, 383n95, 384n112
logos (logic), use in fighting scientific racism, 289–91, 292, 296, 297–301
Lopez de Armesto, Andrew, 171
Lorette mission, 45
Louis, John P., 200
Louisiana (State), 15, 23–24, 76, 275; Board of Education, 283; Constitution of 1864, 265–66, 302; Constitution of 1868, 186, 284–85, 296, 307–9, 311, 313–14, 315, 405n118; Constitution of 1879, 314, 316–17; Constitution of 1898, 334; Grand Coteau, 208–9, 216, 225, 257–58, 395n51; HB261 (2022), 96; House of Representatives, 187–88, 323; Louisiana Club, 314–15; *Louisiana Gazette* (newspaper), 178; *Louisiana Historical Quarterly* (journal), 146, 375n174; Louisiana Purchase, 95, 178–80, 186, 207; Louisiana State University Librar-

ies, 201; Natchitoches, 88, 233–34; Opelousas, 233, 238; Pointe Coupée, 11, 172, 173, 232–33, 274, 381n64; Senate, 196, 323; Superior Council of, 1–4, 343nn1–2, 344n5; Supreme Court, 313, 314, 328, 330; territorial legislature, 380n56. *See also* Jesuits; New Orleans; Upper Louisiana Territory, early Jesuit missionary activity in; Ursulines

The Louisiana Asylum for girls in New Orleans, 227

Louison (enslaved African woman), 145

Louis XIV, 49, 105, 108, 110, 367n58

Louis XV, 72, 91

Louis XVI, 76

Louis XVIII, 199

Louverture, Toussaint, 163, 166

love, as Ursuline pedagogy, 38, 124, 368n65

Loyola, Saint Ignatius, 35

Lugar, Iris, 183

Lugar, Juan, 183

Lusher, Robert, 310

lynching, 320, 326, 330

Maas (Doctor), 269

Madame Grelaud's Seminary for Girls, 167

Maenhaut (Catholic priest), 217–18, 242

Mager, Jean, 224

Mahieu, Madeleine (Sister St. François Xavier), 41, 109–10, 113

Maintenon, Marquise de (Françoise d'Aubignè), 105

Maison Royale de Saint Louis, 105

Mali, Anya, 47, 53

Manesca, John, 167

Mann, Horace, 198, 229

Mantua Academy, 167, 196

manumission, 161, 222, 223, 240, 244, 382n87

marché (contract), 145, 157, 372n140, 373n141

Marching 100, 160, 162

March Revolution, 266–67

Marciacq, Jean Louis, 169, 245

Marest, Gabriel, 68, 356n127

Marianites of the Holy Cross, 208, 257

Marie de l'Incarnation (Marie Guyart), 34, 49–63, 100, 106, 109, 353n67, 353n70, 354n84, 355n110, 364n8; languages and local customs, use of, 55, 58–63; mysticism of, 52–58

Marie de St. Joseph (Ursuline nun), 57, 60

Marigny, Bernard, 240

Marion, Jean (Sister Ste. Michel), 111, 113

Marist fathers, 259

market economy of schools, 235

maroon communities, 86

Marquette, Jacques, 64, 65, 66, 745

marriage, 120, 158, 219, 259, 376n183; intermarriage, 7, 66–67, 68–71, 92, 185–86, 261, 330; plaçage, 212, 213, 221, 249, 387n160, 394n35, 397n93

"Un Marriage de conscience" (Lanusse), 249

Martel, Gustave, 277

Martin (woman teacher of color), 186

Martin, Claude, 49–50, 53, 354n84

Martin, L., 335

Martinet, Hippolite, 320

Martinet, Louis, 339

Martinet, Louis André, 245, 310, 318–24, 325, 327–28, 329, 330, 332, 335

Martinique, 31, 106, 286, 348n8

martyrdom, 54–55, 102, 139, 364n8, 364n15

Mary, Aristide, 245, 301, 310, 316, 324, 405n110

Mary, mother of Jesus, 36–37, 69, 104, 117, 118, 119–20, 129

Masonic Lodges. *See* Freemasonry

Massachusetts, 305–6

Massacre of 1866, 284

Massé, Ennemond, 43, 44

Massy, Claude (Sister Moelle), 111–12, 113, 132

Mathieu, Marie Rose, 184

Mayorquin, Jean Baptiste, 181, 183

Mazureau, Etienne, 197, 384n115

McKenna, Beverly Stanton, 336

McKenna, Dwight, 336

McKinley, William, 335

Mechanics Institute, 284, 321

Mechip8e8a, Dorothée, 7

Melotte, Jeanne (Sister St. André),
    137–38, 147, 149, 152, 157, 373n149,
    374n159
"Mémoir présenté au Congrès des Êtas-
    Unis Amérique par les Habitants de la
    Louisiane" (1804), 178–80
memorization pedagogy, 127, 129,
    369n86
Mercure de France (magazine), 72
Merici, Saint Angela, 36, 100, 117
Mermet, Jean, 86, 356n127
Methodist Church, 267, 289, 378n23,
    400n13
métis marriages, 68
métissage (braiding), 41
métissage (mixed race), 9, 21
Metoyer, Augustin, 233–34
Mexico, 219, 274
Michigamea, 71
Michilimackinac mission, 65, 356n127
microhistories, 28–29
Mina, uprising of, 172
Miro (Governor), 171
Missio Ludovisiana, 106–7
Mission de Sainte-Maire, 45
Mississippian Shatter Zone, 95
Miss Lange's School, 168
Missouri Compromise, 269
Mitchell, Mary Niall, 243, 253, 292, 302
mixed race peoples, 165, 183–84,
    185–86; métis, 9, 21, 41, 68; mulat-
    toes, 140, 152, 159, 173, 225, 279,
    374n159; quadroons, 159, 212, 223,
    226. *See also* Afro-Creoles; Creoles
M'Karaher, James, 200
Mobile, Alabama, 86–87, 91, 202, 268,
    280, 361n196, 361n198, 395n48
mobility, 5, 156, 174, 214
modernism, 24, 37, 53, 99, 105, 286
modernity, conscript of, 21
monogenesis, 58
Monsieur Paul (Questy), 246
Morand, Charles Antoine, 161
Moreau, Julie, 161–62, 188, 382n87
Moreau, Paul, 161, 344n5
Moreau de Saint-Méry, Médéric Louis
    Élie, 165
Moreau-Lislet, Louis, 177, 178, 189,
    380nn58–59, 382n85

Morrissey, Robert, 67, 357n139
Moss, Hilary, 229
Mougoulachas, 93
Mount Carmel Convent Boarding
    School for Free Girls of Color, 258,
    388n174
mulattoes, 140, 152, 159, 173, 225, 279,
    374n159
Müller, Salome, 265
Muro, François, 272
music, as folk pedagogy, 61, 130–33,
    221, 374n150
mysticism, creole, 52–58

NAACP, 326–27
Nanette (enslaved woman), 206, 216
Natchez, 77, 81–82, 86, 93, 374n150,
    375n167; Revolt in 1729, 8, 113–14,
    132, 149, 362n201
Natchitoches, Louisiana, 233–34
National Assembly of France, 10
National Citizens' Rights Association
    (NCRA), 320, 326–27
National Equal Rights League, 295
National Freedmen's Relief Association,
    289
nationalism, 18, 21, 23, 27, 32–33, 63,
    103–4, 176, 341
National Register of Historic Places,
    96–97
National Union Brotherhood Associa-
    tion, 295
native schools, 283
nativism, 255, 267, 270
Navarre, Suzanne, 226, 390n190
Neckere (Bishop), 214–15
négritude movement, 286–87
Negro Act (1740), 2
Nelson, Médard, 317
New England town meeting, 180
New Orleans, Louisiana, 72–75, 174;
    Academy of Science, 298; Battle of,
    12, 275; Board of Assistant Alderman,
    396n66; *City Directory*, 181, 182, 184,
    186, 230, 384n128, 385n134; city fire
    of 1788, 170–71; colonial administra-
    tion in, 107; *Directory and Register*
    (New Orleans, 1822), 194; Faubourg
    Marigny, 169, 181–82, 240, 262–63,

269; Faubourg Tremé, 10, 188–89, 217, 224, 271–72, 321; Jesuits in, 87–94; *New Orleans Bee* (newspaper), 268, 282–83; *New Orleans Democrat* (newspaper), 313; *New Orleans Map* (1732), 144; *New Orleans Medical and Surgical Journal* (journal), 298; *New Orleans Republican* (newspaper), 309; New Orleans University, 318; Public Library, 182, 194, 230; *Times* (newspaper), 300. *See also* College d'Orléans; counterpublic spaces, creole pedagogy of; Haitian Revolution, refugees from; *La Tribune*; Ursuline Academy in New Orleans; Ursulines

newspapers, 281–86, 379n35; advertisements, 163, 169, 184; Black, 400n13, 401n16; as community-based texts, 291–92; reverberations of, 335–37. *See also La Tribune*

New York, 172, 177

New York Abendzeitung (newspaper), 270

Ng-A-Fook, Nicholas, 97

Nicaragua, 219

Nicholas (enslaved child), 145

Nicholas, Armand, 251–52

Nicholls (Governor), 323

Nicolas, Armand, 250–51

Nigeria, 227

night school, 186

normality, 18–19

Nos Hommes et Notre Histoire (Desdunes), 334–35

notes inégales ("swing"), 131–32

Notre-Dame- de-Foy mission, 45

Notre-Dames-des-Anges college/seminary, 45

Nouvelles poésis spirituelles et morales sur les plus beaux airs de la musique françoise et italienne avec la basse (Ursuline music manuscript), 132, 369n101, 370n102

Oblate Rule, 169

Oblate School for Colored Girls, 169

Oblate Sisters of Providence, 168–69, 218, 391n197

Odin (Archbishop), 226

Ohio, 172

Olivier, Pierre, 272

Oneota, 66

Onquilousas, 83

Opelousas, Louisiana, 233, 238

oral traditions, 39, 47–48

Organic Regulations of the College of Orleans (Collège d'Orléans), 189, 190

Orleans Parish School Board, 321

orphanages, 137, 147, 210–11, 226, 241, 374n161, 387n154

orphans, 150, 152–53, 155, 159, 209–10, 242–43. *See also* The Catholic Institute

Our Lady of Victory, 120, 150

paganism, 40, 44, 53, 56, 103, 354n91, 360n176

Page du Pratz, Antoine-Simon Le, 154, 375n167

Pandelly, George: *Pandelly v. Wiltz* (1853), 264–65, 396n66

"Pange Lingua" (St. Thomas Aquinas), 139, 370n120

La Parfaite-Union (Perfect Union) No. 1, 178, 280

Paris Seminary of Foreign Missions, 48

parodies, musical, 130, 132, 369n101, 370n102

Pascagoulas, 76

patriarchy, 155, 156, 210, 394n35

Pawnee, 45

Paxton, John Adams, 194

Peace, Thomas, 47–48

pedagogy, 28–29; deficit pedagogy, 39, 44, 117; double pedagogy, 82; knowledge transmission pedagogy, 27, 36, 37, 127; love, as Ursuline pedagogy, 38, 124, 368n65; memorization pedagogy, 127, 129, 369n86; music, as folk pedagogy, 61, 130–33, 221, 374n150. *See also* creole pedagogies

Pennsylvania Abolition Society (PAS), 167

Périer, Etienne, 135–36

Persévérance Lodge No. 4 (formerly No. 113), 13, 272–73, 275–77, 398n109, 398n111, 399n118

Peruque, Eulalie, 225

Pestalozzian education system, 263

Petit, Mathurin Le, 132, 139–40, 145–47, 157–58, 371n123, 373n145, 374n150; spacial relations and creole communities, 148–56

petite écoles, 105, 128, 369n90

petite nations, 93

Petit Séminaire, 48

Phélypeaux, Jérôme, 75

Philadelphia, Pennsylvania, 166–68, 196, 377n13, 379n35, 384n112

Philippeaux (minister of Louis XIV), 108

Philips, Patrick, 97

phrenology, 167

Picayune (newspaper), 304

Pierrot (enslaved man), 145, 148

Pinar, William, 23

Pinchback, P. B. S., 324

Pind, Jackson, 97

Piron, Myrtil, 325

Pitot, James, 166, 178

Pittman, Philip, 74

plaçage (arranged interracial relationship), 212, 213, 221, 249, 387n160, 394n35, 397n93

"Plan of the City and Suburbs of New Orleans" (New Orleans, 1815), 191

Plessy, Homer, 321, 328–30, 334, 339–40, 408n172

Plessy, Louis, 334

Plessy v. Ferguson (1896), 285, 304, 316, 318, 320; legal preparation for, 324–27; from public to civil rights, 327–35. *See also* Separate Car Act

Plumly, B. Rush, 304

Poché, Felix, 314

Point-au-Chien Tribe, 96, 363n218

Pointe Coupée, Louisiana, 11, 172, 173, 232–33, 274, 381n64

Political Essays (Workman), 176

Pommereu, Marie-Augustine de Sainte-Paule, 100

Pondicherry, India, 106

porosity, 21, 27

postcolonial activism, 286–87

Postel, Guillaume, 51

Powell, Lawrence, 133

power and control, education tool of, 38, 62, 103–4, 105, 136, 263

Poydras Orphan Asylum for Girls, 210, 241, 387n154

The Practice of Everyday Life (de Certeau), 24

La Prairie de la Madeleine mission, 45

Prairie du Rocher mission, 71

Prat, Louis, 143

The Present State of the European Settlements on the Mississippi (Pittman), 74

Preval, Chloé Joachim, 226

Priory of Saint Lô, 102

prisons, 19, 37, 137, 148, 235

private schools, 171, 232–35, 243, 248, 263, 267, 283, 303, 317–18, 404n87, 405n118

The Production of Space (LeFebre), 25

protest and revolutions, 11, 176, 196, 233, 266–67, 274, 279, 311; accommodation *versus*, 310–11, 313, 375n166; American Revolution, 22, 167, 183, 282, 380n59; French Revolution, 22, 172, 178, 197, 208, 248, 261, 378n15, 378n19, 380n59; slave rebellions, 2, 11, 166, 172–73, 187, 274–75, 379n34. *See also* Haitian Revolution

Protestants, 45, 117–18, 209, 210–11, 229, 241, 262, 378n23; Huguenots, 106; Lutherans, 263, 267, 396n72; Methodist Church, 267, 289, 378n23, 400n13; Puritans, 17, 39, 270, 350n32, 351n34, 368n68; Reformation, 16–17, 18–19, 27, 35, 101–2, 103, 105; Second Great Awakening, 270

Prussian education system, 263

psychic spaces, 16

public assistance, 63

public culture, 128, 154, 275

Public Education in the United States (Cubberly), 16

public rights, 15, 32, 97, 118, 162, 180, 291, 307–9, 335–37, 394n45; to civil rights, 327–35, 339–41; during Segregation, 243, 255, 277, 282–85, 288

public schools, 165–66, 170–71, 234, 243, 380n54; "An Act to provide for the establishment of public free schools in the several counties of the Territory" (1806), 180–81; "public" (state-funded, whites only) education, 228–32, 235–36, 238, 243, 249, 256–60, 262–63, 265–66, 283; secularization of education, 103–4, 165–66; University Act of 1805 (supplement 1811), 172–81, 188, 381n64

public schools, integrated, 285, 405n118; *La Tribune*, advocacy by, 289–91, 301–9. *See also Crusader; La Tribune*

public spaces, 275, 276–77, 339–41

public sphere, 32, 37, 50–57, 60, 183–84, 188, 210–11, 234, 290–91, 322–23, 340, 353n73; music in, 61, 130–33, 221, 374n150; during Segregation, 243, 253–54, 258–62, 270, 284–85; in Ursuline schools, 104–6, 109, 115, 137–39, 142, 156; as white space, 228–32, 235–36, 238, 243, 249, 256–60, 262–63, 265–66, 283

punishment, 123–24

Puritans, 17, 39, 270, 350n32, 351n34, 368n68

Pykett, Lyn, 336–37

quadroons (one-fourth Black ancestry), 159, 212, 223, 226

Quakers, 209

Quebec, Canada, 48, 87, 106–7. *See also* Canada

Question de L'Esclavage (Houzeau), 299

Questy, Joanni, 245, 246, 279

Quinipissas, 84

race, 40, 71, 75, 159, 198, 210, 339–41, 345n30; Code Noir, 3–4, 15, 30–34, 46, 73–74, 92, 121, 142, 145, 158, 164–65, 248, 344n10, 349n16, 363n209; fluidity of, 75, 115–18, 140, 170, 184, 186, 206–7, 328; grandfather clause, 334; lynching, 320, 326, 330; Negro Act, 2; racial anxiety, 173–74; racialization, 18, 23, 29, 67, 160, 211, 228–29, 339; racial solidarity, 173–74, 211, 368n75, 369n90; scientific racism, 167, 244, 248, 265, 284, 288–92, 297–302, 333; universal male suffrage, 281, 284, 290, 295, 314. *See also* Africans; Afro-Creoles; colonization; color line; Creoles; francization; free

people of color; Indigenous peoples; Jim Crow; mixed race peoples; segregation; slavery; whiteness

Radical Reconstruction, 227, 235, 285, 316, 320–21

Radical Republican Party, 301, 311, 314–15

Raguet, Gilles Bernard, 108, 137, 361n199

Ramachard, Marguerite Antoinette de (Sister St. Bernard), 147

Ramachard, Marie Therese de (Sister St. François de Paule), 147

Rameau, Jean-Philippe, 72–73, 357n145

Rapley, Elizabeth, 63

Ratio Studiorum, 36

Ray, John, 314–16

Raymond, Gilbert, 226

reconciliation, so-called era of, 97

Reconstruction, 227, 267, 281, 285, 291, 305; Radical Reconstruction, 227, 235, 285, 316, 320–21. *See also La Tribune*

Recovery School District (RSD), 235

Redeemer Democrats, 309–10, 312

redemptionists (indentured servants), 260

Rediker, Marcus, 17

reductions (mission villages), 41, 45

reform, social, 133–38

regional variant of the long nineteenth century, 274–75

Reglemens des religieuses Ursulines de la congrégation de Paris (Ursulines), 37, 116, 123–24, 152

Reign of Terror, 189, 198–99

reimagined citizen, 18

relational space-time, 25–28

Relation du voyage des dames religieuses Ursuline/Relation of the Voyage of the Ursuline Nuns (Ursulines), 99

Relations des Jésuites de la Nouvelle-France (Jesuit annual reports), 42–44, 47, 54, 57, 60, 70, 77, 80–81, 100, 102–3, 352nn48–49

religion, 295, 344n7; Cuban Santeria, 369n92; Haitian Vodou, 369n92; Islam, 165; Judaism, 32, 213, 261–62, 279; paganism, 40, 44, 53, 56, 103,

religion (*continued*)
354n91, 360n176; Quakers, 209. *See
also* Catholic Church; Jesuits; Protestants; Ursuline Academy in New
Orleans; Ursulines
Renaissance, 36, 42
renfermement, 136
republicanism, 27, 170, 173, 177, 202,
212, 269–70, 294, 380n59
Republican Party, 255, 269, 270, 295,
309–10, 397n90; Radical Republican
Party, 301, 311, 314–15
republican school (Haiti), 166
Republic of Letters, European, 76, 94,
109
resegregation, 309–18, 321, 334, 337,
406n135
Rey, Barthelemy, 242
Rhode Island, 172
Ricord, Phillipe, 294
Rightor, Nicholas H., 313–14
Robertson, Thomas B., 196, 384n115
Roberts v. Boston (1849), 289, 305–6
Rochefort, Pierre, 190, 193
Roffignac, Louis Philippe de, 197,
384n115
Rogers, William O., 310
rogue colonialism, 19–20
rogue curriculum, defining, 19–24
Romain, Orfise, 226
Roman law, 33
Roman Sodality of the Blessed Virgin
Mary, 218
Rose, L., 277
Roselius, Christian, 264–65, 279
Roudanez, Jean-Baptiste, 281, 294, 301,
314, 401n16
Roudanez, Louis Charles, 281, 294, 295,
299, 301, 309, 314, 336, 401n16
Rouen, France, 100–102, 106–7, 364n15
Rouensa, Marie, 70
Roup, Charles, 10
Roup, Pierre, 10–13, 16, 20–21, 163,
271–77, 280, 339–40, 345nn21–22
Roup, Pierre, Sr., 10, 273
Rouquette, Adrien, 192, 193, 196,
383n110
Rouquette, Dominique, 196
Rousseau, Jean-Jacques, 200

Rousselon, Etienne, 215, 216, 217, 218,
219, 225
Roussève, Charles, 319, 331
Royal Hospital (New Orleans), 143, 146,
148

Sacred Heart schools, 227, 258, 317,
405n118
sacred objects, 28, 39, 59–60, 83, 119,
129, 139, 157, 368n68; calumet ceremony, 63–64, 67, 73, 79, 84, 360n187
Saint-Ceran, Tullius, 192
Saint Domingue (now Haiti), 10–13,
137, 163–64, 348n8, 377n13. *See also*
Haiti; Haitian Revolution, refugees
from
St. Augustine Church in Natchitoches,
233–34
St. Augustine parish, 161–62, 217–18,
219, 224, 225, 262, 382n87, 388n174
St. Augustine's school in Donaldsonville,
227
St. Charles College, 258, 395n51
St. Claude School for Colored and
White Girls, 162, 205–12, 213–15,
216–17, 218, 241, 386nn145–46,
388n174
St. Frances School for Colored Girls (St.
Frances Academy), 169
St. Joseph's parish, 262
St. Joseph's school in Opelousas, 227,
232
St. Jullien, Marie Charlotte, 152,
374n159
St. Katherine's Church, 332
St. Landry night riders, 233, 238
St. Louis Cathedral, 121, 183, 206–7,
217, 219, 262, 357n141
St. Mary's Academy, 208, 226–27, 241,
390n193
St. Mary's Assumption Church, 262
St. Mary's Chapel, 206, 207, 219
St. Mary's of the Barrens Seminary, 259
St. Mary's School (later Holy Family
Academy) in Baton Rouge, 227
St. Mary's Seminary, 168–69, 378n19
St. Michael's Convent, 225
St. Patrick's Cathedral, 262
St. Patrick's Female Orphan Asylum, 258

St. Paul's Lutheran Church, 263, 267, 396n72

Salaon, Marguerite de (Sister Ste. Thèrése), 110–11, 114, 373n142

Sans, Christian, 263

sauvage ("savage"), 50, 78

Les Sauvages (Rameau), 72, 357n145

Sauve, Pierre, 179

Savonnières de St. Joseph, Marie de, 58

Savry, Joseph, 274

school boards, 204, 309–11, 313–14, 317

schooling (*versus* education), 17–19, 27, 47–48, 95, 358n158

science of education, 18–19, 340

scientific racism, 167, 244, 248, 265, 284, 288–92, 297–302, 333

Scott, David, 21

Scott, Dred, 238–39, 333

Scott, Rebecca, 12, 13, 22, 184, 243, 274–75, 307, 394n45

Scottish Rite Lodges, 276, 399n116, 408n172

Second Great Awakening, 270

secularization of education, 103–4, 165–66. *See also* state support of schools

segregation, 70–71, 95, 143, 160–61; of the Catholic Church, 331–32; desegregation, 296, 309; gendered, 229, 249, 263, 404n87; "public" (state-funded, whites only) education, 228–32, 235–36, 238, 243, 249, 256–60, 262–63, 265–66, 283; racial, pre-Civil War, 209, 216–17, 218–19, 228–32, 391n197; resegregation, 309–18, 321, 334, 337, 406n135

segregation, age of racial, 227, 235, 393n20; Black schools, 95, 160–61, 283–84, 316–18; Black teachers, lack of, 317, 328; tripartite system of, 293, 405n113. *See also* counterpublic spaces, in the age of Segregation; imagination, creole pedagogy of; *Plessy v. Ferguson; La Tribune*

Sejour, Victor, 279

Selles, B., 191

Séminaire des Missions Étrangères de Paris, 48

Senate (Louisiana), 196, 323

Senegal trading company, 101

Separate Car Act (1890), 289, 316, 318, 320–24, 328, 408n168; Citizens' Committee, 316, 321, 324–27, 328–35. *See also Plessy v. Ferguson*

Seton, Elizabeth, 208

shamans, 44

The Shame of the Nation (Kozol), 337

Shaw, John Angier, 263, 396n63

Sillery mission, 45, 65

Sisters of Mt. Carmel (Carmelites), 54, 102, 162, 208, 217, 257, 258, 317, 388n174

Sisters of the Holy Family, 205–6, 212, 218–28, 233, 241–42, 258, 317, 340, 384n127, 385n128, 387n167, 390n194, 391n197; Association of the Holy Family, 221–22, 224; Bayou Road School, 218, 224–25, 226, 228, 249, 390n193; Holy Family archives, 225; Holy Family Boy's School in New Orleans, 227

Sisters of the Sacred Heart, 208, 216, 225, 227, 257–58, 317, 395n51, 405n118

slavery, 5, 15, 20, 23, 86, 185, 286, 290, 358nn146–48, 371n123, 376n181, 376n183, 380n59, 388n170, 395n54; Afro-Creole slaveholders, 222–23, 240, 392n7; Code Noir of 1685 (revised 1724, 1855), 3–4, 15, 30–34, 46, 73–74, 92, 121, 142, 145, 158, 164–65, 248, 344n10, 349n16, 363n209; in early Ursuline schools, 94–95, 101, 111, 150–51, 362n203; Emancipation Proclamation, 282, 283; formerly enslaved people, 226–27, 244, 283–86, 391n197; free-soil principle, 31; of Indigenous peoples, 115, 361n188; Jesuits, role in, 73–75, 89–92, 259–60, 358n147, 395n51; literacy during, 1–4, 46, 213–14, 219, 221, 232, 242, 343n1, 343n4, 344n5, 344n7, 344n14, 387n163, 392n11; manumission, 161, 222, 223, 240, 244, 382n87; rebellions, 2, 11, 166, 172–73, 187, 274–75, 379n34; runaways, 343n2; slave market, 235; at Ursuline Academy in New Orleans, 120–21, 157–60, 240, 371n125, 372n133,

slavery (*continued*)
372n138. *See Also* Africans, enslaved;
anti-slavery; catechism classes; Civil
War; free people of color; Haitian
Revolution
social network analysis, 357n139
social order, 134–38, 140–43, 151–53,
154–56, 210, 314. *See also* class
social space, 25, 211
Société d'Economie et d'Assitance
Mutuelle (Economy and Mutual Aid
Association), 245
Society of the Friends of Blacks, 198
soeur portiere, 125
Souers de Sainte-Famille. *See* Sisters of
the Holy Family
Soul by Soul (Johnson), 235
Soulié brothers (Norbert, Albin, and
Bernard), 272
South Carolina, 2, 86, 174
Southern University, 318, 322
Southwestern Christian Advocate (newspaper), 324–25
sovereignty, Indigenous, 8, 71, 79, 95
spacial relations, 24–29, 148–56
Span, Christopher, 291
spatial codes, 25
Spring Hill College, 259
star cars, 311
star schools, 305
state support of schools, 228–32,
235–36, 237–38, 239, 243, 266, 317;
"public" (state-funded, whites only)
education, 228–32, 235–36, 238, 243,
249, 256–60, 262–63, 265–66, 283
Stern, Laurence, 279, 399n123
Stern, Walter, 266
Stono rebellion of 1739, 2
Straight University, 318, 321, 323, 327;
Board of Trustees, 321, 322
student activism, 250–56, 281–86
subalternity, 20–21, 25
subjectivity, 9, 15–16, 24–26, 133, 212,
223, 271, 340–41; creole, 20–21;
of dehumanization, 20; as individual, 37–38. *See also* global spiritual
universalism
Sublette, Ned, 130, 131–32
Sullivan (Irish teacher), 200

Sulpician Fathers, 168–69, 378n19
Sumner, Chas., 306–7
Superior Council of Louisiana, 1–4,
343nn1–2, 344n5
Supreme Court (Louisiana), 313, 314,
328, 330
Supreme Court (US), 238–39, 313, 315,
322. *See also Plessy v. Ferguson*
syncretism, 39, 79, 81, 83, 119, 127, 129,
132, 369n92. *See Also* creolization;
hybridity

Taensas, 82, 93, 361n191
Taff, Mary Ann, 245
Taiearonk (Chief), 62
Tamarouas, 84
Tanesse, Jacques, 191
Taney (Chief Justice), 238–39
Tanguy de la Boissière, Claude Corentin, 173, 379n35
Tartarin, René, 110, 111, 366n41
taxation, 179, 180–81, 221, 303–4, 317
Te Deum (song), 130
Teinturier (math professor), 190–91
temporality, 27–28, 38, 161, 187
Teresa of Ávila, 54, 225
Terrebonne Parish School Board, 96–97
Theatre Italien, 72
Theatre St. Philippe, 209
Thibodaux Massacre, 322
Thomas, Chazel, 222
Thompson, Shirley Elizabeth, 26, 264,
274, 396n66
Thomy Lafon Orphan's Home, 241
Times (New Orleans, newspaper), 300
Tinchant, Édouard, 185–86
Tinchant, Jacques, 185
Tinchant, Joseph, 185
"To All Who May Be Concerned" (Citizens' Committee), 329
Tocqueville, Alexis de, 211
Tonty/Tonti, Henri, 84, 361n191
Tourgée, Albion W., 318–20, 325–30,
332, 335, 339, 407n160
Tourne, Pascal M., 310
Tranchepain, Marie (Sister St. Augustin), 106–8, 110, 112, 114, 134–37,
366n46, 373n142, 373n149
transatlantic, defining, 20–24

transcultural translation, creole peda-
gogy of, 29, 30–97, 339–41; Father
Paul Du Ru, first Jesuit missionary in
Louisiana, 34, 76–86; global educa-
tional reform movement of Jesuits and
Ursulines, 34–43; Jesuit missionary
activity in Canada, 34, 43–49; Jesuits
in New Orleans and Lower Louisiana,
87–94; reverberations, 95–97. *See also*
Marie de l'Incarnation; Upper Louisiana Territory, early Jesuit missionary
activity in
Transylvania University, 196
Treatise on the Education of Girls
(Fénelon), 104
Tremé, Claude, 162, 188, 214, 382n87,
387n165, 388n174
Trévigne, Paul, 193, 245, 281, 290, 293–
96, 299, 301, 311–16, 383n104
Trévigne, Paul, Jr., 312–13
Trévigne/Treviño, Roderic, 193,
383n104
triangle trade, 20, 22
*La Tribune de la Nouvelle-Orléans/The
New Orleans Tribune* (newspaper),
29, 246, 281–86, 394n35, 401n16,
401n23, 402n58, 402nn35–36; as
advocate for public integrated education, 289–91; Afro-Creole protest
tradition and founding of, 293–97;
fighting scientific racism, 297–301;
newspapers as community-based texts,
291–92; one people and one nation,
advocating for, 301–9; return to battle:
1877–1896, 309–18; reverberations of,
335–37; *L'Union* (newspaper, became
La Tribune), 281, 282, 285, 294, 299,
401n16
Tröhler, Daniel, 340
Trois-Rivières seminary, 45
Trouillot, Michel-Rolph, 27, 379n36
True Delta (newspaper), 303
Truth and Reconciliation Committee
(Canada), 97
tuition system, 180–81, 188–91, 202,
204, 233–34, 242–43, 303, 317,
381n64. *See also* boarding students
Tunicas, 88, 96
Turner, Victor, 139

Turner Societies (Turnvereine), 267–69,
270, 397n78
Turpin, Louis, 4, 7
Turpin, Marie (Sister Ste. Marthe),
4–10, 21, 27, 67, 69, 71, 75, 159, 160,
339–40. *See also* Illinois (Indigenous
peoples); Kaskaskia; Ursulines
tutors, 171, 225, 382n82

Ueber School, 267
Une Folie (opera), 209
unified school system, 283
L'Union (newspaper, became *La Tribune*),
281, 282, 285, 294, 299, 401n16
United States, 95, 159, 170, 172, 175;
Americanization, 176–77, 209, 228–
29, 246, 258, 302; Americans, 171–72,
178, 384n115; Congress, 178–79, 181,
301, 305, 333, 385n133; Constitution,
238–39, 265–66, 301, 312–13, 315,
329–30, 332–33; Freedmen's Bureau,
227, 233, 283–84, 289, 291, 303, 305,
318, 403n76; House of Representatives, 297. *See also* Supreme Court
(US)
universal equality and The Civil War,
281–86
universalism, 286–87, 290, 301–9, 332,
341. *See also* global spiritual universalism; *La Tribune*
universal male suffrage, 281, 284, 290,
295, 314
University Act of 1805 (supplement
1811), 172–81, 188, 381n64
University of Louisiana (now Tulane),
321, 396n57
Upper Creeks (Fort Toulouse), 88
Upper Louisiana Territory, early Jesuit
missionary activity in, 34, 63–75. *See
also* Africans, enslaved; fictive kinship;
intermarriage
urbanization, 174
Ursula, Saint, 100, 138–39
Ursuline Academy in New Orleans,
98–162, 171, 205, 207, 234, 240–41,
258, 366n39; Company of the Indies,
role of, 133–38; creole counterpublic,
creation of, 116–22, 367n60; music as
folk pedagogy, 130–33; reverberations

Ursuline Academy in New Orleans
(*continued*)
of, 160–62; second generation creole
curriculum, 114–15, 122–30, 147,
367n63; slavery, role in, 120–21, 157–
60, 240, 371n125, 372n133, 372n138;
spacial relations and creole communities, 148–56. *See also* disorder,
creole pedagogy of; Hachard, Marie
Madeleine
Ursulines, 4–10, 29, 31–34, 87, 91,
211–12, 215, 228, 257, 317; choir
nuns, 4–5, 8; cloister (clausura), 57,
60–62, 105–6, 108, 112, 125, 147, 151,
355n112, 366n42; convent in Bayeaux,
Normandy, 372n136; convent in
Tours, France, 50, 53–54; convent
school at Rue St. Jacque in Paris,
105, 367n58; converse nuns, 4–5, 9,
57, 111; global educational reform
movement of, 34–43, 47–48; *Lettres
Circulaires*, 130; love, pedagogy of,
38, 124, 368n65; St. Claude School
for Colored and White Girls, 162,
205–12, 213–15, 216–17, 218, 241,
386nn145–46, 388n174; Ursuline
Academy in Quebec, 49, 62–63,
364n8; Ursuline Convent Archives,
New Orleans (UCANO), 362n203.
See also boarding students; catechism
classes; day students; Kaskaskia; Marie
de l'Incarnation; slavery; Turpin,
Marie
Usner, Daniel, 85, 359n159

Value, Victor, 167, 196
van Evrie, John H., 298
Vecque, Josephine, 226
Verdin, Monique, 95
Vida (spiritual autobiography), 54
Vidal, Michel, 295
*Vie de la vénérable mère Marie de
l'Incarnation* (Marie de l'Incarnation),
61
Vigneaux-Lavigne, Joseph, 244–45
Villere school, 312
Vincent de Paul, Saint, 51, 353n67
Vincentians, 51, 259, 353n67
Vine and Olive Colony, 202, 384n123

Visinier (night school teacher), 186
vision of belonging, 271
Vitry (Catholic priest), 92
Vivant, Charles, 181, 183, 186
Voltaire, 31
voting rights, 179, 180, 332, 334; universal male suffrage, 281, 284, 290,
295, 314
Voyage de la Louisiana (Laval), 91

Walker, David, 211
Walker, James C., 321, 327, 329, 330,
332, 334
Wallace, Alfred R., 300
Waloon (French-speaking Belgian), 173
Waples, Rufus, 321
Warmoth, Henry Clay, 309–10
War of 1812, 11, 12, 282
Wars of Religion, 102
Washington, Booker T., 334
Watkins, William, 300
Watrin, Francois Philibert, 75
Weber, Max, 17
Wells, Ida B., 326, 330
Wendat (Huron), 43–47, 53, 56–58,
60, 62, 94, 102, 354n85, 355n102,
355n110, 365n16
Whig Party, 269
White, Sophie, 3
whiteness, 212, 229, 265; white Creole
elite, 174; white flight, 235; white
Francophone exceptionality, 193;
White Leaguers, 312–13; white
passing, 263, 264–65, 320, 327–28,
396n66, 406n135; white privilege,
307; White Redeemers, 309–10, 312;
white superiority, 174, 210, 264, 302;
white-supremacist ideology, 322
whiteness, white men: plaçage, 212, 213,
221, 249, 387n160, 394n35, 397n93;
white male citizenship, 17–18, 23, 29,
138, 211, 238–39, 287
whiteness, white supremacy, 12, 227,
235, 249, 265, 275, 277, 283, 310,
316, 326, 339; lynching, 320, 326,
330; St. Landry night riders, 233, 238;
scientific racism, 167, 244, 248, 265,
284, 288–92, 297–302, 333. *See also*
Separate Car Act

Whitney's New Orleans Directory and
Louisiana and Mississippi Almanac, 1811
(New Orleans): *City Directory*, 181,
182, 184, 186, 230, 384n128, 385n134
Wilder, Craig, 13, 275
Williams, Heather Andrea, 291
Wilson, Samuel, Jr., 146
Wiltz, George, 264–65
witchcraft, 56, 354n91
women, 3, 199, 200; Afro-Creole female
activism, 206; Black female civil rights
activism, 205; enslaved women, 119,
158; femaleness, 212; house mothers,
191; Spanish Creole women, 159;
as teachers, 181, 186, 244, 246, 263;

witchcraft, accusations of, 56, 354n91;
women's rights, 167, 198, 255. *See also*
free women of color; girls, education
of; Indigenous women; Ursulines
Woods, William B., 315
Workman, James, 176–77, 196–97, 200,
202, 234–36, 264, 384n112

Yankee schoolmarm, 291
Yazoos, 88, 149, 362, 374n150
yellow fever epidemics, 209, 268
Young, Iris Marion, 338
Yviguel, Renée (Sister Ste. Marie), 111,
122–23, 146